When you write this well, you don't need boxes to maintain interest...

In the fall of 2000, Harvard sophomore Jay Williams flew to the Sudan where a terrible civil war had resulted in many thousands of deaths. Women and children captured in raids by warring tribes were being enslaved and held for ransom. Working with Christian Solidarity International, Williams was able to pay for the release of 4,000 people. But did Williams do the right thing? It's a serious question and one that is surprisingly complex, both morally and economically. By paying for the release of slaves, could Williams have encouraged more people to be enslaved? If so, by how much? Slavery is an abomination. Because of the terrible effects of slavery, careful thought about the best way to deal with the problem is essential. Perhaps surprisingly, the economic concept of elasticity can help people think clearly about the most effective policies to adopt to end slavery.

Armageddon almost happened on September 29, 2004. We aren't talking about the final battle described in the Bible, but what happened in *Armageddon* the movie. In *Armageddon*, an asteroid is discovered to be on a collision course with Earth and NASA recruits a group of roughneck oil drillers to rocket into space, deflect the asteroid, and save civilization. *Armageddon* the movie is a bit absurd, but it got a few things right. Even an asteroid the size of an apartment building would hit Earth with the force of a 4-megaton nuclear bomb. On September 29, 2004, an asteroid called Toutatis, 2.9 *miles* long by 1.5 *miles* wide, narrowly missed Earth. If Toutatis had hit, it would have meant the end of civilization.

The probability of death by asteroid is remarkably high, by some calculations about the same as death by passenger aircraft crash. How can this be? Although the probability of an asteroid hitting Earth is very small, a lot of people would be killed if one did hit, so the probability of death by asteroid is much larger than most people imagine. It doesn't happen very often but watch out when it does.*

A Price Is a Signal Wrapped Up in an Incentive

How is order produced from freedom of choice? That is a scientific mystery, and prices are the biggest clue to the solution. Prices do much more than tell people how much they must shell out for a burger and fries. Prices are incentives, prices are signals, prices are predictions. To understand the market, you need to better understand prices.

When the price of oil rises, all users of oil are encouraged to economize—perhaps by simply using less but also by thinking about substitutes: everything from electric cars to moving flower cultivation overseas. An increase in the price of oil is also a signal to suppliers to invest more in exploration, to look for alternatives like ethanol, and to increase recycling. Do you know the most recycled product in America? It's asphalt.[9]

Politicians and consumers sometime fail to understand the signaling role of prices. After a hurricane, the prices of ice, generators, and chainsaws often skyrocket. Consumers complain of price gouging, and politicians call for price controls. That's understandable, because it can seem doubly harsh to be hit by a hurricane *and* high prices. But the price system is just doing its job. A skyrocketing price is like a flare being shot into the night sky that shouts—bring ice here! A price control eliminates the signal to bring ice into the devastated area as quickly as possible.

The high price of ice in a hurricane-devastated area signals a profit opportunity for ice suppliers. Buy ice where the price is low and ship it to where the price is high. As the supply of ice in the hurricane-devastated area increases, the price will fall. More generally, price signals and the accompanying profits and losses tell entrepreneurs what areas of the economy consumers want expanded and what areas they want contracted. If consumers want more computers, prices and profits in the computer industry will increase and the industry will expand.

Losses may be an even more important signal than profits. Entrepreneurs who fail to compete with lower costs and better products take losses and their businesses contract or even go bankrupt. Bankruptcy is bad for a business but can be good for capitalism. Ever heard of Smith Corona, Polaroid, Pan Am, or Hechingers? At one point, each of these companies led its industry, but today all are either bankrupt or much smaller than at their peak. In a free market, no firm is so powerful that it does not daily face the

LEY COOPER/CORBIS

Beautiful, uncluttered design with pictures that drive the story...

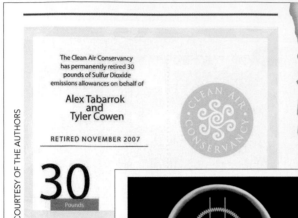

COURTESY OF THE AUTHORS

The Clean Air Conservancy has permanently retired 30 pounds of Sulfur Dioxide emissions allowances on behalf of

Alex Tabarrok and Tyler Cowen

RETIRED NOVEMBER 2007

CLEAN AIR CONSERVANCY

30 Pounds

Externalities

President Nixon said no to commercial holiday lights during the Christmas of 1973.

COURTESY EVERETT COLLECTION

Price Controls

RANDY M. URY/CORBIS

Thomas Edison spent years experimenting with thousands of materials before he discovered that carbonized bamboo filament would make a long-lasting lightbulb. If anyone could have capitalized on his idea, Edison would not have been able to profit from his laborious research and development and perhaps he would not have done the necessary research in the first place.

Profit fuels the fire of invention.

Monopoly

COPYRIGHT © 2007, INDEX FUNDS ADVISORS, IFA.COM

A Devastating Conclusion

Better than the experts?

Investments

ENVISION/CORBIS

How to smuggle sugar

The high price of U.S. sugar has encouraged smuggling and attempts to circumvent the tariff. In the 1980s when the U.S. price was four times the world price, Canadian entrepreneurs created super-high-sugar iced tea. The "tea" was shipped into the United States and then sifted for the sugar, which was resold.

To combat this entrepreneurship, the U.S. government created even more tariffs for

International Trade

MODERN PRINCIPLES:
MICROECONOMICS

Second Edition

Tyler Cowen
George Mason University

Alex Tabarrok
George Mason University

Worth Publishers

Economics is the study of how to get the most out of life.

Tyler and Alex

Senior Publisher: Catherine Woods
Executive Editor: Charles Linsmeier
Senior Acquisitions Editor: Sarah Dorger
Executive Marketing Manager: Scott Guile
Consulting Editor: Paul Shensa
Senior Developmental Editor: Bruce Kaplan
Supplements and Media Editor: Tom Acox
Director of Market Research and Development: Steven Rigolosi
Associate Managing Editor: Lisa Kinne
Editorial Assistant: Mary Walsh
Art Director: Babs Reingold
Cover and Text Designer: Kevin Kall
Project Editor: Anthony Calcara
Photo Editor: Christine Buese
Production Manager: Barbara Anne Seixas
Supplements Production Manager: Stacey Alexander
Supplements Project Editor: Edgar Bonilla
Composition: TSI Graphics
Printing and Binding: RR Donnelley
Cover Image: Image Werks/Corbis and Jim Roof/myLoupe.com

Library of Congress Control Number: 2011936404

ISBN-13: 978-1-4292-3999-8
ISBN-10: 1-4292-3999-9

© 2013, 2010 by Worth Publishers

Printed in the United States of America

First printing 2011

Worth Publishers
41 Madison Avenue
New York, NY 10010
www.worthpublishers.com

ABOUT THE AUTHORS

Tyler Cowen (left) is Holbert C. Harris Professor of Economics at George Mason University. His latest book is *The Great Stagnation*. With Alex Tabarrok, he writes an economics blog at www.marginalrevolution.com. He has published in the *American Economic Review, Journal of Political Economy,* and many other economics journals. He also writes regularly for the popular press, including the *New York Times,* the *Washington Post, Forbes,* the *Wilson Quarterly, Money Magazine,* and many other outlets.

Alex Tabarrok (right) is Bartley J. Madden Chair in Economics at the Mercatus Center at George Mason University and director of research for *The Independent Institute*. His latest book is *Launching the Innovation Renaissance*. His recent research looks at bounty hunters, judicial incentives and elections, crime control, patent reform, methods to increase the supply of human organs for transplant, and the regulation of pharmaceuticals. He is the editor of the books *Entrepreneurial Economics: Bright Ideas from the Dismal Science* and *The Voluntary City: Choice, Community, and Civil Society* among others. His papers have appeared in the *Journal of Law and Economics, Public Choice, Economic Inquiry,* the *Journal of Health Economics,* the *Journal of Theoretical Politics,* the *American Law and Economics Review,* and many other journals. Popular articles have appeared in the *New York Times,* the *Wall Street Journal, Forbes,* and many other magazines and newspapers.

BRIEF CONTENTS

Part 5: Decision Making for Businesses, Investors, and Consumers

CONTENTS

Part 2: The Price System

Part 4: Government

Part 5: Decision Making for Businesses, Investors, and Consumers

PREFACE:
TO THE INSTRUCTOR

Welcome to the second edition of *Modern Principles: Microeconomics.* The response to our first edition was tremendous. Instructors and students responded to our key themes: Make the invisible hand visible. Demonstrate the power of incentives. Present modern models and vivid applications. Make it simpler. These were our goals in writing *Modern Principles: Microeconomics* and they remain our goals in this second edition.

Make the Invisible Hand Visible

One of the most remarkable discoveries of economic science is that under the right conditions the pursuit of self-interest can promote the social good. Nobel laureate Vernon Smith put it this way:

> At the heart of economics is a scientific mystery . . . a scientific mystery as deep, fundamental and inspiring as that of the expanding universe or the forces that bind matter. . . . How is order produced from freedom of choice?

We want students to be inspired by this mystery and by how economists have begun to solve it. Thus, we will explain how markets generate cooperation from people across the world, how prices act as signals and coordinate appropriate responses to changes in economic conditions, and how profit maximization leads to the minimization of industry costs (even though no one intends such an end). We strive to make the invisible hand visible.

In Chapter 7, for example, we show how the invisible hand links romantic American teenagers with Kenyan flower growers, Dutch clocks, British airplanes, Colombian coffee, and Finnish cell phones. We also show how prices signal information and how markets help to solve the *great economic problem* of arranging our limited resources to satisfy as many of our wants as possible.

The focus on the invisible hand or *the price system* continues in Chapter 8. As in other texts, we show how a price ceiling causes a shortage. But a shortage in one market can spill over into other markets (e.g., shortages of oil in the 1970s meant that oil rigs off the coast of California could not get enough oil to operate). In addition, a price ceiling reduces the incentive to move resources from low-value uses to high-value uses, so in the 1970s we saw long lines for gasoline in some states yet *at the same time* gas was plentiful in other states just a few hours away. Price ceilings, therefore, cause a misallocation of resources across markets as well as a shortage within a particular market. We think of Chapters 7 and 8 as a package: Chapter 7 illustrates the price system when it is working and Chapter 8 illustrates what happens when the price system is impeded.

Students who catch even a glimpse of the invisible hand learn something of great importance. Civilization is possible only because under some conditions the pursuit of self-interest promotes the public good.

In discussing the invisible hand, we bring more Hayekian economics into the classroom without proselytizing for Hayekian politics. That is, we want to show how prices communicate information and coordinate action while still recognizing that markets do not always communicate the right information. Thus, our chapters on the price system are rounded out with what we think is an equally interesting and compelling chapter on externalities. The subtitle of Chapter 10, "When Prices Send the Wrong Signals," harkens directly back to Chapter 7. By giving examples where the price signal is right and examples where the price signal is wrong, we convey a sophisticated understanding of the role of prices.

Demonstrate the Power of Incentives

Our second goal in writing *Modern Principles: Microeconomics* is to show—again and again—that incentives matter. In fact, incentives are the theme throughout *Modern Principles*, whether discussing the tragedy of the commons, political economy, or what economics has to say about wise investing. We also include Chapter 21, "Managing Incentives." In this chapter, we explain topics such as the trade-offs between fixed salaries and piece rates, when tournaments work well, and how best to incentivize executives. This chapter can be read profitably by anyone with an interest in *incentive design*—by managers, teachers, even parents! Chapter 21 will be of special interest to business and MBA students (and professors).

Present Modern Models and Vivid Applications

"Modern" is our third goal in writing *Modern Principles: Microeconomics*. For example, we include an entire chapter on price discrimination, in which we cover not just traditional models but also tying and bundling. Students today are familiar with tied goods like cell phones and minutes, or printers and ink, as well as with bundles like Microsoft Office. A modern microeconomics textbook should help students to *understand their world*.

Economics is a powerful tool for understanding the world but too often textbooks end up talking about the supply and demand of ice cream. This textbook is ice cream–free. Whether analyzing the economics of slave redemption, the pricing of AIDS drugs, or the decline of tuna fisheries, we treat economics as important. Startling applications drawn from a wide field are used to illustrate the theory and also to motivate learning.

We also present a modern perspective on the costs and benefits of market power. A significant amount of market power today is tied to innovation, patents, and high fixed costs. Understanding the trade-offs involved with pricing AIDS drugs at marginal cost, for example, is critically important to understanding pharmaceutical policy. Similar issues arise with music, movies, software, chip design, and universities. Our material on monopoly and innovation is consistent with and provides a foundation for modern theories of economic growth (of course, we recommend *Modern Principles: Macroeconomics* to best take advantage of this synergy).

Our chapters on monopoly and price discrimination (Chapters 13 and 14) are filled with business applications, real-world examples, and insightful discussions of policy.

Our game theory chapters (Chapter 15 and 16) are especially geared toward modern real-world choices and problems. Naturally, we cover cartel behavior. We also cover network externalities extensively. In many high-tech and online markets, the value of a good depends on how many other people are using the same good. Students are very familiar with examples such as Facebook and they want to know how the principles of economics apply to these contemporary goods. We even challenge students by showing how the principles of network externalities apply to cultural goods and even to the songs they put on their iPods!

In our chapter on costs (Chapter 11), we jettison some of the old and incorrect rules about when to enter and exit an industry and instead give students a more modern introduction to sunk costs, uncertainty, and the necessity of estimating lifetime expected profits. Our discussion is more modern than in other texts yet it's also simpler and more streamlined, with less focus on the menagerie of cost curves that in other texts chokes off learning.

A modern text needs to place economics in context. We have a whole chapter on normative judgments (Chapter 20). It covers the assumptions behind cost-benefit analysis, the idea of a Pareto improvement, and the ethical judgments that have been used to praise or condemn economic reasoning. Rightly or wrongly, commentators often mix in economic and moral judgments and we teach students to recognize which is which. We stress to the student that economics cannot answer normative issues but the student should be aware of what those normative issues are.

We offer an entire chapter (Chapter 22) on the stock market, a topic of direct practical concern to many students. We teach the basic trade-off between risk and return (no free lunches) and explain why it is a good idea to diversify investments. We also explain the microeconomics of bubbles, which of course bridges to current macroeconomic issues.

We include business examples and topics throughout the text. We cover business issues as diverse as why businesses cluster and how network externalities push businesses to compete "for the market" rather than "in the market," to how successful cartels such as the NBA deal with the incentive to cheat, to how businesses actually go about price discriminating. Our chapter on incentives, already mentioned, is critical for managers in a variety of fields.

Make It Simpler

We also knew that our efforts to reflect modern microeconomics would be wasted if we reached only a small percentage of students. We had to make the material simpler, more compelling, and more intuitive. We had to get to the point right away. We knew that we were writing for a generation that doesn't always have the patience for slow delivery.

Our text is motivated by the following pedagogical guidelines:

> Economics is a set of powerful tools for understanding the world.

> We develop no tools that we do not use to better understand the world.

> Theory is developed alongside real examples.

> Economics is everywhere. Law, management, politics, personal relations— we draw from it all.

> Economics is fun.

Make the invisible hand visible. Demonstrate the power of incentives. Present modern models and vivid applications. Make it simpler. Those are just some of the reasons why we call our text *Modern Principles: Microeconomics*. We have taken recent advances in how economists think and describe microeconomics and we have integrated them throughout the text. We truly seek to get students enthused about the economic way of thinking and to internalize it for the rest of their lives. We hope you will see that this text provides the best coverage of what it means to think like an economist.

Guiding Principles and Innovations: In a Nutshell

Modern Principles offers the following features and benefits:

1. We teach the economic way of thinking.

2. *Modern Principles* has a more intuitive development of markets and their interconnectedness than does any other textbook. More than any other textbook we teach students how the *price system* works.

3. *Modern Principles* helps students to see the invisible hand. We offer an intuitive proof of several "invisible hand theorems." For example, we show that through the operation of incentives and the price system, well-functioning markets will minimize the aggregate sum of the costs of production even though no one intends this result. Local knowledge creates a global benefit.

4. We offer an entire chapter on normative issues. What are some of the normative issues behind the use of markets and market incentives? We stress to the student that this chapter offers more questions than answers.

5. We offer an entire chapter on incentives and how they apply to business decisions, sports, and incentive design. When, for instance, should you reward your employees with a tournament form of compensation, and when a straight salary? Most texts are oddly silent on such practical issues, but it is precisely such issues that interest many students and show them the relevance of the economic way of thinking. We also offer an entire chapter on network goods, which covers Facebook, the tech sector, and music.

6. We offer an entire chapter on the stock market, a topic of concern to many students. We teach the basic trade-off between risk and return and explain why it is a good idea to diversify investments. We also explain the microeconomics of bubbles.

7. Today's students live in a globalized economy. Events in China, India, Europe, and the Middle East affect their lives. *Modern Principles* features international examples and applications throughout, rather than just segregating all of the international topics in a single chapter.

8. Less is more. This is a textbook of *principles*, not a survey or an encyclopedia. A textbook that focuses on what is important helps the student to focus on what is important. There are fewer yet more consistent and more comprehensive models.

9. No tools without applications. Real-world vivid applications are used to develop theory. Applications are not pushed aside into distracting boxes that students do not read.

10. Excel is used as a tool in appendices to help students develop insight, hands-on experience, and modeling ability.

What's New in the Second Edition?

Every book must change with the time and ours has, too. The new edition of *Modern Principles: Microeconomics* includes many additions and structural changes:

- A new Chapter 2, "The Power of Trade and Comparative Advantage," introduces the core ideas of trade and production, using the production possibilities frontier, earlier in the book and gives them greater coverage, for those instructors who want to cover this material before supply and demand.

- "Taxes and Subsidies" now gets its own chapter (Chapter 6), rather than being mixed in with price floors.
- The previous costs chapter has been split up into two new chapters. The first, Chapter 11, "Costs and Profit Maximization Under Competition," covers basic cost issues more thoroughly than before. The second, Chapter 12, "Competition and the Invisible Hand," expands on our previous demonstration of how competition minimizes total costs of production.
- Chapter 15, "Cartels, Oligopolies, and Monopolistic Competition," adds a whole new section on monopolistic competition, with an application to advertising.
- A new Chapter 16 focuses on "The Economics of Network Goods: Competing for Monopoly," with easy-to-teach examples from Facebook and musical songs.
- New Chapter 23, "Consumer Choice," adds extensive coverage of indifference curves, and income and substitution effects, to the book.

Most importantly, we've kept all of the qualities and features that made the first edition so popular.

Tools for Learning

Microeconomics should come across as elegant, intuitive, and unified, falling directly out of real-world experience. Thus, we focus on the core tools of supply and demand and price elasticity, leavened with lots of economic intuition and a dash of game theory. We spend more time on the core tools than do other textbooks, we introduce "no tools without applications," and we focus on tools that we use repeatedly. We spend a lot of time on price elasticity, for example, because in addition to having many important applications (gun buybacks, slave redemption), it is used again in monopoly theory and in the analysis of taxes and subsidies. We relegate income and cross-price elasticity to an appendix because these tools are not used repeatedly.

1. Vivid applications

Nothing sticks with a student like a good example. *Modern Principles* is full of vivid illustrations of core economic principles. From the first sentence in our textbook, "The prisoners were dying of scurvy, typhoid fever, and smallpox, but nothing was killing them more than bad incentives," we strive to draw students into the economic way of thinking and to teach them that economics matters.

2. Simpler graphs

Modern Principles presents microeconomics with fewer curves than you will find in other microeconomics books, yet without skimping on substantive results. This follows from our presentation of integrated and consistent models. For instance, on cost curves we strip the key ideas down to their intuitive essentials. If you look at the clunkier expositions of cost curves—which multiply the number of curves beyond reason—how many students actually learn or remember all of the distinctions presented? Moreover, as we know from the modern theory of investment under uncertainty, the old shut-down "rules" such as $P < AVC$ are wrong, so why present them?[*]

---

[*] On the modern theory of investment under uncertainty, see Dixit, Avinash. 1992. Investment and hysteresis. *Journal of Economic Perspectives* 6(1): 107–132.

We say if the idea is intuitive—as good economics should be—the graph should be intuitive, too. Economics students *do* need to learn how to think in terms of graphs. But that's best done by making graphs manageable, not by making graphs forbidding.

3. No set-off boxes that interrupt the flow of the text

We know that students usually skip these boxes. So we've also skipped them. If the material is important enough for the student to learn, we've put it in the text. If it's not important, we've left it out. We want our pages to look attractive and easy to read. That will get students to read more of the material that really matters.

4. Extensive questions and problems sections

At the end of each chapter, we typically start with "Facts and Tools" questions designed to test knowledge of basic concepts. The next section, "Thinking and Problem Solving," tests whether the student can apply those concepts to examples and also to problems that require a definite solution. The final section, "Challenges," tests whether students understand key concepts in a deep fashion and can apply them to nontrivial examples and problems. If a student can do well in the challenges, he or she has not just memorized some material but is truly thinking like an economist. The multiple tiers for the end-of-chapter material help us teach both different skills and different levels of understanding.

5. Nuggets

The chapter margins offer captioned photos, cartoons, and short informational bits. The examples are chosen because they are memorable and sometimes humorous. Reading a principles textbook is not always sugar, but every now and then it should be fun. The students should look forward to at least some part of the reading and some part of the lesson. We have written *Modern Principles* with this philosophy.

6. Notation

The book has a minimum of notational requirements. Students need to be familiar with simple one-line equations, with basic algebra, and with reading graphs. For help with reading graphs, we offer a useful 14-page appendix. Overall our notation is minimal and standard.

What's in the Chapters?

Part 1: Supply and Demand

We review the key aspects of supply and demand and the price system, done in six chapters. We present incentives as the most important idea in microeconomics. Microeconomics should be intuitive, should teach the skill of thinking like an economist, and should be drawn from examples from everyday life. Along these lines, these chapters run as follows.

Chapter 1: The Big Ideas

What is economics all about? We present the core ideas of incentives, opportunity cost, trade, the importance of economic growth, and thinking on the margin, and some of the key insights of economics such as that tampering with the laws of supply and demand has consequences and good institutions align self-interest with the social interest. The point is to make economics intuitive and compelling and to hook the student with examples from everyday life.

Chapter 2: The Power of Trade and Comparative Advantage

Why is trade so important and why is it a central idea of economics? We introduce ideas of gains from trade, the production possibilities frontier, and comparative advantage to show the student some core ideas behind the economic way of thinking. The key here is to illustrate the power of economic concepts in explaining the prosperity of the modern world. Yet all these topics are covered in greater depth later on, so an instructor can either use this material to entice the student, or postpone the subject and move directly to the supply and demand chapters.

Chapter 3: Supply and Demand

This chapter focuses on demand curves, supply curves, how and why they slope, and how they shift. The chapter presents some basic fundamentals of economic theory, using the central example of the market for oil. We also take special care to illustrate how demand and supply curves can be read "horizontally" or "vertically." That is, a demand curve tells you the quantity demanded at every price and the maximum willingness to pay (per unit) for any quantity.

It takes a bit more work to explain these concepts early on, but students who learn to read demand curves in both ways get a deeper understanding of the curves and they find consumer and producer surplus, taxes, and the analysis of price controls much easier to understand.

Chapter 4: Equilibrium: How Supply and Demand Determine Prices

Market clearing is an essential idea for both microeconomics and macroeconomics. In this chapter, students learn how a well-functioning market operates, how prices clear markets, the meaning of maximizing gains from trade, and how to shift supply and demand curves. The chapter concludes with a section on understanding the price of oil, a topic that recurs throughout the text and our companion volume *Modern Principles: Macroeconomics*.

Chapter 5: Elasticity and Its Applications

Elasticity is often considered a dull topic so we begin this chapter with a shocking story:

> In fall 2000, Harvard sophomore Jay Williams flew to the Sudan where a terrible civil war had resulted in many thousands of deaths. Women and children captured in raids by warring tribes were being enslaved and held for ransom. Working with Christian Solidarity International, Williams was able to pay for the release of 4,000 people. But did Williams do the right thing?

What is a discussion of modern slavery doing in a principles of economics book? We want to show students that economics is a social science, that it asks important questions and provides important answers for people who want to understand their world. We take economics seriously and in *Modern Principles* we analyze serious topics.

Once we have shocked the reader out of his or her complacency, we offer the reader an implicit deal—we are going to develop some technical concepts in economics, which at first may seem dry, but if you learn this material, there is going to be a payoff. We will use the tools to understand the economics of slave redemption as well as why the war on drugs can generate violence, why gun buyback programs are unlikely to work, and how to evaluate proposals to increase drilling in the Arctic National Wildlife Refuge.

Chapter 6: Taxes and Subsidies

We analyze commodity taxes and subsidies, two core topics, to test, refine, and improve an understanding of microeconomics. We have all heard the question "Who pays?" and the statement "Follow the money," but few people understand how to apply these ideas correctly. The economist knows that the final incidence of a tax depends not on the laws of Congress but on the laws of economics, and this can be taught as yet another invisible hand result. Teaching the incidence of taxes and subsidies also gives yet another way of driving home the concept of elasticity, its intuitive meaning, and its real-world importance. We also include in this chapter a timely discussion of wage subsidies to which we compare the minimum wage.

Part 2: The Price System
Chapter 7: The Price System: Signals, Speculation, and Prediction

"A price is a signal wrapped up in an incentive." That's one of the most important ideas of economics, even if it takes a little work from the students. And that is an idea that we drive home in this chapter. Partial equilibrium analysis can sometimes obscure the big picture of markets and how they fit together. General equilibrium analysis, either done mathematically or with an Edgeworth box, captures neither the "marvel of the market" (to use Hayek's phrase) nor the student's interest. We give a fast-paced, intuitive, general equilibrium view of markets and how they tie together. We are linked to the world economy, and goods and services are shipped from one corner of the globe to another, yet without the guidance of a central planner. We show how the price of oil is linked to the price of candy bars. We also show how markets can predict the future, even the future of a movie like *American Pie 2*! For those familiar with Leonard Read's classic essay, this chapter is "I, Pencil" for the twenty-first century.

Chapter 8: Price Ceilings and Price Floors

There is no better way to understand how the price system works than to see what happens when the price system does *not* work very well. That price controls bring shortages is one of the most basic and most solid results of microeconomics. When it comes to price controls, however, the bad consequences extend far beyond shortages. Price controls lead to quality reductions, wasteful lines, excess search, corruption, rent-seeking behavior, misallocated resources, and many other secondary consequences. Price controls are an object lesson in many important economic ideas and we teach the topic as such. Sometimes we're all better off if the university charges more for parking! Price controls also offer a good chance to teach some political economy lessons about why bad economic policies happen in the first place.

Sometimes governments prop up prices instead of keeping them down—the minimum wage for labor is one example, and airline regulation before the late 1970s was another. As with price ceilings, price floors bring misallocated resources, distortions in the quality of the good or service being sold, and rent-seeking. Maybe the government can prop up the price of an airline ticket, as it did in 1974, but each airline will offer lobster dinners to lure away customers.

Chapter 9: International Trade

We build on the basics of international trade—the division of knowledge, economies of scale, and comparative advantage—covered in Chapter 2, to show students how they can use the tools of supply and demand to understand the microeconomics of trade. We consider the costs of protectionism, international trade and market power, trade and wages, and most of all trade and jobs. Is protectionism ever a good idea? The chapter also offers a brief history of globalization as it relates to trade. We emphasize that the principles covering trade across nations are the same as those that govern trade within nations.

Chapter 10: Externalities: When Prices Send the Wrong Signals

When do markets fail or otherwise produce undesired results? Prices do not always signal the right information and incentives, most of all when external costs and benefits are present. A medical patient may use an antibiotic, for instance, without taking into account the fact that disease-causing microorganisms evolve and mutate, and that antibiotic use can in the long run lead to bacteria that are antibiotic-resistant. Similarly, not enough people get flu vaccinations, because they don't take into account how other people benefit from a lower chance of catching a contagious ailment. Private markets sometimes can "internalize" these external costs and benefits by writing good contracts, and we give students the tools to understand when such contracts will be possible and when not. Market contracts, tradable permits, taxes, and command and control are alternative means of treating externalities. Building on our previous understanding of the invisible hand, we consider when these approaches will produce efficient results and when not.

Part 3: Firms and Factor Markets

Chapter 11: Costs and Profit Maximization Under Competition

This chapter makes cost theory *intuitive* once again. Costs are indeed an important economic concept; prices and costs send signals to firms and guide their production decisions, just as a price at Walmart shapes the behavior of consumers. But how exactly does this work? We've all seen textbooks that serve up an overwhelming confusion of different cost curves, all plastered on the same graph and not always corresponding in a simple or direct manner to economic intuition.

This chapter reduces the theory of cost and the theory of production to the essentials. A firm must make three key decisions: What price to set? What quantity to produce? When to enter and exit an industry? A simple notion of average cost suffices to cover decisions of firm entry and exit, while avoiding a tangle of excess concepts. Unlike many books, we stress the importance of "wait and see" and option value strategies. We can show firm-level and industry-level supply responses; constant, decreasing, and increasing cost industries; and how comparative statics differ for these cases.

Chapter 12: Competition and the Invisible Hand

Profit maximization leads competitive firms to produce where $P = MC$, but why is this condition truly important? Most textbooks don't teach the marvelous result that when each firm produces where $P = MC$, total industry costs are minimized. Competitive firms minimize total industry costs despite the fact that no firm intends this result and perhaps never even understands this result. As Hayek says, the minimization of total industry costs is "a product of human action but not of human design." We also show in this chapter how profit and loss signals result in a balancing of industries in a way that solves the great economic problem of getting the most value from our finite resources.

This material is so important that in the second edition we have given it its own chapter. This chapter gives a deeper insight into Adam Smith's invisible hand, and how it relates to profit maximization, than does any other principles text.

Chapter 13: Monopoly

When they can, firms use market power to maximize profit and this chapter shows how. (Some budding entrepreneurs in the class may take this as a how-to manual!) We build on concepts such as cost curves and elasticity to flesh out the economics and also the public policy of monopoly. If you own the intellectual property rights to an important anti-AIDS drug, just how much power do you have? It's good for you, but does this help or hurt broader society? Monopolies sometimes bring higher rates of innovation but in other cases, such as natural monopolies on your water supply, monopolies raise prices and reduce quantity with few societal benefits. Again, formal economic concepts such as elasticity and cost help us see the very real costs and benefits of such regulations as we experience them in our daily lives.

Chapter 14: Price Discrimination

Modern Principles devotes an entire chapter to this topic, which is fun, practical, and contains lots of economics. Students, in their roles as consumers, face (or, as sellers, practice!) price discrimination all the time, and that includes from their colleges and universities—remember in-state vs. out-of-state tuition? A lot of what students already "know" can be turned into more systematic economic intuition, including the concepts of demand and elasticity, and whether marginal cost is rising or falling. The pricing of printers and ink, pharmaceuticals, and cable TV all derive naturally from this analysis. Once students understand price discrimination, their eyes will be open to a world of economics in practice every day.

Chapter 15: Cartels, Oligopolies, and Monopolistic Competition

Can OPEC nations really collude to force up the price of oil? Or is the price of oil set by normal competitive forces of supply and demand in world markets? Understanding when businesses "control price" and when they do not is one of the biggest gaps in understanding between someone with economics training and someone without such training. Cartels usually collapse because of cheating by cartel members, new entrants into the market, and also legal prosecution from governments. Despite the challenges that cartels like OPEC face, many businesses nevertheless would love to cartelize their markets, even if they find it difficult to succeed for very long.

The incentive to cheat on cartels is a key to introducing game theory and also the prisoner's dilemma. We also cover monopolistic competition in depth, focusing on the intuitions behind the concept. We show how monopolistic competition is a good analytic framework for understanding the economics of advertising, a topic that has a strong intuitive relevance for many students.

Chapter 16: The Economics of Network Goods: Competing for Monopoly

Students are eager to understand the world they live in. *Modern Principles* talks not about the market for ice cream but the market for oil, printers and ink, cell phones, Google, Facebook and Match.com. In this chapter, we focus on network goods.

A lot of us use Microsoft Word because so many other people also do. Blu-Ray beat out the HD-DVD standard because again, for reasons of convenience, consumers want to share a common network or system. Markets like this have some unusual properties. They tend to have lots of monopoly and lots of innovation (competition "for the market" versus competition "in the market"), and they change suddenly in fits and starts, rather than gradually. We show the student why Facebook beat out MySpace and the associated economic lessons. How do frequent flyer programs work, why are they profitable, and what does the concept of a contestable market mean for both analysis and policy? How does Match.com work and why do friends so often enjoy the same musical songs? This "hands on" chapter serves up a lot of topics of immediate interest to students and relates them to core microeconomic concepts.

Chapter 17: Labor Markets

Work touches almost all of our lives and most of the fundamental matters and conditions of work are ruled by economics. Wages. Working conditions. Bonuses. Investments in human capital and education. It's the marginal product of labor that has the strongest influence over the wage of a particular job. Risky jobs, like going out on dangerous fishing boats, pay more. Labor unions boost the wages of some workers but will hurt the wages of others. There is also the controversial topic of discrimination in labor markets. We show how some kinds of discrimination may survive while others will tend to fall away, due to the pressure of market forces.

Part 4: Government

Chapter 18: Public Goods and the Tragedy of the Commons

Public goods and externalities help us understand when private property rights do not always lead to good outcomes. The concepts of excludability and non-rivalry help us classify why governments have to provide national defense but why movie theaters are usually left to the private sector.

Why is it that the world is running out of so many kinds of fish? Economics has the best answer and it involves the tragedy of the commons. We show that economics is the single best entry point for understanding many common dilemmas of the environment.

Chapter 19: Political Economy

If economics is so good, why doesn't the world always listen? Political economy is one of the most important topics. Economics has a lot to say about how politics works and the results aren't always pretty. Voters have a rational incentive to be ignorant or underinformed, and the end result is that special interests have a big say over many economic policies. Dairy farmers have a bigger say over milk subsidies than do the people who drink milk, and that is why the United States has milk price supports.

That said, democratic systems still outperform the available alternatives. We present the median voter theorem and also explain why political competition produces results that are at least somewhat acceptable to the "person in the street."

Chapter 20: Economics, Ethics, and Public Policy

Most principles students leave the classroom still underequipped to understand real-world policy debates over economic issues. So often the debate descends into ethics: Are markets fair? Is the distribution of income just? Is it important that individual rights be respected? When is paternalism justified? We do *not* try to provide final, take-away answers to these questions, but we do give the students the tools to unpack how these questions intersect with the economic issues they have been studying.

Should we give physically handicapped individuals better access to public facilities, or should the government simply send them more cash? Should there be a free market in transplantable human organs such as kidneys? For all the power of economics, virtually any public debate on questions like these will quickly bring in lots of ethical questions. We think that students should be familiar with the major ethical objections to "the economic way of thinking," and the strengths and weaknesses of those objections. We introduce the ideas of John Rawls and Robert Nozick, and also the philosophy of utilitarianism. In our view this chapter is an important supplement to the power of economic reasoning.

Part 5: Decision Making for Businesses, Investors, and Consumers

Chapter 21: Managing Incentives

Incentives matter! That may be the key single lesson of economics but a lot of textbooks don't have a complete chapter on incentives. Business applications, sports applications, and personal life all provide plenty of illustrations of economic principles. You get what you pay for, so if you can't measure quality very well, a lot of incentive schemes will backfire. Piece rates make a lot of workers more productive but strong incentives can impose risk on workers and induce them to quit their job altogether. As with grading on a curve, sometimes a boss wishes to pay workers relative to the performance of other workers. A lot of the most important incentives are about pride, fun, and fame, not just money.

Economists can never be doing enough to communicate what they know about incentives to a broader public. By making it easy, we want to increase the incentives here!

Chapter 22: Stock Markets and Personal Finance

The stock market is the one topic that just about every student of economics cares about, and yet it is neglected in many textbooks. We view the stock market as a "teaching moment" as well as an important topic in its own right. What other economic topic commands so much attention from the popular press? Yet not every principles course gives the student the tools to understand media discussions or to dissect fallacies. We remedy that state of affairs. This chapter covers passive versus active investing, the trade-off between risk and return, "how to really pick stocks," diversification, why high fees should be avoided, compound returns, and asset price bubbles. The operation of asset markets is something students need to know if they are to understand today's economy and also the financial crisis.

And, yes, we do offer students some very direct and practical investment advice. Most people should diversify and "buy and hold," and we explain why. In terms of direct, practical value, we try to make this book worth its price!

Chapter 23: Consumer Choice

This chapter adds an extensive and foundational treatment of indifference curves to the book. It starts with the notions of diminishing marginal utility and relative price ratios to derive indifference curves. A budget constraint is added to indifference curves to generate the standard propositions of consumer theory, including marginal rates of substitution, income effects, substitution effects, and the idea of a consumer optimum. The chapter includes novel applications, such as a unique and relevant application to Costco and why a company might charge consumers entry fees for membership.

Alternative Paths through the Book

Modern Principles: Microeconomics has been written with trade-offs in mind and it's easy to pick and choose from among the chapters when time constrains. We offer a few quick suggestions. Chapter 7 is fun to teach but more difficult to test than some of the other chapters. But don't worry, you will find plenty of testable material in other chapters, and for your best students the introduction to the price system in Chapters 7 and 8 will be an eye-opener!

We spend more time on price controls than do other books because we don't confine ourselves to the usual shortage diagram, but we also illustrate the general equilibrium effects of price controls. We have also included a section of advanced material on the losses from random allocation that may be skipped in larger classes or if time constrains.

We have greatly simplified the presentation on cost curves and removed most of production theory, so do take the time to cover monopoly and the chapter on price discrimination. Students love the material on price discrimination because once they understand the concepts, they see the applications all around them. Chapter 16, "The Economics of Network Goods: Competing for Monopoly," is a very appealing chapter for students, and we recommend it for its applications, but if you don't have time, it can be skipped.

Asteroid deflection and the decline of the tuna fisheries are a must, so do cover Chapter 18 on public goods and the tragedy of the commons. Once again, students appreciate the focus on important, real-world applications of the economic way of thinking.

Chapters 19 and 20 on political economy and ethics are optional. If you can teach only one chapter, we think Chapter 19 on political economy has crucial material for avoiding the nirvana fallacy: We should always compare real-world markets with real-world governments when doing political economy. Chapter 20 on ethics works very well in smaller classes with lots of student interaction—we think it important that the philosophy professors are not the ones who get the only say on questions of ethics!

Chapter 21, "Managing Incentives," is fun to teach but it goes beyond the core and can be skipped. We believe this chapter will be especially appropriate for management, MBA, and pre-law students.

We encourage everyone to teach Chapter 22 on stock markets but we have also included this chapter in *Modern Principles: Macroeconomics* so you can choose where it best fits in your lesson plan.

Chapter 23, "Consumer Choice," is for those instructors who wish to cover indifference curves in considerable detail.

Most of all we hope that *Modern Principles* helps you, the teacher, to have fun! We love economics and we have fun teaching economics. We have written this text for people not afraid to say the same. Don't hesitate to email us with your questions, thoughts, and experiences, or just to say hello!

Media and Supplements

ⓧeconportal
FOR MODERN PRINCIPLES OF ECONOMICS
www.youreconportal.com

With *EconPortal* instructors get a complete learning management system, ready to use without hours of prepwork. Students
get easy access to learning resources specific to the course and
the textbook. And virtually every aspect of *EconPortal* is
customizable.

New to *EconPortal*

■ *LearningCurve* Formative Quizzing Engine bringing
adaptive question selection, personalized study plans, and
state-of-the-art question analysis to game-like activities that
keep students engaged.

■ *Launch Pad* Prebuilt Lessons, combining eBook sections
with curated activities, pre-assembled quizzes, and ready-to-
assign homework.

■ **Assignable Videos,** with assessment questions to help
students make connections between what they are studying
and world events.

Also Featuring:

■ A state-of-the-art **Graphing Tool** that replicates the
pencil-and-paper experience by asking students to create
curves, not simply shift them.

■ **The Second Edition Test Bank**, with questions sortable
by level, skill, format, and topic.

■ **All end-of-chapter problems** easily assignable and
automatically gradable.

■ **Student self-assessment resources** tied specifically to
the book.

■ **An HTML-based eBook** that allows for note-taking (both
public and private), custom syllabi (chapters and sections),
highlighting, instructor–student communication, and more!
Also available stand-alone as a low-cost text purchase option
for students.

■ **A Realtime** newsfeed from *The Economist*.

FOR MODERN PRINCIPLES OF ECONOMICS
www.aplia.com/worth

The **Aplia/Worth** partnership combines Worth texts and
eBooks with **Aplia**'s interactive problem sets, news analyses,
tutorials, and economic experiments—all in a format that saves
professors time while encouraging students.

Aplia for *Modern Principles of Economics* Features:

■ **Homework sets** correlated to the text that can be assigned
and graded online. An easy-to-use gradebook tracks results.

■ **Multiple purchase options.** Students can access **Aplia** free
for the first two weeks of the course, then decide if they want
to purchase an eBook or a text package. Students purchasing
an eBook can also purchase a physical text directly from Aplia
at about half off the retail price.

■ **Algorithmic problem sets.** Students can take the tests up
to three times with new iterations of the problems each time.

ALSO AVAILABLE

See The Invisible Hand Resource Bank at stihblog.com
Updated regularly, the Resource Bank correlates posts and
ideas from Cowen and Tabarrok's *Marginal Revolution* blog
to chapters and topics in their textbook (or any principles
of economics text).

Book Companion Site at
worthpublishers.com/cowentabarrok
The companion site serves as a FREE virtual study guide
for students, while providing instructors with a variety of
presentation, assessment, and course management resources.

Instructor's Manual with Solutions
In one convenient resource, instructors get chapter-by-chapter
teaching support, plus suggested in-class and homework
activities, and detailed solutions to all end-of-chapter questions.

Printed Test Bank • Computerized Test Bank
The test bank offers a variety of multiple-choice, true/false,
and short-answer questions—roughly 135 per chapter. The CD
version (Windows and Mac formats on one disc) makes it easy
for instructors to create and customize tests.

Study Guide
The guide provides students with additional opportunities to
reinforce lessons learned in the chapter.

i>clicker
Created for educators, by educators—with
continuous product improvements made through direct
classroom testing and faculty feedback—**i>clicker** is the leading
radio frequency classroom response system. To learn more
about packaging **i>clicker** with this textbook, please contact
your local sales rep or visit **www.iclicker.com**.

Acknowledgments

We are most grateful to the following reviewers, both users and non-users of the first edition, for their careful in-depth chapter reviews used in the development of the second edition of *Modern Principles: Microeconomics*.

Randall Campbell
Mississippi University

Harold Elder
University of Alabama

Patricia Euzent
University of Central Florida

Paul Fisher
Henry Ford Community College

Bradley Hobbs
Florida Gulf Coast University

Kate Krause
University of New Mexico

Daniel Kuo
Orange Coast College

Daniel Lin
American University

Solina Lindahl
California State Polytechnic University

Michael Mace
Sierra College

Michael Makowsky
Towson University

Joan Nix
Queens College, The City University of New York

Zuohong Pan
Western Connecticut State University

Jeff Sarbaum
University of North Carolina at Greensboro

Jonathan Wight
University of Richmond

We are most indebted and grateful to the following focus group participants, reviewers, and class testers for their comments and suggestions in the development of the first edition. Every one of them has contributed to the final product.

Rashid Al-Hmoud
Texas Tech University

Michael Applegate
Oklahoma State University

J. J. Arias
Georgia College and State University

Jim Barbour
Elon University

David Beckworth
Texas State University

Robert Beekman
University of Tampa

Ryan Bosworth
North Carolina State University

Jennifer Brown
Eastern Connecticut State University

Douglas Campbell
University of Memphis

Michael Carew
Baruch College

Shawn Carter
Jacksonville State University

Philip Coelho
Ball State University

Jim Couch
North Alabama University

Scott Cunningham
University of Georgia

Amlan Datta
Texas Tech University

John Dawson
Appalachian State University

Timothy M. Diette
Washington and Lee University

Ann Eike
University of Kentucky

Tisha Emerson
Baylor University

Molly Espey
Clemson University

William Feipel
Illinois Central University

Amanda S. Freeman
Kansas State University

Gary Galles
Pepperdine University

Neil Garston
California State University, Los Angeles

William Gibson
University of Vermont

David Gillette
Truman State University

Lynn G. Gillette
Sierra Nevada College

Stephan F. Gohmann
University of Louisville

Michael Gootzeit
University of Memphis

Carole Green
University of South Florida

Paul Grimes
Mississippi State University

Philip J. Grossman
St. Cloud State University

Darrin Gulla
University of Kentucky

Kyle Hampton
The Ohio State University

Joe Haslag
University of Missouri—Columbia

Sarah Helms
University of Alabama—Birmingham

Matthew Henry
University of Georgia

John Hsu
Contra Costa College

Jeffrey Hummel
San Jose State University

Sarah Jackson
Indiana University of Pennsylvania

Dennis Jansen
Texas A&M University

Bruce Johnson
Centre College

Veronica Kalich
Baldwin Wallace College

Lillian Kamal
University of Hartford

John Keating
University of Kansas

Logan Kelly
Bryant University

Brian Kench
University of Tampa

David Kreutzer
James Madison University

Robert Krol
California State University, Northridge

Gary Lape
Liberty University

Rodolfo Ledesma
Marian College

Jim Lee
Texas A&M University—Corpus Christi

Daniel Lin
American University

Edward Lopez
San Jose State University

Hari Luitel
St. Cloud State University

Douglas Mackenzie
State University of New York— Plattsburgh

Michael Makowsky
Towson University

John Marcis
Coastal Carolina University

Catherina Matraves
Michigan State University

Meghan Millea
Mississippi State University

Stephen Miller
University of Nevada, Las Vegas

Ida Mirzaie
The Ohio State University

David (Mitch) Mitchell
South Alabama University

Ranganath Murthy
Bucknell University

Todd Myers
Grossmont College

Andre Neveu
Skidmore College

Lydia Ortega
San Jose State University

Alexandre Padilla
Metropolitan State College of Denver

Biru Paksha Paul
State University of New York— Cortland

John Perry
Centre College

Gina C. Pieters
University of Minnesota

Dennis Placone
Clemson University

Jennifer M. Platania
Elon University

Brennan Platt
Brigham Young University

William Polley
Western Illinois University

Benjamin Powell
Suffolk University

Margaret Ray
University of Mary Washington

Dan Rickman
Oklahoma State University

Fred Ruppel
Eastern Kentucky University

Mikael Sandberg
University of Florida

Michael Scott
University of Oklahoma

James Self
Indiana University

David Shideler
Murray State University

Mark Showalter
Brigham Young University

Martin Spechler
Indiana University–Purdue University, Indianapolis

David Spencer
Brigham Young University

Richard Stahl
Louisiana State University

Dean Stansel
Florida Gulf Coast University

Liliana V. Stern
Auburn University

Kay Strong
Bowling Green State University— Firelands

Jim Swofford
University of South Alabama

Sandra Trejos
Clarion University of Pennsylvania

Marie Truesdell
Marian College

Norman T. Van Cott
Ball State University

Kristin A. Van Gaasbeck
California State University— Sacramento

Michael Visser
Sonoma State University

Yoav Wachsman
Coastal Carolina University

Doug Walker
Georgia College and State University

Christopher Waller
Notre Dame University

Robert Whaples
Wake Forest University

Mark Wheeler
Western Michigan University

Additional suggestions for improving the manuscript were given by our talented group of supplements authors. We are grateful to all of them:

Jim Swofford
University of South Alabama

John Dawson
Appalachian State University

Benjamin Powell
Suffolk University

Paul Fisher
Henry Ford Community College

Solina Lindahl
California Polytechnic State University

Michael Applegate
Oklahoma State University, Main Campus

David Gillette
Truman State University

David Youngberg
George Mason University

Eli Dourado
George Mason University

Garett Jones
George Mason University

Jennifer Platania
University of West Florida

David Kalist
Shippensburg University of Pennsylvania

Mark Wheeler
Western Michigan University

Bhavneet Walia
Western Illinois University

Sheng Yang
Black Hills State University

Lillian Kamal
University of Hartford

James Self
Indiana University

Kyle Hampton
University of Alaska, Anchorage

Kenneth Slaysman
York College of Pennsylvania

Alanna Holowinsky
Red River College

Irina Pritchett
North Carolina State University

James Watson
University of Colorado—Boulder

Pat Euzent
University of Central Florida

Brett Block
University of Colorado—Boulder

Douglas Campbell
University of Memphis

Ryan Oprea
University of California, Santa Cruz

Margaret apRoberts-Warren
University of California, Santa Cruz

Tyler Watts
Ball State University

We were fortunate to have an eagle-eyed reader of the proofs of the book during the production process. Paul Fisher, Henry Ford Community College, was a careful reader of the page proofs. Paul also contributed numerous new problems and solutions to the second edition. The Mercatus Center supplied an essential work environment. Jane Perry helped us to proof many of the chapters and with Lisa Hill-Corley provided important daily assistance. Teresa Hartnett has done a great job as our agent.

Most of all we are grateful to the team at Worth. The idea for this book was conceived by Paul Shensa, who has seen it through with wise advice from day one until the end. Chuck Linsmeier has been a wonderful publisher and Sarah Dorger has led the editing work and been a joy to work with. Becca Hicks was a delight to work with and introduced us to the key elements of a textbook. Bruce Kaplan, our primary development editor, is the George Martin of book production; he has done a tremendous amount of nitty-gritty work on the manuscript to make every note just right and he has offered excellent counsel throughout.

We are fortunate to have had such a talented production and design group for our book. Anthony Calcara coordinated the entire production process with the help of Lisa Kinne. Kevin Kall created the beautiful interior design and the cover. Christine Buese went beyond the call of duty in tracking down sometimes obscure photos. Barbara Seixas showed a deft hand with the manufacturing aspects of the book. It has been a delight to work with all of them.

The supplements were put together by several people. Tom Acox put together the supplements team and ably brought the supplements and media package to market. Stacey Alexander and Edgar Bonilla helped bring the content to print.

Scott Guile stands out in the marketing of this book. He has been energetic and relentless.

Most of all, we want to thank our families for their support and understanding. Tyler wishes to offer his personal thanks to Natasha and Yana. It is Alex's great fortune to be able to thank Monique, Connor, and Maxwell and his parents for years of support and encouragement.

Tyler Cowen
Alex Tabarrok

1

The Big Ideas

The prisoners were dying of scurvy, typhoid fever, and small-pox, but nothing was killing them more than bad incentives. In 1787, the British government had hired sea captains to ship convicted felons to Australia. Conditions on board the ships were monstrous; some even said the conditions were worse than on slave ships. On one voyage, more than one third of the men died and the rest arrived beaten, starved, and sick. A first mate re-marked cruelly of the convicts, "Let them die and be damned, the owners have [already] been paid for their passage."[1]

The British public had no love for the convicts, but it wasn't prepared to give them a death sentence either. Newspapers edito-rialized in favor of better conditions, clergy appealed to the cap-tains' sense of humanity, and legislators passed regulations requiring better food and water, light and air, and proper medical care. Yet the death rate remained shockingly high. Nothing appeared to be working until an economist suggested something new. Can you guess what the economist suggested?

Instead of paying the captains for each prisoner placed on board ship in Great Britain, the economist suggesting paying for each prisoner that walked off the ship in Australia. In 1793, the new system was implemented and im-mediately the survival rate shot up to 99%. One astute observer explained what had happened: "Economy beat sentiment and benevolence."[2]

The story of the convict ships illustrates the first big lesson that runs through-out this book and throughout economics: *incentives matter.*

By **incentives,** we mean rewards and penalties that motivate behavior. Let's take a closer look at incentives and some of the other big ideas in economics. On first reading, some of these ideas may seem surprising or difficult to under-stand. Don't worry: we will be explaining everything in more detail.

Incentives are rewards and penalties that motivate behavior.

1

We see the following list as the most important and fundamental contributions of economics to human understanding; we call these contributions **Big Ideas**. Some economists might arrange this list in a different manner or order, but these are generally accepted principles among good economists everywhere.

Big Idea One: Incentives Matter

When the captains were paid for every prisoner that they took on board, they had little incentive to treat the prisoners well. In fact, the incentives were to treat the prisoners badly. Instead of feeding the prisoners, for example, some of the captains hoarded the prisoners' food, selling it in Australia for a tidy profit.

When the captains were paid for prisoners who survived the journey, however, their incentives changed. Whereas before, the captains had benefited from a prisoner's death, now the incentive system "secured to every poor man who died at least one sincere mourner."[3] The sincere mourner? The captain, who was at least sincere about mourning the money he would have earned had the poor man survived.

Incentives are everywhere. In the United States, we take it for granted that when we go to the supermarket, the shelves will be stocked with kiwi fruit from New Zealand, rice from India, and wine from Chile. Every day we rely on the work of millions of other people to provide us with food, clothing, and shelter. Why do so many people work for our benefit? In his 1776 classic, *The Wealth of Nations*, Adam Smith explained:

> It is not from the benevolence of the butcher, the brewer, or the baker,
> that we expect our dinner, but from their regard to their own interest.

Do economists think that everyone is self-interested all the time? Of course not. We love our spouses and children just like everyone else! But economists do think that people respond in predictable ways to incentives of all kinds. Fame, power, reputation, sex, and love are all important incentives. Economists even think that benevolence responds to incentives. It's not surprising to an economist, for example, that charities publicize the names of their donors. Some people do give anonymously, but how many buildings on your campus are named Anonymous Hall?

Big Idea Two: Good Institutions Align Self-Interest with the Social Interest

The story of the convict ships hints at a second lesson that runs throughout this book: When self-interest aligns with the broader public interest, we get good outcomes, but when self-interest and the social interest are at odds, we get bad outcomes, sometimes even cruel and inhumane outcomes. Paying the ship captains for every prisoner who walked off the ship was a good payment system because it created incentives for the ship captains to do the right thing, not just for themselves but also for the prisoners and for the government that was paying them.

It's a remarkable finding of economics that under the right conditions markets align self-interest with the social interest. You can see what we mean by thinking back to the supermarket we mentioned above. The supermarket is stocked with products from around the world because markets channel and co-ordinate the self-interest of millions of people to achieve a social good. The farmer who awoke at 5 AM to tend his crops, the trucker who delivered the goods to the market, the entrepreneur who risked his or her capital to build the supermarket—each of these people acted in their own interest, but in so doing, they also acted in your interest.

In a striking metaphor, Adam Smith said that when markets work well, those who pursue their own interest end up promoting the social interest, as if led to do so by an "invisible hand." The idea that the pursuit of self-interest can be in the social interest—that at least sometimes, "greed is good"—was one of the most surprising discoveries of economic science, and after several hundred years this insight is still not always appreciated. Throughout this book, we emphasize ways in which individuals acting in their self-interest produce outcomes that were not part of their intention nor design, but which never-theless have desirable properties.

Markets, however, do not always align self-interest with the social interest. Sometimes the invisible hand is absent, not just invisible. Market incentives, for example, can be too strong. A firm that doesn't pay for the pollution that it emits into the air has too great an incentive to emit pollution. Fishermen sometimes have too strong an incentive to catch fish, thereby driving the stock of fish into collapse. In other cases, market incentives are too weak. Did you get your flu shot this year? The flu shot prevents you from getting the flu (usually) but it also reduces the chances that other people will get the flu. When deciding whether to get a flu shot, did you take into account the social interest or just your self-interest?

When markets don't properly align self-interest with the social interest, an-other important lesson of economics is that government can sometime improve the situation by changing incentives with taxes, subsidies, or other regulations.

Big Idea Three: Trade-offs Are Everywhere

Vioxx users were outraged when in September 2004 Merck withdrew the ar-thritis drug from the market; at the time a new study showed that Vioxx could cause strokes and heart attacks. Vioxx had been on the market for five years and had been used by millions of people. Patients were angry at Merck and at the Food and Drug Administration (FDA). How could the FDA, which is charged with ensuring that new pharmaceuticals are safe and effective, have let Vioxx onto the market? Many people demanded more testing and safer phar-maceuticals. Economists worried that approved pharmaceuticals could become too safe.

Too safe! Is it possible to be too safe?! Yes, because trade-offs are every-where. Researching, developing, and testing a new drug cost time and re-sources. On average, it takes about 12 years and $900 million to bring a new drug to market. More testing means that approved drugs will have fewer side effects, but there are two important trade-offs: *drug lag* and *drug loss*.

Testing takes time so more testing means that good drugs are delayed, just like bad drugs. On average, new drugs work better than old drugs. So the longer it takes to bring new drugs to market, the more people are harmed who could have benefited if the new drugs had been approved earlier.[4] You can die because an unsafe drug is approved—you can also die because a safe drug has *not yet* been approved. This is *drug lag*.

Testing not only takes time, it is costly. The greater the costs of testing, the fewer new drugs there will be. The costs of testing are a hurdle that each potential drug must leap if it is to be developed. Higher costs mean a higher hurdle, fewer new drugs and fewer lives saved. You can die because an unsafe drug is approved—you can also die because a safe drug is *never* developed. This is *drug loss*.

Thus, society faces a trade-off. More testing means the drugs that are (eventually) approved will be safer but it also means more drug lag and drug loss. When thinking about FDA policy, we need to look at both sides of the trade-off if we are to choose wisely.

Trade-offs are closely related to another important idea in economics, opportunity cost.

Opportunity Cost

The **opportunity cost** of a choice is the value of the opportunities lost.

Every choice involves something gained and something lost. The **opportunity cost** of a choice is the value of the opportunities lost. Consider the choice to attend college. What is the cost of attending college? At first, you might calculate the cost by adding together the price of tuition, books, and room and board—that might be $15,000 a year. But that's not the opportunity cost of attending college. What opportunities are you losing when you attend college?

The main opportunity lost when you attend college is (probably) the opportunity to have a full-time job. Most of you reading this book could easily get a job earning $25,000 a year or maybe quite a bit more (Bill Gates was a college dropout). If you spend four years in college, that's $100,000 that you are giving up to get an education. The opportunity cost of college is probably higher than you thought. Perhaps you ought to ask more questions in class to get your money's worth! (But go back to the list of items we totaled earlier—tuition, books, and room and board—one of these items should *not* count as part of the opportunity cost of college. Which one? Answer: Room and board is not a cost of college if you would have to pay for it whether you go to college or not.)

The concept of opportunity cost is important for two reasons. First, if you don't understand the opportunities you are losing when you make a choice, you won't recognize the real trade-offs that you face. Recognizing trade-offs is the first step to making wise choices. Second, most of the time people do respond to changes in opportunity costs—*even when money costs have not changed*—so if you want to understand behavior, you need to understand opportunity cost.

What would you predict, for example, would happen to college enrollment during a recession? The price of tuition, books, and room and board doesn't fall during a recession but the opportunity cost of attending college does fall. Why? During a recession, the unemployment rate increases so it's harder to get a high-paying job. That means you lose less by attending college when the unemployment rate is high. We, therefore, predict that college enrollments increase when the unemployment rate increases; in opportunity costs terms, it is cheaper to go to college. Figure 1.1 shows that this is correct—when the unemployment rate is unusually high (above trend), the college enrollment rate tends to be unusually high as well. The reverse is also true: When the economy is booming and the unemployment rate is unusually low, the college enrollment rate tends to be low as well. Of course, many other factors other than the unemployment rate influence college enrollment rates so the relationship

FIGURE 1.1

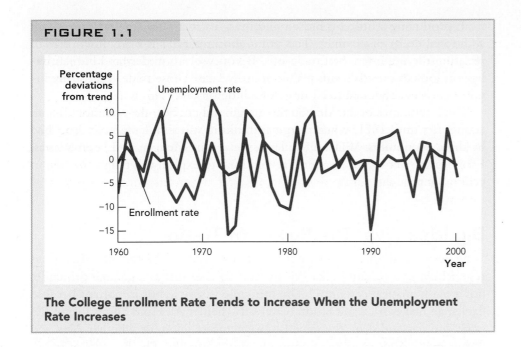

The College Enrollment Rate Tends to Increase When the Unemployment Rate Increases

is not exact, but Figure 1.1 shows that as a general tendency, the enrollment rate tends to be unusually high when the unemployment rate is unusually high.

Big Idea Four: Thinking on the Margin

Robert is cruising down Interstate-80 toward Des Moines, Iowa. Robert wants to get to his destination quickly and safely and he doesn't want to get a speeding ticket. The speed limit is 70 mph but he figures the risk of a ticket is low if he travels just a little bit faster, so Robert sets the cruise control to 72 mph. The road is straight and flat, and after 20 minutes he hasn't seen another car, so he thumbs it up a few clicks to 75. As he approaches Des Moines, Robert spots a police cruiser and thumbs it down to 70. After Des Moines it's nothing but quiet corn fields once again, so he thumbs it up to 72. Crossing the state line into Nebraska, Robert notices that the speed limit is 75, so he thumbs it up to 77 before thumbing it down again as he approaches Omaha.

Robert and his thumb illustrate what economists mean by thinking on the margin. As Robert drives, he constantly weighs benefits and costs and makes a decision: A little bit faster or a little bit slower?

Thinking on the margin is just making choices by thinking in terms of marginal benefits and marginal costs, the benefits and costs of a little bit more (or a little bit less). Most of our decisions in life involve a little bit more of something or a little bit less, and it turns out that thinking on the margin is also useful for understanding how consumers and producers make decisions. Should the consumer buy a few more apples or a few less? Should the oil well produce a few more barrels of oil or a few less?

In this book, you will find lots of talk about marginal choices, which includes marginal cost (the additional cost from producing a little bit more), marginal revenue (the additional revenue

Thinking on the margin: A little bit faster? Or a little bit slower?

from producing a little bit more), and marginal tax rates (the tax rate on an additional dollar of income). This point about margins is really just a way of restating the importance of trade-offs. If you wish to understand human behavior, look at the trade-offs people actually face. Those trade-offs usually involve choices about a little bit more or a little bit less.

The importance of thinking on the margin did not become commonplace in economics until 1871, when marginal thinking was simultaneously described by three economists: William Stanley Jevons, Carl Menger, and Leon Walras. Economists refer to the "marginal revolution" to explain this transformation in economic thought.

Big Idea Five: The Power of Trade

When Alex and Shruti trade, both of them are made better off. (Alex does regret buying a certain polka-dot sweater so take this as a general principle, not a mathematical certainty.) The principle is simple but important because exchange makes Alex and Shruti better off whether Alex and Shruti live in the same country and share the same language and religion, or whether Alex and Shruti live worlds apart geographically and culturally. The benefits of trade, however, go beyond those of exchange. The real power of trade is the power to increase production through specialization.

Few of us could survive if we had to produce our own food, clothing, and shelter (let alone our own cell phones and jet aircraft). Self-sufficiency is death. We survive and prosper only because specialization increases productivity. With specialization, the auto mechanic learns more about cars and the thoracic surgeon learns more about hearts than either could if each one of them needed to repair both cars and hearts. Through the division of knowledge, the sum total of knowledge increases and in this way so does productivity.

Trade also allows us to take advantage of economies of scale, the reduction in costs created when goods are mass-produced. No farmer could ever afford a combine thresher if he was growing wheat only for himself, but when a farmer grows wheat for thousands, a combine thresher reduces the cost of bread for all.

A surprising feature of trade is that everyone can benefit from trade, even those who are not especially productive. The reason is that especially productive people can't do everything! Martha Stewart may be able to iron a blouse better than anyone else in the world, but she still hires people to do her ironing because for her an hour of ironing comes at the price of an hour spent running her business. Given the choice of spending an hour ironing or running her business, Martha Stewart is better off running her business. In other words, Martha Stewart's *opportunity cost* of ironing is very high.

The theory of comparative advantage says that when people or nations specialize in goods in which they have a low opportunity cost, they can trade to mutual advantage. Thus, Martha Stewart can benefit by buying ironing services even from people who are not as good at ironing as she is. Notice that the better Martha Stewart gets at running her business, the greater her cost of ironing. So when Martha becomes more productive, this increases her demand to trade. In a similar way, the greater the productivity of American business in producing jet aircraft or designing high-technology devices, the greater will be our demand to trade for textiles or steel ingots.

Big Idea Six: The Importance of Wealth and Economic Growth

Every year, several hundred million people contract malaria. In mild cases, malaria causes extensive fever, chills, and nausea. In severe cases, malaria can cause kidney failure, coma, brain damage and, for about a million people a year—mostly children—death. Today, we think of malaria as a "tropical" disease but malaria was once common in the United States. George Washington caught malaria, as did James Monroe, Andrew Jackson, Abraham Lincoln, Ulysses S. Grant, and James A. Garfield. Malaria was present in America until the late 1940s, when the last cases were wiped out by better drainage, removal of mosquito breeding sites, and the spraying of insecticides. The lesson? Wealth—the ability to pay for the prevention of malaria—ended malaria in the United States and wealth comes from economic growth, so the incidence of malaria is not just about geography—it's also about economics.

Malaria is far from the only problem that diminishes with wealth and economic growth. In the United States, one of the world's richest countries, 993 out of every 1,000 children born survive to the age of 5. In Liberia, one of the world's poorest countries, only about 765 children survive to age 5 (i.e., 235 of every 1,000 children die before seeing their fifth birthday). Overall, it's the wealthiest countries that have the highest rates of infant survival.

Indeed, if you look at most of the things that people care about, they are much easier to come by in wealthier economies. Wealth brings us flush toilets, antibiotics, higher education, the ability to choose the career we want, fun vacations, and of course a greater ability to protect our families against catastrophes. Wealth also brings women's rights and political liberty, at least in most (but not all) countries. Wealthier economies lead to richer and more fulfilled human lives. In short, *wealth matters, and understanding economic growth is one of the most important tasks of economics.*

Big Idea Seven: Institutions Matter

If wealth is so important, what makes a country rich? The most proximate cause is that wealthy countries have lots of physical and human capital per worker and they produce things in a relatively efficient manner, using the latest technological knowledge. But why do some countries have more physical and human capital and why is it organized well using the latest technological knowledge? In a word, incentives, which of course brings us back to Big Idea One.

Entrepreneurs, investors, and savers need incentives to save and invest in physical capital, human capital, innovation, and efficient organization. Among the most powerful institutions for supporting good incentives are property rights, political stability, honest government, a dependable legal system, and competitive and open markets.

Consider South and North Korea. South Korea has a per capita income more than 10 times greater than its immediate neighbor, North Korea. South Korea is a modern, developed economy but in North Korea people still starve or can go for months without eating meat. And yet both countries were equally poor in 1950 and, of course, the two countries share the same language and cultural and historical background. What differs is their economic systems and the incentives at work.

Macroeconomists are especially interested in the incentives to produce new ideas. If the world never had any new ideas, the standard of living eventually would stagnate. But entrepreneurs innovate with iPhones, soil fertilizer, the Prius, and many other discoveries. Just about any device you use in daily life is based on a multitude of ideas and innovations, the life-blood of economic growth. New ideas, of course, require incentives and that means an active scientific community and the freedom and incentive to put new ideas into action. Ideas also have peculiar properties. One apple feeds one man but one idea can feed the world. Ideas, in other words, aren't used up when they are used and that has tremendous implications for understanding the benefits of trade, the future of economic growth, and many other topics.

Big Idea Eight: Economic Booms and Busts Cannot Be Avoided but Can Be Moderated

We have seen that growth matters and that the right institutions foster growth. But no economy grows at a constant pace. Economies advance and recede, rise and fall, boom and bust. In a recession, wages fall and many people are thrown into miserable unemployment. Unfortunately, we cannot avoid all recessions. Booms and busts are part of the normal response of an economy to changing economic conditions. When the weather is bad in India, for example, crops fail and the economy grows more slowly or perhaps it grows not at all. The weather doesn't much affect the economy in the United States, but the U.S. economy is buffeted by other unavoidable shocks.

Although some booms and busts are part of the normal response of an economy to changing economic conditions, not all booms and busts are normal. The Great Depression (1929–1940) was not normal, but rather it was the most catastrophic economic event in the history of the United States. National output plummeted by 30 percent, unemployment rates exceeded 20 percent, and the stock market fell to less than a third of its original value. Almost overnight the United States went from confidence to desperation. The Great Depression, however, didn't have to happen. Most economists today believe that if the government, especially the U.S. Federal Reserve, had acted more quickly and more appropriately, the Great Depression would have been shorter and less deep. At the time, however, the tools at the government's disposal—monetary and fiscal policy—were not well understood.

Today, the tools of monetary and fiscal policy are much better understood. When used appropriately, these tools can reduce swings in unemployment and GDP. Unemployment insurance can also reduce some of the misery that accompanies a recession. The tools of monetary and fiscal policy, however, are not all-powerful. At one time it was thought that these tools could end all recessions, but we know now that this is not the case. Furthermore, when used poorly, monetary and fiscal policy can make recessions worse and the economy more volatile.

A significant task of macroeconomic theory is to understand both the promise and the limits of monetary and fiscal policy in smoothing out the normal booms and busts of the macroeconomy.

Big Idea Nine: Prices Rise When the Government Prints Too Much Money

Yes, economic policy can be useful but sometimes policy goes awry, for instance, when **inflation** gets out of hand. Inflation, one of the most common problems in macroeconomics, refers to an increase in the general level of prices. Inflation makes people feel poorer but, perhaps more important, rising and especially volatile prices make it harder for people to figure out the real values of goods, services, and investments. For these and other reasons, most people (and economists) dislike inflation.

Inflation is an increase in the general level of prices.

But where does inflation come from? The answer is simple: Inflation comes about when there is a sustained increase in the supply of money. When people have more money, they spend it, and without an increase in the supply of goods, prices must rise. As Nobel laureate Milton Friedman once wrote: "Inflation is always and everywhere a monetary phenomenon."

The United States, like other advanced economies, has a central bank that in the United States is called the Federal Reserve. The Federal Reserve has the power and the responsibility to regulate the supply of money in the American economy. This power can be used for good, such as when the Federal Reserve holds off or minimizes a recession. But the power also can be used for great harm if the Federal Reserve encourages too much growth in the supply of money. The result will be inflation and economic disruption.

In Zimbabwe, the government ran the printing presses at full speed for many years. By the end of 2007, prices were rising at an astonishing rate of 150,000 percent per year. The United States has never had a problem of this scope or anything close to it but inflation remains a perennial concern.

Amazingly, the inflation rate in Zimbabwe kept rising. In January of 2008, the government had to issue a 10 million dollar bank note (worth about 4 U.S. dollars) and a year later they announced a 20 *trillion* dollar note that bought about what 10 million dollars had a year earlier. In early 2009, the inflation rate leaped to billions of percent per month! Finally, in April of 2009 the government stopped issuing the Zimbabwean dollar altogether and permitted trade using foreign currencies such as the South African rand and U.S. dollar.

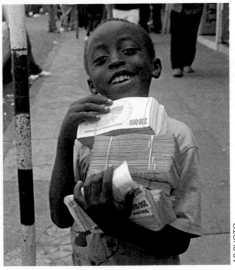

A billionaire in Zimbabwe

Big Idea Ten: Central Banking Is a Hard Job

The U.S. central bank, the Federal Reserve Bank ("the Fed"), is often called on to combat recessions. But this is not always easy to do. Typically, there is a lag—often of many months—between when the Fed makes a decision and when the effects of that decision on the economy are known. In the meantime, economic conditions have changed so you should think of the Fed as shooting at a moving target. No one can foresee the future perfectly and so the Fed's decisions are not always the right ones.

As mentioned above, too much money in the economy means that inflation will result. But not enough money in the economy is bad as well and can lead to a recession or a slowing of economic growth. These ideas are an important and extensive topic in macroeconomics, but the key problem is that a low or falling money supply forces people to cut their prices and wages and this adjustment doesn't always go smoothly.

The Fed is always trying to get it "just right," but some of the time it fails. Sometimes the failure is a mistake the Fed could have avoided, but other times it simply isn't possible to always make the right guess about where the world is headed. Thus, in some situations the Fed must accept a certain amount of either inflation or unemployment. Central banking relies on economic tools, but in the final analysis it is as much an art as a science.

Most economists think that the Fed does more good than harm. But if you are going to understand the Fed, you have to think of it as a highly fallible institution that faces a very difficult job.

The Biggest Idea of All: Economics Is Fun

When you put all these ideas and others together, you see that economics is both exciting and important. Economics teaches us how to make the world a better place. It's about the difference between wealth and poverty, work and unemployment, happiness and squalor. Economics increases your understanding of the distant past, present events, and future possibilities.

As you will see, the basic principles of economics hold everywhere, whether it is in a rice paddy in Vietnam or a stock market in São Paulo, Brazil. No matter what the topic, the principles of economics apply to all countries, not just to your own. Moreover, in today's globalized world, events in China and India influence the economy in the United States, and vice versa. For this reason, you will find that our book is truly international and full of examples and applications from Algeria to Zimbabwe.

But economics is also linked to everyday life. Economics can help you think about your quest for a job, how to manage your personal finances, and how to deal with debt, inflation, a recession, or a bursting stock market bubble. In short, economics is about understanding your world.

We are excited about economics and we hope that you will be too. Perhaps some of you will even become economics majors. If you are thinking about majoring, you might want to know that a bachelors degree in economics is one of the best-paying degrees, with starting salaries just behind chemical and nuclear engineering. That reflects the value of an economics degree and the world's recognition of that value. But if your passion lies elsewhere, that's okay too; a course in the principles of economics will take you a long way toward understanding your world. With a good course, a good professor, and a good textbook, you'll never look at the world the same way again. So just remember: *See the Invisible Hand. Understand Your World.*

▫ CHAPTER REVIEW

KEY CONCEPTS

Incentives, p. 1

Opportunity cost, p. 4

Inflation, p. 9

FACTS AND TOOLS

1. A headline[5] in the *New York Times* read: "Study Finds Enrollment Is Up at Colleges Despite Recession." How would you rewrite this headline now that you understand the idea of opportunity cost?

2. When bad weather in India destroys the crop harvest, does this sound like a fall in the total "supply" of crops or a fall in people's "demand" for crops? Keep your answer in mind as you learn about economic booms and busts later on.

3. How much did national output fall during the Great Depression? According to the chapter, which government agency might have helped to avoid much of the Great Depression had it acted more quickly and appropriately?

4. The chapter lists four things that entrepreneurs save and invest in. Which of the four are actual objects, and which are more intangible, like concepts or ideas or plans? Feel free to use Wikipedia or some other reference source to get definitions of unfamiliar terms.

5. Who has a better incentive to work long hours in a laboratory researching new cures for diseases: a scientist who earns a percentage of the profits from any new medicine she might invent, or a scientist who will get a handshake and a thank you note from her boss if she invents a new medicine?

6. In the discussion of Big Idea Five, the chapter says that "self-sufficiency is death" because most of us would not be able to produce for ourselves the food and shelter that we need to survive. In addition to *death*, however, one could also say that self-sufficiency is *boredom* or *ignorance*. How does specialization and trade help you to avoid boredom and ignorance?

THINKING AND PROBLEM SOLVING

1. In recent years, Zimbabwe has had hyperinflation, with prices tripling (or more!) every month. According to what you learned in this chapter, what do you think the government can do to end this hyperinflation?

2. Some people worry that machines will take jobs away from people, making people permanently unemployed. In the United States, only 150 years ago most people were farmers. Now, machines do almost all of the farm work and fewer than 2% of Americans are farmers, yet that 2% produces enough food to feed the entire country while still exporting food overseas.

   a. What happened to all of those people who used to work on farms? Do you think most adult males in the United States are unemployed nowadays, now that farm work is gone?

   b. Some people say that it's okay for machines to take jobs, since we'll get jobs fixing the machines. Just from looking around, do you think that most working Americans are earning a living by fixing farm equipment? If not, what do you think most working people are doing instead? (We'll give a full answer later in this book.)

3. Let's connect Big Ideas Six and Nine: Do you think that people in poor countries are poor because they don't have enough money? In other words, could a country get richer by printing more pieces of paper called "money" and handing those out to its citizens?

4. Nobel Prize winner Milton Friedman said that a bad central banker is like a "fool in the shower." In a shower, of course, when you turn the faucet, water won't show up in the showerhead for a few seconds. So if a "fool in the shower" is always making big changes in the temperature based on how the water feels *right now*, the water is likely to swing back and forth between too hot and too cold. How does this apply to central banking?

5. According to the United Nations, there were roughly 300 million humans on the planet a thousand years ago. Essentially all of them were poor by modern standards: They lacked antibiotics, almost all lacked indoor plumbing, and none traveled faster than a horse or a river could carry them. Today, between 1 and

3 billion humans are poor out of about 7 billion total humans. So, over the last thousand years, what has happened to the *fraction* of humans who are poor: Did it rise, fall, or stay about the same? What happened to the total *number* of people living in deep poverty: Rise, fall, or no change?

CHALLENGES

1. We claim that part of the reason the Great Depression was so destructive is because economists didn't understand how to use government policy very well in the 1930s. In your opinion, do you think that economists during the Great Depression would have agreed? In other words, if you had asked them why the Depression was so bad, would they have said, "Because the government ignored our wise advice," or would they have said, "Because we don't have any good ideas about how to fix this"? What does your answer tell you about the confidence of economists and other experts?

2. Some problems that economists try to solve are easy *as economic problems* but hard *as political problems*. Medical doctors face similar kinds of situations: Preventing most deaths from obesity or lung cancer is easy *as a medical problem* (eat less, exercise more, don't smoke) but hard *as a self-control problem*. With this in mind, how is ending hyperinflation like losing 100 pounds?

3. As Nobel Prize winner and *New York Times* columnist Paul Krugman has noted, the field of economics is a lot like the field of medicine: They are fields where knowledge is limited (both are new as real scientific disciplines), and where many cures are quite painful ("opportunity cost"), but where regular people care deeply about the issues. What are some other ways that economics and medicine are alike?

4. Economics is sometimes called "the dismal science." Of the big ideas in this chapter, which sound "dismal"—like bad news?

2

The Power of Trade and Comparative Advantage

Chaos, conflict, and war may dominate the news, but it's heartening to know that there is also an astounding amount of world *cooperation*. The next time you are in your local supermarket, stop and consider how many people cooperated to bring the fruits of the world to your table: kiwis from New Zealand, dried apricots from Turkey, dates from Egypt, mangoes from Mexico, bananas from Guatemala. How is it that farmers in New Zealand wake up at 5 AM to work hard tending their fields so that you, on the other side of the world, may enjoy a kiwi with your fruit salad?

This chapter is about a central feature of our world, trade. It's about how you eat reasonably well every day yet have little knowledge of farming, it's about how you cooperate with people whom you will never meet, and it's about how civilization is made possible.

We will focus on three of the benefits of trade:

1. Trade makes people better off when preferences differ.

2. Trade increases productivity through specialization and the division of knowledge.

3. Trade increases productivity through comparative advantage.

Trade and Preferences

In September 1995, Pierre Omidyar, a 28-year old computer programmer, finished the code for what would soon become eBay. Searching around for a test item, Omidyar grabbed a broken laser pointer and posted it for sale with a starting price of $1. The laser pointer sold for $14.83. Astonished, Omidyar contacted the winning bidder to make sure he understood that the laser pointer was broken. "Oh yes," the bidder replied, "I am

13

eBay profits by making buyers and sellers happy.

a collector of broken laser pointers." At that instant, Omidyar knew eBay was going to be a huge success. Within just a few years, he would become one of the richest men in the United States.

Today, eBay operates in more than 30 countries and earns billions of dollars in revenue. eBay's revenues, however, are a small share of the total value that is created for the hundreds of millions of buyers and sellers who trade everything on eBay from children's toys to the original Hollywood sign. Trade creates value by moving goods from people who value them less to people who value them more. Sam, for example, was going to trash the old Fisher Price garage that his kids no longer play with. Instead, Sam sells it on eBay to Jen who pays $65.50. What had been worth nothing is now worth at least $65.50. Value has been created. Trade makes Sam better off, Jen better off, and it makes eBay, the market maker who brought Sam and Jen together, better off. Trade makes people with different preferences better off.

Specialization, Productivity, and the Division of Knowledge

Simple trades of the kind found on eBay create value, but the true power of trade is discovered only when people take the next step, specialization. In a world without trade, no one can afford to specialize. People will specialize in the production of a single good only when they are confident that they will be able trade that good for the many other goods that they need. Thus, as trade develops, so does specialization and specialization turns out to vastly increase productivity.

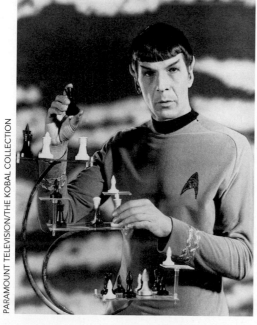

Contra Episode 61, even Spock's brain could not come close to running a modern economy. For this reason, some economists consider "Spock's Brain" to be the worst *Star Trek* episode *ever*.

How long could you survive if you had to grow your own food? Probably not very long. Yet most of us can earn enough money in a single day spent doing something other than farming to buy more food than we could grow in a year. Why can we get so much more food through trade than through personal production? The reason is that specialization greatly increases productivity. Farmers, for example, have two immense advantages in producing food compared to economics professors or students: Since they specialize, they know more about farming than other people, and because they sell large quantities, they can afford to buy large-scale farming machines. What is true for farming is true for just about every field of production—specialization increases productivity. Without specialization and trade, we would each have to produce our own food as well as other goods, and the result would be mass starvation and the collapse of civilization.

The human brain is limited and there is much to know. Thus, it makes sense to divide knowledge across many brains and then trade. In a primitive agricultural economy in which each person or household farms for themselves, each person has about the same knowledge as the person next door. In this case, the combined knowledge of a society of 1 million people barely exceeds that of a single person.[1] A society run with the knowledge of one brain is a poor and miserable society.

In a modern economy, many millions of times more knowledge is used than could exist in a single brain. In the United States, for example, we don't just have doctors—we have neurologists, cardiologists, gastroenterologists, gynecologists, and urologists, to name just a few of the many specializations in medicine. Knowledge increases productivity so specialization increases total output. All of this knowledge is productive, however, only because each person can specialize in the production of one good and then trade for all other desired goods. Without trade, specialization is impossible.

The extent of specialization in a modern economy explains why no one knows the full details of how even the simplest product is produced. A Valentine's Day rose may have been grown in Kenya, flown to Amsterdam on a refrigerated airplane, and trucked to Topeka by drivers staying awake with Colombian coffee. Each person in this process knows only a small part of the whole, but with trade and market coordination, they each do their part and the rose is delivered without anyone needing to understand the whole process.

The extent of specialization in modern society is remarkable. We have already mentioned the many specializations in medicine. We also have dog walkers, closet organizers, and manicurists. It's common to dismiss the latter jobs as frivolous, but trade connects all markets. It's the dog walkers, closet organizers, and manicurists who give the otolaryngologists—specialists in the nose, ear, and throat—the time they need to perfect their skills.

The division of knowledge increases with specialization and trade. Economic growth in the modern era is primarily due to the creation of new knowledge. Thus, one of the most momentous turning points in the division of knowledge happens when trade is extensive enough to support large numbers of scientists, engineers, and entrepreneurs, all of whom specialize in producing new knowledge.

Every increase in world trade is an opportunity to increase the division of knowledge and extend the power of the human mind. During the Communist era, for example, China was like an island cut off from the world economy: 1 billion people who neither traded many goods nor many ideas with the rest of the world. The fall of the Berlin Wall and the opening to the world economy of China, Russia, Eastern Europe, and other nations greatly adds to the productive stock of scientists and engineers and is one of the most promising signs for the future of the world. Billions of minds have been added to the division of knowledge and cooperation around the world has been extended further than ever before.

Consider the many ideas and innovations that make life better, from antibiotics, to high-yield, disease-resistant wheat, to the semiconductor. Insofar as those goods have originated in one place and then been spread around the world, improving the lives of millions or billions, it is because of trade.

Reducing trade barriers, Berlin 1989

REUTERS/CORBIS

Comparative advantage: It's a good thing

Martha Stewart may be the world's best ironer but she doesn't do her own ironing. Every hour Martha spends ironing is an hour less she has to run her billion-dollar business. The cost of ironing is too high for Martha Stewart, even if she is the world's best.

Martha can be most productive if she does what she does *most* best.

Absolute advantage is the ability to produce the same good using fewer inputs than another producer.

A **production possibilities frontier** shows all the combinations of goods that a country can produce given its productivity and supply of inputs.

Comparative Advantage

A third reason to trade is to take advantage of differences. Brazil, for example, has a climate ideally suited to growing sugar cane, China has an abundance of low-skilled workers, and the United States has one of the best-educated workforces in the world. Taking advantage of these differences suggests that world production can be maximized when Brazil produces sugar, China assembles iPads, and the United States devotes its efforts to designing the next generation of electronic devices.

Taking advantage of differences is even more powerful than it looks. We say that a country has an **absolute advantage** in production if it can produce the same good using fewer inputs than another country. But to benefit from trade, a country need not have an absolute advantage in production. For example, even if the United States did have the world's best climate for growing sugar, it might still make sense for Brazil to grow sugar and for the United States to design iPads, if the United States had a bigger advantage in designing iPads than it did in growing sugar.

Here's another example of what economists call comparative advantage. Martha Stewart doesn't do her own ironing. Why not? Martha Stewart may, in fact, be the world's best ironer but she is also good at running her business. If Martha spent more time ironing and less time running her business, her blouses might be pressed more precisely but that would be a small gain compared with the loss from having someone else run her business. It's better for Martha if she specializes in running her business and then trades some of her income for other goods, such as ironing services, and of course many other goods and services as well.

The Production Possibility Frontier

The idea of comparative advantage is subtle but important. In order to give a precise definition, let's explore comparative advantage using a simple model. Suppose that there are just two goods, computers and shirts, and one input, labor. Assume that in Mexico, it takes 12 units of labor to make one computer and 2 units of labor to produce one shirt, and suppose that Mexico has 24 units of labor. Mexico, therefore, can produce 2 computers and 0 shirts or 0 computers and 12 shirts, or they can have any combination of computers and shirts along the line in the left panel of Figure 2.1 labeled Mexico's PPF. Mexico's PPF, short for Mexico's **production possibilities frontier**, shows all the combinations of computers and shirts that Mexico can produce given its productivity and supply of inputs.

Similarly, assume that there are 24 units of labor in the United States but that in the United States it takes 1 unit of labor to produce either good. The U.S., therefore, can produce 24 computers and 0 shirts, or 0 computers and 24 shirts, or any combination along the U.S. PPF shown in the right panel of Figure 2.1.

In its simplest form, a PPF illustrates trade-offs. If Mexico wants to produce more shirts, it must produce fewer computers, and vice versa: It moves along its PPF. That's just another way of restating the fundamental principles of scarcity and opportunity cost.

FIGURE 2.1

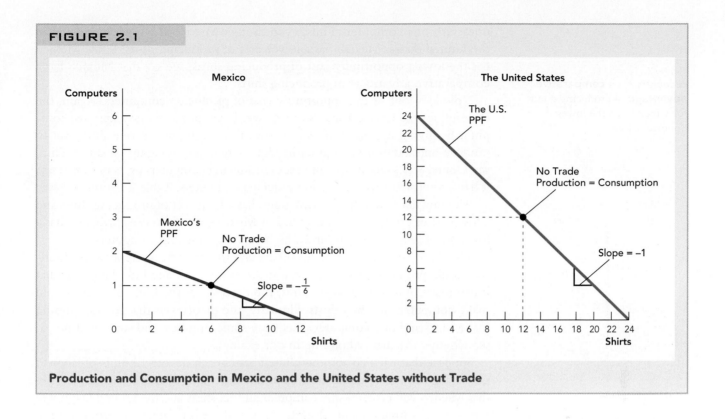

Production and Consumption in Mexico and the United States without Trade

Opportunity Costs and Comparative Advantage

In fact, there is a close connection between opportunity costs and the PPF. Looking first at the U.S. PPF in the right panel of Figure 2.1, notice that the slope, the rise over the run, is $-24/24 = -1$. In other words, for every additional shirt the United States produces, it must produce one fewer computer. One shirt has an opportunity cost of one computer and vice versa.

Now consider Mexico's PPF. The rise over the run is $-2/12 = -1/6$. In other words, for every additional shirt that Mexico produces, it must produce 1/6th less of a computer. Once again, the slope of the PPF tells us the opportunity cost. In Mexico one shirt costs 1/6th of a computer, or 1 computer costs 6 shirts. We summarize the opportunity costs in Table 2.1.

Now here is the key. The (opportunity) cost of a shirt in the United States is one computer but the (opportunity) cost of a shirt in Mexico is just

TABLE 2.1 Opportunity Costs

Country	Opportunity Cost of 1 Computer	Opportunity Cost of 1 Shirt	
Mexico	6 Shirts	1/6 of a Computer	Mexico is the low-cost producer of shirts.
United States	1 Shirt	1 Computer	

The United States is the low-cost producer of computers.

A country has a **comparative advantage** in producing goods for which it has the lowest opportunity cost.

one-sixth of a computer. Thus, even though Mexico is less productive than the United States, Mexico has a lower cost of producing shirts! Since Mexico has the lowest opportunity cost of producing shirts, we say that Mexico has a **comparative advantage** in producing shirts.

Now let's look at the opportunity cost of producing computers. Again, the trade-off for the United States is easy to see: It can produce one additional computer by giving up one shirt so the cost of one computer is one shirt. But to produce one additional computer in Mexico requires giving up six shirts! Thus, the United States has the lowest cost of producing computers or, economists say, it has a comparative advantage in producing computers. Table 2.1 summarizes.

We now know that the United States has a high cost of producing shirts and a low cost of producing computers. For Mexico, it's the reverse: Mexico has a low cost of producing shirts and a high cost of producing computers.

The theory of comparative advantage says that to increase its wealth a country should produce the goods it can make at low cost and buy the goods that it can make only at high cost. Thus, the theory says the United States should make computers and buy shirts. Similarly, the theory says that Mexico should make shirts and buy computers. Let's use some numbers and some pictures to see whether the theory holds up in our example.

Suppose that Mexico and the United States each devote 12 units of labor to producing computers and 12 units to producing shirts. We can see from the PPFs that Mexico will produce one computer and six shirts and the United States will produce 12 computers and 12 shirts. At first, there is no trade, so production in each country is equal to consumption. We show the production–consumption point of each country with a black dot in Figure 2.1. Now, can Mexico and the United States make themselves better off through trade? Yes.

Imagine that Mexico moves 12 units of its labor out of computer production and into shirt production. Thus, Mexico specializes completely by allocating all 24 units of its labor to shirt production, thereby producing 12 shirts. Similarly, suppose that the United States moves 2 units of its labor out of shirt production and into computers—thus producing 14 computers and 10 shirts. Production in Mexico and the United States is now shown by the green points in Figure 2.2.

So to finish the story, can you now see a way in which both Mexico and the United States can be made better off? Sure! Imagine that the United States trades one computer to Mexico in return for three shirts. Mexico is now able to consume one computer and nine shirts (three more shirts than before trade), while the United States is able to consume 13 computers (one more than before trade) and 13 shirts (one more than before trade).

Amazingly, both Mexico and the United States can now consume outside of their PPFs. In other words, before trade, Mexico could not have consumed one computer and nine shirts because this was outside of their PPF. Similarly, before trade, the United States could not have consumed 13 computers and 13 shirts. But with trade, countries are able to increase their consumption beyond the range that was possible without trade.

Thus, when each country produces according to its comparative advantage and then trades, total production and consumption increase. Importantly, both Mexico and the United States gain from trade even though the United States is more productive than Mexico at producing *both* computers and shirts.

The theory of comparative advantage not only explains trade patterns but it also tells us something remarkable: A country (or a person) will *always* be the low-cost seller of some good. The reason is clear: The greater the advantage

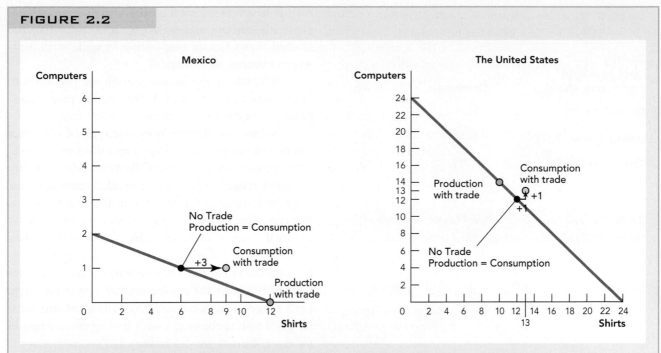

FIGURE 2.2

Production and Consumption in Mexico and the United States with Trade With no trade, Mexico produces and consumes 1 computer and 6 shirts and the United States produces and consumes 12 computers and 12 shirts. With specialization, Mexico produces 0 computers and 12 shirts and the United States produces 14 computers and 10 shirts. By trading 3 shirts for 1 computer, Mexico increases its consumption (compared to the no-trade situation) by 3 shirts and the United States increases its consumption by 1 computer and 1 shirt.

a country has in producing A, the greater the cost to it of producing B. If you are a great pianist, the cost to you of doing anything else is very high. Thus, the greater your advantages in being a pianist, the greater the incentive you have to trade with other people for other goods. It's the same way for countries. The more productive the United States is at producing computers, the greater its demand will be to trade for shirts. Thus, countries with high productivity can always benefit by trading with lower-productivity countries, and countries with lower productivity need never fear that higher-productivity countries will outcompete them in the production of all goods.

When people fear that a country can be outcompeted in everything, they are making a common mistake, namely confusing absolute advantage with comparative advantage. A producer has an absolute advantage over another producer if it can produce more output from the same input. But what makes trade profitable is differences in comparative advantage, and a country will always have some comparative advantage.

Thus, everyone can benefit from trade. From the world's greatest genius down to the person of below average ability, no person or country is so productive or so unproductive that they cannot benefit from inclusion in the worldwide division of labor. The theory of comparative advantage tells us something vital about world trade and about world peace. Trade unites humanity.

Comparative Advantage and Wages

Comparative advantage is a difficult story to grasp. Most of the world hasn't got it yet so don't be too surprised if it takes you some time as well. You

TABLE 2.2 Consumption in Mexico and the United States (No Specialization or Trade)

Country labor allocation (computers, shirts)	Computers	Shirts
Mexico (12, 12)	1	6
United States (12, 12)	12	12
Total Consumption	13	18

TABLE 2.3 Consumption in Mexico and the United States (Specialization and Trade)

Country	Computers	Shirts
Mexico	1	9 = 6 + 3
United States	13 = 12 + 1	13 = 12 + 1
Total Consumption	14	22

may at first be bothered by the fact that we did not explicitly discuss wages. Won't a country like the United States be uncompetitive in trade with low-wage countries like Mexico?

In fact, wages are in our model, we just need to bring them to the surface. Doing so will provide another perspective on comparative advantage.

In our model, there is only one type of labor that can be used to produce either computers or shirts. In a free market, all workers of the same type will earn the same wage.* So, in this model there is just one wage in Mexico and one wage in the United States. We can calculate the wage in Mexico by summing up the total value of *consumption* in Mexico and dividing by the number of workers.† We can perform a similar calculation for the United States. To do this, we need only a price for computers and a price for shirts. Let's suppose that computers sell for $300 and shirts for $100 (this is consistent with trading one computer for three shirts as we did earlier). Let's look first at the situation with no trade (see Table 2.2). The value of Mexican consumption is 1 × $300 plus 6 × $100 for a total of $900. Since there are 24 workers, the average wage is $37.50. The value of U.S. consumption is 12 × $300 + 12 × $100 = $4,800 so the U.S. wage is $200.

Now consider the situation with trade (see Table 2.3). The value of Mexican consumption is now 1 × $300 + 9 × $100 = $1,200 for a wage of $50, while the U.S. wage is now $216.67 (check it!). Wages in both countries have gone up, just as expected.

But notice that the wage in Mexico is lower than the wage in the United States, both before and after trade. The reason is that the productivity of labor is lower in Mexico. Ultimately, it's the productivity of labor that determines the wage rate. Specialization and trade let workers make the most of what they have—it raises wages as high as possible given productivity—but trade does not directly increase productivity.‡ Trade makes both Einstein and his less clever accountant better off, but it doesn't make the accountant a skilled scientist like Einstein.

In summary, workers in the United States often fear trade because they think that they cannot compete with low-wage workers in other countries. Meanwhile, workers in low-wage countries fear trade because they think that they cannot compete with high productivity countries like the United States! But differences in wages reflect differences in productivity. High-productivity countries

* In a free market, the same good will tend to sell for the same price everywhere. Imagine that the wages in computer manufacturing exceed the wages in shirt manufacturing. Everyone wants a higher wage so workers in the shirt industry will try to move to the computer industry. As the supply of workers in computer manufacturing increases, however, wages in the computer sector will fall. And, as the supply of workers in shirt manufacturing decreases, wages in that sector will increase. Only when workers of the same type are paid the same wage is there no incentive for workers to move.

† We calculate the value of consumption because at the end of the day workers care about what they consume, not what they produce.

‡ Trade can increase productivity by improving the division of knowledge, and diffusing information about advanced production techniques. These advantages of trade are important but the logic of comparative advantage does not require an increase in productivity.

have high wages, low-productivity countries have low wages. Trade means that workers in both countries can raise their wages to the highest levels allowed for by their respective productivities.

Adam Smith on Trade

Notice that we have so far talked about trade without distinguishing it much from "international trade." Adam Smith had an elegant summary connecting the argument for trade to that for international trade:

> It is the maxim of every prudent master of a family never to attempt to make at home what it will cost him more to make than to buy. The tailor does not attempt to make his own shoes, but buys them of the shoemaker. The shoemaker does not attempt to make his own clothes, but employs a tailor. What is prudence in the conduct of every private family can scarce be folly in that of a great kingdom. If a foreign country can supply us with a commodity cheaper than we ourselves can make it, better buy it of them with some part of the produce of our own industry employed in a way in which we have some advantage.[2]

BETTMANN/CORBIS

Adam Smith (1723–1790), author of the *Wealth of Nations* and one of the greatest economists of all time. When Smith could not finish teaching one semester, he told his students he would refund their tuition. When the students refused the refund saying they had learned so much already, Smith wept. We, however, will not refund the purchase price of this book even if you only read half of it. We are not as good economists as was Adam Smith.

Trade and Globalization

Having trouble understanding the theory of trade? GrowingStars.com offers online tutors who are available 24 hours a day, 7 days a week to help you understand difficult topics in economics.* GrowingStars tutors ought to understand international trade: The tutors live in India.[3]

Decreases in transportation costs, integration of world markets, and increased speed of communication have made the world a smaller place. But globalization is not new; rather, it has been a theme in human history since at least the Roman Empire, which knit together different parts of the world in a common economic and political area. When these trade networks later fell apart, the subsequent era was named "The Dark Ages."

Later, the European Renaissance arose from revitalized trade routes, the rebirth of commercially based cities, and also the spread of science from China, India, and the Middle East. Periods of increased trade, and the spread of ideas, have been among the best for human progress. As economist Donald Boudreaux puts it: "Globalization is the advance of human cooperation across national boundaries."[4]

☐ Takeaway

Simple trade makes people better off when preferences differ, but the true power of trade occurs when trade leads to specialization. Specialization creates enormous increases in productivity. Without trade, the knowledge used by an

CHECK YOURSELF

> What does specialization do to productivity? Why?

> How does trade let us benefit from the advantages of specialization?

> Alex Rodriguez is a premier baseball player. Being so athletic, he also would be very good at mowing his lawn, much better than Harry who mows lawns for a living. Why would Alex Rodriguez pay Harry to do his lawn rather than do it himself?

*We are using GrowingStars as an example of globalization. We have not evaluated the services of GrowingStars or any online tutors and make no recommendation for or against any such service.

entire economy is approximately equal to the knowledge used by one brain. With specialization and trade, the total sum of knowledge used in an economy increases tremendously and far exceeds that of any one brain.

International trade is trade across political borders. The theory of comparative advantage explains how a country, just like a person, can increase its standard of living by specializing in what it can make at low (opportunity) cost and trading for what it can make only at high cost. When we apply the logic of opportunity cost to trade, we discover that everyone has a comparative advantage in something so everyone can benefit from inclusion in the worldwide market.

□CHAPTER REVIEW

KEY CONCEPTS

Absolute advantage, p. 16

Production possibilities frontier, p. 16

Comparative advantage, p. 18

FACTS AND TOOLS

1. Use the idea of the "division of knowledge" to answer the following questions:

   a. Which country has more knowledge: Utopia, where in the words of Karl Marx, each person knows just enough about hunting, fishing, and cattle raising to "hunt in the morning, fish in the afternoon, [and] rear cattle in the evening," or Drudgia, where one-third of the population learns only about hunting, one-third only about fishing, and one-third only about cattle raising?

   b. Which planet has more knowledge: Xeroxia, each of whose 1 million inhabitants knows the same list of 1 million facts, or Differentia, whose 1 million inhabitants each know a different set of 1 million facts? How many facts are known in Xeroxia? How many facts are known in Differentia?

2. In the *Wealth of Nations*, Adam Smith said that one reason specialization makes someone more productive is because "a man commonly saunters a little in turning his hand from one sort of employment to another." How can you use this observation to improve your pattern of studying for your four or five college courses this semester?

3. "Opportunity cost" is one of the tougher ideas in economics. Let's make it easier by starting with some simple examples. In the examples below, find the opportunity cost: Your answer should be a *rate*, as in "1.5 widgets per year" or "6 lectures per month." Ignoring Adam Smith's insight from the previous question, assume that these relationships are simple linear ones, so that if you put in twice the time, you get twice the output, and half the time yields half the output.

   a. Erin has a choice between two activities: She can repair one transmission per hour or she can repair two fuel injectors per hour. What is the opportunity cost of repairing one transmission?

   b. Katie works at a customer service center and every hour she has a choice between two activities: answering 200 telephone calls per hour or responding to 400 emails per hour. What is the opportunity cost of responding to 400 phone calls?

   c. Deirdre has a choice between writing one more book this year or five more articles this year. What is the opportunity cost of writing half of a book this year, in terms of articles?

4. a. American workers are typically paid much more than Chinese workers. *True or false:* This is largely because American workers are typically more productive than Chinese workers.

   b. Julia Child, an American chef (and World War II spy) who reintroduced French cooking to Americans in the 1960s, was paid much more than most American chefs. *True or false:* This was largely because Julia Child was much more productive than most American chefs.

5. According to the *Wall Street Journal* (August 30, 2007, "In the Balance"), it takes about 30 hours to assemble a vehicle in the United States. Let's use that fact plus a few invented numbers to sum up the global division of labor in auto manufacturing. In international economics, "North" is shorthand for the high-tech developed countries of East Asia, North America, and Western Europe, while "South" is shorthand for the rest of the world. Let's use that shorthand here.

   a. Consider the productivity table below: Which region has an absolute advantage at making high-quality cars? And low-quality cars?

	Number of Hours to Make One High-Quality Car	Number of Hours to Make One Low-Quality Car
North	30	20
South	60	30

   b. Using the information in the productivity table above, estimate the opportunity cost of making high- or low-quality cars in the North and in the South. Which region has a comparative advantage (i.e., lowest opportunity cost) for manufacturing high-quality cars? For low-quality cars?

	Opportunity Cost of Making One High-Quality Car	Opportunity Cost of Making One Low-Quality Car
North	____ low-quality cars	____ high-quality cars
South	____ low-quality cars	____ high-quality cars

   c. There are 1 million hours of labor available for making cars in the North, and another 1 million hours of labor available for making cars in the South. In a no-trade world, let's assume that two-thirds of the auto industry labor in each region is used to make high-quality cars and one-third is used to make low-quality cars. Solve for how many of each kind of car will be produced in the North and South, and add up to determine the total global output of each type of car. (Why will both kinds of cars be made? Because the low-quality cars will be less expensive.)

	Output of High-Quality Cars	Output of Low-Quality Cars
North		
South		
Global output		

   d. Now, allow specialization. If each region completely specializes in the type of car in which it holds the comparative advantage, what will the global output of high-quality cars be? Of low-quality cars? In the table below, report your answers. Is global output in each kind of car higher than before? (We'll solve a problem with the final step of trade in the Thinking and Problem Solving section.)

	Output of High-Quality Cars	Output of Low-Quality Cars
North		
South		
Global output		

6. Conan O'Brien has been a talk show host since 1993, but he began his career in comedy as a writer: first at the *Harvard Lampoon* while in college, then eventually at *Saturday Night Live* and *The Simpsons*. Given that he is such an accomplished comedy writer, it might be surprising to learn that his current talk show staff includes over a dozen writers. How can you explain this using the material covered in the chapter? Is Conan not capable enough a writer to write his own show, or is there some other explanation? Suppose none of Conan's writers are as funny a writer as he is; is it still possible that hiring a writing staff makes the show funnier?

THINKING AND PROBLEM SOLVING

1. Fit each of the following examples into one of these reasons for trade:

   I. *Division of knowledge*

   II. *Comparative advantage*

   a. Two recently abandoned cats, Bingo and Tuppy, need to quickly learn how to catch mice in order to survive. If they also remain well groomed, they stand a better chance of surviving: Good grooming reduces the risk of disease and parasites. Each cat could go it alone, focusing almost exclusively on learning to catch mice. The alternative would be for Bingo to specialize in learning how to groom well and for Tuppy to specialize in learning how to catch mice well.

   b. Former President Bill Clinton, a graduate of Yale Law School, hires attorneys who are less skilled than himself to do routine legal work.

2. Nobel laureate Paul Samuelson said that comparative advantage is one of the few ideas in economics that is both "true and not obvious." Since it's not obvious, we should practice with it a bit. In each of the cases below, who has the absolute advantage at each task, and who has the comparative advantage?

   a. In 30 minutes, Kana can either make miso soup or she can clean the kitchen. In 15 minutes, Mitchell can make miso soup; it takes Mitchell an hour to clean the kitchen.

   b. In one hour, Ethan can bake 20 cookies or lay the drywall for two rooms. In one hour, Sienna can bake 100 cookies or lay the drywall for three rooms.

   c. Kara can build two glass sculptures per day or she can design two full-page newspaper advertisements per day. Sara can build one glass sculpture per day or design four full-page newspaper ads per day.

   d. Data can write 12 excellent poems per day or solve 100 difficult physics problems per day. Riker can write one excellent poem per day or solve 0.5 difficult physics problems per day.

3. The federal education reform law known as No Child Left Behind requires every state to create standardized tests that measure whether students have mastered key subjects. Since the same test is given to all students in the same grade in the state, this encourages all schools within a state to cover the same material. According to the division of knowledge model, what are the costs of this approach?

4. In this chapter, we've often emphasized how specialization and exchange can create more *output*. But sometimes the output from voluntary exchange is difficult to measure and doesn't show up in GDP statistics. In each of the following cases, explain how the two parties involved might be able to make themselves *both* better off just by making a voluntary exchange.

   a. Alan received two copies of *Gears of War* as birthday gifts. Burton received two copies of *Halo* as birthday gifts.

   b. Jeb has a free subscription to *Field and Stream* but isn't interested in hunting. George has a free subscription to the *Miami Herald* but isn't all that interested in Florida news.

   c. Pat has a lot of love to give, but it is worthless unless received by another. Terry is in the same sad situation.

5. Here's another specialization and exchange problem. This problem is wholly made-up, so that you won't be able to use your intuition about the names of countries or the products to figure out the answer.

   a. Consider the productivity table below: Which country has an absolute advantage at making rotids? At making taurons?

	Number of Hours to Make One Rotid	Number of Hours to Make One Tauron
Mandovia	50	100
Ducennia	150	200

   b. Using the information in the productivity table above, estimate the opportunity cost of making rotids and taurons in Mandovia and Ducennia. Which country has a comparative advantage at manufacturing rotids? At making taurons?

	Opportunity Cost of Making One Rotid	Opportunity Cost of Making One Tauron
Mandovia	____taurons	____rotids
Ducennia	____taurons	____rotids

c. There are 1 billion hours of labor available for making products in Mandovia, and 2 billion hours of labor available for making products in Ducennia. In a no-trade world, let's assume that half the labor in each country gets used to make each product. (In a semester-long international trade course, you'd build a bigger model that would determine just how the workers are divided up according to the forces of supply and demand.) Fill in the table.

	Output of Rotids	Output of Taurons
Mandovia		
Ducennia		
Total output		

d. Now, allow specialization. If each country completely specializes in the product in which it holds the comparative advantage, what will the total output of rotids be? Of taurons? Is total output of each product higher than before?

	Output of Rotids	Output of Taurons
Mandovia		
Ducennia		
Total output		

e. Finally, let's open up trade. Trade has to make both sides better off (or at least no worse off), and in this problem as in most negotiations, there's more than one price that can do so (just think about haggling over the price of a car or a house). Let's pick out a case that makes one side better off, and leaves the other side just as well off as in a no-trade world. The price both sides agree to is three rotids for two taurons. Ship 5 million taurons in one direction, and 7.5 million rotids in the other direction (you'll have to figure out on your own which way the trade flows). In the table below, calculate the amount that each country gets to consume. Which country is better off under this set of prices? Which one is exactly as well off as before?

	Consumption of Rotids	Consumption of Taurons
Mandovia		
Ducennia		
Total consumption		

f. This time, the trade negotiations turn out differently: It's two rotids for one tauron. Have the correct country ship 10 million rotids, have the other send 5 million taurons, and fill out the table below. One way to make sure you haven't made a mistake is to make sure that "total consumption" is equal to "total output" from part d: We can't create rotids and taurons out of thin air! Are both countries better off than if there were no trade? Which country likes this trade deal better than the deal from part e?

	Consumption of Rotids	Consumption of Taurons
Mandovia		
Ducennia		
Total consumption		

6. Many people talk about manufacturing jobs leaving the United States and going to other places, like China. Why isn't it possible for all jobs to leave the United States and go overseas (as some people fear)?

7. Suppose the table below shows the number of labor hours needed to produce airplanes and automobiles in the United States and South Korea, but one of the numbers is unknown.

	Number of Hours to Produce One Airplane	Number of Hours to Produce One Auto
South Korea	2,000	?
United States	800	5

a. Without knowing the number of labor hours required to produce an auto in South Korea, you can't figure out which country has the comparative advantage in which good. Can you give an example of a number for the empty cell of the table that would give the United States the comparative advantage in the production of airplanes? What about South Korea?

b. Who has the absolute advantage in the production of airplanes? What about autos?

c. What exact number would you have to place in the empty cell of the table for it to be impossible that trade between the United States and South Korea could benefit both nations?

CHALLENGES

1. In the computers and shirts example from the chapter, the United States traded one computer to Mexico in exchange for three shirts. This is not just an arbitrary ratio of shirts to computers, however. Let's explore the *terms of trade* a little bit more.

   a. Why is trading away a computer for three shirts a good trade for the United States? Why is it also a good deal for Mexico?

   b. What if instead the agreed upon terms of trade was one computer for eight shirts—would this trade still benefit both the U.S. and Mexico?

   c. What is the maximum (and minimum) number of shirts that a computer can trade for if the U.S. and Mexico are both to benefit from the trade?

2. Go to *www.Ted.com* and watch Thomas Thwaites's talk, "How I built a toaster—from scratch." How much money and time do you think Thwaites spent building his toaster? How long do you think it would have taken Thwaites to earn enough money in, say, a minimum wage job to buy a toaster? Comment on the division of labor and the importance of specialization in increasing productivity.

3

Supply and Demand

The world runs on oil. Every day about 82 *million* barrels of "black gold" flow from the earth and the sea to fuel the world's demand. Changes in the demand for and supply of oil can plunge one economy into recession while igniting a boom in another. In capitals from Washington to Riyadh, politicians carefully monitor the price of oil and so do ordinary consumers. Gasoline is made from oil so when world events like war in the Middle East disrupt the oil supply, prices at the corner gas station rise. The oil market is arguably the single most important market in the world.

The most important tools in economics are supply, demand, and the idea of equilibrium. Even if you understand little else, you may rightly claim yourself economically literate if you understand these tools. Fail to understand these tools and you will understand little else. In this chapter, we use the supply and demand for oil to explain the concepts of supply and demand. In the next chapter, we use supply, demand, and the idea of equilibrium to explain how prices are determined. So pay attention: This chapter and the next one are important. Really important.

The Demand Curve for Oil

How much oil would be demanded if the price of oil were $5 per barrel? What quantity would be demanded if the price were $20? What quantity would be demanded if the price were $55? A demand curve answers these questions. A **demand curve** is a function that shows the quantity demanded at different prices.

In Figure 3.1 on the next page, we show a hypothetical demand curve for oil and a table illustrating how a demand curve can be constructed from information on prices and quantities demanded. The demand curve tells us, for example, that at a price of $55 per barrel buyers are willing and able to buy

A **demand curve** is a function that shows the quantity demanded at different prices.

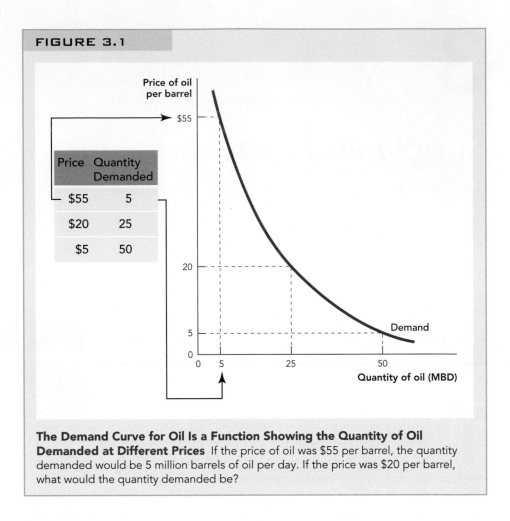

FIGURE 3.1

Price of oil per barrel

Price	Quantity Demanded
$55	5
$20	25
$5	50

The Demand Curve for Oil Is a Function Showing the Quantity of Oil Demanded at Different Prices If the price of oil was $55 per barrel, the quantity demanded would be 5 million barrels of oil per day. If the price was $20 per barrel, what would the quantity demanded be?

The **quantity demanded** is the quantity that buyers are willing and able to buy at a particular price.

5 million barrels of oil a day or, more simply, at a price of $55 the **quantity demanded** is 5 million barrels a day (MBD).

Demand curves can be read in two ways. Read "horizontally," we can see from Figure 3.2 that at a price of $20 per barrel demanders are willing and able to buy 25 million barrels of oil per day. Read "vertically," we can see that the maximum price that demanders are willing to pay for 25 million barrels of oil a day is $20 per barrel. Thus, demand curves tell us the quantity demanded at any price or the maximum willingness to pay (per unit) for any quantity. Some applications are easier to understand with one reading than with the other so you should be familiar with both.

Okay, a demand curve is a function that shows the quantity that demanders are willing to buy at different prices. But what does the demand curve *mean*? And why is the demand curve negatively sloped; that is, why is a greater quantity of oil demanded when the price is low?

Oil has many uses. A barrel of oil contains 42 gallons, and a little over half of that is used to produce gasoline (19.5 gallons) and jet fuel (4 gallons). The remaining 18.5 gallons are used for heating and energy generation and to make products such as lubricants, kerosene, asphalt, plastics, tires, and even rubber duckies (which are actually made not from rubber but from vinyl plastic).

Oil, however, is not equally valuable in all of its uses. Oil is more valuable for producing gasoline and jet fuel than it is for producing heating or rubber duckies. Oil is very valuable for transportation because in that use oil has few substitutes. There

FIGURE 3.2

Reading a Demand Curve in Two Different Ways
Horizontal Reading: At a price of $20 per barrel, buyers are willing to buy 25 million barrels of oil per day.
Vertical Reading: The maximum price that demanders are willing to pay to purchase 25 million barrels of oil per day is $20 per barrel.

is no reasonable substitute for oil as jet fuel, for example, and although some hybrids like the Prius are moderately successful, pure electric cars remain costly and inconvenient. There are more substitutes for oil in heating and energy generation. In these fields, oil competes directly or indirectly against natural gas, coal, and electricity. Within each of these fields are also more and less valuable uses. It's more valuable, for example, to raise the temperature in your house on a winter's day from 40 degrees to 65 degrees than it is to raise the temperature from 65 degrees to 70 degrees. Vinyl has high value as wire wrapping because it is fire retardant, but we can probably substitute wooden toy boats for rubber duckies.

The fact that oil is not equally valuable in all of its uses explains why the demand curve for oil has a negative slope. When the price of oil is high, consumers will choose to use oil *only* in its most valuable uses (e.g., gasoline and jet fuel). As the price of oil falls, consumers will choose to also use oil in its less and less valued uses (heating and rubber duckies). Thus, a demand curve summarizes how millions of consumers choose to use oil given their preferences and the possibilities for substitution. Figure 3.3 illustrates these ideas with a demand curve for oil.

FIGURE 3.3

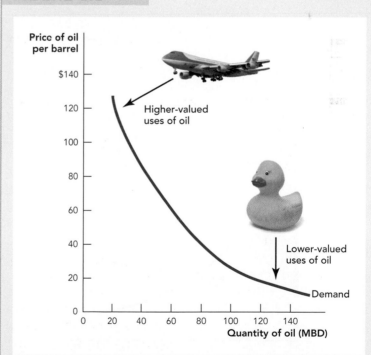

The Demand for Oil Depends on the Value of Oil in Different Uses When the price of oil is high, oil will only be used in its higher-valued uses. As the price of oil falls, oil will also be used in lower-valued uses.

(Top photo: EuroStyle Graphics/Alamy)
(Bottom: Lew Robertson/Corbis)

In summary, a demand curve is a function that shows the quantity that demanders are willing and able to buy at different prices. The lower the price, the greater the quantity demanded—this is often called the "law of demand."

Consumer Surplus

Consumer surplus is the consumer's gain from exchange, or the difference between the maximum price a consumer is willing to pay for a certain quantity and the market price.

Total consumer surplus is measured by the area beneath the demand curve and above the price.

If a consumer, say, the president of the United States, is willing to pay $80 per barrel to fuel his jet plane but the price of oil is only $20 per barrel, then the president earns a consumer surplus of $60 per barrel. If Joe is willing to pay $25 and the price of oil is $20 per barrel, then Joe earns a consumer surplus of $5 per barrel. **Consumer surplus** is the consumer's gain from exchange. Adding up consumer surplus for each consumer and for each unit, we can find **total consumer surplus.** On a graph, *total consumer surplus is the shaded area beneath the demand curve and above the price* (see Figure 3.4).

It's often convenient to approximate demand and supply curves with straight lines—this makes it easy to calculate areas like consumer surplus. The right panel of Figure 3.4 simplifies the left panel. Now we can calculate consumer surplus using a little high school geometry. Recall that the area of a triangle is $\frac{\text{base} \times \text{height}}{2}$. The base of the consumer surplus triangle is 90 million barrels and the height is $60 = \$80 - \$20$, so consumer surplus equals $2,700 million ($\frac{1}{2} \times 90$ million $\times \$60$).

FIGURE 3.4

Total Consumer Surplus Is the Area Beneath the Demand Curve and Above the Price
Total consumer surplus is the sum of consumer surplus of all buyers, the area beneath the demand curve and above the price. In the right panel, we show that consumer surplus is easy to calculate with a linear demand curve.

What Shifts the Demand Curve?

The demand curve for oil tells us the quantity of oil that people are willing to buy at a given price. Assume, for example, that at a price of $25 per barrel, the world demand for oil is 70 million barrels per day. An increase in demand means that at a price of $25, the quantity demanded increases to, say, 80 million barrels per day. Or, equivalently, it means that the maximum willingness to pay for 70 million barrels increases to say $50 per barrel. The left panel of Figure 3.5 shows an increase in demand. *An increase in demand shifts the demand curve outward, up and to the right.*

The right panel of Figure 3.5 shows a decrease in demand. *A decrease in demand shifts the demand curve inward, down and to the left.*

FIGURE 3.5

Shifting the Demand Curve An increase in demand shifts the demand curve outward, up and to the right. A decrease in demand shifts the demand curve inward, down and to the left.

What kinds of things will increase or decrease demand? Unfortunately for economics students, a lot of things! Here is a list of some important demand shifters:

Important Demand Shifters

> Income
> Population
> Price of substitutes
> Price of complements
> Expectations
> Tastes

If you must, memorize the list. But keep in mind the question, "What would make people willing to buy a greater quantity at the same price?" Or equivalently,

"What would make people willing to pay more for the same quantity?" With these questions in mind, you should always be able to come up with a fairly good list on your own.

Here are some examples of demand shifters in action.

Income When people get richer, they buy more stuff. In the United States, people buy bigger cars when their income increases and big cars increase the demand for oil. When income increases in China or India, many people buy their first car and that too increases the demand for oil. Thus, an increase in income will increase the demand for oil exactly as shown in the left panel of Figure 3.5.

> A **normal good** is a good for which demand increases when income increases.

When an *increase* in income *increases* the demand for a good, we say the good is a **normal good.** Most goods are normal; for example, cars, electronics, and restaurant meals are normal goods. Can you think of some goods for which an increase in income will *decrease* the demand? When we were young economics students, we didn't have a lot of money to go to expensive restaurants. For 50 cents and some boiling water, however, we could get a nice bowl of instant Ramen noodles. Ah, good times. When our income increased, however, our demand for Ramen noodles decreased—we don't buy Ramen noodles anymore! A good like Ramen noodles for which an *increase* in income *decreases* the demand is called an **inferior good.** What goods are you consuming now that you probably wouldn't consume if you were rich? Economic growth is rapidly increasing the incomes of millions of poor people in China and India. What goods do poor people consume in these countries today that they will consume less of 20 years from now?

> An **inferior good** is a good for which demand decreases when income increases.

Population More people, more demand. That's simple enough. Things get more interesting when some subpopulations increase more than others. The United States, for example, is aging. Today the 65-year-old and older crowd makes up about 13 percent of the population. By 2030, 19.4 percent of the population will be 65 years or older. In fact, demographers estimate that by 2030, 18.2 million people in the United States will be over 85 years of age![1] What sorts of goods and services will increase in demand with this increase in population? Which will decrease in demand? Entrepreneurs want to know the answers to these questions because big profits will flow to those who can anticipate new and expanded markets.

Demographics and Demand
The number of old people in the United States is increasing. How will this increase in the elderly population shift the demand curve for different goods?

Price of Substitutes Natural gas is a substitute for oil in some uses such as heating. Suppose that the price of natural gas goes down. What will happen to the quantity of oil demanded? When the price of natural gas goes down, some people will switch from oil furnaces to natural gas, so the quantity of oil demanded will decrease—the demand curve shifts down and to the left. Figure 3.6 illustrates.

More generally, a decrease in the price of a **substitute** will decrease demand for the other good. A decrease in the price of Pepsi, for example, will decrease the demand for Coca-Cola. A decrease in the price of rental apartments will reduce the demand for condominiums. Naturally, an increase in the price of a substitute will increase demand for the other substituted good.

> If two goods are **substitutes**, a decrease in the price of one good leads to a decrease in demand for the other good.

Price of Complements **Complements** are things that go well together: French fries and ketchup, sugar and tea, DVD movies and DVD players. More technically, good A is a complement to good B if greater consumption of A encourages greater consumption of B. Ground beef and hamburger buns are complements. Suppose the price of beef goes down. What happens to the demand for hamburger buns? If the price of beef goes down, people buy more ground beef and they also increase their demand for hamburger buns; that is,

> If two goods are **complements**, a decrease in the price of one good leads to an increase in the demand for the other good.

MARK HAMILTON/ZEFA/CORBIS

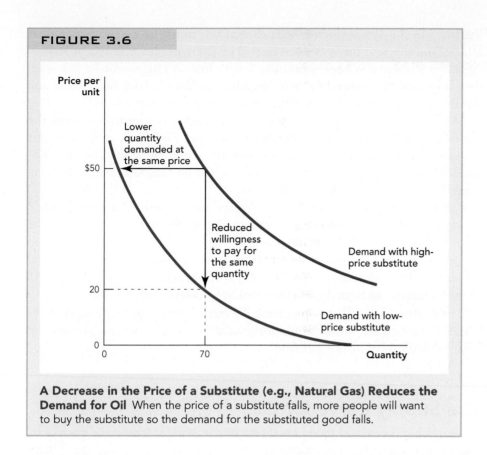

FIGURE 3.6

A Decrease in the Price of a Substitute (e.g., Natural Gas) Reduces the Demand for Oil When the price of a substitute falls, more people will want to buy the substitute so the demand for the substituted good falls.

the demand curve for hamburger buns shifts up and to the right. A supermarket having a sale on ground beef, for example, will also want to stock up on hamburger buns.

A decrease in the price of a complement increases the demand for the complementary good. An increase in the price of a complement decreases the demand for the complementary good. It sounds complicated, so just remember that ground beef and hamburger buns are complements and you should be able to work out the relationship.

Expectations In July 2007, a construction worker in the oil fields of southern Nigeria was kidnapped. On hearing the news, oil prices around the world jumped to record high levels.[2] Was a single construction worker so critical to the world supply of oil? No. What spooked the world's oil markets was the fear that the kidnapping was the beginning of large-scale disruption in the Niger Delta, Nigeria's main oil-producing region and the base for many anti-government rebels. Fear of future disruptions increased the demand for oil as businesses and governments worked to increase their emergency stockpiles. In other words, *the expectation of a reduction in the future oil supply increased the demand for oil today.*

You have probably responded to expectations about future events in a similar way. When the weather forecaster predicts a big storm, many people rush to the stores to stock up on storm supplies. In the week before Hurricane Katrina hit New Orleans, for example, sales of flashlights increased by 700 percent and battery sales increased by 250 percent compared with the week before.[3]

Expectations are powerful—they can be as powerful in affecting demand (and supply) as events themselves.

Tastes In the 1990s, doctors warned that too much fat could lead to heart attacks and demand for beef decreased. The 2001 publication of *Dr. Atkins' New Diet Revolution,* a book promising weight loss on a high-protein, low-carb diet, increased the demand for beef. Steakhouses like Outback Steakhouse and the Brazilian-inspired Fogo De Chão started to appear everywhere.

Michael Jordan's popularity and his six NBA championships with the Chicago Bulls created a huge increase in demand for Nike's innovative Air Jordans. Demand for the shoes was so high that some young boys became victims of "shoe jackings." Changes in tastes caused by fads, fashions, and advertising can all increase or decrease demand.

Can tastes change something like the demand for oil? Sure. The environmental movement has made people more aware of global climate change and how the consumption of oil adds carbon dioxide to the atmosphere. As a result, the demand for hybrid cars has increased, more people are recycling things like plastic bags, and nuclear power is once again being discussed as an alternative source of energy. All of these changes can be understood as a change in tastes or preferences.

The bottom line is that while many different factors can shape market demand, most of these factors should make intuitive sense. After all, you are, on a daily basis, part of market demand.

CHECK YOURSELF

> Economic growth in India is raising the income of Indian workers. What do you predict will happen to the demand for automobiles? What about the demand for charcoal bricks for home heating?

> As the price of oil rises, what do you predict will happen to the demand for mopeds?

The **supply curve** is a function that shows the quantity supplied at different prices.

The **quantity supplied** is the amount of a good that sellers are willing and able to sell at a particular price.

The Supply Curve for Oil

How much oil would oil producers supply to the world market if the price of oil were $5 per barrel? What quantity would be supplied if the price were $20? What quantity if the price were $55? A supply curve for oil answers these questions.

The **supply curve** for oil is a function showing the quantity of oil that suppliers would be willing and able to sell at different prices, or, more simply, the supply curve shows the **quantity supplied** at different prices. Figure 3.7 shows a hypothetical supply curve for oil. The price is on the vertical axis and the quantity of oil is on the horizontal axis. The table beside the graph shows how a supply curve can be constructed from a table of prices and quantities supplied.

The supply curve tells us, for example, that at a price of $20 the quantity supplied is 30 million barrels of oil a day.

As with demand curves, supply curves can be read in two ways. Read "horizontally," Figure 3.8 shows that at a price of $20 per barrel suppliers are willing to sell 30 million barrels of oil per day. Read "vertically," the supply curve tells us that to produce 30 million barrels of oil a day, suppliers must be paid at least $20 per barrel. Thus, the supply curve tells us the maximum quantity that suppliers will supply at different prices or the minimum price at which suppliers will sell different quantities. The two ways of reading a supply curve are equivalent, but some applications are easier to understand with one reading than with the other so you should be familiar with both.

Our hypothetical supply curve is not realistic because we just made up the numbers. But now that we know the technical meaning of a supply curve—*a function that shows the quantity that suppliers would be willing to sell at different prices*—we can easily explain its economic meaning.

Saudi Arabia, the world's largest oil producer, produces about 10 million barrels of oil per day. Surprisingly, the United States is not far behind, producing nearly 9 million barrels per day. But there is one big difference between Saudi oil and U.S. oil: U.S. oil costs much more to produce. The United States has

FIGURE 3.7

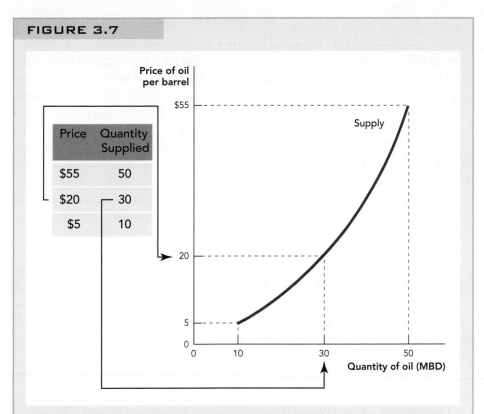

The Supply Curve for Oil Is a Function Showing the Quantity of Oil Supplied at Different Prices If the price of oil was $20 per barrel, the quantity of oil supplied would be 30 million barrels of oil per day. How much oil would suppliers be willing and able to sell at $55?

FIGURE 3.8

Reading a Supply Curve in Two Different Ways
Horizontal Reading: At a price of $20 per barrel, suppliers are willing to sell 30 million barrels of oil per day.
Vertical Reading: To produce 30 million barrels of oil a day, suppliers must be paid at least $20 per barrel.

been producing major quantities of oil since early 1901 when, after drilling to a depth of 1,020 feet, mud started to bubble out of an oil well dug in Spindletop, Texas. Minutes later the drill bit exploded into the air and a fountain of oil leapt 150 feet into the sky. It took nine days to cap the well, and in the process a million barrels of oil were spilt. No one had ever seen so much oil. Within months the price of oil dropped from $2 per barrel to just 3 cents per barrel.[4]

It's safe to say that the United States will never see another gusher like Spindletop. Today the typical new well in the United States is drilled to a depth of more than 1 mile. Instead of gushing, most of the wells must be pumped or flooded with water to push the oil to the surface.[5] All of this makes oil production in the United States much more expensive than it used to be and much more expensive than in Saudi Arabia, where oil is more plentiful than anywhere else in the world.

In Saudi Arabia, lifting a barrel of oil to the surface costs about $2. Costs in Iran and Iraq are only slightly higher. Nigerian and Russian oil can be extracted at a cost of around $5 and $7 per barrel, respectively. Alaskan oil costs around $10 to extract. Oil from Britain's North Sea costs about $12 to extract. There is more oil in Canada's tar sands than in all of Iran, but it costs about $22.50 per barrel to get the oil out of the sand.[6] In the continental United States, one of the oldest and most developed oil regions in the world, lifting costs are about $27.50. At a price of $40 per barrel, it becomes profitable to "sweat" oil out of Oklahoma oil shale.

Putting all of this together, we can construct a simple supply curve for oil. At a price of $2 per barrel, the only oil that would be profitable to produce would be oil from the lowest-cost wells in places like Saudi Arabia. As the price of oil rises, oil from Iran and Iraq become profitable. When the price reaches $5, Nigerian and then Russian producers begin to just break even. As the price rises yet further toward $10, Alaskan oil starts to break even and then become profitable. North Sea, Canadian, and then Texan oil fields come online and increase production as the price rises further. At higher prices, it becomes profitable to extract oil using even more exotic technologies or deeper wells in more inhospitable parts of the world. Figure 3.9 illustrates.

What's important to understand about Figure 3.9 is that as the price of oil rises, it becomes profitable to produce oil using methods and from regions of the world with higher costs of production. The higher the price of oil, the deeper the wells.

In summary, a supply curve is a function that shows the quantity that suppliers would be willing to sell at different prices. The higher the price, the greater the quantity supplied—this is often called the "law of supply."

FIGURE 3.9

The Supply Curve for Oil As the price of oil rises, it becomes profitable to extract oil from more costly sources. Thus, as the price of oil rises, the quantity of oil supplied increases.

(Top photo: Dan Lamont/Corbis)
(Bottom: Bettmann/Corbis)

Producer Surplus

Figure 3.9 suggests two other concepts of importance. If the price of oil is $40 per barrel and Saudi Arabia can produce oil at $2 per barrel, then we say that Saudi Arabia earns a **producer surplus** of $38 per barrel. Similarly, if the price of oil is $40 per barrel and Nigeria can produce at $5 a barrel, Nigeria earns a producer surplus of $35 per barrel. Adding the producer surplus for each producer for each unit, we can find total producer surplus. Fortunately, this is easy to do on a diagram. *Total producer surplus is the shaded area above the supply curve and below the price* (see Figure 3.10).

Producer surplus is the producer's gain from exchange, or the difference between the market price and the minimum price at which a producer would be willing to sell a particular quantity.

Total producer surplus is measured by the area above the supply curve and below the price.

What Shifts the Supply Curve?

The second important concept suggested by Figure 3.9 is the connection between the supply curve and costs. What happens to the supply curve when the cost of producing oil falls? Suppose, for example, that a technological innovation in oil drilling such as sidewise drilling allows more oil to be produced at the same cost. What happens to the supply curve? The supply curve tells us how much suppliers are willing to sell at a particular price. The new technology makes some oil fields profitable that were previously unprofitable, so *at any price* suppliers are now willing to supply a greater quantity. Equivalently, the new technology lowers costs, so suppliers will be willing to sell any given quantity at a lower price. Either way economists say that a decrease in costs increases supply. In terms of the diagram, *a decrease in costs mean that the supply curve shifts down and to the right.* The left panel of Figure 3.11 illustrates. Of course, *higher costs mean that the supply curve shifts in the opposite direction, up and to the left* as illustrated in the right panel of Figure 3.11.

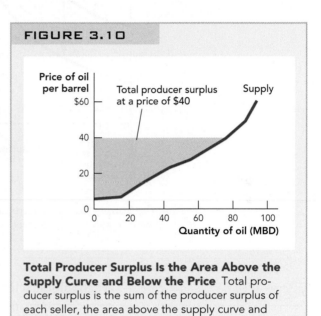

FIGURE 3.10

Total Producer Surplus Is the Area Above the Supply Curve and Below the Price Total producer surplus is the sum of the producer surplus of each seller, the area above the supply curve and below the price.

Once you know that a decrease in costs shifts the supply curve down and to the right and an increase in costs shifts the supply curve up and to the left, then you really know everything there is to know about supply shifts. It can take a little practice, however, to identify the many factors that can change costs. Here are some important supply shifters:

Important Supply Shifters

> Technological innovations and changes in the price of inputs

> Taxes and subsidies

> Expectations

> Entry or exit of producers

> Changes in opportunity costs

It can also help in analyzing supply shifters to know that sometimes it's easier to think of cost changes as shifting the supply curve right or left, and other times it's a little easier to think of cost changes as shifting the supply curve up or down. These two methods of thinking about supply shifts are equivalent and correspond to the two methods of reading a supply curve, the horizontal and vertical readings, respectively. We will give examples of each method as we examine some cost shifters in action.

FIGURE 3.11

Shifting the Supply Curve A decrease in costs increases supply, shifting the supply curve down and to the right. An increase in costs decreases supply, shifting the supply curve up and to the left.

Technological Innovations and Changes in the Price of Inputs We have already given an example of how improvements in technology can reduce costs, thus increasing supply. A reduction in input prices also reduces costs and thus has a similar effect. A fall in the wages of oil rig workers, for example, will reduce the cost of producing oil, shifting the supply curve down and to the right as in the left panel of Figure 3.11. Alternatively, an increase in the wages of oil rig workers will increase the cost of producing oil, shifting the supply curve up and to the left as in the right panel of Figure 3.11.

Taxes and Subsidies We can get some practice using up or down shifts to analyze a cost change by examining the effect of a $10 oil tax on the supply curve for oil. As far as firms are concerned, a tax on output is the same as an increase in costs. If the government taxes oil producers $10 per barrel, this is exactly the same to producers as an increase in their costs of production of $10 per barrel.

In Figure 3.12, notice that before the tax, firms require $40 per barrel to sell 60 million barrels of oil per day (point *a*). How much will firms require to sell the same quantity of oil when there is a tax of $10 per barrel? Correct, $50. What firms care about is the take-home price. If firms require $40 per barrel to sell 60 million barrels of oil, that's what they require regardless of the tax. When the government takes $10 per barrel, firms must charge $50 to keep their take-home price at $40. Thus, in Figure 3.12, notice that the $10 tax shifts the supply curve up by exactly $10 at *every point* along the curve.

It's important to avoid one possible confusion. All we have said so far is that a $10 tax shifts the supply curve for oil up by $10. We haven't said anything about the effect of a tax on the *price* of oil—that's because we have not yet analyzed how market prices are formed. We are saving that topic for Chapter 4.

How does a subsidy, a tax-benefit, or write-off shift the supply curve? We will save that analysis for the end of chapter problems but here's a hint: A subsidy is the same as a negative or "reverse" tax.

Expectations   Suppliers who expect that prices will increase in the future have an incentive to sell less today so that they can store goods for future sale. Thus, the expectation of a future price increase shifts today's supply curve to the left as illustrated in Figure 3.13. The shifting of supply in response to price expectations is the essence of *speculation,* the attempt to profit from future price changes.

Entry or Exit of Producers   When the United States signed the North American Free Trade Agreement (NAFTA), reducing barriers to trade among the United States, Mexico, and Canada, Canadian producers of lumber entered the U.S. market and increased the supply of lumber. We can most easily think about this as a shift to the right of the supply curve.

In Figure 3.14 on the next page, the domestic supply curve is the supply curve for lumber before NAFTA. The curve labeled domestic supply plus Canadian imports is the supply curve for lumber after NAFTA allowed Canadian firms to sell in the United States with fewer restrictions. The entry of more firms meant that at any price a greater quantity of lumber was available; that is, the supply curve shifted to the right.*

In a later chapter, we discuss the effects of foreign trade at greater length.

Changes in Opportunity Costs   The last important supply shifter, changes in opportunity costs, is the trickiest to understand. Recall from Chapter 1 that when the unemployment rates increase, more people tend to go to college. If you can't get a job, you aren't giving up many good opportunities by going to college. Thus, when the unemployment rate increases, the (opportunity) cost of college falls and so more people attend college. Notice that to understand how people behave, you must understand their opportunity costs.

FIGURE 3.12

A Tax on Industry Output Shifts the Supply Curve Up by the Amount of the Tax   When suppliers pay no tax, they are willing to supply 60 million barrels a day (MBD) of oil for a price of $40 per barrel. If they must pay a tax of $10 per barrel, they will be willing to supply 60 MBD for $10 more, or $50 a barrel. Thus, a tax shifts the supply curve up by the amount of the tax.

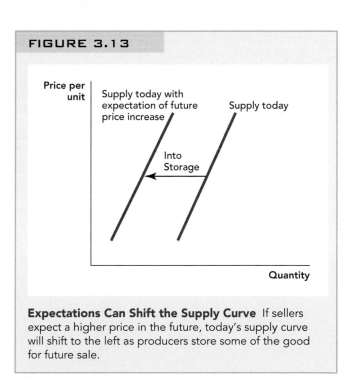

FIGURE 3.13

Expectations Can Shift the Supply Curve   If sellers expect a higher price in the future, today's supply curve will shift to the left as producers store some of the good for future sale.

---

* It is equally correct to think of new entrants as shifting the supply curve down. Remember, it's ultimately costs that shift supply and what increases supply is entry of *lower-cost* producers. Industry costs fell when Canadian producers entered the market because many Canadian producers had lower costs than some U.S. producers. As lower-cost Canadian producers entered the industry, higher-cost U.S. producers exited the industry and industry costs decreased, thus shifting the supply curve down.

FIGURE 3.14

Entry Increases Supply The entry of lower-cost producers increases supply, thus shifting the supply curve to the right and down.

Now suppose that a farmer is currently growing soybeans but that he could also use his land to grow wheat. If the price of *wheat* increases, then the farmer's opportunity cost of growing soybeans increases and the farmer will want to shift land from soybean production into the more profitable alternative of wheat production. As land is taken out of soybean production, the supply curve for soybeans shifts up and to the left.

In Figure 3.15, notice that before the increase in the price of wheat, farmers would be willing to supply 2,800 million bushels of soybeans at a price of $5 per bushel (point *a*). But when the price of wheat increases, farmers are only willing to supply 2,000 million bushels of soybeans at a price of $5 per bushel because an alternative use of the land (growing wheat) is now more valuable. Equivalently, before the increase in the price of wheat, farmers were willing to sell 2,800 million bushels of soybeans for $5 per bushel, but after their opportunity costs increase, farmers require $7 per bushel to sell the same quantity (point *c*).

Similarly, a decrease in opportunity costs shifts the supply curve down and to the right. If the price of wheat falls, for example, the opportunity cost of growing soybeans falls and the supply curve for soybeans will shift down and to the right. It's just another example of a running theme throughout this chapter, namely that both supply and demand respond to incentives.

FIGURE 3.15

Higher (Opportunity) Costs Reduce Supply An increase in the price of wheat increases the opportunity cost of growing soybeans, which shifts the supply curve of soybeans up and to the left.

☐ Takeaway

In this chapter, we have presented the fundamentals of the demand curve and the supply curve. The next chapter and much of the rest of this book build on these fundamentals. We thus give you fair warning. If you do not understand this chapter and the next, you will be lost!

Key points to know are that a demand curve is a function that shows the quantity demanded at different prices. In other words, a demand curve shows how customers respond to higher prices by buying less and to lower prices by buying more. Similarly, a supply curve is a function that shows the quantity supplied at different prices. In other words, a supply curve shows how producers respond to higher prices by producing more and to lower prices by producing less.

The difference between the maximum price a consumer is willing to pay for a product and the market price is the consumer's gain from exchange or consumer surplus. The difference between the market price and the minimum price at which a producer is willing to sell a product is the producer's gain from exchange or producer surplus. You should be able to identify total consumer and producer surplus on a diagram, again as we have outlined in the chapter.

When it comes to what shifts the supply and demand curves, we have listed some factors in this chapter. Yes, you should know these lists but more fundamentally you should know that an increase in demand *means* that buyers want a greater quantity at the same price or, equivalently, they are willing to pay a higher price for the same quantity. Thus, anything that causes buyers to want more at the same price or be willing to pay more for the same quantity increases demand. In a pinch, just think about some of the factors that would cause you to want more of a good at the same price or that would make you willing to pay more for the same quantity.

Similarly, an increase in supply *means* that sellers are willing to sell a greater quantity at the same price or, equivalently, they are willing to sell a given quantity at a lower price. Again, what would make you willing to sell more of a good for the same price or sell the same quantity for a lower price? (Here's a hint—you might be willing to do this if your costs had fallen.) Supply and demand curves are not just abstract constructs, they also shape your life.

In the next chapter, we will use supply curves and demand curves to answer one of the most crucial questions in economics: How is the price of a good determined?

☐ CHAPTER REVIEW

KEY CONCEPTS

Demand curve, p. 27

Quantity demanded, p. 28

Consumer surplus, p. 30

Total consumer surplus, p. 30

Normal good, p. 32

Inferior good, p. 32

Substitutes, p. 32

Complements, p. 32

Supply curve, p. 34

Quantity supplied, p. 34

Producer surplus, p. 37

Total producer surplus, p. 37

FACTS AND TOOLS

1. When the price of a good increases, the quantity demanded _____. When the price of a good decreases, the quantity demanded _____.

2. When will people search harder for substitutes for oil: When the price of oil is high or when the price of oil is low?

3. Your roommate just bought an iPod for $200. She would have been willing to pay $500 for a machine that could store and replay that much music. How much consumer surplus does your roommate enjoy from the iPod?

4. What are three things that you'll buy less of once you graduate from college and get a good job? What kinds of goods are these called?

5. When the price of Apple computers goes down, what probably happens to the demand for Windows-based computers?

6. **a.** When the price of olive oil goes up, what probably happens to the demand for corn oil?

   b. When the price of petroleum goes up, what probably happens to the demand for natural gas? To the demand for coal? To the demand for solar power?

7. **a.** If everyone thinks that the price of tomatoes will go up next week, what is likely to happen to demand for tomatoes today?

   b. If everyone thinks that the price of gasoline will go up next week, what is likely to happen to the demand for gasoline today? (*Note:* Is this change in demand caused by consumers or by gas station owners?)

8. Along a supply curve, if the price of oil falls, what will happen to the quantity of oil supplied? Why?

9. If the price of cars falls, are carmakers likely to make more cars or fewer cars, according to the supply curve? (Notice that the "person on the street" often thinks the opposite is true!)

10. When is a pharmaceutical business more likely to hire highly educated, cutting-edge workers and use new, experimental research methods: When the business expects the price of its new drug to be low or when it expects the price to be high?

11. Imagine that a technological innovation reduces the costs of producing high-quality steel. What happens to the supply curve for steel?

12. When oil companies expect the price of oil to be higher next year, what happens to the supply of oil today?

13. Do taxes usually increase the supply of a good or reduce the supply?

THINKING AND PROBLEM SOLVING

1. Consider the following supply curve for oil. Note that MBD stands for "millions of barrels per day," the usual way people talk about the supply of oil:

   a. Based on the above supply curve, fill in the table below:

Price	Quantity Supplied
$12	
	40

   b. If the price for a barrel of oil was $15, how much oil would oil suppliers be willing to supply?

   c. What is the lowest price at which suppliers of oil would be willing to supply 20 MBD?

2. From the following table of prices per 100 pencils and quantities supplied (in hundreds of pencils), draw the supply curve for pencils:

Price	Quantity Supplied
$5	20
$15	40
$25	50
$35	55

3. Suppose LightBright and Bulbs4You were the only two suppliers of 60-watt lightbulbs in Springfield. Draw the supply curve for the 60-watt lightbulb industry in Springfield from the following tables for the two companies. To create this "light bulb industry supply curve," note that you'll add up the *total* number of bulbs that the industry will supply at a price of $1 (15 bulbs), and then do the same for the prices of $5, $7, and $10.

Price	Bulbs Supplied by LightBright	Bulbs Supplied by Bulbs4You
$1	10	5
$5	15	7
$7	25	15
$10	35	20

4. Using the following diagram, identify and calculate total producer surplus if the price of oil is $50 per barrel. Recall that for a triangle, Area = (1/2) × Base × Height. (You never thought you'd use that equation unless you became an engineer, did you?)

5. In Sucrosia, the supply curve for sugar is as follows:

Price (per 100 pound bag)	Quantity
$30	10,000
$50	15,000
$70	20,000

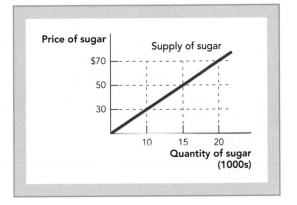

Under pressure from nutrition activists, the government decides to tax sugar producers with a $5 tax per 100 pound bag. Using the figure above, draw the new supply curve. After the tax is enacted, what price will bring forth quantities of 10,000? 15,000? 20,000? Give your answers in the table below:

Price (per 100 pound bag)	Quantity
	10,000
	15,000
	20,000

6. Consider the farmers talked about in the chapter who have land that is suitable for growing both wheat and soybeans. Suppose all farmers are currently farming wheat but the price of soybeans rises dramatically.

   a. Does the opportunity cost of producing wheat rise or fall?

b. Does this shift the supply curve for wheat (as in one of the panels of Figure 3.11), or is it a movement along a fixed supply curve?

What direction is this shift or movement? Illustrate your answer on the figure below:

7. Consider the following demand curve for oil:

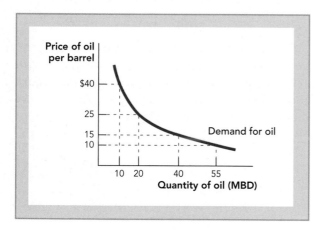

a. Using the above demand curve, fill in the following table:

Price	Quantity Demanded
	55
$25	

b. If the price was $10, how much oil would be demanded?

c. What is the maximum price (per barrel) demanders will pay for 20 million barrels of oil?

8. From the following chart, draw the demand curve for pencils (in hundreds):

Price	Quantity Demanded (in hundreds)
$5	60
$15	45
$25	35
$35	20

9. If the price of glass dramatically increases, what are we likely to see a lot less of: glass windows or glass bottles? Why?

10. Let's think about the demand for plasma TVs.

a. If the price for a 50″ plasma TV is $2,010, and Newhart would be willing to pay $3,000, what is Newhart's consumer surplus?

b. Consider the figure below for the total demand for plasma TVs. At $2,010 per TV, 1,200 TVs were demanded. What would be the total consumer surplus? Calculate the total and identify it on the diagram.

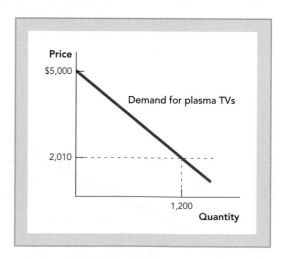

c. Where is Newhart in the figure above?

11. If income increases and the demand for good X shifts as shown below, then is good X a normal or inferior good? Give an example of a good like good X.

12. Assume that butter and margarine are substitutes. What will happen to the demand curve for butter if the price of margarine increases? Why?

13. Cars and gasoline are complements. What will happen to the demand curve for gasoline if the price of cars decreases? Why? (*Hint:* What happens to the quantity demanded of cars?)

14. Suppose that the supply curve for solar panels is as shown in the diagram:

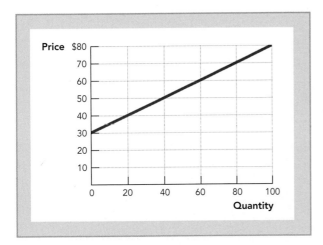

The government decides that it would like to increase the quantity of solar panels in use, so it offers a $20 subsidy per panel to producers. Draw the new supply curve. As a hint, remember our analysis of how a tax affects supply, as shown in Figure 3.12, and bear in mind that a subsidy can be thought of as a "negative tax."

CHALLENGES

1. Michael is an economist. He loves being an economist so much that he would do it for a living even if he only earned $30,000 per year. Instead, he earns $80,000 per year. (*Note:* This is the average salary of new economists with a Ph.D. degree.) How much producer surplus does Michael enjoy?

2. The economist Bryan Caplan recently found a pair of $10 arch supports that saved him from the pain of major foot surgery. As he stated on his blog (econlog.econlib.org), he would have been willing to pay $100,000 to fix his foot problem, but instead he only paid a few dollars.

   a. How much consumer surplus did Bryan enjoy from this purchase?

   b. If the sales tax was 5 percent on this product, how much revenue did the government raise when Bryan bought his arch supports?

   c. If the government could have taxed Bryan based on his *willingness to pay* rather than on how much he *actually* paid, how much sales tax would Bryan have had to pay?

3. For most young people, working full time and going to school are substitutes: You tend to do one or the other. When it's tough to find a job, does that raise the opportunity cost of going to college or does it lower it? When it's tough to find a job, does the demand for college rise or fall?

4. What should happen to the "demand for speed" (measured by the average speed on highways) once airbags are included on cars?

5. The industrial areas in northeast Washington, D.C., were relatively dangerous in the 1980s. Over the last two decades, the area has become a safer place to work (although there are still several times more violent crimes per person in these areas compared with another D.C. neighborhood, Georgetown). When an area becomes a safer place to work, what probably happens to the "supply of labor" in that area?

4

Equilibrium: How Supply and Demand Determine Prices

In Chapter 3, we introduced the supply curve and the demand curve. In that chapter, we wrote things like "if the price is $20 per barrel, the quantity supplied will be 50 million barrels per day (MBD)" and "if the price is $50, the quantity demanded will be 120 MBD." But how is price determined?

We are now ready for the big event: equilibrium. Figure 4.1 puts the supply curve and demand curve for oil together in one diagram. Notice the one point where the curves meet. The price at the meeting point is called the equilibrium price and the quantity at the meeting point is called the equilibrium quantity.

The equilibrium price is $30 and the equilibrium quantity is 65 MBD. What do we mean by equilibrium? We say that $30 and 65 are the equilibrium price and quantity because at any other price and quantity, economic forces are put in play that push prices and quantities toward these values. The equilibrium price and quantity are the only price and quantity that in a free market are stable. The sketch at right gives an intuitive feel for what we mean by equilibrium— the force of gravity pulls the ball down the side of the bowl until it comes to a state of rest. We will now explain the economic forces that push and pull prices toward their equilibrium values.

Equilibrium and the Adjustment Process

Imagine that demand and supply were as in Figure 4.1 on the next page, but the price was $50, above the equilibrium price of $30—we would then have the situation depicted in the left panel of Figure 4.2 on page 49.

Thinking About Equilibrium

FIGURE 4.1

Price Is Determined by Supply and Demand Equilibrium occurs when the quantity demanded equals the quantity supplied. The quantity demanded equals the quantity supplied only when the price is $30 and the quantity exchanged is 65; hence, $30 is the equilibrium price and 65 the equilibrium quantity.

A **surplus** is a situation in which the quantity supplied is greater than the quantity demanded.

At a price of $50, suppliers want to supply 100, but at that price the quantity demanded by buyers is just 32, which creates an excess supply or **surplus** of 68. What will suppliers do if they cannot sell all of their output at a price of $50? Hold a sale! Each seller will reason that by pricing just a little bit below his or her competitors, he or she will be able to sell much more. *Competition will push prices down whenever there is a surplus.* As competition pushes prices down, the quantity demanded will increase and the quantity supplied will decrease. Only at a price of $30 will equilibrium be restored because only at that price does the quantity demanded (65) equal the quantity supplied (65).

A **shortage** is a situation in which the quantity demanded is greater than the quantity supplied.

What if price is below the equilibrium price? The right panel of Figure 4.2 shows that at a price of $15 demanders want 95 but suppliers are only willing to sell 24, which creates an excess demand or **shortage** of 71. What will sellers do if they discover that at a price of $15, they can easily sell all of their output and still have buyers asking for more? Raise prices! Buyers also have an incentive to offer higher prices when there is a shortage because when they can't buy as much as they want at the going price, they will try to outbid other buyers by offering sellers a higher price. *Competition will push prices up whenever there is a shortage.* As prices are pushed up, the quantity supplied increases and the quantity demanded decreases until at a price of $30 there is no longer an incentive for prices to rise and equilibrium is restored.

The **equilibrium price** is the price at which the quantity demanded is equal to the quantity supplied.

If competition pushes the price down whenever it is above the **equilibrium price** and it pushes the price up whenever it is below the equilibrium price, what happens at the equilibrium price? *The equilibrium price is stable because at the equilibrium price the quantity demanded is exactly equal to the quantity supplied.* Because every buyer can buy as much as he or she wants at the equilibrium price, buyers

FIGURE 4.2

A Surplus Drives Prices Down At a price of $50 there is a surplus of oil. When there is a surplus, sellers have an incentive to decrease their price and buyers have an incentive to offer lower prices. The price decreases until at $30 the quantity demanded equals the quantity supplied and there is no longer an incentive for price to fall.

A Shortage Drives Prices Up At a price of $15 there is a shortage of oil. When there is a shortage, sellers have an incentive to increase the price and buyers have an incentive to offer higher prices. The price increases until at $30 the quantity supplied equals the quantity demanded and there is no longer an incentive for the price to rise.

don't have an incentive to push prices up. Since every seller can sell as much as he or she wants at the equilibrium price, sellers don't have an incentive to push prices down. Of course, buyers would like lower prices, but any buyer who offers sellers a lower price will be scorned. Similarly, sellers would like higher prices, but any seller who tries to raise his or her asking price will quickly lose customers.

Who Competes with Whom?

Sellers want higher prices and buyers want lower prices so the person in the street often thinks that sellers compete *against* buyers.

But economists understand that regardless of what sellers want, what they do when they compete is lower prices. *Sellers compete with other sellers.* Similarly, buyers may want lower prices but what they do when they compete is raise prices. *Buyers compete with other buyers.*

If the price of a good that you want is high, should you blame the seller? Not if the market is competitive. Instead, you should "blame" other buyers for outbidding you.

Gains from Trade Are Maximized at the Equilibrium Price and Quantity

Figure 4.3 provides another perspective on the market equilibrium. Consider Panel A. At a price of $15 suppliers will voluntarily produce 24 MBD. But notice that this is only enough oil to satisfy some of the buyers' wants. Which ones? The buyers will allocate what oil they have to their

FIGURE 4.3

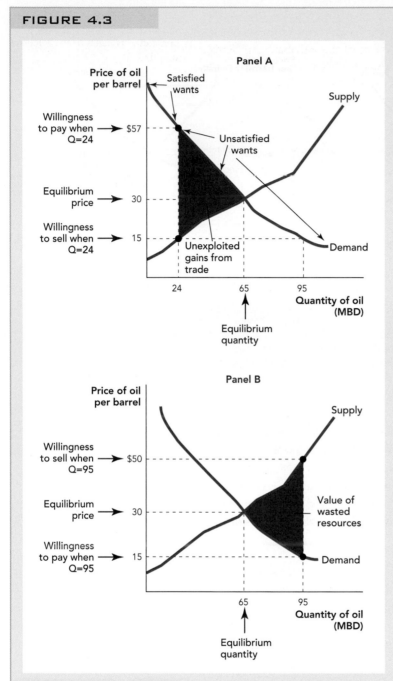

At the Equilibrium Quantity There Are No Unexploited Gains from Trade Nor Any Wasteful Trades

Panel A: Unexploited gains from trade exist when quantity is below the equilibrium quantity. Buyers are willing to pay $57 for the 24th unit and sellers are willing to sell the 24th unit for $15, so not trading the 24th unit leaves $42 in unexploited gain from trade. Only at the equilibrium quantity are there no unexploited gains from trade.

Panel B: Resources are wasted at quantities greater than the equilibrium quantity. Sellers are willing to sell the 95th unit for $50, but buyers are willing to pay only $15 so selling the 95th unit wastes $35 in resources. Only at the equilibrium quantity are there no wasted resources.

highest-valued wants. In Panel A of Figure 4.3, the 24 MBD of oil will be used to satisfy the wants labeled "Satisfied Wants." All other wants will remain unsatisfied. Now suppose that suppliers could be induced to sell just one more barrel of oil. How much would buyers be willing to pay for this barrel of oil? We can read the value of this additional barrel of oil by the height of the demand curve at 24 MBD. Buyers would be willing to pay up to $57 (or $56.99 if you want to be very precise), the value of the first unsatisfied want for an additional barrel of oil when 24 MBD are currently being bought. How much would sellers be willing to accept for one additional barrel of oil? We can read the lowest price at which sellers are willing to sell an additional barrel of oil by the height of the supply curve at 24 MBD. (Since sellers will be just willing to sell an additional barrel of oil when it covers their additional costs, we can also read this as the cost of producing an additional barrel of oil when 24 MBD are currently being produced.) Sellers would be willing to sell an additional barrel of oil for as little as $15.

Buyers are willing to pay $57 for an additional barrel of oil, and sellers are willing to sell an additional barrel for as little as $15. Trade at any price between $57 and $15 can make both buyers and sellers better off. There are potential gains from trade so long as buyers are willing to pay more than sellers are willing to accept. Now notice that *there are unexploited gains from trade at any quantity less than the* **equilibrium quantity.** Economists believe that in a free market unexploited gains from trade won't last for long. We expect, therefore, that in a free market the quantity bought and sold will increase until the equilibrium quantity of 65 is reached.

We have shown that gains from trade push the quantity toward the equilibrium quantity. What about a push for trade coming from the other direction? In a free market, why won't the quantity bought and sold *exceed* the equilibrium quantity?

Now consider Panel B of Figure 4.3. Suppose that for some reason suppliers produce a quantity of 95 MBD. At a quantity of 95, it costs suppliers $50 to produce the last barrel of oil (say, by squeezing it out of the Athabasca tar sands). How much is that barrel of oil worth to buyers? Again, we can read this from the height of the demand curve at 95 MBD. It's only $15 (they get a few extra rubber duckies). So if quantity supplied exceeds the equilibrium quantity, it costs the sellers more to produce a barrel of oil than that barrel of oil is worth to buyers.

In a free market, suppliers won't spend $50 to produce something they can sell for at most $15—that's a recipe for bankruptcy.* We expect, therefore, that in a free market, the quantity bought and sold will decrease until the equilibrium quantity of 65 MBD is reached.

Suppliers won't try to drive themselves into bankruptcy, but if they did, would this be a good thing? Even at the equilibrium quantity, buyers have unsatisfied wants. Wouldn't it be a good idea to satisfy even more wants? No. The reason is that resources are wasted if the quantity exceeds the equilibrium quantity.

Imagine once again that suppliers were producing 95 units, and thus were producing many barrels of oil whose cost exceeded their worth. This would be a loss not just to the suppliers but also to society. Producing oil takes resources—labor, trucks, pipes, and so forth. Those resources, or the value of those resources, could be used to produce something people really are willing to pay for—economics textbooks, for example, or iPods. If we waste resources producing barrels of oil for $50 that are only worth $15, we have fewer resources to produce goods that cost only $32 but that people value at $75. We have only a limited number of resources and getting the most out of those resources means producing neither too little of a good (as in Panel A of Figure 4.3) nor too much of a good (as in Panel B). Markets can help us to achieve this goal.

Figure 4.3 shows why in a free market there tends not to be unexploited gains from trade—at least not for long—or wasteful trades. Put these two things together and we have a remarkable result. *A free market maximizes the gains from trade.* The gains from trade can be broken down into producer surplus and consumer surplus, so we can also say that *a free market maximizes producer plus consumer surplus.*

Figure 4.4 illustrates how the gains from trade—producer plus consumer surplus—are maximized at the equilibrium price and quantity. Maximizing the gains from trade, however, requires more than just producing at the equilibrium price and quantity. In addition, goods must be produced at the lowest possible cost and they must be used to satisfy the highest value demands. In Figure 4.4, for example, notice that every seller has lower costs than every non-seller. Also, every buyer has a higher willingness to pay for the good than every non-buyer.

Imagine if this claim were not true; suppose, for example, that Joe is willing to pay $50 for the good and there are two sellers: Alice with costs of $40 and Barbara with costs of $20. It's possible that Joe and Alice could make a deal, splitting the gains from trade of $10. At a price of $44, for example, Joe could earn $6 in consumer surplus ($50–$44) and Alice could earn $4 in producer surplus ($44–$40). But this trade would not maximize the gains from trade because if Joe and Barbara trade, the gains from trade are much higher, $30. Over time, both Joe and Barbara will figure this out, so in equilibrium,

The **equilibrium quantity** is the quantity at which the quantity demanded is equal to the quantity supplied.

---

* Can you think of when suppliers might do this? What about if they were being subsidized by the government? In that case, the buyers might value the good less than the cost to sellers, but so long as the government makes up the difference, the sellers will be happy to sell a large quantity. See Chapter 6 for more on subsidies.

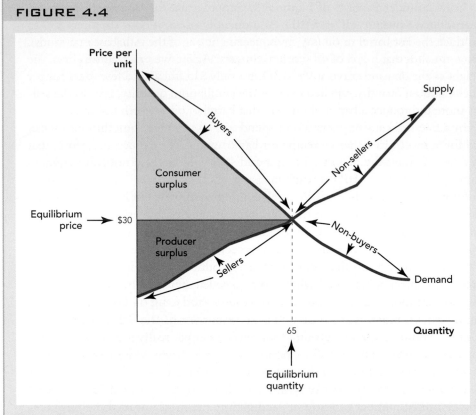

FIGURE 4.4

A Free Market Maximizes Producer Plus Consumer Surplus (the Gains from Trade) A free market maximizes the gains from trade because (1) buyers are willing to pay more for the good than non-buyers, (2) sellers are willing to sell the good at a lower price than non-sellers, and (3) there are no mutually profitable deals between non-sellers and non-buyers.

we expect Joe to trade with Barbara, not Alice. Thus, when we say that a free market maximizes the gains from trade, we mean three closely related things:

1. The supply of goods is bought by the buyers with the highest willingness to pay.
2. The supply of goods is sold by the sellers with the lowest costs.
3. Between buyers and sellers, there are no unexploited gains from trade and no wasteful trades.

Together, these three conditions imply that the gains from trade are maximized.

One of the remarkable lessons of economics is that under the right conditions, the pursuit of self-interest leads not to chaos but to a beneficial order. The maximization of the gains from trade in markets populated solely by self-interested individuals is one application of this central idea.

CHECK YOURSELF

> As the price of cars goes up, which marketplace wants will be the first to stop being satisfied? Give an example.

> In the late 1990s, telecommunication firms laid a greater quantity of fiber-optic cable than the market equilibrium quantity (as proved by later events). Describe the nature of the losses from too much investment in fiber-optic cable. What market incentives exist to avoid these losses?

Does the Model Work? Evidence from the Laboratory

It's easy to see the equilibrium price and quantity when we draw textbook supply and demand curves, but in a real market the demanders and sellers do not know the true curves. Moreover, the conditions required to maximize the gains from trade are quite sophisticated. So how do we know whether the model really works?

In 1956, Vernon Smith launched a revolution in economics by testing the supply and demand model in the lab. Smith's early experiments were simple. He took a group of undergraduate students and broke them into two groups, buyers and sellers. Buyers were given a card that indicated their maximum willingness to pay. Sellers were given a card that indicated their cost, the minimum price at which they would be willing to sell. The buyers and sellers were then instructed to call out bids and offers ("I will sell for $3.00" or "I will pay $1.50"). Each student could earn a profit by the difference between their willingness to pay or sell and the contract price. For example, if you were a buyer and your card said $3.00 and you were able to make a deal with a seller to buy for $2.00, then you would have made a $1.00 profit.

The students knew only their own willingness to pay or to sell, but Vernon Smith knew the actual shape of the supply and demand curves. Smith knew the curves because he knew exactly what cards he had handed out. Data from one of Smith's first experiments are shown in Figure 4.5. Smith handed out 11 cards to sellers and 11 to buyers. The lowest-cost seller had costs of 75 cents, the next lowest-cost seller had costs of $1.00. Thus, at any price below 75 cents the quantity supplied on the market supply curve was zero, between 75 cents and $1 the quantity supplied was 1 unit, between $1.00 and $1.25, the next highest cost, 2 units, and so forth. Looking at the figure can you see how many units were demanders willing to buy at a price of $2.65? At a price of $2.65, the quantity demanded is 3 units. (To test yourself, identify, by their willingness to pay, exactly which three buyers are willing to buy at a price of $2.65.)

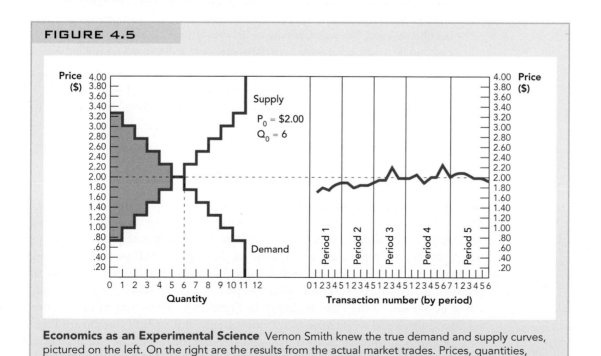

FIGURE 4.5

Economics as an Experimental Science Vernon Smith knew the true demand and supply curves, pictured on the left. On the right are the results from the actual market trades. Prices, quantities, and the gains from trade all converged quickly to those predicted by economic theory.

Source: Smith, Vernon. 1962. An experimental study of competitive market behavior. *Journal of Political Economy* V **70**(2): 111–137.

The idea of economics as an experimental science came to Vernon Smith in a fit of insomnia in 1956. Nearly 50 years later, Smith was awarded the 2002 Nobel Prize in Economics.

Smith knew from the graph that the equilibrium price and quantity as predicted by the supply and demand model were $2.00 and 6 units, respectively. But what would happen in the real world? Smith ran his experiment for 5 periods, each period about 5 minutes long. The right side of the figure shows the price for each completed trade in each period. The prices quickly converged toward the expected equilibrium price and quantity so that in the last period the average price was $2.03 and the quantity exchanged was 6 units.

Smith's market converged rapidly to the equilibrium price and quantity exactly as predicted by the supply and demand model. But recall that the model also predicts that a free market will maximize the gains from trade. Remember our conditions for efficiency, which in this context are that the supply of goods must be bought by the demanders with the highest willingness to pay, the supply of goods must be sold by the suppliers with the lowest costs, and the quantity traded should be equal to 6 units, neither more nor less.

So what happened in Smith's test of the market model? In the final period, 6 units were bought and sold and the buyers had the six highest valuations and the sellers the six lowest costs—exactly as predicted by the supply and demand model. Producer plus consumer surplus or total surplus was maximized. In fact, in the entire experiment only once was a seller with a cost greater than equilibrium price able to sell and only once was a buyer with a willingness to pay less than the equilibrium price able to buy—so total surplus was very close to being maximized throughout the experiment.

Vernon Smith began his experiments thinking that they would prove the supply and demand model was wrong. Decades later he wrote:

> I am still recovering from the shock of the experimental results. The outcome was unbelievably consistent with competitive price theory. . . . But the results *can't* be believed, I thought. It must be an accident, so I must take another class and do a new experiment with different supply and demand schedules.[1]

Many thousands of experiments later, the supply and demand model remains of enduring value. In 2002, Vernon Smith was awarded the Nobel Prize in Economics for establishing laboratory experiments as an important tool in economic science.

Shifting Demand and Supply Curves

Another way of testing the supply and demand model is to examine the model's predictions about what happens to equilibrium price and quantity when the supply or demand curves shift. Even if the model doesn't give us precise predictions (outside of the lab), we can still ask whether the model helps us to understand the world.

Imagine, for example, that technological innovations reduce the costs of producing a good. As we know from Chapter 3, a fall in costs shifts the supply curve down and to the right as shown in Figure 4.6. The result of lower costs is a lower price and an increase in quantity. Begin at the Old Equilibrium Price and Quantity at point *a*. Now a decrease in costs shifts the Old Supply curve down and to the right out to the New Supply curve. Notice at the Old Equilibrium Price there is now a surplus—in other words, now that their costs have fallen, suppliers are willing to sell more at the old price than demanders are willing to buy. The excess supply, however, is temporary. Competition

FIGURE 4.6

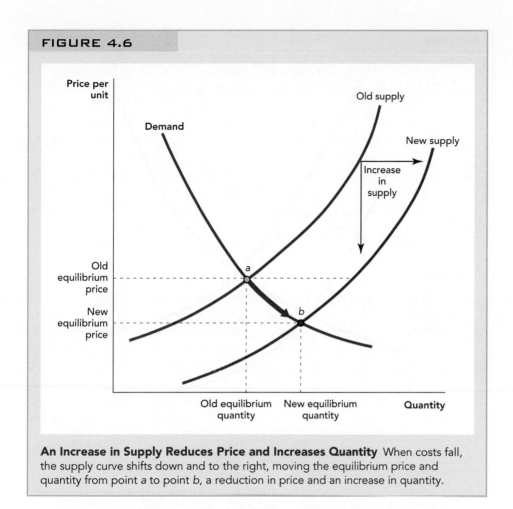

An Increase in Supply Reduces Price and Increases Quantity When costs fall, the supply curve shifts down and to the right, moving the equilibrium price and quantity from point *a* to point *b*, a reduction in price and an increase in quantity.

between sellers pushes prices down, and as prices fall, the quantity demanded increases. Prices fall and quantity demanded increases until the New Equilibrium Price and Quantity are established at point *b*. At the new equilibrium, the quantity demanded equals the quantity supplied.

We can see this process at work throughout the economy. As technological innovations reduce the price of computer chips, for example, prices fall and the quantity of chips—used in everything from computers to cell phones to toys—increases.

What about a decrease in supply? A decrease in supply will raise the market price and reduce the market quantity, exactly the opposite effects to an increase in supply. But don't take our word for it. Draw the diagram. The key to learning demand and supply is not to try to memorize everything that can happen. Instead, focus on learning how to use the tools. If you know how to use the tools, you can deduce what happens to price and quantity for any configuration of demand and supply and for any set of shifts simply by drawing a few pictures.

Figure 4.7 shows the same process for an increase in demand. Begin with the Old Equilibrium Price and Quantity at point *a*. Now suppose that demand increases to New Demand. As a result, the price and quantity are driven up to the New Equilibrium Price and Quantity at point *b*. Notice this time we omitted discussion of the temporary transition. So here's a good test of your knowledge. Can you explain *why* the price and quantity demanded increased with an increase in demand? *Hint*: What happens at the Old Equilibrium Price after demand has increased to New Demand?

FIGURE 4.7

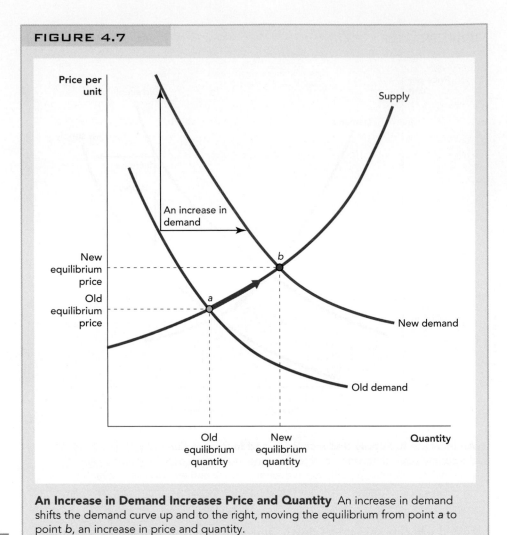

An Increase in Demand Increases Price and Quantity An increase in demand shifts the demand curve up and to the right, moving the equilibrium from point *a* to point *b*, an increase in price and quantity.

CHECK YOURSELF

> Flooding in Iowa destroys some of the corn and soybean crop. What will happen to the price and quantity for each of these crops?

> Resveratrol, which is found in the plant Japanese knotweed (and is also a component of red wine), has recently been shown to increase life expectancy in worms and fish. What are your predictions about the price and quantity of Japanese knotweed grown?

> With the increase in gasoline prices, demand has shifted away from large cars and SUVs, and toward hybrid cars such as the Prius. Draw a graph showing the supply and demand for hybrid cars before and after an increase in the price of gasoline. What do you predict will happen to the price of hybrids as the price of gasoline rises?

Of course, if we can analyze an increase in demand, then a decrease in demand is just the opposite: A decrease in demand will tend to decrease price and quantity. Once again, draw the diagram!

Do you recall the list of demand and supply shifters that we presented in Chapter 3? We can now put all that knowledge to good use. With demand, supply, and the idea of equilibrium, we have powerful tools for analyzing how changes in income, population, expectations, technologies, input prices, taxes and subsidies, alternative uses of industry inputs, and other factors will change market prices and quantities. In fact, with our tools of demand, supply, and equilibrium, we can analyze and understand *any* change in *any* competitive market.

Terminology: Demand Compared with Quantity Demanded and Supply Compared with Quantity Supplied

Sometimes economists use very similar words for quite different things. (We're sorry but unfortunately it's too late to change terms.) In particular, there is a big difference between demand and quantity demanded. For example, an increase in the quantity demanded is a movement *along* a fixed demand curve. An increase in demand is a *shift* of the entire demand curve (up and to the right).

Don't worry: You are *already* familiar with these differences; we just need to point them out to you and explain the associated differences in terminology. Panel A of Figure 4.8 is a repeat of Figure 4.6, showing that an increase in supply reduces the equilibrium price and increases the equilibrium quantity. But now we emphasize something a little different—the increase in supply pushes the

FIGURE 4.8

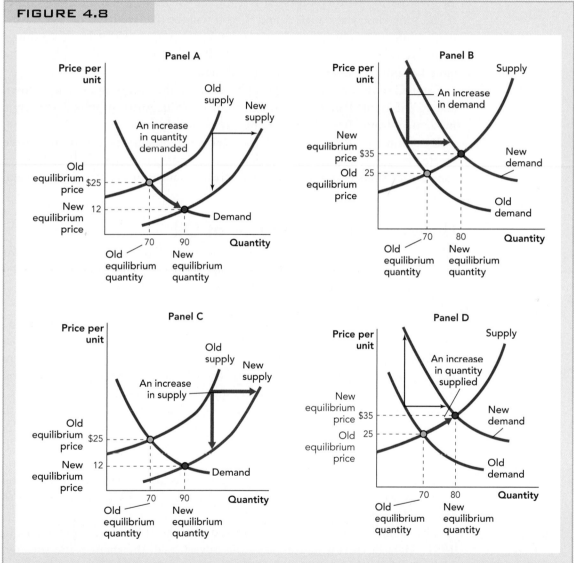

An Increase in Quantity Demanded Compared with an Increase in Demand, and an Increase in Supply Compared with an Increase in Quantity Supplied

Panel A: An increase in quantity demanded is a movement along a fixed demand curve caused by a shift in the supply curve.

Panel B: An increase in demand is a shift in the demand curve up and to the right.

Panel C: An increase in supply is a shift in the supply curve down and to the right.

Panel D: An increase in quantity supplied is a movement along a fixed supply curve caused by a shift in the demand curve.

price down, thereby causing an increase in the *quantity demanded* from 70 units to 90 units. Notice that the increase in the quantity demanded is a movement along the demand curve. In Panel A, the demand has not changed, only the quantity demanded. Notice also that changes in the quantity demanded are always caused by changes in supply. In other words, *shifts* in the supply curve cause movements *along* the demand curve.

Panel B is a repeat of Figure 4.7 and it shows an *increase in demand*. Notice that an increase in demand is a shift in the entire demand curve up and to the right. Indeed, we can also think about an increase in demand as the creation of a new demand curve, appropriately labeled New Demand.

Similarly, an increase in supply is a *shift* of the entire supply curve, whereas an increase in quantity supplied is a movement *along* a fixed supply curve. If you look closely at Panels A and B, you will see that we have already shown you a shift in supply and a change in quantity supplied! But to make things clear, we repeat the analysis for supply in Panels C and D: The graphs are the same but now we emphasize different things.

Panel C shows an increase in supply, a shift in the entire supply curve down and to the right. Panel D shows an increase in quantity supplied, namely a movement from 70 to 80 units along a fixed supply curve.

By comparing Panels A and C, we can see that shifts in the supply curve create changes in quantity demanded. And by comparing Panels B and D, we can see that shifts in the demand curve create changes in the quantity supplied.

Understanding the Price of Oil

We can use the supply and demand model to understand some of the major events that have determined the price of oil over the past half-century. Figure 4.9 shows the *real price* of oil in 2005 dollars between 1960 and 2005. (The real price corrects prices for inflation.)

From the early twentieth century to the 1970s, the demand for oil increased steadily, but major discoveries and improved production techniques meant that the supply of oil increased at an even faster pace, leading to modest declines in price. Contrary to popular belief, slightly declining prices over time are common for minerals and other natural resources supplied under competitive conditions.

Although the streets of Baghdad were paved with tar as early as the eighth century, the discovery and development of the modern oil industry in the Middle East were made primarily by U.S., Dutch, and British firms much later. For many decades, these firms controlled oil in the Middle East, giving local governments just a small cut of their proceeds. It's hard to take your oil well and leave the country, however, so the major firms were vulnerable to taxes and nationalization.

The Iranian government nationalized the British oil industry in Iran in 1951.* The Egyptians nationalized the Suez Canal, the main route through which oil flowed to the West, in 1956, leading to the Suez Crisis—a brief war that pitted Egypt against an alliance of the United Kingdom, France, and Israel. Further nationalizations and increased government control of the oil industry occurred throughout the 1960s and early 1970s.

---

* The nationalization was reversed in 1953 when the government of Mohammad Mosaddeq was toppled by a CIA-backed coup that brought the king, Mohammad Reza Pahlavi, back to power. The coup would have repercussions a quarter-century later with the coming of the Iranian Revolution, when the American-backed government was overthrown by Islamic radicals.

FIGURE 4.9

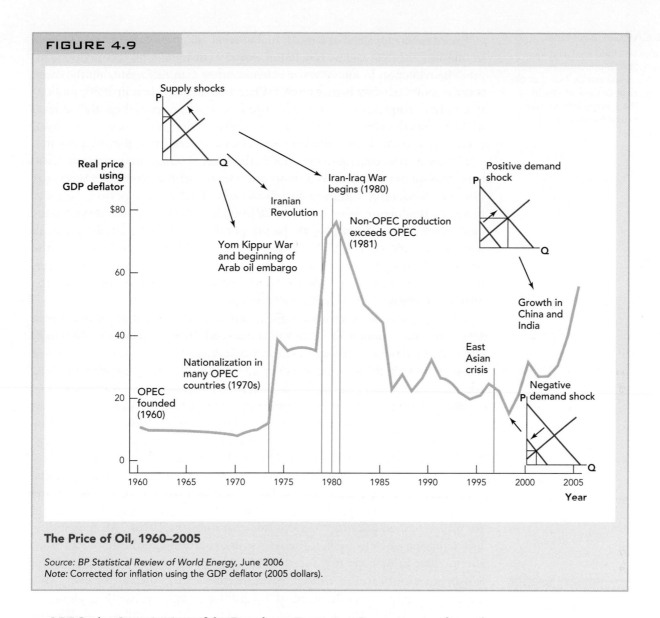

The Price of Oil, 1960–2005

Source: BP Statistical Review of World Energy, June 2006
Note: Corrected for inflation using the GDP deflator (2005 dollars).

OPEC, the Organization of the Petroleum Exporting Countries, was formed in 1960.[†] Initially, OPEC restricted itself to bargaining with the foreign nationals for a larger share of their oil revenues. By the early 1970s, however, further nationalizations in the OPEC countries made it possible for OPEC countries to act together to reduce supply and raise prices.

A triggering event for OPEC was the Yom Kippur War. Egypt and Syria attacked Israel in 1973 in an effort to regain the Sinai Peninsula and the Golan Heights, which Israel had captured in 1967. In an effort to punish Western countries that had supported Israel, a number of Arab exporting nations cut oil production. Supply had been increasing by about 7.5 percent per year in the previous decade, but between 1973 and 1974 production was dead flat. Prices shot up, increasing in real dollars from $14.50 to $46 per barrel in just one year. The large increase in price from a small decline in supply (relative to what it would have been without the cut in production) demonstrated how much the world depended on oil.

[†] OPEC was founded by Iran, Iraq, Kuwait, Saudi Arabia, and Venezuela, later joined by Qatar (1961), Indonesia (1962), Libya (1962), United Arab Emirates (1967), Algeria (1969), Nigeria (1971), Ecuador (1973–1992), and Gabon (1975–1994). Ecuador rejoined OPEC in 2007, Angola joined in 2007, and Indonesia left in 2008.

►►SEARCH ENGINE
Statistics on world energy prices, consumption, production, reserves, and other areas can be found at the **BP Statistical Review of World Energy.** The **Energy Information Administration** focuses on the United States.

Prices stabilized, albeit at a much higher level, after 1974, but political unrest in Iran in 1978 followed by revolution in 1979 cut Iranian oil production. This time the reduction in supply was accidental rather than deliberate, but the result was the same—sharply higher prices. When Iraq attacked Iran in 1980, production in both countries diminished yet again, pushing prices to their highest level in the twentieth century—$75.31 in 2005 dollars. Prices might have been driven even higher if demand had not been reduced by a recession in the United States.

Higher prices attract entry. In 1972, the United Kingdom produced 2,000 barrels of oil per day. By 1978, with the opening of the North Sea wells, the UK was producing 1 million barrels per day. In the same period, Norway increased production from 33,000 to 287,000 barrels per day and Mexico doubled its production from 506,000 barrels per day to just over 1 million barrels per day. By 1982, non-OPEC production exceeded OPEC production for the first time since OPEC was founded. Iranian production also began to recover, increasing by 1 million barrels per day in 1982. Prices began to fall during the 1980s and 1990s.

Prices can also fluctuate with shifts in demand. A sharp fall in prices came in 1997 when the economy of South Korea (the tenth largest economy in the world) and that of Indonesia, Thailand, and other East Asian countries went into a severe recession. Income fell, reducing the demand for oil and reducing oil prices. As these countries recovered, however, the demand for oil increased along with prices.

The economies of China and India have surged in the early twenty-first century to the point where millions of people are for the first time in the history of their country able to afford an automobile. In 1949, the Communists confiscated all the private cars in China. As late as 2000, there were just 6 million cars in all of China, but by 2010 more vehicles were bought in China than in the United States, almost 18 million in that one year alone. Total highway miles quadrupled between 2000 and 2010.[2] This increased demand for oil has pushed prices up to levels not seen since the 1970s.* Moreover, unlike temporary events such as the Iranian Revolution and the Iran-Iraq War, the increase in demand in China and in other newly developing nations will not reverse soon. In the United States, there's nearly one car for every two people. China has a population of 1.3 billion people, so there is plenty of room for growth in the number of cars and thus the demand for oil. What is your prediction for future oil prices?

CHECK YOURSELF

> In Figure 4.9, you will notice a jump in oil prices around 1991. What happened in this year to increase price? Was it a supply shock or a demand shock?

> In Figure 4.9, during what period would you include a small figure for positive supply shocks (increases in supply?) Explain the causes behind the positive supply shocks and the effect of these shocks on the price of oil.

☐ Takeaway

Now that you have finished reading this chapter, you should read it again. Really. Understanding supply and demand is critical to understanding economics, and in this chapter we have covered the most important aspects of the supply and demand model, namely how supply and demand together determine equilibrium price and quantity. You should understand, among other ideas, the following:

1. Market competition brings about an equilibrium in which the quantity supplied is equal to the quantity demanded.

---

* Improved technology is continually lowering the cost of discovering and producing oil (shifting the supply curve down and to the right), so what has happened in recent years is not simply an increase in demand but an increase in demand that has outstripped the increase in supply.

2. Only one price/quantity combination is a market equilibrium and you should be able to identify this equilibrium in a diagram.

3. You should understand and be able to explain the incentives that enforce the market equilibrium. What happens when the price is above the equilibrium price? Why? What happens when the price is below the equilibrium price? Why?

4. Gains from trade are maximized at the equilibrium price and quantity and no other price/quantity combination maximizes the gains from trade.

5. You should know from Chapter 3 the major factors that shift demand and supply curves and from this chapter be able to explain and predict the effect of any such shift on the equilibrium price and quantity.

6. A "change in demand [the demand curve]" is not the same thing as "a change in quantity demanded"; a "change in supply [the supply curve]" is not the same thing as "a change in quantity supplied."

Most important, you should be able to work with supply and demand to answer questions about the world.

□ CHAPTER REVIEW

KEY CONCEPTS

Surplus, p. 48

Shortage, p. 48

Equilibrium price, p. 48

Equilibrium quantity, p. 51

FACTS AND TOOLS

1. If the price in a market is above the equilibrium price, does this create a surplus or a shortage?

2. When the price is above the equilibrium price, does greed (in other words, self-interest) tend to push the price down or does it push it up?

3. Jon is on eBay, bidding for a first edition of the influential Frank Miller graphic novel *Batman: The Dark Knight Returns*. In this market, who is Jon competing with: the seller of the graphic novel or the other bidders?

4. Now, Jon is in Japan, trying to get a job as a full-time translator; he wants to translate English TV shows into Japanese and vice versa. He notices that the wage for translators is very low. Who is the "competition" that is pushing the wage down: Does the competition come from businesses who hire the translators or from the other translators?

5. Jules wants to purchase a Royale with cheese from Vincent. Vincent is willing to offer this tasty burger for $3. The most Jules is willing to pay for the tasty burger is $8 (after all, his girlfriend is a vegetarian, so he doesn't get many opportunities for tasty burgers).

a. How large are the potential gains from trade if Jules and Vincent agree to make this trade? In other words, what is the sum of producer and consumer surplus if the trade happens?

b. If the trade takes place at $4, how much producer surplus goes to Vincent? How much consumer surplus goes to Jules?

c. If the trade takes place at $7, how much producer surplus goes to Vincent? How much consumer surplus goes to Jules?

6. What happened in Vernon Smith's lab? Choose the right answer:

a. The price and quantity were close to equilibrium but gains from trade were far from the maximum.

b. The price and quantity were far from equilibrium and gains from trade were far from the maximum.

c. The price and quantity were far from equilibrium but gains from trade were close to the maximum.

d. The price and quantity were close to equilibrium and gains from trade were close to the maximum.

7. When supply falls, what happens to quantity demanded in equilibrium? (This should get you to notice that both suppliers and demanders change their behavior when one curve shifts.)

8. a. When demand increases, what happens to price and quantity in equilibrium?

b. When supply increases, what happens to price and quantity in equilibrium?

c. When supply decreases, what happens to price and quantity in equilibrium?

d. When demand decreases, what happens to price and quantity in equilibrium?

9. a. When demand increases, what happens to price and quantity in equilibrium?

b. When supply increases, what happens to price and quantity in equilibrium?

c. When supply decreases, what happens to price and quantity in equilibrium?

d. When demand decreases, what happens to price and quantity in equilibrium?

No, this is not a mistake. Yes, it is that important.

10. What's the best way to think about the rise in oil prices in the 1970s, when wars and oil embargoes wracked the Middle East? Was it a rise in demand, a fall in demand, a rise in supply, or a fall in supply?

11. What's the best way to think about the rise in oil prices in the last 10 years, as China and India have become richer: Was it a rise in demand, a fall in demand, a rise in supply, or a fall in supply?

THINKING AND PROBLEM SOLVING

1. Suppose the market for batteries looks as follows:

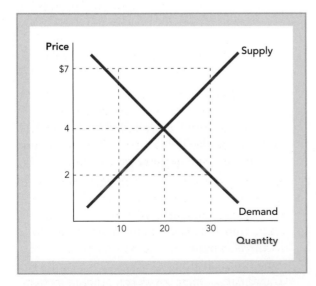

What is the equilibrium price and quantity?

2. Consider the following supply and demand tables for bread. Draw the supply and demand curves for this market. What is the equilibrium price and quantity?

Price of One Loaf	Quantity Supplied	Quantity Demanded
$0.50	10	75
$1	20	55
$2	35	35
$3	50	25
$5	60	10

3. If the price of a one-bedroom apartment in Washington, D.C., is currently $1,000 per month, but the supply and demand curves look as follows, then is there a shortage or surplus of apartments? What would we expect to happen to prices? Why?

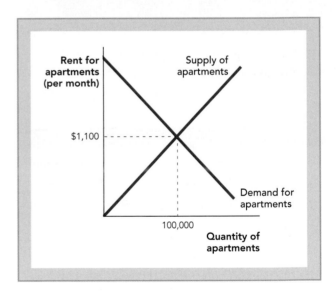

4. Determine the equilibrium quantity and price without drawing a graph.

Price of Good X	Quantity Supplied	Quantity Demanded
$22	100	225
$25	115	200
$30	130	175
$32	150	150
$40	170	110

5. In the figure below, how many pounds of sugar are sellers willing to sell at a price of $20? How much is demanded at this price? What is the buyer's willingness to pay when the quantity is 20 lb? Is this combination of $20 per pound and a quantity of 20 lb an equilibrium? If not, identify the unexploited gains from trade.

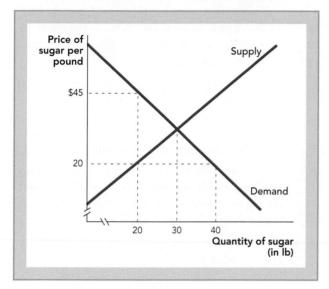

6. The market for marbles is represented in the graph below. What is the total producer surplus? The total consumer surplus? What are the total gains from trade?

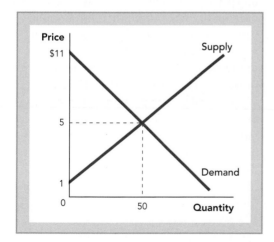

7. Suppose you decided to follow in Vernon Smith's footsteps and conducted your own experiment with your friends. You give out 10 cards, 5 cards to buyers with the figures for willingness to pay of $1, $2, $3, $4, and $5, and 5 cards to sellers with the amounts for costs of $1, $2, $3, $4, and $5. The rules are the same as Vernon Smith implemented.

   a. Draw the supply and demand curves for this market. At a price of $3.50, how many units are demanded? And supplied?

   b. Assuming the market works as predicted, and the market moves to equilibrium, will the buyer who values the good at $1 be able to purchase? Why or why not?

8. If the price of margarine decreases, what happens to the demand for butter? What happens to the equilibrium quantity and price for butter? What would happen if butter and margarine were not substitutes? Use a supply and demand diagram to support your answer.

9. The market for sugar is diagramed below:

   a. What would happen to the equilibrium quantity and price if the wages of sugar cane harvesters increased?

   b. What if a new study was published that emphasized the negative health effects of consuming sugar?

10. If a snowstorm was forecast for the next day, what would happen to the demand for snow shovels? Is this a change in quantity demanded or a change in demand? This shift in the demand curve would affect the price; would this cause a change in quantity supplied or a change in supply?

11. In 2002, the Atkins diet, which emphasized eating more meat and fewer grains, became very popular. What do you suppose that did to the price and quantity of bread? Use supply and demand analysis to support your answer.

12. In recent years, there have been news reports that toys made in China are unsafe. When those news reports show up on CNN and Fox News, what probably happens to the demand for toys made in China? What probably happens to the equilibrium price and quantity of toys made in China? Are Chinese toymakers probably better or worse off when such news comes out?

CHALLENGES

1. For many years, it was illegal to color margarine yellow (margarine is naturally white). In some states, margarine manufacturers were even required to color margarine pink! Who do you think supported these laws? Why? *Hint:* Your analysis in question 8 from the previous section is relevant!

2. Think about two products: "safe cars" (a heavy car such as a BMW 530xi with infrared night vision, four-wheel antilock brakes, and electronic stability control), and "dangerous cars" (a lightweight car such as _____ [name removed for legal reasons, but you can fill in as you wish]).

   a. Are these two products substitutes or complements?

   b. If new research makes it easier to produce safe cars, what happens to the supply of safe cars? What will happen to the equilibrium price of safe cars?

   c. Now that the price of safe cars has changed, how does this impact the demand for dangerous cars?

   d. Now let's tie all of these links into one simple sentence:

   "In a free market, as engineers and scientists discover new ways to makes cars safer, the number of dangerous cars sold will tend to _____."

3. Many clothing stores often have clearance sales at the end of each season. Using the tools you learned in this chapter, can you think of an explanation why?

4. **a.** If oil executives read in the newspaper that massive new oil supplies have been discovered under the Pacific Ocean but will likely only be useful in 10 years, what is likely to happen to the supply of oil *today*? What is the likely equilibrium impact on the price and quantity of oil *today*?

   b. If oil executives read in the newspaper that new solar-power technologies have been discovered but will likely only become useful in 10 years, what is likely to happen to the supply of oil *today*? What is the likely equilibrium impact on the price and quantity of oil *today*?

   c. What's the short version of the above scenarios? Fill in the blank: If we learn *today* about promising *future* energy sources, today's price of energy will _____ and today's quantity of energy will _____.

5. Economists often say that prices are a "rationing mechanism." If the supply of a good falls, how do prices "ration" these now-scarce goods in a competitive market?

6. When the crime rate falls in the area around a factory, what probably happens to wages at that factory?

7. Let's take the idea from the previous question and use it to explain why businesses sometimes try to make their employees happy. If a business can make a job seem fun (by offering inexpensive pizza lunches) or at least safe (by nagging the city government to put police patrols around the factory), what probably happens to the supply of labor? What happens to the equilibrium wage if a factory or office or laboratory becomes a great place where people "really want to work"? How does this explain why the hourly wage for the typical radio or television announcer is only $13 per hour, lower than almost any other job in the entertainment or broadcasting industry?

5

Elasticity and Its Applications

In the fall of 2000, Harvard sophomore Jay Williams flew to the Sudan where a terrible civil war had resulted in many thousands of deaths. Women and children captured in raids by warring tribes were being enslaved and held for ransom. Working with Christian Solidarity International, Williams was able to pay for the release of 4,000 people. But did Williams do the right thing? It's a serious question and one that is surprisingly complex, both morally and economically. By paying for the release of slaves, could Williams have encouraged more people to be enslaved? If so, by how much? Slavery is an abomination. Because of the terrible effects of slavery, careful thought about the best way to deal with the problem is essential. Perhaps surprisingly, the economic concept of elasticity can help people think clearly about the most effective policies to adopt to end slavery.

In this chapter, we develop the tools of demand and supply elasticity. To be honest, at first these tools will seem rather dry and technical. Stick with us, however, and you will see how the concept of elasticity is useful for dealing with important questions such as how best to help people held as slaves for ransom, why the war on drugs can generate violence, why gun buyback programs are unlikely to work, and how to evaluate proposals to increase drilling in the Arctic National Wildlife Refuge (ANWR).

In Chapter 4, we discussed how to shift the supply and demand curves to produce *qualitative* predictions about changes in prices and quantities. Estimating elasticities of demand and supply is the first step in *quantifying* how changes in demand and supply will affect prices and quantities.

The Elasticity of Demand

The **elasticity of demand** measures how responsive the quantity demanded is to a change in price; more responsive equals more elastic.

When the price of a good increases, individuals and businesses will buy less. But how much less? A lot or a little? The **elasticity of demand** measures how responsive the quantity demanded is to a change in price—the more responsive quantity demanded is to a change in the price, the more elastic is the demand curve. Let's start by comparing two different demand curves.

In Figure 5.1, when the price increases from $40 to $50, the quantity demanded decreases from 100 to 20 along demand curve E but only from 100 to 95 along demand curve I—thus, demand curve E is more elastic than demand curve I.

FIGURE 5.1

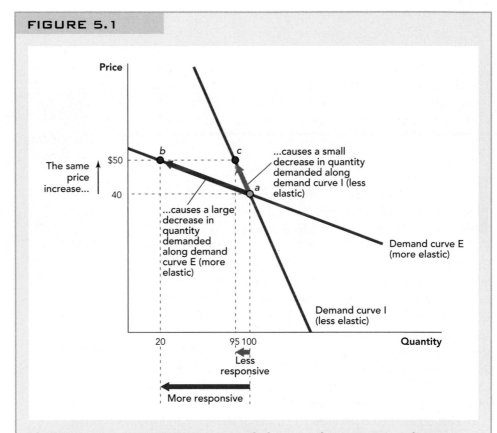

The More Responsive Quantity Demanded Is to a Change in Price, the More Elastic Is the Demand Curve Beginning at point *a*, an increase in price from $40 to $50 causes a big decrease in quantity demanded along demand curve E, from 100 units to 20 units at point *b*. But the same increase in price causes only a small decrease in quantity demanded along demand curve I from 100 to 95 units at point *c*. Since the quantity demanded is more responsive to a change in price along demand curve E, demand curve E is more elastic than demand curve I.

Elasticity is not the same thing as slope, but they are related and for our purposes you won't make any mistakes if you follow the elasticity rule:

Elasticity rule: If two linear demand (or supply) curves run through a common point, then at any given quantity the curve that is flatter is more elastic.

Determinants of the Elasticity of Demand

Of the two curves in Figure 5.1, which do you think would best represent the demand curve for oil?

The demand curve for oil is not very elastic, which means that the quantity demanded falls by only a little even when the price increases by a lot. Thus, demand curve I would best represent the demand curve for oil. The demand for oil is not very elastic because there are *few substitutes* for oil in its major use, transportation.

The fundamental determinant of the elasticity of demand is how easy it is to substitute one good for another. The fewer substitutes for a good, the less elastic the demand. The more substitutes for a good, the more elastic the demand.

When the price of oil goes up people grumble, but few stop using cars, at least not right away. But what happens to the elasticity of the demand for oil over time? The demand for oil tends to become more elastic over time because the more time people have to adjust to a price change, the better they can substitute one good for another. In other words, there are more *substitutes* for oil in the long run than in the short run. Since the OPEC oil price increases in the 1970s (see Figure 4.9 in Chapter 4), the U.S. economy has slowly substituted away from oil by moving toward other sources of energy such as coal, nuclear, and hydroelectric. It took many years, but today the U.S. economy uses about half the amount of oil per dollar of GDP than it did in the 1970s.[1]

In the long run, there are even substitutes for oil in transportation. One reason that mopeds are more popular and SUVs less popular in Europe than in the United States is that taxes make the price of gasoline much higher in Europe than in the United States. Europeans have adjusted by buying more mopeds and smaller cars and driving fewer miles—Americans would do the same if the price of gasoline were expected to increase permanently.

If the price of oil increases by a significant amount for a long period, then even the organization of cities will change as people move from suburbia toward apartments and townhouses located closer to work. It may seem odd to think of moving closer to work as a "substitute for oil," but people adjust to price increases in many ways and economists think of all these adjustments as involving substitutes. If the price of cigarettes goes up and people decide to satisfy their oral cravings by chewing carrots, then carrots are a substitute for cigarettes.

In short, the more time people have to adjust to a change in price, the more elastic the demand curve will be.

Let's compare the demand for Orange Crush, a particular brand of orange soda, with the demand for orange soda. There are many good substitutes for Orange Crush, including Orangina, Fanta, and Slice (Wikipedia lists 24 types of orange soda). As a result, the demand for Orange Crush is very elastic because even a small increase in the price of Orange Crush will result in a large decrease in the quantity demanded as people switch to the substitutes. The demand curve for orange soda, however, is less elastic because there are fewer substitutes for orange soda than there are for Orange Crush and the substitutes such as root beer or cola are not as good. We illustrate this in Figure 5.2 on the next page. The general point is that the demand for a specific brand of a product is more elastic than the demand for a product category. We will come back to this point when we look in more depth at competition and monopoly in Chapters 12 and 13.

FIGURE 5.2

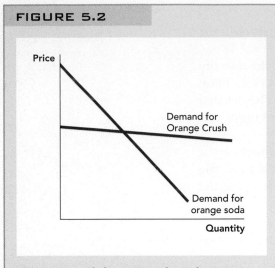

The More and the Better the Substitutes, the More Elastic the Demand There are more substitutes for a particular brand of orange soda, such as Orange Crush, than there are for orange soda. Thus, the demand for Orange Crush is more elastic than the demand for orange soda.

TABLE 5.1 Some Factors Determining the Elasticity of Demand

Less Elastic	More Elastic
Fewer substitutes	More substitutes
Short run (less time)	Long run (more time)
Categories of product	Specific brands
Necessities	Luxuries
Small part of budget	Large part of budget

What counts as a good substitute depends on a buyer's preferences, as well as on objective properties of the good. If the price of Coca-Cola increases at the supermarket, many people will buy Pepsi but others will keep on buying Coca-Cola because for them Pepsi is *not* a good substitute. So, some people have a more elastic demand for Coca-Cola, while other people have a less elastic demand. A closely related idea is that demand is less elastic for goods that people consider to be "necessities" and is more elastic for goods that are considered "luxuries." Of course, for some people their morning coffee at Starbucks is a necessity and for others it's a luxury. Let's summarize by saying that the demand for necessities—however a person defines that term—tends to be less elastic and the demand for luxuries tends to be more elastic.

The higher a person's income, the less concerned they are likely to be with the price of an item; thus, higher income makes demand less elastic. In 2008, the price of wheat tripled, and many people all around the world bought less bread. But neither of the authors of this book cut back much on his consumption of bread. The price of bread is too small a portion of our budgets to worry very much about its price, so our consumption of bread is not very elastic. On the other hand, when the price of housing increases, we buy smaller houses just like everyone else. Thus, the larger the share of a person's budget devoted to a good, the more elastic his or her demand for that good is likely to be.

We summarize the determinants of the elasticity of demand in Table 5.1.

Calculating the Elasticity of Demand

The elasticity of demand has a precise definition with important properties. The elasticity of demand is the percentage change in the quantity demanded divided by the percentage change in price.

$$\text{Elasticity of demand} = E_d = \frac{\text{Percentage change in quantity demanded}}{\text{Percentage change in price}}$$

$$= \frac{\%\Delta Q_{Demanded}}{\%\Delta Price}$$

where Δ (delta) is the mathematical symbol for "change in."

> If the price of oil increases by 10% and over a period of several years the quantity demanded falls by 5%, then the long-run elasticity of demand for oil is $-5\%/10\% = -0.5$, or 0.5 in absolute terms.

> If the price of Minute Maid orange juice falls by 10% and the quantity of Minute Maid orange juice demanded increases by 17.5%, then the elasticity of demand for Minute Maid OJ is $17.5\%/-10\% = -1.75$, or 1.75 in absolute terms.[2]

Elasticities of demand are always negative because when the price goes up, the quantity demanded always goes down (and vice versa), which is why economists sometimes drop the negative sign and work with the absolute value instead.

When the absolute value of the elasticity is less than 1, the demand is not very elastic or economists say the demand is **inelastic;** if it is greater than 1, economists say that demand is **elastic;** and if it is exactly equal to 1, economists say that demand is **unit elastic.** So in our calculations above, oil has inelastic demand and Minute Maid orange juice has elastic demand.

Using the Midpoint Method to Calculate the Elasticity of Demand

To calculate an elasticity, you need to know how to calculate the percentage change in quantity and the percentage change in price. That is a bit trickier than it sounds. To see why, let's suppose that you observe the price and quantity pairs shown in the table at the right (careful readers will note that these points correspond to points *a* and *b* along demand curve E in Figure 5.1).

If you think of moving from point *a* to point *b* (let's call this moving from "before" to "after"), then the quantity demanded falls from 100 to 20 so the change in quantity demanded is −80. What is the percentage change in quantity demanded?

If the beginning quantity Q_{Before} is 100 and the ending quantity Q_{After} is 20, it seems natural to calculate the percentage change in quantity like this:

The **elasticity of demand** is a measure of how responsive the quantity demanded is to a change in price. It is computed by

$$E_d = \frac{\%\Delta Q_{Demanded}}{\%\Delta Price}$$

$|E_d| > 1 = $ **Elastic**

$|E_d| < 1 = $ **Inelastic**

$|E_d| = 1 = $ **Unit Elastic**

	Price	Quantity Demanded
Point *a*	$40	100
Point *b*	$50	20

$$\frac{\Delta Q}{Q} = \frac{Q_{After} - Q_{Before}}{Q_{Before}} = \frac{20 - 100}{100} = \frac{-80}{100} = -0.8 = -80\%$$

But now think of moving from point *b* to point *a*. In this case, quantity demanded increases from 20 to 100 and it now seems natural to calculate the percentage change in quantity like this:

$$\frac{\Delta Q}{Q} = \frac{Q_{After} - Q_{Before}}{Q_{Before}} = \frac{100 - 20}{20} = \frac{80}{20} = 4 = 400\%$$

In the first case, we are thinking of a percentage decrease in quantity and in the second of a percentage increase in quantity so it's easy to see why one number is negative and the other positive. But why are the numbers so different when we are calculating exactly the same change?

The different values occur because the base of the calculation changes. If you are driving 100 mph and decrease speed to 20 mph, it's natural to say that your speed went down by 80% because you calculate using a base of 100. But if you are driving 20 mph and you increase speed to 100 mph, it's natural to say that you increased your speed by 400% since you now use 20 as the base. Economists would like to calculate the same number for elasticity whether the quantity (or speed) decreases from 100 to 20 or increases from 20 to 100.

To avoid problems with the choice of base, economists calculate the percentage change in quantity by dividing the change in quantity by the *average or midpoint quantity*—the base is thus the same whether you think about quantity as increasing or decreasing.

Here is the formula:

$$\text{Elasticity of demand} = E_d = \frac{\%\Delta Q_{Demanded}}{\%\Delta Price}$$

$$= \frac{\dfrac{\text{Change in quantity demanded}}{\text{Average quantity}}}{\dfrac{\text{Change in price}}{\text{Average price}}} = \frac{\dfrac{Q_{After} - Q_{Before}}{(Q_{After} + Q_{Before})/2}}{\dfrac{P_{After} - P_{Before}}{(P_{After} + P_{Before})/2}}$$

In this case, we calculate the percentage change in quantity demanded as $\dfrac{-80}{(100 + 20)/2} \times 100 = -133.3\%$ and we also use the midpoint formula for the percentage change in price, which is $\dfrac{(50 - 40)}{(50 + 40)/2} \times 100 = 22.2\%$. With these two numbers, we can now calculate the elasticity of demand over this portion of the demand curve:

$$E_d = -133.3\%/22.2\% = -6$$

Notice that the absolute value of the elasticity, 6, is greater than 1 so the demand is elastic over this range.

It's most important that you understand the concept of elasticity. To calculate an elasticity, don't worry too much; just remember where the formula is located and plug in the numbers. In the second appendix to this chapter, we show how to create a simple Excel spreadsheet to calculate elasticity so you need not even worry about making calculation mistakes (at least not on your homework!).

Total Revenues and the Elasticity of Demand

A firm's revenues are equal to price per unit times quantity sold.

$$\text{Revenue} = \text{Price} \times \text{Quantity, or } R = P \times Q$$

Elasticity measures how much Q goes down when P goes up, so you might suspect that there is a relationship between elasticity and revenue. Indeed, the relationship is remarkably useful: If the demand curve is inelastic, then revenues go up when the price goes up. If the demand curve is elastic, then revenues go down when the price goes up.

Let's give some intuition for this result. Imagine that the demand curve is inelastic, thus not responsive to price. This means that when P goes up by a lot, Q goes down by a little, like this

$$\underset{\downarrow}{\overset{\uparrow}{P \times Q}}$$

So when the demand curve is inelastic, what will happen to revenues? If P goes up by a lot and Q goes down by a little, then revenues will go up

FIGURE 5.3

Elasticities and Revenues When the price increases, what happens to total revenue? If demand is inelastic, an increase in price increases revenues. In the left panel, an increase in the price from $40 to $50 increases revenues from $4,000 to $4,750 so demand is inelastic. If the demand is elastic, then an increase in price decreases revenues. In the right panel, an increase in price from $40 to $50 decreases revenues from $4,000 to $1,000 so demand is elastic.

$$\uparrow \quad \uparrow$$
$$R = P \times Q$$
$$\downarrow$$

Thus, when the demand curve is inelastic, revenues go up when the price goes up and, of course, revenues will go down when the price goes down.

We can also show the relationship in a diagram. Figure 5.3 shows an inelastic demand curve on the left and an elastic demand curve on the right.* Revenue is $P \times Q$ so revenue is equal to the area of a rectangle with height equal to price and width equal to the quantity; for example, when the price is $40 and the quantity is 100, revenues are $4,000, or the area of the blue rectangle (note that the blue and green rectangles overlap).

In both diagrams, the blue rectangles show revenue at a price of $40 and the green rectangles show revenues at the higher price of $50. Compare the size of the green and blue rectangles when the demand curve is inelastic (on the left) and when the demand curve is elastic (on the right). What do you see? When the demand curve is inelastic, an increase in price increases revenues (the green rectangle

---

* These curves are the same curves as in Figure 5.1 so they run through a common point and thus we can apply our elasticity rule, which tells us that at any given quantity the flatter curve is more elastic than the steeper curve.

is bigger than the blue rectangle), but when the demand curve is elastic, an increase in price decreases revenues (the green rectangle is smaller than the blue rectangle).

Of course, the relationships hold in reverse as well. If the demand curve is inelastic, a price decrease causes a decrease in revenues, and if the demand curve is elastic, a price decrease causes an increase in revenues.

Can you guess what happens to revenues when price increases or decreases when the demand curve is unit elastic? Right, nothing! When the demand curve is unit elastic, a change in price is exactly matched by an equal and opposite percentage change in quantity so revenues stay the same. Unit elasticity is the dividing point between elastic and inelastic curves.

You should be able to use all of these relationships on an exam. Table 5.2 summarizes what we have covered so far.

TABLE 5.2 Elasticity and Revenue

Absolute Value of Elasticity	Name	How Revenue Changes with Price
$|E_d| < 1$	Inelastic	Revenue and price move together.
$|E_d| > 1$	Elastic	Revenue and price move in opposite directions.
$|E_d| = 1$	Unit Elastic	Revenue stays the same when price changes.

If you must, memorize the table. At least one of your textbook authors, however, can never remember the relationship between elasticity and total revenue. So, instead of memorizing the relationship, he always derives it by drawing little diagrams like those in Figure 5.3. If you can easily duplicate these diagrams, you too will always be able to answer questions involving elasticity and total revenue.

Applications of Demand Elasticity

Let's put to work what you have learned so far about demand elasticity. Here are two applications.

How American Farmers Have Worked Themselves Out of a Job   Using the same inputs of land, labor, and capital, American farmers can produce more than twice as much food today as they could in 1950—that's an amazing increase in productivity. The increase in productivity means that Americans can produce more food per person today than in 1950. But how much more food can Americans eat? Although it doesn't always seem this way, Americans want to consume only so much more food even if the price falls by a lot. So what type of demand curve does this suggest? An inelastic demand curve; and remember, when the demand curve is inelastic, a fall in price means a fall in revenues.

The left panel of Figure 5.4 shows how the American farmer has worked himself (and herself) out of a job. Increases in farming productivity have reduced cost, shifting the supply curve down and reducing the price of food. But since the demand curve for food is inelastic, the quantity of food demanded has increased by a smaller percentage than the price has fallen. As a result, farming revenues have declined. Notice that in the left panel of Figure 5.4,

FIGURE 5.4

Farming/Computer Chips Productivity improvements have increased the supply of food and the supply of computer chips, thus reducing the prices of these goods. The demand for food, however, is inelastic, while the demand for computer chips is elastic. As a result, the decrease in the price of food has driven down farm revenues, while the decrease in the price of computer chips has driven up computer chip revenues.

the blue rectangle (farm revenues today) is smaller than the green rectangle (revenues in 1950)—just as we showed in Figure 5.3.

Increases in productivity, however, do not always mean that revenue falls. In the last several decades, productivity has increased in computer chips even faster than in farming. But as the price of computer chips has fallen, the quantity of computer chips demanded has increased even more. Computer chips are now not just in computers but in phones, televisions, automobiles, and toys. As a result, revenues for the computer chip industry have increased and made computing a larger share of the American economy. What type of demand curve does this suggest? An elastic demand curve. The right panel in Figure 5.4 illustrates how an increase in productivity in computing has shifted the supply curve down and reduced prices, but the quantity of computer chips demanded has increased by an even greater percentage than the price has fallen. As a result, computer chip revenues have increased.

The lesson is that whether a demand curve is elastic or inelastic has a tremendous influence on how an industry evolves over time. If you want to be in on a growing industry, it helps to know the elasticity of demand.

Why the War on Drugs Is Hard to Win

It's hard to defeat an enemy that grows stronger the more you strike against him or her. (See the movies *Rocky I, II, III, IV, V,* and *VI.*) The war on drugs is like that. We illustrate with a simple model.

The U.S. government spends over $33 billion a year arresting over 1.5 million people and deterring the supply of drugs with police, prisons, and border patrols.[*] This, in turn, increases the cost of smuggling and dealing drugs. (The war on drugs also increases the costs of buying drugs. We could include this factor in our model, but to keep the model simple, we will focus on increases in the costs of supplying drugs.) When costs go up,

---

[*]See Miron, Jeffrey A. 2004. *Drug War Crimes: The Consequences of Prohibition* (Oakland, CA: Independent Institute) and MacCoun, Robert J. and Peter Reuter. 2001. *Drug War Heresies: Learning from Other Vices, Times, and Places* (Cambridge, UK: Cambridge University Press) for two good analyses of the war on drugs from an economic perspective.

FIGURE 5.5

The Drug War Is Hard to Win Because Seller Revenues Increase with Greater Enforcement Without drug prohibition, the market equilibrium is at point *a* with seller revenues given by the blue area. Prohibition raises the costs of supply, pushing up the supply curve and moving the equilibrium to point *b*. At point *b*, seller revenues are the larger green area. Prohibition in this graph reduces the quantity of drugs consumed a little, from $Q_{no\ pro}$ to Q_{pro} but it raises seller revenues by a lot.

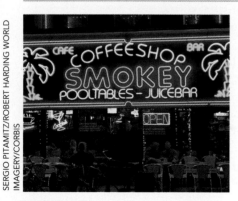

High Prices?

How do we know how much prohibition has raised the price of illegal drugs? In the Netherlands, small quantities of marijuana can be bought openly at "coffee shops" and the price is roughly the same as it is in the United States.

It may seem surprising that prohibition doesn't raise prices more, but prohibition raises some costs of selling illegal drugs while lowering others. Marijuana shops in the Netherlands, for example, pay taxes, while most drug dealers in the United States do not.

suppliers require a higher price to supply any given quantity so the supply curve shifts up—in Figure 5.5 from "Supply with no prohibition" to "Supply with prohibition."[†]

The most important assumption in Figure 5.5 is that the demand curve is inelastic. It's hard to get good data on how the quantity of drugs demanded varies with the price, but most studies suggest that the demand for illegal drugs is quite inelastic, approximately 0.5. Inelastic demand is also plausible from what we know intuitively about how much people are willing to pay for drugs even when the price rises. Economists have much better data on the elasticity of demand for cigarettes, which one can think of as the elasticity of demand for the drug nicotine and it too is about 0.5.[3]

What happens to seller revenues when the demand curve is inelastic and the price rises? (Review Figure 5.3 if you don't know immediately.) When the demand curve is inelastic, an increase in price increases seller revenues. In Figure 5.5, the blue rectangle is seller revenues at the no prohibition price; the much larger green rectangle is seller revenues with prohibition. Prohibition increases the cost of selling drugs, which raises the price, but at a higher price, revenues from drug selling are greater even if the quantity sold is somewhat smaller.

The more effective prohibition is at raising costs, the greater are drug industry revenues. So, more effective prohibition means that drug sellers have more money to buy guns, pay bribes, fund the dealers, and even research and develop new technologies in drug delivery (like crack cocaine). It's hard to beat an enemy that gets stronger the more you strike against him or her.

The war on drugs is difficult to win, but that doesn't necessarily mean that it's not worth fighting. Nobel Prize-winning economist Gary S. Becker, however, suggests a change in tactics. Suppose drugs were legal but taxed, much as alcohol is today. Becker suggests that the tax could be set so that it raised seller costs exactly as much as did prohibition (in Figure 5.5 simply relabel "Supply with prohibition" as "Supply with tax"). Since the tax raises costs by the same amount, the quantity of drugs sold would be the same under the tax as under prohibition. The only difference would be that instead of increasing seller revenues, a tax would increase government revenues (by the green rectangle *not* including the

---

[†]Note that we have assumed that the supply of drugs is perfectly horizontal, which is plausible for an agricultural product whose production can be expanded or contracted very easily without an increase in costs. We discuss the elasticity of supply at greater length in the next section.

overlap with the blue rectangle). Many of the unfortunate spillovers of the war on drugs—things like gangs, guns, and corruption—could be greatly reduced under a "legal but taxed" system.[*]

Let's turn now to the elasticity of supply.

The Elasticity of Supply

When the price of a good like oil increases, suppliers will increase the quantity supplied, but by how much? Will the quantity supplied increase by a lot or by a little? The **elasticity of supply** measures how responsive the quantity supplied is to a change in price. To see the intuition, let's take a look at Figure 5.6, which shows two different supply curves.

CHECK YOURSELF

> Which is more elastic, the demand for computers or the demand for Dell computers?
> The elasticity of demand for eggs has been estimated to be 0.1. If the price of eggs increases by 10%, what will happen to the total revenue of egg producers or in other words the total spending on eggs? Will it go up or down?
> If a fashionable clothing store raises its prices by 25%, what does that suggest about the store's estimate of the elasticity of demand for its products?

The **elasticity of supply** measures how responsive the quantity supplied is to a change in price.

FIGURE 5.6

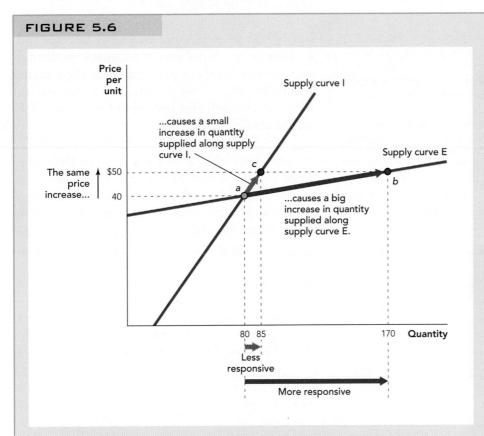

The More Responsive Quantity Supplied Is to a Change in Price, the More Elastic the Supply Curve Beginning at point *a*, an increase in price from $40 to $50 causes a small increase in quantity supplied along supply curve I, from 80 to 85 units (at point *c*). But the same increase in price causes a big increase in quantity supplied along supply curve E, from 80 to 170 units (at point *b*). Since the quantity supplied is more responsive to a change in price, supply curve E is more elastic than supply curve I.

In Figure 5.6, when the price increases from $40 to $50, the quantity supplied increases from 80 to 85 along supply curve I but a much larger amount from 80 to 170 along supply curve E. Since the quantity supplied is more responsive to a change in price, supply curve E is more elastic than supply curve I.

---

[*]On the benefits of a tax system for currently illegal drugs, see Becker, Gary S., Kevin M. Murphy, and Michael Grossman. 2006. The market for illegal goods: The case of drugs. *Journal of Political Economy 114*(1): 38–60.

FIGURE 5.7

A perfectly inelastic supply curve

Price

Quantity

The supply of Picasso paintings is very inelastic.

A perfectly elastic supply curve

Price

Quantity

The supply of toothpicks is very elastic.

The Elasticity of Supply of Toothpicks and Picasso Paintings The supply of Picasso paintings is very inelastic because Picasso won't paint any more no matter how high the price rises. The supply of toothpicks is very elastic because it's easy for suppliers to make more in response to even a small increase in price.

Guernica—never again.

Detail of painting by Pablo Picasso

Determinants of the Elasticity of Supply

Which supply curve, supply curve I or supply curve E, do you think would better represent the supply curve for oil? Even large increases in the price of oil will not increase the quantity of oil supplied by very much because it's not easy to quickly increase the production of oil. Producing more oil requires time and a significant increase in the costs of exploration and drilling. Thus, the supply curve for oil is not very elastic (we could also say inelastic) and would be better represented by supply curve I.

The fundamental determinant of the elasticity of supply is how quickly per-unit costs increase with an increase in production. If increased production requires much higher per-unit costs, then supply will be less elastic—or inelastic. If production can increase with constant per-unit costs, then supply will be elastic.

It's usually difficult to increase the supply of raw materials like oil, coal, and gold without increasing costs—remember from Chapter 3 that the higher the price, the deeper the mine—so the supply of raw materials is often not very elastic. The supply for manufactured goods is usually more elastic since production can often be increased at the same cost per unit by building more factories. To fully understand the elasticity of supply, let's consider two goods that represent polar cases of the elasticity of supply: Picasso paintings and toothpicks.

Picasso won't be painting any more *Guernica*s no matter how high the price of his paintings rises so the supply of Picasso paintings is not at all elastic—perfectly inelastic would be a good working assumption.* A perfectly inelastic supply curve is a vertical line. We show an example in the left panel of Figure 5.7, which indicates that even a very large increase in price won't increase the quantity supplied.

Toothpick manufacturers, however, can increase the supply of toothpicks without an increase in their costs per toothpick by cutting down just a few more trees and running them through the mill. Thus, a small increase in the price of toothpicks will generate a large increase in quantity supplied; that is, the supply of toothpicks will be very elastic—perfectly elastic would be a good working assumption. A perfectly elastic supply curve is flat, which indicates that even a tiny increase in price increases the quantity supplied by a very large amount. We show a perfectly elastic supply curve in the right panel of Figure 5.7.

It's easy to expand the supply of toothpicks because even if the toothpick industry doubles in size, the increases in the demand for wood will be negligible, so the toothpick industry can expand without pushing up the price of its primary input, wood. But if the housing industry were to double in

---

*Why isn't the supply of Picasso paintings perfectly inelastic for certain? The supply of newly created Picasso paintings is perfectly inelastic, but with a higher price more people will be induced to sell their Picasso paintings so the market supply of Picasso paintings will be very inelastic but not necessarily perfectly inelastic.

size, the demand for wood would increase dramatically, and since it takes time to plant and harvest new trees, the price of wood and thus the price of houses would increase in the short run. More generally, supply is more elastic when the industry can be expanded without causing a big increase in the demand for that industry's inputs.

A closely related point is that the local supply of a good is much more elastic than the global supply. The supply of oil to the world is inelastic because world production won't increase without a significant increase in the cost of production per barrel. But imagine that more people move to Austin, Texas, increasing the demand for oil in that city. It's very easy to ship more oil to Austin from other parts of the United States so the supply of oil to Austin is well approximated by a perfectly elastic supply curve.

As with demand, supply tends to be more elastic in the long run than in the short run because in the long run, suppliers have more time to adjust. Suppliers can respond to an increase in the price of bicycles fairly quickly by running currently existing factories at higher capacity. Given more time, however, suppliers can increase output at lower cost by building new factories.

For some goods, it's almost impossible to increase output much in the short run. The best Scotch whisky, for example, is aged in oak barrels for 10, 20, or even 30 years. If the price of such high-quality Scotch whisky increases today, it will be at least 10 years before supply can increase.

We summarize the primary factors that determine the elasticity of supply in Table 5.3.

TABLE 5.3 Primary Factors Determining the Elasticity of Supply	
Less Elastic	**More Elastic**
Difficult to increase production at constant unit cost (e.g., some raw materials)	Easy to increase production at constant unit cost (e.g., some manufactured goods)
Large share of market for inputs	Small share of market for inputs
Global supply	Local supply
Short run	Long run

Calculating the Elasticity of Supply

The elasticity of supply also has a precise definition. The **elasticity of supply** is the percentage change in the quantity supplied divided by the percentage change in price.

Examples:

> If the price of cocoa rises by 10% and the quantity supplied increases by 3%, then the elasticity of supply for cocoa is $\frac{3\%}{10\%} = \mathbf{0.3}$.

> If the price of coffee falls by 10% and the quantity supplied of coffee falls by 1.5%, then the elasticity of supply for coffee is $\frac{-1.5\%}{-10\%} = \mathbf{0.15}$.[4]

Using the Midpoint Method to Calculate the Elasticity of Supply As with demand elasticities, it's important to calculate percent changes for supply

The **elasticity of supply** is a measure of how responsive the quantity supplied is to a change in price. It is computed by

$$E_s = \frac{\%\Delta Q_{Supplied}}{\%\Delta Price}$$

elasticities using the midpoint method. Here is the midpoint formula for the elasticity of supply.

$$\text{Elasticity of supply} = E_s = \frac{\%\Delta Q_{Supplied}}{\%\Delta Price}$$

$$= \frac{\dfrac{\text{Change in quantity supplied}}{\text{Average quantity}}}{\dfrac{\text{Change in price}}{\text{Average price}}} = \frac{\dfrac{Q_{After} - Q_{Before}}{(Q_{After} + Q_{Before})/2}}{\dfrac{P_{After} - P_{Before}}{(P_{After} + P_{Before})/2}}$$

Applications of Supply Elasticity

Let's examine two important issues in public policy, gun buybacks and slave redemption. In both cases, understanding the elasticity of supply is critical if people are to evaluate these policies wisely.

Gun Buyback Programs   The police in Washington, D.C., bought over 6,000 guns, *no questions asked*, from anyone coming to one of their gun buy-backs held between August 1999 and December 2000. The program got a big assist from then President Clinton and the Department of Housing and Urban Development, which paid most of the buyback's $528,000 cost. Millions of dollars more were spent buying guns in Chicago, Sacramento, Seattle, and dozens of other cities around the country.[5]

The theory of gun buybacks is that gun buybacks (1) reduce the number of guns in circulation and (2) reductions in the number of guns in circulation reduces crime. It's not obvious that point (2) is true—guns are used for self-defense as well as for crime so fewer guns could mean more crime. But we don't have to decide that controversial question here because simple economic theory suggests that point (1) is false—gun buybacks in a city like Washington, D.C., are unlikely to reduce the number of guns in circulation. Let's see why.

We can analyze the effect of this program with a few questions. What kinds of guns are most likely to be sold at the gun buyback, high-quality or low-quality guns? And, what is the elasticity of supply of such guns to a city like Washington, D.C.?

What type of gun is most likely to be sold at a gun buyback? The best gun to sell at a buyback is one that you can't sell anywhere else, so buybacks attract low-quality guns. In one Seattle buyback, 17% of the guns turned in didn't even fire.[6]

Now here is the key question: What is the elasticity of supply of low-quality guns to a city like Washington, D.C.? Recall from Table 5.3 that local supply curves are typically more elastic than global or national supply curves. It's estimated that there are 150 to 200 million guns in the United States so there are plenty of low-quality guns. So many that the supply of such guns to Washington, D.C., will be very elastic—elastic enough to make perfectly elastic a good working assumption.

Now that we know that the supply of low-quality guns to Washington, D.C., is very elastic, let's draw the diagram and analyze the policy. In Figure 5.8, we draw a perfectly elastic supply curve. With no buyback, the price of a low-quality, used gun is $84 and 1,000 guns are traded in Washington. The gun buy back program increases the demand for used guns, shifting the demand curve outward, and the increase in demand pushes up the quantity of guns supplied in Washington, D.C., to 6,000 units. But the supply is so elastic that the price of guns doesn't increase so even though the police buy 5,000 guns, the quantity of guns traded on the streets stays at 1,000. In other words, there is no net change in the number of guns on the streets of D.C.

If this seems difficult to believe, imagine that instead of guns, the Washington police decided to buy back shoes. Remember, the idea of a gun buyback is to reduce the number of people in Washington, D.C., with guns. Now, do you think that a shoe buyback would reduce the number of people in Washington, D.C., with shoes? Of course not. What will happen? People will sell their old shoes, the ones they don't wear anymore. Some enterprising individuals might even buy old shoes from thrift shops and sell those to the police. (In one Oakland gun buyback, some enterprising gun dealers from Reno, Nevada, drove to Oakland and sold the police more than 50 low-quality guns.[7]) The shoe buyback is unlikely to cause people to go shoeless, and for the same reasons a gun buyback is unlikely to cause people to go gunless.

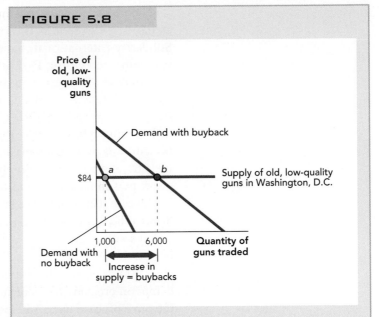

FIGURE 5.8

Elasticity and Gun Buybacks In the initial equilibrium at point *a*, 1,000 low-quality guns are traded. When police buy guns, the demand for guns increases, but since the supply of guns to a local region is very elastic, the street price of guns does not increase. As a result, the police can buy as many guns as they want, but there is no decrease in guns on the street.

The key point is that if the police can't drive up the price of guns, then they can't reduce the quantity of guns demanded on the streets. And the price of guns is determined not in Washington, D.C., but in the national market for guns where millions of guns are bought and sold so a police buyback of 5,000 guns is too small to influence the price.

It's even possible that gun buybacks will *increase* the number of guns in circulation. Suppose that gun buybacks become a common and permanent feature of the market for guns. Before the gun buyback, a purchaser of a new gun expects that it will eventually wear out or otherwise fall in value until it becomes worthless. But when gun buybacks are common, someone buying a gun knows that if it stops working, he can always sell it to the government. A buyback makes new guns more valuable; now they come with an insurance policy protecting against declines in value, which increases the demand for new guns.[8] You have probably experienced the same effect—students are more willing to buy an expensive textbook if they know they can easily sell it at the end of the semester—but do keep this book forever!

Given the economic analysis, it's not surprising that studies of gun buybacks have shown them to be completely ineffective at reducing crime.[9]

The Economics of Slave Redemption

Let's return to our opening example. Recall that Harvard sophomore Jay Williams flew to the Sudan in fall 2000 to buy the freedom of people who had been enslaved. Working with Christian Solidarity International, Williams was able to buy and free 4,000 people. Donations came from all over the United States, including a fourth-grade class in Denver.[10]

Jay Williams (right) in the Sudan.

The policy of slave redemption has been controversial. Some groups such as Christian Freedom International, equally as humanitarian as Christian Solidarity International, have argued that slave redemption can make a bad situation even worse. Perhaps surprisingly, at the heart of the controversy is the concept of the elasticity of supply. If groups who pay to free people from slavery increase the demand for slaves, what effect will this have on the price of slaves and on the incentives of those who traffic in people?

In Figure 5.9, we show the best case for slave redemption, when the supply curve is perfectly inelastic (vertical). When the supply curve is perfectly inelastic, there is a fixed number of slaves no matter what the price. As a result, every person ransomed and freed is one less slave held in captivity. This may be the case that people like Jay Williams were implicitly thinking of when they flew to the Sudan.

Let's take a closer look at Figure 5.9. Before the slave redemption program begins, the price of a slave is $15, a realistic number for slaves in Sudan, and there are 1,000 slaves bought and held in captivity every year (point *a*). With the redemption program, the demand for slaves increases (shifts outward), which pushes the price of slaves up to $50 (point *b*). Now here is the key: At a price of $50, the quantity of slaves demanded by potential slave owners decreases to 200 (point *c*). The remaining 800 slaves are bought and freed by the redeemers. Because there is no increase in the quantity supplied in this case, every slave purchased means one less person held in slavery. Note that slave redemption works by driving up the price of slaves so high that potential owners cannot afford to buy slaves. In other words, to work well, slave redeemers must outbid potential slave owners.

Unfortunately, the supply of slaves is unlikely to be perfectly inelastic. We return to one of the primary lessons of this book, incentives. When people en-

FIGURE 5.9

Slave Redemption Works Best When the Supply Curve for Slaves Is Perfectly Inelastic In the initial equilibrium at point *a*, potential slave owners purchase 1,000 slaves at a price of $15. The increase in demand from the redeemers pushes up the price of slaves to $50 at point *b*. At the higher price, the quantity of slaves demanded by potential slave owners is just 200 so the redeemers are able to free 800 slaves. Since there is no increase in the quantity supplied, every slave purchased is a slave freed.

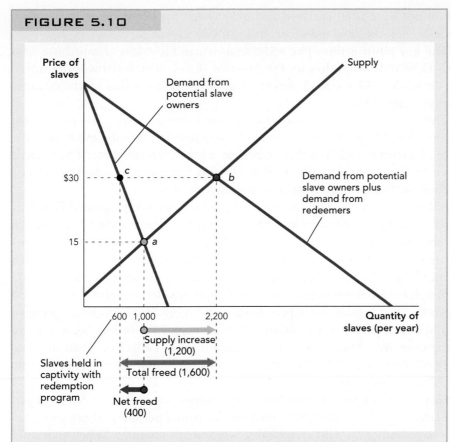

FIGURE 5.10

Slave Redemption When the Supply Curve Is Not Perfectly Inelastic When the slave redeemers enter the market, the demand for slaves increases and the price rises from $15 at point *a* to $30 at point *b*. At the higher price, potential slave owners demand just 600 slaves, or 400 fewer than before—that's the good aspect of slave redemption. But at the higher price, slave traffickers increase the quantity of slaves supplied from 1,000 to 2,200. The slave redeemers free 1,600 slaves, but 1,200 of these people would not have been enslaved had it not been for the increase in demand; thus, on net just 400 slaves are freed.

ter the market to buy back slaves and increase the price of slaves, they increase the incentive to capture more slaves.

Figure 5.10 analyzes the more realistic case when the supply curve is not perfectly inelastic. In the initial equilibrium, the price of slaves is $15 and potential owners buy 1,000 slaves (point *a*). When the redeemers enter the market, the demand for slaves increases and the price increases from $15 to $30 (point *b*). The price of slaves does not increase as much as when the supply curve was perfectly inelastic because some of the increased demand for slaves is met by a greater quantity supplied. At a price of $30, the quantity of slaves demanded by potential owners falls from 1,000 to 600 (point *c*), but notice also that the total number of people captured by human traffickers increases by 1,200 to 2,200 (point *b*). Of these 2,200, 1,600 are freed by the redeemers, leaving 600 held in captivity.

Let's summarize: Before redemption, 1,000 slaves were demanded by slave owners. After redemption, demand has dropped to 600 slaves from these slave owners. This is the good result of the redemption program. But due to the higher price of slaves, slave traffickers increase the quantity of slaves from 1,000 to 2,200. The redeemers free 1,600 of these 2,200 slaves, but 1,200 of these would not have been enslaved had it not been for the increase in demand. Thus, on net, the slave redeemers free just 400 slaves.

The key point is this: The additional demand for slaves from those who wish to free slaves pushes up the price of slaves, which reduces the quantity demanded—that's good. But the higher price also pushes up the quantity supplied—that's bad.

Thus, slavery redemption programs create a true dilemma. The groups that buy freedom can reduce the number of slaves held in captivity, but only at the price of increasing the number of people who are enslaved for at least some time. An economist can point to this dilemma but economics does not offer a solution (and unfortunately neither does anyone else).

Is there any evidence on the effect of slave redemption programs? Remember that one sign of whether the redemption program is working is how much the program increases the price of slaves. Higher prices mean that the redeemers are outbidding potential slave traffickers. Data on slave prices in the Sudan are unreliable, but the fragmentary data that do exist are not encouraging. Although the redemption program initially appeared to raise prices, prices soon began to fall.[11] Recall that supply tends to be more elastic in the long run—thus, the data on prices are consistent with a supply curve that became more elastic over time. Since redemption programs are less effective when the elasticity of supply is greater, the data on prices suggest that the program became less effective over time.

Finally, let us note some further complications. Slavery in the Sudan is part of a larger civil war—the government in Khartoum permits and even encourages slave traffickers who attack the government's enemies. When redeemer groups buy slaves, they are funding not simply slave traffickers but shock troops in a civil war. Guns bought with money received from selling slaves can be used to kill as well as to enslave. Even if we concluded that slave redemption was on average good for the slaves, it might not be good once we account for all of the *external effects* of enriching slave raiders. (We explain the idea of external effects at greater length in Chapter 10.)

Ultimately, the only way to truly end slavery is to raise the punishment for buying or selling slaves so high that there is no longer a market for slaves. Doing this in the Sudan will require an end to the civil war and the establishment of the rule of law.*

Using Elasticities for Quick Predictions (Optional)

Economists are often asked to predict how shifts in demand and supply will change market prices. Two simple price-change formulas make it possible to make quick predictions for price changes using elasticities.[12]

> Percent change in price from a shift in demand $= \dfrac{\text{Percent change in demand}}{|E_d| + E_s}$

> Percent change in price from a shift in supply $= -\dfrac{\text{Percent change in supply}}{|E_d| + E_s}$

*For more on the difficult ethics and economics of slave redemption, see the essays in Kwame Anthony Appiah and Martin Bunzl. 2007. *Buying Freedom: The Ethics and Economics of Slave Redemption*. (Princeton, NJ: Princeton University Press). See especially, Chapter 1, "Some Simple Analytics of Slave Redemption," by Dean S. Karlan and Alan B. Krueger, for an incisive economic analysis that we have drawn on.

CHECK YOURSELF

> A computer manufacturer makes an experimental computer chip that critics praise, leading to a huge increase in the demand for the chip. How elastic is supply in the short run? What about the long run?

> Will the same increase in the demand for housing increase prices more in Manhattan or in Des Moines, Iowa?

These formulas are approximations that work well when the percent change in demand or supply is small, say, 10% or less.[13] Let's apply the formula to an interesting problem.

How Much Would the Price of Oil Fall if the Arctic National Wildlife Refuge Were Opened Up for Drilling?

The Arctic National Wildlife Refuge (ANWR) is the largest of Alaska's 16 national wildlife refuges. It is believed to contain significant deposits of petroleum. Former President George W. Bush argued in favor of drilling in ANWR.

> Increasing our domestic energy supply will help lower gasoline prices and utility bills. We can and should produce more crude oil here at home in environmentally responsible ways. The most promising site for oil in America is a 2,000 acre site in the Arctic National Wildlife Refuge, and thanks to technology, we can reach this energy with little impact on the land or wildlife.[14]

At what price should we drill for oil in ANWR?

Some environmentalists disagree about whether the oil can be produced in environmentally responsible ways. We will leave that debate to others. What do economists say about the former president's assertion that "Increasing our domestic energy supply will help lower gasoline prices and utility bills"? An increase in supply will lower prices, but by how much?

The Department of Energy's Energy Information Service (EIS) predicts that production from ANWR will average about 800,000 barrels per day, or a little bit less than 1% of worldwide oil production (86 million barrels per day in 2010 and increasing slowly over time). Let's be generous and suppose that ANWR increases world supply by 1%. Since the elasticity of demand for oil is about −0.5 and in the long run the best estimate of the elasticity of supply is about 0.3, using our price formula, we have

$$\text{Percent change in price of oil from a 1\% increase in supply} = -\frac{1\%}{0.5 + 0.3}$$
$$= -1.25\%$$

A 1.25% fall in price won't seem like very much when *you* are gassing up at the pump but don't forget that *every user of oil in the world* will benefit from the fall in price—so a fall of 1.25% is nothing to sneeze at.

So should we drill for oil in ANWR or not? The answer will depend on the value of conservation, the costs of drilling for oil (including the costs of a potential oil spill such as occured in the Gulf of Mexico), and the price and quantity of oil that can be recovered. Not an easy calculation!

☐ Takeaway

The elasticity of demand measures how responsive the quantity demanded is to a change in price—the more responsive, the more elastic the demand. Similarly, the elasticity of supply measures how responsive the quantity supplied is to a change in price—the more responsive, the more elastic the supply.

In Chapter 4, we learned how to shift the supply and demand curves to produce *qualitative* predictions about changes in prices and quantities. Estimating elasticities of demand and supply is the first step in *quantifying* how changes in demand and supply will affect prices and quantities. You should know how to calculate elasticities of demand and supply using data on prices and quantities.

The elasticity of demand tells you how revenues respond to changes in price along a demand curve. If the $|E_d| < 1$, then price and revenue move together, and if $|E_d| > 1$, then price and revenue move in opposite directions. We used these relationships to explain why decreases in the price of food have made farming a smaller share of the economy, but decreases in the price of computer chips have made computing a larger share of the economy. We also used the same relationship to explain why the war on drugs can strengthen the very people it is trying to weaken.

You don't need to do statistical studies of demand and supply to get useful information about elasticities. Once you understand the concept, a little common sense will tell you that the supply curve for low-quality guns in Washington, D.C., is very elastic. And, if you can reason that the supply of low-quality guns to Washington, D.C., is very elastic, a little economics will tell you that gun buyback programs are a waste of taxpayer dollars. Similar reasoning suggests how slave redemption programs might harm more people than they benefit.

Elasticity is a bit dry but it's a useful concept and it will appear again in this book when we come to discuss taxes in Chapter 6 and monopoly in Chapter 13.

□ CHAPTER REVIEW

KEY CONCEPTS

Elasticity of demand, p. 66

Inelastic, p. 69

Elastic, p. 69

Unit elastic, p. 69

Elasticity of supply, p. 75

FACTS AND TOOLS

1. For each of the following pairs, which of the two goods is more likely to be inelastically demanded and why? Table 5.1 should help:

   a. Demand for tangerines vs. demand for fruit

   b. Demand for beef next month vs. demand for beef over the next decade

   c. Demand for Exxon gasoline at the corner of 7th and Grand vs. demand for gasoline in the entire city

   d. Demand for insulin vs. demand for vitamins

2. For each of the following pairs, which of the two goods is more likely to be elastically supplied? Table 5.3 should help:

   a. Supply of apples over the next growing season vs. supply of apples over the next decade

   b. Supply of construction workers in Binghamton, NY, vs. supply of construction workers in New York state

   c. Supply of breakfast cereal vs. supply of food

   d. Supply of gold vs. supply of computers

3. Indicate whether the demand for the good would become more elastic or less elastic after each of the following changes. (Note that in each of these cases, the demand curve may also shift inward or outward, but in this question we are interested in whether the demand becomes more or less elastic.) Briefly justify your answer.

   a. The demand curve for soap after wide understanding that bacteria and other organisms cause and spread disease

   b. The demand curve for coal after the invention of nuclear power plants

c. The demand curve for cars as more employers allow employees to telecommute

d. The demand curve for a new television during an economic boom

4. For each of the following, indicate if the supply for the good would become more elastic or less elastic as a result of each change and briefly justify your answer (once again, in each case the supply curve will also shift, but we are interested in changes in the elasticity).

a. The supply curve for diamonds if a new process for *manufacturing* diamonds is created

b. The supply curve for food if pesticides and fertilizers were banned

c. The supply curve for plastic if a very large share of oil output was used to make plastic

d. The supply curve for nurses after several years of increasing wages in nursing

5. Let's work out a few examples to get a sense of what elasticity of demand means in practice. Remember that in all of these cases, we're moving along a fixed demand curve—so think of supply increasing or decreasing, while the demand curve is staying in the same place.

a. If the elasticity of demand for college textbooks is −0.1 and the price of textbooks increases by 20%, how much will the quantity demanded change, and in what direction?

b. In your answer to part a, was your answer in percentages or in total number of textbooks?

c. If the elasticity of demand for spring break packages to Cancun is −5, and if you notice that this year in Cancun the quantity of packages demanded increased by 10%, then what happened to the price of Cancun vacation packages?

d. In your college town, real estate developers are building thousands of new student-friendly apartments close to campus. If you want to pay the lowest rent possible, should you hope that demand for apartments is elastic or inelastic?

e. In your college town, the local government decrees that thousands of apartments close to campus are uninhabitable and must be torn down next semester. If you want to pay the lowest rent possible, should you hope that demand for apartments is elastic or inelastic?

f. If the elasticity of demand for ballpoint pens with blue ink is −20, and the price of ballpoint pens with blue ink rises by 1%, what happens to the quantity demanded?

g. What's an obvious substitute for ballpoint pens with blue ink? (This obvious substitute explains why the demand is so elastic.)

6. It's an important tradition in the Santos family that they eat the same meal at their favorite restaurant every Sunday. By contrast, the Chen family spends exactly $50 for their Sunday meal at whatever restaurant sounds best.

a. Which family has a more elastic demand for restaurant food?

b. Which family has a unit elastic demand for restaurant food? (*Hint*: How would each family respond to an increase in food prices?)

7. The U.S. Department of Agriculture (USDA) has been concerned that Americans aren't eating enough fruits and vegetables, and they've considered coupons and other subsidies to encourage people—especially lower-income people—to eat these healthier foods. Of course, if people's demand for fruits and vegetables is perfectly inelastic, then there's no point in giving out coupons (Thought question: Why?). If instead the demand is only somewhat elastic, there may be better ways to spend taxpayer dollars.

This is clearly a situation where you'd want to know the elasticity of fruit and vegetable demand: If people respond a lot to small changes in price, then government-funded fruit and vegetable coupons *could* make poorer Americans a lot healthier, which *might* save taxpayers money *if* they don't have to pay for expensive medical treatments for unhealthy eaters. There are a lot of links in this chain of reasoning—all of which are covered in more advanced economics courses—but the first link is whether people actually have elastic demand for fruits and vegetables. The USDA's Economic Research Service employs economists to answer these sorts of questions, and a recent report contained the following estimated elasticities (*Source:* Diansheng Dong and Biing-Hwan Lin. 2009. "Fruit and Vegetable Consumption by Low-Income Americans: Would a Price Reduction Make a Difference?" In *Economic Research Report* 70, USDA).

Fruit	Elasticity of Demand
Apple	−0.16
Banana	−0.42
Grapefruit	−1.02
Grapes	−0.91
Orange	−1.14

a. Based on these demand elasticity estimates, which fruit is most inelastically demanded? Which is most elastically demanded?

b. For which of these fruits would a 10% drop in price cause an increase in total revenue from the sale of that fruit?

c. If the government could only offer "10% off" coupons for three of these fruits, and it wanted to have the biggest possible effect on quantity demanded, which three fruits should get the coupons?

d. Overall, the authors found that for the average fruit, the elasticity of demand was about −0.5. Is the demand for fruit elastic or inelastic?

8. On average, old cars pollute more than newer cars. Therefore, every few years, a politician proposes a "cash for clunkers" program: The government offers to buy up and destroy old, high-polluting cars. If a "cash for clunkers" program buys 1,000 old, high-polluting cars, is this the same as saying that there are 1,000 fewer old, high-polluting cars on the road? Why or why not?

9. As we noted in the chapter, many economists have estimated the short-run and long-run elasticities of oil demand. Let's see if a rise in the price of oil hurts oil revenues in the long run. Cooper, the author cited in this chapter, found that in the United States, the long-run elasticity of oil demand is −0.5.

a. If the price of oil rises by 10%, how much will the quantity of oil demanded fall: By 5%, by 0.5%, by 2%, or by 20%?

b. Does a 10% rise in oil prices increase or decrease total revenues to the oil producers?

c. Some policymakers and environmental scientists would like to see the United States cut back on its use of oil in the long run. We can use this elasticity estimate to get a rough measure of how high the price of oil would have to permanently rise in order to get people to make big cuts in oil consumption. How much would the price of oil have to permanently rise in order to cut oil consumption by 50%?

d. France has the largest long-run elasticity of oil demand (−0.6) of any of the large, rich countries, according to Cooper's estimates. Does this mean that France is better at responding to long-run price changes than other rich countries, or does it mean France is worse at responding?

10. Figure 5.3 and Table 5.2 both set out some important but tedious rules. Let's practice them, since they are quite likely to be on an exam. For each of the cases below, state whether the demand curve is relatively steep or flat, and whether a *fall* in price will raise total revenue or lower it. In this case, note that we present the elasticity in terms of its absolute value.

a. Elasticity of demand = 0.2

b. Elasticity of demand = 2.0

c. Elasticity of demand = 10.0

d. Elasticity of demand = 1.1

e. Elasticity of demand = 0.9

11. A lot of American action movies are quests to eliminate a villain. If in real life villains are elastically supplied (like guns for buyback programs), should we care whether the hero captures a particular villain? Why or why not?

THINKING AND PROBLEM SOLVING

1. During the Middle Ages, the African city of Taghaza quarried salt in 200-pound blocks to be sent to the salt market in Timbuktu, in present-day Mali. Travelers report that Taghazans used salt instead of wood to construct buildings.

Compared with other towns without big salt mines, was the demand for *wood* more elastic or less elastic in Taghaza? How do you know?

2. Suppose that drug addicts pay for their addiction by stealing: So the higher the total revenue of the illegal drug industry, the higher the amount of theft. If a government crackdown on drug suppliers leads to a higher price of drugs, what will happen to the amount of stealing if the demand for drugs is elastic? What if the demand for drugs is inelastic?

3. Henry Ford famously mass-produced cars at the beginning of the twentieth century, starting Ford Motor Company. He made millions because mass production made cars cheap to make, and he passed some of the savings to the consumer in the form of a low price. Cars became a common sight in the United States thereafter. Keeping total revenue and its relationship with price in mind, do you expect the demand for cars to be elastic or inelastic given the story of Henry Ford?

4. In Chapter 10, you'll see that we recently purchased permits to pollute the air with sulfur dioxide (SO_2). We didn't use the permits: Instead, we threw them out. In other words, we bought permits for the same reason the government buys guns in gun buyback programs—to prevent what we bought from being used. As we discussed in the chapter, gun buyback programs have failed. So why is our plan to buy permits more likely to get SO_2 out of the air than the government's plan to get guns off the street?

5. How might elasticities help to explain why people on vacation tend to spend more for food and necessities than the local population?

6. In the short run, the price elasticity of the demand and supply of electricity can be very low.

    a. How might revenue for the electricity industry change if one power plant were shut down for maintenance, reducing supply?

    b. If one power company owned many power plants, would it have a short-term incentive to keep all of its plants running, or could it have a short-term incentive to shut down a power plant now and then?

7. Immigration is a fact of life in the United States. This will lead to a big boost in the labor supply. What field would you rather be in: a field where the demand for your kind of labor is elastic or a field where the demand for your kind of labor is inelastic?

8. In the world of fashion, the power to imitate a trendy look is the power to make money. Stores such as H&M and Forever 21 focus on imitating fashions wherever possible: As soon as they see that a new look is coming along, something people are willing to pay a high price for, they start cranking out that look. Do these imitation-centered stores make the supply of clothing more elastic or less elastic? How can you tell?

9. Let's practice the midpoint formula. Calculate the elasticity of demand for each of the following goods or services.

Good or Service	Beginning Price	Beginning Quantity	Ending Price	Ending Quantity	Elasticity
Daily movie ticket sales in Denver, Colorado	$6	50,000	$10	40,000	
Weekly milk sales at Loma Vista Elementary School	$1	1,000	$1.50	800	
Weekly round-trip ticket sales, New York to San Francisco	$500	10,000	$1,000	9,000	
Annual student enrollments, Upper Tennessee State University	$6,000	40,000	$9,000	39,000	

CHALLENGES

1. In this chapter, we've emphasized that the elasticity of supply is higher in the long run than in the short run. In a lot of cases, this is surely true: If you see that jobs pay more in the next state over, you won't move there the next week but you might move there next year. But sometimes the short-run elasticity will be *higher* than the long-run elasticity.

   Austan Goolsbee found an interesting example of this when he looked at the elasticity of income of highly paid executives with respect to taxes. In 1993, then President Clinton passed a law raising income taxes. This tax hike was fully expected: He campaigned on it in 1992.

   a. What do you expect happened to executive income in the first year of the tax increases? What about in subsequent years?

      Here's a hint: Top executives have a lot of power over when they get paid for their work: They can ask for bonuses a bit earlier, or they can cash out their stock options a bit earlier. Literally, this isn't their "labor supply," it's more like their "income supply."

   (*Source:* Goolsbee, Austan. 2000. What happens when you tax the rich? Evidence from executive compensation. *Journal of Political Economy* **108**(2): 352–378. For a book on the topic written by a leading economist, see Joel Slemrod, ed. 2000. *Does Atlas Shrug?* Cambridge, MA: Harvard University Press).

   b. Goolsbee estimated that the short-run elasticity of "income supply" for these executives was 1.4, while the long-run elasticity of "income supply" was 0.1. (*Note*: Goolsbee used a variety of statistical methods to look for these elasticities, and all came to roughly the same result.) If taxes pushed down their take-home income by 10%, how much would this cut the amount of income supplied in the short run? In the long run?

   c. You are a newspaper reporter. Your editor tells you to write a short story with this title: "Goolsbee's research proves that tax hikes make the rich work less." Make your case in one sentence.

   d. You are a newspaper reporter. Your editor tells you to write a short story with this title: "Goolsbee's research proves that tax hikes have little effect on work by the wealthy." Make your case in one sentence.

   e. Which story is more truthful?

2. We saw that a gun buyback program was unlikely to work in Washington, D.C. If the entire United States ran a gun buyback program, would that be better at eliminating guns or worse? Why? What about if the gun buyback was also accompanied by a law making (at least some) guns illegal?

3. Using the data from the ANWR example, what will be the percentage increase in quantity supplied if ANWR raises supply by 1%? No, this isn't a trick question, and the formula is already there in the chapter. Why isn't this number just 1%?

Other Types of Elasticities

Economists often compute elasticities any time one variable is related to another variable. Klick and Tabarrok, for example, find that a 50% increase in the number of police on the streets reduces automobile theft and theft from automobiles by 43%, so the elasticity of auto crime with respect to police is $-43\%/50\% = -0.86$. Gruber studies church attendance and he finds an interesting relationship: The more people give to their church, the less likely they are to attend! In other words, people regard money and time as substitutes and those who give more of one are likely to give less of the other. Gruber calculates that a 10% increase in giving leads to an 11% decline in attendance or an elasticity of attendance with respect to giving of $-11\%/10\% = -1.1$.[15]

Thus, any time there is a relationship between two variables A and B, you can always express the relationship in terms of an elasticity. Two other frequently used elasticities in economics are the cross-price elasticity of demand and the income elasticity of demand.

The Cross-Price Elasticity of Demand

The cross-price elasticity of demand measures how responsive the quantity demanded of good A is to the price of good B.

Cross-price elasticity of demand $=$

$$\frac{\text{Percentage change in quantity demanded of good } A}{\text{Percentage change in price of good } B} = \frac{\%\Delta Q_{Demanded, A}}{\%\Delta P_{Price, B}}$$

Given data on the quantity demanded of good A at two different prices of good B, the cross-price elasticity can be calculated using the following formula:

$$\frac{\dfrac{\text{Change in quantity demanded } A}{\text{Average quantity } A}}{\dfrac{\text{Change in price } B}{\text{Average price } B}} = \frac{\dfrac{Q_{After, A} - Q_{Before, A}}{(Q_{After, A} + Q_{Before, A})/2}}{\dfrac{P_{After, B} - P_{Before, B}}{(P_{After, B} + P_{Before, B})/2}}$$

The cross-price elasticity of demand is closely related to the idea of substitutes and complements. If the cross-price elasticity is positive, an increase in the price of good B increases the quantity of good A demanded so the two goods are substitutes. If the cross-price elasticity is negative, an increase in the price of good B decreases the quantity of good A demanded so the two goods are complements.

> If the cross-price elasticity >0, then goods A and B are substitutes.
> If the cross-price elasticity <0, then goods A and B are complements.

The Income Elasticity of Demand

The income elasticity of demand measures how responsive the quantity demanded of a good is with respect to changes in income.

$$\text{Income elasticity of demand} = \frac{\text{Percentage change in quantity demanded}}{\text{Percentage change in income}}$$

$$= \frac{\%\Delta Q_{Demanded}}{\%\Delta_{Income}}$$

As usual, given data on the quantity demanded at two different income levels, the income elasticity of demand can be calculated as

$$\frac{\dfrac{\text{Change in quantity demanded}}{\text{Average quantity}}}{\dfrac{\text{Change in income}}{\text{Average income}}} = \frac{\dfrac{Q_{After} - Q_{Before}}{(Q_{After} + Q_{Before})/2}}{\dfrac{I_{After} - I_{Before}}{(I_{After} + I_{Before})/2}}$$

The income elasticity of demand can be used to distinguish normal from inferior goods. Recall from Chapter 3 that when an *increase* in income *increases* the demand for a good, we say the good is a *normal good*. And a good like Ramen noodles, for which an *increase* in income *decreases* the demand, is called an *inferior good*.

> If the income elasticity of demand > 0, then the good is a normal good.

> If the income elasticity of demand < 0, then the good is an inferior good.

Sometimes economists also distinguish normal from "luxury" goods, where a luxury good is defined as one where, say, a 10% increase in income causes more than a 10% increase in the quantity of the good demanded. Thus,

> If the income elasticity of demand > 1, then the good is a luxury good.

Using Excel to Calculate Elasticities

Let's use a spreadsheet to compute the elasticity of demand along the two demand curves illustrated in Figure 5.1.

The first step is to input the basic data into the spreadsheet. For the demand curve labeled demand curve I, we have Q Before=100, Q After=95, P Before=$40, and P After=$50 and for the demand curve labeled demand curve E, we have Q Before=100, Q After=20, P Before=$40, and P After=$50. (By the way, it doesn't matter which price-quantity pair you call before and which after.) Your spreadsheet should like look Figure A5.1.

FIGURE A5.1

	A	B	
1	Q Before	Q After	
2	100	95	
3	P Before	P After	
4	40	50	
5			
6			
7	Q Before	Q After	
8	100	20	
9	P Before	P After	
10	40	50	
11			

Now remember our formula for calculating an elasticity:

$$\text{Elasticity of demand} = E_d = \frac{\%\Delta Q_{Demanded}}{\%\Delta Price} = \frac{\dfrac{Q_{After} - Q_{Before}}{(Q_{After} + Q_{Before})/2}}{\dfrac{P_{After} - P_{Before}}{(P_{After} + P_{Before})/2}}$$

Let's input the formula in two parts: the %ΔQ on the top and %ΔPrice on the bottom, as in Figure A5.2.

FIGURE A5.2

	C2	▼	f_x	=(B2-A2)/((B2+A2)/2)*100	
	A	B	C	D	E
1	Q Before	Q After	%Change in Quantity		
2	100	95	-5.12821		
3	P Before	P After	%Change in Price		
4	40	50	22.22222		
5					
6					
7	Q Before	Q After	%Change in Quantity		
8	100	20	-133.333		
9	P Before	P After	%Change in Price		
10	40	50	22.22222		
11					

Notice the formula in cell C2, $= (B2 − A2)/(B2 + A2/2) \times 100$, that's the percentage change in quantity along demand curve I. There is a similar formula in C4 for the percentage change in price and then these are repeated for demand curve E.

We can then finish off the spreadsheet by dividing C2/C4 and taking the absolute value, which gives us Figure A5.3.

FIGURE A5.3

	F2	▼	f_x	=ABS(C2/C4)		
	A	B	C	D	E	F
1	Q Before	Q After	%Change in Quantity			
2	100	95	-5.12821		Elasticity	0.230769
3	P Before	P After	%Change in Price			
4	40	50	22.22222			
5						
6						
7	Q Before	Q After	%Change in Quantity			
8	100	20	-133.333		Elasticity	6
9	P Before	P After	%Change in Price			
10	40	50	22.22222			
11						

Fortunately, the answer is consistent with what we said earlier in the chapter! Along this region of the curve labeled demand curve I, the elasticity is $0.231 < 1$ or inelastic, and along this region of demand curve E, the elasticity is $6 > 1$ or elastic.

6

Taxes and Subsidies

"If you're super-wealthy, it's a good year to die," so argued one estate planner in 2010. In 2010, the U.S. estate tax temporarily disappeared, giving the very wealthy a big tax break, so long as they died. George Steinbrenner was one billionaire who timed it right. The owner of the New York Yankees, worth an estimated $1.1 billion, died in 2010, leaving the IRS next to nothing. If Steinbrenner had died in 2009 or 2011, he would have likely owed about $500 million.

The temporarily disappearing estate tax created some peculiar incentives. In 2009, it paid to keep wealthy grandma on life support until at least January 1, 2010, but in 2010, it was financially better to pull the plug. Could financial incentives really make a difference in when people die? Before you answer, it may help to know that in the last week of 1999, New York hospitals reported fewer deaths than usual. The following week there were more deaths than usual. Why? Could it be that people willed themselves to live to see the dawn of the twenty-first century? People also show a small but noticeable trend to live until after their birthdays or other major events.

If death can be postponed for major events, then why not postpone death to save on taxes? In fact, two economists, Wojciech Kopczuk and Joel Slemrod, found that in Australia a $10,000 reduction in the estate tax can postpone death by about a week! (To be fair, however, it could also be that the heirs to the inheritance alter death certificates so as to lower their taxes.)

If all this seems a bit macabre, don't worry— not only can deaths be postponed for tax reasons, births can also be advanced. Parents get a tax deduction for dependents like children, and so long as the child is born before the clock strikes midnight on December 31st, the family gets the deduction for the entire year. Thus, compared with a child born in early January, a child born in late

December can save parents thousands of dollars. Journalist David Leonhardt wrote about this incentive in *The New York Times*:

> Unless you're a cynic, or an economist, I realize you might have trouble believing that the intricacies of the nation's tax code would impinge on something as sacred as the birth of a child. But it appears that you would be wrong.

Not only are more children born in late December than in early January, but also the extra births appear to be clustered among those who have the most to gain from a tax deduction, exactly as a cynic or an economist would predict. Leonhardt coined the term "national birth day" to indicate the day of the year on which the largest number of births occurs. For a long time, "national birth day" was around mid-September (probably because it was cold and dark the previous December!). But amazingly, as induced labor, Caesarian sections, and taxes have all increased, the day of the year on which the largest number of births occur has now moved to late December![1]

In this chapter, we examine taxes and also subsidies, which are payments from the government for production. The analysis will draw on our understanding of demand and supply and also on our understanding of elasticity from the last chapter.

Commodity Taxes

Commodity taxes are taxes on goods. Well-known commodity taxes include those on fuel, liquor, and cigarettes, although in the United States most commodities are taxed in one way or another. We will emphasize the following truths about commodity taxation:

1. Who ultimately pays the tax does *not* depend on who writes the check to the government.

2. Who ultimately pays the tax *does* depend on the relative elasticities of demand and supply.

3. Commodity taxation raises revenue and reduces the gains from trade (creates deadweight loss).

Who Ultimately Pays the Tax Does Not Depend on Who Writes the Check

Imagine that the government is considering a tax on apples. The government can collect the tax in either of two different ways (assume that each method is equally costly to implement). The government can tax apple sellers $1 for every basket supplied, or they can tax apple buyers $1 for every basket of apples bought. Which tax scheme is better for apple buyers?

Surprisingly, the answer is that the tax has exactly the same effects whether it is "paid" for by sellers or "paid" for by buyers. It is one of the great insights of economics that who ultimately pays a tax is determined not by the laws of Congress but by the laws of supply and demand.

Let's consider the effect of a $1 tax on apple sellers, which we analyze beginning with Panel A of Figure 6.1 below. As we discussed in Chapter 3, as far as sellers are concerned, a tax is the same as an increase in costs. Thus, if with no tax, sellers require a minimum of $1 per basket to sell 250 baskets of apples, then with a $1 tax they will require $2 per basket to sell the same quantity—$1 for their regular costs and $1 for their tax cost. Similarly, if with no tax, sellers require a minimum of $3 per basket to sell 1,250 baskets, then with a $1 tax they will require $4 per basket. Following through on this logic, we see that a $1 tax shifts the supply curve up at every quantity by exactly $1.

Panel B of Figure 6.1 adds a demand curve to show the effect of the tax on the market for apples. With no tax, the equilibrium is at point a with a price of $2 per basket and a quantity of 700. If apple sellers must pay a $1 tax for every basket supplied, the supply curve shifts up by $1 and the new equilibrium is at point b with a higher price of $2.65 and a smaller quantity consumed of 500.

Students are sometimes surprised that a $1 tax does not necessarily raise the price by $1. To see why, imagine that the price did rise by $1. In that case, the price would rise to $3 at point c. But is point c an equilibrium?

FIGURE 6.1

A Tax on Apple Sellers
Panel A: A $1 tax on apple sellers shifts the supply curve up by $1.
Panel B: A $1 tax on apple sellers shifts the supply curve up by $1, changing the equilibrium from point a to point b.

No. Point *c* is not an equilibrium because at point *c*, the quantity supplied is greater than the quantity demanded. In other words, apple sellers in this market find that if they try to pass all of the tax onto apple buyers by raising the price to $3 per basket, there are not enough buyers to purchase 700 baskets, so sellers have excess supply. What incentives does this create? As they compete to obtain buyers, sellers must bid the price down. As the price falls, sellers supply fewer apples until the new equilibrium is reached at point *b*.

With the tax, buyers pay $2.65 per basket and sellers receive $1.65 per basket ($2.65 minus the $1 tax they must send to the government). Notice that the difference between the price that buyers pay and the price that sellers receive is equal to the tax. In fact, so long as the tax doesn't drive the industry out of existence, it will always be the case that

The tax = Price paid by buyers − Price received by sellers

What happens if instead of taxing sellers, the government taxes buyers? We illustrate beginning with Panel A of Figure 6.2. Imagine that before the tax buyers were willing to pay up to $4 per basket to purchase 100 baskets. If buyers must pay a $1 tax *on top of the price,* what is the most that they will now be willing to pay? Correct, $3. That is, if the buyers value the apples at $4 per basket but they must pay a tax of $1 to the government, then the most the buyers will be willing to pay the apple suppliers is $3 per basket (since the total price including the tax will now be $4). Similarly, if before the tax buyers were willing to pay up to $2 per basket to purchase 700 baskets, then after the $1 tax they will be willing to pay to the sellers at most $1 per basket for the same quantity. Following through on this logic, we see that a tax of $1 on buyers shifts the demand curve down at every quantity by $1.

FIGURE 6.2

A Tax on Apple Buyers
Panel A: A $1 tax on apple buyers shifts the demand curve down by $1.
Panel B: A $1 tax on apple buyers shifts the demand curve down by $1, changing the equilibrium from point *a* to point *d*.

Panel B shows the market for apples. With no tax, the equilibrium is at point *a* with a price of $2 and a quantity of 700. With the $1 tax on apple buyers, the demand curve shifts down by $1 and the new equilibrium is at point *d* with a price of $1.65 and a quantity of 500.

Notice that with the tax, apple buyers pay a total price of $2.65 ($1.65 in market price plus $1 tax) and apple sellers receive $1.65. In other words, the price buyers pay, the price sellers receive, and the quantity traded (500 baskets) are identical to what they were when the tax was placed on apple sellers.

We can see what is going on by also showing in Panel B of Figure 6.2 a dotted supply curve, the supply curve *if* there were a $1 tax on sellers (exactly as in Figure 6.1). If the $1 tax is placed on sellers, the equilibrium is at point *b*. If the tax is placed on buyers, the equilibrium is at point *d*. The only difference between points *b* and *d* is that when the tax is placed on suppliers, the market price ($2.65) *includes* the tax, but when the tax is placed on buyers, the market price ($1.65) does not include the tax. The tax must be paid, however, so in either case the final price paid by buyers is $2.65 and the final price received by sellers is $1.65.

We have just shown something quite surprising. Who pays a tax does not depend on who must send the check to the government. Don't be fooled; a tax on apple sellers has exactly the same effects as a tax on apple buyers.

Who Ultimately Pays the Tax Depends on the Relative Elasticities of Supply and Demand

We have just seen that whether the $1 apple tax is placed on buyers or sellers, the price to buyers ends up being $2.65 and the price received by sellers ends up being $1.65. But why is it that with the tax, buyers pay 65 cents more ($2.65 − $2), while sellers receive 35 cents less ($2 − $1.65)? What determines how the burden of the tax is shared between buyers and sellers? To answer this question, we introduce the *wedge shortcut*.

The Wedge Shortcut　The most important effect of a tax is to drive a tax wedge between the price paid by buyers and the price received by sellers. Recall that

$$\text{The tax} = \text{Price paid by buyers} - \text{Price received by sellers}$$

If we focus on the wedge aspect of a tax, we can simplify our tax analysis. In Figure 6.3, instead of shifting curves, we start with a tax of $1 and we "push" this vertical "tax wedge" into the diagram until the top of the wedge just touches the demand curve and the bottom of the wedge just touches the supply curve. The top of the wedge at point *b* gives us the price paid by the buyers ($2.65), the bottom of the wedge at point *d* gives us the price received by sellers ($1.65), and the quantity at which the wedge "sticks" is 500 baskets, exactly as before.

Using the wedge shortcut, we show that whether buyers or sellers pay a tax is determined by the relative elasticities of demand and supply. Recall from Chapter 5 that the elasticity of demand measures how responsive the quantity demanded is to a change in price and the elasticity of supply measures how

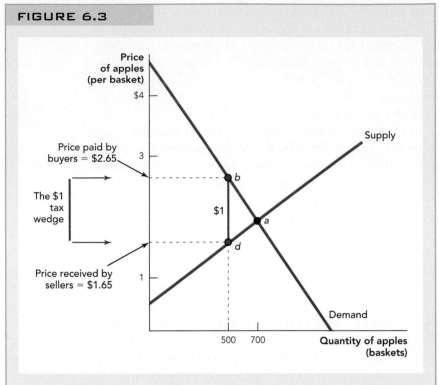

FIGURE 6.3

The Tax Wedge If the tax is $1, the price paid by the buyers must be $1 higher than the price received by the sellers. Driving a $1 tax wedge into the diagram shows us the new equilibrium must be where the price paid by the buyers is $2.65, the price received by the sellers is $1.65, and the quantity traded is 500.

responsive the quantity supplied is to a change in price. We show that *when demand is more elastic than supply, demanders pay less of the tax than sellers. When supply is more elastic than demand, suppliers pay less of the tax than buyers.*

In Panel A of Figure 6.4, we draw a demand curve that is more elastic than the supply curve. So who will pay most of the tax? Sellers. To see why sellers will pay most of the tax, push the tax wedge into the diagram. Notice that at the quantity that the tax wedge sticks, the price paid by buyers is only a small amount above the price with no tax. The price received by sellers, however, falls well below the price with no tax. Thus, when demand is more elastic than supply, buyers pay less of the tax than sellers.

In Panel B of Figure 6.4, we draw a supply curve that is more elastic than the demand curve. So who will pay most of the tax? Buyers. To see why buyers will pay most of the tax, take the tax wedge and push it into the diagram. At the point that the wedge "sticks," notice that the price paid by buyers has risen far above the price with no tax. The price received by sellers, however, has fallen only just below the price with no tax. Thus, when supply is more elastic than demand, buyers pay more of the tax.

The intuition for these results is simple. An elastic demand curve means that demanders have lots of substitutes and you can't tax someone who has a good substitute because they will just buy the substitute! Thus, when demand is elastic, sellers will end up paying most of the tax. An elastic supply curve has a similar interpretation. It means that the workers and capital in the industry can easily find work in another industry—so if you try to tax an industry with an elastic

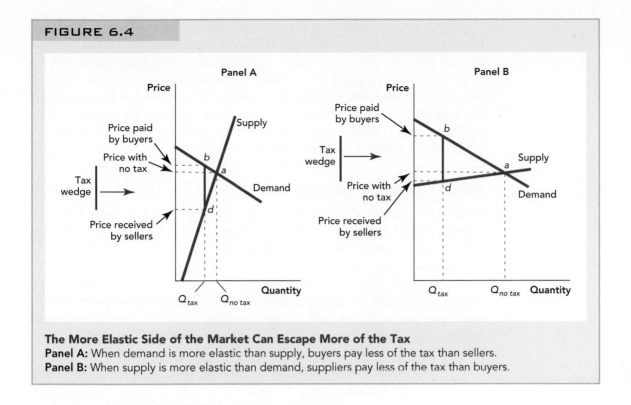

FIGURE 6.4

The More Elastic Side of the Market Can Escape More of the Tax
Panel A: When demand is more elastic than supply, buyers pay less of the tax than sellers.
Panel B: When supply is more elastic than demand, suppliers pay less of the tax than buyers.

supply curve, the industry inputs will escape to other industries. Just remember, therefore, that *elasticity = escape*. So long as the industry is not taxed out of existence, someone must pay the tax, so whether buyers or sellers pay most depends on who can escape the best—that is, which curve is *relatively* more elastic.

Bearing in mind our rule that the more elastic side of the market can better escape the tax, let's take a look at some taxes to see whether it is buyers or sellers who will bear the greater burden.

Health Insurance Mandates and Tax Analysis

Imagine that the government requires firms to provide their workers with health insurance. It's good to have health insurance and it's even better if someone else is paying for it. But who really pays? This law requires that firms buy health insurance for every worker hired so we can think of the law as a tax on labor. Who pays the tax? As we now know, who pays more of the tax depends on whether supply or demand is more elastic. So consider, is it easier for firms to escape the tax by not employing or for workers to escape the tax by not working?

Can firms escape the tax? Yes, in a lot of ways. If the tax on labor gets too high, firms can substitute capital (machines) for labor, they can move overseas, or they can close up shop altogether. Can workers escape the tax? It's not so easy. Most workers would continue to work even if their wages were lower because the costs of leaving the labor force are high. Thus, for most workers, the elasticity of labor supply is low (this is especially true for working-age men; men nearing retirement and married women tend to have higher elasticities of labor supply). The demand for labor, therefore, is likely to be more elastic than the supply of labor. Remember that when demand is more elastic than supply, then sellers (i.e., workers = sellers of labor) will pay most of the tax in the form of lower wages. This is the situation depicted in Panel A of Figure 6.4.

Just because workers bear the costs of a law requiring firms to purchase health insurance, doesn't mean that the law is a bad idea. It's quite reasonable to want everyone in society to have health insurance and requiring employers to purchase health insurance is one way, albeit not necessarily the best way, to move toward this goal. What is important is that citizens not be fooled into thinking that the law is a free lunch at the expense of their employer. Tax analysis is useful because it helps us to see the true benefits and costs of economic policy and thus to choose wisely.

Who Pays the Cigarette Tax?

States tax cigarettes at rates ranging from $2.57 per pack in New Jersey to 7 cents per pack in South Carolina (2009 rates). Who ultimately pays the cigarette tax? Buyers or sellers? As usual, who pays depends on the relative elasticities of demand and supply.

As you might expect, given the addictive nature of nicotine, smokers have an inelastic demand for cigarettes, around −0.5. What about suppliers? Before you answer, remember that we are analyzing *state* cigarette taxes so the relevant question is how easily can a cigarette manufacturer escape a state tax?

A manufacturer can easily escape a state tax by selling elsewhere. In fact, because it's so easy for a cigarette manufacturer to ship its product around the country, the elasticity of supply to any one state is very large, which means that buyers will bear almost all of the tax—as illustrated in Panel B of Figure 6.4.

If the price paid by buyers increases by almost the amount of the tax, then the price received by sellers must be almost the same in all states regardless of the tax. To see why this makes sense, imagine what would happen if manufacturers earned less money per pack selling cigarettes in a high-tax state like New Jersey than in a low-tax state like South Carolina. If this happened, manufacturers would ship fewer cigarettes to New Jersey and more to South Carolina, and this would continue until the after-tax price was the same in both states.

We can easily test this theory. A pack of cigarettes sold for about $3.35 in South Carolina and $6.45 in New Jersey (2009), so the price to buyers was nearly twice as high in New Jersey as in South Carolina. But the after-tax price received by sellers was about the same, $3.28 in South Carolina ($3.35 − $0.07) vs. $3.88 in New Jersey ($6.45 − $2.57). (The small differences can probably be accounted for by other costs of doing business that differ between New Jersey and South Carolina.)

By the way, one argument for high cigarette taxes is that the government should discourage smoking. State taxes, however, are a bad method of discouraging smoking in the United States. A New Jersey tax will discourage smoking by residents of New Jersey but, as we have seen, to escape the NJ tax, cigarette manufacturers will ship more cigarettes to other states, which pushes cigarette prices down in those states, thereby increasing the quantity demanded. A New Jersey tax, therefore, will decrease smoking in New Jersey but this will be partially offset by increased smoking in other states. It's more difficult for cigarette

What a drag it is being taxed
Heavy taxes encourage smokers to smoke fewer cigarettes, but they also encourage smokers to choose cigarettes with higher nicotine levels. High cigarette taxes have also been shown to increase smoking intensity—when taxes are high, smokers inhale more deeply and they smoke down to the butt.

ENVISION/CORBIS

manufacturers to escape federal taxes than state taxes so if the goal is to reduce national consumption, a federal tax is superior to a state tax.

A Commodity Tax Raises Revenue and Reduces the Gains from Trade (Creates Deadweight Loss)

A tax generates revenues for the government but also reduces the gains from trade. In the left panel of Figure 6.5, we show the apple market with no tax; the equilibrium price is $2 and the equilibrium quantity is 700. Consumer surplus is shown in green and producer surplus is shown in blue. As we emphasized in Chapter 4, in a free market trade occurs whenever the buyer's willingness to pay exceeds the supplier's willingness to sell (i.e., whenever the demand curve lies above the supply curve). A free market maximizes the gains from trade, the sum of consumer and producer surplus.

In the right panel, we show the same market with a $1 tax (this is identical to Figure 6.3 only this time we have labeled some of the areas). The tax is $1 per basket and 500 baskets are traded, so tax revenues are shown by the purple rectangle and are equal to $500 = $1 × 500.

The tax decreases consumer and producer surplus, as you can see by comparing the green and blue areas in the left and right panels. *Some* of the consumer and producer surplus is transferred to the government in the form of tax revenues, but notice

FIGURE 6.5

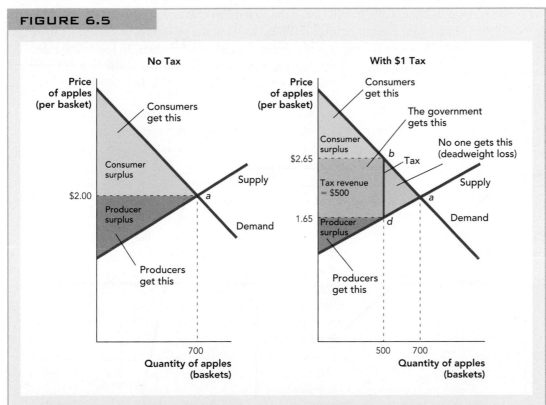

A Tax Generates Revenue and Creates a Deadweight Loss With no tax, producer plus consumer surplus is maximized in the left panel. With the tax, consumer surplus and producer surplus are smaller and tax revenues are larger. But tax revenues increase by less than producer and consumer surplus fall. As a result, the tax creates a net loss or deadweight loss shown by the gray area (triangle abd) in the right panel.

that consumer and producer surplus together decrease by more than government revenue increases—the difference is the gray triangle (abd) labeled "deadweight loss."

To understand why a tax creates a deadweight loss, let's take a simple case. Imagine that you are willing to pay $50 for a bus ride to New York City when the price of a ticket is $40. Thus, you take the trip and earn $10 in consumer surplus ($50 − $40). Now suppose the government imposes a $20 tax, which increases the price of the ticket to $60. Do you take the trip? No, since the price of the ticket now exceeds your willingness to pay, you do not go to New York City. Thus, you lose $10 in consumer surplus. Does the government gain any tax revenue? No. Your loss of $10 is not compensated for by any increase in government revenue and, thus, is a deadweight loss. In short, the deadweight loss of a tax is the lost gains from the trips (trades) that do not occur because of the tax.

A key factor determining deadweight loss is the elasticities of supply and demand. Figure 6.6, for example, shows that the deadweight loss from taxation is larger the more elastic the demand curve. To understand why, remember that deadweight loss is the lost gains from trade. If the demand curve is relatively elastic, as in the left panel of Figure 6.6, then the tax deters a lot of trades, Q_{tax} is much less than $Q_{no\ tax}$, so the lost gains from trade are large. It's just like the bus story—if the demand curve is elastic, then the tax means many lost bus trips.

If the demand is relatively inelastic, however, as in the right panel of Figure 6.6 then the tax does not deter many trades. Notice that Q_{tax} is only slightly smaller than $Q_{no\ tax}$. Since nearly the same number of trades occur, there are few lost gains from trade. Again, let's go back to the bus. Imagine that you were willing to pay $100 to go to New York. In that case, if the government taxes you $20, you still take the trip. True, your consumer surplus falls by $20, but the government's revenues increased by $20—since the trip was not deterred, there is no deadweight loss in this case.

The same intuition also explains why the deadweight loss from taxation (holding tax revenue constant) is lower the less elastic the supply

FIGURE 6.6

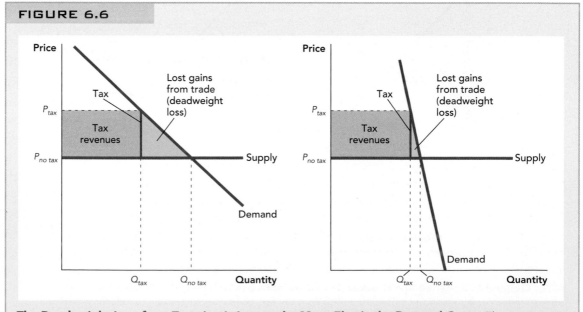

The Deadweight Loss from Taxation Is Larger the More Elastic the Demand Curve The tax rate and tax revenues are the same but the deadweight loss is larger in the left panel where the demand curve is more elastic.

curve. If the supply curve is elastic, then the tax deters many trades, but if the supply curve is inelastic, there is little deterrence and, thus, few lost gains from trade.

Even though taxes create a deadweight loss, they also pay for beneficial goods and services. In Chapter 18, we discuss in more detail when the goods that taxation provides are likely to have benefits that exceed the deadweight loss caused by taxation.

◄------

Subsidies

A subsidy is a reverse tax: Instead of taking money away from consumers (or producers), the government gives money to consumers (or producers). The close connection between subsidies and taxes means that their effects are analogous. We emphasize the following facts about commodity subsidies:

1. Who gets the subsidy does *not* depend on who gets the check from the government.

2. Who benefits from a subsidy *does* depend on the relative elasticities of demand and supply.

3. Subsidies must be paid for by taxpayers and they create inefficient *increases* in trade (deadweight loss).

With a tax, the price paid by the buyers exceeds the price received by sellers. A subsidy reverses this relationship so the price received by sellers exceeds the price paid by buyers, the difference being the amount of the subsidy. In other words:

The subsidy = Price received by sellers − Price paid by buyers

We can analyze subsidies using the same wedge shortcut as before, except now we push the wedge from the right side of the diagram toward the left side. In Figure 6.7 on the next page, we show that with a $1 subsidy, sellers of apples will receive $2.40 per basket, but buyers will pay only $1.40, the difference of $1 being the subsidy amount.

A subsidy means that the sellers are receiving more than buyers are paying, so who is making up the difference? Taxpayers. The cost to taxpayers is the amount of the subsidy times the number of units subsidized. In Figure 6.7, this is $1 × 900 or $900.

Just like a tax, a subsidy also creates a deadweight loss. A tax creates a deadweight loss because with the tax, some beneficial trades fail to occur. A subsidy creates a deadweight loss for the reverse reason: With the subsidy, some non-beneficial trades do occur. In Figure 6.7, notice that for the baskets between 700 and 900, the supply curve lies above the demand curve (i.e., line segment *ab* lies above line segment *ad*). The height of the supply curve tells us the cost of producing these baskets. The height of the demand curve tells us the value of these baskets to buyers. Producing baskets for which the cost exceeds the value creates waste, a deadweight loss measured by the triangle *abd*. In other words, the resources used to produce those extra baskets have an opportunity cost, and they could produce more value in some other part of the economy.

As with taxes, the wedge analysis shows that it doesn't make a difference whether buyers are subsidized $1 for every unit bought or sellers are subsidized $1 for every unit sold.

CHECK YOURSELF

> Suppose that the government taxes insulin producers $50 per dose produced. Who is likely to ultimately pay this tax?

> Although the government taxes almost everything, would the government rather tax items that have relatively inelastic or relatively elastic demands and supplies? Why?

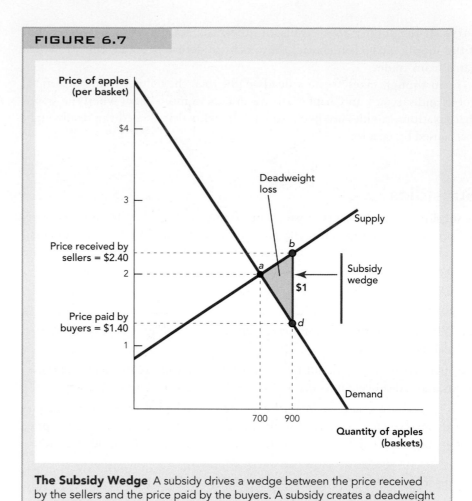

FIGURE 6.7

The Subsidy Wedge A subsidy drives a wedge between the price received by the sellers and the price paid by the buyers. A subsidy creates a deadweight loss (triangle abd).

Similarly, we showed that who bears the burden of a tax depends on the relative elasticities of supply and demand. Exactly the same forces determine who gets the benefit of a subsidy. The rule is simple: Whoever bears the burden of a tax receives the benefit of a subsidy. Figure 6.8 illustrates the intuition for the case where the elasticity of supply is less than the elasticity of demand. In this case, suppliers bear the burden of the tax but receive the benefit of a subsidy.

Let's analyze two examples of subsidies in action.

King Cotton and the Deadweight Loss of Water Subsidies

In California, Arizona, and other western states, there are very large subsidies to water used in agriculture. In California, for example, cotton, alfalfa, and rice farmers in the Central Valley area typically pay $20–$30 an acre-foot for water that costs $200–$500 an acre-foot (an acre-foot is the amount of water needed to cover 1 acre 1 foot deep). The difference is made up by a government subsidy.

Farmers use the subsidized water to transform desert into prime agricultural land. But turning a California desert into cropland makes about as much sense as building greenhouses in Alaska! America already has plenty of land on which cotton can be grown cheaply. Spending billions of dollars to dam rivers and transport water hundreds of miles to grow a crop that can be grown more cheaply in Georgia is a waste of resources, a deadweight loss. The water used to grow

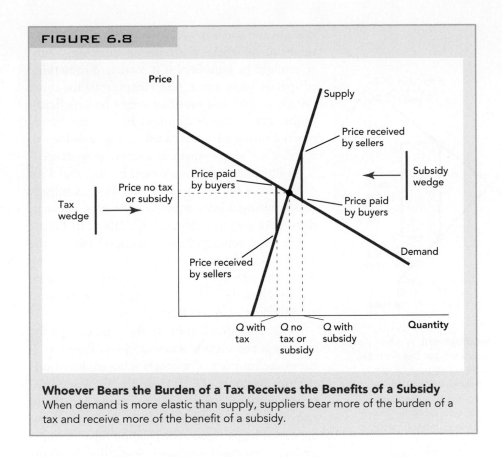

FIGURE 6.8

Whoever Bears the Burden of a Tax Receives the Benefits of a Subsidy
When demand is more elastic than supply, suppliers bear more of the burden of a tax and receive more of the benefit of a subsidy.

California cotton, for example, has much higher value producing silicon chips in San Jose or as drinking water in Los Angeles than it does as irrigation water.

Recall from Chapter 4 that one of the conditions for maximizing the gains from trade in a free market is that there are no wasteful trades. We can now see how in some situations a subsidy can create wasteful trades.

The waste created by water subsidies is compounded with a variety of agricultural subsidies. Some farmers in the Central Valley are "double-dippers"—they use subsidized water to grow subsidized cotton. Some are even "triple-dippers"—they use subsidized water to grow subsidized corn to feed cows to produce subsidized milk!

Who benefits from the water subsidy? Is it California cotton suppliers or cotton buyers? Remember that suppliers receive more of the benefit of a subsidy than buyers when the elasticity of demand is greater than the elasticity of supply (as in Figure 6.8). Can you explain why the elasticity of demand for California cotton is much greater than the elasticity of supply? The elasticity of demand for *California* cotton is very high since cotton grown elsewhere is almost a perfect substitute. In other words, the price of cotton is determined on the world market for cotton and California production is too small to have much of an influence on the world price. It's not surprising, therefore, that it's not cotton consumers who lobby for water subsidies but the farmers in California's Central Valley. Central Valley California farmers are politically powerful and they have been subsidized since 1902!

Wage Subsidies

It's difficult to see why California cotton should be subsidized when cotton from Georgia (or India, China, or Pakistan) is just as good, but subsidies are

FIGURE 6.9

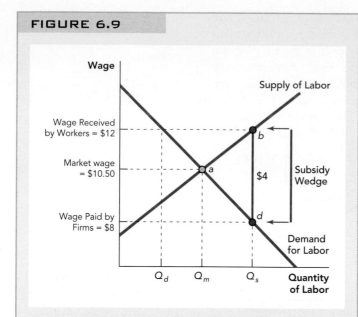

A Subsidy to Wages Increases Employment A subsidy to firms that hire low-wage workers drives a wedge between the wage received by workers ($12) and the wage paid by firms ($8). The subsidy increases the wages received by workers and reduces the wage paid by firms. As a result, employment increases from Q_m to Q_s. The cost of the subsidy to the government is the subsidy amount, $4, times the number of workers employed, Q_s.

CHECK YOURSELF

> To promote energy independence, the U.S. government provides a subsidy to corn growers if they convert the corn to ethanol, a fuel used in some cars. Because of this subsidy, what happens to the quantity supplied of ethanol, and what happens to the price received by corn growers and the price paid by ethanol buyers?

> The U.S. government subsidizes college education in the form of Pell grants and lower-cost government Stafford loans. How do these subsidies affect the price of college education? Which is relatively more elastic: supply or demand? Who benefits the most from these subsidies: suppliers (colleges) or demanders of education (students)?

not always bad for social welfare. Just as a tax might be beneficial if it reduced smoking, a subsidy might be beneficial if it increased something of special importance (see Chapter 10 for more on when taxes and subsidies might be beneficial). Nobel Prize winner Edmund Phelps, for example, is a strong advocate of using wage subsidies to increase the employment of low-wage workers.

In Phelps's plan, firms would be subsidized for every low-wage worker that they hire. A subsidy makes hiring a low-wage worker even cheaper, thus increasing the demand for labor. In Figure 6.9, a wage subsidy drives a wedge between the wage received by workers and the wage paid by firms. The subsidy increases the wage received by workers and decreases the wage paid by firms so employment increases from Q_m to Q_s.

Wage subsidies can be costly. The cost of the subsidy is the subsidy amount ($4 in Figure 6.9) times the number of workers who are hired under this program (Q_s in Figure 6.9). Wage subsidies, however, could have offsetting benefits to taxpayers, making their total cost less than it first appears. Phelps argues, for example, that if wages and employment among low-skilled workers were higher, welfare payments would be lower. He also suggests that encouraging work among those with the least skills would reduce crime, drug dependency, and the culture of "rational defeatism" that keeps many people in poverty.

The United States does have one program that is similar to a wage subsidy. It's called the Earned Income Tax Credit (EITC). The EITC is a cash subsidy to the earnings of low-income workers. The main difference between the EITC and a Phelps wage subsidy is that Phelps would like to subsidize all low-wage workers. The EITC, however, is targeted at families with children—the subsidy is much smaller for workers without children. The EITC has been successful at increasing employment among single mothers but it doesn't do much for single men.

In his book *Rewarding Work*, Phelps argues that wage subsidies are a better way to help low-skill workers than the minimum wage. We will return to this question in Chapter 8 when we take up price ceilings and price floors.

□ Takeaway

We used supply and demand to explain the effects of taxes and subsidies. Using the wedge shortcut, you should be able to show that taxes decrease the quantity traded, subsidies increase the quantity traded, and both taxes and subsidies create a deadweight loss. Surprisingly, we showed that the burden of a tax and the benefit of a subsidy do not depend on who sends or receives the government check. Instead, who bears the burden of a tax and who receives the benefit of a subsidy depends on the relative elasticities of supply and demand. In particular, if you remember that *elasticity = escape*, then you will know that the side of the market (buyers or sellers) with the more elastic curve will escape more of the tax. We also showed that elasticities of demand and supply determine the deadweight loss of a tax. The more elastic either the demand or the supply curve is, the more a tax deters trade, and the more trades that are deterred, the greater the deadweight loss (for a given amount of tax revenue).

The tools of supply and demand are very powerful. In this chapter, we have shown how we can use these tools to understand taxes and subsidies.

□ CHAPTER REVIEW

FACTS AND TOOLS

1. As we saw in Chapter 4, economists' idea of "equilibrium" borrows a lot from physics. Let's push the physics metaphors a bit further. Here, we focus just on the supply side. For each set of words in brackets, circle the correct choice:

   a. When the government subsidizes an activity, resources such as labor, machines, and bank lending will tend to gravitate [toward/away from] the activity that is subsidized and will tend to gravitate [toward/away from] activity that is not subsidized.

   b. When the government taxes an activity, resources such as labor, machines, and bank lending will tend to gravitate [toward/away from] the activity that is taxed and will tend to gravitate [toward/away from] activity that is not taxed.

2. Junk food has recently been criticized for being unhealthy and too cheap, enticing the poor to adopt unhealthy lifestyles. Suppose that the state of Oklakansas imposes a tax on junk food.

   a. What needs to be true for the tax to actually deter people from eating junk food: Should junk food demand be elastic or should it be inelastic?

   b. If the Oklakansas government wants to strongly discourage people from eating junk food, when will it need to set a higher tax rate: When junk food demand is elastic or when it is inelastic?

   c. But hold on a moment: The supply side matters as well. If junk food supply is highly elastic—perhaps because it's not

that hard to start selling salads with low-fat dressing instead of mayonnaise- and cheese-laden burgers—does that mean that a junk food tax will have a bigger effect than if supply were inelastic? Or is it the other way around?

   d. Let's combine these stories now: If a government is hoping that a small tax can actually discourage a lot of junk food purchases, it should hope for:

   I. Elastic supply and inelastic demand
   II. Elastic supply and elastic demand
   III. Inelastic supply and elastic demand
   IV. Inelastic supply and inelastic demand

3. As we saw in the chapter, a lot turns on elasticity. Decades ago, Washington, DC, a fairly small city, wanted to raise more revenue by increasing the gas tax. Washington, DC, shares borders with Maryland and Virginia, and it's very easy to cross the borders between these states without even really noticing: The suburbs just blend together.

   a. How elastic is the demand for gasoline *sold at stations within DC?* In other words, if the price of gas in DC rises, but the price in Maryland and Virginia stays the same, will gasoline sales at DC stations fall a little, or will they fall a lot?

   b. Take your answer in part **a** into account when answering this question. So, when Washington, DC, increased its gasoline tax, how much revenue did it raise: Did it raise a little bit of revenue, or did it raise a lot of revenue?

c. How would your answer to **b** change if DC, Maryland, and Virginia all agreed to raise their gas tax simultaneously? These states have heavily populated borders with each other, but they don't have any heavily populated borders with other states.

4. In Figure 6.5, what is the total revenue raised by the tax, in dollars? What is the deadweight loss from the tax, in dollars? (*Note:* You've seen the formula for the latter before. We'll let you look around a little for this one.)

5. a. Once again: Why does the text say that *elaticity = escape*? (This is worth remembering: Elasticity is one of the toughest ideas for most economics students.)

b. Which two groups of workers did we say have a relatively high elasticity of labor supply? Keep this in mind as politicians debate raising or lowering taxes on different types of workers: These two groups are the ones most likely to make big changes in their behavior.

6. Suppose that Maria is willing to pay $40 for a haircut, and her stylist Juan is willing to accept as little as $25 for a haircut.

a. What possible prices for the haircut would be beneficial to both Maria and Juan? How much total surplus (that is, the sum of consumer and producer surplus) would be generated by this haircut?

b. If the state where Maria and Juan live instituted a tax on services that included a $5 per haircut tax on stylists and barbers, what happens to the range of haircut prices that benefit both Maria and Juan? Will the haircut still happen? Will this tax alter the total economic benefit of this haircut?

c. What if instead the tax was $20?

THINKING AND PROBLEM SOLVING

1. Some people with diabetes absolutely need to take insulin on a regular basis to survive. Pharmaceutical companies that make insulin could find a lot of other ways to make some money.

a. If the U.S. government imposes a tax on insulin producers of $10 per cubic

centimeter of insulin, payable every month to the U.S. Treasury, who will bear most of the burden of the tax: Insulin producers, people with diabetes, or can't you tell with the information given?

b. Suppose instead that because of government corruption, the insulin manufacturers convince the U.S. government to pay the insulin makers $10 per cubic centimeter of insulin, payable every month *from* the U.S. Treasury. Who will get most of the benefit of this subsidy: Insulin producers, people with diabetes, or can't you tell with the information given?

2. Let's see if we can formulate any real laws about the economics of taxation. Which of the following *must* be true, as long as supply and demand curves have their normal shape (i.e., they aren't perfectly vertical or horizontal, and demand curves have a negative slope while supply curves have a positive slope). More than one may be true.

If there is a tax:

a. The equilibrium quantity must fall, and the price that buyers pay must rise.

b. The equilibrium quantity must rise, and the price that sellers pay must rise.

c. The equilibrium quantity must fall, and the price that sellers receive must fall.

d. The equilibrium quantity must rise, and the price that buyers receive must fall.

(*Note:* The correct answer(s) to this question was(were) actually controversial until Nobel laureate Paul Samuelson created a simple mathematical proof in his legendary graduate textbook, *Foundations of Economic Analysis*.)

3. Using the following diagram, use the wedge shortcut to answer these questions:

a. If a tax of $2 were imposed, what price would buyers pay and what price would suppliers receive? How much revenue would be raised by the tax? How much deadweight loss would be created by the tax?

b. If a subsidy of $5 were imposed, what price would buyers pay and what price would suppliers receive? How much would the subsidy cost the government? How much deadweight loss would be created by the subsidy?

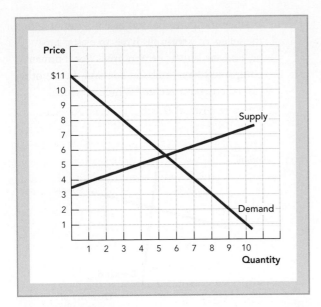

4. When governments are trying to raise tax revenue, they sometimes attempt to target higher-income people, since they are in a better position to bear the burden of a tax. However, it can be very difficult to earn tax revenue from wealthy people.

   a. Consider the progressive nature of the U.S. federal income tax system: It's designed so that higher incomes are taxed at higher tax rates. Thinking about the elasticity of labor supply, why might it be more difficult to collect tax revenue from a wealthy individual than from a poor person, all else equal?

   b. Another way governments have tried to collect taxes from the wealthy is through the use of luxury taxes, which are exactly what they sound like: taxes on goods that are considered luxuries, like jewelry or expensive cars and real estate. What is true about the demand for luxuries? Consider jewelry. Is a luxury tax more likely to hurt the buyers of jewelry, or the sellers of jewelry?

   c. The chapter began by discussing another tax that targets wealthy individuals: the estate tax. Comment on the effectiveness of this tax (in terms of government revenue), considering the demand of wealthy individuals for leaving an inheritance.

5. Consider the supply and demand diagram below. In this market, the government subsidizes the production of this good, and the subsidy wedge is indicated.

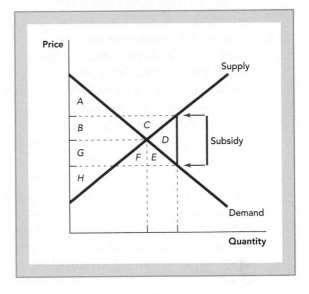

   a. Without the subsidy, which area(s) represent the total gains from trade?

   b. After the subsidy, which area(s) represent consumer surplus? Which area(s) represent producer surplus? Which area(s) represent total government spending on this subsidy?

   c. Which area(s) in part **b** showed up in the answer to more than one of the questions? Can you explain this?

6. As we learned in Chapter 4, the competitive market equilibrium maximizes gains from trade. Taxes and subsidies, by altering the market outcome, reduce the gains from trade. Does this happen primarily because of the impact of taxes and subsidies on *prices*, or the impact of taxes and subsidies on *quantities*?

CHALLENGES

1. Let's apply the economics of taxation to romantic relationships.

   a. What does it mean to have an inelastic demand for your boyfriend or girlfriend? How about an elastic demand?

b. Sometimes relationships have taxes. Suppose that you and your boyfriend or girlfriend live one hour apart. Using the tools developed in the chapter, how can you predict which one of you will do most of the driving? That is, which one of you will bear the majority of the relationship tax?

2. a. In the opening scene of the classic Eddie Murphy comedy *Beverly Hills Cop,* Axel Foley, a Detroit police officer, is stopping a cigarette smuggling ring. Of course, smugglers don't pay the tax when the cigarettes crossed state lines. Which way do you suspect the smugglers were moving the cigarettes, based on economic theory? From the high-tax North to the low-cost South, or vice versa?

b. In our discussion of taxation, we've acted as if it were effortless to pass and enforce tax laws. But of course, law enforcement officials including the Internal Revenue Service put a lot of effort into enforcing tax laws. Let's think for a moment about what kind of taxes are easiest to collect, just based on the basic ideas we've covered. Who will make the most effort to escape a tax: The party who is elastic or the party who is inelastic? (*Hint:* It doesn't matter whether we're talking about suppliers or demanders.)

(*Note:* Public administration researchers know the most about this topic. Carolyn Webber and Aaron Wildavsky's surprisingly enjoyable classic, *A History of Taxation and Expenditure in the Western World,* sets out just how difficult it's been for most Western governments to collect taxes.)

3. Let's get some practice with the "wedge trick," and use it to learn about the relationship between subsidies and lobbying. The U.S. government has many subsidies for alternative energy development: Some are just called subsidies, some are called tax breaks instead. Either way, they work just like the subsidies we studied in this chapter. We'll look at the market for windmills.

a. In the two figures below, one is a case where the sellers of windmills have an elastic supply and the buyers of windmills (local power companies) have inelastic demand. In the other case, the reverse is true. Which is which?

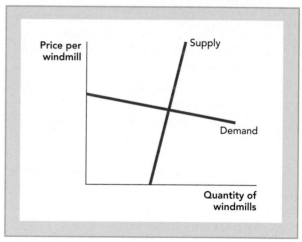

b. In which case will a subsidy cut the price paid by the buyers the most: When demand is elastic or when it is inelastic? (It'll be easiest if you use the "wedge trick.") Is this the first or second graph?

c. In which case will a subsidy increase the price received by the sellers the most: When supply is elastic or when it is inelastic? Again, which graph is this?

d. Now look at how producer surplus and consumer surplus change in these two cases. To see this, remember that producer surplus is the area *above* the supply curve and below the price, and consumer surplus is the area *below* the demand curve and above the price. So in the first graph, who gets the lion's share of any subsidy-driven extra surplus: suppliers or demanders? Is that the inelastic group or the elastic group? In other words, whose surplus triangle gets bigger faster as the quantity increases? (You might try shading in these triangles just to be sure.)

e. Now it's time for the second graph. Again, who gets the lion's share of any subsidy-driven extra surplus: suppliers or demanders? Is that the inelastic group or the elastic group?

f. There's going to be a pattern here in parts **d** and **e:** The more [elastic or inelastic?] side of the market gets most of the extra surplus from the subsidy.

g. When Congress gives subsidies for the alternative energy market, it is hoping that a small subsidy can get a big increase in output: In other words, they are hoping that the equilibrium quantity will be *elastic*. At the same time, the groups most likely to lobby Congress for a big alternative energy subsidy are going to be the groups that get the most extra surplus from any subsidy.

After all, if the subsidy doesn't give them much surplus, they're not likely to ask Congress for it.

So here's the big question: Will the groups that are most likely to *lobby for* a subsidy be the same groups that are most likely to *respond to* the subsidy? (*Note:* This is a general lesson about the incentives for lobbying: It's not just a story about the alternative energy industry.)

4. As you learned in the chapter, the elasticities of demand and supply are crucial in determining how the burden of a tax (or the benefit of a subsidy) is divided between buyers and sellers. Under what conditions for supply or demand would a seller actually be able to avoid bearing any of the burden of a tax? Under what conditions would a subsidy benefit only the sellers of a good?

5. In the chapter, most of the taxes we discussed were equal to a certain dollar amount per unit. In this case, a tax on sellers results in a parallel upward shift of the supply curve; a tax on buyers results in a parallel downward shift of the demand curve. In reality, however, many taxes are expressed as a percentage. Graphically, how would you show a 100% tax on the sellers of a good? How would you show a 100% tax on the buyers of a good? One of the results of this chapter is that it doesn't matter on whom the tax is levied—the result is the same. Show graphically that this also applies to *percentage* taxes.

7

The Price System: Signals, Speculation, and Prediction

A price is a signal wrapped up in an incentive. That may sound a little abstract, but it's one of the most fundamental insights in economics. Prices convey important information and they create an incentive to respond to that information in socially useful ways. In this chapter, you'll see how one market influences another and then how an entire series of markets in a global economy fit together. Prices are the key force integrating markets and motivating entrepreneurs. We will have plenty of examples in this chapter, but keep your eye on the primary theme: The price system creates rich connections between markets and enable societies to mobilize vast amounts of knowledge toward common ends, yet without a central planner.

Markets Link the World

Let's take a closer look at the story of just one product. It's Valentine's Day. You have just given your boyfriend or girlfriend a beautiful, single-stemmed rose, one of 180 million that will be sold today.[1] Where did the rose come from and how did it get into your hands?

Chances are good that your rose was grown in Kenya in the Lake Naivasha area to the northwest of Nairobi.[2] Over 50,000 tons of roses are grown in Kenya every year, almost all for export. The Kenyan women who do most of the fieldwork know very little about the strange Western celebration of love called Saint Valentine's Day, but they don't have to. What they do know is that they get paid more when the roses are debudded so that they bloom just in time for delivery on February 14.

No one wants to give (or receive) a wilted rose, so everyone involved in the rose business has an incentive to move quickly. In a matter of hours after

Kenyan woman harvesting roses.

A small part of the world's largest flower market in Aalsmeer, Holland.

The world is linked in fascinating ways. In Peru, workers roam the hillsides collecting millions of female cochineal bugs from their cactus pad nests. After dunking in hot water, drying and grinding, the bugs make an excellent red dye. The dye is used to color many products including yogurt (look for carmine in the ingredients), red Smarties, and even lipstick!

picking, the roses travel in cooled trucks from the field to the airport in Nairobi, where they are loaded onto refrigerated aircraft. Within a day, the flowers are in Aalsmeer, Holland.

Aalsmeer is the home of the world's largest flower market. On a typical working day, 20 million flowers are flown into this tiny Dutch town. The flowers are paraded in lots before large clocks, clocks that measure not time but prices. Beginning with a high price, the clocks quickly tick downward until a bidder stamps a button indicating that he or she is willing to buy at that price. By the end of the day, 20 million flowers have been sold, and they are once again packed onto cooled airplanes to be flown to the world's buyers in London, Paris, New York, and Topeka. From Kenya to your girlfriend's or boyfriend's hand in 72 hours.[3]

The worldwide market links romantic American teenagers with Kenyan flower growers, Dutch clocks, British airplanes, Colombian coffee (to keep the pilots awake), Finnish cell phones, and much, much more. To bring just one product to your table requires the co-operative effort of millions.

Moreover, this immense cooperation is voluntary and undirected. Each of millions of people acting in his or her own self-interest play a role, but no one knows the full story of how a Kenyan rose becomes a gift of love in Topeka because the full story is too complex. Nevertheless, every Valentine's Day you can count on the fact that your local florist will have roses for sale.

The market is the original Web, and it's more dense, interconnected, and alive with intelligence than its computer analog.

Markets Link to One Another

In Chapters 3 and 4, we showed how the supply and demand for oil determine the price of oil. Now we return to oil but this time as an example of how shifts in supply and demand in one market ripple across the worldwide market, changing distant people and products in ways that no one can foresee.

The Kenyan flower industry was one unforeseen consequence of changes in the market for oil. Prior to the 1970s, roses were grown in American greenhouses. Higher prices for oil raised heating costs so much that it became cheaper to grow roses in warm countries and ship them to cold countries.* If roses had been heavier, the higher costs of transportation might have outweighed the lower costs of heating, but even with higher fuel costs, transportation costs in the modern world have been falling.

It's not obvious that the right way to respond to an increased scarcity of oil is to move flower production from California to Kenya. No one planned such a response in advance. Instead, creative entrepreneurs responded to the increase in the price of oil in ways that no

---

* The shift of flower production from America to Kenya and other equatorial countries like Colombia and Ecuador in the 1980s is part of a trend. Two decades earlier, declines in transportation costs and relative increases in the relative costs of heating, land, and labor moved flower production from New York and Pennsylvania to Florida and California. On the evolution of the cut flower industry, see Mendez, Jose A. 1991. *The Development of the Colombian Cut Flower Industry.* The World Bank. WPS 660.

one predicted or planned. Entrepreneurs are constantly on the lookout for ways to lower costs, and their cost-cutting measures link markets that at first seem like they are a world away.

From Oil to Candy Bars and Brick Driveways

How does the price of oil affect the price of candy bars? One way is obvious: Higher energy costs increase the cost of producing most products, including candy bars. But the market also links oil and candy bars in more subtle ways. For instance, ethanol is the active ingredient in alcoholic beverages, but it's also a good fuel that can be made from a variety of crops like corn or sugar cane. Brazil is the largest producer and consumer of fuel ethanol in the world, so much so that it has managed to reduce its gasoline consumption by 40% by adopting flexible fuel vehicles that can run on ethanol, gasoline, or any combination of the two.[4] Brazil is also the largest producer of sugar in the world.

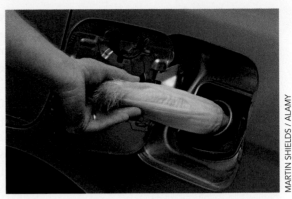

Surprised? Corn and oil are substitutes.

Can you see the connection between the price of oil and the price of candy bars now? As the price of oil has increased, the Brazilians have shifted sugar cane from sugar production to ethanol production, thereby holding down fuel costs but increasing the price of sugar.[5]

What about brick driveways? A 42-gallon barrel of crude oil is refined into approximately 19.5 gallons of gasoline, 9.7 gallons of fuel oil, 4 gallons of jet fuel, 1.4 gallons of asphalt, and a number of other products.[6] To some extent, these divisions are fixed. (Asphalt is what you get after you separate out the other products.) But oil refiners do have some flexibility, and when the price of gasoline is relatively high, it pays for them to pull every last drop of gasoline out of a barrel of crude, leaving less crude to make the remaining products. A higher price of gasoline, therefore, means a reduced supply of asphalt. A reduced supply of asphalt pushes up the price of asphalt. When the price of oil rose to $70 a barrel in 2006, for example, the price of using asphalt to pave an average-sized driveway rose by $300.[7] Seeing the higher price, homeowners turned to substitutes such as concrete, cobblestones, and brick.

Solving the Great Economic Problem

Markets around the world are linked to one another. A change in supply and demand in one market can influence markets for entirely different products thousands of miles away. But what does all this linking accomplish? The **great economic problem** is to arrange our limited resources to satisfy as many of our wants as possible. Let's imagine that war in the Middle East reduces the supply of oil. We must economize on oil. But how? It would be foolish to reduce oil equally in all uses—oil is more valuable in some uses than in others. We want to shift oil out of low-valued uses, where we can do without or where good substitutes for oil exist, so that we can keep supplying oil for high-valued uses, where oil has few good substitutes.

One way to make this shift would be for a central planner to issue orders. The central planner would order so much oil to be used in the steel industry, so much for heating, and so much for Sunday driving. But how would the central planner know the value of oil in each of its millions of uses? No one knows for certain all the uses of oil, let alone which uses of oil are high-valued uses and

CHECK **YOURSELF**

> The U.S. government offers a subsidy for converting corn to ethanol. If farmers receive a higher price for turning corn into ethanol, what will happen to the price of corn used in cornbread? How will cafeterias and restaurants respond?

> Sawdust is used for bedding milk cows. What did the end of the housing boom in 2007 do to the price of milk? Search for "sawdust" at http://www.MarginalRevolution.com if you need a hint.

The **great economic problem** is to arrange our limited resources to satisfy as many of our wants as possible.

which are low-valued uses. Is the oil used to produce steel more valuable than the oil used to produce vegetables? Even if steel is worth more than vegetables, the answer isn't obvious because electricity might be a good substitute for oil in producing steel but not for producing vegetables. To estimate the value of oil in different uses, therefore, the central planner would have to gather information about all the uses of oil and all of the substitutes for oil in each use (and all of the substitutes for the substitutes!). Using this information, the central planner would then have to somehow compute the optimal allocation of oil and then send out thousands of orders directing oil to its many uses in the economy.

The task of central planning is impossibly complex and we haven't yet discussed incentives. Why would anyone have an incentive to send truthful information to the central planner? Each user of oil would surely announce that its use is the high-valued use for which no substitute is possible. And what incentive would the central planner have to actually direct oil to its high-value uses?

The U.S. government briefly tried to centrally plan the allocation of oil during the 1973–1974 oil crisis. President Nixon even went so far as to forbid gas stations from opening on Sundays in an attempt to reduce Sunday driving! We describe the consequences of this approach to the oil crisis at greater length in the next chapter. The Soviet Union and China went much further than the United States and tried to centrally plan entire economies. Central planning on a large scale, however, failed and has now been abandoned throughout virtually all the world (Cuba and North Korea, both very poor countries, are the exceptions).

The central planning approach failed because of problems of *information* and *incentives*. We need a better approach.

Users of oil have a lot of information about the value of oil in their own uses, much more information than could ever be communicated to a central planner. We need to take advantage of this information without attempting to communicate it to a central bureaucracy. Ideally, each user of oil would compare the value of oil in their use with the value of oil in alternative uses, and each user of oil would have an incentive to give up the oil if it has a lower value in their use than in alternative uses. This is exactly what the price system accomplishes.

Let's go back to the person thinking about whether to pave the driveway with asphalt or brick. This person knows the value of a paved driveway, but he or she doesn't know what uses the asphalt has elsewhere in the economy. They do know the price of asphalt, and *in a free market, the price of asphalt is equal to the value of the asphalt in its next highest-value use.* Take a look at Figure 7.1, which is just the now-familiar supply and demand diagram. Remember that the value of a good in its various uses is given by the height of the demand curve. Notice that the equilibrium price splits the uses of the good into two—above the equilibrium price are the high-value, satisfied demands; below the price are the low-value, unsatisfied demands. Now what is the value of the highest-value demand that is *not* satisfied? It's just equal to the market price (or if you like, "just below" the market price). In other words, if one more barrel of oil became available, the highest-value use of that barrel would be to satisfy the first presently unsatisfied demand. The market price tells us the value of the good in its next highest-valued use.

Opportunity cost. The true cost of a motorcycle is not its money price but rather a lawnmower. The true cost is the *opportunity cost*—what the resources that went into the motorcycle could have produced had the motorcycle not been built.

It is part of the marvel of a free market that, under the right conditions, the money price of the motorcycle exactly represents the value of the resources that went into producing the motorcycle, namely the value those resources would have had in their next highest-valued use.

FIGURE 7.1

The Market Price and Opportunity Cost The market price splits the uses of oil into two. Above the price are the uses of oil whose value is greater than the price; in a free market, these demands will be satisfied. Below the price are the uses of oil whose value is less than the price; in a free market, these are the unsatisfied demands. Notice the value of oil in the first unsatisfied demand is just slightly below the market price.

(Top photo: EuroStyle Graphics/Alamy)
(Bottom: Lew Robertson/Corbis)

When a consumer compares the price of asphalt to the value of asphalt for paving his driveway, he is comparing *the value of asphalt on his driveway to its opportunity cost.* And remember, because markets are linked, the price of asphalt is linked to the price of oil, and the price of oil is linked to the demand for automobiles in China and the supply of ethanol and the price of sugar. . . . So when the consumer compares the value of asphalt in paving his driveway to the price of asphalt, he may be comparing the value of asphalt in paving his driveway to the value of 500 gallons of gasoline used by a motorist in Brazil. Or, in other words, when you decide whether to drive to school or take the bus, you are deciding whether your use of oil is more valuable than the billions of other uses of oil in the world that are presently unsatisfied!

The market solves the information problem by collapsing all the relevant information in the world about the uses of oil into a single number, the price. As Nobel laureate Friedrich Hayek wrote:[*]

> The most significant fact about this system is the economy of knowledge with which it operates . . . by a kind of symbol [the price], only

---

[*] Hayek's classic paper, The use of knowledge in society, is deep but easy to read. You can find it online by searching for "Hayek use of knowledge in society." The original citation is Hayek, Friedrich A., 1945. The use of knowledge in society. *American Economic Review XXXV*, (4):519–530.

HULTON ARCHIVE/GETTY IMAGE

Friedrich A. Hayek (1899–1992) explained the marvel of the price system.

the most essential information is passed on and passed on only to those concerned. . . . The marvel is that in a case like that of a scarcity of one raw material, without an order being issued, without more than perhaps a handful of people knowing the cause, tens of thousands of people whose identity could not be ascertained by months of investigation, are made to use the material or its products more sparingly; i.e., they move in the right direction.

In addition to solving the information problem, the price system also solves the incentive problem. It's in a consumer's interest to pay attention to prices! When the price of an oil product like asphalt increases, consumers have an incentive to turn to substitutes like bricks and, in so doing, they free up oil to be used elsewhere in the economy where it is of higher value.

The worldwide market accomplishes this immense task of allocating resources without any central planning or control. No one knows or understands all the links between oil, sugar, and brick driveways, but the links are there and the market works even without anyone's understanding or knowledge. Amazed by what he saw, Adam Smith said the market works as if "an invisible hand" guided the process.

Nobel laureate Vernon Smith, whom we met in Chapter 4, put it this way:

At the heart of economics is a scientific mystery: How is it that the pricing system accomplishes the world's work without anyone being in charge? Like language, no one invented it. None of us could have invented it, and its operation depends in no way on anyone's comprehension or understanding of it. . . . The pricing system—How is order produced from freedom of choice?—is a scientific mystery as deep, fundamental and inspiring as that of the expanding universe or the forces that bind matter.[8]

CHECK YOURSELF

> Peanuts are used primarily for food dishes, but they are also used in bird feed, paint, varnish, furniture polish, insecticides, and soap. Rank these uses from higher to lower value taking into account in which use the peanuts are critical and in which uses there are good substitutes. Don't obsess over this: We know you are not a peanut expert, but see if you can come up with a sense of higher and lower value.

> Imagine that there is a large peanut crop failure in China, which produces more than one-third of the world's supply. Which of the uses that you ranked in the previous question will be cut back?

A Price Is a Signal Wrapped Up in an Incentive

How is order produced from freedom of choice? That is a scientific mystery, and prices are the biggest clue to the solution. Prices do much more than tell people how much they must shell out for a burger and fries. Prices are incentives, prices are signals, prices are predictions. To understand the market, you need to better understand prices.

When the price of oil rises, all users of oil are encouraged to economize—perhaps by simply using less but also by thinking about substitutes: everything from electric cars to moving flower cultivation overseas. An increase in the price of oil is also a signal to suppliers to invest more in exploration, to look for alternatives like ethanol, and to increase recycling. Do you know the most recycled product in America? It's asphalt.[9]

Politicians and consumers sometime fail to understand the signaling role of prices. After a hurricane, the prices of ice, generators, and chainsaws often skyrocket. Consumers complain of price gouging, and politicians call for price controls. That's understandable, because it can seem doubly harsh to be hit by a hurricane *and* high prices. But the price system is just doing its job. A skyrocketing price is like a flare being shot into the night sky that shouts—bring ice here! A price control eliminates the signal to bring ice into the devastated area as quickly as possible.

The high price of ice in a hurricane-devastated area signals a profit opportunity for ice suppliers. Buy ice where the price is low and ship it to where the price is high. As the supply of ice in the hurricane-devastated area increases, the price will fall. More generally, price signals and the accompanying profits and losses tell entrepreneurs what areas of the economy consumers want expanded and what areas they want contracted. If consumers want more computers, prices and profits in the computer industry will increase and the industry will expand.

Losses may be an even more important signal than profits. Entrepreneurs who fail to compete with lower costs and better products take losses and their businesses contract or even go bankrupt. Bankruptcy is bad for a business but can be good for capitalism. Ever heard of Smith Corona, Polaroid, Pan Am, or Hechingers? At one point, each of these companies led its industry, but today all are either bankrupt or much smaller than at their peak. In a free market, no firm is so powerful that it does not daily face the market test. As a result, *in a successful economy there will be many unsuccessful firms.*

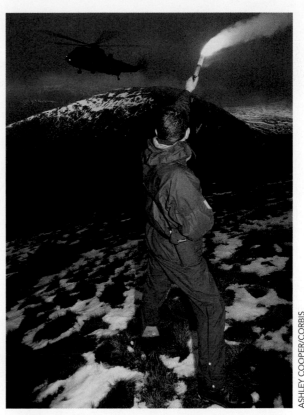

ASHLEY COOPER/CORBIS

A skyrocketing price is a signal to bring resources here!

Speculation

Suppose that you expect that a war in the Middle East is likely next year and that, if it should occur, the supply of oil will decrease, thereby pushing up the price of oil. How could you profit from your expectation? The way to make money is to buy low and sell high, so you should buy oil today when the price is low, hold the oil in storage, and then sell it next year after war breaks out, when the price is higher. Figure 7.2 on the next page shows this process, which is called **speculation**. We have used vertical supply curves, meaning that the amount of oil is fixed, to simplify the diagram.

The top panel shows what happens without speculation. Production today is high and today's price is low (point *a*). Future production, however, will be disrupted by the war, pushing up the future price (point *b*). Notice that without speculation, the war disrupts the oil market and prices jump from point *a* to point *b*.

The bottom panel shows what happens with speculation. Speculators buy oil today and they put it into storage—this reduces the quantity available for consumption today and pushes up today's price (point *c*). Next year, however, when the war occurs, production is low but consumption is higher than it would have been without speculation and prices are lower because the speculators sell oil from their inventories (point *d*). Notice that with speculation, preparations are made for any disruption in oil production and oil prices are smoothed.

CHECK YOURSELF

> Imagine that whenever the supply of oil rose or fell, the government sent text messages to every user of oil asking them to use more or less oil as the case warranted. Suppose that the messaging system worked very well. Is such a messaging system likely to allocate resources as well as prices? Why or why not? What is the difference between the message system and the price system?

> Firms in the old Soviet Union never went bankrupt. How do you think this influenced the rate of innovation and economic growth?

Speculation is the attempt to profit from future price changes.

FIGURE 7.2

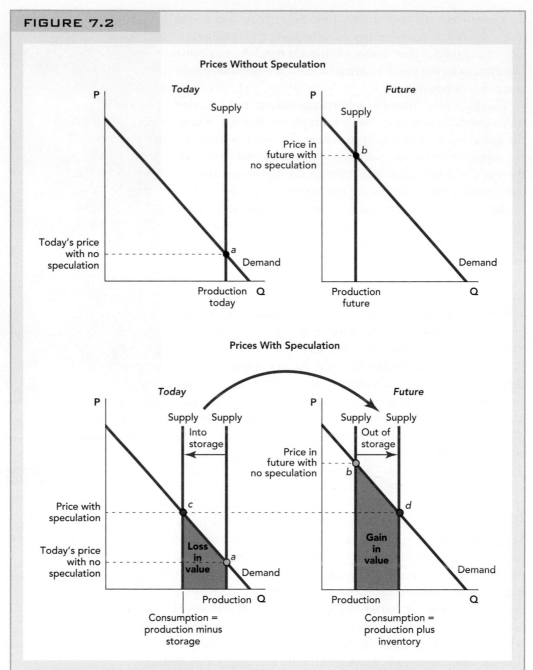

Prices Without Speculation

Today

Future

Prices With Speculation

Today

Future

Speculation Tends to Smooth Prices over Time and Increase Welfare The top panel shows the price of oil, oil consumption, and oil production in an economy without speculation. In the panel on the left, Today, the equilibrium is at point *a*, the price is low, and oil consumption and production are high. In the panel on the right, Future, the price of oil is high because the disruption has reduced the production of oil. Since no oil was stored from the previous period, the consumption of oil is also reduced.

The bottom panel shows what happens with speculation. In the left panel, labeled *Today*, oil speculators buy oil and put it into storage, pushing up the price of oil and reducing consumption today—thus, the equilibrium shifts from point a to point c. In the future when the price of oil is high (at point *b*), speculators sell their oil from storage. The oil flowing out of storage pushes the price down and allows people to consume more oil even though production is low.

The value of oil to consumers (in blue) falls today when oil is put into storage, but rises by an even larger amount in the future when oil is in short supply and speculators move their stocks out of storage.

Speculators raise prices today but lower prices in the future. As a result, speculators have an image problem because the media often report when speculators raise prices but rarely do they report when speculators lower prices. Overall, however, society is better off from speculation because speculators move oil from when it has low value (today) and move it to when it has high value (the future). When producers put oil in storage, society doesn't get to consume that oil so some wants become unsatisfied—the loss in value from these unsatisfied wants is measured by the blue area in the (bottom) left panel of Figure 7.2 (once again, the value of the good in its various uses is measured by the height of the demand curve). But when the speculators sell that oil in the future, consumption increases—more wants are satisfied—and the value of this increase in consumption is measured by the much larger blue area in the right panel. Thus, when speculators are right, they move oil from today, where it has low value, to the future, where the value of oil is much higher—in the process making society better off.

Speculators, of course, don't always guess correctly. But speculators put their money where their mouth is. They have strong incentives to be as accurate as possible because when they are wrong, they lose money—a lot of money. Furthermore, bad speculators soon find themselves poor. Anyone who is able to be a speculator for a long time is either very, very lucky or just very good. So, on net, speculators tend to make prices more informative, even though in particular instances many speculators are wrong.

A careful observer of Middle East politics might have very good information about the probability of war in the Middle East but have no easy way to store oil. Fortunately, the market provides a way to speculate in oil without having to build oil tanks in your backyard.

A speculator can buy oil **futures**. Oil futures are contracts to buy or sell a given quantity of oil at a specified price with delivery set at a specified time and place in the future. On the New York Mercantile Exchange (NYMEX), you can buy futures for light, sweet crude oil to be delivered in Cushing, Oklahoma, at 30, 36, 48, 72, or 84 months in the future at a price agreed on today. What makes futures contracts important is that despite specifying delivery and acceptance in Cushing, almost all futures contracts actually settle in cash.

Futures are standardized contracts to buy or sell specified quantities of a commodity or financial instrument at a specified price with delivery set at a specified time in the future.

Let's see how this works. Suppose Tyler believes that the price of oil will be higher in the future than what other people are expecting. Tyler buys an oil contract that gives him the right to 1,000 barrels of oil to be delivered (in Cushing) 30 months in the future. Tyler agrees that on delivery he will pay the seller, Alex, $50 per barrel or $50,000. Similarly, Alex has agreed to deliver 1,000 barrels of oil in Cushing in 30 months. Thirty months from now, Tyler's expectation is proven correct—the actual or "spot" price of oil is $82. If Tyler went to Cushing, he could physically accept the oil from Alex, give him $50,000 and then turn around and sell the oil to someone else for $82 per barrel for a profit of $32 per barrel or $32,000. Instead of doing that, however, Tyler and Alex could agree to *cash settlement*. Alex has agreed to give Tyler 1,000 barrels of oil, which are currently worth $82,000, for a price of $50,000. Instead of giving Tyler the oil, suppose that Alex gives Tyler the cash difference, $32,000, and they call it even. The advantage of cash settlement is that Tyler and Alex can both speculate on the price of oil without ever accepting or delivering oil. Moreover, neither

Tyler nor Alex ever have to go to Cushing, which is sadly lacking in good ethnic restaurants.*

Futures markets are used not only for speculation but also for reducing risk. An airline that wants to know in advance what its fuel costs are going to be next year can lock in the price by buying oil on the futures market. Instead of buying futures, farmers can sell futures. A soybean farmer plants the crop today but does not harvest it until next year when the soybean price could be quite different than today's spot price. To avoid the price risk, the farmer can sell futures, that is, agree to sell so many soybeans at harvest time at a price agreed on today. Futures markets are also common in currencies. Suppose that Ford expects to sell 1,000 cars in Germany for 25,000 euros each. At the end of the year, how many dollars will Ford make? Ford doesn't know because the euro/dollar exchange rate can fluctuate. By selling euro futures, Ford can lock in the exchange rate.

Signal Watching

Speculators who think that a war in the Middle East is likely will buy oil futures, pushing up the futures price (the price agreed on today for delivery in the future). If the futures price is much higher than the spot or current price, that is a sign that smart people with their own money on the line think that supply disruptions may soon occur. Futures prices for oil, currencies, and many commodities can be found in a newspaper or online, so anyone who wants to forecast events in the Middle East can benefit from reading price signals.

Futures prices can be extraordinarily informative about future events. The major factor determining the price of orange juice futures, for example, is the weather. If bad weather is expected to cause a frost destroying many oranges, the price of OJ futures will be high. If good weather and a bumper crop are expected, the price will be low. The economist Richard Roll found that the futures price for OJ was so sensitive to the weather that it could be used to improve the predictions of the National Weather Service![10]

It's not hard to see the future if you know where to look. In December 1991, the United Nations and the Worldwatch Institute warned that wheat would be very scarce in the coming year. Economist Paul Heyne looked in the newspaper and found that on that day the price of wheat was $4.05 a bushel. But the futures price for the following December was $3.51. Speculators, unlike the Worldwatch Institute, were not forecasting increased scarcity. In whose

DOUGLAS PULSIPHER/ ACCLAIM IMAGES

Markets see the future with futures markets.

---

* Technically, this describes a forward contract. The difference between forward and futures contracts is not important for making the point that cash settlement allows anyone to speculate in oil even if he or she neither wants nor has any oil to trade.

The technical difference between futures and forwards is that in a futures contract the buyer and the seller do not contract directly but rather each works through a middleman, the New York Mercantile Exchange (NYMEX). NYMEX guarantees that neither the buyer nor the seller will cheat on the deal. NYMEX does this by *marking the contract to market* on a daily basis, which means that there is a small cash settlement every day until the final day. For example, if the day after Tyler and Alex signed the contract the spot price moved to $51, then Alex would have to pay some extra money to NYMEX. If the day after the contract was signed, the spot price moved to $49, then Tyler would have to pay some extra money to NYMEX. NYMEX holds onto the money, keeping a running tab, until the final day when it releases the total to the party with the net gain. In this way, NYMEX's losses are limited even if one party refuses to honor the deal.

forecast would you put more confidence: that of the Worldwatch Institute or that of wheat speculators? Why?*

The futures price of oil can be used to predict war in the Middle East, but that is a side benefit of the futures market and not its purpose. Factors other than war (e.g., the decisions of OPEC, oil discoveries, and the demand for oil) also affect oil futures, so the futures price of oil is a *noisy signal* of war in the Middle East. A phone line with static—that's a noisy signal. Electrical engineers work to increase the signal-to-noise ratio on cell phones. More recently, economic engineers have begun to design markets to increase the signal-to-noise ratio of prices.

Prediction Markets

If markets are good at predicting the future even though they evolved to do something else, imagine how useful they might be if they were designed to predict. Beginning in the late 1980s, economic engineers began to design **prediction markets,** speculative markets designed so that prices can be interpreted as probabilities and used to make predictions.[11]

A **prediction market** is a speculative market designed so that prices can be interpreted as probabilities and used to make predictions.

The best known prediction market is the Iowa Electronic Markets. The Iowa market lets traders use real money to buy and sell "shares" of political candidates. During the 2008 election, for example, traders on the Iowa Electronic Markets could buy shares in John McCain and Barack Obama. A share in Barack Obama, for example, would pay $1 if Barack Obama won the election and nothing otherwise. Suppose that the market price of an Obama share is 75 cents. What does this market price suggest about the probability of Barack Obama winning the election?

To answer this question, think about each share as a bit like a lottery ticket. The ticket pays $1 if Obama wins and nothing if he loses. How much would you be willing to pay for this lottery ticket if Obama has a 20% chance of winning? How much would you be willing to pay for this lottery ticket if Obama has a 75% chance of winning? If Obama has a 20% chance of winning, then a lottery ticket that pays $1 if he wins, and nothing otherwise, is worth about 20 cents on average (0.2 × $1). If Obama has a 75% chance of winning, then the lottery ticket is worth about 75 cents (0.75 × $1). Thus, working backward, if we see that people are willing to pay 75 cents for an Obama lottery ticket, we can infer that they think that Obama has about a 75% probability of winning the election. In this way, we can use market prices to predict elections!

The Iowa markets correctly predicted the Obama win in 2008 and they were very close about Obama's vote share as well. The future can never be predicted perfectly, but in some 20 years of predicting U.S. and foreign elections, primaries, and other political events, the Iowa markets have proven to be more accurate than alternative institutions such as polls.[12] In tight elections, professional bond traders—who often have millions of dollars riding on postelection economic policies—monitor the Iowa markets for clues about future events.

Hewlett-Packard has used a similar market approach to help predict future hardware sales. Members of HP's sales team bought and sold shares that paid

---

* By the way, Heyne's forecast was correct—wheat was not especially scarce in 1992. Did you put your confidence in the right place?

off when sales fell within a certain range. A typical security would pay out $1, if and only if future sales were, say, between 10,000 and 15,000 units. Another might pay off if sales were between 15,000 and 20,000 units. The market contained 10 types of securities—a range broad enough to include all the relevant possible sales outcomes.

By examining the prices of all 10 shares, HP could assign a probability to any combination of outcomes. For example, if the price of the 5,000–10,000 unit sales security was 10 cents and the price of the 10,000–15,000 unit sales security was 20 cents, this suggests that the probability of selling 5,000–15,000 units was 30%.

HP compared the forecasts made by the prediction market with its own official forecasts and with actual sales figures. In 15 out of 16 trials, the mean market-based prediction was significantly closer to the actual sales figure than the official forecast. In the one remaining trial, the mean market-based prediction and the official forecast were equally close. Encouraged by these results, HP created its own experimental economics laboratory.

Another advantage of prediction markets is that they encourage traders to put their money where their mouths are *not*. Although the members of a company's sales team may know better than anyone that next quarter's sales will be lower than expected, they rarely have incentives to relay this information to their bosses.

Prediction markets can help to overcome the "yes-man" phenomenon that makes it difficult for information to move from the field and into the hands of the senior decision makers.

The Hollywood Stock Exchange (http://www.HSX.com) is also proving that the innovative use of markets can be profitable. The Hollywood Exchange lets traders buy and sell shares and options in movies, music, and Oscar contenders. Trading on the Hollywood Exchange is conducted in make-believe "Hollywood Dollars," but the goal of the HSX—which is owned by a subsidiary of the Wall Street firm Cantor Fitzgerald—is profit. Some 800,000 people trading on HSX for fun have proven that HSX prices are reliable predictors of future film profits. Figure 7.3 graphs market predictions of opening revenues on the *x*-axis against actual opening revenues on the *y*-axis. If all predictions were perfect, then predicted revenues would be exactly equal to actual revenues and all the observations would lie on the 45-degree red line. No one can predict the future perfectly, of course. Movies above the red line did better than predicted and movies below the red line did worse than predicted. The market predicted that *The Adventures of Pluto Nash,* a 2002 movie starring Eddie Murphy, would take in opening weekend revenues of over $10 million. In fact, *The Adventures* was the biggest financial bomb of all time with costs of $100 million and revenues of $4.41 million, just over half of that generated on the opening weekend before word of mouth sent it straight to the reject pile. Director Spike Lee's *The Original Kings of Comedy,* however, was an unexpected hit with actual opening revenues of nearly $12 million compared to predicted revenues of just $4.7 million. Although market predictions are sometimes a little high and sometimes a little low, they are centered around the 45-degree line, which means that they are correct on average. The market, for example, predicted that *American Pie 2* would have opening revenues of $45.1 million and actual revenues were $45.3 million. Perhaps the biggest sign of the accuracy of the HSX market is that HSX sells its data to Hollywood studios eager to improve their predictions about future blockbusters.

FIGURE 7.3

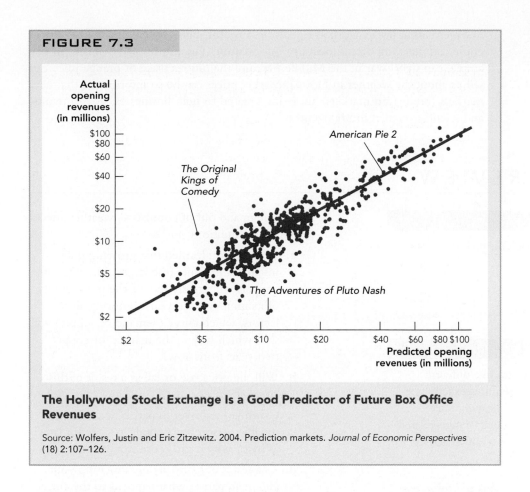

The Hollywood Stock Exchange Is a Good Predictor of Future Box Office Revenues

Source: Wolfers, Justin and Eric Zitzewitz. 2004. Prediction markets. *Journal of Economic Perspectives* (18) 2:107–126.

The use of prediction markets is expanding rapidly, but what's important for our purposes is that prediction markets help to illustrate how *all* markets work. Market prices are signals that convey valuable information. Buyers and sellers have an incentive to pay attention to and respond to prices and in so doing they direct resources to their highest-value uses. That means everyone can make the most out of limited resources.

☐ Takeaway

No market is an island. Markets are linked geographically, through time and across different goods. The price of gasoline at your local gasoline station is linked to the market for oil in China. The price of oil today is linked to the expectations about the market for oil in the future and, through investment, to the market for oil in the past. Markets in one good are linked to markets in other goods. The supply and demand of flowers, asphalt, and candy bars are all linked through the worldwide market.

The worldwide market is neither designed nor, because it is so complex, is it ever completely understood. The market acts like a giant computer to arrange our limited resources to satisfy as many of our wants as possible. Prices are the heart of the market process. Prices signal the value of resources to consumers, suppliers, and entrepreneurs, and they encourage everyone to take appropriate actions to respond to scarcity and changing circumstances.

Free market prices work as signals because through buying and selling, prices come to reflect important pieces of information. The futures price of oil, for example, can signal war in the Middle East and the futures price of orange juice can tell us about the weather in Florida. Market prices can be so informative that new markets (prediction markets) are being created to help businesses, governments, and scientists predict future events.

□ CHAPTER REVIEW

KEY CONCEPTS

The great economic problem, p. 115

Speculation, p. 119

Futures, p. 121

Prediction market, p. 123

FACTS AND TOOLS

1. a. Suppose you'd like to do five different things, each of which requires exactly one orange. Complete the following table, ranking your highest-valued orange-related activity (1) to your lowest-valued activity (5).

Activity	Rank of Preference
Give a friend the orange.	
Throw the orange at a person you don't like.	
Eat the orange.	
Squeeze the orange to drink the juice.	
Use the orange as decorative fruit.	

b. Suppose the price per orange is high enough that you buy only four. What activity do you not do?

c. How low would the price of oranges have to fall for you to purchase five oranges? What does the price at which you would just purchase the fifth orange tell us about the value you receive from the fifth-ranked activity?

2. The supply and demand for copper change constantly. New sources are discovered, mines collapse, workers go on strike, products that use it wane in and out of popularity, weather affects shipping conditions, and so on.

a. Suppose you learned that growing political instability in Chile (the largest producer of copper) will greatly reduce the productivity of its mines in two years. Ignoring all other factors, which curve (demand or supply) will shift which way in the market for copper two years from now?

b. Will the price rise or fall as a result of this curve shift?

c. Given your answer in part b, would a reasonable person buy copper to store for later? Why or why not? Ignore storage costs.

d. As a result of many people imitating your choice in part c, what happens to the current price of copper?

e. Does the action in parts c and d encourage people to use more copper today or less copper today?

3. In this chapter, we noted that successful economies are more likely to have many failing firms. If a nation's government instead made it impossible for inefficient firms to fail by giving them loans, cash grants, and other bailouts to stay in business, why is that nation likely to be poor? (*Hint:* Steven Davis and John Haltiwanger. 1999. "Gross Job Flows." In *Handbook of Labor Economics* (Amsterdam: North-Holland) found that in the United States, 60% of the increase in U.S. manufacturing efficiency was caused by people moving from weak firms to strong firms.)

4. For you, personally, what is your opportunity cost of doing this homework?

5. Suppose you are bidding on a used car and someone else bids above the highest amount that you are willing to pay. What can you say for sure about that person's monetary value of the good compared to yours?

6. Sometimes speculators get it wrong. In the months before the Persian Gulf War, speculators drove up the price of oil: The average price in October 1990 was $36 per barrel, more than double its price in 1988. Oil speculators, like many people around the world, expected the Gulf War to last for months, disrupting the oil supply throughout the Gulf region. Thus, speculators either bought oil on the open market (almost always at the high speculative price) or they already owned oil and just kept it in storage. Either way, their plan was the same: to sell it in the future, when prices might even be higher.

As it turned out, the war was swift: After one month of massive aerial bombardment of Iraqi troops and a 100-hour ground war, then President George H. W. Bush declared a cessation of hostilities. Despite the fact that Saddam Hussein set fire to many of Kuwait's oil fields, the price of oil plummeted to about $20 per barrel, a price at which it remained for years.

In 1991, speculators bet that a war against Saddam Hussein's regime would raise the price of oil for years. Wrong decade, perhaps.

a. Is buying oil for $36 a barrel and selling it for $20 per barrel a good business plan? How much profit did speculators earn, or how much money did they lose, on each barrel?

b. Why did the speculators follow this plan?

c. When the speculators sold their stored oil in the months after the war, did this massive resale tend to increase the price of oil or decrease it?

d. Do you think that many consumers complained about speculators or even realized that speculators were influencing the price of oil in spring 1991?

7. You manage a department store in Florida, and one winter day you read in the newspaper that orange juice futures have fallen dramatically in price. Should your store stock up on more sweaters than usual, or should your store stock up on more Bermuda shorts?

8. Take a look at Figure 7.3. If investors in the Hollywood Stock Exchange were too optimistic on average, would the dots tend to cluster above the red diagonal line or below it? How can you tell?

9. Let's see if the forces of the market can be as efficient as a benevolent dictator. Since laptop computers are increasingly easy to build and since they allow people to use their computers wherever they like, an all-wise benevolent dictator would probably decree that most people buy laptops rather than desktop computers. This is especially true now that laptops are about as powerful as most desktops. In answering questions a–c, answer in words as well as by shifting the appropriate curves in the figures below.

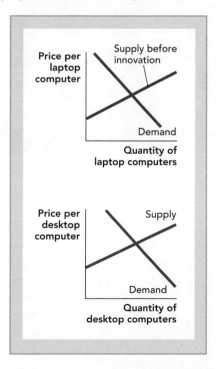

a. Since it's become much easier to build better laptops in recent years, laptop supply has increased. What does this do to the price of laptops?

b. Laptops and desktops are substitutes. Now that the price of laptops has changed, what does this do to the demand for desktop computers?

c. And how does that affect the quantity supplied of desktop computers?

d. Now let's look at the final result: Once it became easier to build good laptops, did "invisible hand" forces push more of society's resources into making laptops and push resources away from making desktops? (*Note:* Laptop sales first outnumbered desktop sales in 2008.)

THINKING AND PROBLEM SOLVING

1. Andy enters into a futures contract, allowing him to sell 5,000 troy ounces of gold at $1,000 per ounce in 36 months. After that time passes, the market price of gold is $950 per troy ounce. How much does Andy make or lose?

CRAIG AURNESS/CORBIS

2. Two major-party presidential candidates are running against each other in the 2016 election. The Democratic Party candidate promises more money for corn-based ethanol research, and the Republican Party candidate promises more money for defense contractors. In the weeks before the election, defense stocks take a nosedive.

a. Who is probably going to win the election: the pro-ethanol candidate or the pro–defense spending candidate?

b. We talked about how price signals are sometimes noisy. Think of two or three other markets you might want to look at to see if your answer to part a is correct.

3. Circa 1200 BCE, a decreasing supply of tin due to wars and the breakdown of trade led to a drastic increase in the price of bronze in the Middle East and Greece (tin being necessary for its production). It is around this time that blacksmiths developed iron- and steel-making techniques (as substitutes for bronze).

a. How is the increasing price of bronze a signal?

b. How is the increasing price an incentive?

c. How do your answers in parts a and b help explain why iron and steel became more common around the same time as the increase in price?

d. After the development of iron, did the supply or demand for bronze shift? Which way did it shift? Why?

4. In 1980, University of Maryland economist Julian Simon bet Stanford entomologist Paul Ehrlich that the price of any five metals of Ehrlich's choosing would fall over 10 years. Ehrlich believed that resources would become scarcer over time as the population grew, while Simon believed that people would find good substitutes, just as earlier people developed iron as a substitute for scarce bronze. The price of all five metals that Ehrlich chose (nickel, tin, tungsten, chromium, and copper) fell over the next 10 years and Simon won the bet. Ehrlich, an honorable man, sent a check in the appropriate amount to Simon.

a. What does the falling price tell us about the relative scarcity of these metals?

b. What *could have* shifted to push these prices down: demand or supply? And would demand have increased or decreased? And supply?

5. In this chapter, we explored how prices tie all goods together. To illustrate this idea, suppose new farming techniques drastically increased the productivity of growing wheat.

a. Given this change, how would the price of wheat change?

b. Given your answer in part a, how would the price of cookbooks specializing in recipes using wheat flour change?

c. Given your answer in part b, how would the price of paper change?

d. Given your answer in part c, how would the price of pencils change? (*Hint:* Are paper and pencils substitutes or complements?)

e. Given your answer in part d, how would the quantity of graphite (used in pencils) consumed change?

6. The "law of one price" states that if it's easy to move a good from one place to another, the price of identical goods will be the same because traders will buy low in one region and sell high in another. How is our story about the effect of speculators similar to the lesson about the "law of one price"?

7. Let's build on this chapter's example of asphalt. Suppose a new invention comes along that makes it easier and much less expensive to recycle clothing: Perhaps a new device about the size of a washing machine can bleach, reweave, and redye cotton fabric to closely imitate any cotton item you see in a fashion magazine. Head into the laundry room, drop in a batch of old clothes, scan in a couple of pages from *Vogue*, and come back in an hour.

a. If you think of the "market for clothing" as "the market for new clothing," does this shift the demand or the supply curve, and in which direction?

b. If you think of the "market for clothing" as "the market for clothing, whether it's new or used," does this shift the demand or the supply curve, and in which direction?

c. What will this do to the price of new, unrecycled clothing?

d. After this invention, will society's scarce productive resources (machines, workers, retail space) flow *toward* the "new clothing" sector or away from it?

(*Note:* This question might sound fanciful but three-dimensional printers, which can create plastic or plaster prototypes of small items such as toys, cups, etc., have fallen dramatically in price. Every day, you're getting just a little bit closer to having your own personal *Star Trek* replicator.)

8. Robin is planning to ask Peggy to the Homecoming dance. Before he asks her, he wants to know what the chances are that she'll say "yes." Robin is a scientist so he considers two paths to estimate the probability that Peggy will say yes.

I. Ask 10 of his friends, "Do you think she'll really say yes?"

II. Tell another 10 of his friends, "I'm starting a betting market. I'll pay $10 if she says yes, $0 if she says no. I'm only offering this bet once, to the highest bidder. Start bidding against each other for a chance at $10!"

a. According to the evidence in this chapter, one of these methods will work better. Which one, and why?

b. If the highest bid from Group II is $1 (along with a few lower bids of $0.75, $0.50, and zero), then roughly what's the chance that Peggy will say yes to Robin?

c. If the highest bid from Group II quickly shoots up to about $9, then what's the chance that Peggy will say yes to Robin?

9. A classic essay about how markets link to each other is entitled "I, Pencil," written by Leonard E. Read (his real name). It is available for free online at the *Library of Economics and Liberty*. As you might suspect, it is written from the point of view of a pencil. One line is particularly famous: "No single person on the face of this earth knows how to make me." Based on what you've learned in this chapter about how markets link the world, how is this true?

CHALLENGES

1. In *The Fatal Conceit*, economist Friedrich A. Hayek, arguing against central planning, wrote: "The curious task of economics is to demonstrate to men how little they really know about what they imagine they can design." In other words, people generally assume that they can plan out the best procedure for producing a good (such as the Valentine's Day rose mentioned at the beginning of the chapter), but as we learned, that's not true. What are some of the different roles that the price system plays in creating this order? (*Hint:* Key words are "links," "signals," and "incentives.")

2. One question that economics students often ask is "In a market with a lot of buyers and sellers, who sets the price of the good?" There are two possible correct answers to this question: "Everyone" and "No one." Choose one of the two as your answer, and explain in one or two sentences why you are correct.

3. This chapter emphasized the ability of an orderly system to emerge without someone explicitly designing the entire system. How does the evolution of language illustrate a type of spontaneous order?

4. Are you in favor of "price gouging" during natural disasters? Why or why not?

5. What is the opportunity cost of the economics profession?

8

Price Ceilings and Floors

On a quiet Sunday in August 1971, President Richard Nixon shocked the nation by freezing all prices and wages in the United States. It was now illegal to raise prices—even if both buyers and sellers voluntarily agreed to the change. Nixon's order, one of the most significant peacetime interventions into the U.S. economy ever to occur, applied to almost all goods, and even though it was supposed to be in effect for only 90 days, it would have lasting effects for more than a decade.

In Chapter 7, we explained how a price is "a signal wrapped up in an incentive"; that is, we explained how prices signal information and create incentives to economize and seek out substitutes. We also explained how markets are linked geographically, across different products, and through time. In this chapter, we show how price controls—laws making it illegal for prices to move above a maximum price (price ceilings) or below a minimum price (price floors)—interfere with all of these processes. We begin by explaining how a price control affects a single market, and then we turn to how price controls delink some markets and link others in ways that are counterproductive.

Price Ceilings

Nixon's price controls didn't have much effect immediately because prices were frozen near market levels. But the economy is in constant flux and market prices soon shifted. At the time of the freeze, prices were rising because of inflation, so the typical situation came to resemble that in Figure 8.1, with the controlled price below the uncontrolled or market equilibrium price.

FIGURE 8.1

Price Ceilings Create Shortages At the controlled price, the quantity demanded exceeds the quantity supplied, creating a shortage.

A **price ceiling** is a maximum price allowed by law.

A shortage of vinyl in 1973 forced Capitol Records to melt down slow sellers so they could keep pressing Beatles' albums.

When the maximum price that can be legally charged is below the market price, we say that there is a **price ceiling**. Economists call it a price ceiling because prices cannot legally go higher than the ceiling. Price ceilings create five important effects:

1. Shortages
2. Reductions in product quality
3. Wasteful lines and other search costs
4. A loss of gains from trade
5. A misallocation of resources

Shortages

When prices are held below the market price, the quantity demanded exceeds the quantity supplied. Economists call this a shortage. Figure 8.1 shows that the shortage is measured by the difference between the quantity demanded at the controlled price and the quantity supplied at the controlled price. Notice also that the lower the controlled price is relative to the market equilibrium price, the larger the shortage.

In some sectors of the economy, shortages appeared soon after prices were controlled in 1971. Increased demand in the construction industry, for example, meant that price controls hit that sector especially hard. Ordinarily, increased demand for steel bars, for example, would increase the price of steel bars, encouraging more production. But with a price ceiling in place, demanders could not signal their need to suppliers nor could they provide suppliers with an incentive to produce more. As a result, shortages of steel bars, lumber, toilets (for new homes), and other construction inputs were common. By 1973, there were shortages of wool, copper, aluminum, vinyl, denim, paper, plastic bottles, and more.

Reductions in Quality

At the controlled price, demanders find that there is a shortage of goods—they cannot buy as much of the good as they would like. Equivalently, at the controlled price, sellers find that there is an excess of demand or, in other words, *sellers have more customers than they have goods*. Ordinarily, this would be an opportunity to profit by raising prices, but when prices are controlled, sellers can't raise prices without violating the law. Is there another way that sellers can increase profits? Yes. It's much easier to evade the law by cutting quality than by raising price, so when prices are held below market levels, quality declines.

Thus, even when shortages were not apparent, quality was reduced. Books were printed on lower-quality paper, 2″ × 4″ lumber shrank to 1⅝″ × 3⅝″, and new automobiles were painted with fewer coats of paint. To help deal with the shortage of paper, some newspapers even switched to a smaller font size.[1]

Another way quality can fall is with reductions in service. Ordinarily, sellers have an incentive to please their customers, but when prices are held below market levels, sellers have more customers than they need *or want*. Customers without potential for profit are just a pain so when prices cannot rise, we can expect service quality to fall. The full service gasoline station, for example, disappeared with price controls in 1973, and instead of staying open for 24 hours, gasoline stations would close whenever the owner wanted a lunch break.

Wasteful Lines and Other Search Costs

The most serious shortage during the 1970s was for oil. The OPEC embargo in 1973 and the reduction in supply caused by the Iranian Revolution in 1979 increased the world price of oil, as we saw in Chapter 4. In the United States, however, price controls on domestically produced oil had not been lifted and thus the United States faced intense shortages of oil and the classic sign of a shortage, lines.

Figure 8.2 focuses on the third consequence of controlling prices below market prices: wasteful lines.

TETRA IMAGES/CORBIS

The Great Matzo Ball Debate

In 1972, AFL-CIO boss George Meany complained that the number of matzo balls in his favorite soup had sunk from four to three, in effect raising the price.

C. Jackson Grayson, chairman of the U.S. Price Commission, was worried about the bad publicity, so on *Face the Nation* he triumphantly held aloft a can of Mrs. Adler's soup claiming that his staff had opened many cans and concluded there were still four balls per can.

Whoever was right about the soup, Meany was certainly the better economist: Price ceilings reduce quality.

FIGURE 8.2

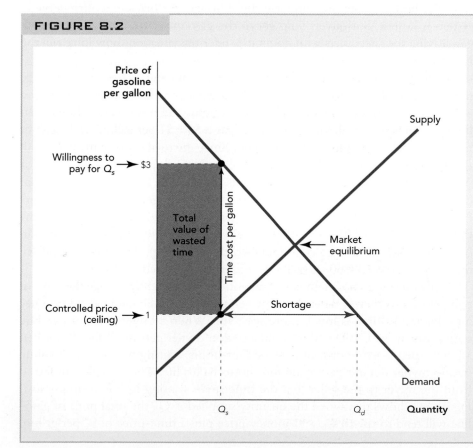

Price Ceilings Create Wasteful Lines At the controlled price, the quantity of gasoline supplied is Q_s and buyers are willing to pay as much as $3 for a gallon of gasoline. But the maximum price that sellers can charge is $1. The difference between what buyers are willing to pay and what sellers can charge encourages buyers to line up to buy gasoline. Buyers will line up until the total price of gasoline, the out-of-pocket price plus the time cost, increases to $3 per gallon. Time spent waiting in line is wasted time. The total value of wasted time is given by the time cost per gallon multiplied by the quantity of gallons bought.

When the quantity demanded exceeds the quantity supplied, someone is going to be disappointed.

IMAGE100/CORBIS

At the controlled price of $1, sellers supply Q_s units of the good. How much are demanders willing to pay (per unit) for these Q_s units? Recall that the demand curve shows the willingness to pay, so follow a line from Q_s up to the demand curve to find that demanders are willing to pay $3 per unit for Q_s units. The price controls, however, make it illegal for demanders to offer sellers a price of $3, but there are other ways of paying for gas.

Knowing that there is a shortage, some buyers might bribe station owners (or attendants) to fill up their tanks. Suppose that the average tank holds 20 gallons. Buyers would then be willing to pay $60 for a fill-up, the legal price of $20 plus a $40 under-the-table bribe. Thus, if bribes are common, the total price of gasoline—the legal price plus the bribe price—will rise to $3 per gallon ($60/20 gallons).

Corruption and bribes can be common, especially when price controls are long-lasting, but they were not a major problem during the gasoline shortages of the 1970s. Nevertheless, the total price of gasoline did rise well above the controlled price. Instead of competing by paying bribes, buyers competed by their willingness to wait in line. Remember that at the controlled price the quantity of gasoline demanded is greater than the quantity supplied, so some buyers are going to be disappointed—they are going to get less gasoline than they want and some buyers may get no gasoline at all. Buyers will compete to avoid being left with nothing. Let's assume that all gasoline station owners refuse bribes. Unfortunately, honesty does not eliminate the shortage. A "first-come, first-served" system is honest, but buyers who get to the gasoline station early will get the gas, leaving the latecomers with nothing. Under this situation, how long will the lineups get?

Suppose that buyers value their time at $10 an hour and, as before, the average fuel tank holds 20 gallons. Eager to obtain gas during the shortage, a buyer arrives at the station early, perhaps even before it opens, and must wait in line for an hour before he is served. His total price of gas is $30: $1 per gallon for 20 gallons in out-of-pocket cost plus $10 in time cost. Since the total value of the gas is $60, that's still a good deal. But if it's a good deal for him, it's probably a good deal for other buyers, too, so the next time he wants to fill up, he is likely to discover that others have preceded him and now he has to wait longer. How much longer? Following the logic to its conclusion, we can see that the line will lengthen until the total cost for 20 gallons of gasoline is $60: $20 in cash paid to the station owner plus $40 in time costs (4 hours worth of waiting). The price per gallon, therefore, rises to $3 ($60/20 gallons)—exactly as occurred with bribes!

Price controls do not eliminate competition. They merely change the form of competition. Is there a difference between paying in bribes and paying in time? Yes. Paying in time is much more wasteful. When a buyer bribes a gasoline station owner $40, at least the gasoline station owner gets the bribe. But when a buyer spends $40 worth of time or four hours waiting in line, the gasoline station owner doesn't get to add four hours to his life. The bribe is transferred from the buyer to the seller, but the time spent waiting in line is simply lost. Figure 8.2 shows that when the quantity supplied is Q_s, the total price of gasoline will tend to rise to $3: a $1 money price plus a time-price of $2 per gallon.

FIGURE 8.3

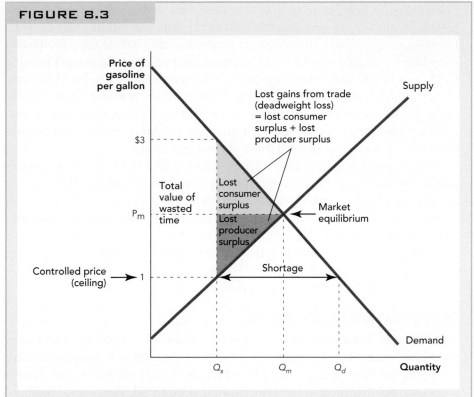

A Price Ceiling Reduces the Gains from Trade At the controlled price, Q_s units are supplied and buyers are willing to pay just slightly less than $3 for an additional gallon of gasoline that sellers are willing to sell for just slightly more than $1. Although mutually profitable, these trades are illegal. If all mutually profitable trades were legal, the gains from trade would increase by the green plus blue triangle.

The total amount of waste from waiting in line is given by the shaded area, the per gallon time price ($2) multiplied by the number of gallons bought (Q_s).★

Lost Gains from Trade

Price controls also reduce the gains from trade. In Figure 8.3, at the quantity supplied Q_s, how much would demanders pay for one *additional* gallon of gasoline? The willingness to pay for a gallon of gas at Q_s is $3, so demanders would be willing to pay just a little bit less, say, $2.95, for an additional gallon. How much would suppliers require to sell an additional gallon? Supplier cost is read off the supply curve, so reading up from the quantity Q_s to the supply curve, we find that the willingness to sell at Q_s is $1; suppliers would be willing to supply an additional unit for just a little bit more, say, $1.05.

Demanders are willing to pay $2.95 for an additional gallon of gas, suppliers are willing to sell an additional gallon for $1.05, and so there is $1.90 of

---

★ We need to qualify this slightly. If *every* buyer has a time value of $10 per hour, then the total time wasted will be the area as shaded in the diagram. If some buyers have a time value lower than $10, say, $5 per hour, they will wait in line for four hours, paying $20 in out-of-pocket costs but only $20 in time costs. If these buyers value the gasoline as high as does the marginal buyer, at $60 for 20 gallons, they will earn what economists call a "rent" of $20; thus, not all of the rectangle would be wasted. Regardless of whether all of the rectangle or just some of the rectangle is wasted, it's important to see that (1) price ceilings generate shortages and lineups, (2) the lineups mean that the total price of the controlled good is higher than the controlled price (and perhaps even higher than the uncontrolled price), and (3) the time spent waiting in line is wasted.

potential gains from trade to split between them. But it's illegal for suppliers to sell gasoline at any price higher than $1. Buyers and sellers want to trade, but they are prevented from doing so by the threat of jail. If the price ceiling were lifted and trade were allowed, the quantity traded would expand from Q_s to Q_m and buyers would be better off by the green triangle labeled "Lost consumer surplus," while sellers would be better off by the blue triangle labeled "Lost producer surplus." But with a price ceiling in place, the quantity supplied is Q_s and together the lost consumer and producer surplus are lost gains from trade (economists also call this a **deadweight loss**).

> A **deadweight loss** is the total of lost consumer and producer surplus when not all mutually profitable gains from trade are exploited. Price ceilings create a deadweight loss.

Recall from Chapter 4 that we said that in a free market the quantity of goods sold maximizes the sum of consumer and producer surplus. We can now see that in a market with a price ceiling, the sum of consumer and producer surplus is not maximized because the price control prevents mutually profitable gains from trade from being exploited.

In addition to these losses, price controls cause a misallocation of scarce resources; let's see how that works in more detail.

Misallocation of Resources

In Chapter 7, we explained how a price is a signal wrapped up in an incentive. Price controls distort signals and eliminate incentives. Imagine that it's sunny on the West Coast of the United States, but on the East Coast there is a cold winter that increases the demand for heating oil. In a market without price controls, the increase in demand in the East pushes up prices in the East. Eager for profit, entrepreneurs buy oil in the West, where the oil is not much needed and the price is low, and they move it to the East, where people are cold and the price of oil is high. In this way, the price increase in the East is moderated and supplies of oil move to where they are needed most.

Now consider what happens when it is illegal to buy or sell oil at a price above a price ceiling. No matter how cold it gets in the East, the demanders of heating oil are prevented from bidding up the price of oil, so there's *no signal* and *no incentive* to ship oil to where it is needed most. Price controls mean that oil is misallocated. Swimming pools in California are heated, while homes in New Jersey are cold. In fact, this was exactly what occurred in the United States, especially in the harsh winter of 1972–1973.

Once again recall from Chapter 4 that we said that in a free market the supply of goods is bought by the demanders who have the highest willingness to pay. We can now see that in a market with a price ceiling demanders with the highest willingness to pay have no easy way to signal their demands nor do suppliers have an incentive to supply their demands. As a result, in a controlled market goods are misallocated.

Price controls cause resources to be misallocated not just geographically, but also across different uses of oil. Recall

Distorted signals cause resources to be misallocated.

FOGSTOCK LLC/PHOTOLIBRARY

FIGURE 8.4

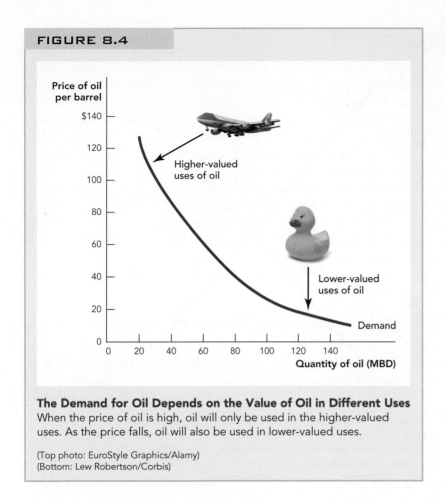

The Demand for Oil Depends on the Value of Oil in Different Uses
When the price of oil is high, oil will only be used in the higher-valued uses. As the price falls, oil will also be used in lower-valued uses.

(Top photo: EuroStyle Graphics/Alamy)
(Bottom: Lew Robertson/Corbis)

from Chapter 3 that the demand curve for oil shows the uses of oil from the highest-valued uses to the lowest-valued uses. In case you forgot, Figure 8.4 shows the key idea: High-valued uses are at the top of the curve and low-valued uses at the bottom. Without market prices, however, we have no guarantee that oil will flow to its highest-valued uses. As we have just seen, in a situation with price controls, it's possible to have plenty of oil to heat swimming pools in California (hello, rubber ducky!) and not enough oil for heating cold homes in New Jersey. Similarly, in 1974 *Business Week* reported, "While drivers wait in three-hour lines in one state, consumers in other states are breezing in and out of gas stations."[2]

Figure 8.5 on the next page illustrates the problem more generally. As we know, at the controlled price, the quantity demanded Q_d exceeds the quantity supplied Q_s and there is a shortage. Ideally, we would like to allocate the quantity of oil supplied Q_s, to its highest-valued uses; these are illustrated at the top of the demand curve by the thick line. But the potential consumers of the oil with the highest-valued uses are legally prevented from signaling their high value by offering to pay oil suppliers more than the controlled price. Oil suppliers, therefore, have no incentive to supply oil to just the highest-valued uses. Instead, oil suppliers will give the oil to any user who is willing to pay the controlled price—but most of these users of oil have lower-valued uses. Like the lines at the gas station, it's first-come, first-served. In fact, the only uses of oil that definitely will not be satisfied are the least-valued uses. (Why not? The users with the least-valued uses are not even willing to pay the controlled price.)

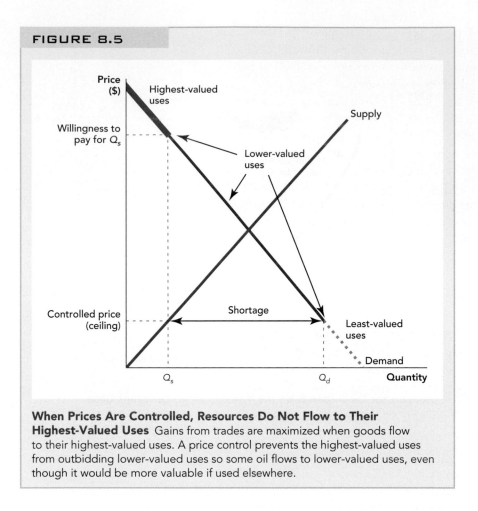

FIGURE 8.5

When Prices Are Controlled, Resources Do Not Flow to Their Highest-Valued Uses Gains from trades are maximized when goods flow to their highest-valued uses. A price control prevents the highest-valued uses from outbidding lower-valued uses so some oil flows to lower-valued uses, even though it would be more valuable if used elsewhere.

When a crisis in the Middle East reduces the supply of oil, the price system rationally responds by reallocating oil from lower-valued uses to the highest-value uses. In contrast, when the supply of oil is reduced and there are price ceilings, oil is allocated according to random and often trivial factors. The shortage of heating oil in 1971, for example, was exacerbated by the fact that President Nixon happened to impose price controls in *August* when the price of heating oil was near its seasonal low.[3] Since the price of heating oil was controlled at a low price, while gasoline was controlled at a slightly higher price, it was more profitable to turn crude oil into gasoline than into heating oil. As winter approached, the price of heating oil would normally have risen and refiners would have turned away from gasoline production to the production of heating oil, but price controls removed the incentive to respond rationally.

Advanced Material: The Loss from Random Allocation If there were no misallocation, then under a price control consumer surplus would be the area between the demand curve and the price up to the quantity supplied, the green area in Figure 8.6. (Of course, some of this surplus will likely be eaten up by bribes, time spent waiting in line, and so forth as we discussed above.)

Under a price control, however, the good is not necessarily allocated to the highest-valued uses. As a result, consumer surplus will be less than the green area—but how much less? The worst-case scenario would occur if all the goods were allocated to the lower-valued uses, but that seems unlikely.

A more realistic assumption is that under price controls, goods are allocated randomly so that a high-valued use is as likely as a low-valued use to be satisfied.

In Figure 8.7 on the next page we show two uses. The highest-valued use has a value of $30 and the lowest-valued use has a value of $6. Now imagine that one unit of the good is allocated randomly between these two uses. Thus, with a probability of 1/2, it will be allocated to the use with a value of 30, and with a probability of 1/2, it will be allocated to the use with a value of 6. On average, how much value will this unit create? The average value will be

$$\text{Average value} = \frac{1}{2} \times \$30 + \frac{1}{2} \times \$6 = \$18$$

Extending this logic, it can be shown that if every use between the highest-valued use and the lowest-valued use is *equally* likely to be satisfied, then the average value is $18. Thus on average, a randomly allocated unit of the good will create a value of $18. If there are, say, 10 units allocated, then the total value of those units will be $10 \times \$18 = \$180$. Since the average value is $18 and the controlled price is

FIGURE 8.6

In a Free Market Goods Flow to Their Highest-Value Uses If all units of the good are allocated to the highest-valued uses, then consumer surplus is the area between the demand curve and the price up to the quantity supplied.

$6, consumer surplus is the green area in Figure 8.7 labeled total consumer surplus under random allocation. But notice that the green area in Figure 8.7, consumer surplus under random allocation, is much less than the green area in Figure 8.6, consumer surplus under allocation to the highest value uses. The difference is the red area in Figure 8.7, the loss due to random allocation.

Misallocation and Production Chaos Shortages in one market create breakdowns and shortages in other markets, so the chaos of price controls expands even into markets without price controls. In ordinary times, we take it for granted that products will be available when we want them, but in an economy with many price controls, shortages of key inputs can appear at any time. In 1973, for example, million dollar construction projects were delayed because a few thousand dollars worth of steel bar was unavailable.[4]

Perhaps the height of misallocation occurred when shortages of steel drilling equipment made it difficult to expand oil production; this mistake took place even as the United States was undergoing the worst energy crisis in its history.[5]

As the shortages and misallocations grew worse, schools, factories, and offices were forced to close, and the government stepped in to allocate oil by command. President Nixon ordered gasoline stations to close between 9 PM Saturday and 12:01 AM Monday.[6] The idea was to prevent "wasteful" Sunday driving, but the ban simply encouraged people to fill their tanks earlier. Daylight savings time and a national 55 mph speed limit were put into place (the latter not to be repealed until 1995). Some industries, such as agriculture, were given priority treatment for fuel allocation, while others were forced to endure cutbacks. Fuel for noncommercial aircraft, for example, was cut by 42.5% in November of

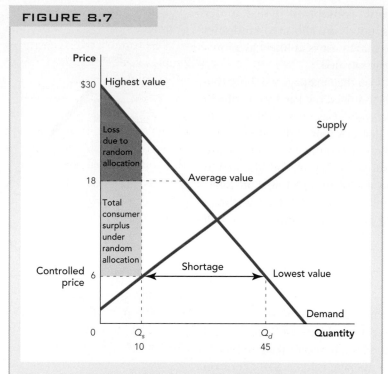

FIGURE 8.7

Consumer Surplus Falls Under Random Allocation When there is a price control, the buyers with the highest-valued uses cannot outbid other buyers, so goods will flow to *any* buyer willing to pay more than the controlled price of $6. If goods are allocated randomly to buyers with values between $30 and $6, the average value will be $18. Consumer surplus under random allocation is the green area. If goods were allocated to the highest-valued uses, consumer surplus would be larger, the red plus green areas. Thus, a price control misallocates resources, reducing consumer surplus.

1973, sending the local economy of Wichita, Kansas, where aircraft producers Cessna, Beech, and Lear were located, into a tailspin.[7]

Some of these ideas for conserving fuel were probably sensible while others were not, but without market prices, it's hard to tell which is which. The subtlety of the market process in allocating oil and taking advantage of links between markets is difficult, even impossible, to duplicate. C. Jackson Grayson was chairman of President Nixon's Price Commission, but after seeing how controls worked in practice, he said:

> Our economic understanding and models are simply not powerful enough to handle such a large and complex economic system better than the marketplace.[8]

The End of Price Ceilings

Price controls for most goods were lifted by April 1974, but controls on oil remained in place. Over the next seven years, controls on oil would be eased but at the price of substantial increases in complexity and bureaucracy. In September 1973, for example, price controls were lifted on new oil. "New oil" was defined as oil produced on a particular property in excess of the amount that had been produced in 1972. Decontrol of new

President Nixon said no to commercial holiday lights during the Christmas of 1973.

oil was a good idea because it increased the incentive to develop new deposits. The two-tier system, however, also created wasteful gaming as firms shut down some oil wells only to drill "new" wells right next door.[9] The battle between entrepreneurs and regulators was met with increasingly complex rules. Thus, the two-tier program was extended to three tiers, then five, then eight, then eleven.

Price controls on oil ended as abruptly as they had begun when on the morning of January 20, 1981, Ronald Reagan was inaugurated as president, and before lunch with Congress, he performed his first act as president—eliminating all controls on oil and gasoline. As expected, the price of oil in the United States rose a little but the shortage ended overnight. Within a year, prices began to fall as supply increased and within a few years they were well below the levels of 1979. Fluctuations in the price of oil have continued to occur, of course, but since the ending of controls, there has been no shortage of oil in the United States.

CHECK YOURSELF

> Nixon's price controls set price ceilings below the market price. What would have happened if the price ceilings had been set above market prices?

> Under price controls, why were the shortages of oil in some local markets much more severe than in others?

Rent Controls (Optional Section)

A **rent control** is a price ceiling on rental housing, such as apartments, so everything we have learned about price ceilings also applies to rent controls. Rent controls create shortages, reduce quality, create wasteful lines and increase the costs of search, cause a loss of gains from trade, and misallocate resources.

A **rent control** is a price ceiling on rental housing.

Shortages

Rent controls usually begin with a "rent freeze," which prohibits landlords from raising rents. Since rent controls are often put into place when rents are rising, the situation quickly comes to look like Figure 8.8, with the controlled rent below the market equilibrium rent.

FIGURE 8.8

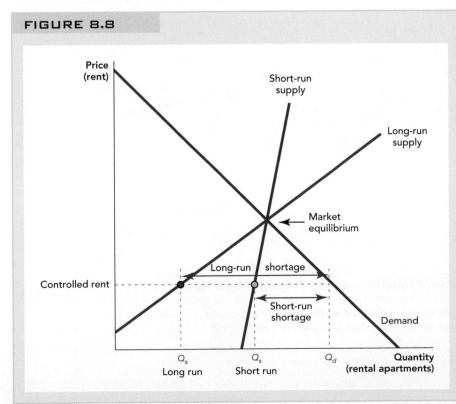

Rent Control Creates Larger Shortages in the Long Run than in the Short Run A rent control below the equilibrium price generates a shortage. The short-run shortage is small since the apartment units are already built. In the long run, fewer new units are built and old apartments are torn down or turned into condominiums so the long-run shortage is much greater.

Apartments are long-lasting goods that cannot be shipped elsewhere, so when rent controls are first imposed, owners of apartment buildings have few alternatives but to absorb the lower price. In other words, the short-run supply curve for apartments is inelastic. Thus, Figure 8.8 shows that even though the rent freeze may result in rents well below the market equilibrium level, there is only a small reduction in the quantity supplied in the short run.

In the long run, however, fewer new apartment units are built and older units are turned into condominiums or torn down to make way for parking garages or other higher-paying ventures. Thus, the long-run supply curve is much more elastic than the short-run supply curve, and the shortage grows over time from the short-run shortage to the long-run shortage.

Although old apartment buildings can't disappear overnight, future apartment buildings can. Developers look for profits over a 30-year or longer time frame, so even a modest rent control can sharply reduce the value of new apartment construction. Developers who fear that rent controls are likely will immediately end their plans to build. In the early 1970s, for example, rent control was debated in Ontario, Canada, and put into place in 1975. In the five years before controls were put into place, developers built an average of 27,999 new apartments per year. In the five years after controls were put into place, developers built only 5,512 apartments per year. Figure 8.9 graphs the number of new apartment starts and the number of new house starts per year from 1969 to 1979. The sharp drop in new apartment construction in the years when rent controls first started to be debated is obvious. But perhaps the drop was due to other factors like the state of the economy. To test for this possibility,

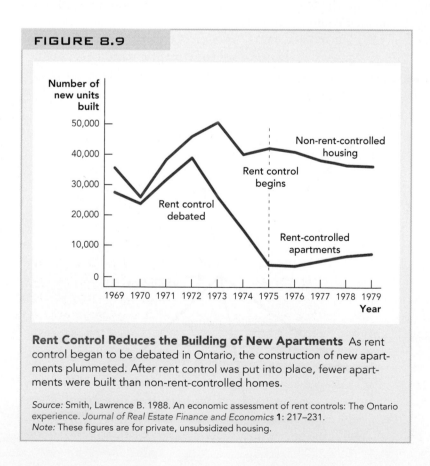

FIGURE 8.9

Rent Control Reduces the Building of New Apartments As rent control began to be debated in Ontario, the construction of new apartments plummeted. After rent control was put into place, fewer apartments were built than non-rent-controlled homes.

Source: Smith, Lawrence B. 1988. An economic assessment of rent controls: The Ontario experience. *Journal of Real Estate Finance and Economics* **1**: 217–231.
Note: These figures are for private, unsubsidized housing.

we also graph the number of new houses that were built annually during this time. The demand for houses and the demand for apartments respond similarly to the economy, but price controls on houses were never debated or imposed. We can see from Figure 8.9 that prior to 1972 the number of new apartment starts was similar to the number of new house starts. But when rent control became a possibility, apartment construction fell but the construction of houses did not. Thus, it's likely that rent control and not the general state of the economy (which would also have affected house starts) was responsible for the sharp drop in the number of new apartments built.

Reductions in Product Quality

Rent controls also reduce housing quality, especially the quality of low-end apartments. When the price of apartments is forced down, owners attempt to stave off losses by cutting their costs. With rent controls, for example, owners mow the lawns less often, replace lightbulbs more slowly, and don't fix the elevators so quickly. When the controls are strong, cheap but serviceable apartment buildings turn into slums and then slums turn into abandoned and hollowed-out apartment blocks. In Manhattan, for example, 18% of the rent-controlled housing is "dilapidated or deteriorating," a much higher percentage than in the uncontrolled sector.[10] Rent controls in European countries have tended to be more restrictive than in the United States, leading the economist Assar Lindbeck to remark, "Rent control is the most effective method we know for destroying a city, except for bombing it."[11] Lindbeck, however, was wrong, at least according to Vietnam's foreign minister who in 1989 said, "The Americans couldn't destroy Hanoi, but we have destroyed our city by very low rents."[12]

Wasteful Lines, Search Costs, and Lost Gains from Trade

Lines for apartments are not as obvious as for gasoline, but finding an apartment in a city with extensive rent controls usually involves a costly search. New Yorkers have developed a number of tricks to help them, as Billy Crystal explained in the movie *When Harry Met Sally:*

> What you do is, you read the obituary column. Yeah, you find out who died, and go to the building and then you tip the doorman. What they can do to make it easier is to combine the obituaries with the real estate section. Say, then you'd have "Mr. Klein died today leaving a wife, two children, and a spacious three-bedroom apartment with a wood-burning fireplace."

Search can be especially costly for people that landlords think are not "ideal renters." At the controlled price, landlords have more customers than they have apartments, so they can pick and choose among prospective renters. Landlords prefer to rent to people who are seen as being more likely to pay the rent on time and not cause trouble for other tenants, for example, older, richer couples without children or dogs. Landlords might also discriminate on racial or other grounds. Indeed, a landlord who doesn't like your looks can turn you down and immediately rent to the next person in line. Landlords can discriminate even if there are no rent controls, but without rent controls, the vacancy rate will be higher because the quantity of apartments will be larger and turnover will be more common, so landlords who turn down prospective renters will lose money as they wait for their ideal renter. Rent controls reduce the price of discrimination, so remember the law of demand: When the

A rent-controlled apartment—furnished.

COURTESY DON FLECK

price of discrimination falls, the quantity of discrimination demanded will increase.

Bribing the landlord or apartment manager to get a rent-controlled apartment is also common. Bribes are illegal but they can be disguised. An apartment might rent for $500 a month but come with $5,000 worth of "furniture." Renters refer to these kind of tie-in sales as paying "key money," as in the rent is $500 a month but the key costs extra. Nora Ephron, the screenwriter for *When Harry Met Sally*, lived for many years in a five-bedroom luxury apartment that thanks to rent control cost her just $1,500 a month. She did, however, have to pay $24,000 in key money to get the previous renter to move out!

The analysis of lost gains from trade from rent controls is exactly the same as we showed in Figure 8.3 for price controls on gasoline. At the quantity supplied under rent control, demanders are willing to pay more for an apartment than sellers would require to rent the apartment. If buyers and sellers were free to trade, they could both be better off, but under rent control, these mutually profitable trades are illegal and the benefits do not occur.

Misallocation of Resources

As with gasoline, apartments under rent control are allocated haphazardly—some people with a high willingness to pay can't buy as much housing as they want, even as others with a low willingness to pay consume more housing than they would purchase at the market rate. The classic example is the older couple who stay in their large rent-controlled apartment even after their children have moved out. It's a great deal for the older couple, but not so good for the young couple with children who as a result are stuck in a cramped apartment with nowhere to go.

Economists can estimate the amount of misallocation by comparing the types of apartments that renters choose in cities like New York, which has had rent controls since they were imposed as a "temporary" measure in World War II, with the types of apartments that people choose in cities like Chicago, which has a free market in rental housing. In one recent study of this kind, Edward Glaeser and Erzo Luttmer found that as many as 21% of the renters in New York City live in an apartment that has more or fewer rooms than they would choose if they lived in a city without rent controls.[13] This misallocation of resources creates significant waste and hardship.

Rent Regulation

In the 1990s, many American cities with rent control changed policy and began to eliminate or ease rent controls. Some economists refer to these new policies not as rent control but as "rent regulation." A typical rent regulation limits price increases without limiting prices. Prices increases, for example, might be limited to, say, 10% per year. Thus, rent regulations can protect tenants from sharp increases in rent, while still allowing prices to rise or fall over several years in response to market forces. Rent regulation laws usually also allow landlords to pass along cost increases so the incentive to cut back on maintenance is reduced. Economists are almost universally opposed to rent controls but some economists think that moderate rent regulation could have some benefits.[14]

Arguments for Price Controls

Without price controls on oil in 1973, some people might not have been able to afford to heat their homes. Without rent controls, some people may not be able to afford appropriate housing. It's not obvious that the poor are better off with shortages than with high prices. Nevertheless, *if* price controls were the *only* way to help the poor, then this would be an argument in favor of price controls.

Price controls, however, are never the only way to help the poor and they are rarely the best way. If affordable housing is a concern, for example, then a better policy than rent controls is for the government to provide housing vouchers. Housing vouchers, which are used extensively in the United States, give qualifying consumers a voucher worth, say, $500 a month that can be applied to any unit of housing.[15] Unlike rent controls, which create shortages, vouchers *increase* the supply of housing. Vouchers can also be targeted to consumers who need them, whereas rent controls in New York City have subsidized millionaires.

There are a few other sound arguments for price controls. The best case for price controls is to discipline monopolies. Alas, this explanation does not fit price controls on gasoline, apartments, bread, or almost all of the goods that price controls are routinely placed on. We will look at this special case more extensively in Chapter 13.

One of the primary reasons for price controls may be that the public, unlike economists, does not see the consequences of price controls. People who have not been trained in economics rarely connect lineups with price controls. During the gasoline shortages of the 1970s, probably not one American in ten understood the connection between the controls and the shortage—most consumers blamed big oil companies and rich Arab sheiks. Americans are not alone in blaming shortages on foreigners. The demand for price controls is a recurring and common event in history. Consider, for example, the situation in Iraq in 2003:

> The line of cars waiting to fill up at the Hurreya gas station on Monday snaked down the right lane of a busy thoroughfare, around a traffic circle, across a double-decker bridge spanning the Tigris River and along a potholed side street leading to one of Iraq's three oil refineries.
>
> At the end, almost two miles from the station, was Mohammed Adnan, a taxi driver who could not comprehend why he would have to wait seven hours to fuel his mud-spattered Chevrolet Beretta. "This is Iraq," he noted wryly. "Don't we live on a lake of oil?". . .
>
> "Maybe it's the black marketeers," Adnan said. "They're taking all our fuel."
>
> Bayar was more certain. "It's the refineries," he said. "They're not producing enough gasoline."
>
> The driver of the next car in line scoffed at both explanations. "It's the Americans, for sure," said Hassan Jawad Mehdi. "They are taking our oil back to America."[16]

Iraq, 2003. Gasoline was a bargain at 5 cents a gallon. If you could afford the wait.

PAULA BRONSTEIN/GETTY IMAGES

In the former Soviet Union, never-ending shortages meant that lining up for hours to get bread, shoes, or other goods was normal.

PETER TURNLEY/CORBIS

Each of these explanations might help to explain why Iraq in 2003 was producing less gasoline than before the war. But reductions in supply create high prices, not shortages. To generate a shortage, you need a price control, and in Iraq in 2003 the price of gasoline was controlled at 5 cents per gallon.[17]

Universal Price Controls

We have seen that price controls in the United States caused shortages, lineups, delays, quality reductions, misallocations, bureaucracy, and corruption. And the U.S. experience with extensive price controls was short, just a few months for most goods, and a few years for oil and a handful of other goods. What would happen if price controls on all goods remained in place for a lengthy period of time? An economy with permanent, universal price controls is in essence a "command economy," much as existed in the Communist countries prior to the fall of the Berlin Wall. In *The Russians*, Hedrick Smith described what it was like for consumers living in the Soviet Union in 1976:[18]

> The list of scarce items is practically endless. They are not permanently out of stock, but their appearance is unpredictable . . . . Leningrad can be overstocked with cross-country skis and yet go several months without soap for washing dishes. In the Armenian capital of Yerevan, I found an ample supply of accordions but local people complained that they had gone for weeks without ordinary kitchen spoons or tea samovars. I knew a Moscow family that spent a frantic month hunting for a child's potty while radios were a glut on the market. . . .
>
> The accepted norm is that the Soviet woman daily spends two hours in line, seven days a week . . . . I have known of people who stood in line 90 minutes to buy four pineapples . . . three and a half hours to buy three large heads of cabbage only to find the cabbages were gone as they approached the front of the line, 18 hours to sign up to purchase a rug at some later date, all through a freezing December night to register on a list for buying a car, and then waiting 18 months for actual delivery, and terribly lucky at that.

The never-ending shortage of goods in the Soviet Union suggests another reason why price controls are not eliminated even when doing so would make most people better off. Shortages were beneficial to the very same party elite who controlled prices. With all goods in permanent shortage, how did anyone in the Soviet Union obtain goods? By using *blat*. *Blat* is a Russian word meaning one has connections that can be used to get favors. As Hedrick Smith put it:

> In an economy of chronic shortages and carefully parceled-out privileges, blat is an essential lubricant of life. The more rank and power one has, the more blat one normally has . . . each has access to things or services that are hard to get and that other people want or need.

Consider the manager of a small factory that produces radios. Music may be the food that feeds people's souls but the manager would also like some beef. Shortages mean that the manager's salary is almost useless in helping him to obtain beef but what does he have of value? He has access to radios. If the manager can find a worker in a beef factory who loves music, he will have *blat*, a connection and something to trade. Even if he can't find someone with the exact opposite wants as he has, access to radios gives the manager power because people will want to do favors for him. But notice that the manager of the radio factory only has *blat* because of a shortage of radios. If radios were easily available at the market price, then the manager's access would no longer be of special value. The manager of the radio factory wants low prices because then he can legally buy radios at the official price and use them to obtain goods that he wants. Ironically, the managers and producers of beef, purses, and televisions all want shortages of their own good even though all would benefit if the shortages of all goods were eliminated.

Blat is a Russian word but it's a worldwide phenomena. Even in the United States, where by world standards corruption is low, *blat* happens. During the 1973–1974 oil crisis, for example, when the Federal Energy Office controlled the allocation of oil, it quickly became obvious that the way to get more oil was to use *blat*. Firms began to hire former politicians and bureaucrats who used their connections to help the firms get more oil. Today, the *blat* economy is much larger—about half of all federal politicians who leave office for the private sector become lobbyists.

Price Floors

When governments control prices, it is usually with a price ceiling designed to keep prices below market levels, but occasionally the government intervenes to keep prices above market levels. Can you think of an example? Here's a hint. Buyers usually outnumber sellers, so it's probably no accident that governments intervene to keep prices below market levels more often than they intervene to keep prices above market levels. The most common example of a price being controlled above market levels is the exception that proves the rule because it involves a good for which sellers outnumber buyers. Here's another hint. You own this good.

The good is labor, and the most common example of a price controlled above the market level is the minimum wage.

When the minimum price that can be legally charged is above the market price, we say that there is a **price floor**. Economists call it a price floor because prices cannot legally go below the floor. Price floors create four important effects:

1. Surpluses
2. Lost gains from trade (deadweight loss)
3. Wasteful increases in quality
4. A misallocation of resources

A **price floor** is a minimum price allowed by law.

Surpluses

Figure 8.10 on the next page graphs the demand and supply of labor and shows how a price held above the market price creates a surplus, a situation where the quantity of labor supplied exceeds the quantity demanded. We have a special word for a surplus of labor: unemployment.

The idea that a minimum wage creates unemployment should not be surprising. If the minimum wage did not create unemployment, the solution to poverty would be easy—raise minimum wages to $10, $20, or even $100 an hour! But at a high enough wage, none of us would be worth employing.

Can a more moderate minimum wage also create unemployment? Yes. A minimum wage of $7.25 an hour, the federal minimum in 2009, won't affect most workers who, because of their productivity, already earn more than $7.25 an

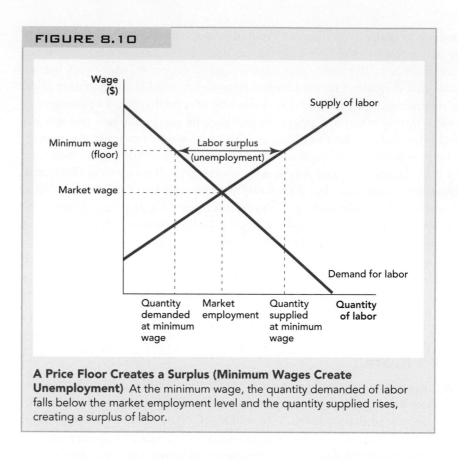

FIGURE 8.10

A Price Floor Creates a Surplus (Minimum Wages Create Unemployment) At the minimum wage, the quantity demanded of labor falls below the market employment level and the quantity supplied rises, creating a surplus of labor.

hour. In the United States, for example, more than 95% of all workers paid by the hour already earn more than the minimum wage. A minimum wage, however, will decrease employment among low-skilled workers. The more employers have to pay for low-skilled workers, the fewer low-skilled workers they will hire.

Young people, for example, often lack substantial skills and are more likely to be made unemployed by the minimum wage. About a quarter of all workers earning the minimum wage are teenagers (ages 16–19) and about half are less than 25 years of age.[19] Studies of the minimum wage verify that the unemployment effect is concentrated among teenagers.[20]

In addition to creating surpluses, a price floor, just like a price ceiling, reduces the gains from trade.

Lost Gains from Trade

Notice in Figure 8.11 that at the minimum wage employers are willing to hire Q_d workers. Employers would hire more workers if they could offer lower wages and, importantly, workers would be willing to work at lower wages if they were allowed to do so. If employers and workers could bargain freely, the wage would fall and the quantity of labor traded would increase to the level of market employment. Notice that at the market employment level, the gains from trade increase by the green and blue triangles. The green triangle is the increase in consumer surplus (remember that in this example it is the employers who are the consumers of labor) and the blue triangle is the increase in producer (worker) surplus.

Although the minimum wage creates some unemployment and reduces the gains from trade, the influence of the minimum wage in the American economy is very small. Even for the young, the minimum wage is not very important because although most workers earning the minimum wage are young, most

FIGURE 8.11

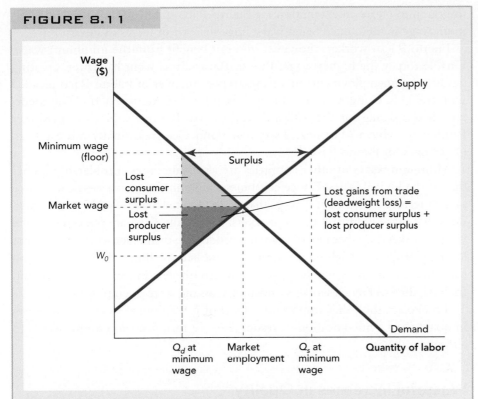

A Price Floor Reduces the Gains from Trade At the minimum wage, employers are willing to hire more workers at just less than the minimum wage and workers are willing to work additional hours for just more than W_0. Although mutually profitable, these trades are illegal. If all mutually profitable trades were legal, the gains from trade would increase by the green plus blue triangles.

young workers earn more than the minimum wage. As we noted above, a majority of workers earning the minimum wage are younger than 25 years old but 93.9% of workers younger than 25 earn more than the minimum wage.[21]

These facts may surprise you. The minimum wage is hotly debated in the United States. Democrats often argue that the minimum wage must be raised to help working families. Republicans respond that a higher minimum wage will create unemployment and raise prices as firms pass on higher costs to customers. Neither position is realistic. At best, the minimum wage will raise the wages of some teenagers and young workers whose wages would increase anyway as they improve their education and become more skilled. At worst, the minimum wage will raise the price of a hamburger and create unemployment among teenagers, many of whom will simply choose to stay in school longer (not necessarily a bad thing). The minimum wage debate is more about rhetoric than reality.

Even though small increases in the U.S. minimum wage won't change much, large increases would cause serious unemployment. A large increase in the minimum wage is unlikely in the United States, but it has happened elsewhere. In 1938, Puerto Rico was surprised to discover that it was bound by a minimum wage set well above the Puerto Rican average wage for unskilled labor.

Puerto Rico has a peculiar political status; it's an unincorporated U.S. territory classified as a commonwealth. In 1938, Congress passed the Fair Labor Standards Act, which set the first U.S. minimum wage at 25 cents an hour. At the time, the average wage in the United States was 62.7 cents an hour, but in Puerto Rico many workers were earning just 3 to 4 cents an hour. Congress, however, had forgotten to create an exemption for Puerto Rico so what was a modest minimum wage in the United States was a huge increase in wages in Puerto Rico.

Puerto Rican workers, however, did not benefit from the minimum wage. Unable to pay the higher wage, Puerto Rican firms went bankrupt, creating devastating unemployment. In a panic, representatives of Puerto Rico pleaded with the U.S. Congress to create an exemption for Puerto Rico. "The medicine is too strong for the patient," said Puerto Rican Labor Commissioner Prudencio Rivera Martinez. Two years later Congress finally did establish lower rates for Puerto Rico.[22]

Minimum wages in other countries are also sometimes considerably higher than in the United States. France combines a high minimum wage—nearly twice as high relative to the median wage than in the United States—with labor regulations that make it difficult to fire workers. As a result, firms are reluctant to hire young workers both because they are less productive than older workers, and thus less employable at a high minimum wage, and because hiring someone that you can't fire is more risky when the person doesn't have a history of employment. In 2005, 23% of French workers under 25 years old were unemployed.

To explain the other important effects of price floors—wasteful increases in quality and a misallocation of resources—we turn from minimum wages to airline regulation.

Wasteful Increases in Quality

Many years ago, flying on an airplane was extremely pleasurable; seats were wide, service was attentive, flights weren't packed, and the food was good. So airplane travel in the United States must have gotten worse, right? No, it has gotten better. Let's explain.

The Civil Aeronautics Board (CAB) extensively regulated airlines in the United States from 1938 to 1978. No firm could enter or exit the market, change prices, or alter routes without permission from the CAB. The CAB kept prices well above market levels, sometimes even denying requests by firms to lower prices!

We know that prices were kept above market levels because the CAB only had the right to control airlines operating *between* states. In-state airlines were largely unregulated. Using data from large states like Texas and California, it was possible to compare prices on unregulated flights to prices on regulated flights of the same distance. Prices on flights between San Francisco and Los Angeles, for example, were half the price of similar-length flights between Boston and Washington, D.C.

In Figure 8.12, firms are earning the CAB-regulated fare on flights that they would be willing to sell at the much lower price labeled "Willingness to sell." Initially, therefore, regulation was a great deal for the airlines, who took home the red area as producer surplus.

A price floor means that prices are held *above* market levels, so firms want more customers. The price floor, however, makes it illegal to compete for more customers by lowering prices. So how do firms compete when they cannot lower prices? Price floors cause firms to compete by offering customers higher quality.

When airlines were regulated, for example, they competed by offering their customers bone china, fancy meals, wide seats, and frequent flights. Sounds good, right? Yes, but don't forget that the increase in quality came at a price. Would you rather have a fine meal on your flight to Paris or a modest meal and more money to spend at a real Parisian restaurant?

FIGURE 8.12

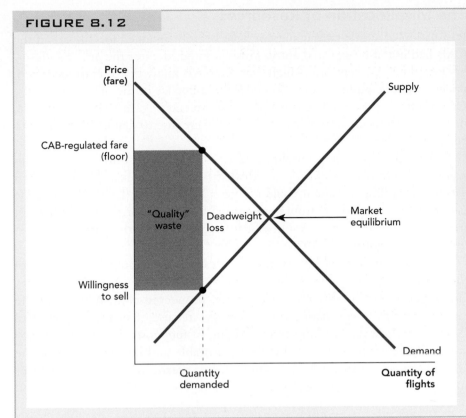

A Price Floor Creates Quality Waste At the CAB-regulated fare, price is well above a seller's willingness to sell. Sellers cannot compete by offering lower prices so they compete by offering higher quality. Higher quality raises costs and reduces seller profit. Buyers enjoy the higher quality, but would prefer less quality at a lower price. Thus, the price floor encourages sellers to waste resources by producing more quality than buyers are willing to pay for.

If consumers were willing to pay for fine meals on an airplane, airlines would offer that service. But if you have flown recently, you know that consumers would rather have a lower price. An increase in quality that consumers are not willing to pay for is a wasteful increase in quality. Thus, as firms competed by offering higher quality, the initial producer surplus was wasted away in frills that consumers liked but would not be willing to pay for—hence, the red area in Figure 8.12 is labeled "Quality" waste.

Airline costs increased over time for another reason. The producer surplus initially earned by the airlines was a tempting target for unions who threatened to strike unless they got their share of the proceeds. The airlines didn't put up too much of a fight because, when their costs rose, they could apply to the CAB for an increase in fares, thus passing along the higher costs to consumers. Many of the problems that older airlines have faced in recent times are due to generous pension and health benefits, which were granted when prices of flights were regulated above market levels.

By 1978, costs had increased so much that the airlines were no longer benefiting from regulation and were willing to accede to deregulation.[23] Deregulation lowered prices, increased quantity, and reduced wasteful quality competition.[24] Deregulation also reduced waste and increased efficiency in another way—by improving the allocation of resources.

Despite being more efficient than its rivals, airline regulation prevented Southwest from entering the national market until deregulation in 1978. Today, Southwest Airlines is one of the largest airlines in the world.

MUSEUM OF FLIGHT/CORBIS

The Misallocation of Resources

Regulation of airline fares could not have been maintained for 40 years if the CAB had not also regulated entry. Firms wanted to enter the airline industry because the CAB kept prices high, but the CAB knew that if entry occurred, prices would be pushed down. So under the influence of the older airlines, the CAB routinely prevented new competitors from entering. In 1938, for example, there were 16 major airlines; by 1974, there were just 10 despite 79 requests to enter the industry.

Restrictions on entry misallocated resources because low-cost airlines were kept out of the industry. Southwest Airlines, for example, began as a Texas-only airline because it could not get a license from the CAB to operate between states. (Lawsuits from competitors also nearly prevented Southwest from operating in Texas.) Southwest was able to enter the national market only after deregulation in 1978.

The entry of Southwest was not just a case of increasing supply. One of the virtues of the market process is that it is open to new ideas, innovations, and experiments. Southwest, for example, pioneered consistent use of the same aircraft to lower maintenance costs, greater use of smaller airports like Chicago's Midway, and long-term hedging of fuel costs. Southwest's innovations have made it one of the most profitable and largest airlines in the United States. Southwest's innovations have spread, in turn, to other firms such as JetBlue Airways, easyJet (Europe), and WestJet (Canada). Regulation of entry didn't just increase prices; it increased costs and reduced innovation. Deregulation improved the allocation of resources by allowing low-cost, innovative firms to expand nationally. Deregulation is the major reason why, today, flying is an ordinary event for most American families, rather than the province of the wealthy.

CHECK YOURSELF

> The European Union guarantees its farmers that the price of butter will stay above a floor. The floor price is often above the market equilibrium price. What do you think has been the result of this?

> The United States has set a price floor for milk above the equilibrium price. Has this led to shortages or surpluses? How do you think the U.S. government has dealt with this? (*Hint*: Remember the cartons of milk you had in elementary school and high school? What was their price?)

☐ Takeaway

Price ceilings have several important effects: They create shortages, reductions in quality, wasteful lines and other search costs, a loss of gains from trade, and a misallocation of resources.

After reading this chapter, you should be able to explain all of these effects to your uncle. Also, to do well on the exam, you should be able to draw a diagram showing the price ceiling and correctly labeling the shortage. On the same diagram, can you locate the wasteful losses from waiting in line and the lost gains from trade? Review Figures 8.2 and 8.3 if you are having trouble with these questions. You should also understand why a price ceiling reduces product quality and how price ceilings misallocate resources, not just in the market with the price ceiling but potentially throughout the economy.

Price floors create surpluses, a loss of gains from trade, wasteful increases in quality, and a misallocation of resources.

After reading this chapter, you should be able to explain all of these effects to your aunt. Can you show, using the tools of supply and demand, why a price floor creates a surplus, a deadweight loss, and a wasteful increase in quality? You should be able to label these areas on a diagram. You should also be able to explain how price floors cause resources to be misallocated.

◻ CHAPTER REVIEW

KEY CONCEPTS

Price ceiling, p. 132

Deadweight loss, p. 136

Rent control, p. 141

Price floors, p. 147

FACTS AND TOOLS

1. How does a free market eliminate a shortage?

2. When a price ceiling is in place keeping the price below the market price, what's larger: quantity demanded or quantity supplied? How does this explain the long lines and wasteful searches we see in price-controlled markets?

3. Suppose that the quantity demanded and quantity supplied in the market for milk is as follows:

Price per Gallon	Quantity Demanded	Quantity Supplied
$5	1000	5000
$4	2000	4500
$3	3500	3500
$2	4100	2000
$1	6000	1000

   a. What is the equilibrium price and quantity of milk?

   b. If the government places a price ceiling of $2 on milk, will there be a shortage or surplus of milk? How large will it be? How many gallons of milk will be sold?

4. If a government decides to make health insurance affordable by requiring all health insurance companies to cut their prices by 30%, what will probably happen to the number of people covered by health insurance?

5. The Canadian government has wage controls for medical doctors. To keep things simple, let's assume that they set one wage for all doctors: $100,000 per year. It takes about 6 years to become a general practitioner or a pediatrician, but it takes about 8 or 9 years to become a specialist like a gynecologist, surgeon, or ophthalmologist. What kind of doctor would you want to become under this system? (*Note:* The actual Canadian system does allow specialists to earn a bit more than general practitioners, but the difference isn't big enough to matter.)

6. Between 2000 and 2008, the price of oil increased from $30 per barrel to $140 per barrel, and the price of gasoline in the United States rose from about $1.50 per gallon to more than $4.00 per gallon. Unlike in the 1970s when oil prices spiked, there were no long lines outside gas stations. Why?

7. Price controls distribute resources in many unintended ways. In the following cases, who will probably spend more time waiting in line to get scarce, price-controlled goods? Choose one from each pair:

   a. Working people or retired people?

   b. Lawyers who charge $800 per hour or fastfood employees who earn $8 per hour?

   c. People with desk jobs or people who can disappear for a couple of hours during the day?

8. In the chapter, we discussed how price ceilings can put goods in the wrong *place*, as when too little heating oil wound up in New Jersey during a harsh winter in the 1970s. Price controls can also put goods in the wrong *time* as well. If there are price controls on gasoline, can you think of some periods during which the shortage will get worse? Here's a hint: Gas prices typically rise during the busy Memorial Day and Labor Day weekends.

9. a. Consider Figure 8.8. In a price-controlled market like this one, when will consumer surplus be larger: in the short run or in the long run?

   b. In this market, supply is more elastic, more flexible, in the long run. In other words, in the longer term, landlords and homebuilders can find something else to do for a living. In light of this and in light of the geometry of producer surplus in this figure, do rent controls hurt landlords and homebuilders more in the short run or in the long run?

10. Business leaders often say that there is a "shortage" of skilled workers, and so they argue that immigrants need to be brought in to do these jobs. For example, a recent AP article was entitled "New York farmers fear a shortage of skilled workers," and went on to point out that a special U.S. visa program, the H-2A program, "allows employers to hire foreign workers temporarily if they show that they were not able to find U.S. workers for the jobs."

(*Source:* Thompson, Carolyn. May 13, 2008. N.Y. farmers fear a shortage of skilled workers. *Associated Press.*)

    a. How do unregulated markets cure a "labor shortage" when there are no immigrants to boost the labor supply?

    b. Why are businesses reluctant to let unregulated markets cure the shortage?

11. **a.** If the government forced all bread manufacturers to sell their products at a "fair price" that was half the current, free-market price, what would happen to the quantity supplied of bread?

    b. To keep it simple, assume that people must wait in line to get bread at the controlled price. Would consumer surplus rise, fall, or can't you tell with the information given?

    c. With these price controls on bread, would you expect bread *quality* to rise or fall?

12. A review of the jargon: Is the minimum wage a "price ceiling" or a "price floor"? What about rent control?

13. How do U.S. business owners change their behavior when the minimum wage rises? How does this impact teenagers?

14. The basic idea of deadweight loss is a willing buyer and a willing seller can't find a way to make an exchange. In the case of the minimum wage law, the reason they can't make an exchange is because it's illegal for the buyer (the firm) to hire the seller (the worker) at any wage below the legal minimum. But how can this really be a "loss" from the worker's point of view? It's obvious why business owners would love to hire workers for less than the minimum wage, but if all companies obey the minimum wage law, why are some workers still willing to work for less than that?

THINKING AND PROBLEM SOLVING

1. In rich countries, governments almost always set the fares for taxi rides. The prices for taxi rides are the same in safe neighborhoods and in dangerous neighborhoods. Where is it easier to find a cab? Why? If these taxi price controls were ended, what would probably happen to the price and quantity of cab rides in dangerous neighborhoods?

2. When the United States had price controls on oil and gasoline, some parts of the United States had a lot of heating oil, while other states had long lines. As in the chapter, let's assume that winter oil demand is higher in New Jersey than in California. If there had been no price controls, what would have happened to the prices of heating oil in New Jersey and in California and how would "greedy businesspeople" have responded to these price differences?

3. On January 31, 1990, the first McDonald's opened in Moscow, capital of the then Soviet Union. Economists often described the Soviet Union as a "permanent shortage economy," where the government kept prices permanently low in order to appear "fair."

"An American journalist on the scene reported the customers seemed most amazed at the 'simple sight of polite shop workers . . . in this nation of commercial boorishness.'"

(*Source:* http://www.history.com/this-day-in-history.do?action=Article&id=2563.)

    a. Why were most Soviet shop workers "boorish" when the McDonald's workers in Moscow were "polite"?

    b. What does your answer to the previous question tell you about the power of economic incentives to change human behavior? In other words, how entrenched is "culture"?

McDonald's in Moscow: The First Day

4. Let's count the value of lost gains from trade in a regulated market. The government decides it wants to make basic bicycles more affordable, so it passes a law requiring that all one-speed bicycles sell for $30, well below the market price. Use the data below to calculate the lost gains from trade, just as in Figure 8.3. Supply and demand are straight lines.

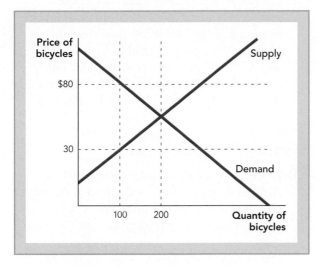

a. What is the total value of wasted time in the price-controlled market?

b. What is the value of the lost gains from trade?

c. Note that we haven't given you the original market price of simple bicycles—why don't you need to know it? (*Hint:* The answer is a mix of geometry and economics.)

5. During a crisis such as Hurricane Katrina, governments often make it illegal to raise the price of emergency items like flashlights and bottled water. In practice, this means that these items get sold on a first-come, first-served basis.

a. If a person has a flashlight that she values at $5, but its price on the black market is $40, what gains from trade are lost if the government shuts down the black market?

b. Why might a person want to sell a flashlight for $40 during an emergency?

c. Why might a person be willing to pay $40 for a flashlight during an emergency?

d. When will entrepreneurs be more likely to fill up their pickup trucks with flashlights and drive into a disaster area: when they can sell their flashlights for $5 each or when they can sell them for $40 each?

6. A "black market" is a place where people make illegal trades in goods and services. For instance, during the Soviet era, it was common for American tourists to take a few extra pairs of Levi's jeans when visiting the Soviet Union: They would sell the extra pairs at high prices on the illegal black market.

Consider the following claim: "Price-controlled markets tend to create black markets." Let's illustrate with the figure below. If there is a price ceiling in the market for cancer medication of $50 per pill, what is the *widest* price range within which you can *definitely* find both a buyer and a seller who would be willing to illegally exchange a pill for money? (There is only one correct answer.)

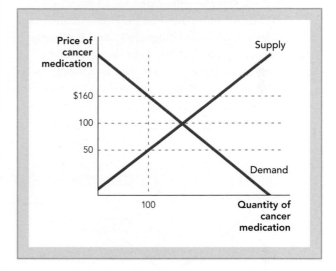

7. So, knowing what you know now about price controls, are you in favor of setting a $2 per gallon price ceiling on gasoline? Create a pro-price control and an anti-price control answer.

8. a. As we noted, Assar Lindbeck once said that short of aerial bombardment, rent control is the best way to destroy a city. What do you think Lindbeck might mean by this?

b. How does paying "key money" to a landlord reduce the severity of Lindbeck's "bombardment"?

9. In the town of Freedonia, the government declares that all street parking must be free: There can be no parking meters. In an almost identical town of Meterville, parking costs $5 per hour (or $1.25 per 15 minutes).

a. Where will it be easier to find parking: in Freedonia or Meterville?

b. One town will tend to attract shoppers who hate driving around looking for parking. Which one?

c. Why will the town from part b also attract shoppers with higher incomes?

10. In the late 1990s, the town of Santa Monica, California, made it illegal for banks to charge people ATM fees. As you probably know, it's almost always free to use your own bank's ATMs, but there's usually a fee charged when you use another bank's ATM. (*Source:* The war on ATM fees, *Time,* November 29, 1999.) As soon as Santa Monica passed this law, Bank of America stopped allowing customers from other banks to use their ATMs: In bank jargon, B of A banned "out-of-network" ATM usage.

In fact, this ban only lasted for a few days, after which a judge allowed banks to continue to charge fees while awaiting a full court hearing on the issue. Eventually, the court declared the fee ban illegal under federal law. But let's imagine the effect of a full ban on out-of-network fees.

a. In the figure below, indicate the new price per out-of-network ATM transaction after the fee ban. Also clearly label the shortage.

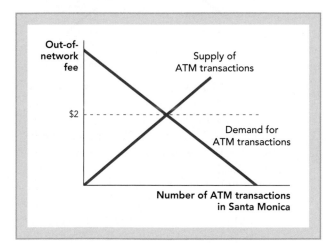

b. Calculate the exact amount of producer and consumer surplus in the out-of-network ATM market in Santa Monica after the ban. How large is producer surplus? How large is consumer surplus?

11. Consider Figure 8.9. Your classmate looks at that chart and says, "Apartment construction slowed down years before rent control was passed, and after rent control was passed, more apartments were built. Rent control didn't cut

the number of new apartments, it raised it. This proves that rent control works." What is wrong with this argument?

12. Rent control creates a shortage of housing, which makes it hard to find a place to live. In a price-controlled market, people have to waste a lot of time trying to find these scarce, artificially cheap products. Yet Congressman Charles B. Rangel, the chairman of the powerful House Ways and Means Committee, lived in *four* rent-stabilized apartments in Harlem. Why are powerful individuals often able to "find" price-controlled goods much more often than the nonpowerful? What does this tell us about the political side effects of price controls? (*Source:* Republicans question Rangel's tax break support, *The New York Times,* November 25, 2008.)

13. In the 1970s, AirCal and Pacific Southwest Airlines flew only within California. As we mentioned, the federal price floors didn't apply to flights within just one state. A major route for these airlines was flying from San Francisco to Los Angeles, a distance of 350 miles. This is about the same distance as from Chicago, Illinois, to Cleveland, Ohio. Do you think AirCal flights had nicer meals than flights from Chicago to Cleveland? Why or why not?

14. President Jimmy Carter didn't just deregulate airline prices. He also deregulated much of the trucking industry, as well. Trucks carry almost all of the consumer goods that you purchase, so almost every time you purchase something, you're paying money to a trucking company.

a. Based on what happened in the airline industry after prices were deregulated, what do you think happened in the trucking industry after deregulation? You can find some answers here: http://www.econlib.org/ Library/Enc1/TruckingDeregulation.html. For another look that is critical of trucking deregulation, but comes to basically the same answers, see Michael Belzer, 2000. *Sweatshops on Wheels: Winners and Losers in Trucking Deregulation.* Thousand Oaks, CA: SAGE.

b. Who do you think asked Congress and the president to keep price floors for trucking: consumer groups, retail shops like Wal-Mart, or the trucking companies?

15. Suppose you're doing some history research on shoe production in ancient Rome, during the reign of the famous Emperor Diocletian. Your records tell you how many shoes were produced each year in the Roman Empire, but it doesn't tell you the price of shoes. You find a document that says that in the year 301, Emperor Diocletian issued an "edict on prices," but you don't know whether he imposed price *ceilings* or price *floors*—your Latin is a little rusty. However, you can clearly tell from the documents that the number of shoes actually exchanged in markets fell dramatically, and that both potential shoe sellers and potential shoe buyers were unhappy with the edict. With the information given, can you tell whether Diocletian imposed a ceiling or a floor? If so, which is it? (Yes, there really was an edict of Diocletian, and Wikipedia has excellent coverage of ancient Roman history.)

16. In the market depicted below there is either a price ceiling or a price floor—surprisingly, it doesn't matter which one it is: Whether it's an $80 price floor or a $30 price ceiling, the chart looks the same.

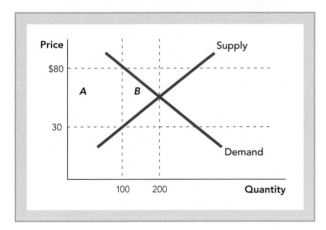

In the chart, there's a rectangle and a triangle. One represents the value lost from the "deals that don't get made" and one represents the value lost from "the deals that do get made." Which is which?

17. We noted that in the 1970s price floors on airline tickets caused wasteful increases in the quality of airline trips. Does the minimum wage cause wasteful increases in the quality of workers? If so, how? In other words, how are minimum-wage workers like airplane trips?

CHALLENGES

1. If a government decided to impose price controls on gasoline, what could it do to avoid the time wasted waiting in lines? There is surely more than one solution to this problem.

BETTMANN/CORBIS

2. In New York City, some apartments are under strict rent control, while others are not. This is a theme in many novels and movies about New York, including *Bonfire of the Vanities* and *When Harry Met Sally*. One predictable side effect of rent control is the creation of a black market. Let's think about whether it's a good idea to allow this black market to exist.

a. Harry is lucky enough to get a rent-controlled apartment for $300 per month. The market rent on such an apartment is $3,000 per month. Harry himself values the apartment at $2,000 per month, and he'd be quite happy with a regular $2,000 per month New York apartment. If he stays in the apartment, how much consumer surplus does he enjoy?

b. If he illegally subleases his apartment to Sally on the black market for $2,500 per month and instead rents a $2,000 apartment, is he better off or worse off than if he obeyed the law?

3. Suppose that the market for coats can be described as follows:

Price	Quantity Demanded (millions)	Quantity Supplied (millions)
$120	16	20
$100	18	18
$80	20	16
$60	22	14

a. What are the equilibrium price and quantity of coats?

b. Suppose the government sets a price ceiling of $80. Will there be a shortage, and if so, how large will it be?

c. Given that the government sets a price ceiling of $80, how much will demanders be willing to pay per unit of the good (i.e., what is the true price)? Suppose that people line up to get this good and that they value their time at $10 an hour. For how long will people wait in line to obtain a coat?

4. Let's measure consumer surplus if the government imposes price controls and goods ended up being randomly allocated among those consumers willing to pay the controlled price. If the demand and supply curves are as in the figure below, then:

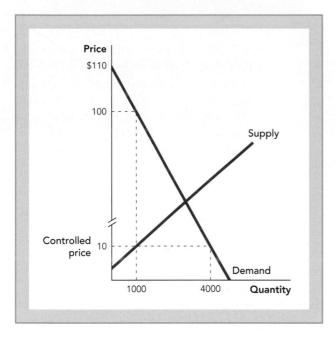

a. What is consumer surplus under the price control?

b. What would consumer surplus be if the quantity supplied were 1,000 but the goods were allocated to the highest-value users?

5. Antibiotics are often given to people with colds (even though they are not useful for that purpose), but they are also used to treat life-threatening infections. If there was a price control on antibiotics, what do you think would happen to the allocation of antibiotics across these two uses?

6. In a command economy such as the old Soviet Union, there were no prices for almost all goods. Instead, goods were allocated by a "central planner." Suppose that a good like oil becomes more scarce. What problems would a central planner face in reallocating oil to maximize consumer plus producer surplus?

7. Labor unions are some of the strongest proponents of the minimum wage. Yet in 2008, the median full-time union member earned $886 per week, an average of over $22 per hour (http://www.bls.gov/news.release/union2.nr0 .htm). Therefore, a rise in the minimum wage doesn't directly raise the wage of many union workers. So why do unions support minimum wage laws? Surely, there's more than one reason why this is so, but let's see if economic theory can shed some light on the subject.

a. Skilled and unskilled labor are substitutes: For example, imagine that you can hire four low-skilled workers to move dirt with shovels at $5 an hour, or you can hire one skilled worker at $24 an hour to move the same amount of dirt with a skid loader. Using the tools developed in Chapter 3, what will happen to the demand for skilled labor if the price of unskilled labor increases to $6.50 per hour?

b. If the minimum wage rises, will that increase or decrease the demand for the average union worker's labor? Why?

c. Now, let's put the pieces together: Why might high-wage labor unions support an increase in the minimum wage?

9

International Trade

Economics textbooks should never have chapters on "international trade." The word "international" suggests that international trade is a special type of trade requiring new principles and arguments. But when Joe and Frank trade, Joe and Frank are made better off. When Joe and Francisco trade, Joe and Francisco are made better off. The politics are different but the economics doesn't change much if Frank lives in El Paso and Francisco lives in Ciudad Juarez. International trade is trade.

In Chapter 2, we discussed the "big picture" view of trade and why trade is generally beneficial. To recap:

1. Trade makes people better off when preferences differ.

2. Trade increases productivity through specialization and the division of knowledge.

3. Trade increases productivity through comparative advantage.

All of these reasons hold for trade between nations as well as trade within nations. What is different in this chapter is that we will focus our analysis on a single market. Using the tools of supply and demand, we will discuss the prices at which trade occurs and how trade in a single market affects consumers and producers in that market. We will also show how to analyze restrictions on trade, such as tariffs and quotas. We close by evaluating some of the arguments, both economic and political, against international trade.

Analyzing Trade with Supply and Demand

Let's look at trade—and trade restrictions—using tools that you are already familiar with: demand and supply.

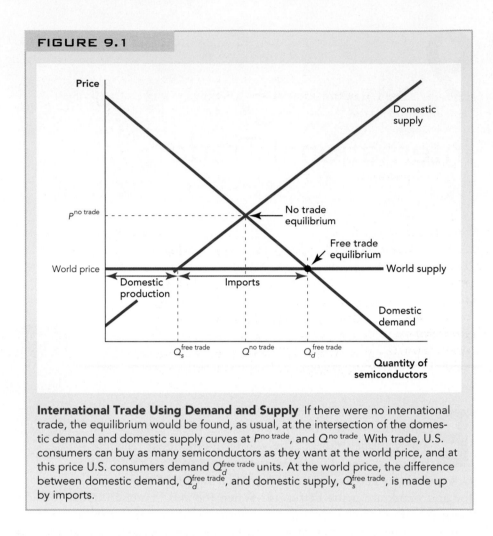

FIGURE 9.1

International Trade Using Demand and Supply If there were no international trade, the equilibrium would be found, as usual, at the intersection of the domestic demand and domestic supply curves at $P^{\text{no trade}}$, and $Q^{\text{no trade}}$. With trade, U.S. consumers can buy as many semiconductors as they want at the world price, and at this price U.S. consumers demand $Q_d^{\text{free trade}}$ units. At the world price, the difference between domestic demand, $Q_d^{\text{free trade}}$, and domestic supply, $Q_s^{\text{free trade}}$, is made up by imports.

Figure 9.1 shows a domestic demand curve and a domestic supply curve for semiconductors. If there were no international trade, the equilibrium would be, as usual, at $P^{\text{no trade}}$, $Q^{\text{no trade}}$. Suppose, however, that this good can also be bought in the world market at the world price. To simplify, we will assume that the U.S. market is small relative to the world market, so U.S. demanders can buy as many semiconductors as they want without pushing up the world price. In terms of our diagram, the world supply curve is flat (perfectly elastic) at the world price.

Given that U.S. consumers can buy as many semiconductors as they want at the world price, how many will they buy? As usual, we read the quantity demanded off the domestic demand curve so at the world price, U.S. consumers will demand $Q_d^{\text{free trade}}$ semiconductors. How many semiconductors will be supplied by *domestic* suppliers? As usual, we read the quantity supplied off the domestic supply curve so domestic suppliers will supply $Q_s^{\text{free trade}}$ units. Notice that $Q_d^{\text{free trade}} > Q_s^{\text{free trade}}$, so where does the difference come from? From imports. In other words, with international trade, domestic consumption is $Q_d^{\text{free trade}}$ units; $Q_s^{\text{free trade}}$ of these units are produced domestically and the remainder, $Q_d^{\text{free trade}} - Q_s^{\text{free trade}}$, are imported.

Analyzing Tariffs with Demand and Supply

Many countries, including the United States, restrict international trade with tariffs, quotas, or other regulations that burden foreign producers but not domestic producers—this is called **protectionism**. A **tariff** is simply a tax on imports.

Protectionism is the economic policy of restraining trade through quotas, tariffs, or other regulations that burden foreign producers but not domestic producers.

A **tariff** is a tax on imports.

A **trade quota** is a restriction on the quantity of foreign goods that can be imported: Imports greater than the quota amount are forbidden or heavily taxed.

Figure 9.2 shows how to analyze a tariff. The figure looks imposing but it's really the same as Figure 9.1 except that now we analyze domestic consumption, production, and imports before and after the tariff. Before the tariff, the situation is exactly as in Figure 9.1, $Q_d^{\text{free trade}}$ units are demanded, $Q_s^{\text{free trade}}$ units are supplied by domestic producers, and imports are $Q_d^{\text{free trade}} - Q_s^{\text{free trade}}$.

The tariff is a tax on imports so—just as you learned in Chapter 3—the tariff (tax) shifts the world supply curve up by the amount of the tariff. For example, if the world price of semiconductors is $2 per unit and a new tariff of $1 per semiconductor is imposed, then the world supply curve shifts up to $3 per unit.

At the new, higher price of semiconductors, two things happen. First, there is an increase in the domestic production of semiconductors as domestic suppliers respond to the higher price by increasing production. In the diagram, domestic production increases from $Q_s^{\text{free trade}}$ to Q_s^{tariff}. Second, there is a decrease in domestic consumption from $Q_d^{\text{free trade}}$ to Q_d^{tariff} as domestic consumers respond to the higher price by buying fewer semiconductors. Since the quantity produced by domestic suppliers rises and the quantity demanded by domestic consumers falls, the quantity of imports falls. Specifically, imports fall from $Q_d^{\text{free trade}} - Q_s^{\text{free trade}}$ to the smaller amount $Q_d^{\text{tariff}} - Q_s^{\text{tariff}}$.

Figure 9.2 illustrates one more important idea. A tariff is a tax on imports so tariffs raise tax revenue for the government. The revenue raised by a tariff is

A **trade quota** is a restriction on the quantity of goods that can be imported: Imports greater than the quota amount are forbidden or heavily taxed.

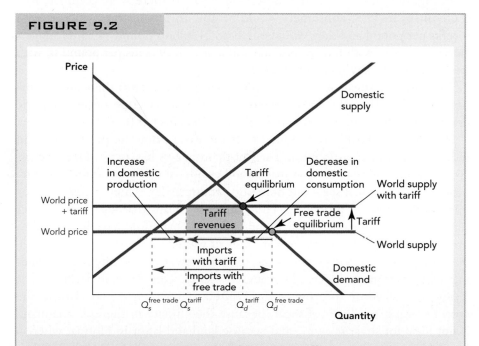

FIGURE 9.2

International Trade Using Demand and Supply: Tariffs A tariff shifts the world supply curve up by the amount of the tariff, thus raising the world price. In response to the higher price, consumers reduce their purchases from $Q_d^{\text{free trade}}$ to Q_d^{tariff} and domestic suppliers increase their production from $Q_s^{\text{free trade}}$ to Q_s^{tariff}. Since domestic consumption decreases and domestic production increases, the quantity of imports falls from $Q_d^{\text{free trade}} - Q_s^{\text{free trade}}$ to $Q_d^{\text{tariff}} - Q_s^{\text{tariff}}$.

The government collects revenues from the tariff equal to the tariff × the quantity of imports, which is shown as the blue area.

the tariff amount times the quantity of imports (the quantity taxed). Thus, in Figure 9.2 the tariff revenue is given by the blue area.

The Costs of Protectionism

Now that we know that a tariff on an imported good will increase domestic production and decrease domestic consumption, we can analyze in more detail the costs of protectionism. The U.S. government, for example, greatly restricts the amount of sugar that can be imported into the United States. As a result, U.S. consumers pay more than double the world price for sugar—in the early 2000s, U.S. consumers paid about 20 cents per pound of sugar compared with a world price of around 9 cents per pound. So, let's look in more detail at the costs of sugar protectionism.

To simplify our analysis, we make two assumptions. First, we assume that the tariff is so high that it completely eliminates all sugar imports. Although a small amount of sugar is allowed into the United States at a low tariff rate, anything above this small amount is taxed so heavily that no further imports occur. Our assumption that the tariff eliminates all sugar imports is not a bad approximation to what actually happens. Second, we assume that if we had complete free trade, all sugar would be imported. This is also a reasonable assumption because, as we will explain shortly, sugar can be produced elsewhere at much lower cost than in the United States. Making these two assumptions will focus attention on the key ideas. See Challenge Question 1 in the end-of-chapter questions for a more detailed analysis.

In Figure 9.3, we show the market for sugar. If there were complete free trade in sugar, U.S. consumers would be able to buy at the world price of 9 cents per pound and they would purchase 24 billion pounds. U.S. producers cannot compete with foreign producers at a price of 9 cents per pound so with free trade all sugar would be imported.

The tariff on sugar imports is so high that with the tariff there are no imports and the U.S. price of sugar—found at the intersection of the domestic demand and domestic supply curve—rises to 20 cents per pound.

Recall that a tariff has two effects: It increases domestic production and reduces domestic consumption. Each of these effects has a cost. First, the increase in domestic production may sound good—and it is good for domestic producers as we shall see—but domestic producers have higher costs of production than foreign producers. Thus, the tariff means that sugar is no longer supplied by the lowest-cost sellers and resources that could have been used to produce other goods and services are instead wasted producing sugar. Second, due to higher costs, the price of sugar rises and fewer people buy sugar, reducing the gains from trade. Let's look at each of these costs in more detail.

Sugar costs more to grow in the United States than in, say, Brazil, the world's largest producer of sugar, because the climate in the U.S. mainland is not ideal for sugar growing and because land and labor in Florida, where a lot of U.S. sugar is grown, have many alternative uses that are high in value. Sugar farmers in Florida, for example, have to douse their land with expensive fertilizers to increase production—in the process creating environmental damage in the Florida Everglades.[1] The excess resources—the fertilizer, land, and labor—that go into producing U.S. sugar could have been used to produce other goods like oranges and theme parks for which the United States and Florida are better suited.

▶▶SEARCH ENGINE

Information on sugar and the U.S. sugar tariff can be found from the *USDA Economic Research Service, Sugar Briefing Room.*

FIGURE 9.3

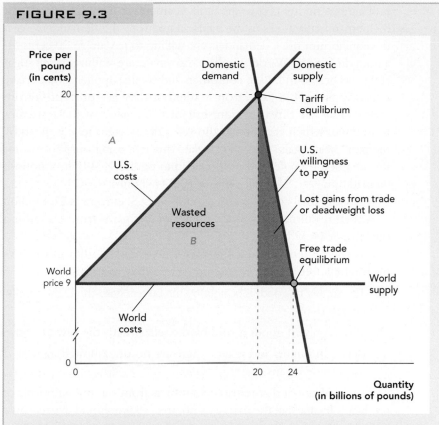

A Restriction on Trade Wastes Resources and Creates Lost Gains from Trade With free trade, domestic production of sugar is 0 billion pounds. When imports are restricted, the domestic industry expands to 20 billion pounds, but U.S. costs are above world costs so the expansion of the domestic industry creates wasted resources (area *B*). At the higher price of sugar, less sugar is bought so the import restriction also creates lost gains from trade (area *C*).

Recall from Chapter 3 that the supply curve tells us the cost of production so at the equilibrium price the cost of producing an additional pound of sugar in the United States is exactly 20 cents. In other words, in the United States it takes 20 cents worth of resources like land and labor to produce one additional pound of sugar. That same pound of sugar could be bought in the world market for just 9 cents so the tariff causes 11 cents worth of resources to be wasted in producing that last pound of sugar.

The total value of wasted resources is shown in Figure 9.3 by the yellow area labeled "Wasted resources"; that area represents the difference between what it costs to produce 20 billion pounds of sugar in the United States and what it would cost to buy the same amount from abroad. We can calculate the total value of wasted resources using our formula for the area of a triangle.

The height of the yellow triangle is 20 − 9 or 11 cents per pound, the base is 20 billion pounds, so the area is 110 billion cents, or $1.1 billion. The sugar tariff wastes $1.1 billion worth of resources.

Notice that if the sugar tariff were eliminated, the price of sugar in the United States would fall to the world price of 9 cents per pound and U.S. production would drop from 20 billion pounds to 0 pounds. It's important to see that the reduction in U.S. production is a *benefit* of eliminating the tariff because it frees up resources that can be used to produce other goods and services.

How to smuggle sugar

The high price of U.S. sugar has encouraged smuggling and attempts to circumvent the tariff. In the 1980s when the U.S. price was four times the world price, Canadian entrepreneurs created super-high-sugar iced tea. The "tea" was shipped into the United States and then sifted for the sugar, which was resold.

To combat this entrepreneurship, the U.S. government created even more tariffs for sugar-containing products like iced tea, cake mixes, and cocoa.

Source: Economic Report of the President 1986, Chapter 4.

There is another cost to the tariff. Remember from Chapter 3 that the demand curve tells us the value of goods to the demanders, so at the equilibrium price demanders are willing to pay up to 20 cents for a pound of sugar. World suppliers, however, are willing to sell sugar at 9 cents per pound. U.S. consumers and world suppliers could make mutually profitable gains from trade, but they are prevented from doing so by the threat of punishment. The value of the lost gains from trade, which economists also call a deadweight loss, is given by the pink area. Again, we can calculate this area using our formula for the area of a triangle ($(20 - 9)$ cents per pound $\times$ 4 billion pounds divided by 2) = 22 billion cents or $0.22 billion.

Thus, the total cost of the sugar tariff to U.S. citizens is $1.1 billion of wasted resources plus $0.22 billion of lost gains from trade for a total loss of $1.32 billion.

Do you remember from Chapter 4 the three conditions that explain why a free market is efficient? Here they are again:

1. The supply of goods is bought by the buyers with the highest willingness to pay.

2. The supply of goods is sold by the sellers with the lowest costs.

3. Between buyers and sellers, there are no unexploited gains from trade or any wasteful trades.

A tariff or quota that restricts consumers from trading with foreign producers means that the market is not free, so we should expect some of the conditions in our list to be violated. In this case, conditions 2 and 3 are violated. A tariff reduces efficiency because the supply of goods is no longer sold by the sellers with the lowest costs, and with a tariff, there are unexploited gains from trade between buyers and sellers.

Some of these benefits of trade may sound fairly abstract, but for a lot of people, they are a matter of life and death. If Brazilian sugar cane farmers could sell more of their products to U.S. consumers, many more of the farmers could afford to eat better or to improve their housing with proper water and sewage. But don't think the United States is the only party at fault here. The Brazilian government places a lot of tariffs on foodstuffs from the United States and for many Brazilians, including the very poor, this makes food more expensive. The end result is that U.S. consumers pay a high price for sugar and poor Brazilians have less to eat and less money to spend when they need to take their kids to the doctor.

Winners and Losers from Trade

We can arrive at this same total loss in another revealing way. The sugar tariff raises the price of sugar to U.S. consumers, which reduces consumer surplus. Recall from Chapter 3 that consumer surplus is the area underneath the demand curve and above the price. Thus, consumer surplus with the tariff is the area above the price of 20 cents and below the demand curve (not all of which is shown in Figure 9.3). As the price falls from 20 cents to 9 cents, consumer surplus increases by area $A + B + C$, which has a value (check it!) of $2.42 billion. Or, put differently, the tariff costs consumers $2.42 billion in lost consumer surplus.

The tariff increases price, which increases producer surplus, the area above the supply curve and below the price. Thus, the tariff increases U.S. producer surplus by area A, which has a value of $1.10 billion.

Notice that U.S. consumers lose more than twice as much from the tariff as U.S. producers gain. The total loss to U.S. citizens is the $2.42 billion loss to consumers minus the $1.10 billion gain to producers, for a total loss of $1.32 billion a year, *exactly as we found before.*

Our two methods of analyzing the cost of the sugar tariff are equivalent, but they emphasize different things. The first method calculates social loss directly and emphasizes where the loss comes from: wasted resources and lost gains from trade. The second method focuses on *who* gains and *who* loses. Domestic producers gain but U.S. consumers lose even more.

Why does the government support the U.S. sugar tariff when U.S. consumers lose much more than U.S. producers gain? One clue is that the costs of the sugar tariff are spread over millions of consumers so the costs per consumer are small. The benefits of the tariff, however, flow to a small number of producers, each of whom benefits by millions of dollars. As a result, the producers support and lobby for the tariff much more actively than consumers oppose the tariff.

The costs of all this lobbying point our attention to yet another cost of protectionism. When a country erects a lot of tariffs against foreign competition, the producers in that country will spend a lot of their time, energy, and money lobbying the government for protection. Those same resources could be spent on production and innovation, not lobbying. Protectionism tends to create a society that pits one interest group against the other and seeds social discord. Free trade, in contrast, creates incentives for people to cooperate toward common and profitable ends.

> **CHECK YOURSELF**
>
> > Who benefits from a tariff? Who loses?
> > Why does trade protectionism lead to wasted resources?
> > If there are winners and losers from trade restrictions, why do we hear more often from the people who gain from trade restrictions than from the people who lose?

Arguments Against International Trade

It would take several books to analyze all the arguments against international trade. We will take a closer look at some of the most common arguments:

> Trade reduces the number of jobs in the United States.

> It's wrong to trade with countries that use child labor.

> We need to keep certain industries at home for reasons of national security.

> We need to keep certain "key" industries at home because of beneficial spillovers onto other sectors of the economy.

> We can increase U.S. well-being with strategic trade protectionism.

Trade and Jobs

When the United States reduces tariffs and imports more shirts from Mexico, the U.S. shirt industry will contract. As a result, many people associate free trade deals with lost jobs. As economists, however, we want to trace the impact of lower tariffs beyond the most immediate and visible effects. So let's trace what happens when a tariff is lowered, paying particular attention to the effect on jobs.

When the price of shirts falls, U.S. consumers have more money in their pockets that they can use to buy other goods. The increased consumer spending on Scotch tape, bean bag chairs, x-ray tests, and thousands of other goods leads to increased jobs in these industries. These jobs gains may be more difficult to see than the job losses in the U.S. shirt industry but they are no less real. But what about the money that is now going to Mexican shirt producers instead of to U.S. shirt producers? Isn't it better to "Buy American" and keep this money at home?

When Mexican producers sell shirts in the United States, they are paid in dollars. But what do Mexicans want dollars for? Ultimately, everyone sells in order to buy. Mexican producers might use their dollars to buy U.S. goods. In this case, the increased U.S. spending on imports of Mexican shirts leads directly to increased Mexican spending on U.S. goods (i.e., U.S. exports).

But what happens if the Mexican shirt producers want to buy Mexican goods or European goods rather than U.S. goods? In order to buy Mexican or European goods, the Mexican shirt producers will need pesos or euros. Fortunately, they can trade their dollars for pesos or euros on the foreign exchange market. Suppose the Mexicans trade their dollars to someone in Germany who in return gives them euros. Why would a German want to trade euros for dollars? Remember that people sell in order to buy. Thus, Germans want dollars so that they can buy U.S. goods or U.S. assets. So once again, the increased spending on Mexican shirt imports leads to an increase in U.S. exports (in this case, to Germany) and thus an increase in jobs in U.S. exporting industries.

Our thought experiment reveals an important truth: *We pay for our imports with exports*. Think about it this way: Why would anyone sell us goods if not to get goods in return? Thus, trade does not eliminate jobs—it moves jobs from import-competing industries to export industries. And remember: Although trade does not change the number of jobs, it does raise wages, as we demonstrated in Chapter 2 on comparative advantage.

Of course, it's traumatic to lose a job and not all workers can easily transfer from shirt making to the industries that expand with trade. But in a dynamic and growing economy, job loss and job gain are two sides of the same coin. Thomas Edison ended the whale oil industry with his invention of the electric lightbulb in 1879. This was bad for whalers but good for people who like to read at night (and very good for the whales). The phonograph destroyed jobs in the piano industry (darn that Edison, again!), CDs destroyed jobs in the record industry, and today MP3s are destroying jobs in the CD industry. And, yet somehow with all these jobs being destroyed, employment and the standard of living keep trending upward.

Job destruction is ultimately a healthy part of any growing economy, but that doesn't mean we have to ignore the costs of transitioning from one job to another. Unemployment insurance, savings, and a strong education system can help workers respond to shocks. Trade restrictions, however, are not a good way to respond to shocks. Trade restrictions save *visible* jobs, but they destroy jobs that are just as real but harder to see.

BOYER/ROGER VIOLLET/GETTY IMAGES

Thomas Edison, destroyer of jobs or benefactor of humanity? Yes.

Child Labor

Is child labor a reason to restrict trade? In part, this is a question of ethics on which reasonable people can disagree, but our belief, for which we will give reasons, is that the answer is no.

In 1992, labor activists discovered that Walmart was selling clothing that had been made in Bangladesh by subcontractors who had employed some child workers. Senator Tom Harkin angrily introduced a bill in Congress to prohibit firms from importing any products made by children under the age of 15. Harkin's bill didn't pass, but in a panic the garment industry in Bangladesh dismissed 30,000 to 50,000 child workers. A success? Before we decide, we need to think about what happened to the children who were thrown out of work. Where did these children go? To the playground? To school? To a better job? No. Thrown out of the garment factories, the children went to work elsewhere, many at jobs like prostitution with worse conditions and lower pay.[2]

In 2009, about 18% of all children aged 5–14 around the world worked for a significant number of hours. The vast majority of these children worked in agriculture, often alongside their parents, and not in export industries. Restrictions on trade, therefore, cannot directly reduce the number of child workers, and by making a poor country poorer, trade restrictions may increase the number of child workers. In fact, studies have shown that more openness to trade increases income and reduces child labor.[3]

Child labor is more common in poor countries and it was common in nineteenth-century Great Britain and the United States when people were much poorer than today. Child labor declined in the developed world as people got richer.

The Pin Factory

Lewis Hine photograph of bowling alley boys in New Haven, CT. Circa 1910.

FIGURE 9.4

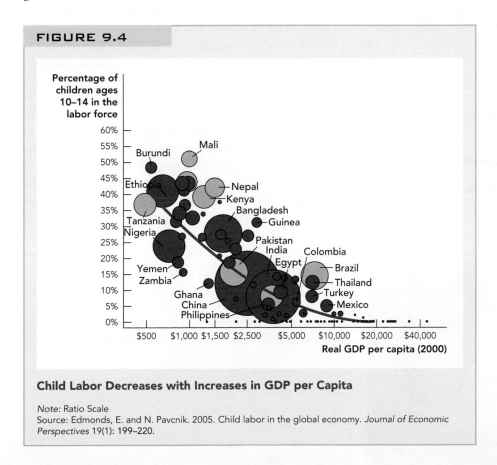

Child Labor Decreases with Increases in GDP per Capita

Note: Ratio Scale
Source: Edmonds, E. and N. Pavcnik. 2005. Child labor in the global economy. *Journal of Economic Perspectives* 19(1): 199–220.

The forces that reduced child labor in the developed world are also at work in the developing world. The vertical axis of Figure 9.4 shows the percentage of children ages 10–14 who are laboring in 132 countries across the world. Real GDP per capita is shown on the horizontal axis. The size of the circles is proportionate to the total number of child laborers, so although the percentage of child laborers is much higher in Burundi (48.5%) than in India (12%), there are many more child laborers in India. The lesson of Figure 9.4 is that economic growth reduces child labor.

The real cause of child labor is poverty, not trade. Thus, to reduce child labor, we should focus on reducing poverty rather than on reducing trade; putting up trade barriers is likely to be ineffective or even counterproductive.

Governments and nonprofits from the developed world can help developing countries reduce child labor by helping them to improve the quality of schooling and to lower the opportunity cost of education. In Bangladesh, at about the same time that child workers were being thrown out of work by the Harkin bill, the government introduced the Food for Education program. The program provides a free monthly stipend of rice or wheat to poor families who have at least one child attending school that month. The program has been very successful at encouraging school attendance. Even more important, increased education of children today means richer parents tomorrow—parents who will no longer feel crushed by the forces of poverty, or in other words parents who will have enough wealth to feed their children *and* send them to school.[4]

Trade and National Security

If a good is vital for national security but domestic producers have higher costs than foreign producers, it can make sense for the government to tax imports or subsidize the production of the domestic industry. It may make sense, for example, to support a domestic vaccine industry. In 1918, more than a quarter of the U.S. population got sick with the flu and more than 500,000 died, sometimes within hours of being infected. The young were especially hard-hit and, as a result, life expectancy in the United States dropped by 10 years. No place in the world was safe, as between 2.5% to 5% of the entire world population died from the flu between 1918 and 1920. Producing flu vaccine requires an elaborate process in which robots inject hundreds of millions of eggs with flu viruses. In an ordinary year, there are few problems with buying vaccine produced in another country, but if something like the 1918 flu swept the world again, it would be wise to have significant vaccine production capacity in the United States.[5]

Don't be surprised, however, if every domestic producer in trouble claims that their product is vital for national security. Everything from beeswax to mohair, not to mention steel and computer chips, has been protected in the name of national security.

More generally, it's common for protectionists to lobby under the guise of some other motive. Many people, for example, are legitimately concerned about working conditions in developing countries, but does it surprise you that U.S. labor unions are often the biggest lobbyists for bills to restrict trade on behalf of "oppressed foreign workers"?

Vital for National Security?

In 1954 the U.S. government declared that mohair, the fleece of the Angora goat, was vital for national security (it can be used to make military uniforms). For nearly 40 years mohair producers received millions of dollars in annual payments. Finally, after much ridicule, the program was eliminated in 1993 . . . only to be reestablished in 2002. Hard to believe? Yes, but we aren't kidding around.

NORM EGGERT

As Youssef Boutros-Ghali, Egypt's former minister for trade, put it, "The question is why all of a sudden, when third world labor has proved to be competitive, why do industrial countries start feeling concerned about our workers? . . . It is suspicious."[6]

Key Industries

Another argument that in principle could be true is the "it's better to produce computer chips than potato chips" argument. The idea is that the production of computer chips is a key industry because it generates spillovers, benefits that go beyond the computer chips themselves (see Chapter 10 for more on spillovers). Protectionism isn't the best policy in this case (in theory, a subsidy would work better), but if a subsidy isn't possible, then protectionism might be a second best policy with some net benefits.

The words "in principle" and "might" are well chosen. The "computer chips are better than potato chips" argument can't be faulted on logic alone, but it's not very compelling. To address this particular example, most computer chips today are cheap, mass-manufactured commodities. The United States rightly doesn't specialize in this type of manufacturing and is better off for it, even though this used to be a common argument for protectionism against foreign computer chips.

Walmart: SuperProductivity

Surprisingly, the biggest factor in the productivity boom of the 1990s was not a Silicon Valley high-tech firm but improvements in the retail and wholesale sector. Walmart alone was responsible for one-eighth of these productivity gains and Walmart innovations in warehouse logistics, wireless bar code scanning, and database integration spread throughout the retail industry.

Computer chips may be better than potato chips, but apparently *selling* potato chips is best of all.[7]

Second, it is difficult to know which industries are the ones with the really important spillovers. In the late 1980s, many pundits argued that HDTV would be a technology driver for many related industries. Japan and the European Union subsidized their producers to the tune of billions of dollars. The United States lagged behind. In the end, however, Japan and the EU chose an analog technology that is now considered obsolete and HDTV has yet to produce significant benefits for the broader economy, even if it does give you a really nice picture at home.

Strategic Trade Protectionism

In some cases, it's possible for a country to use tariffs and quotas to grab a larger share of the gains from trade than would be possible with pure free trade policy. The idea is for the government to help domestic firms to act like a cartel when they sell to international buyers. Oddly, the way to do this is to limit or tax exports. A tax or limit on exports reduces exports but can drive up the price enough so that net revenues increase. Of course, this can only work if international buyers have few substitutes for the domestic good. Could this work in practice? Yes, in many ways OPEC is a possible example. OPEC limits exports, and because the demand for oil is inelastic, this increases oil revenues.

Oil is a special good, however, because it is found in large quantities in just a few places in the world. The United States would have a much harder time using strategic trade protectionism because there are more substitutes for U.S.-produced goods. The U.S. economy, or any advanced economy, would also have another problem. Oil is Saudi Arabia's only significant export so when that nation raises the price of oil, the rest of the world can't threaten to retaliate by putting tariffs on

Saudi Arabia's other exports. But if the United States were to try to grab a larger share of the gains from trade, in, say, computers, other countries could respond with tariffs on our grain exports. A trade war could easily make both countries worse off. Trying to divide the pie in your favor usually makes the pie smaller.

□ Takeaway

We have shown in this chapter how to use demand and supply curves to analyze trade and the costs of trade protectionism.

Restrictions on trade waste resources by transferring production from low-cost foreign producers to high-cost domestic producers. Restrictions on trade also prevent domestic consumers from exploiting gains from trade with foreign producers. Domestic producers can benefit from trade restrictions, but domestic consumers lose more than the producers gain. Trade restrictions sometimes persist because the benefits from restrictions are often concentrated on small groups who lobby for protection, while the costs of restrictions are spread over millions of consumers and can be small for each individual.

We have set out various common arguments for restricting trade. Some of these arguments are valid, but they are usually of limited applicability.

□ CHAPTER REVIEW

KEY CONCEPTS

Protectionism, p. 160

Tariff, p. 160

Trade quota, p. 161

FACTS AND TOOLS

1. The Japanese people currently pay about four times the world price for rice. If Japan removed its trade barriers so that Japanese consumers could buy rice at the world price, who would be better off and who would be worse off: Japanese consumers or Japanese rice farmers? If we added all the gains and losses to the Japanese, would there be a net gain or net loss? Who would make a greater effort lobbying, for or against, this reduction in trade barriers: Japanese consumers or Japanese rice farmers?

2. The supply curve for rice in Japan slopes upward, just like any normal supply curve. If Japan eliminated its trade barriers to rice, what would happen to the number of workers employed in the rice-producing industry in Japan: Would it rise or fall? What would these workers probably do over the next year or so? Will they ever work again?

3. In Figure 9.3, consider triangles *B* and *C*. One of these could be labeled "Workers and machines who could be better used in another sector of the economy," while the other could be labeled "Consumers who have to pay more than necessary for their product." Which is which?

4. In his book *The Choice*, economist Russ Roberts asks how voters would feel about a machine that could convert wheat into automobiles.

   a. Do you think that voters would complain that this machine should be banned, since it would destroy jobs in the auto industry?

   b. Would this machine, *in fact,* destroy jobs in the auto industry? If so, would roughly the same number of jobs eventually be created in other industries?

   c. Here is Roberts's punch line: If voters were told that the wonder machine was in fact just a cargo ship that exported wheat and imported autos from a foreign country, how would voters' attitudes toward this machine change?

5. Spend some time driving in Detroit, MI—the Motor City—and you're sure to see bumper stickers with messages like "Buy American" or "Out of a job yet? Keep buying foreign!" or "Hungry? Eat your foreign car!" Explain these

bumper stickers in light of what you've learned in this chapter. Who is hurt by imported automobiles? Who benefits?

6. This chapter pointed out that trade restrictions on sugar cause U.S. consumers to pay more than twice the going world price for sugar. However, you are very unlikely to ever encounter bumper stickers that say things like "Out of money yet? Keep taxing foreign sugar!" or "Hungry? It's probably because domestic sugar is so expensive!" Why do you think it is that these bumper stickers are not popular?

7. Of the three conditions that explain why a free market is efficient (from Chapter 4), which condition or conditions cease to hold in the case of a tariff on imported goods? Which condition or conditions continue to hold even in the case of a tariff on imports?

THINKING AND PROBLEM SOLVING

1. **a.** Just to review: Back in Chapter 8, we illustrated price ceilings with a horizontal line below the equilibrium price. Did price ceilings create surpluses or shortages?

   b. The horizontal line in Figure 9.1 doesn't represent a surplus or a shortage. What does it represent?

   c. Figure 9.1 considers the case of a country that can buy as many semiconductors as it wants at the same world price. Why do people in this country only buy $Q_d^{\text{free trade}}$ units? Why don't they buy more of this inexpensive product?

2. Figure 9.1 looks at a case where the world price is below the domestic no-trade price. Let's look at the case where the world price is *above* the domestic no-trade price. We'll work with the market for airplanes shown in the figure below.

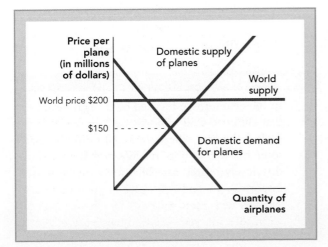

a. In the figure, use the Quantity axis to label $Q_s^{\text{free trade}}$ and $Q_d^{\text{free trade}}$. This is somewhat similar to Figure 9.1.

b. What would you call the gap between $Q_s^{\text{free trade}}$ and $Q_d^{\text{free trade}}$?

c. Also following Figure 9.1, label "domestic consumption" and "domestic production."

d. Will domestic airplane buyers—airlines and delivery companies like FedEx—have to pay a higher or a lower price under free trade compared with the no-trade alternative? Will domestic airplane buyers purchase a higher or a lower quantity of planes if there's free trade in planes?

e. Based on your answer to part d, would you expect domestic airplane demanders to support free trade in planes or oppose it?

3. In the text, we discuss sugar farmers in Florida who use unusually large amounts of fertilizer to produce their crops; they do so because their land isn't all that great for sugar production. If we translate this into the language of the supply curve, would these Florida sugar farms be those on the lower-left part of a supply curve, or those along the upper right of the supply curve? Why?

4. According to Chinese government statistics, China imported 140,000 sedans in 2007. Let's see what would happen to consumer and producer surplus if China were to ban sedan imports. To keep things simple, let's assume that if sedan imports were banned, the equilibrium price of sedans (holding quality constant!) would rise by $5,000.

   a. In the figure below, shade the area that represents the total gains when sedan imports are allowed into China.

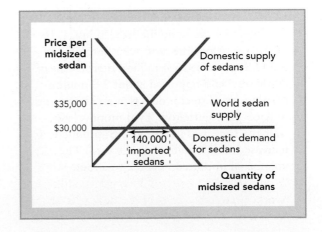

b. Once China bans the import of sedans, what is the dollar value of the lost gains from trade? (*Hint:* The chapter provides the formula.)

c. If sedan imports are banned, Chinese sedan producers will be better off and Chinese sedan consumers will be worse off. A polygon in the figure shows the surplus that will shift from consumers to producers. Write the word "transfer" in this polygon. (*Hint:* It's not the area you calculated in part b.)

5. Many people will tell you that, whenever possible, you should always buy U.S.-made goods. Some will go further and tell you to spend your money on goods produced in your own state whenever possible. (Just do a simple Google search for "Buy [any state]" and you'll find a Web site encouraging this kind of thinking.) The idea is that if you spend money in your state, you help the economy of *your* state, rather than the economy of some other state. By the same logic, shouldn't one buy only goods produced in one's own city? Or on one's own street? Where does this thinking lead to? And how does it relate to Big Idea Five from Chapter 1?

6. Some people argue for protectionism by pointing out that other countries with whom we trade engage in "unfair trade practices," and that we should retaliate with our own protectionist measures. One such policy is the policy of some countries to subsidize exporting industries. India, for example, subsidizes its steel industry. Obviously, U.S. steel producers are hurt by this policy and would like to restrict imported steel from India. Is this a good reason to place tariffs on Indian steel? Why or why not?

7. In March 2002, then President George W. Bush put a tariff on imported steel as a means of protecting the domestic steel industry. In February, before the tariff went into effect, the U.S. produced 7.4 million metric tons of crude steel and imported about 2.8 million metric tons of steel products at an average price of $363 per metric ton. Two months later, after the tariff was in effect, U.S. production increased to 7.9 million metric tons. The volume of imported steel fell to about 1.7 million metric tons, but the price of the imported steel rose to about $448 per metric ton. The supply and demand diagram below shows this situation (along with an estimated no-trade domestic equilibrium at a price of $625 per metric ton and a quantity of 8.9 million metric tons).

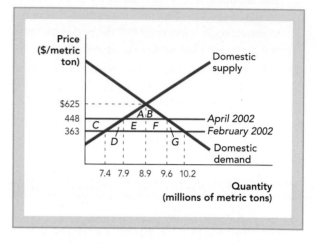

Determine which areas on the graph represent each of the following:

a. The increase in producer surplus gained by U.S. steel producers as a result of the tariff

b. The loss in consumer surplus suffered by U.S. steel consumers as a result of the tariff

c. The revenue earned by the government because of the tariff

d. The gains from trade that are lost (the deadweight loss) because of the tariff

8. For each of the four parts of Question #7 above, calculate the *values* of these areas in dollars. How much of the deadweight loss is due to the overproduction of steel by higher-cost U.S. steel producers, and how much is due to the underconsumption of steel by U.S. steel consumers?

CHALLENGES

1. In the chapter, we focused on a sugar tariff that eliminated all imports. Let's now take a look at the case where the sugar tariff eliminates some but not all imports. We will also examine the closely related case of a quota on sugar imports.

The figure below shows a tariff on sugar that raises the U.S. price to 20 cents per pound but at that price some sugar is imported even after the tariff.

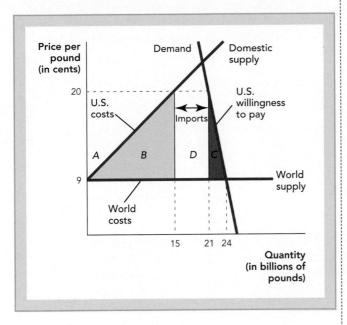

a. Label the free trade equilibrium, the tariff equilibrium, wasted resources, lost gains from trade, and tariff revenues.

b. Now imagine that instead of a tariff, the U.S. government uses a quota that forbids imports of sugar greater than 6 billion pounds. (Equivalently, imagine a tariff that is zero on the first 6 billion pounds of imports but then jumps to a prohibitive level after that quantity of imports—this is closer to how the system works in practice.) Under the quota system what does area D represent? Would importers of sugar prefer a tariff or a quota?

c. The sugar quota is allocated to importing countries based on imports from these countries between 1975 and 1981 (with some subsequent adjustments). For example, in 2008 Australia was given the right to export 87 thousand metric tons of sugar to the United States at a very low tariff rate, while Belize was given the right to export 11.5 thousand metric tons of sugar to the United States at a very low tariff rate. How do you think these rights are allocated to firms within the sugar-exporting countries?

d. Discuss how the quota and the way it is allocated could create a misallocation of resources that would further reduce efficiency relative to a tariff that resulted in the same quantity of imports.

2. In a 2005 Washington Post article ("The Road to Riches Is Called K Street"), Jeffrey Birnbaum noted that there were 35,000 registered lobbyists in Washington, DC, people whose primary job is asking the federal government for something. A lobbyist who comes with long experience as an aide to a powerful politician will earn at least $200,000 per year. Many lobbyists (not all) are attempting to restrict trade in order to turn consumer surplus into producer surplus.

a. Let's focus just on the lobbyists who are restricting trade. If the United States were to amend the Constitution to permanently ban all tariffs and trade restrictions, these lobbyists would lose their jobs, and they'd have to leave Washington to get "real jobs." Would this job change raise U.S. productivity or lower it?

b. Would most of these lobbyists likely earn more after the amendment was enacted or less?

c. How can you reconcile your answers to parts a and b?

3. Let's think a little more about Thinking and Problem Solving question 4. If quality weren't held constant, what would you expect to happen to the additional Chinese sedans produced after the import ban? Would they be as good as the ones that used to be imported? (Hint: Which types of sedans do you think that China imports? Low-quality or high-quality? Why?)

4. One of the assumptions made in the chapter was that the U.S. market for sugar was small relative to the overall world market for sugar, so that when the United States entered the world market for sugar, and U.S. buyers began to buy imported sugar, the price did not change. If we relax this assumption, how do you think that would affect Figure 9.1? How would the outcome differ from the outcome under the assumption of the relatively small market?

10

Externalities: When Prices Send the Wrong Signals

On a sunny day in June 1924, a young man developed a blister on his toe after playing a game of tennis. A week later, he was dead from a bacterial infection. The young man had been given the best medical care possible: He was the son of the president of the United States. President Coolidge wept when he learned that all the "power and the glory of the presidency" could not prevent the death of his son from a simple blister.

The president's son, Calvin Jr., was probably killed by a bacterium called *Staphylococcus aureus* or *staph* for short. Penicillin could easily have cured him, but penicillin was not discovered until 1928. When penicillin and other antibiotics became widely available in the 1940s, they were hailed as miracle drugs. Dying from a blister became a thing of the past—until recently.

Staph has evolved. Today it is resistant to penicillin and some "superbug" strains are resistant to almost all antibiotics. In 2007, five healthy high school athletes died from infections much like those that killed Calvin Jr. Multidrug-resistant *Staphylococcus aureus* is now spreading around the globe.

Antibiotic resistance is a product of evolution. Any population of bacteria includes some bacteria with unusual traits, such as the ability to resist an antibiotic's attack. When a person takes an antibiotic, the drug kills the defenseless bacteria, leaving the unusually strong bacteria behind. Without competition for resources, these stronger bacteria multiply rapidly. When the same antibiotic is applied again and again, the stronger bacteria get even stronger until after many generations of bacteria, the antibiotic loses its power to perform miracles.

Evolution is a powerful force so it was inevitable that staph would grow resistant to penicillin eventually, but staph has grown more resistant more quickly than was necessary. The problem is that antibiotics are overused.

A private cost is a cost paid by the consumer or the producer.

Antibiotic users get all the benefits of antibiotics but they do not bear all of the costs. The person who demands an antibiotic must pay a **private cost** for the antibiotic, the market price. But because bacteria spread widely, each use of an antibiotic creates a small increase in bacterial resistance, which raises the probability that other people could die from a simple infection. For example, when a teenager takes tetracycline for acne, there is an increase in antibiotic-resistant bacteria on the skin of *other* members of his or her family. Antimicrobial detergents that are washed down the sink enter into the environment where they increase the proportion of resistant bacteria for us all. Almost half of all antibiotics are used on farm animals, not to treat disease but primarily because they increase and accelerate growth. Bacteria that develop resistance on the farm travel onto and into human beings, where they may cause incurable infections.

In a sense, each use of antibiotics pollutes the environment with more resistant and stronger bacteria. Thus, each use of antibiotics creates an **external cost,** a cost that is paid not by the consumers or producers of antibiotics but by bystanders to the transaction. The **social cost** of antibiotic use is the cost to everyone: the private cost plus the external cost.

An external cost is a cost paid by people other than the consumer or the producer trading in the market.

The social cost is the cost to everyone: the private cost plus the external cost.

Since the external cost is not paid by consumers or producers, it is not built into the price of antibiotics. So when patients or farmers choose whether to use more antibiotics, they compare their private benefits with the market price, but they ignore the external costs just as a factory will ignore the cost of the pollution that it emits into the atmosphere (assuming there are no regulations forbidding this). Since antibiotic users ignore some relevant costs of their actions, antibiotics are overused. Alternatively stated, since the price of antibiotics does not include all the costs of using antibiotics, the price sends an imperfect signal—the price is too low and so antibiotics are overused. Thus, the problem of antibiotic resistance is about evolution *and* economics. Evolution drives antibiotic resistance, but the process is happening much faster than we would like because antibiotic users do not take into account the external costs of their choices.

External Costs, External Benefits, and Efficiency

This chapter is about products, like antibiotics, for which some of the costs or benefits of the product fall on bystanders. These costs or benefits are called external costs or external benefits or, for short, **externalities.** (External costs are sometimes also called negative externalities, and external benefits are sometimes also called positive externalities.) When externalities are significant, markets work less well and government action can increase social surplus.

Externalities are external costs or external benefits that fall on bystanders.

In Chapter 4, we showed that a market equilibrium maximizes consumer plus producer surplus (the gains from trade). But maximizing consumer plus producer surplus isn't so great if bystanders are harmed in the process. Everyone counts, not just the consumers and producers of a particular product. So, when we evaluate how well a market with externalities is working, we want to look at **social surplus,** namely consumer surplus plus producer surplus plus everyone else's surplus.

Social surplus is consumer surplus plus producer surplus plus everyone else's surplus.

To show why a market with externalities *does not* maximize *social surplus,* it's useful to briefly review why a market equilibrium *does* maximize *consumer plus producer surplus* (see also Chapter 4). The key is to remember that you can read the value of the *n*th unit of a good from the height of the demand curve and the cost of the *n*th unit of a good from the height of the supply curve.

For example, imagine that buyers and sellers are currently exchanging 99 units of a good. What is the value to buyers and the costs to sellers of one additional unit, the 100th unit? In Figure 10.1, you can read the value to buyers from the height of the demand curve at the 100th unit, namely $22. You can read the cost to sellers from the height of the supply curve at the 100th unit, namely $10. Since the value of the 100th unit exceeds the additional cost of the 100th unit, there is an incentive to trade, namely an opportunity to increase consumer and producer surplus. Following this logic, trade is mutually profitable up until the 210th unit is sold. The value to buyers of the 210th unit is $13 and the cost to sellers of producing that additional unit is $13 so at this point there are no further incentives to trade. If any fewer units were traded, gains from trade would be left on the table. If any more units were traded, the cost of those units would exceed their value. Thus, gains from trade are maximized at the market equilibrium of 210 units.

Let's call the price and quantity that maximize social surplus the **efficient equilibrium.** If there are no significant externalities, the market equilibrium is also the efficient equilibrium (because if there are no significant external costs or benefits, maximizing producer plus consumer surplus is the same as maximizing everyone's surplus). But if there are significant externalities, the market equilibrium is no longer the efficient equilibrium, as we will now show.

FIGURE 10.1

Reviewing Gains from Trade The value of the 100th unit to buyers is $22. The cost of the 100th unit to sellers is $10. At the 100th unit, there is a $12 gain from exchange. Gains from trade are maximized when a total of 210 units are exchanged. Notice that the value of the 210th unit is just equal to the cost of the 210th unit.

The **efficient equilibrium** is the price and quantity that maximizes social surplus.

External Costs

The left panel of Figure 10.2 on the next page shows the market equilibrium for antibiotics. As usual, the market equilibrium maximizes consumer plus producer surplus. But now the use of antibiotics creates an external cost, a cost to people who are neither buying nor selling antibiotics. At the market equilibrium, the price of a round of antibiotics—such as your doctor would prescribe to cure an infection—is $5 and we will assume that the external cost of antibiotic use is $7, a number that is consistent with a recent study of the matter.[1] The private cost plus the external cost is the social cost of antibiotic use.

In the right panel of Figure 10.2, we add the external cost to the supply curve to show the social cost curve. The social cost curve takes into account *all* of the costs of antibiotic use so it's the social cost curve that we use to figure out the **efficient quantity,** the quantity that maximizes social surplus. The efficient quantity $Q_{Efficient}$ is found where the demand curve intersects the social cost curve.

To see exactly why the market equilibrium is *not* efficient, let's consider the value to buyers and the social costs of the Q_{Market} unit of the good. The height of the demand curve at the Q_{Market} unit (the black arrow labeled "Private value") tells us that this unit has a private value of $5. The height of the social cost curve at Q_{Market} (the green arrow labeled "Social cost") tells us that this unit has a social cost of $12. Thus, producing this unit creates a social loss or deadweight loss of $7. Following this logic, you can see that reducing output increases social surplus so long as the social cost of an additional prescription of

The **efficient quantity** is the quantity that maximizes social surplus.

FIGURE 10.2

Panel A

Panel B

When External Costs Are Significant, Output Is Too High
Panel A: The market equilibrium is found, as usual, where the supply and demand curves intersect. The market equilibrium maximizes consumer plus producer surplus.
Panel B: We add external costs to the supply curve to find the social cost curve. Notice that the social cost of the Q_{Market} unit exceeds the private value of this unit. The efficient equilibrium is found where the social cost and demand curves intersect. $Q_{Efficient}$ is less than Q_{Market} so the market overproduces goods with significant external costs.

antibiotics exceeds the buyer value, that is, so long as the social cost curve lies above the demand curve. Thus, to maximize social surplus, output should be reduced to $Q_{Efficient}$, the point at which the social cost curve intersects the demand curve and where the social costs of an additional unit just equal the value.

A final way of illustrating the overuse of antibiotics is to notice that *if* the users did bear all the costs of antibiotic use, that is, *if* the private cost included the $7 external cost, then the supply curve would shift upward and would be the same as the social cost curve. The market equilibrium would then be the same as the efficient equilibrium, that is, buyers would purchase $Q_{Efficient}$ units. But for determining efficient quantities, *who* bears the costs is irrelevant—*costs are costs regardless of who bears them.* Thus, $Q_{Efficient}$ is the efficient quantity when antibiotic users pay all of the costs *and* when they pay only some of the costs— the only difference is that when other people bear some of the costs, antibiotic users purchase more antibiotics, so $Q_{Market} > Q_{Efficient}$.

The last way of explaining why antibiotics are overused suggests one potential solution to the problem of external costs. If antibiotic users had to pay a tax just equal to the external costs, $7, they would demand only the amount $Q_{Efficient}$. Remember from Chapter 6 that we can analyze a tax by shifting the supply curve up by the amount of the tax. Thus, in Figure 10.2, notice that a tax set equal to the level of the external cost would shift the supply curve up so that it exactly overlays the social cost curve. The market quantity would then fall from Q_{Market} to $Q_{Efficient}$. Thus, a tax set equal to the external cost would once again mean that the market equilibrium was the efficient equilibrium!

A tax on an ordinary good increases deadweight loss, as we discussed in Chapter 6, but a tax on a good with an external cost reduces deadweight loss and raises revenue. For these reasons, there is a strong argument for taxing goods with external costs. Such taxes are often called **Pigouvian taxes,** after the economist Arthur C. Pigou (1877–1959) who first focused attention on externalities and how they might be corrected with taxes. We will return to look at solutions to external cost problems in more detail after we have examined a parallel issue, external benefits.

A **Pigouvian tax** is a tax on a good with external costs.

External Benefits

An **external benefit** is a benefit to people other than the consumers or the producers trading in the market. Consider, for example, another medical good, vaccines. Vaccines benefit the person who is vaccinated but they also create an external benefit for other people because people who have been vaccinated are less likely to harbor and spread disease-causing viruses.[*]

An **external benefit** is a benefit received by people other than the consumers or producers trading in the market.

In a typical year, for example, some 36,000 Americans die from the flu, a contagious respiratory disease caused by influenza viruses. Fortunately, millions of Americans get a yearly vaccination—a "flu shot"—that is usually effective at preventing the flu. Flu viruses spread from person to person when someone who *already has the flu* coughs or sneezes. As a result, when one person gets a flu shot, the expected number of people who get the flu falls by more than one. So getting a flu shot is a real public service. Get a flu shot. The life you save may not be your own.

So what's the problem? The problem is not the millions of Americans who get a flu shot—it's the even larger number of Americans who don't get one. When an individual compares the private costs and benefits of getting a flu shot, it may be quite sensible not to get one. It takes time to get a shot, it costs money, and there is often a slight fever and ache associated with the vaccine itself. The problem is that the person getting the shot bears all these costs but doesn't receive all the benefits. As a result, fewer people get flu shots than is efficient.

In Figure 10.3 on the next page, for example, we show the demand and supply of vaccines. Demanders compare their private value of vaccines with their private costs and purchase Q_{Market} units at the price P_{Market}. Vaccination, however, reduces the probability that a disease spreads so there are external benefits from vaccination. The social value curve counts *all* the benefits of vaccine use, the private value plus the external benefits, so the efficient quantity is found where the social value curve intersects the supply curve.

To see exactly why the market equilibrium is not efficient, consider in Figure 10.3 the private and social value of the Q_{Market} unit of vaccination. This unit has a private cost of $20 (the black arrow labeled "Private cost"), but it has a social value of $40 (the green arrow labeled "Social value"). Thus, consuming more units would increase social surplus. Following this logic, you can see that increasing output increases social surplus so long as the social value of an additional flu shot exceeds the private cost, that is, so long as the social value curve is above the supply curve. Thus, to maximize social surplus, output should increase to $Q_{Efficient}$, the unit for which social value just equals the costs of production.

A final way of illustrating the underuse of vaccines is to notice that *if* people who got a flu shot did receive all the benefits of vaccination, then their

---

[*] An antibiotic could also have an external benefit in the case of infections that can be easily transmitted. Not all infections are easily transmitted, however, and the external costs due to antibiotic resistance appear to be much larger than any external benefits.

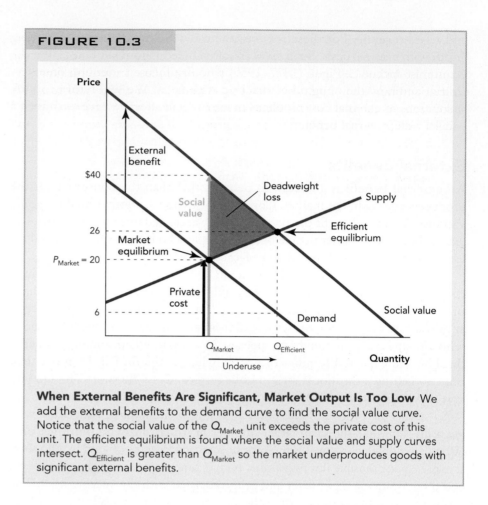

FIGURE 10.3

When External Benefits Are Significant, Market Output Is Too Low We add the external benefits to the demand curve to find the social value curve. Notice that the social value of the Q_{Market} unit exceeds the private cost of this unit. The efficient equilibrium is found where the social value and supply curves intersect. $Q_{Efficient}$ is greater than Q_{Market} so the market underproduces goods with significant external benefits.

demand curve would shift upward by $20 and would be the same as the social value curve. The market equilibrium would then be the same as the efficient equilibrium, that is, buyers would purchase $Q_{Efficient}$ units. But for determining efficiency, *who* receives the benefits is irrelevant—benefits are benefits regardless of who receives them. Thus, $Q_{Efficient}$ is the efficient quantity when vaccine users receive all of the benefits of vaccination *and* when they receive only some of the benefits—the only difference is that when other people receive some of the benefits, fewer people purchase flu shots, so $Q_{Market} < Q_{Efficient}$.

The last way of thinking about the problem of external benefits also suggests one potential solution. If every time someone was vaccinated, they were given a subsidy of $20, the monetary equivalent of the external benefit, they would demand the amount $Q_{Efficient}$. Recall from Chapter 6 that we can analyze a subsidy by shifting up the demand curve by the amount of the subsidy. Thus, in Figure 10.3, notice that a subsidy set equal to the level of the external benefit would shift the demand curve up and increase the market quantity from Q_{Market} to $Q_{Efficient}$. In other words, if set correctly, a subsidy will make the market equilibrium equal to the efficient equilibrium. In addition, unlike in Chapter 6 where we looked at subsidies on ordinary goods, a subsidy on a good with an external benefit will reduce deadweight loss, thereby increasing social surplus.

A **Pigouvian subsidy** is a subsidy on a good with external benefits.

A subsidy on a good with an external benefit is often called a **Pigouvian subsidy,** again after Pigou, who first discussed these issues. Another way of thinking about Pigouvian taxes and subsidies is to recall from Chapter 7 that market prices are signals. But when there are external costs or benefits, the market price sends the wrong signal. If there are external costs, the market price is too low, thus resulting in overconsumption. A Pigouvian tax increases the price so that the after-tax price sends the correct signal. Similarly, if there are external benefits, the market price is too high, thus resulting in underconsumption. A Pigouvian subsidy reduces the price so that the after-subsidy price sends the correct signal.

Let's look in more detail at how to solve problems caused by external costs or benefits. We will discuss private solutions to problems created by externalities and three types of solutions involving government: taxes and subsidies (which we have mentioned already), command and control, and tradable permits.

Private Solutions to Externality Problems

In a classic paper on externalities, the Nobel Prize-winning economist James Meade wrote that the market for honey was inefficient. As they make honey, bees pollinate fruits and vegetables, which is an important benefit to farmers. Since pollination is an external benefit of honey production, Meade argued there was too little honey being made.

Meade was right about the bees, but wrong about the market for honey. Bee pollination is a thriving business for which beekeepers are paid. In fact, in the United States, beekeepers manage around half a billion bees that they truck around the country to rent out to farmers. Since farmers pay beekeepers to pollinate their crops, the "external benefit" becomes internalized—the beekeepers earn money from the pollination of fruits and vegetables and so expand production toward the efficient quantity, the quantity that takes into account the benefits of bees for honey production and for fruit and vegetable production.[2]

The market in pollination is quite sophisticated. When bees pollinate almonds, for example, the honey that they produce doesn't taste good so beekeepers charge almond growers $75 per colony of bees, but they only charge apple growers $25 per colony because the honey produced tastes better and can be sold. In this way, the price of pollination adjusts to take into account not only the external benefit of honey production on fruit production but also the external benefit of fruit production on honey production.

The lesson of the bees is that our earlier story was a bit too pessimistic. The market equilibrium can be efficient even when there are externalities, *if* there is systematic trading in those externalities. To see which externalities the market can handle, let's take a closer look at why the market for pollination works reasonably well.

The market for pollination works because transaction costs are low and property rights are clearly defined. **Transaction costs** are all the costs necessary to reach an agreement. The costs of identifying and bringing buyers and sellers together, bargaining, and drawing up a contract are all transaction costs. Transaction costs are low for beekeepers and farmers because farms are large and bees don't fly that far. So when a beekeeper places bees in the center of a large farm, the beekeeper and the farmer know that the bees will pollinate the crops owned by the farmer who is paying and not pollinate some other farmer's crops. As a result, the externality from bees is limited to one farmer at a time and can be internalized with one transaction.

CHECK YOURSELF

> In our discussion of Pigouvian taxes, we assumed that the government set the correct tax to achieve the efficient equilibrium. What if government overshoots and adds a tax that is too high? Will the equilibrium quantity be higher or lower than the efficient equilibrium?

> In our discussion of Pigouvian subsidies, we assumed that government set the correct subsidy amount to achieve the efficient equilibrium. What if the government undershoots and provides a subsidy that is too low? Will the equilibrium quantity be higher or lower than the efficient equilibrium?

Bees create external beenefits.

STEFFEN SCHMIDT/ EPA/CORBIS

Transaction costs are all the costs necessary to reach an agreement.

Property rights over farms and bees are also clearly defined. Everyone knows that the beekeeper has the right to the benefits created by bee pollination, so if the farmer wants bees to pollinate his crops, he must pay the beekeeper. This works for beekeepers and farmers, but as you will see, property rights in other externalities are not as clearly defined and this makes transactions more difficult; you might say that unclear property rights are a type of transaction cost, since they make it harder to trade.

It's not so difficult for beekeepers to trade with farmers, but how many transactions would it take to internalize the external benefit created when someone has a flu shot? When one person is vaccinated, thousands of other people benefit by a small amount, especially if the vaccinated person spends a lot of time in airports. When Alex has the flu and coughs while boarding a plane, he could spread the flu virus to dozens of other people, each of whom could in turn pass it on to many others. If Alex receives a flu shot, all these people are better off. In theory, if each of these people paid Alex a small amount for getting a flu shot, Alex would be more likely to get a flu shot. But the transaction costs of arranging a deal like this are enormous—simply to identify the beneficiaries is difficult and getting thousands of them to send a check to Alex is next to impossible (trust us, we have tried!).

What about property rights? We assumed above that other people might be willing to pay Alex to get a flu shot because the flu shot creates an external benefit. But when Alex spreads the flu, he imposes an external cost on other people. Maybe Alex should have to pay other people when he doesn't get a flu shot! Even when other transaction costs are low, if property rights are not well defined—who should have to pay whom—it will be difficult to solve externality problems with bargaining.

The **Coase theorem** posits that if transaction costs are low and property rights are clearly defined, private bargains will ensure that the market equilibrium is efficient even when there are externalities.

Ronald Coase, another Nobel Prize winner, summarized the situations in which markets alone can solve the externality problems in what has come to be called the **Coase theorem**. The Coase theorem says that if transaction costs are low and property rights are clearly defined, then private bargains will ensure that the market equilibrium is efficient even when there are externalities. In other words, in these cases trading makes sure that just the right amount of the externality is produced. If there were either too little or too much of the externality, trading would push the quantity to the optimum level.

Recall that in a free market, the quantity of goods sold maximizes the sum of consumer and producer surplus. If the conditions of the Coase theorem are met, we can replace this with the even stronger conclusion that in a free market, the quantity of goods sold will maximize social surplus, the sum of consumer, producer, and everyone else's surplus.

But the conditions of the Coase theorem are often *unlikely* to be met. Transaction costs for many externalities are high and property rights are often not clearly defined. Thus, markets alone will *not* solve all externality problems.

The importance of the Coase theorem lies not in suggesting that markets alone might solve externality problems, but in suggesting a solution—the creation of new markets. If property rights can be clearly defined and transaction costs reduced, then a market for externalities might develop. If such a market does develop, we know from the Coase theorem that it will have all the efficiency properties of ordinary markets. Not only will this market maximize social surplus (consumer + producer + everyone else's surplus), but it will also ensure that the supply of goods will be bought by the demanders with the highest willingness to pay and sold by the suppliers with the lowest costs.

Government can play a role in defining property rights and reducing transaction costs. In fact, in recent years governments have helped to create working markets in many externalities, verifying the insights of the Coase theorem. Below, we discuss one of these new markets, a market in the right to emit pollution.

Government Solutions to Externality Problems

We have already discussed one kind of government solution to externality problems, namely taxes and subsidies. Two other solutions are also common: command and control and tradable allowances for the activity in question. We will look at both of these solutions in the context of another externality, acid rain, and we will also offer some comparisons with taxes and subsidies.

Acid rain damages forests and lakes, it corrodes metal and stone, and in the form of particulates, it creates haze and increased lung diseases such as asthma and bronchitis. Acid rain is caused when sulfur dioxide (SO_2) and nitrogen oxides (NO_x) are released into the atmosphere. A majority of SO_2 and a significant fraction of NO_x are created in the process of generating electricity from coal. Let's look at how the government has reduced the external cost of acid rain.

Command and Control

When external costs are significant, we know that $Q_{Market} > Q_{Efficient}$, so the most obvious (but not necessarily the best) method to reduce the external cost of electricity generation is for the government to order firms to use (or make) less electricity. This is called a command and control method. Command and control methods are not always efficient. The government, for example, issued a command and control regulation that required manufacturers to make clothes washers that use less electricity. *Consumer Reports* reviewed the clothes washers produced under this new standard and the reviewers were not happy with the results:[3]

> Not so long ago you could count on most washers to get your clothes very clean. Not anymore. Our latest tests found huge performance differences among machines. Some left our stain-soaked swatches nearly as dirty as they were before washing. For best results, you'll have to spend $900 or more.

> What happened? As of January [2007], the U.S. Department of Energy has required washers to use 21 percent less energy, a goal we wholeheartedly support. But our tests have found that traditional top-loaders, those with the familiar center-post agitators, are having a tough time wringing out those savings without sacrificing cleaning ability, the main reason you buy a washer.

The problem with command and control is that there are typically many methods to achieve a goal and the government may not have enough information to choose the least costly method. Let's suppose, for example, that the Department of Energy's regulation on clothes washers reduces electricity consumption by 1% (this number is too large but it will do for our purposes). Now let's compare command and control with a tax on electricity consumption that causes people to reduce their electricity consumption by *exactly the same amount, 1%*.[4] Faced with an increase in price, how would people choose to reduce their electricity consumption?

CHECK YOURSELF

> You want to hold a Saturday night party at your house but are worried that your elderly neighbors will complain to the police about the noise. Suggest a solution to this problem using what you know about the Coase theorem.

> Consider a factory near you that pollutes. What are the transaction costs involved in you and your neighbors negotiating with the factory to reduce the pollution? Is a private solution possible?

If the price of electricity increased, some people would choose to cut back on electricity by turning their lights off more often or by switching to lower-consumption fluorescent lightbulbs. Other people would respond by turning down the heat or the air conditioning, or by buying a cover for their pool, or by installing insulation in their attic. The ways in which people would reduce electricity consumption are as different as the people themselves. But notice that probably very few people would respond to an increase in the price of electricity by spending a *lot* more on a clothes washer that saves electricity or by buying a clothes washer that saves electricity but doesn't clean very well. Thus, the government's method of reducing electricity consumption is not the lowest-cost method.

A tax on electricity can reduce the consumption of electricity by exactly the same amount as a regulation on clothes washers but a tax will cost less. The tax costs less because a tax gives people the flexibility to reduce consumption in the way that is least costly to them. Recall from Chapter 7 that prices are signals. A tax on electricity sends a signal to every user of electricity that says "Economize!" But the tax leaves it to each person to use his or her local knowledge and unique preferences to choose the least costly method of economizing.

It's better to reduce electricity consumption with a tax than with a regulation on clothes washers, but we can do even better. After all, we don't really want to reduce *electricity*—we want to reduce *pollutants* like SO_2 and NO_x. It's true that pollutants are a by-product of electricity generation but there are many ways of reducing SO_2 and NO_x other than by producing less electricity. Thus, taxing the pollutants directly is a better way of creating incentives to reduce pollution than is taxing electricity. Taxing the pollutants directly gives firms the maximum flexibility to adopt the least costly methods of reducing pollution. Remember it's the pollutants that are creating the external cost so taxing the pollutants sends the right signal.

Command and control is not always a bad idea. The advantage of using incentives like taxes to control an externality is flexibility. The government corrects the price with a tax or subsidy so the price sends the right signal and people adapt using their own information and preferences (with all the benefits of the price system that we described in Chapters 4 and 7). But flexibility is not always desirable. Consider, for example, one of the great triumphs of humanity—the eradication of smallpox. Smallpox killed 300–500 million people in the twentieth century alone. As late as 1967, 2 million people died and millions more were scarred and blinded from smallpox, but in that year the World Health Organization (WHO) launched a program of mass vaccination, intensive surveillance, and immediate quarantine. The WHO program relied on command and control because so long as *any* reservoir of smallpox remained anywhere on the planet, the virus could reemerge and spread worldwide. To be successful, the WHO could not rely on taxes because it needed everyone to follow its policies—flexibility was not desirable. Fortunately, the WHO program was successful and by 1978 smallpox was extinct—the first and so far the only human infectious disease to be stopped dead in its tracks.[*]

The bottom line is that command and control can be useful if the best approach to a problem is well known and if success requires very strong compliance. If it's important to control the externality at the least possible

---

[*] Command and control continues to be used today in handling other infectious diseases. Before registering for classes, for example, school-age children and college and university students must show that they have had their MMR vaccine (preventing measles, mumps, rubella).

cost and if the government doesn't have full information, then more flexible approaches such as taxes and subsidies are preferable.

Tradable Allowances

Another type of command and control program is to require that firms reduce pollutants by a specific quantity. In the 1970s, for example, the government limited SO_2 from all generators of electricity to a maximum rate. The problem with this approach is that because of differences in location, fuel, and technology, it's much cheaper to reduce emissions of SO_2 from some firms than from others. By treating all firms the same, the government reduced flexibility and increased the cost of eliminating a given amount of pollution.

A simple example illustrates the problem with quantity restrictions and a potential solution. Suppose that there are two firms. We begin with a command and control regulation that limits each firm to 100 tons of SO_2 emissions in a year. Now imagine that reducing pollution at High-Cost Industries is expensive, so High could save $1,100 if it were allowed to produce 101 tons of SO_2 instead of being limited to 100 tons. Low-Cost Industries can control its pollution quite cheaply, so if Low reduces its pollution level even further to 99 tons, its costs increase by only $200.

Now imagine that the CEOs of High and Low approach the head of the Environmental Protection Agency with a proposal. The CEOs suggest that High be allowed to increase its pollution level by 1 ton to 101 tons. High will also pay $500 to Low. In return, Low will cut its pollution level by 1 ton to 99 tons. It's clear why High and Low want the deal—it's profitable. High cuts its pollution control costs by $1,100 for which it pays $500 for a net increase in profit of $600. Low increases its pollution control costs by $200, but it receives a $500 payment for a net increase in profit of $300. But should the EPA accept this deal?

Yes, if the EPA cares about social surplus, it should accept the deal. Notice that pollution stays exactly the same, 200 units, so the deal does not harm the environment. The deal, however, does increase profits by $900 ($600 to High and $300 to Low). Should the EPA care about firm profits? Maybe not directly, but notice *why* profits increase in this example. Profits increase because the costs of reducing pollution fall. By trading, the firms reduce the cost of eliminating the last unit of pollution from $1,100 to just $200—a $900 fall in costs and that represents an increase in resources available to society.

So, we can now ask our question in a different way. Should the EPA care about decreasing the costs of reducing pollution? Of course, the answer is yes. If we can reduce the same amount of pollution at lower cost, that means more resources are available for other goods. And, the lower the costs of eliminating pollution, the more pollution it makes sense to eliminate.

What we have shown is that trading pollution allowances is like a new technology that reduces pollution at lower cost. The EPA should always be in favor of new technologies to reduce pollution and so it should also be in favor of trades in the right to pollute.

Tradable Allowances in Practice   A formal version of the tradable allowances system that we have just described was created by the Clean Air Act of 1990. Under this reform, the EPA distributes pollution allowances to generators of electricity, and each allowance gives the owner the right to emit 1 ton of SO_2. Firms may trade allowances as they see fit and they have organized sophisticated markets in tradable allowances. Firms can even bank allowances for future use.

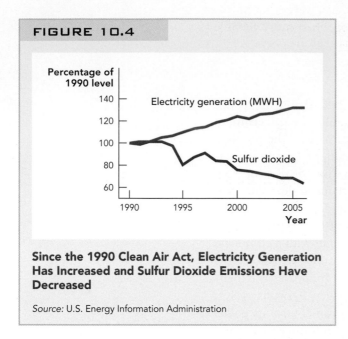

FIGURE 10.4

Percentage of 1990 level

Since the 1990 Clean Air Act, Electricity Generation Has Increased and Sulfur Dioxide Emissions Have Decreased

Source: U.S. Energy Information Administration

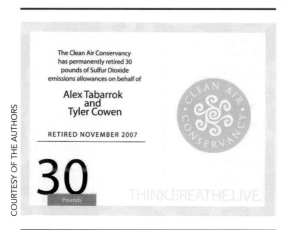

The EPA monitors each firm's emissions of SO_2, and it also tracks how many allowances each firm owns so no firm can emit more pollution than it has allowances. Congress sets the total number of allowances.

The EPA's tradable allowances program has been very successful, as SO_2 emissions have been reduced by more than 5 million tons or 35% since 1990. Air quality has improved and illness has been reduced.[5] The number of allowances was scheduled to fall so that by 2010, SO_2 emissions from power plants were roughly half what they were in 1980. Remarkably, as shown in Figure 10.4, electricity generation has increased even as SO_2 emissions have decreased.

The EPA's system of tradable allowances is a successful application of the Coase theorem. Recall that the Coase theorem says that markets can internalize externalities when transaction costs are low and property rights are clearly defined. The Clean Air Act of 1990 clearly defined rights to emit SO_2, and the EPA has reduced transaction costs by distributing the allowances, monitoring emissions, and creating a database that tracks ownership. Trading in markets has then allocated the allowances among firms in the way that minimizes the costs of reducing pollution.

One of the most interesting aspects of the market in rights to emit sulfur dioxide is that anyone can participate in this market, not just generators of electricity. We bought the rights to emit 30 pounds of SO_2. We don't intend to emit any pollutants; rather, we bought the rights and ripped them up in order to create more clean air. Environmentalists and industry often oppose one another, but when markets in externalities are created, environmentalists can buy pollutants and industry is happy to sell—as always, trade makes both parties better off.

An important result of the SO_2 trading program is that firms that generate electricity from relatively clean sources such as solar power can make money by selling their pollution allowances. In contrast, firms that generate electricity from relatively dirty sources must buy allowances. In essence, clean energy is subsidized and dirty energy is taxed—thus, a program of tradable allowances correctly reflects the fact that clean energy has lower social costs than dirty energy.

The success of the acid rain program in reducing SO_2 emissions at low cost and concern over global climate change motivated President Barack Obama to propose a tradable allowances plan for carbon dioxide, a greenhouse gas that contributes to global warming. Tradable allowances in carbon dioxide would change the economics of all energy, not just electricity, and would create incentives for firms to move toward nuclear, solar, and biomass fuels that contribute less to global warming. Since global warming is a worldwide problem, tradable allowances ideally would be distributed and bought and sold on a worldwide basis. As of yet, however, not enough cooperation exists in the world community to establish such a system. Why not? Transaction costs again—in moving to a tradable allowance system, some countries and industries will be harmed and others will benefit. If moving to such a system would prevent global climate change, the overall outcome is good, but even if the overall outcome is good, no one wants to bear a large share of the costs.

Comparing Tradable Allowances and Pigouvian Taxes—Advanced Material

There is a close relationship between using Pigouvian taxes and tradable allowances to solve externality problems. A tax set equal to the level of the external cost is equivalent to tradable allowances, where the number of allowances is set equal to the efficient quantity. To achieve the efficient equilibrium in Figure 10.5, for example, the government can either use taxes to raise the price to the efficient price or it can use allowances to reduce the quantity to the efficient quantity. The equilibrium is identical no matter which method is used.

Differences between Pigouvian taxes and tradable allowances do occur when there is uncertainty. Imagine, for example, that we know any quantity above a certain threshold level of SO_2 will acidify thousands of lakes and thus cause an environmental disaster. Any level below the threshold, however, will be acceptable or at least tolerable. In this case, tradable allowances are best because we can set the allowance below the threshold level and be certain that we will avoid disaster. If we set a tax, however, and we don't know the exact position of the supply curve, then we could easily set the tax too low, leading to SO_2 emissions above the threshold level. A fixed quantity, even if tradable, is like a command and control regulation, and just as in our discussion of eliminating smallpox, the best argument for command and control is when flexibility is not a virtue.

On the other hand, sometimes we know a lot about the cost that a unit of SO_2 creates, but we aren't sure about the efficient quantity of pollution because demand and supply are changing. If the supply curve in Figure 10.5 were to shift down, for example, if the cost of producing electricity falls, the efficient quantity will increase. With a Pigouvian tax, the adjustment to the new equilibrium occurs automatically, but with allowances we could be stuck with a quantity of allowances that is much lower than the new efficient quantity. In this case, a Pigouvian tax is best because it can more easily adjust to changes in demand and supply.

The second difference between taxes and pollution allowances is not economic but political. With a tax, firms must pay the government for each ton of pollutant that they emit. With pollution allowances, firms must either use the pollution allowances that they are given or, if they want to emit more, they must buy allowances from other firms. Either way, firms that are given allowances in the initial allocation get a big benefit compared with having to pay taxes. Thus, some people say that pollution allowances equal corrective taxes plus corporate welfare.

FIGURE 10.5

Comparing Tradable Allowances and Pigouvian Taxes If we knew the exact positions of the supply and demand curves, then we could always use tradable allowances to hit the efficient quantity or a tax to hit the efficient price and the equilibrium would be identical.

That's not necessarily the best way of looking at the issue, however. First, allowances need not be given away; they could be auctioned to the highest bidder, as under some proposed tradable allowance programs for carbon dioxide—this would also raise significant tax revenue. To make progress against global warming, moreover, may require building a political coalition. A carbon tax pushes one very powerful and interested group, the large energy firms, into the opposition. If tradable allowances are instead given to firms initially, there is a better chance of bringing the large energy firms into the coalition. Perhaps it's not fair that politically powerful groups must be bought off, but as Otto von Bismarck, Germany's first chancellor, once said, "Laws are like sausages, it is better not to see them being made." We can only add that producing both laws and sausages requires some pork.

☐ Takeaway

In a free market, the quantity of goods sold maximizes consumer plus producer surplus. When the consumers and producers bear all the significant costs and benefits of trading, the market quantity is also the efficient quantity. But when there are external costs or benefits, the market quantity is not the efficient quantity. If it doesn't bear all the costs of pollution, an electricity generator will emit too much pollution. If a person doesn't receive all the benefits of a flu shot, he or she will choose too few flu shots.

There are three types of government solutions to externality problems: taxes and subsidies, command and control, and tradable allowances. Market prices do not correctly signal true costs and benefits when there are significant external costs or benefits. Taxes and subsidies can adjust prices so that they do send the correct signals. When external costs are significant, the market price is too low, so an optimal tax raises the price. When external benefits are significant, the market price is too high, so an optimal subsidy lowers the price.

Command and control solutions can work but are often high-cost because they are inflexible and do not take advantage of differences in the costs and benefits of eliminating and producing the externality.

The Coase theorem explains that the ultimate source of the externality problem is too few markets. If property rights can be clearly defined and transaction costs reduced, then markets in the externality will solve the problem and will do so at the lowest cost. In recent years, successful markets have been created in the right to emit sulfur dioxide, and new markets are being proposed to reduce the gases that contribute to global warming.

☐ CHAPTER REVIEW

KEY CONCEPTS

Private cost, p. 176

External cost, p. 176

Social cost, p. 176

Externalities, p. 176

Social surplus, p. 176

Efficient equilibrium, p. 177

Efficient quantity, p. 177

Pigouvian tax, p. 179

External benefit, p. 179

Pigouvian subsidy, p. 180

Transaction costs, p. 181

Coase theorem, p. 182

FACTS AND TOOLS

1. Let's sort the following eight items into private costs, external costs, private benefits, or external benefits. There's only one correct answer for each of questions a–h.

   a. The price you pay for an iTunes download

   b. The benefit your neighbor receives from hearing you play your pleasant music

   c. The annoyance of your neighbor because she doesn't like your achingly conventional music

   d. The pleasure you receive from listening to your iTunes download

   e. The price you pay for a security system for your home

   f. The safety you enjoy as a result of having the security system

   g. The crime that is more likely to occur to your neighbor once a criminal sees a "Protected by alarm" sticker on your window

   h. The extra safety your neighbor might experience because criminals tend to stay away from neighborhoods that have a lot of burglar alarms

2. If the students at your school started saying "thank you" to friends who got flu shots, would this tend to reduce the undersupply of people who get flu shots? Why or why not?

3. a. Consider a factory, located in the middle of nowhere, producing a nasty smell. As long as no one is around to experience the unpleasant odor, are any externalities produced?

   b. Suppose that a family moves in next door to the smelly factory. Do we now have an externalities problem? If so, who is causing it: the factory by producing the smell, the family by moving in next door, or both?

   c. Suppose that the family clearly possesses the right to a pleasant-smelling environment. Does this mean that the factory will be required to stop producing the bad smell? What could happen instead? There are many right answers. (*Hint*: Think about the Coase theorem. Actually, it's *always* a good idea to think about the Coase theorem, whether the topic is smelly factories, labor-management

disputes, international peace negotiations, or divorce settlements.)

4. Considering what we've learned about externalities, should human-caused global warming be *completely* stopped? Explain, using the language of social benefits and social costs.

5. In the following cases, the markets are in equilibrium, but there are externalities. In each case, determine whether there is an external benefit or cost and estimate its size. Finally, decide between a tax or a subsidy as a simple way to compensate for the externality. Fill out the table below with your answers.

   a. In the market for automobiles, the private benefit of one more small SUV is $20,000 and the social cost of one more small SUV is $30,000.

   b. In the market for fashionable clothes, the marginal social benefit of one more dress per person is $100, and the marginal private benefit is $500. Bonus: Can you tell an externality story that makes sense of these numbers?

   c. In the market for really good ideas, ideas that will dramatically change the world for the better, the private benefit of one more really good idea (from speaker's fees, book sales, patents, etc.) is $1,000,000. The marginal social benefit is $100,000,000.

Case	External Cost or Benefit?	Size of External Benefit (or Cost if Negative)	Tax It or Subsidize It?
a. SUVs			
b. Fashionable clothes			
c. Ideas			

6. In which cases are the Coase theorem's assumptions likely to be true? In other words, when will the parties be likely to strike an efficient bargain? How do you know?

   a. My neighbor wants me to cut down an ugly shrub in my front yard. The ugly shrub, of course, imposes an external cost on him and on his property value.

   b. My neighbors all would love for me to get that broken-down Willys Jeep off my front lawn. It's been years now, after all.

And would it be too much for me to paint the house and fill up that 6-foot deep ditch in the front yard? The whole neighborhood is annoyed.

c. A coal-fired electricity plant dumps its leftover hot water into the nearby lake, killing the naturally occurring fish. Thousands of homes line the banks of the lake.

d. A coal-fired electricity plant dumps its leftover hot water into the nearby river, killing the naturally occurring fish downstream. There is one large fishery 1 mile downstream affected by this. After that, the water cools enough so it's not a problem.

7. With electricity, we saw that it was important to tax the pollutant rather than the final product itself. In the following cases, will the proposed taxes actually hit at the source of the external cost, or will it only land an inefficient glancing blow? What kind of tax might be better?

a. Gas-guzzling cars create more pollution, so the government should tax big SUVs at a higher rate.

b. All-night liquor stores seem to generate unruly behavior in nearby neighborhoods, so owners of all-night liquor stores should pay higher property taxes.

c. Bell-bottom jeans insist on coming back every few years, and their ugliness creates external costs for all who see them. Therefore, bell-bottom jeans should be taxed heavily.

d. American parents are worried about their children hearing too much profanity on television. Congress decides to tax TV shows based on the number of profane words used on the shows.

8. When the government expands the number of pollution allowances, does that increase the cost of polluting or cut it? What about when the number of pollution allowances is cut back?

9. Maxicon is opening a new coal-fired power plant, but the government wants to keep pollution down.

a. Based on what we've seen in this chapter, which is a more efficient way to reduce pollution: commanding Maxicon to use one particular air-scrubbing technology that will reduce pollution by 25% or commanding Maxicon to reduce pollution by 25%?

b. If a corrupt government just grants Maxicon all of the (tradable) pollution permits in the entire nation (even though there are many energy companies), does this guarantee that Maxicon will engage in an enormous amount of pollution? Why or why not?

THINKING AND PROBLEM SOLVING

1. When someone is sick, the patient's decision to take an antibiotic imposes costs on others—it helps bacteria evolve resistance faster. But it also gives free benefits to others: It may slow down the spread of infectious disease the same way that vaccinations do. Thus, antibiotics can create external *costs* as well as external *benefits*. In theory, these could cancel each other out, so that just the right amount of antibiotics are being used. But economists think that on balance, there is overuse of antibiotics, not underuse. Why? Here's one hint—think on the margin!

2. A flu shot typically costs about $25–$50 but some firms offer their employees free flu shots. Why might a firm prefer to offer its employees free flu shots if the alternative is an equally costly wage increase?

3. "The environment is priceless." What evidence do you have that this statement is incorrect?

4. Cultural influences often create externalities, for good and ill. A happy movie might make people smile more, which improves the lives of people who don't see the movie. A fashion trend for tight-fitting clothing might hurt the body image of people who think they won't look good in the trendy clothing.

Let's consider the market for one cultural good that unrealistically raises expectations about the opposite sex: the romance novel. In romance novels, men are dangerous yet safe, wealthy yet never at work, they ride high-speed motorcycles yet never get in terrible accidents, they look fantastic even though they never waste endless hours at the gym, and so on. (Of course, advertising that focuses on sexy female models may also unrealistically raise expectations about the opposite sex so feel free to change our example as you see best.)

a. Consider the market below. Romance novels impose an external cost on men, who have to try to live up to these unrealistic expectations.

Illustrate the effect of this external cost on the figure below.

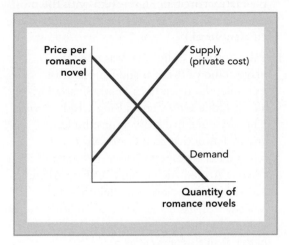

b. Illustrate on the above figure the deadweight loss from the externality, before a tax or other solution is imposed.

c. If the government decides to compensate for the externality by imposing a tax on romance novels, should the tax be high enough to stop everyone from reading the novels? Why or why not?

d. Show graphically how big the tax should be per novel.

e. As long as the government spends the money efficiently, does it matter what the government spends the money from the "romance novel tax" on? In other words, could the government just use the money to pay for necessary roads and bridges, or does it need to spend the money to fix the harmful social effects of romance novels?

5. Green Pastures Apartments wants to build a playground to increase demand for its larger-sized apartments but is worried that it will be overcrowded with tenants from the Still Waters Mobile Estates and Twin Pines Townhomes developments nearby.

   a. What type of externality is the playground: external cost or external benefit?

   b. What type of compromise might Green Pastures be able to make with Still Waters and Twin Pines so that all three developments will benefit from the playground? More than one answer is possible, but give just one based on reasoning from this chapter.

6. In Chapter 6, we said that taxes create deadweight losses. When we tax goods with external costs should we worry about deadweight losses? Why or why not?

7. Economists have found that increasing the proportion of girls in primary and secondary school leads to significant improvement in students' cognitive outcomes (Victor Lavy and Analia Schlosser. 2007. "Mechanisms and Impacts of Gender Peer Effects at School," NBER Working Paper 13292). One key channel seems to be that, on average, boys create more trouble in class, which makes it harder for everyone to learn. In newspaper English, we'd say that "boys are a tax on every child's education."

   a. Using the tools of this chapter, do girls in a classroom provide external costs or benefits? What about boys?

   b. Just based on this study, if you are a parent of a boy, would you rather your son be in a class with mostly boys or mostly girls? What if you are the parent of a girl?

   c. Who should be taxed in this situation? Can you see any problems implementing this tax?

8. In the example of honeybees, we said that the farmers pay the beekeepers for pollination services. But why don't the beekeepers pay the fruit farmers? After all, the beekeepers need the fruit farmers to make honey, so why does the payment go one way and not the other? (*Hint:* The almond example has some clues.)

9. A government is deciding between command and control solutions versus tax and subsidy solutions to solve an externality problem. In each case, explain why you think one is better, using arguments from the chapter.

   a. Suppose that whales are threatened with extinction because a large number of people like to eat whale meat. Governments are torn between banning all whaling except for certain religious ceremonies, and heavily taxing all whale meat. Assume there are only a few countries in the world that consume whale meat, and that they have fairly efficient governments.

   b. Fires create external costs because they spread from one building to another. Should governments encourage subsidies to sprinkler systems or should they just mandate that everyone have sprinklers?

c. Pets who procreate can create external costs due to problems with stray animals. Strays are extremely common on the streets of poor countries. Sterilization can solve the problem, but is a tax/subsidy or command and control a better method to encourage sterilization? Does the best solution depend on the sex of the animal?

CHALLENGES

1. Before Coase presented his theorem, economists who wanted economic efficiency argued that people should be responsible for the damage they do—they should pay for the social costs of their actions. This advice fits nicely with notions of personal responsibility. Explain how the Coase theorem refutes this older argument.

2. A government is torn between selling annual pollution allowances and setting an annual pollution tax. Unlike in the messy real world, this government is quite certain that it can achieve the same price and quantity either way. It wants to choose the method that will pull in more government tax revenue. Is selling allowances better for revenues or is setting a pollution tax better, or will both raise exactly the same amount of revenue? (*Hint:* Recall that tax revenue is a rectangle. Compare the size of the tax rectangle in Figure 10.5 with the most someone will pay for the right to pollute at the efficient level.)

3. Palm Springs, California, was once the playground of the rich and famous—for example, the town has a Frank Sinatra Drive, a Bob Hope Drive, and a Bing Crosby Drive. The city once had a law against building any structure that could cast a shadow on anyone else's property between 9 AM and 3 PM (*Source:* Armen Alchian and William Allen. 1964. *University Economics*, Belmont, CA: Wadsworth). What are some alternatives to this command and control solution? Are they any better than this approach?

4. At indoor shopping malls, who makes sure that no business plays music too loud, no store is closed too often, and that the common areas aren't polluted with garbage? What incentive does this party have to prevent these externalities? Does your answer help explain why parents are quite happy to let their preteen and teen children stroll the malls, as in the Kevin Smith movie *Mallrats*?

11

Costs and Profit Maximization Under Competition

Drive through the Texas countryside and standing alone in a field of wheat, you will often see a nodding donkey. In Texas, a nodding donkey isn't an animal but an oil pump. Most oil comes from giant oil fields, but in the United States there are over 400,000 "stripper oil wells," oil wells that produce 10 barrels or less per day. That's not much per well, but it adds up to nearly a million barrels of oil a day or about 19% of all U.S. production.[1]

Imagine that you are the owner of a stripper oil well and that you want to maximize your profit. Three questions present themselves:

> What price to set?

> What quantity to produce?

> When to enter and exit the industry?

These three questions are basic to any firm. In this chapter, we will be looking at how to answer these questions in a competitive industry. In later chapters, we will look at these questions for a monopolist.

What Price to Set?

The first question of the three we set out above—what price should a firm set?—is the easiest to answer because under some conditions, the firm doesn't set prices; it simply accepts the price that is given by the market. So, let's start with the pricing decision.

What Price to Set?   If the price of oil is $50 per barrel, will you be able to sell your oil for $100 a barrel? Of course not. Oil is pretty much the same

A Nodding Donkey

CORBIS

193

FIGURE 11.1

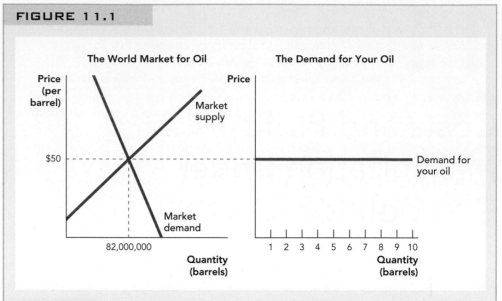

Market Demand and Firm Demand The price of oil is determined in the world market for oil. You cannot sell oil at a price above the market price. At the market price, you can sell as many barrels as you want.

wherever it is found in the world (this is not quite true but it's close enough for our purposes), so even your mother probably won't pay much extra just because it's *your* oil. Thus, you can't charge appreciably more than $50 a barrel. What about charging a lower price? You could charge less but why would you? The world market for oil is so large that you can easily sell all that you can produce at the market price. Thus, your pricing decision is easy; you can't sell *any* oil at a price above the market price and you can sell *all* your oil at the market price. Thus to maximize profit, you sell at the market price.

To better understand this result, let's recall an insight about the elasticity of demand from Chapter 5: The more and the better the substitutes, the more elastic the demand. With more than 400,000 oil wells in the United States alone, the substitutes for oil from your well are so plentiful that a useful approximation is to think of the demand for your oil as perfectly elastic (flat) at the world price. In Figure 11.1, we compare the world market for oil on the left with the demand for *your* oil on the right.

The price of oil is determined in the world market, where approximately 82 million barrels are bought and sold every day. Your stripper well, however, can at best produce a tiny fraction of world demand, perhaps 10 barrels of oil per day. As a result, the world price of oil won't change by a noticeable amount whether you produce 2, 7, or 10 barrels of oil a day.* This is why in the right panel of Figure 11.1, we draw the demand curve for your oil as flat at the market price—whether you choose to sell 2, 7, or 10 barrels, the price is the same: $50 per barrel.

---

*How much is not a noticeable amount? Recall from Chapter 5 that the elasticity of demand is $E_D = \dfrac{\%\Delta Q}{\%\Delta P}$ or rearranging $\%\Delta P = \dfrac{\%\Delta Q}{E_D}$. Suppose that the elasticity of demand for oil is 0.5. This means that a 10% increase in the quantity of oil will reduce price by $20\% = \dfrac{10\%}{0.5}$. An increase in the supply of oil of 10 barrels a day is a percentage increase of $\dfrac{10}{82,000,000} \times 100 = 0.0012195122\%$, so price falls by $\dfrac{0.000012195122}{0.5} = 0.0000243902439\%$. At a price of $50 per barrel, this means that an increase in 10 barrels of oil would reduce price to 49.9999987, that is, it would not be noticeable.

Your job as an entrepreneur is greatly simplified if you don't have to decide on the price, and so is our job as economists trying to understand firm behavior. Thus, in this chapter, we are going to simplify by assuming that the demand for a firm's product is perfectly elastic at the market price.

A stripper well doesn't have much influence on the price of oil because there's nothing special about oil from a particular producer, and there are many buyers and sellers of oil, each small relative to the total market. Generalizing, a perfectly elastic demand curve for firm output is a reasonable approximation when the product being sold is similar across different firms and there are many buyers and sellers, each small relative to the total market. The markets for gold, wheat, paper, steel, lumber, cotton, sugar, vinyl, milk, trucking, glass, Internet domain name registration, and many other goods and services satisfy these conditions.

In addition, don't forget another lesson from Chapter 5: Demand curves are more elastic in the long run. We define the **long run** as the time after all exit and entry has occurred, and the **short run** as the period before exit and entry can occur. Imagine that you are the owner of the only grocery store in a small town. Can you raise prices to exorbitant levels, reasoning that everyone needs food and you are the only seller? In the short run, you probably could. But if you raise prices too high, other sellers will set up shop and your business will be wiped out. Thus, even when there aren't many sellers, there are sometimes many *potential sellers* so a perfectly elastic demand curve can be a reasonable assumption even in a market with a few firms, at least in the long run.

> The **long run** is the time after all exit or entry has occurred.

> The **short run** is the period before exit or entry can occur.

Summarizing, economists say that an industry is competitive (or sometimes "perfectly competitive") when firms don't have much influence over the price of their product. This is a reasonable assumption under at least the following conditions:

> The product being sold is similar across sellers.

> There are many buyers and sellers, each small relative to the total market.

and/or

> There are many potential sellers.

When *do* firms have a lot of influence on the price of their product? We will be saying more about this in a later chapter on monopoly. Briefly, for purposes of comparison, a firm selling a unique product for which there are neither many other sellers nor potential sellers has considerable freedom to choose its price. An example would be a firm with a patent on a uniquely useful pharmaceutical. Similarly, a firm that controls a large share of the market for a homogeneous product could also have significant control over the price. The Saudis, for example, have significant control over the price of oil because their output is a significant share of the total market output. We will analyze how firms choose price and output under these conditions in Chapters 13 through 16.

A competitive firm will sell its output at the market price, but what quantity will it choose to produce?

What Quantity to Produce?

What quantity of oil should the owner of a stripper well produce if she wants to maximize profit? Profit is total revenue minus total cost, so the owner wants to maximize the difference between total revenue and total costs.

CHECK YOURSELF

> In a competitive market, what happens when a firm prices its product above the market price? Below the market price?

> What kind of demand elasticity curve does the competitive firm face?

> How can a firm that produces oil face a very elastic demand curve when the demand for oil is inelastic?

$$\text{Profit} = \pi = \text{Total Revenue} - \text{Total Cost}$$

Total revenue, *TR*, is price times quantity sold: $TR = P \times Q$

Total cost is the cost of producing a given quantity of output.

An **explicit cost** is a cost that requires a money outlay.

An **implicit cost** is a cost that does not require an outlay of money.

Economic profit is total revenue minus total costs including implicit costs.

Accounting profit is total revenue minus explicit costs.

Total revenue is fairly easy to understand. **Total revenue** is simply price times quantity ($P \times Q$). If the price of oil is $50 per barrel, then total revenues are $50 per day if 1 barrel is produced per day, $100 if 2 barrels are produced, $150 if 3 barrels are produced, and so forth.

Total costs, however, are more tricky. First, we have to remember that total costs include opportunity costs, not just money costs. Second, understanding the profit maximization decision will require us to distinguish among many different costs—not just total costs, but also average costs, marginal costs, fixed costs, and a few others. Keeping all these different costs straight in our minds will take some effort.

Don't Forget: Opportunity Costs!

Total costs include explicit money costs and also implicit opportunity costs, the costs of foregone alternatives. Imagine that Lian runs a flower shop. Each month she spends $10,000 buying flowers from a wholesaler. The cost of flowers is an **explicit cost** of running her shop, like rent and electricity, which she pays out of pocket by writing a check. But these are not her only costs. If Lian weren't selling flowers, let's suppose that she could be working as a patent attorney earning $7,000 a month. Lian is giving up something of value when she works as a florist, namely the opportunity to earn $7,000 a month—that's also a cost of running a flower shop, even though she is not writing anybody a check. It is an **implicit cost**. When deciding whether she would rather be a florist or a patent attorney, for example, Lian needs to take into account all of her costs, including opportunity costs.

Here is another example. Imagine that Alex and Tyler each decide to drill an oil well in their backyard, which costs $200,000. Alex borrows the $200,000 from a bank at a 5% annual rate of interest so Alex must pay the bank $10,000 per year ($10,000 = 0.05 \times $200,000). Tyler pays the $200,000 out of a small inheritance he received from a rich uncle. Each well produces $15,000 worth of oil annually. Which well is more profitable?

At the end of every year, Alex pockets $5,000 ($15,000 in revenue minus $10,000 in interest cost), while Tyler pockets $15,000. It's tempting to conclude that Tyler's well is more profitable, but that would be a mistake. Tyler could have left his $200,000 in the bank, and at a 5% rate of interest, he would have earned $10,000 a year in income. Tyler's opportunity cost is the $10,000 in income he gave up when he invested his money in drilling the oil well. Thus, once we take into account all costs, including opportunity costs, Alex and Tyler's wells are equally profitable.

The economic definition of profit differs from the accounting definition of profit because accountants typically don't take into account all opportunity costs. As a result, **economic profits** are typically less than **accounting profits**. Why is the distinction between accounting and economic profit important? Because firms want to maximize economic profit, not accounting profit.

Let's look again at Alex and Tyler and their oil wells. Suppose that the price of oil fell, so that instead of earning revenues of $15,000, each oil well earned revenues of just $6,000. In Alex's case, he has to pay the bank $10,000 in interest annually so it's obvious that Alex is losing $4,000 a year. In reality, we know that from an economic point of view, Tyler is in exactly the same situation—his oil well is also economically unprofitable. If Tyler just looks at his accounting profits, however, he will see a profit of $6,000, which may cause him to be complacent and perhaps even to invest more in the oil industry!

In fact, the situation that we have just described is not uncommon. The steel producer Bethlehem Steel, for example, had positive accounting profits for a long time even though it suffered economic losses. Bethlehem Steel was once the second largest producer of steel in the United States and it had a lot of built-up capital (factories, buildings, and other assets) as well as substantial revenues. Bethlehem Steel's capital was like the inheritance that Tyler received from a rich uncle. Bethlehem, however, was not able to use that capital efficiently. As a result, Bethlehem was destroying value every year even as it made a (small) accounting profit.

Calculating economic profit is important for entrepreneurs who must always think about the future. Is this the best use of our firm's assets? What am I giving up by following this strategy? Could these assets be used to make more profit if I used them in another way? Economic profit is also what stock market investors want to keep an eye on. Careful stock market investors, for example, had calculated that Bethlehem Steel was not making an economic profit and, as a result, they had sold their shares long before Bethlehem went bankrupt in 2001.

Maximizing Profit

Okay, from here on, we will take it for granted that our measure of total costs includes opportunity costs. Let's now return to a typical stripper oil supplier. The table in Figure 11.2 on the next page shows total revenues and total costs as barrels of oil produced increase from 0 to 10 barrels.

Total cost is simply the cost of producing a given quantity of output. Let's break total cost into two components. To produce oil, the firm must drill the well and then it must pump the oil out of the ground and deliver it to customers. Let's assume that the firm borrows the money that it needs to drill the well and, as a result, it must pay interest of $30 per day on its loan (we use interest costs per day to make a comparison with barrels of oil produced per day more convenient). Notice that the firm must pay $30 per day even if it pumps no oil; hence, the entry in the table for Total Cost for 0 barrels of oil is $30. In fact, the firm must pay $30 per day for its loan however many barrels of oil it produces. Thus, we say that the firm has $30 per day of **fixed costs**, costs that do not vary with output.

Fixed costs are costs that do not vary with output.

The firm must pay additional costs when it runs the oil pump. To pump the oil, the firm must pay for electricity, maintenance, costs for the barrels to store the oil, trucking costs to deliver the oil, and so forth. These costs are called **variable costs**, since they vary with output. Total costs are therefore equal to fixed costs plus variable costs.

Variable costs are costs that do vary with output.

$$\text{Total Cost } (TC) = \text{Fixed Costs } (FC) + \text{Variable Costs } (VC)$$

Profit is the difference between total revenue and total cost, and it is shown in the fourth column. Thus, to find the maximum profit, one method is to look for the quantity that maximizes $TR - TC$. Using the table in Figure 11.2, we can see that the profit maximizing quantity is 8 barrels of oil per day.

It turns out to be useful, especially in order to create graphs, to use a second method to find the quantity that maximizes profit. Instead of looking at

FIGURE 11.2

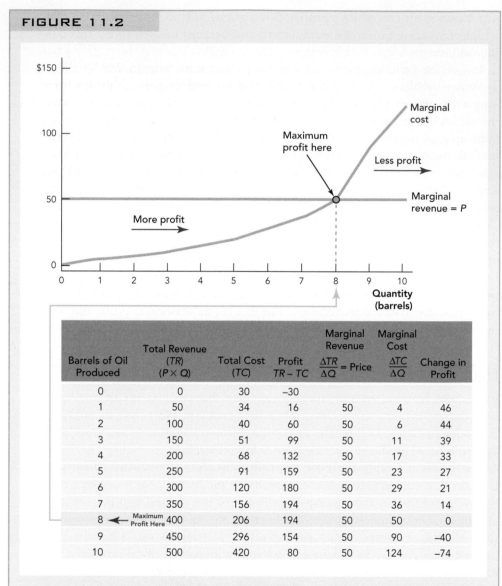

Barrels of Oil Produced	Total Revenue (TR) (P × Q)	Total Cost (TC)	Profit TR − TC	Marginal Revenue $\frac{\Delta TR}{\Delta Q}$ = Price	Marginal Cost $\frac{\Delta TC}{\Delta Q}$	Change in Profit
0	0	30	−30			
1	50	34	16	50	4	46
2	100	40	60	50	6	44
3	150	51	99	50	11	39
4	200	68	132	50	17	33
5	250	91	159	50	23	27
6	300	120	180	50	29	21
7	350	156	194	50	36	14
8 ← Maximum Profit Here	400	206	194	50	50	0
9	450	296	154	50	90	−40
10	500	420	80	50	124	−74

Profit Is Maximized by Producing until MR = MC To maximize profit, a firm compares the revenue from selling an additional unit, marginal revenue (for a firm in a competitive industry, this is equal to the price) to the costs of selling an additional unit, marginal cost. Profit increases from an additional sale whenever *MR* > *MC* so profit is maximized by producing up until the point where *MR* = *MC*.

Marginal revenue, MR, is the change in total revenue from selling an additional unit.

$$MR = \frac{\Delta TR}{\Delta Q}$$

For a firm in a competitive industry *MR*=Price.

Marginal cost, MC, is the change in total cost from producing an additional unit.

total revenue and total cost, we compare the increase in revenue from selling an additional barrel of oil, called **marginal revenue**, to the increase in cost from selling an additional barrel, called **marginal cost**. To maximize profit, we will show that the owner wants to keep producing oil so long as Marginal Revenue > Marginal Cost, which means that the last drop of oil the firm produces should be the one where Marginal Revenue = Marginal Cost. Let's walk through this argument.

Marginal revenue is the change in total revenue from selling an additional barrel of oil. Suppose that the price of a barrel of oil is $50. Then what is marginal revenue? If the owner sells an additional barrel of oil, his or her revenues increase by $50, so marginal revenue is just equal to $50, the price. That was easy because we assumed that the price of oil doesn't change as the firm sells more barrels; in other words, we used our assumption that a stripper oil well is in a competitive industry and thus faces a perfectly elastic demand curve at the market price. Thus, we have a simple rule: For a firm in a competitive industry, $MR = P$.

Marginal cost is the change in total cost from producing an additional barrel of oil. The owner of a small oil well has some choice about whether to produce a little bit more or a little bit less. The owner, for example, can increase the pump rate and produce more oil per day but only by spending more on electricity, maintenance, and the more frequent pickup and shipping of the oil. The extra costs that come with a little additional production are called marginal costs. Notice, for example, that if the well produces 2 barrels of oil per day, then Total Cost = \$40, and if the well produces 3 barrels per day, then Total Cost = \$51. Thus, producing the third barrel of oil increases costs by \$11, that is, the marginal cost of the third barrel of oil is \$11.

At some point, marginal costs must increase because you can only get so much blood out of a stone and only so much oil out of rock. The well, for example, cannot be pumped more than 24 hours a day. As the well reaches capacity, the marginal cost of an additional barrel approaches infinity!

We can now use the data in Figure 11.2 to find the profit-maximizing quantity using our second method. The owner should keep producing additional barrels so long as the revenue from producing an additional barrel exceeds the cost of producing an additional barrel. The first barrel of oil that the firm produces adds \$50 to revenue and \$4 to costs, so $MR > MC$, and by producing that barrel, the firm can add \$46 to profit. On the second barrel, the marginal revenue is \$50 and the marginal cost is \$6, so producing that barrel adds \$44 to profit. Following through on this logic, we can see that each additional barrel of oil adds to profit up until the eighth barrel. If the firm produces the ninth barrel of oil, however, it adds \$50 to revenue but \$90 to costs, so the firm will not want to produce the ninth barrel. Thus, the profit-maximizing quantity is 8 barrels of oil. Notice that the profit-maximizing quantity is where $MR = MC$ and since $MR = P$ for a competitive firm, we can also say that the profit-maximizing quantity for a competitive firm is where $P = MC$.

To maximize profit, a firm in a competitive industry increases output until $P = MC$.

Students are often confused by why economists say that the profit-maximizing output is 8 barrels instead of 7 barrels. Why produce the eighth barrel where $P = MC$ and therefore no addition to profit? Consider the graph above the table. Notice that wherever $P > MC$, producing additional barrels means more profit, and wherever $MC > P$, producing fewer barrels means more profit. Now think about producing oil not in barrels but in drops. Then the graph says that at 7.9999 barrels, you still want to add a drop or two, but at 8.0001 barrels, you want to take away a drop or two. The reason we say profit is maximized where $P = MC$ is that $P = MC$ is the "just right" point between too little and too much.

As the price changes, so does the profit-maximizing quantity. When the price is \$50, the profit-maximizing quantity is 8. If the price of oil rises to \$100 per barrel, then the firm will expand production. But by how much? The firm will expand until it is once again maximizing profit when $P = MC$. In Figure 11.3 on the next page, we show how the firm expands production along its MC curve as the price of oil increases from \$50 to \$100 per barrel.

We have now answered our second question: To maximize profit, the firm should produce the quantity such that $MR = MC$, which for a firm in a competitive industry means produce up until $P = MC$.

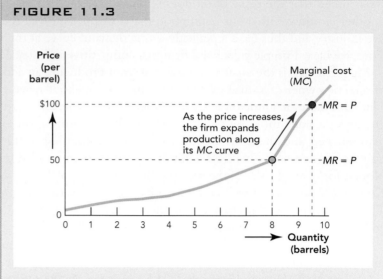

FIGURE 11.3

As the Price Changes So Does the Profit-Maximizing Quantity
The profit-maximizing quantity is found where $P = MC$. At a price of $50, the profit-maximizing quantity is 8. As the price rises to $100, the firm expands. At $100, the profit-maximizing quantity is approximately 9.4 barrels per day.

CHECK YOURSELF

> Let's check our $MR = MC$ rule for maximizing profit. Look at the last column in Figure 11.2, which shows the change in profit. When the firm produces 4 barrels rather than 3, how much additional profit is made? How about when it goes from 7 barrels to 8 barrels? From 8 barrels to 9 barrels? Now look at the MR and MC columns and find the profit-maximizing quantity. How does it compare with what you observe in the last column of the table?

The **average cost** of production is the cost per barrel, that is, the total cost of producing Q barrels divided by Q:
$$AC = \frac{TC}{Q}.$$

Profits and the Average Cost Curve

We have shown that the firm maximizes profits by producing the quantity such that $P = MC$, but a firm can maximize profits and still have low profits or even losses. Just because the firm is doing the best it can doesn't mean that it is doing very well. We would like, therefore, to be able to show profits in a diagram. To do this, we need to introduce the average cost curve.

The **average cost** of production is simply the cost per barrel, that is, the average cost of producing Q barrels of oil is the total cost of producing Q barrels divided by Q: $AC = \frac{TC}{Q}$. For example, in Figure 11.4, we can read from the table that the total cost of producing 6 barrels of oil per day is $120; thus, the cost per barrel is $120/6 = $20. Figure 11.4 computes average cost (in the last column) and graphs the average cost curve alongside the price and marginal cost curves.

With a little bit of work, we can now show profit on our graph. Recall that

$$\text{Profit} = \text{Total Revenue} - \text{Total Cost} = TR - TC$$

so we can also write

$$\text{Profit} = \left(\frac{TR}{Q} - \frac{TC}{Q}\right) \times Q$$

or

$$\text{Profit} = (P - AC) \times Q$$

(To get to the last statement, notice that we used the two definitions, $TR = P \times Q$ and $AC = \frac{TC}{Q}$.)

FIGURE 11.4

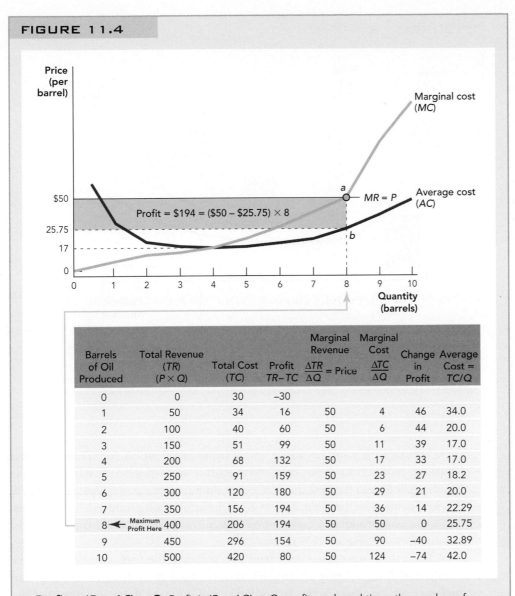

Barrels of Oil Produced	Total Revenue (TR) ($P \times Q$)	Total Cost (TC)	Profit TR–TC	Marginal Revenue $\frac{\Delta TR}{\Delta Q}$ = Price	Marginal Cost $\frac{\Delta TC}{\Delta Q}$	Change in Profit	Average Cost = TC/Q
0	0	30	−30				
1	50	34	16	50	4	46	34.0
2	100	40	60	50	6	44	20.0
3	150	51	99	50	11	39	17.0
4	200	68	132	50	17	33	17.0
5	250	91	159	50	23	27	18.2
6	300	120	180	50	29	21	20.0
7	350	156	194	50	36	14	22.29
8 ← Maximum Profit Here	400	206	194	50	50	0	25.75
9	450	296	154	50	90	−40	32.89
10	500	420	80	50	124	−74	42.0

Profit = (P − AC) × Q Profit is $(P - AC) \times Q$, profit per barrel times the number of barrels produced. When the price is $50 and 8 barrels of oil are produced, profit is shown on the graph as the shaded area. Notice that the price is the height of point *a*, AC is the height of point *b*, so that the area $(a - b) \times Q$ is equal to profit or $194 = (\$50 - \$25.75) \times 8$.

The last statement says that profit is equal to the average profit per barrel $(P - AC)$ times the number of barrels sold Q.

We already know that 8 barrels is the profit-maximizing quantity when the price is $50, but now we can show profit on our graph. To illustrate profit, begin at a quantity of 8 barrels and move up to find the price of $50 at point *a*. Now reading down from point *a*, find the average cost from the *AC* curve at point *b*, which is $25.75. (You can also check this by examining the table below the diagram for the *AC* of producing 8 barrels.) The average profit per barrel, $P - AC$, is ($50 − $25.75) or $24.25 per barrel. Finally, since production is 8 barrels, the total profit is $(P - AC) \times Q$ or $24.25 × 8 = $194 per day, the shaded area in the diagram.

FIGURE 11.5

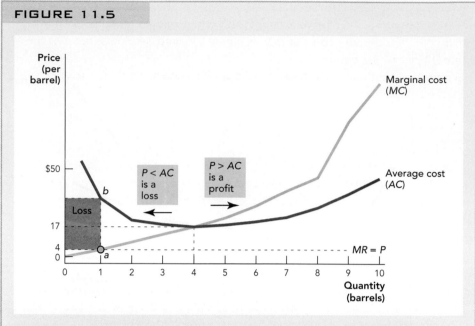

Maximum Profit Can Be a Loss At a price of $4, the firm maximizes profit by choosing, as always, the quantity such that P = MC. At a price of $4, the profit maximizing output is 1 barrel but even though the firm is maximizing profit, the maximum profit is a loss since P < AC. Notice that at any price below $17 (where P < AC), the firm is making a loss.

As we said earlier, just because a firm is maximizing profits doesn't mean that it is making profits. If the price of oil were to drop to $4 per barrel, what happens? Price equals $4 and the best the firm could do is produce at P = MC. Looking at the MC column in the table, MC = $4 at 1 barrel of oil produced. So at a price of $4, the firm produces 1 barrel of oil. But at this price, the firm is taking a loss because P < AC. Figure 11.5 illustrates.

What is the lowest price per barrel that will give the firm a profit (not make a loss)? The firm will stop making a loss only when price is no longer less than average cost. Looking at the last column in Figure 11.4, we can see that the firm will be making a loss if the price of oil is anywhere below $17. Recall that profit is $(P - AC) \times Q$, thus—assuming that the firm is profit-maximizing so P = MC at all times—when P > AC, the firm is making a profit, and when P < AC, the firm is making a loss. The minimum point of the AC curve is at $17, so at any price below $17 the firm must be taking a loss.

One more technical point is worth noting. Take a look again at Figure 11.5 and notice that the marginal cost curve meets the average cost curve at the minimum of the average cost curve. This is not an accident but a mathematical necessity. We won't delve into this in detail, but suppose that your average grade in a class is 75% and that on the next test, the marginal test, you earn a grade below your average, 60%. What happens to your average grade? It falls. So whenever your marginal grade is below your average grade, your average falls. Now suppose that your average grade is 75% and on the next test, the marginal test, you earn a grade above your average, 80%. What happens to your average? It rises. So whenever your marginal grade is above your average grade, your average rises. What is true for your average and marginal grade is equally true for average and marginal cost. So think about what must happen around the point where the *MC* and *AC* curves meet. When marginal cost is just below average cost, the average cost curve is falling, and when marginal cost is just above average cost, the average cost curve is rising, so *AC* and *MC* must meet at the minimum of the *AC* curve.

We are now ready to turn to our third question, when should the firm enter or exit the industry?

Entry, Exit, and Shutdown Decisions

We now know that a firm will be profitable when $P > AC$ and unprofitable when $P < AC$. Firms seek profits so the basic idea is very simple. In the long run, firms will enter profitable industries ($P > AC$) and exit unprofitable industries ($P < AC$). Notice that at the intermediate point, when $P = AC$, profits are zero and there is neither entry nor exit.

In Figure 11.5, we can see that at a price of $4, the firm is taking losses. Thus, in the long run, this firm will exit the industry. In fact, at any price below $17, the firm will be making a loss at any output level. Thus at any price below $17, the firm will exit the industry in the long run. At any price above $17, firms will be making profits and other firms will enter the industry.

Only when $P = AC$, in this case when $P = \$17$, will firms be making zero profits, and there will be no incentive to either enter or exit the industry. Students often wonder why firms would remain in an industry when profits are zero. The problem is the language of economics. By **zero profits**, economists mean what everyone else means by *normal profits*. Remember that average cost includes wages and payments to capital, so even when the firm earns "zero profits," labor and capital are being paid enough to keep them in the industry. Thus, when we say that a firm is earning zero profits, we mean that the price of output is just enough to pay labor and capital their ordinary opportunity costs.

Zero profits, or normal profits, occur when $P = AC$. At this price the firm is covering all of its costs, including enough to pay labor and capital their ordinary opportunity costs.

The Short-Run Shutdown Decision

In the long run, a firm will exit an industry if price falls below average cost, but exit typically takes some time. To exit the stripper well industry, for example, the well must be either sold to another investor or dismantled, closed, and sealed.

Even when exit takes some time, a firm can typically shut down more quickly, that is, produce zero output. A stripper well can stop pumping oil, for example, before the well is fully sealed and the capital scrapped.

When should a firm shut down? Surprisingly, a firm may not want to shut down even when $P < AC$. The reason is that shutdown does not immediately eliminate all costs. Consider, for example, a hotel in Cape Cod. During the summer months, there are plenty of tourists and the hotel is profitable. But during the winter months, there are fewer tourists and revenues don't cover all of the hotel's costs. Should the hotel shut down in the winter? Not necessarily. If the hotel shuts down in the winter, it can reduce its variable costs—the hotel won't have to pay its bellmen and cleaning staff, for example. But the hotel still must pay its fixed costs, the costs that do not vary with output, such as rent on the land and the interest on the loan that the firm took out to construct the hotel. If revenues in the winter are large enough to cover the firm's variable costs—the bellmen and the cleaning staff—and *some* of the firm's fixed costs, the firm will make a smaller loss staying open than closing, so even though the hotel is unprofitable in the winter, it's in the firm's interest not to shut down

TABLE 11.1 A Firm Should Stay Open in the Short Run if It Can Cover Its Variable Costs

Decision	Fixed Costs	Variable Costs	Winter Revenues	Profits
Shut down	100	0	0	−100
Stay open	100	50	75	−75

the hotel. Table 11.1 provides a simple illustration. Notice that if the hotel shuts down in the winter, its variable costs are zero but so are its revenues—if the hotel stays open, its variable costs increase to 50, but revenues increase to 75, so by staying open, the firm covers its variable costs and some of its fixed costs, and this reduces the hotel's winter losses.

Entry and Exit with Uncertainty and Sunk Costs

The entry and exit rules that we have given are useful for understanding the principles of economics, but there are significant complications that we have ignored that firms in the real world must take into account. We said above that if $P < AC$, the firm will want to exit in the long run, and if $P > AC$, the firm will want to enter. To be more precise, however, a firm should exit when $P < AC$ only if it expects P to remain below AC for a substantial period of time, and it should enter only if $P > AC$ and it expects P to stay above AC for a substantial period.

Let's return to our oil firm to illustrate. We said above that if the price of oil rises to just above $17, the firm will enter the industry (since at this point, $P > AC$) but entering the industry means drilling an oil well. The costs of drilling an oil well are **sunk costs** (literally!), which means that once paid, these costs can never be recovered. If the price of oil rises to, say, $18 but then quickly falls back below $17, the oil firm is unlikely to make enough money to cover its sunk costs. Thus, for entry to be profitable, the price must rise above $17 and the firm must *expect* the price to stay above $17 for long enough for the firm to cover the costs of entry, that is, drilling the well.

For exactly the same reasons, it doesn't always make sense to exit an industry immediately when $P < AC$ or even when $TR < $ Variable Costs.

Imagine, for example, that to exit, you have to pay fired workers a severance payment, and suppose that when you hire new workers, you have to spend resources training them. If you hold onto your workers during bad times, you can avoid these hiring and firing costs. So, *if* you expect your firm to be profitable in the future, it can sometimes make sense to keep workers on, even when it is not profitable to do so today.

Let's generalize the above ideas. If a firm could instantly and without cost enter and exit an industry then our simple rule—enter when $P > AC$ and exit when $P < AC$—would be exactly correct. But when it's costly to enter and exit and there is uncertainty about future prices, firms must estimate the effect of their decisions on their *lifetime expected profit*. That's not an easy calculation. It can cost Exxon $100 million to drill an oil well off the Gulf of Mexico. Whether such an oil well will be profitable depends on the price of oil over perhaps the next 20 years. Since the price of oil is volatile, the price may have to rise to a very high level before Exxon makes the leap and sinks its money into an expensive well.

Notice that if a firm is highly uncertain about future prices, it will often pay to adopt a wait-and-see attitude. A short delay has small costs but big benefits if a short delay will reveal more information about future prices. The microeconomics of entry and exit can help to explain macroeconomic events, such as why uncertainty about the national economy can cause many firms to reduce investment at the same time.

A **sunk cost** is a cost that once incurred can never be recovered.

In short, whenever there is uncertainty and sunk costs to entering or exiting an industry, the best entry or exit decision requires a forecast of future prices and the correct decision is not always obvious from simply looking at current revenues and costs.

Entry, Exit, and Industry Supply Curves

Now that we have examined the *MC* curves for competitive firms and their entry and exit decisions, we can put these all together to derive the industry supply curve, which you have been working with since Chapter 3. Supply curves can slope upward, be flat, or in rare circumstance even slope downward. We will show that the slope of the supply curve can be explained by how costs change as industry output increases or decreases.

In an **increasing cost industry**, costs increase with greater industry output and this generates an upward-sloping supply curve. In a **constant cost industry**, costs do not change with changes in industry output and this generates a flat supply curve. In a **decreasing cost industry**, costs decrease with greater industry output and this generates a downward-sloping supply curve. Decreasing cost industries are rare.

Let's start with constant cost industries, which are conceptually the simplest.

Constant Cost Industries

Consider the industry of domain name registrars. Web pages on the Internet have a conventional name, called a domain name, such as eBay.com, MarginalRevolution.com, or the Web page for the National Bureau of Economic Research which has the domain name NBER.org. But the conventional names are just masks for more difficult-to-remember numbers called IP (Internet Protocol) addresses. When you type www.NBER.org into a browser, the browser sends a message to the Domain Name System (DNS), which looks up and returns the corresponding IP address, in this case http://66.251.72.129/. The IP address tells your browser where to find the information that is posted by the NBER. So, in order to work, every domain name must be registered with the DNS and assigned an IP address. Domain name registrars are firms that manage and register domain names.

The domain name registration industry has two important characteristics. First, domain name registration satisfies all of the conditions for a competitive industry.

> The product being sold is similar across sellers.

> There are many buyers and sellers, each small relative to the total market.

> There are many potential sellers.

As far as the user is concerned, there is little difference between registering with GoDaddy.com or GetRealNames.com so the product is similar across sellers. There are many buyers and many sellers. There are hundreds of registrars in the United States alone. Indeed, GoDaddy.com is based in the United States and GetRealNames.com is based in India; thus, there is *world* free trade in domain name registration. Furthermore, not only are there many competitors in the industry, but just about anyone in the world can become an accredited registrar with an investment of a few thousand dollars, so there are many potential competitors.

Increasing cost industry is an industry in which industry costs increase with greater output; shown with an upward sloped supply curve.

Constant cost industry is an industry in which industry costs do not change with greater output; shown with a flat supply curve.

Decreasing cost industry is an industry in which industry costs decrease with an increase in output; shown with a downward sloped supply curve.

The second important characteristic of the domain name industry is that the major input for domain name registration is a bank of computers, but all the computers of all the domain name registrars in all the world don't add up to much compared with the world supply of computers. The domain name industry, therefore, can expand without pushing up the prices of its major inputs and thus without raising its own costs. An industry that can expand or contract without changing the prices of its inputs is called a constant cost industry.

These two characteristics, free entry and the fact that the industry demands only a small share of its major inputs, produce the following properties: (1) The price for domain name registration is quickly driven down to the average cost of managing and assigning a domain name, so profits are quickly driven to normal levels; and (2) because average costs don't change much when the industry expands or contracts, the price of domain name registration doesn't change much when the industry expands or contracts so the long-run supply curve is very elastic (flat).

Let's examine these characteristics in turn. One of the largest registrars is GoDaddy.com, which charges $6.99 to register a domain name for one year. What would happen if it raised its price to $14.95 a year? GoDaddy would quickly lose a significant fraction of its business. New customers would choose other firms, and since domains must be renewed every few years, old customers would soon also switch. As a result of this competition, GoDaddy and every other firm in the industry price their services at near average cost and earn a zero or normal profit.

Now consider what happens when the demand for domain names increases. In 2005, there were more than 60 million domain names. Just one year later, there were more than 100 million domain names. If the demand for oil nearly doubled, the price of oil would rise dramatically, but despite nearly doubling in size, the price of registering a domain name has not increased. When an increase in demand hits a constant cost industry, the price rises in the short run as each firm moves up its MC curve. But the expansion of old firms and the entry of new firms quickly push the price back down to average cost.

Figure 11.6 illustrates how a constant cost industry responds to an increase in demand. The figure looks imposing, but if we consider it in steps, the logic of the story will be clear. In the top panel, we have the initial equilibrium. On the left-hand side of the panel, we illustrate the industry. The market price is P_{lr} ($6.99 in the case of domain name registration), the market quantity is Q_1, and the quantity demanded is exactly equal to the quantity supplied so the industry is in equilibrium. On the right-hand side of the panel, we have a typical firm in the industry. The firm is profit-maximizing because $P = MC$ and it is making a zero or normal profit because $P = AC$. Note that the industry output is Q_1 but the firm output is q_1, which indicates that each firm in the industry produces only a small share of total industry output.

In the middle panel on the left, we illustrate an increase in demand from Old Demand to New Demand. In the short run, the increase in demand increases price to P_{sr}, $7.99, where New Demand and Short Run Supply meet. The industry quantity increases to Q_{sr}. Where does the increase in quantity come from? It comes from many firms in the industry, each of which produces a little bit more by increasing production along its MC curve. In the middle panel on the right, we show that the typical firm in the industry expands to q_{sr}, and since the price is above average cost, the firm earns profits as illustrated by the shaded area $(P - AC) \times q_{sr}$.

FIGURE 11.6

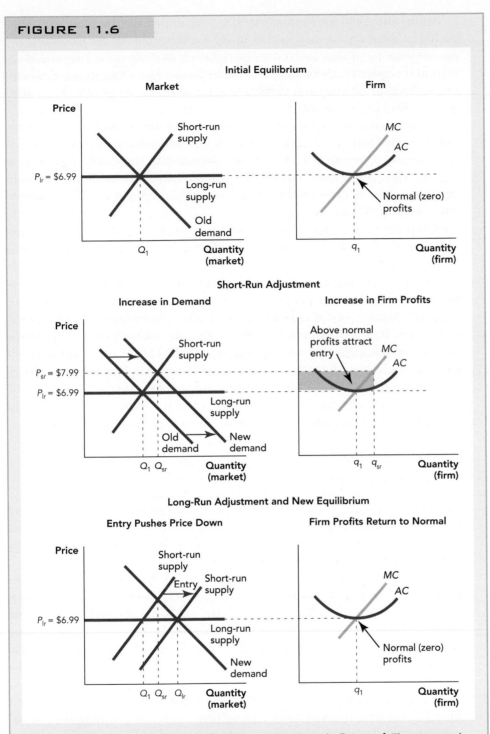

How a Constant Cost Industry Adjusts to an Increase in Demand The top panel shows the initial industry and firm equilibrium. The market price for domain name registration is $6.99 and each firm is making a normal profit. In the middle panel, the demand for registration increases, which pushes up the market price to $7.99. In the short run, each firm in the industry expands along its *MC* curve and thus market quantity increases to Q_{sr}. Each firm earns above-normal profits. In the bottom panel, the above-normal profits attract entry. As more firms enter the industry, the short-run supply curve shifts to the right and as it does price falls. Firms continue to enter and the price continues to fall until price returns to $6.99. At that price, firms are once again earning normal (zero) profits since $P = AC$.

Before turning to the bottom panel, let's remember that the short run is the period before entry (or exit) occurs. In the middle panel, we are illustrating the *first* response to an increase in demand, which is that the price rises and every firm in the industry responds by increasing production along its marginal cost curve. (Indeed, the short-run supply curve is simply the sum of the *MC* curves for each firm in the industry.)

The increase in price generates above-normal profits for each firm in the industry. Notice that above-normal profits attract new investment and entry. Entry is the *second* response to the increase in demand. In some industries, like the domain name registration industry, entry might take a matter of a few months or even as little as a few weeks, while in other industries it could take several years before significant entry occurs.

When entry does occur, the short-run supply curve shifts to the right, and as it does, the price falls and profits are reduced. Entry doesn't stop until profits return to normal levels so entry continues until price is pushed down to *AC*. In the long run, after all entry and exit have occurred, profits have returned to normal.

Since the prices of the industry inputs don't change when the industry expands, the *AC* curve of each firm in the industry doesn't change, so in the new industry, equilibrium price is again equal to P_{lr}, $6.99. Although the typical firm produces q_1, just as it did before the increase in demand, the industry quantity has increased to Q_{lr} because there are now more firms in the industry.

Thus, the key to a constant cost industry is that it is small relative to its input markets, so when the industry expands, it does not push up the price of its inputs and thus industry costs do not increase.

Increasing Cost Industries

In an increasing cost industry, costs rise as industry output increases. The oil industry is an increasing cost industry because greater quantities of oil can only be produced by using more expensive methods such as drilling deeper, drilling in more inhospitable spots, or extracting the oil from tar sands.

To illustrate, let's focus on just two firms. Firm 1 is the firm that we examined earlier. Its oil is located near the surface, so its average costs are low and it enters the industry when the price of oil rises to just $17. Firm 2's oil, however, is located deeper than Firm 1's, and so Firm 2's fixed costs of drilling are higher and its average cost curve is higher than that of Firm 1. As a result, Firm 2 will not enter the industry until the price of oil reaches $29. We can now build the industry supply curve.

At any price below $17, what is the quantity supplied? Zero. At a price less than $17, the firm is losing money so no firm enters the industry, and the industry supply curve, indicated in the rightmost panel of Figure 11.7 by the red line, shows a quantity supplied of zero. When the price of oil hits $17, Firm 1 enters the industry at its profit-maximizing quantity of 4 barrels of oil and thus industry supply at a price of $17 jumps to 4 barrels. As the price rises, Firm 1 expands along its *MC* curve and so does industry supply. When the price hits $29, Firm 2 enters the industry with its profit-maximizing quantity of 5 barrels of oil. To find the quantity supplied by the industry, we sum the quantity supplied by each firm in the industry. At a price of $29, Firm 1 supplies 6 barrels of oil and Firm 2 supplies 5 barrels of oil, so industry supply is 11 barrels of oil. As the price rises further, both firms now expand along their respective

FIGURE 11.7

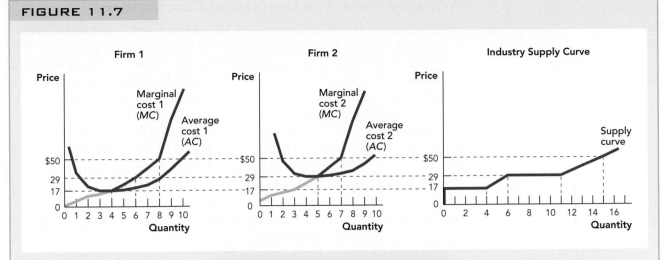

	Firm 1	Firm 2	Industry Output
P<$17	0	0	0
P=$17	4	0	4
P=$29	6	5	11
P=$50	___	___	15

To Find the Quantity Supplied by the Industry, Add the Quantities Supplied by Each Firm in the Industry At any price below $17, profits for both Firm 1 and Firm 2 are negative so industry output is 0. At a price of $17, Firm 1 enters the industry with a profit-maximizing quantity of 4 barrels so industry output jumps to 4 barrels. As price rises further, Firm 1 expands along its *MC* curve. At a price of $29, Firm 2 enters the industry with a profit-maximizing quantity of 5 barrels so total industry output is 11 barrels (6 from Firm 1 and 5 from Firm 2). As price rises further, both firms expand along their marginal cost curve. At any price, industry output is the sum of each firm's output. At a price of $50, what quantity does Firm 1 produce? What quantity does Firm 2 produce? Fill in the table and check that the production from Firm 1 and Firm 2 add up to industry output.

MC curves. Once again, industry supply at any price is found by adding up the quantity supplied by each firm at that price. Thus at a price of $50, Firm 1 produces 8 barrels of oil and Firm 2 produces 7 barrels of oil, so industry supply at a price of $50 is 15 barrels of oil.

Our explanation of the supply curve is simply a more detailed version of the account in Chapter 3. At a low price, the only oil that is profitable to exploit is the oil that can be recovered at low cost from places like Saudi Arabia. As the price of oil rises, it becomes profitable to supply oil from the North Sea, the Athabasca tar sands, and other higher-cost sources. The analysis in Chapter 3 focused on how a higher price encourages entry from higher-cost producers. This chapter adds to the entry story the idea that as the price increases, each firm expands output by moving along its marginal cost curve.

More generally, any industry that buys a large fraction of the output of an increasing cost industry will also be an increasing cost industry. The gasoline industry, for example, is an increasing cost industry because greater demand for gas will push up the price of oil, which in turn raises the price of gas. The electricity industry is an increasing cost industry because greater demand for electricity requires more coal, and coal is an increasing cost industry for the same reasons as oil.

A Special Case: The Decreasing Cost Industry

In a constant cost industry, firm costs are constant as the industry expands, and thus, the long-run supply curve is flat. In an increasing cost industry, firm costs increase as the industry expands, and thus, the supply curve slopes upward. Could firm costs decrease as the industry expands, creating a decreasing cost industry with a downward-sloping supply curve? Yes. To see how, we must ask the question: Why is Dalton, Georgia, the "carpet capital of the world"?

An amazing 72% of the $12 billion worth of carpets produced in the United States every year are produced in Dalton and the surrounding area. Dalton is home to 150 carpet plants and hundreds of machine shops, cotton mills, dye plants, and other related industries. Why Dalton? Dalton is not like Saudi Arabia, as it has no outstanding natural advantages for producing carpets, so why is Dalton the carpet capital of the world? The answer is nothing more than an accident of history that launched a virtuous circle.

The Dalton carpet industry began in 1895 with one teenage girl who crafted an especially beautiful bedspread for her brother's wedding. Wedding guests saw the bedspread and asked her to make more. To meet the demand, she hired workers and trained them in her innovative techniques. As demand grew even further, these workers and others went into business for themselves, creating a bedspread industry. The skills needed to make bedspreads were also useful for making carpets, so carpet firms began to locate in Dalton. With so many carpet firms located in Dalton, it became profitable to open trade schools to teach carpet-making skills. In turn, the trade schools made it even more cost-efficient for carpet firms to move to Dalton. Similarly, machine shops, cotton mills, and dye plants moved to Dalton to be close to their customers, and the ready access to machine shops, cotton mills, and dye plants made it even less costly for carpet firms to make carpets in Dalton. The resulting virtuous circle made Dalton the cheapest place to make carpets in the United States—not because Dalton had natural advantages but because it was cheaper to make carpets in a place where there already were a lot of carpet makers.

Decreasing cost industries are important, but very special because costs cannot decrease forever. Dalton became the cheapest place to produce carpets in the United States many years ago and that is unlikely to change any time soon. But if the demand for carpets were to increase today, the costs of making carpets in Dalton would increase, not fall further. The costs of making carpets in Dalton fell when the local industry expanded from 1 to 50 firms, but they didn't fall by nearly as much when the industry expanded from 50 to 100 firms.

Economists use the idea of a decreasing cost industry to explain the history of industry clusters: not just carpets in Dalton, Georgia, but computer technology in Silicon Valley, movie production in Hollywood, and flower distribution in Aalsmeer, Holland. Once the cluster is established, however, constant or increasing costs are the norm. If the demand for carpet were to increase today, for example, the price of carpets would rise, not fall.

CHECK YOURSELF

> Is the automobile manufacturing industry a constant cost, increasing cost, or decreasing cost industry? Why?

> Where are most U.S. films made? Why do you think the film industry is concentrated in such a small region?

Industry Supply Curves: Summary

In summary, if the industry is small relative to its input markets so the industry can expand without pushing up its costs, the supply curve will be flat; we call this a constant cost industry. In an increasing cost industry, costs increase with

FIGURE 11.8

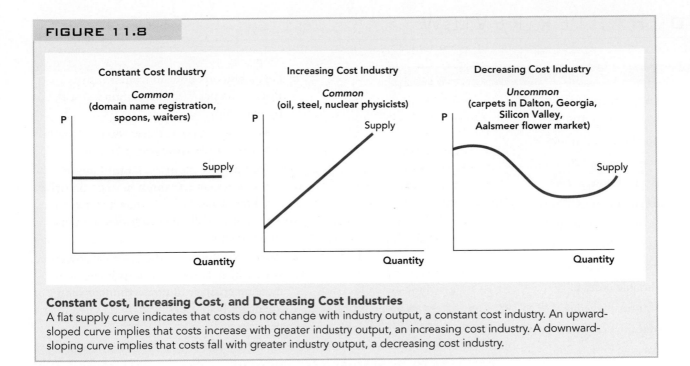

Constant Cost, Increasing Cost, and Decreasing Cost Industries
A flat supply curve indicates that costs do not change with industry output, a constant cost industry. An upward-sloped curve implies that costs increase with greater industry output, an increasing cost industry. A downward-sloping curve implies that costs fall with greater industry output, a decreasing cost industry.

industry output and the supply curve slopes upward. Industry supply curves can even slope downward but this is rare and temporary, although the idea of a decreasing cost industry is important for explaining the existence of industry clusters. Figure 11.8 illustrates the three possibilities.

☐ Takeaway

We have now answered the three questions with which we opened the chapter. What price to set? Answer: A firm in a competitive industry sets price at the market price. What quantity to produce? Answer: To maximize profit, a competitive firm should produce the quantity that makes $P = MC$. When to exit and enter an industry? Answer: In the long run, the firm should enter if $P > AC$ and exit if $P < AC$.

A competitive industry is one where the product being sold is similar across sellers; there are many buyers and sellers, each small relative to the total market; and/or there are many potential sellers.

We have also shown how profit maximization and entry and exit decisions are the foundation of supply curves. In an increasing cost industry, costs rise as more firms enter so supply curves are upward-sloping. In a constant cost industry, costs remain the same as firms enter so the long-run supply curve is flat. And in the rare case of a decreasing cost industry, costs fall as firms enter so supply curves are downward-sloping.

□ CHAPTER REVIEW

KEY CONCEPTS

FACTS AND TOOLS

1. You've been hired as a management consultant to four different companies in competitive industries. They're each trying to figure out if they should produce a little more output or a little bit less in order to maximize their profits. The firms all have typical marginal cost curves: They rise as the firm produces more.

   Your staff did all the hard work for you of figuring out the price of each firm's output and the marginal cost of producing one more unit of output *at their current level of output*. However, they forgot to collect data on how much each firm is actually producing at the moment. Fortunately, that doesn't matter. In your final report, you need to decide which firms should produce more output, which should produce less, and which are producing just the right amount:

   a. WaffleCo, maker of generic-brand frozen waffles. Price = $4 per box, marginal cost = $2 per box.

   b. Rio Blanco, producer of copper. Price = $32 per ounce, marginal cost = $45 per ounce.

   c. GoDaddy.com, domain name registry. Price = $5 per Web site, marginal cost = $2 per Web site.

   d. Luke's Lawn Service. Price: $80 per month, marginal cost = $120 per month.

2. In the competitive electrical motor industry, the workers at Galt Inc. threaten to go on strike. To avoid the strike, Galt Inc. agrees to pay its workers more. At all other factories, the wage remains the same.

   a. What does this do to the marginal cost curve at Galt Inc.? Does it rise, does it fall, or is there no change? Illustrate your answer in the figure below.

   b. What will happen to the number of motors produced by Galt Inc.? Indicate the "before" and "after" levels of output on the *x*-axis in the figure above.

   c. In this competitive market, what will the Galt Inc. labor agreement do to the price of motors?

   d. Surely, more workers will *want* to work at Galt Inc. now that it pays higher wages. Will more workers *actually* work at Galt Inc. after the labor agreement is struck? Why or why not?

3. In Figure 11.6, you saw what happens in the long run when demand rises in a constant-cost industry. Let's see what happens when demand falls in such an industry: For instance, think about the market for gasoline or pizza in a small city after the city's biggest textile mill

shuts down. In the figure below, indicate the price and quantity of output at three points in time:

I. In the long run, before demand falls

II. In the short run, after demand falls

III. In the long run, after demand falls

Also, answer the following questions about the market's response to this fall in demand.

a. When will the marginal cost of production be lowest: At stage I, II, or III?

b. When firms cut prices, they often do so in dramatic ways. During which stage will the local pizza shops offer "Buy one, get one free" offers? During which stage will the local gas station be more likely to offer "Free car wash with fill-up?"

c. When is $P > AC$? $P < AC$? $P = AC$?

d. Restating the previous question: When are profits positive? Negative? Zero?

e. Roughly speaking, will the long-run response mostly involve firms leaving the industry, or will it mostly involve individual firms shrinking? The "firm" column of Figure 11.6 should help you with the answer.

4. We mentioned that carpet manufacturing looks like a decreasing cost industry. In American homes, carpets are much less popular than they were in the 1960s and 1970s, when "wall-to-wall carpeting" was fashionable in homes. Suppose that carpeting became even less popular than it is today: What would this fall in demand probably do to the price of carpet in the long run?

5. Replacement parts for classic cars are expensive, even though these parts aren't any more complicated than parts for new cars.

a. What kind of industry is the market for old car parts: an increasing cost industry, a constant cost industry, or a decreasing cost industry? How can you tell?

b. If people began recycling old cars more in the United States—repairing them rather than sending them off to junkyards—would the cost of spare parts probably rise or probably fall in the long run? Why do you think so?

6. Arguing about economics late one night in your dorm room, your friend says, "In a free market economy, if people are willing to pay a lot for something, then businesses will charge a lot for it." One way to translate your friend's words into a model is to think of a product with highly inelastic demand: items like life-saving drugs or basic food items. Let's consider a market where costs are roughly constant: perhaps they rise a little or fall a little as the market grows, but not by much.

a. In the long run, is your friend right?

b. In the long run, what has the biggest effect on the price of a good that people really want: the location of the average cost curve or the location of the demand curve?

7. a. In the highly competitive TV manufacturing industry, a new innovation makes it possible to cut the average cost of a 50-inch plasma TV from $1,000 to $400. Most TV manufacturers quickly adopt this new innovation, earning massive short-run profits. In the long run, what will the price of a 50-inch plasma TV be?

b. In the highly competitive memory key industry, a new innovation makes it possible to cut the average cost of a 20-megabyte memory key, small enough to fit in your pocket, from $5 to $4. In the long run, what will the price of a 20-megabyte memory key be?

c. Assume that the markets in parts a and b are both constant cost industries. If demand rises massively for these two goods, why won't the price of these goods rise in the long run?

d. In constant cost industries, does demand have any effect on price in the long run?

e. When average cost falls in *any* competitive industry, regardless of cost structure, who gets 100% of the benefits of cost cutting in the long run: consumers or producers?

8. On January 27, 2011, the price of Ford Motor Company stock hit an almost 10-year high at $18.79 per share. (Two years prior, in January 2009, Ford stock was trading for about a *tenth* of that price.)

   a. Suppose that on January 27, 2011, you owned 10,000 shares of Ford stock (a small fraction of the almost 3.8 billion shares). Suppose you offered to sell your stock for $18.85 per share, just slightly above the market price. Would you have been successful?

   b. What if, on January 27, 2011, you wanted to sell your 10,000 shares of Ford stock but you reduced your asking price to $18.75 per share? Would you have found a lot of willing buyers?

   c. What do your answers for parts a and b tell you about the demand curve that you, as an individual seller of Ford stock, face?

9. In November 2010 Netflix announced a new lower price for streaming video direct to home televisions. At the time, Netflix had no serious competitors—Netflix's share of the digital download market was more than 60% (the second firm's was only 8%). Just three months later, Amazon announced that it was entering the market for streaming video. How are these two announcements related?

10. The chapter pointed out that whenever money is used to purchase capital, interest costs are incurred. Sometimes those costs are explicit—like when Alex borrowed the money from the bank—and sometimes those costs are implicit—like when Tyler had to forgo the interest he could have earned had he left his funds in a savings account. If an economist and accountant calculated Alex and Tyler's costs, for whom would they have identical numbers and for whom would the numbers differ?

THINKING AND PROBLEM SOLVING

1. Suppose Sam sells apples in a competitive market, apples picked from his apple tree. Assume all apples are equal in quality, but grow at different heights on the tree. Sam, being fearful of heights, demands greater compensation

the higher he goes: So for him, the cost of grabbing an apple rises higher and higher, the higher he must climb, as shown in the Total Cost column below. The market price of an apple is $0.50.

   a. What is Sam's marginal revenue for selling apples?

   b. Which apples does Sam pick first? Those on the low branches or high branches? Why?

   c. Does this suggest that the marginal cost of apples is increasing, decreasing, or staying the same as the quantity of apples picked increases? Why?

   d. Complete the table below.

Apples	Total Cost	Marginal Cost	Marginal Revenue	Change in Profit
1	$0.10	$0.10	$0.50	$0.40
2	$0.22			
3	$0.50			
4	$1.00			
5	$1.73			
6	$2.78			

   e. How many apples does Sam pick?

2. How long is the "long run?" It will vary from industry to industry. How long would you estimate the long run is in the following industries?

   a. The market for pretzels and soda sold from street carts in the Wall Street financial district in New York

   b. The market for meals at newly trendy Korean porridge restaurants

   c. The market for electrical engineers

   d. After 1999, the market for movies that are suspiciously similar to *The Matrix*

3. In this chapter, we discussed the story of Dalton, Georgia, and its role as the "carpet capital of the world." A similar story can be used to explain why some 60% of the motels in the United States are owned by people of Indian origin or why, as of 1995, 80% of doughnut shops in California were owned by Cambodian immigrants. Let's look at the latter case. In the 1970s, Cambodian immigrant Ted Ngoy began

working at a doughnut shop. He then opened his own store (and later stores).*

Ngoy was drawn to the doughnut industry because it required little English, startup capital, or special skills. Speaking the same language as your workers, however, helps a lot.

a. As other Cambodian refugees came to Los Angeles fleeing the tyrannical rule of the Khmer Rouge, which group—the refugees or existing residents—was Ngoy more likely to hire from? Why?

b. Did this make it more or less likely that other Cambodian refugees would open doughnut shops? Why?

c. As more refugees came in, did this encourage a virtuous cycle of Cambodian-owned doughnut shops? Why?

d. At this point in the story, what sort of cost industry (constant, increasing, or decreasing) would you consider doughnut shops owned by Cambodians to be? Why?

e. Why did this cycle not continue forever? What kind of cost structure are Californian doughnut shops probably in now?

4. Ralph opened a small shop selling bags of trail mix. The price of the mix is $5, and the market for trail mix is very competitive. Ralph's cost curves are shown in the figure below.

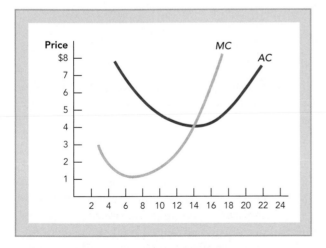

a. At what quantity will Ralph produce? Why?

b. When the price is $5, shade the area of profit or loss in the graph provided and calculate Ralph's profit or loss (round up).

c. If all other sellers of trail mix have the same marginal and average costs as Ralph, should he expect more or fewer competitors in the future? In the long run, will the price of trail mix rise or fall? How do you know? What will the price of trail mix be in the long run?

5. In the competitive children's pajama industry, a new government safety regulation raises the average cost of children's pajamas by $2 per pair.

a. If this is a constant cost industry, then in the long run, what exactly happens to the price of children's pajamas?

b. If this is an increasing cost industry, will the long-run price of pajamas rise by more than $2 or less? (*Hint:* The long-run supply curve will be shaped just like an ordinary supply curve from the first few chapters. If you treat this like a $2 tax per pair, you'll get the right answer.)

c. If this is an increasing cost industry, how much will this new safety regulation change the average pajama maker's profits in the long run?

d. Given your answer to part c, why do businesses in competitive industries often oppose costly new regulations?

6. In the ancient Western world, incense was one of the first commodities transported long distances. It grew only in the south of the Arabian Peninsula (modern-day Yemen, known then as Arabia Felix), which was transported by camel to Alexandria and the Mediterranean civilizations, notably the Roman Republic. As the republic expanded into a richer and larger empire, the demand for incense grew and planters in Arabia added a second and then a third annual crop (though this incense was not as high of a quality). Cultivation also crossed to the Horn of Africa (modern-day Oman) even though such fields were farther away from Rome.[2]

a. How does the lower quality of the additional annual crops illustrate incense as an increasing cost industry? (*Hint:* Think in terms of an amount of good crop produced per unit of currency.)

b. How does the added distance of incense grown in the Horn of Africa illustrate incense as an increasing cost industry?

---

* Not only are 60% of the small motels and hotels in the United States owned by East Indians, nearly a third of these owners have the surname Patel; see http://news.bbc.co.uk/2/hi/south_asia/3177054.stm. The story of Cambodian doughnut shops in Los Angeles is from Postrel, Virginia. 1999. *The Future and Its Enemies.* New York: Touchstone, pp. 49–50.

c. It's more costly to grow incense in Eastern Africa than in Arabia Felix. Which region would you expect to see more incense grown in?

7. You run a small firm. Two management consultants are offering you advice. The first says that your firm is losing money on every unit that you produce. To reduce your losses, the consultant recommends that you cut back production. The second consultant says that if your firm sells another unit, the price will more than cover your increase in costs. In order to reduce losses, the second consultant recommends that you should increase production.

a. As an economist, can you explain why both facts that the consultants rely on could be true?

b. Which consultant is offering the correct advice?

8. Paulette, Camille, and Hortense each own wineries in France. They produce inexpensive, mass-market wines. Over the last few years, such wines sold for 7 euros per bottle; but with a global recession, the price has fallen to 5 euros per bottle. Given the information below, let's find out which of these three winemakers (if any) should shut down temporarily until times get better. *Remember:* Whether or not they shut down, they still have to keep paying fixed costs for at least some time (that's what makes them "fixed").

To keep things simple, let's assume that each winemaker has calculated the optimal quantity to produce if they decide to stay in business; your job is simply to figure out if she should produce that amount or just shut down.

Annual Income Statement When Price = 5 euros				
Winemaker	Fixed Costs	Variable Costs	Recession Revenues	Profits
Paulette	50,000	80,000	120,000	
Camille	100,000	40,000	70,000	
Hortense	200,000	250,000	200,000	

a. First, calculate each winemaker's profit.

b. Which of these women, if any, earned a profit?

c. Who should stay in business in the short run? Who should shut down?

d. Fill in the blank: Even if profit is negative, if revenues are _____ variable costs, then it's best to stay open in the short run.

e. For which of these wineries, if any, is $P > AC$? You don't need to calculate any new numbers to answer this.

9. Suppose Carrie decides to lease a photocopier and open up a black-and-white photocopying service in her dorm room for use by faculty and students. Her total cost, as a function of the number of copies she produces per month, is given in the table below:

Number of Photocopies per Month	Total Cost	Fixed Cost	Variable Cost	Total Revenue	Profit
0	$100				
1,000	$110				
2,000	$125				
3,000	$145				
4,000	$175				
5,000	$215				
6,000	$285				

a. Fill in the missing numbers in the table, assuming that Carrie can charge 5 cents per black-and-white copy.

b. How many copies per month should Carrie sell?

c. If the lease rate on the copier were to increase by $50 per month, how would that impact Carrie's profit-maximizing level of output? How would this $50 increase in the lease rate affect Carrie's profit? What will she do when it is time to renew her lease?

10. Let's explore the relationship between marginal and average a little more. Suppose your grade in your economics class is composed of 10 quizzes of equal weight. You start off the semester well, then your grades start to slip a little, but then you get back into the swing of things, your

grades pick up, and you finish off the semester with a bang. Your 10 quiz grades, in order, are: 82, 74, 68, 72, 77, 83, 86, 88, 90, and 100. Graph your *marginal* grades, along with your *average* grade, after each quiz. What do you notice about the relationship between *marginal* and *averages*? Your grades start improving with your fourth quiz grade; does your average also start increasing with your fourth quiz grade? Why or why not?

11. Given the cost function for Simon, a housepainter in a competitive local market, below, answer the questions that follow. (You may want to calculate average cost.)

Number of Rooms Painted per Week	Total Cost
0	$100
1	$120
2	$125
3	$145
4	$200
5	$300
6	$460

What is the minimum price per room at which Simon would be earning positive economic profit? At prices below this price, what will Simon's long run plan be?

12. Sandy owns a firm with annual revenues of $1,000,000. Wages, rent, and other costs are $900,000.

   a. Calculate Sandy's accounting profit.

   b. Suppose that instead of being an entrepreneur, Sandy could get a job with one of the following annual salaries (i) $50,000; (ii) $100,000; or (iii) $250,000. Assume that a job would be as satisfying to Sandy as being an entrepreneur. Calculate Sandy's economic profit under each of these scenarios.

CHALLENGES

1. The demand for most metals tends to increase over time. Moreover, as we discussed in this chapter and also in Chapter 5, these types of natural resource industries tend to be increasing cost industries. And yet the price of metals compared with other goods has tended to fall slowly over time (albeit with many spikes in between). The following figure, for example, shows an index of prices for aluminum, copper, lead, silver, tin, and zinc from 1900 to 2003 (adjusted for inflation). The trend is downward. Why do you think this is the case?

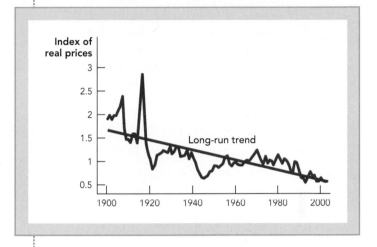

2. Frequent moviegoers often note that movies are rarely based on original ideas. Most of them are based on a television series, a video game, or, most commonly, a book. Why? To help you answer this question, start with the following.

   a. Does a movie or a book have a higher fixed cost of production?

   b. In 2005, American studios released 563 movies[3] and American publishers produced 176,000 new titles.[4] How does your answer in part a explain such a wide difference? Which is riskier: publishing a book or producing a movie?

   c. How does the difference in fixed costs and risk of failure explain why so many movies are based on successful books? As a result, where do you expect to see more innovative plots, dialogues, and characters: in novels or movies?

3. a. In the nineteenth century, economist Alfred Marshall wrote about decreasing cost industries, writing in his *Principles of Economics* (available free online) that "when an industry has thus chosen a locality for itself . . . .[t]he mysteries of the trade become no mysteries; but are as it were in the air."

In Chapter 10, we had a concept for benefits that are not internal to a firm but are "as it were in the air." What specific concept from Chapter 10 is at work in a business cluster?

b. In the twenty-first century, economist Michael Porter of the Harvard Business School writes about decreasing cost industries, as well: He calls them "business clusters." Porter's work has been very influential among city and town governments that argue carefully targeted tax breaks and subsidies can attract investment and create a business cluster in their town, which will subsequently reap the benefits of decreasing costs. Is this argument correct? Be careful, it's tricky!

4. In Kolkata, India, it is very common to see beggars on the streets. Imagine that the visitors and residents of Kolkata become more generous in their donations; what will be the effect on the standard of living of beggars in Kolkata? Answer this question using supply and demand, making assumptions as necessary.

5. Just to make sure you've gotten enough practice using the different formulas in this chapter, let's try a challenging exercise with them. Very little information is given in the table below, but surprisingly, there's enough information for you to fill in all of the missing values—if you remember all of the relationships and can think of creative ways to use them.

Quantity	Total Cost	Fixed Cost	Variable Cost	Average Cost	Marginal Cost	Total Revenue	Profit
0				—	—		−$80
10					$4		
20	$200						
30			$240			$450	
40							
50				$13.60	$20		

Using Excel to Graph Cost Curves

We can use a spreadsheet such as Excel to take some of the drudgery out of graphing and calculating things like marginal revenue and marginal cost. In Figure A11.1, we show some of the data from the chapter on revenues and costs for the oil well. Notice that in cell B5 we show the Excel formula "=$A$2*A5," which takes the price from cell A2 and multiplies it by the quantity in cell A5 to produce total revenue. We then copy and paste this formula into the remainder of the column. We use the $ sign in $A$2 to tell Excel not to adjust the cell reference when we copy and paste (A5 doesn't have dollar signs so it is automatically adjusted to A6, A7, etc. when we copy and paste).

FIGURE A11.1

	B5	▾	*fx* =$A$2*A5	
	A	B	C	D
1	Price			
2	50			
3				
4	Barrels of Oil Produced	Total Revenue (P * Q)	Total Cost	
5	0	0	30	
6	1	50	34	
7	2	100	40	
8	3	150	51	
9	4	200	68	
10	5	250	91	
11	6	300	120	
12	7	350	156	
13	8	400	206	
14	9	450	296	
15	10	500	420	
16				

With total revenue and total cost input, it's easy to create the other data that we need. Profit is just total revenue minus total cost, which in Figure A11.2 we show in column D. Marginal revenue and marginal cost are defined as $MR = \dfrac{\Delta TR}{\Delta Q}$ and $MC = \dfrac{\Delta TC}{\Delta Q}$. We show in cell F4 how to implement these formulas in Excel. The formula "= (C4 − C3)/(A4 − A3)" takes the cost of producing 2 barrels of oil from cell C4 and subtracts the cost of producing 1 barrel of oil from C3; we then divide by the increase in the number of barrels as we move from producing 1 to 2 barrels. In this case, $MC = (40 − 34)/(2 − 1) = 6$. The formula for MR is entered into Excel in a similar manner.

FIGURE A11.2

	F4	▼		f_x =(C4-C3)/(A4-A3)			
	A	B	C	D	E	F	G
1	Barrels of Oil Produced	Total Revenue (P * Q)	Total Cost	Profit	Marginal Revenue (Price)	Marginal Cost	
2	0	0	30	-30			
3	1	50	34	16	50	4	
4	2	100	40	60	50	6	
5	3	150	51	99	50	11	
6	4	200	68	132	50	17	
7	5	250	91	159	50	23	
8	6	300	120	180	50	29	
9	7	350	156	194	50	36	
10	8	400	206	194	50	50	
11	9	450	296	154	50	90	
12	10	500	420	80	50	124	
13							
14							

Average cost is $AC = \dfrac{TC}{Q}$ and we show this calculation in Figure A11.3.

FIGURE A11.3

	G13	▼		f_x =C13/A13			
	A	B	C	D	E	F	G
1	Price						
2	50						
3							
4	Barrels of Oil Produced	Total Revenue (P * Q)	Total Cost	Profit	Marginal Revenue (Price)	Marginal Cost	Average Cost
5	0	0	30	-30			
6	1	50	34	16	50	4	34
7	2	100	40	60	50	6	20
8	3	150	51	99	50	11	17
9	4	200	68	132	50	17	17
10	5	250	91	159	50	23	18.2
11	6	300	120	180	50	29	20
12	7	350	156	194	50	36	22.28571
13	8	400	206	194	50	50	25.75
14	9	450	296	154	50	90	32.88889
15	10	500	420	80	50	124	42
16							

It's now easy to graph *MR, MC,* and *AC.* By highlighting the Marginal Revenue, Marginal Cost, and Average Cost columns, including the labels, and clicking Insert and then Line Chart, we can produce a graph similar to that shown in Figure A11.4 (to get the exact graph, you must also tell Excel to use the barrel numbers in Column 1 on the *x*-axis—you can do this by clicking on the graph, clicking Select Data, and then Edit, Horizontal (Category) Axis Labels; this is for Excel 2007, Excel 2003 works similarly).

Remember that the profit–maximizing quantity is found where $MR = MC$. You can check this by looking at the table. You can see what happens to the profit–maximizing quantity when price changes simply by changing the price in cell A2; the graph will change automatically.

FIGURE A11.4

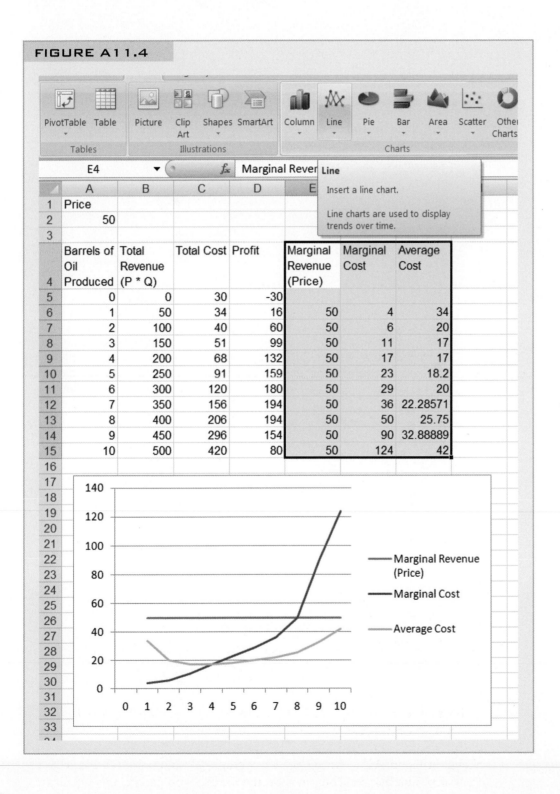

12

Competition and the Invisible Hand

In Chapter 7, we explained how the price system—the signaling and incentive system—solves the great economic problem of arranging our limited resources to satisfy as many of our wants as possible. We showed how markets connect the world in a great cooperative endeavor, and how price signals and the accompanying profits and losses create incentives for entrepreneurs to direct labor and capital to their highest value uses. Chapter 7 was a "big picture" view of markets. In Chapter 11, we took a closer look at firms and showed that to maximize profit, a firm wants to (1) produce the quantity such that $P = MC$, (2) enter industries where $P > AC$, and (3) exit industries where $P < AC$. In this chapter, we connect these two perspectives on markets.

We also return in this chapter to the invisible hand. Recall Big Idea Two from Chapter 1, namely the metaphor of the invisible hand. With the right institutions, individuals acting in their self-interest can generate outcomes that are neither part of their intention nor design but that nevertheless have desirable properties. In this chapter, we show exactly this: How the conditions for profit maximization under competition lead entrepreneurs to produce outcomes that they neither intend nor design but that nevertheless have desirable properties.

In particular, we show that the $P = MC$ condition for profit maximization in a competitive market balances production across firms in an industry in just the way that minimizes the total industry costs of production. Second, we show that the entry ($P > AC$) and exit ($P < AC$) signals balance production across different industries in just the way that maximizes the total value of production.

Invisible Hand Property 1: The Minimization of Total Industry Costs of Production

We know from the previous chapter that a firm in a competitive industry increases output until $P = MC$. What's even more important is that every firm in the same industry faces the *same* price. Thus, in a competitive market with N firms, the following will be true:

$$P = MC_1 = MC_2 = ... = MC_N$$

where MC_1 is the marginal cost of firm 1, MC_2 is the marginal cost of firm 2, and so forth. To understand the importance of this condition, let's briefly consider a seemingly different problem. Suppose that you own two farms on which to grow corn. Farm 1 is in a hilly region that is costly to seed and plow. Farm 2 is on land ideal for growing corn. The marginal cost of growing corn on each of these farms is illustrated in Figure 12.1.

Let's say that you would like to grow 200 bushels. It might seem that the lowest-cost way to produce 200 bushels is to produce all 200 bushels on Farm 2. After all, the marginal costs of production on Farm 2 are lower than on Farm 1 for any level of output.

Assume that you did produce all 200 bushels on Farm 2 and no bushels on Farm 1. Can you see a way of lowering your total costs of production?

Let's think in marginal terms. Instead of producing all 200 bushels on Farm 2, what would happen to your total costs of production if you produced, say, 197 bushels on Farm 2 and 3 bushels on Farm 1? Notice from Figure 12.2 that when you produce less on Farm 2, your costs of production decrease by the shaded area labeled *A*—this is the marginal cost of producing those last few bushels on Farm 2. By instead producing those bushels on Farm 1, your costs increase by area *B*, the marginal cost of production on Farm 1. But area *B* is

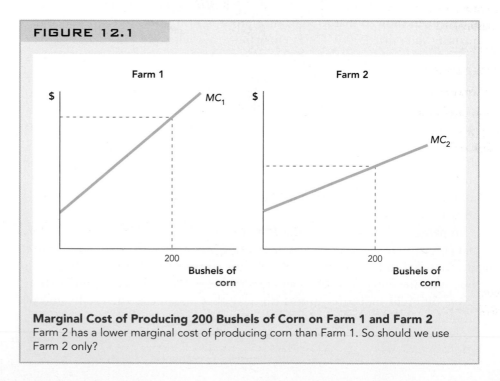

FIGURE 12.1

Marginal Cost of Producing 200 Bushels of Corn on Farm 1 and Farm 2
Farm 2 has a lower marginal cost of producing corn than Farm 1. So should we use Farm 2 only?

FIGURE 12.2

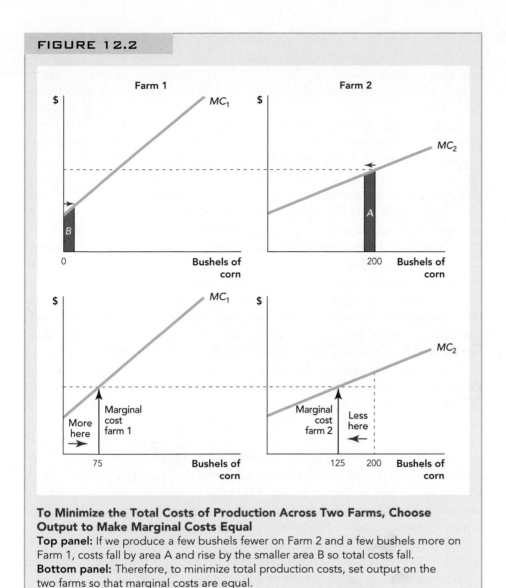

To Minimize the Total Costs of Production Across Two Farms, Choose Output to Make Marginal Costs Equal
Top panel: If we produce a few bushels fewer on Farm 2 and a few bushels more on Farm 1, costs fall by area A and rise by the smaller area B so total costs fall.
Bottom panel: Therefore, to minimize total production costs, set output on the two farms so that marginal costs are equal.

less than area A, so by switching some production from Farm 2 to Farm 1, your total costs of producing 200 bushels of corn goes down.

How far can you extend this logic? Clearly, you should continue producing fewer bushels on Farm 2 and more on Farm 1 if the marginal costs of production on Farm 2 exceed those on Farm 1; that is, produce less on Farm 2 and more on Farm 1 if $MC_2 > MC_1$. By the same logic, you should switch production from Farm 1 to Farm 2 if $MC_1 > MC_2$. Put these two statements together and it follows that the way to minimize the total costs of production is to produce just so much on each farm so that the marginal costs of production are equalized, $MC_1 = MC_2$. In the bottom panel of Figure 12.2, we show that the cost-minimizing way to produce 200 bushels of corn is to produce 75 bushels on Farm 1 and 125 bushels on Farm 2.

Now comes the really important part. If you own both farms, you can act as a "central planner" and allocate production across the two farms so that the marginal costs of production are equal and thus the total costs of production are minimized. But now suppose that Farm 1 is in North Carolina and Farm 2 is in Iowa, and let's say Farm 1 is owned by Sandy and Farm 2 by Pat. Let's further suppose that Sandy and Pat will live their entire lives without ever meeting. Is there any way to organize production so that the output is split in exactly the way that you would split it if you owned both farms? Yes, there is.

Sandy and Pat sell their corn in the same market so each of them sees the same price of corn. How will Sandy maximize profits? How will Pat maximize profits? To maximize profits, Sandy will set $P = MC_1$ and Pat will set $P = MC_2$, but this means that $MC_1 = MC_2$! But we know from above that if $P = MC_1 = MC_2$, then the total costs of production are minimized. Amazingly, in pursuit of their own profit, Sandy and Pat will allocate output across their two farms in exactly the way that a central planner would to minimize the total costs of production!

It's remarkable that a free market could mimic an ideal central planner. What's even more remarkable is that a free market can allocate production across the two farms to minimize total costs even when an ideal central planner could not! Imagine, for example, that only Sandy knows MC_1 and that only Pat knows MC_2. For a free market, this is no problem, and Sandy and Pat, each acting in their own self-interest, choose the output levels that minimize total costs. But a central planner cannot allocate production correctly if it lacks knowledge of MC_1 and MC_2.

The insight that a free market minimizes the total costs of production is one of the most surprising and deepest in all of economics. In a famous phrase in *The Wealth of Nations*, Adam Smith described a similar situation saying that each individual "in this, as in many other cases, [is] led by an invisible hand to promote an end which was no part of his intention." Sandy and Pat don't intend to minimize the total costs of producing 200 bushels of corn; they intend only to make a profit. But this beneficial outcome is the result of their action. Indeed, until Adam Smith and other economists began to study markets, not only did no one intend to minimize industry costs, no one even *knew* that individuals acting to maximize their own profits would minimize industry costs.

Friedrich Hayek, a Nobel Prize–winning economist we discussed in Chapter 7, said that properties like the minimization of the total costs of production were "products of human action but not of human design."

Invisible Hand Property 1 says that even though no actor in a market economy intends to do so, in a free market $P = MC_1 = MC_2 = ... = MC_N$ and, as a result, the total industry costs of production are minimized.

Invisible Hand Property 1 provides another perspective on free trade. In Chapter 9, we explained how free trade increased wealth by letting the United States buy goods from the lowest-cost producers. We can now see this in another way. Remember that costs are minimized when $MC_1 = MC_2$ so costs are *not* minimized when $MC_1 \neq MC_2$. Now imagine that Farm 1 and Farm 2 are in different countries with no free trade between them. Sandy and Pat, therefore, face *different* prices for corn. Since Sandy and Pat face different prices, $MC_1 \neq MC_2$ and thus the total costs of producing corn cannot be at a minimum.

The Invisible Hand

CHECK YOURSELF

> If the *MC* of production on Sandy's farm is higher than on Pat's farm, how should production be rearranged to minimize the total costs of production?

Invisible Hand Property 2: The Balance of Industries

Invisible Hand Property 1 tells us that in a competitive industry, the total industry costs of production are minimized. But we could minimize the total costs of producing corn and still have too much or too little corn. It's good to know that if 20 or 200 million bushels of corn are produced, we get those bushels at the lowest cost, but how many bushels is the right amount? It's the second invisible hand property that ensures the right amount of corn is produced.

Consider two industries, the car industry and the computer industry. Both industries use labor and capital to produce goods. Labor and capital, however, are limited. Recall from Chapter 7 that the great economic problem is to arrange our limited resources to satisfy as many of our wants as possible. So how do we allocate our limited labor and capital across the computer and car industry to satisfy as many of our wants as possible?

Profit in the computer industry is total revenue minus total cost. Total revenue measures the value of the output of the computer industry, the computers. Total cost measures the value of the inputs to the computer industry, the labor and capital. High profits, therefore, mean that outputs of high value are being created from inputs of low value. Profit is a signal that our limited labor and capital are being used productively in satisfying our wants.

Now suppose that the computer industry is more profitable than the car industry—then a unit of labor and capital in the computer industry is creating more value than in the car industry. What we would like, therefore, is for labor and capital to move from the car industry to the computer industry. Or, in other words, to use our limited resources most effectively, we would like resources to flow from low-profit industries to high-profit industries.

Of course, moving labor and capital from low-profit to high-profit industries is exactly what entrepreneurs would like to do! Recall that our condition to enter an industry is $P > AC$, but as we showed in Chapter 11, that's equivalent to $TR > TC$ (divide both sides of $TR > TC$ by Q). So, in a competitive market, the incentives that entrepreneurs have to seek profit and avoid losses align with the social incentive to move labor and capital out of low-value industries and into high-value industries.

Notice that profits encourage entry, but what happens to price and profits when firms enter an industry? As firms enter, supply increases and the price declines, which reduces profits. Losses encourage exit, but what happens to price and profits when firms exit an industry? As firms exit, supply decreases and the price increases, which increases profit (reduces losses). Thus, there is a tendency for the profit rate in all competitive industries to go to zero (normal profits). Since the profit rate tends to the same level in the car and the computer and all other industries, the marginal value of resources in all industries is the same. That's just another way of saying that the total value of production is maximized because if the profit rate in one industry were greater than in another, total value would increase if resources were to move from the less profitable to the more profitable industry.

Invisible Hand Property 1 showed how self-interest worked to minimize the total costs of, say, corn production. Invisible Hand Property 2 shows how the self-interest of entrepreneurs causes them to enter and exit the car, computer, corn, apple, and other industries in such a way that the total value of all production is maximized. An implication of Invisible Hand Property 2 is that the profit rate in all competitive industries tends toward the same level.

Creative Destruction

Although the profit rate in all competitive industries tends toward the same level, that's just a tendency. Change is constant—tastes change, technologies change, and new ideas are always being tested—so there are always some profitable industries that are popping up and some unprofitable industries, as well. So the great economic problem is never solved completely, but in a dynamic economy, resources are always moving toward an increase in the value of production. In a dynamic economy, entrepreneurs listen to price signals and they move capital and labor from unprofitable industries to profitable industries.

These dynamics illustrate a general feature of competitive markets that we call the **elimination principle:** *Above-normal profits are eliminated by entry and below-normal profits are eliminated by exit.*

> According to the **elimination principle**, above-normal profits are eliminated by entry and below-normal profits are eliminated by exit.

The elimination principle says that above-normal profits are temporary. Great ideas are soon adopted by others; they diffuse throughout the economy and became commonplace—and no one profits from the commonplace. Since no one profits from the commonplace *to earn above-normal profits, an entrepreneur must innovate.*

The economist Joseph Schumpeter was eloquent on this point. In textbooks, he said, competition is about pushing price down to average cost:

> [But] in capitalist reality as distinguished from its textbook picture, it is not that kind of competition which counts but the competition from the new commodity, the new technology, the new source of supply, the new type of organization . . . competition which commands a decisive cost or quality advantage and which strikes not at the margins of the profits and the outputs of the existing firms but at their foundations and their very lives. . . .
>
> This process of Creative Destruction is the essential fact about capitalism.[1]

PHOTO BY CAMERON QUINN

Profits pop up all the time, but in a dynamic economy, the entry of new firms quickly whacks them down again.

Thus, the elimination principle serves as both a warning and an opportunity to entrepreneurs. Stand still and fall behind. Leap ahead and profits may follow. In a dynamic economy, there is a constant dance between elimination and innovation. Above-normal profits are constantly being eliminated by competition, and new sources of profit are constantly being created through innovation.

The Invisible Hand Works with Competitive Markets

We have shown in this chapter that competitive markets have some desirable "invisible hand" properties, but don't forget that the invisible hand works only in certain circumstances. For the competitive process to work, for example, it's important that prices accurately signal costs and benefits. But we already know from Chapter 10 on externalities that prices do not always accurately signal costs and benefits. We can now see from another perspective why this is a problem. If prices don't accurately signal costs and benefits, then Invisible Hand Property 2 won't work perfectly and there will not be an ideal balance between industries. We will get too few resources in some industries and too many resources in other industries.

Similarly, if markets are not competitive, then the invisible hand doesn't work so well. We will be taking up the problem of monopoly in Chapter 13 and oligopoly (a few firms but not many) in Chapter 15, but we can point to the basic issue here. Monopolists and oligopolists earn above-normal profits. We know that if an industry earns above-normal profits, we would like resources to move to that industry, but without the pressure of the competitive process, not enough resources will move and profits will not be eliminated. We can see right away, therefore, that output will be too low in a monopoly or in an oligopoly.

We will also be showing in Chapter 18 on public goods and the tragedy of the commons that for some types of goods, self-interest either doesn't align with the social interest or sometimes it may align in the wrong direction. All this remind us of the basic point: Good institutions align self-interest with the social interest, but good institutions are sometimes hard to find or create.

□ Takeaway

Invisible Hand Property 1 says that by producing where $P = MC$, the self-interested, profit-seeking behavior of entrepreneurs results in the minimization of the total industry costs of production even though no entrepreneur intends this result. Invisible Hand Property 2 says that entry and exit decisions not only work to eliminate profits, they work to ensure that labor and capital move across industries to optimally balance production so that the greatest use is made of our limited resources.

The elimination principle tells us that above-normal profits are eliminated by entry and below-normal profits are eliminated by exit. Perhaps even more importantly, the elimination principle tells us that to earn above-normal profits, a firm must innovate.

Competitive markets do a good job of aligning self-interest with the social interest, but not all markets are competitive.

Joseph Schumpeter (1883–1950)
In his youth, Schumpeter said he wanted to be "the greatest lover in Vienna, the best horseman in Europe, and the greatest economist in the world." He later claimed to have achieved two of the three, adding that he and horses just didn't get along.

BETTMANN/CORBIS

□ CHAPTER REVIEW

KEY CONCEPTS

Elimination principle, p. 228

FACTS AND TOOLS

1. Entrepreneurs shift capital and labor across industries in pursuit of profit. Let's look at this a little more closely. Suppose there are two industries: a high-profit industry, Industry H, and a low-profit industry, Industry L. Answer the questions below about these two industries.

   a. If the two industries have similar costs, then what must be true about prices in the two industries?

   b. What does your answer to part a imply about the value of the output in the two industries?

   c. If labor and capital are moved from Industry L to Industry H, what is given up? What is gained?

   d. Suppose instead that the prices in the two industries were identical. In this case, what must be true about the costs in the two industries?

   e. What does your answer to part d imply about the amounts of capital and labor required to produce one unit of output in each industry?

   f. If labor and capital are moved from Industry L to Industry H, are more units of output lost in Industry L or gained in Industry H?

2. Suppose that two industries, the pizza industry and the calzone industry, are equally risky, but rates of return on capital investments are only 5% in the pizza industry and 8% in the calzone industry.

Which way will capital flow—from the pizza industry to the calzone industry, or from the calzone industry to the pizza industry?

3. We've claimed that the efficient way to spread out work across firms in the same industry is to set the marginal cost of production to be the same across firms. Let's see if this works in an example.

Consider a competitive market for rolled steel (measured by the ton) with just two firms: SmallCo and BigCo. If we wanted to be more realistic, we could say there were 100 firms like SmallCo and 100 firms like BigCo, but that would just make the math harder without generating any insight. The two firms have marginal cost schedules like this:

	Marginal Cost	
Q	SmallCo	BigCo
1	$10	$10
2	$20	$10
3	$30	$10
4	$40	$10
5	$50	$20
6	$60	$30
7	$70	$40
8	$80	$50

a. We'll ignore the fixed costs of starting up the firms just to make things a little simpler. What is the total cost at each firm of producing each level of output? Fill in the table.

	Total Cost	
Q	SmallCo	BigCo
1	$10	$10
2	$30	$20
3	$60	
4		
5		
6		
7		
8		

b. What's the cheapest way to make 11 tons of steel? 5 tons?

c. What would the price have to be in this competitive market for these two firms to produce a total of 11 tons of steel? 5 tons?

d. Suppose that a government agency looked at BigCo and SmallCo's cost curves. Which firm looks like the low-cost producer to a government agency? Would it be a good idea, an efficient policy, for the government to shut down the high-cost producer? In other words, could a government intervention do better than the invisible hand in this case?

e. Let's make part d more concrete: What would the total cost be if BigCo were the only firm in the market, and it had to produce 7 tons of rolled steel? What would marginal and total costs be if SmallCo and BigCo let the invisible hand divvy up the work between them?

4. Let's review the basic mechanism of the elimination principle.

a. When demand rises in Industry X, what happens to profits? Do they rise, fall, or remain unchanged?

b. When that happens, do firms, workers, and capital tend to enter Industry X, or do they tend to leave?

c. Does this tend to increase short-run supply in Industry X or reduce it?

d. In the long run, after this rise in demand, what will profits typically be in Industry X?

THINKING AND PROBLEM SOLVING

1. The elimination principle discussed in this chapter tells us what we can expect in the long run from perfectly competitive markets: zero (normal) profits across industries. If this were the case, and this fate were unavoidable, going into business would seem to be a fairly dismal choice, given that the end result of normal profits is known right out of the gate. Despite this, we constantly see entrepreneurs working hard to earn profits. Is this a waste of time, given what we know about the elimination principle? Is the fate of zero profit unavoidable? What would Joseph Schumpeter say about all of this?

2. How can the market mechanism guarantee that the marginal cost of production will be the same across all firms if those firms have different owners, are in different locations, and have unique cost functions known only to the firms themselves? Why don't these different firms need to have one shared owner or one shared manager to coordinate this "equal marginal cost" condition?

3. We've seen already from this chapter that dividing up output over multiple producers—even when one has higher costs than the other—can lead to lower industry costs, so long as output is divided up such that $MC_1 = MC_2 = MC_N$. You've already done some practice in Facts and Tools question 3 above with cost functions presented as tables. Let's try to see how this works graphically.

Take a look at the two marginal cost functions below.

MC of Firm 1

MC of Firm 2

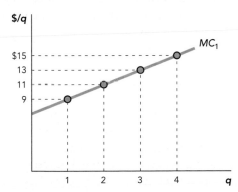

Based on the graphs of these two marginal cost functions, fill in the table below, for industry-wide marginal cost, assuming that production is divided up among the two firms

according to Invisible Hand Principle 1. Then, create a graph of the industry marginal cost curve. To help you get started, take a look at the table and answer the following questions. Which firm produces the first unit of industry output? Which firm produces the second unit of industry output? Why?

Quantity	Industry-Wide MC
1	$6
2	$9
3	
4	
5	
6	
7	
8	

4. In the process of creative destruction, what gets destroyed?

Firms

Workers

Machines

Buildings

Business plans

Valuable relationships

Or some combination of these? The chapter itself contains quite a few ideas about how to answer this question, but you'll have to think hard about the "opportunity cost" for each item on the list.

5. Every year, American television introduces many new shows, only about one-third of which survive past their first season.[2] The few shows that last, however, prove to be very profitable.

   a. How does creative destruction explain why studios bother to make new shows if most of them will fail?

   b. In 2000, CBS premiered *Survivor*, an immensely popular reality show about everyday people living on an island. How did CBS and other networks respond to this surprise hit?

c. What happened over the next several years to profits from *Survivor*? You don't need to check CBS's financial statements to get the answer; use the elimination principle!

6. Let's suppose that the demand for allergists increases in California. How does the invisible hand respond to this demand? There is more than one correct answer to this question: Try to come up with two or three.

CHALLENGES

1. Now let's take a look at the equations for the marginal cost functions that are graphed in Thinking and Problem-Solving question 3, and see if we can combine them into one equation for industry-wide marginal cost. This is what the two equations for the graphs in the question look like:

$$MC_1 = 2 + 4q_1$$
$$MC_2 = 7 + 2q_2$$

Can you create an industry marginal cost equation that shows MC_{Total} as a function of q_{Total} instead of just q_1 or q_2?

a. First, solve both equations for q.

b. Now, replace MC_1 and MC_2 with MC_{Total}, since Invisible Hand Principle 1 tells us that marginal cost will be equal for all of the firms in the industry.

c. Next, write an equation for q_{Total}, which is just $q_1 + q_2$.

d. Finally, solve the equation for MC_{Total}. Now you have created an industry marginal cost function from the cost functions of two different firms in the industry. (If you compare this equation to your answers for Thinking

and Problem-Solving question 3, you'll see that the marginal cost is a little different when you use the equation. This is, in part, because this equation assumes you can produce *partial* units at either firm, whereas your graph was based on the assumption that only *whole* units were produced.)

2. Let's take a look at Invisible Hand Principle 2 in action using a mathematical example. Suppose an industry is characterized by the equations in the table below. (We're going to assume all individual firms are identical to make this problem a little simpler.)

Demand	$Q_D = 100 - 2P$
Individual firm's supply	$q_S = 0.5 + 0.1P$
Market supply with n firms	$Q_S = n \times q_S$ $= 0.5n + 0.1nP$
Individual firm's average cost	$AC = 5q_S - 5 + (24.2/q_S)$

a. Suppose there are 24 firms in this industry. What is the equation for market supply? What is the equilibrium price and quantity (this can be found by setting $Q_D = Q_S$)? How much profit is each firm earning? According to the elimination principle, what should occur in this industry over time?

b. Suppose there are 35 firms in this industry. Answer the same questions from part a above.

c. The elimination principle says that profits will be eliminated in the long run, which means that $AC = P$. Using that fact, figure out how many firms will be in this industry in the long run (solve for n).

13

Monopoly

O n June 5, 1981, the Centers for Disease Control and Prevention reported that a strange outbreak of pneumonia was killing young, healthy homosexual men in Los Angeles. Alarm spread as similar reports streamed in from San Francisco, New York, and Boston. What had at first looked like a disease peculiar to homosexual men turned out to be a worldwide killer caused by HIV (the human immunodeficiency virus). Since 1981, AIDS (acquired immune deficiency syndrome) has killed more than 28 million people.

There is no known cure for AIDS, but progress has been made in treating the disease. In the United States, deaths from AIDS dropped by approximately 50% between 1995 and 1997. The major cause of the falling death rate was the development of new drugs called combination antiretrovirals, such as Combivir.[1] The drugs only work, however, if one can afford to take them, and they are expensive. A single pill of Combivir costs about $12.50—at two per day, every day, that's nearly $10,000 per year.[2] If you have the money, $10,000 a year is a small price to pay for life, but there are 35 million people worldwide living with HIV and most of them don't have $10,000.[3]

If HIV drugs were expensive because production costs were high, economists would have little to say about drug pricing. But it costs less than 50 cents to produce a pill of Combivir—thus, the price of one pill is about 25 times higher than the cost.[4] In earlier chapters, we emphasized how competitive markets drive the price of a good down to marginal cost. Why hasn't

The cause of AIDS, the human immunodeficiency virus (HIV).

that process worked here? There are three reasons why HIV drugs are priced well above cost.

1. Market power
2. The "you can't take it with you" effect
3. The "other people's money" effect

The primary reason that AIDS drugs are priced well above costs is monopoly or market power, the subject of this chapter. The "you can't take it with you" and "other people's money" effects, which we will also discuss in this chapter, make market power especially strong in the pricing of pharmaceuticals.

Market Power

GlaxoSmithKline (GSK), the world's largest producer of AIDS drugs, owns the patent on Combivir. A patent is a government grant that gives the owner the exclusive rights to make, use, or sell the patented product. GlaxoSmithKline, for example, is the only legal seller of Combivir. Even though the formula to manufacture it is well known and easily duplicated, competitors who try to make Combivir or its equivalent will be jailed, at least in the United States and other countries where the patent is enforced.

> **Market power** is the power to raise price above marginal cost without fear that other firms will enter the market.
>
> A **monopoly** is a firm with market power.

GSK's patent on Combivir gives GSK **market power,** the power to raise price above marginal cost without fear that other competitors will enter the market. A **monopoly** is simply a firm with market power.

India does not recognize the Combivir patent, so in that country competition prevails and an equivalent drug sells for just 50 cents per pill.[5] Thus, economics correctly predicts that competition will drive price down to the marginal cost of production; it's just that GSK's patent prevents competition from operating.

Patents are not the only source of market power. Government regulations other than patents, as well as economies of scale, exclusive access to an important input, and technological innovation can all create firms with market power. We discuss the sources of market power and appropriate responses at greater length later on in this chapter. For now, we want to ask how a firm will use its market power to maximize profit.

How a Firm Uses Market Power to Maximize Profit

We know that a firm with market power will price above cost—but how much above cost? Even a firm with no competitors faces a demand curve, so as it raises its price, it will sell fewer units. Higher prices, therefore, are not always better for a seller—raise the price too much and profits will fall. Lower the price and profits can increase. What is the profit-maximizing price?

> **Marginal revenue, MR,** is the change in total revenue from selling an additional unit.
>
> **Marginal cost, MC,** is the change in total cost from producing an additional unit. To maximize profit, a firm increases output until $MR = MC$.

To maximize profit, a firm should produce until the revenue from an additional sale is equal to the cost of an additional sale. This is the same condition that we discovered in Chapter 11: produce until **marginal revenue** equals **marginal cost** ($MR = MC$). In Chapter 11, however, calculating marginal revenue was easy because even if a small oil well increases production significantly, the effect on the world price of oil is so small it can be ignored. For a small firm, therefore, the revenue from the sale of an additional unit is the market price ($MR = $ Price). But when a firm's output of a product is large relative to the entire market's output of that product (or very close substitutes), a significant increase in the firm's output will cause the market price of that product to fall. When the Saudis boost oil production, for example, the price of oil falls. Thus, for a firm that produces a large share of the market's total output of a product, the revenue from the sale of an additional unit is less than the current market price ($MR <$ Price).

To understand how a firm with market power will price its product, we need to calculate marginal revenue for a firm that is large enough to influence the price of its product.

We show how to calculate marginal revenue in the table in the left panel of Figure 13.1. Suppose that at a price of $16 the quantity demanded is 2 units, so that total revenue is $32 (2 × $16). If the monopolist reduces the price to $14, it can sell 3 units for a total revenue of $42 (3 × $14). Marginal revenue, the change in revenue from selling an additional unit, is therefore $10 ($42 − $32). Thus, we can always calculate MR by looking at the change in total revenue when production changes by one unit.

The right panel of Figure 13.1 shows another way of thinking about marginal revenue. When the monopolist lowers its price from $16 to $14, it makes one additional sale, which increases revenues by $14—the green area. But to make that additional sale, the monopolist had to lower its price by $2, so it loses

FIGURE 13.1

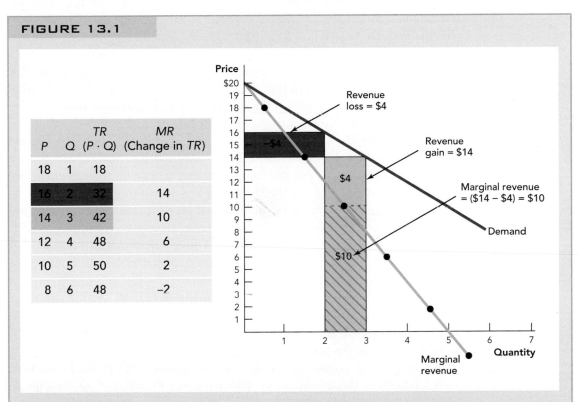

P	Q	TR (P · Q)	MR (Change in TR)
18	1	18	
16	2	32	14
14	3	42	10
12	4	48	6
10	5	50	2
8	6	48	−2

Marginal Revenue The table on the left shows that marginal revenue is the change in total revenue when quantity sold increases by 1 unit. When the quantity sold increases from 2 units to 3 units, for example, total revenue increases from $32 to $42 so marginal revenue, the change in total revenue, is $10.
The figure on the right shows how we can break down the change in total revenue into two parts. When the firm lowers the price from $16 to $14, it sells one more unit and so there is a gain in revenue of $14, but since the firm had to lower the price, it loses $2 on each of its two previous sales so there is a revenue loss of $4. Thus, marginal revenue is the revenue gain on new sales plus the revenue loss on previous sales.

FIGURE 13.2

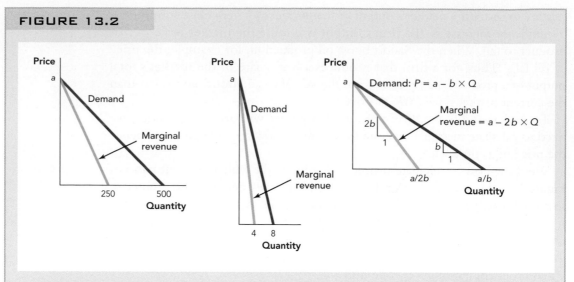

The MR Shortcut When the demand curve is a straight line, the marginal revenue curve begins at the same point on the vertical axis as the demand curve and has twice the slope.

$2 on *each* of the two units that it was selling at the higher price for a revenue loss of $4—the red area. Marginal revenue is the revenue gain (green, $14) plus the revenue loss (red, −$4) or $10 (green striped area). Notice that *MR* ($10) is less than price ($14)—once again, this is because to sell more units, the monopolist must lower the price so there is a loss of revenue on previous sales.

Now that you understand the idea of marginal revenue, here's a shortcut for finding marginal revenue. If the demand curve is a straight line, then the marginal revenue curve is a straight line that begins at the same point on the vertical axis as the demand curve but with twice the slope.[6] Figure 13.2 shows three demand curves and their associated marginal revenue curves. Notice that if the demand curve cuts the horizontal axis at, say, Z, then the marginal revenue curve will always cut the horizontal axis at half that amount, $Z/2$.

Figure 13.3 sketches the demand, marginal revenue, marginal cost, and average cost curve for a firm with market power, like GlaxoSmithKline. GSK maximizes profit by producing the quantity where $MR = MC$. In Figure 13.3, this is at point a, a quantity of 80 million units. What is the maximum price at which the monopolist can sell 80 million units? To find the maximum that consumers will pay for 80 million units, remember that we read up from the quantity supplied of 80 million units to the *demand curve* at point b. Consumers are willing to pay as much as $12.50 per pill when the quantity supplied is 80 million pills, so the profit-maximizing price is $12.50.

We can also use Figure 13.3 to illustrate the monopolist's profit. Remember from Chapter 11 that profit can be calculated as $(P - AC) \times Q$. At a quantity of 80 million units, the price is $12.50 (point b), the average cost (AC) is $2.50 (point c), and thus profit is ($12.50 − $2.50) × 80 million units or $800 million, as illustrated by the green rectangle. (By the way, the fixed costs of producing a new pharmaceutical are very large so the minimum point of the AC curve occurs far to the right of the diagram.) Recall that a competitive firm earns zero or normal profits but a monopolist uses its market power to earn positive or *above-normal* profits.

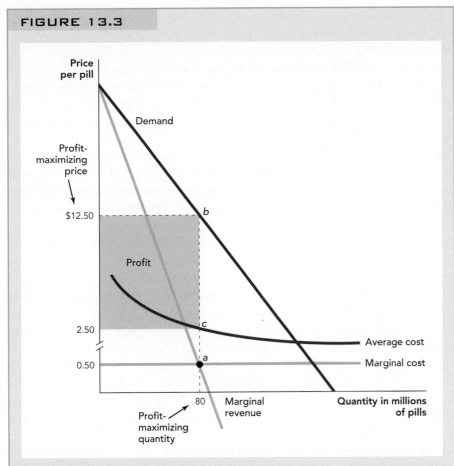

FIGURE 13.3

How a Monopolist Maximizes Profit To maximize profit, the monopolist produces until $MR = MC$ (point a). Reading down from point a, we find the profit-maximizing quantity, 80 million pills. Reading upward from point a, we find the profit-maximizing price on the demand curve, $12.50. Profit is $(P - AC) \times Q$ and is given by the green rectangle.

The Elasticity of Demand and the Monopoly Markup

Market power for pharmaceuticals can be especially powerful because of the two other effects we mentioned earlier: the "you can't take it with you" effect and the "other people's money" effect. If you are dying of disease, what better use of your money do you have than spending it on medicine that might prolong your life? If you can't take it with you, then you may as well spend your money trying to stick around a bit longer. Consumers with serious diseases, therefore, are *relatively insensitive to the price of life-saving pharmaceuticals.*

Moreover, if you are willing to spend *your* money on pharmaceuticals, how do you feel about spending *other people's money*? Most patients in the United States have access to public or private health insurance, so pharmaceuticals and other medical treatments are often paid by someone other than the patient. Thus, both the "you can't take it with you" and the "other people's money" effects make consumers with serious diseases relatively insensitive to the price of life-saving pharmaceuticals—that is, they will continue to buy in large quantities even when the price increases.

If GlaxoSmithKline knows that consumers will continue to buy Combivir even when it increases the price, how do you think it will respond? Yes, it will increase the price! When consumers are relatively insensitive to the price, what sort of demand curve do we say consumers have? An inelastic demand curve. The "you can't take it with you" effect and the "other people's money" effect make the demand curve more *inelastic*. Thus, we say that the more inelastic the demand curve, the more a monopolist will raise its price above marginal cost.

Is it ethically wrong for GSK to raise its price above marginal cost? Perhaps, but keep in mind that in the United States, it costs nearly a billion dollars to research and develop the average new drug. Once we better understand how monopolies price, we will return to the question of what, if anything, should be done about market power.

Figure 13.4 illustrates that the more inelastic the demand curve, the more a monopolist will raise its price above marginal cost. On the left side of the figure, the monopolist faces a relatively elastic demand curve, and on the right side a relatively inelastic demand curve. As usual, the monopolist maximizes profit by choosing the quantity at which $MR = MC$ and the highest price that consumers will pay for that quantity. Notice that even though the marginal cost curve is identical in the two panels, the markup of price over marginal cost is much higher when the demand curve is relatively inelastic.

Remember from Chapter 5 that the fewer substitutes that exist for a good, the more inelastic the demand curve. With that in mind, consider the following puzzle. In December 2006, American Airlines was selling a flight from Washington, DC, to Dallas for $733.30. On the same day, it was selling a flight from Washington to San Francisco for $556.60. That's a little puzzling. You would expect the shorter flight to have lower costs, and Washington is much closer to Dallas than to San Francisco. The puzzle,

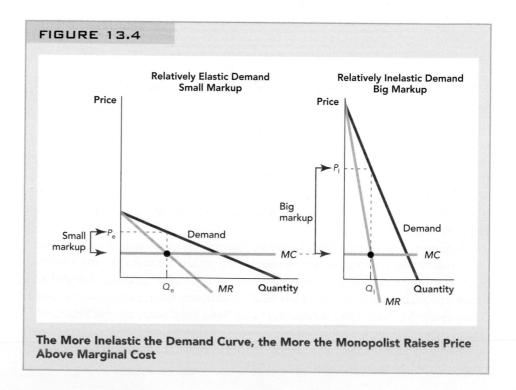

FIGURE 13.4

The More Inelastic the Demand Curve, the More the Monopolist Raises Price Above Marginal Cost

however, is even deeper. The flight from Washington to San Francisco stopped in Dallas. In fact, the Washington-to-Dallas leg of the journey was on exactly the same flight![7]

Thus, a traveler going from Washington to Dallas was being charged nearly $200 *more* than a traveler going from Washington to Dallas and then on to San Francisco even though both were flying to Dallas on the same plane. Why?

Here's a hint. Each of the major airlines flies most of its cross-country traffic into a hub, an airport that serves as a busy "node" in an airline's network of flights, and most hubs are located near the center of the country. Delta's hub, for example, is in Atlanta. So if you fly cross-country on Delta, you will probably travel through Atlanta. United's hub is in Chicago and American Airlines has its hub in Dallas. Have you solved the puzzle yet?

Of the flights into the Dallas-Fort Worth airport, 84% are on American Airlines, so if you want to fly from Washington to Dallas at a convenient time, you have few choices of airline. But if you want to fly from Washington to San Francisco, you have many choices. In addition to flying on American Airlines, you can fly Delta, United, or Jet Blue. Since travelers flying from Washington to Dallas have few substitutes, their demand curve is inelastic, like the demand curve in the right panel of Figure 13.4. Since travelers flying from Washington to San Francisco have many substitutes, their demand curve is more elastic, like the one in the left panel of Figure 13.4. As a result, travelers flying from Washington to Dallas (inelastic demand) are charged more than those flying from Washington to San Francisco (elastic demand).

You are probably asking yourself why someone wanting to go from Washington to Dallas doesn't book the cheaper flight to San Francisco and then exit in Dallas? In fact, clever people try to game the system all the time—but don't try to do this with a round-trip ticket or the airline will cancel your return flight. As a matter of contract, most airlines prohibit this and similar practices—their profit is at stake!

The Costs of Monopoly: Deadweight Loss

What's wrong with monopoly? The question may seem absurd—isn't it the high prices? Not so fast. The high price is bad for consumers, but it's good for the monopolist. And what's so special about consumers? Monopolists are people, too. So if we want to discover whether monopoly is good or bad, we need to count the gains to the monopolist equally with the losses to consumers. It turns out, however, that the monopolist gains less from monopoly pricing than the consumer loses. So monopolies are bad—they are bad because, compared with competition, monopolies reduce *total surplus*, the total gains from trade (consumer surplus plus producer surplus).

In Figure 13.5 on the next page, we compare total surplus under competition with total surplus under monopoly. In the left panel, the competitive equilibrium price and quantity are P_c and Q_c. We also label Q_c the optimal quantity because it is the quantity that maximizes total surplus (recall from Chapter 4 that a competitive market maximizes total surplus). For simplicity, we assume a constant cost industry so the supply curve is flat ($MC = AC$) and producer surplus is zero. Total surplus is thus the same as consumer surplus and is shown by the blue triangle.

CHECK YOURSELF

> As a firm with market power moves down the demand curve to sell more units, what happens to the price it can charge on all units?

> What type of demand curve does a firm with market power prefer to face for its products: relatively elastic or inelastic? Why?

FIGURE 13.5

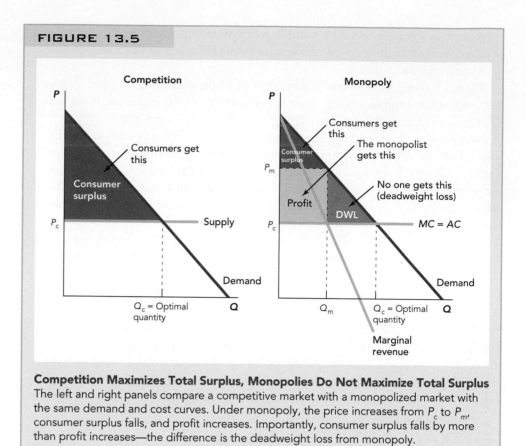

Competition Maximizes Total Surplus, Monopolies Do Not Maximize Total Surplus
The left and right panels compare a competitive market with a monopolized market with the same demand and cost curves. Under monopoly, the price increases from P_c to P_m, consumer surplus falls, and profit increases. Importantly, consumer surplus falls by more than profit increases—the difference is the deadweight loss from monopoly.

The right panel shows how a monopolist with the same costs would behave. Setting $MR = MC$, the monopolist produces Q_m, which is much less than Q_c, and prices at P_m. Consumer surplus is now the much smaller blue triangle. Now here is the key point: *Some* of the consumer surplus has been transferred to the monopolist as profit, the green area. But some of the consumer surplus is not transferred, it goes to neither the consumers nor to the monopolist; it goes to no one and is lost. We call the lost consumer surplus *deadweight loss*.

To better understand deadweight loss, remember that the height of the demand curve tells you how much consumers are willing to pay for the good, and the height of the marginal cost curve tells you the cost of producing the good. Now notice that in between the amount that the monopolist produces, Q_m, and the amount that would be produced under competition, Q_c, the demand curve is above the marginal cost curve. In other words, consumers value the units between Q_m and Q_c more than their cost; so if these units were produced, total surplus would increase. But the monopolist does not produce these units. Why not? Because to sell these units, the monopolist would have to lower its price; and if it did so, the increase in revenue would not cover the increase in costs, that is, MR would be less than MC, so the monopolist's profit would decrease.

Let's look at deadweight loss in practice. GlaxoSmithKline prices Combivir at $12.50 a pill, the profit-maximizing price. There are plenty of consumers who can't pay $12.50 a pill but would gladly pay more than the marginal cost of 50 cents a pill. Deadweight loss is the value of the Combivir sales that do not occur because the monopoly price is above the competitive price.

CHECK YOURSELF

> Does the monopolist price its product above or below the price of a competitive firm?

> Does the monopolist produce more or less than competitive firms? Why?

The Costs of Monopoly: Corruption and Inefficiency

Sadly, around the world today, many monopolies are government-created and born of corruption. Indonesian President Suharto (in office from 1967 to 1998), for example, gave the lucrative clove monopoly to his playboy son, Tommy Suharto. Cloves may sound inconsequential, but they are a key ingredient in Indonesian cigarettes, and the monopoly funneled hundreds of millions of dollars to Tommy. A lot of rich playboys buy Lamborghinis—Tommy bought the entire company.

Monopolies are especially harmful when the goods that are monopolized are used to produce other goods. In Algeria, for example, a dozen or so army generals each control a key good. Indeed, the public ironically refers to each general by the major commodity that they monopolize—General Steel, General Wheat, General Tire, and so forth.

Steel is an input into automobiles, so when General Steel tries to take advantage of his market power by raising the price of steel, this increases costs for General Auto. General Auto responds by raising the price of automobiles even more than he would if steel were competitively produced. Similarly, General Steel raises the price of steel even more than he would if automobiles were competitively produced. Throw in a General Tire, a General Computer, and, let's say, a General Electric and we have a recipe for economic disaster. Each general tries to grab a larger share of the pie, but the combined result is that the pie gets much, much smaller.

Monopoly profit.

Compare a competitive market economy with a monopolized economy: Competitive producers of steel work to reduce prices so they can sell more. Reduced prices of steel result in reduced prices of automobiles. Cost savings in one sector are spread throughout the economy, resulting in economic growth. In a monopolized economy, in contrast, the entire process is thrown into reverse. Each firm wants to raise its prices, and the resulting cost increases are spread throughout the economy, resulting in poverty and stagnation.

One of the great lessons of economics is to show that good institutions channel self-interest toward social prosperity, whereas poor institutions channel self-interest toward social destruction. Business leaders in the United States are no less self-interested than generals in Algeria. So why are the former a mostly positive force, while the latter are a mostly negative force? It's because competitive markets channel the self-interest of business leaders toward social prosperity, whereas the political structure of Algeria channels self-interest toward social destruction.

The Benefits of Monopoly: Incentives for Research and Development

GlaxoSmithKline prices its AIDS drugs above marginal cost. If GSK didn't have a monopoly, competition would push prices down, more people could

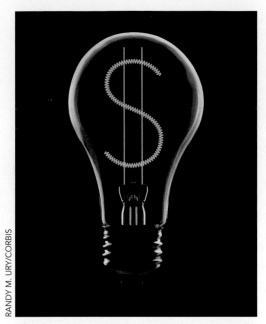

RANDY M. URY/CORBIS

Thomas Edison spent years experimenting with thousands of materials before he discovered that carbonized bamboo filament would make a long-lasting lightbulb. If anyone could have capitalized on his idea, Edison would not have been able to profit from his laborious research and development and perhaps he would not have done the necessary research in the first place.

Profit fuels the fire of invention.

afford to buy Combivir, and total surplus would increase (i.e., deadweight loss would decline). So isn't the solution to the monopoly problem obvious? Open up the industry to competition by refusing to enforce the firm's patent or force GlaxoSmithKline to lower its price.

In fact, many countries pursue one or the other of these policies. India, for example, has traditionally not offered strong patent protection, and Canada controls pharmaceutical prices. India's and Canada's policies have successfully kept pharmaceutical prices low in those countries. Many people argue that the United States should also control pharmaceutical prices. Unfortunately, the story is not so simple. We need to revisit our question, what's wrong with monopoly?

In the United States, researching, developing, and successfully testing the average new drug cost nearly 1 billion dollars.[8] Firms must be compensated for these expenses if people expect them to invest in the discovery process. But if competition pushes the price of a pill down to the marginal cost, nothing will be left over for the cost of invention. And he who has no hope of reaping will not sow.

Patents are one way of rewarding research and development. Look again at Figure 13.3, which shows the green rectangle of monopoly profit. It's precisely the expectation (and hope) of enjoying that monopoly profit that encourages firms to research and develop new drugs.

If pharmaceutical patents are not enforced, the number of new drugs will decrease. India is poor and Canada is small, so neither contributes much to the global profit of pharmaceutical firms. But if the United States were to limit pharmaceutical patents significantly or to control pharmaceutical prices, the number of new drugs would decrease significantly.[9] But new drugs save lives. As noted in the introduction, antiretrovirals like Combivir were the major cause of the 50% decrease in AIDS deaths in the United States in the mid-1990s. We should be careful that in pushing prices closer to marginal cost, we do not lose the new drug entirely.

In evaluating pharmaceutical patents, you should keep in mind that patents don't last forever. A patent lasts for at most 20 years, and by the time a new drug is FDA-approved, its effective life is typically only 12–14 years. Once the drug goes off patent, generic equivalents appear quickly and the deadweight loss is eliminated as price falls.

Pharmaceuticals are not the only goods with high development costs and low marginal costs. Information goods of all kinds often have the same cost structure. Video games like Halo, Madden NFL, and The Sims, have typical development costs of $7 million to $10 million; Grand Theft Auto IV cost more than $100 million to develop. Once the code has been written, however, the marginal cost of printing a manual and writing a DVD or CD might be $2. Prices, typically $40–$60, are therefore well above marginal costs. Since prices exceed marginal costs, there is a deadweight loss, which in theory could be reduced by a price control. Reducing prices, however, would reduce the incentive to research and develop new games. What would you rather have: Pong at $2, or, for $50 a game, a constant stream of new and better games?

Video games may seem trivial, but the trade-off between lower prices today at the expense of fewer new ideas in the future is a central one in modern economies. In fact, modern theories of economic growth emphasize that monopoly—*when it increases innovation*—may increase economic growth.

Nobel Prize-winning economic historian Douglass North argues that economic growth was slow and sporadic until laws, including patent laws, were created to protect innovation:

> [T]hroughout man's past he has continually developed new techniques, but the pace has been slow and intermittent. The primary reason has been that the incentives for developing new techniques have occurred only sporadically. Typically, innovations could be copied at no cost by others and without any reward to the inventor or innovator. The failure to develop systematic property rights in innovation up until fairly modern times was a major source of the slow pace of technological change.[10]

Patent Buyouts—A Potential Solution?

Is there a way to eliminate the deadweight loss without reducing the incentive to innovate? Economist Michael Kremer has offered one speculative idea.[11] Take a look again at Figure 13.3. The green profit rectangle is the value of the patent to the patent owner, $800 million. Suppose that the government were to offer to buy the rights to the patent at, say, $850 million? The monopolist would be eager to sell at this price. What would the government do with the patent? Rip it up! If the government ripped up the patent, competitors would enter the field, drive the price down to the average cost of production, and eliminate the deadweight loss. In other words, Combivir would fall from $12.50 a pill to 50 cents a pill, and more of the world's poor could afford to be treated for AIDS.

The great virtue of Kremer's proposal is that it reduces the price of new drugs without reducing the incentive to develop more new drugs. Indeed, by offering more than the potential profit, the government could even increase the incentive to innovate! As usual, however, there is no such thing as a free lunch. To buy the patent, the government must raise taxes, and we know from Chapter 6 that taxes, just like monopolies, create deadweight losses. Also determining the right price to buy the patent is not easy and some people worry that corruption could be a problem.

Kremer's idea has never been tried on a widespread basis, but despite these problems, economists are becoming increasingly interested in patent buyouts and the closely related idea of prizes as a way to encourage innovation without creating too much deadweight loss.

HANDOUT/EPA/CORBIS

Eyes on the Prize

Prizes are another way of rewarding research and development without creating monopolies. *SpaceShipOne*, pictured here, won the $10 million Ansari X Prize for being the first privately developed manned rocket capable of reaching space and returning in a short time. Netflix, the DVD distribution firm, offered and paid a $1 million prize for improvements to its movie recommendation system. The Department of Defense has sponsored prizes for driverless vehicles and Congress recently established the H-Prize for advances in hydrogen technology.

CHECK YOURSELF

> Name some firms with market power that plausibly encourage innovation. Name some firms with market power that do not seem to encourage innovation.

> If we rewarded innovation with prizes instead of patents, how large do you think the prize should be for a new cancer drug?

Economies of scale are the advantages of large-scale production that reduce average cost as quantity increases.

A **natural monopoly** is said to exist when a single firm can supply the entire market at a lower cost than two or more firms.

Economies of Scale and the Regulation of Monopoly

Governments are not the only source of market power. Monopolies can arise naturally when **economies of scale** create circumstances where one large firm (or a handful of large firms) can produce at lower cost than many small firms. When a single firm can supply the entire market at lower cost than two or more firms, we say that the industry is a **natural monopoly.**

A subway is a natural monopoly because it would cost twice as much to build two parallel subway tunnels than to build one, but even though costs would be twice as high, output (the number of subway trips) would be the same. Utilities such as water, natural gas, and cable television are typically natural monopolies because in each case it's much cheaper to run one pipe or cable than to run multiple pipes or cables to the same set of homes.

In Figure 13.5, we compared competitive firms with an *equal cost* monopoly and showed that total surplus was higher under competition. The comparison between competitive firms and natural monopoly is more difficult. Even though natural monopolies produce less than the optimal quantity, competitive firms would also produce less than the optimal quantity because they could not take advantage of economies of scale.

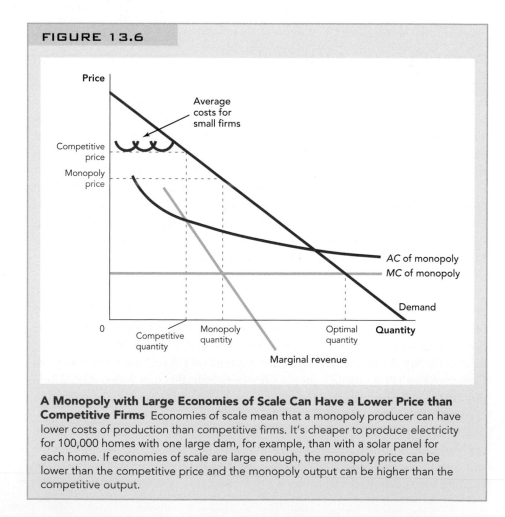

FIGURE 13.6

A Monopoly with Large Economies of Scale Can Have a Lower Price than Competitive Firms Economies of scale mean that a monopoly producer can have lower costs of production than competitive firms. It's cheaper to produce electricity for 100,000 homes with one large dam, for example, than with a solar panel for each home. If economies of scale are large enough, the monopoly price can be lower than the competitive price and the monopoly output can be higher than the competitive output.

FIGURE 13.7

A Price Control on a Monopoly Can Increase Output Without regulation, the monopoly maximizes profit by choosing P_m, Q_m. If the government imposes a price control at P_R, the monopolist chooses Q_R, a larger quantity. The optimal price is at $P = MC$, but at this price the monopolist is making a loss and will exit the industry. The lowest price that will keep the monopolist in the industry is $P = AC$ at point a. At that price, the monopolist makes a zero (normal) profit.

If the economies of scale are large enough, it's even possible for price to be lower under natural monopoly than it would be under competition. Figure 13.6 shows just such a situation. Notice that the average cost curve for the monopoly is so far below the average cost curves of the competitive firms, that the monopoly price is below the competitive price. It's possible, for example, for every home to produce its own electric power with a small generator or solar panel, but the costs of producing electricity in this way would be higher than buying electricity produced from a dam even if the dam was a natural monopoly.

Is there any way to have our cake and eat it too? That is, is there a way to have prices equal to marginal cost and to take advantage of economies of scale?

In theory the answer is yes, but it's not easy. In Chapter 8, we showed that a price control set below the market price would create a shortage. But surprisingly, when the market price is set by a monopolist, a price control can increase output. Let's see how.

Suppose that the government imposes a price control on the monopolist at level P_R, as in Figure 13.7. Imagine that the monopolist sells two units and suppose it wants to sell a third. What is the marginal revenue on the third unit? It's just P_R. In fact, when the price is set at P_R, the monopolist can sell up to Q_R units without having to lower the price. Since the monopolist doesn't have to lower the price to sell more units, the marginal revenue for each unit up to

Q_R is P_R. Notice that we have drawn the new marginal revenue curve in Figure 13.7 equal to P_R in between 0 and Q_R (after that point, to sell an additional unit, the monopolist has to lower the price on all previous units so the *MR* curve jumps down to the level of the old *MR* curve and becomes negative). Now the problem is simple because, as always, the monopolist wants to produce until $MR = MC$, so Q_R is the profit-maximizing quantity.

Notice that the monopolist produces *more* as the government-regulated price of its output *falls*.

So what price should the government set? Since the optimal quantity is found where $P = MC$, the natural answer is that the government should set $P_R = MC$. Unfortunately, that won't work when economies of scale are large because if the price is set equal to marginal cost, the monopolist will be making a loss. Remember that Profit $= (P - AC) \times Q$ so setting P_R equal to marginal cost creates a loss illustrated by the red area in Figure 13.7.

The government could subsidize the monopolist to make up for the loss when $P_R = MC$ but, once again, taxation has its own deadweight losses. If the government set $P_R = AC$ at point *a*, where the *AC* curve intersects the demand curve, the monopolist would just break even; output would then be larger than the monopoly quantity but less than the optimal quantity. This seems like a fairly good solution, but there are other problems with regulating a monopolist. When the monopolist's profits are regulated, it doesn't have much incentive to increase quality with innovative new products or to lower costs. The strange history of cable TV regulation and California's ill-fated efforts at electricity deregulation illustrate some of the real problems with regulating and deregulating monopolies.

I Want My MTV

Regulation of retail subscription rates for cable TV seemed to keep prices low in the early years of television, when there were basically only three channels, ABC, CBS, and NBC. In the 1970s, however, new technology made it possible for cable operators to offer 10, 20, or even 30 channels. But if subscription rates were fixed at the low levels, thereby limiting profit rates, the cable operators would have little incentive to add channels. Recognizing this, Congress lifted caps on pay TV rates in 1979 and on all cable television in 1984.

Deregulation of cable TV rates led to higher prices, just as the theory of natural monopoly predicts, but something else happened—the number of television stations and the quality of programming increased dramatically. And, contrary to natural monopoly theory, consumers seemed to appreciate the new channels more than they disliked the higher prices. This is evident because even as prices rose, more people signed up for cable television.[12]

Congress re-regulated "basic cable" rates in 1992 but left "premium channels" unregulated. *Wayne's World* was the result. Let's explain: Cable operators were typically required to carry a certain number of channels in the basic package, but they had some choice over which channels were included in the package. So when basic cable was re-regulated, the cable operators moved some of the best channels to their unregulated premium package. To fill the gaps in the basic package, they added whatever programs were cheap, including television shows created by amateurs

Quality comes at a price.

on a shoestring budget. *Wayne's World,* a *Saturday Night Live* comedy sketch, mocked the proliferation of these amateur cable shows.

Rates were mostly deregulated again in 1996. Not entirely coincidentally, this was the first year that HBO won an Emmy. Today, "basic tier cable" is regulated by local governments, but anything beyond the most basic service is predominantly free of regulation and cable companies can charge a market rate. As before, prices have risen since deregulation, but so have the number of television channels and the quality of programming.

If you like *True Blood, Boardwalk Empire,* and *Dexter,* then cable deregulation has worked well. Deregulation of electricity, however, has proven shocking.

Electric Shock

Government ownership is another potential solution to the natural monopoly problem. In the United States, there are some 3,000 electric utilities, and two-thirds of them are government-owned (the remainder are heavily regulated). Government ownership of utilities began early in the twentieth century with municipalities owning local distribution companies. In the 1930s, the federal government became a major generator of electricity with the construction of the then largest manmade structures ever built, the Hoover Dam in 1936 and the even larger Grand Coulee Dam in 1941.

Government ownership and regulation worked reasonably well for several decades in providing the United States with cheap power. Without the discipline of competition or a profit motive, however, there is a tendency for a government-run or regulated monopoly to become inefficient. Why reduce costs when costs can be passed on to customers? In the 1960s and 1970s, multibillion dollar cost overruns for the construction of nuclear power plants drew attention to industry inefficiencies as the price of power increased.

Historically, a single firm handled the generation, long-distance transmission, and local distribution of electricity. In the 1970s, however, new technologies reduced the average cost of generating electricity at small scales (in Figure 13.6 you can think of the curves labeled "Average costs for small firms" as moving down). Although the transmission and distribution of electricity remained natural monopolies, the new technologies meant that the generation of electricity was no longer a natural monopoly. Economists began to argue that unbundling generation from transmission and distribution could open up electricity generation to competitive forces, thereby reducing costs.

The Hoover Dam
The natural monopoly that lights Las Vegas.

California's Perfect Storm

Hoping to benefit from lower costs and greater innovation, California deregulated wholesale electricity prices in 1998. In the first two years after deregulation, all appeared well. In fact, as the new century was born, California was booming. In Silicon Valley, college students in computer science were being turned into overnight millionaires and billionaires. In 2000, personal income in California rose by a whopping 9.5%. Higher incomes and an unusually hot summer increased the demand for electricity. But California's generating capacity, which was old and in need of repair, began to strain. To meet the demand, California had to import power from other states, but other states had little to spare. Hot weather was pushing up demand throughout the West and the supply of hydroelectric power had fallen by approximately 20% because of low snowfall the previous winter.

All of these forces and more smashed together in the summer of 2000 to double, triple, quadruple, and finally quintuple the wholesale price of electricity from an average in April of $26 per megawatt hour (MWh) to an August high of $141 per MWh. Prices declined modestly in the fall but jumped again in the winter, reaching for one short period a price of $3,900 per MWh and peaking in December at an average monthly price of $317 per MWh—about 10 times higher than the previous December's rate.[13] Worse yet, when not enough power was available to meet the demand, blackouts threw more than 1 million Californians off the grid and into the dark. The new century wasn't looking so bright after all.

Mother Nature was not the only one to blame for California's troubles. The combination of increased demand, reduced supply, and a poorly designed deregulation plan had created the perfect opportunity for generators of electricity to exploit market power.

When the demand for electricity is well below capacity, each generator has very little market power. If a few generators had shut down in 1999, for example, the effect on the price would have been minimal because the power from those generators could easily have been replaced with imports or power from other generators. Thus, in 1999, each generator faced an elastic demand for its product. In 2000, however, every generator was critical because nearly every generator needed to be up and running just to keep up with demand. Electricity is an unusual commodity because it is expensive to store, and if demand and supply are ever out of equilibrium, the result can be catastrophic blackouts. Thus, when demand is near capacity, a small decline in supply leads to much higher prices as utilities desperately try to buy enough power to keep the electric grid up and running. Thus, in 2000, the demand curve facing each generator was becoming very inelastic. And what happens to the incentive to increase price when demand becomes inelastic? Do you remember the lesson of Figure 13.4, also pictured at left in Figure 13.8?

In the summer and winter of 2000, demand was near capacity and *every* generator was facing an inelastic demand curve. A firm that owned only one generating plant couldn't do much to exploit its market power: If it shut down its plant, the price of electricity would rise but the firm wouldn't have any power to sell! Many firms, however, owned more than one generator, and in 2000, this created a terrible incentive. A firm with four generators could shut down one, say, for "maintenance and repair," and the price of electricity would rise by so much that the firm could make more money selling the power

FIGURE 13.8

Relatively Elastic Demand, Small Markup

Relatively Inelastic Demand, Big Markup

produced by its three operating generators than it could if it ran all four! Suspiciously, far more generators were taken off-line for "maintenance and repair" in 2000 and early 2001 than in 1999.[14]

California was not the only state to restructure its electricity market in the late 1990s. Other states such as Texas and Pennsylvania had opened up generation to competition and have seen modestly lower electricity prices. Restructuring has also occurred in Britain, New Zealand, Canada, and elsewhere, but California's experience has demonstrated that unbundling generation from transmission and distribution, which remain natural monopolies, is tricky.

Other Sources of Market Power

Table 13.1 summarizes some of the sources of market power. In addition to patents, government regulation and economies of scale, monopolies may be created whenever there is a significant **barrier to entry**, something that raises the cost to new firms of entering the industry. One firm, for example, might own an input that is difficult to duplicate. Saudi Arabia, for example, has some market power in the market for oil because the demand for oil is inelastic and Saudi Arabia controls a significant fraction of the world's oil supply. What makes oil special is that oil is found in large quantities in only a few places in the world so a single firm in the right place can monopolize a significant share of the total supply. The market power of Saudi Arabia is enhanced when instead of competing with other suppliers, it joins with them to form a cartel, a group of firms that acts in concert to maximize total profits. We analyze cartels at greater length in Chapter 15.

Brands and trademarks can also give a firm market power because the prestige of owning the real thing cannot be easily duplicated. Timex watches tell the time as well as a Rolex, but only the Rolex signals wealth and status.

Monopolies may also arise when a firm innovates and produces a product that no other firm can immediately duplicate. In 2006, Apple had a 70% share in the market for MP3 players even though Apple's iPod had many competitors—the iPod was simply better than its rivals.[15] As with patent

CHECK YOURSELF

> Look at Figure 13.7. If regulators controlled the price at $P = AC$, at point a how much would the monopolist produce? Is this better for consumers, the monopolist, or society than the unregulated monopoly quantity?

> Telephone service used to be a natural monopoly. Why? Is it a natural monopoly today? Discuss how technology can change what is and isn't a natural monopoly.

Barriers to entry are factors that increase the cost to new firms of entering an industry.

TABLE 13.1 Some Sources of Market Power

Sources of Market Power	Example
Patents	GSK's patent on Combivir
Laws preventing entry of competitors	Indonesian clove monopoly, Algerian wheat monopoly, U.S. Postal Service
Economies of scale	Subways, cable TV, electricity transmission, major highways
Hard to duplicate inputs	Oil, diamonds, Rolex watches
Innovation	Apple's iPod, Wolfram's Mathematica software, eBay

monopolies, monopolies produced by innovation involve a trade-off: iPods are priced higher than they would be if Apple had better competitors, but Apple would have less incentive to innovate if it didn't expect to earn monopoly profits.

Takeaway

After reading this chapter, you should be able to find marginal revenue given either a demand curve or a table of prices and quantities (as in Figure 13.1). Given a demand and marginal cost curve, you should be able to find and label the monopoly price, the monopoly quantity, and deadweight loss. With the addition of an average cost curve, you should be able to find and label monopoly profit. You should also be able to demonstrate why the markup of price over marginal cost is larger the more inelastic the demand—this relationship will also be useful in the next chapter.

What makes monopoly theory interesting and a subject of debate among economists is that it's not always obvious whether monopolies are good or bad. Instead, we are faced with a series of trade-offs. Patent monopolies, such as the one on Combivir, create a trade-off between deadweight loss and innovation. The monopolist prices its product above marginal cost, but without the prospect of monopoly profits, there might be no product at all.

Natural monopolies also involve trade-offs, this time between deadweight loss and economies of scale. Deadweight loss means that monopoly is not optimal, but when economies of scale are large, competitive outcomes aren't optimal either. Regulating monopoly seems to offer an escape from this trade-off, but as we saw in our analysis of cable TV and electricity regulation, the practice of regulation is much more complicated than the theory. Cable TV regulation kept prices low but it kept quality low as well. Overall, deregulation of cable television rates worked surprisingly well, at least according to the consumers who flocked to cable even as rates rose. In contrast, electricity deregulation left California at the mercy of firms wielding market power.

Economists don't always agree on the best way to navigate the trade-offs between deadweight loss, innovation, and economies of scale. Many monopolies, however, perhaps most on a world scale, are "unnatural"—they neither support innovation nor take advantage of economies of scale—instead they are created to transfer wealth to politically powerful elites. For these monopolies, economics does offer guidance—open the field to competition! Alas, economics offers less clear guidance about how to convince the elites to follow the advice of economists.

CHAPTER REVIEW

KEY CONCEPTS

Market power, p. 234

Monopoly, p. 234

Marginal revenue, *MR*, p. 234

Marginal cost, *MC*, p. 234

Economies of scale, p. 244

Natural monopoly, p. 244

Barriers to entry, p. 249

FACTS AND TOOLS

1. In the following diagram, label the marginal revenue curve, the profit-maximizing price, the profit-maximizing quantity, the profit, and the deadweight loss.

2. a. Consider a market like the one illustrated in Figure 13.5, where all firms have the same average cost curve. If a competitive firm in this market tried to set a price above the minimum point on its average cost curve, how many units would it sell?

b. If a monopoly did the same thing, raising its price above average cost, what would happen to the number of units it sells: Does it rise, fall, or remain unchanged?

c. What accounts for the difference between your answers to parts a and b?

3. a. In the textbook *The Applied Theory of Price,* D. N. McCloskey refers to the equation $MR = MC$ as the rule of rational life. Who follows this rule: monopolies, competitive firms, or both?

b. Rapido, the shoe company, is so popular that it has monopoly power. It's selling 20 million shoes per year, and it's highly profitable. The marginal cost of making extra shoes is quite low, and it doesn't change much if the company produces more shoes. Rapido's marketing experts tell the CEO of Rapido that if it *decreased* prices by 20%, it would sell so many more shoes that profits would rise. If the expert is correct, at its current output, is $MC > MR$, is $MC = MR$, or is $MR > MC$?

c. If Rapido's CEO follows the expert's advice, what will this do to marginal revenue: Will it rise, fall, or be unchanged? Will Rapido's total revenue rise, fall, or be unchanged?

d. Apollo, another highly profitable shoe company, also has market power. It's selling 15 million shoes per year, and it faces marginal costs quite similar to Rapido's. Apollo's marketing experts conclude that if the company *increased* prices by 20%, profits would rise. For Apollo, is $MC > MR$, is $MC = MR$, or is $MR > MC$?

4. a. When selling e-books, music on iTunes, and downloadable software, the marginal cost of producing and selling one more unit of output is essentially zero: $MC = 0$. Let's think about a monopoly in this kind of market. If the monopolist is doing its best to maximize profits, what will marginal revenue equal at a firm like this?

b. All firms are trying to maximize their profits $(TR - TC)$. The rule from part a tells us that in the special case where marginal cost is zero, "profit maximization" is equivalent to which of the following statements?

"Maximize total revenue"

"Minimize total cost"

"Minimize average cost"

"Maximize average revenue"

5. a. What's the rule: Monopolists charge a higher markup when demand is highly elastic or when it's highly inelastic?

b. What's the rule: Monopolists charge a higher markup when customers have many good substitutes or when they have few good substitutes?

c. For the following pairs of goods, which producer is more likely to charge a bigger markup? Why?

i. Someone selling new trendy shoes, or someone selling ordinary tennis shoes?

ii. A movie theater selling popcorn or a New York City street vendor selling popcorn?

iii. A pharmaceutical company selling a new powerful antibiotic or a firm selling a new powerful cure for dandruff?

6. a. An answer you can find on the Internet: How high did *SpaceShipOne* fly when it won the Ansari X Prize?

b. How much did it cost to develop *SpaceShipOne*? Was the $10 million prize enough to cover the costs? Why do you think Microsoft cofounder Paul Allen invested so much money to win the prize? Do Allen's motivations show up in our monopoly model?

7. Which of the following is true when a monopoly is producing the profit-maximizing quantity of output? More than one may be true.

Marginal revenue = Average cost

Total cost = Total revenue

Price = Marginal cost

Marginal revenue = Marginal cost

8. a. Consider a typical monopoly firm like that in Figure 13.3. If a monopolist finds a way to cut marginal costs, what will happen: Will it pass along some of the savings to the consumer in the form of lower prices, will it paradoxically raise prices to take advantage of these fatter profit margins, or will it keep the price steady?

b. Is this what happens when marginal costs fall in a competitive industry, or do competitive markets and monopolies respond differently to a fall in costs?

9. a. Where will profits be higher: when demand for a patented drug is highly inelastic or when demand for a patented drug is highly elastic? (Figure 13.4 may be helpful.)

b. Which of those two drugs are more likely to be "important?" Why?

c. Now, consider the lure of profits: If a pharmaceutical company is trying to decide what kind of drugs to research, will it be lured toward inventing drugs with few good substitutes or drugs with many good substitutes?

d. Is your answer to part c similar to what an all-wise, benevolent government agency would do, or is it roughly the opposite of what an all-wise, benevolent government agency would do?

10. True or False?

a. When a monopoly is maximizing its profits, price is greater than marginal cost.

b. For a monopoly producing a certain amount of output, price is less than marginal revenue.

c. When a monopoly is maximizing its profits, marginal revenue equals marginal cost.

d. Ironically, if a government regulator sets a fixed price for a monopoly *lower* than the unregulated price, it is typically *raising* the marginal revenue of selling more output.

e. In the United States, government regulation of cable TV cut down the price of premium channels to average cost.

f. When consumers have many options, monopoly markup is lower.

g. A patent is a government-created monopoly.

THINKING AND PROBLEM SOLVING

1. In addition to the clove monopoly discussed in this chapter, Tommy Suharto, the son of Indonesian President Suharto (in office from 1967 to 1998), owned a media conglomerate, Bimantara Citra. In their entertaining book, *Economic Gangsters* (Princeton University Press, 2008), economists Raymond Fisman and Edward Miguel compared the stock price of Bimantara Citra with that of other firms on Indonesia's stock exchange around July 4, 1996, when the government announced that President Suharto was traveling to Germany for a health checkup. What do you think happened to the price of Bimantara Citra shares relative to other shares on the Indonesian stock exchange? Why? What does this tell us about corruption and monopoly power in Indonesia?

2. a. Sometimes, our discussion of marginal cost and marginal revenue unintentionally hides the real issue: the entrepreneur's quest to maximize total profits. Here is information on a firm:

Demand: $P = 50 - Q$ Fixed cost = 100
Marginal cost = 10

Using this information, calculate total profit for each of the values in the table below, and then plot total profit in the figure below. Clearly label the amount of maximum profit and the quantity that produces this level of profit.

Quantity	Total Revenue	Total Cost	Total Profit
18			
19			
20			
21			
22			
23			

b. If the fixed cost increased from 100 to 200, would that change the shape of this curve at all? Also, would it shift the location of the curve to the left or right? Up or down? How does this explain why you can ignore fixed costs most of the time when thinking about a monopoly's decision-making process?

3. When a sports team hires an expensive new player or builds a new stadium, you often hear claims that ticket prices have to rise to cover the new, higher cost. Let's see what monopoly theory says about that. It's safe to treat these new expenses as fixed costs: something that doesn't change if the number of customers rises or falls. You have to pay A-Rod the same salary whether people show up or not, you have to make the interest payments on the new Yankee Stadium whether the seats are filled or not. Treat the local sports team as a monopoly in this question, and to keep it simple, let's assume there is only one ticket price.

a. As long as the sports team is profitable, will a mere rise in fixed costs raise the equilibrium ticket price, lower the equilibrium ticket price, or have no effect whatsoever on the equilibrium ticket price? Why?

b. In fact, it seems common in real life for ticket prices to rise after a team raises its fixed costs by building a fancy new stadium or hiring a superstar player: In recent years, it's happened in St. Louis and San Diego's baseball stadiums. What's probably shifting to make this happen? Name *both* curves, and state the direction of the shift.

c. So, do sports teams spend a lot of money on superstars so that they can pass along the costs to the fans? Why *do* they spend a lot on superstars, according to monopoly theory? (*Note:* Books like *Moneyball* and *The Baseball Economist* apply economic models to the national pastime, and it's common for sports managers to have solid training in economic methods.)

4. Earlier we mentioned the special case of a monopoly where $MC = 0$. Let's find the firm's best choice when more goods can be produced at no extra cost. Since so much e-commerce is close to this model—where the fixed cost of inventing the product and satisfying government regulators is the only cost that matters—the $MC = 0$ case will be more important in the future than it was in the past. In each case, be sure to see whether profits are positive! If the "optimal" level of profit is negative, then the monopoly should never start up in the first place; that's the only way it can avoid paying the fixed cost.

a. $P = 100 - Q$ Fixed cost = 1,000

b. $P = 2,000 - Q$ Fixed cost = 900,000 (Driving the point home from part a.)

c. $P = 120 - 12Q$ Fixed cost = 1,000

5. **a.** Just based on self-interest, who is more likely to support strong patents on pharmaceuticals: young people or old people? Why?

b. Who is more likely to support strong patent and copyright protection on video games: people who really like old-fashioned videogames or people who want to play the best, most advanced video games?

c. How are parts a and b really the same question?

6. "Common sense" might say that a monopolist would produce more output than a competitive industry facing the same marginal costs. After all, if you're making a profit, you want to sell as much as you can, don't you? What's wrong with this line of reasoning? Why do monopolistic industries sell *less* than competitive industries?

7. In the early part of the twentieth century, it was cheaper to travel by rail from New York to San Francisco than it was to travel from New York to Denver, even though the train to San Francisco would stop in Denver on the way.

   a. Denver is a city in the mountains. Suggest alternate ways to get there from New York without taking the train.

   b. San Francisco is a city on the Pacific Ocean. Suggest alternate ways to get there from New York without taking the train.

   c. Why was San Francisco cheaper?

   d. How is this story similar to the one told in this chapter about prices for flights from Washington, DC, to either Dallas or San Francisco?

8. This chapter told the story of how the 2000 California energy shortage was aggravated by price deregulation.

   a. Suppose you are an entrepreneur who is interested in building a power plant to take advantage of the high prices for energy. Seeing rising energy costs, would price deregulation make it more or less likely you would build a new power plant? Why?

   b. It's very difficult to build and operate a new power plant largely because new plants have to comply with a long list of environmental and safety regulations. Compared with a world with fewer such regulations, how do these rules change the average cost of building and operating a power plant? Why?

   c. Do these regulations make it more or less likely that you will build a new power plant? Why?

   d. Do these regulations increase or decrease the market power of power plants that already exist?

9. The lure of spices during the medieval period wasn't driven merely by the desire to improve the taste of food (Europe produced saffron, thyme, bay leaves, oregano, and other spices for that). The lure of nutmeg, mace, and cloves came from their mystique. Spices became a symbol of prestige (just as Gucci and Ferrari are today). Most Europeans didn't even know that they grew in the tiny chain of islands that is called the Spice Islands today.

   a. Suppose you grow much of the spices in the Spice Islands. Knowing that few people could compete with you, how would you adjust your production to maximize your profits?

   b. Suppose you heard rumors that the Europeans to whom you often sell are also becoming fascinated by the mechanical clock, a new invention that was spreading across Europe as a new novelty and as yet another symbol of prestige. How would this change your optimal production? Why?

   c. Once Europeans made contact with the Americas, a new, high-status novelty arose: chocolate. Was this good news or bad news for you, the monopolist in the Spice Islands?

10. China developed gunpowder, paper, the compass, water-driven spinning machines, and many other inventions long before its European counterparts. Yet the Chinese did not adopt cannons, industrialization, and many other applications until *after* the West did.

   a. Suppose you are an inventor in ancient China and suddenly realize that the fireworks used for celebration could be enlarged into a functioning weapon. It would take time and money to develop, but you could easily sell the cutting-edge result to the government. If there is a strong patent system, would you put a big investment into developing this technology? Why or why not?

   b. Suppose there were no patent system, but you could still sell your inventions to the government. Compared with a world with a good patent law, would you be more inclined, less inclined, or about equally inclined to invest in technological development? Why?

CHALLENGES

1. a. For the following three cases, calculate

   i. The marginal revenue curve

   ii. The level of output where $MR = MC$ (i.e., set the equation from i equal to marginal cost and solve for Q)

    iii. The profit-maximizing price (i.e., plug your answer from equation ii into the demand curve)

    iv. Total revenue and total cost at this level of output (something you learned in Chapter 11)

    v. What entrepreneurs really care about—total profit.

      Case A: Demand: $P = 50 - Q$
      Fixed cost = 100   Marginal cost = 10

      Case B: Demand: $P = 100 - 2Q$
      Fixed cost = 100   Marginal cost = 10

      Case C: Demand: $P = 100 - 2Q$
      Fixed cost = 100   Marginal cost = 20

  b. What's the markup in each case? Measure it two ways: first in dollars, as price minus marginal cost, and then as a percentage markup [$100 \times (P - MC)/MC$, reported as a percent].

  c. If you solved part b correctly, you found that when costs rose from case B to case C, the monopolist's optimal price increased. Why didn't the monopolist charge that same higher price when costs were lower? After all, it's a monopolist, so it can charge what price they want. Explain in language that your grandmother could understand.

2. In Challenges question 1, what was the deadweight loss of monopoly in each of the three cases? (*Hint:* Where does the marginal cost curve cross the demand curve? The same place it does under competition.) Is this number measured in dollars, in units of the good, or in some other way?

3. a. In 2006, Medicare Part D was created to subsidize spending on prescription drugs. What effect would you expect this expansion to have on pharmaceutical prices? What principle in the chapter would explain this result?

  b. Given your answer in part a, what effect would you predict on pharmaceutical research and development?

  c. Whatever answer you gave in part a, can you think of an argument for the opposite prediction? *Hint:* In writing the Part D law, Congress said that subsidized drug plans must cover all pharmaceuticals in some "protected" classes, such as AIDS drugs, but in other areas subsidized plans could pick

and choose which drugs to offer. Understanding this difference may lead to different predictions.

4. In 1983, Congress passed the Orphan Drug Act, which gave firms that developed pharmaceuticals to treat rare diseases (diseases with U.S. patient populations of 200,000 people or fewer) the exclusive rights to sell their pharmaceutical for 7 years, basically an extended patent life. In other words, the act gave greater market power to pharmaceutical firms who developed drugs for rare diseases. Perhaps surprisingly, a patient organization, the National Organization for Rare Disorders (NORD), lobbied for the act. Why would a patient group lobby for an act that would increase the price of pharmaceuticals to its members? Why do you think the act was specifically for rare diseases?

5. For Kremer's patent buyout proposal (mentioned in the chapter) to work, the government needs to pay a price that's high enough to encourage pharmaceutical companies to develop new drugs. How can the government find out the right price? Through an auction, of course. In Kremer's plan, it works roughly like this: The government announces that it will hold an auction the next time that a company invents a powerful anti-AIDS drug. Once the drug has been invented and thoroughly tested, the government holds the auction. Many firms compete in the auction—just like on eBay—and the highest bid wins.

Now comes the twist: After the auction ends, a government employee rolls a six-sided die. If it comes up "1," then the highest bidder gets the patent, it pays off the inventor, and it's free to charge the monopoly price. If the die comes up "2" through "6," then the government pays the inventor whatever the highest bid was, and then it tears up the patent. The auction had to be held to figure out how much to pay, but most of the time it's the government that does the paying. Similarly, most of the time, citizens get to pay marginal cost for the drug, but one-sixth of all new drugs will still charge the monopoly price.

  a. In your opinion, would taxpayers be willing to pay for this?

  b. Using Figure 13.5 to guide your answer, what polygon(s) would these firms' bid be equal to?

c. If the government wins the die roll, what *net* benefits do consumers get, using Figure 13.5's polygons as your answer? (Be sure to subtract the cost of the auction!)

6. a. Let's imagine that the firm with cost curves illustrated in the left panel of the figure below is a large cable TV provider. Assuming that the firm is free to maximize profit, label the profit-maximizing price, quantity, and the firm's profit.

b. Now assume that the firm is regulated and that the regulator sets the price so that the firm earns a normal (zero) profit. What price does the regulator set and what quantity does the firm sell? (Label this price and quantity on the diagram.)

c. Which price and quantity pair do consumers prefer, that in part a or b? Do consumers benefit from price regulation?

d. Imagine that the cable TV provider can invest in fiber optic cable (high-definition), better programming, movie downloading, or some other service that increases the demand for the product, as shown in the right panel. If the firm were regulated as in part b, do you think it would be more or less likely to make these investments?

e. Given your answer in part d, revisit the question of price regulation and make an argument that price regulation could harm consumers once you take into account dynamic factors. Would this argument apply to all consumers or just some? If so, which ones?

14

Price Discrimination

After months of investigation, Interpol police swooped down on an international drug syndicate operating out of Antwerp, Belgium. The syndicate had been smuggling drugs from Kenya, Uganda, and Tanzania into the port of Antwerp for distribution throughout Europe. Smuggling had netted the syndicate millions of dollars in profit. The drug being smuggled? Heroin? Cocaine? No, something more valuable, Combivir. Why was Combivir, the anti-AIDS drug we introduced in Chapter 13, being illegally smuggled from Africa to Europe when Combivir was manufactured in Europe and could be bought there legally?[1]

The answer is that Combivir was priced at $12.50 per pill in Europe and, much closer to cost, about 50 cents per pill in Africa. Smugglers who bought Combivir in Africa and sold it in Europe could make approximately $12 per pill, and they were smuggling millions of pills. But this raises another question. Why was GlaxoSmithKline (GSK) selling Combivir at a much lower price in Africa than in Europe? Remember from Chapter 13 that GSK owns the patent on Combivir and thus has some market power over pricing. In part, GSK reduced the price of Combivir in Africa for humanitarian reasons, but lowering prices in poor countries can also increase profit. In this chapter, we explain how a firm with market power can use **price discrimination**—selling the same product at different prices to different customers—to increase profit.

> **Price discrimination** is selling the same product at different prices to different customers.

Price Discrimination

Figure 14.1 shows how price discrimination can increase profit. In the left panel we show the market for Combivir in Europe and in the right panel the market in Africa. The demand curve in Africa is much lower and more elastic (price sensitive) than in Europe because, on average, Africans are poorer than Europeans.

257

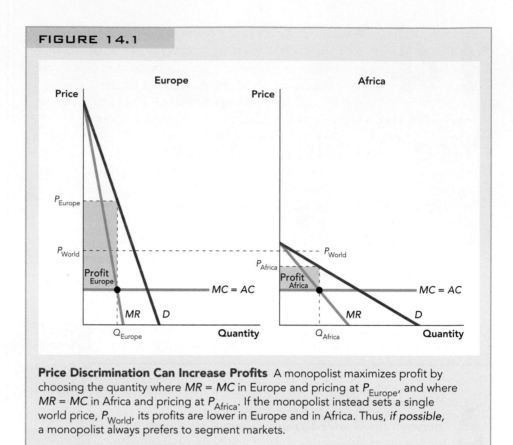

FIGURE 14.1

Price Discrimination Can Increase Profits A monopolist maximizes profit by choosing the quantity where *MR* = *MC* in Europe and pricing at P_{Europe}, and where *MR* = *MC* in Africa and pricing at P_{Africa}. If the monopolist instead sets a single world price, P_{World}, its profits are lower in Europe and in Africa. Thus, *if possible*, a monopolist always prefers to segment markets.

Now let's suppose for the moment that Europe is the only market. What price should GSK set? We know from Chapter 13 that the profit-maximizing quantity is found where marginal revenue equals marginal cost. From *MR* = *MC* in the left panel, we find that the profit-maximizing quantity is Q_{Europe}. The profit-maximizing price is the highest price that consumers will pay to purchase Q_{Europe} units, which we label P_{Europe}. Profit is given by the green area labeled $\text{Profit}_{\text{Europe}}$.

Similarly, if Africa were the only market, GSK would choose the profit-maximizing quantity Q_{Africa} and the profit-maximizing price P_{Africa}, which would generate profit in the amount $\text{Profit}_{\text{Africa}}$.

But what price should GSK set if it wants to have a single "world price" for both Europe and Africa? If GSK wants a single world price, it should lower the price in Europe and raise the price in Africa, setting a price somewhere between P_{Europe} and P_{Africa}, say, at P_{World}. (In a more advanced class, we would solve for the exact profit-maximizing world price, but that level of detail is not necessary here.)

But remember that P_{Europe} is the profit-maximizing price in Europe and P_{Africa} is the profit-maximizing price in Africa, so by lowering the price in Europe, GSK must be reducing profit in Europe. Similarly, by raising the price in Africa, GSK must be reducing profit in Africa. Thus, profit at the single price P_{World} must be less than when GSK sets two different prices earning the combined profit: $\text{Profit}_{\text{Europe}} + \text{Profit}_{\text{Africa}}$.

We have now arrived at the first principle of price discrimination: *(1a) If the demand curves are different, it is more profitable to set different prices in different markets than a single price that covers all markets.*

We also know from Chapter 13 and from Figure 14.1 how a monopolist should set prices. Recall that the more inelastic the demand curve, the higher the profit-maximizing price. In this case, the demand for Combivir is more inelastic (less sensitive to price) in the European market than in the African market, so the price is higher in Europe. This really isn't an independent principle; it's an implication of profit maximization, as we showed in Chapter 13. But it's a useful reminder, so we will add to our first principle: (*1b*) *To profit maximize, the monopolist should set a higher price in markets with more inelastic demand.*

The first principle of price discrimination tells us that GSK wants to set a higher price for Combivir in Europe than in Africa. But we also know from the introduction that setting two different prices for Combivir encourages drug smuggling. Smugglers buy Combivir at P_{Africa} and sell at P_{Europe}, which leaves fewer sales for GSK. A smuggler's profit comes out of GSK's pocket.

If smuggling is extensive, GSK will end up selling most of its output at P_{Africa}, which is less profitable than if GSK set a single world price. Thus, if GSK can't stop the drug smugglers, it will abandon its attempt at price discrimination and will instead set a single price—perhaps a single world price such as P_{World} or, if the African market is small, GSK may abandon Africa altogether and set a single price of P_{Europe}.

Smuggling is a special example of a more general (and legal) process that economists call **arbitrage**—buying low in one market and selling high in another market. Thus, we arrive at the second principle of price discrimination: (*2*) *Arbitrage makes it difficult for a firm to set different prices in different markets, thereby reducing the profit from price discrimination.*

We summarize the principles of price discrimination.

> **Arbitrage** is taking advantage of price differences for the same good in different markets by buying low in one market and selling high in another market.

The Principles of Price Discrimination

1a. If the demand curves are different, it is more profitable to set different prices in different markets than a single price that covers all markets.

1b. To maximize profit, the firm should set a higher price in markets with more inelastic demand.

2. Arbitrage makes it difficult for a firm to set different prices in different markets, thereby reducing the profit from price discrimination.

The first principle tells us that a firm *wants* to set different prices in different markets. The second principle tells us that a firm may not be *able* to set different prices in different markets. To succeed at price discrimination, the monopolist must prevent arbitrage.

Preventing Arbitrage

If it wants to profit from price discrimination, GSK must prevent Combivir that it sends to Africa from being resold in Europe. GSK has a number of tools to discourage smuggling. GSK, for example, sends red Combivir pills to Africa and sells white Combivir in Europe. If GSK detectives find red Combivir in Europe, they know that a GSK distributor has broken its agreement. Using special bar codes on each package, GSK can then track the smuggled pills back to the distributor who was supposed to distribute them in Africa. Interpol is called in to make arrests.

Markets can differ in more ways than geographically. Rohm and Haas is a producer of plastics. One of its plastics, methyl methacrylate (MM), was used in industry and also in dentistry as a material for

THE KOBAL COLLECTION/WALT DISNEY

Region codes prevent DVDs bought in India from being played on U.S. players. The codes help studios to price discriminate by discouraging arbitrage from low-price regions to high-price regions. Many consumers modify their players so that they can play DVDs from any region. Is this pirating?

dentures. MM had lots of substitutes as an industrial plastic but few as a denture material, so Rohm and Haas sold MM for industrial uses at 85 cents per pound and sold a slightly different version designed for dentures at $22 per pound. At these prices, it wasn't long before enterprising individuals started buying industrial MM and converting it to denture MM. Just like GSK, Rohm and Haas needed a way to prevent arbitrage between the two markets.

One bold thinker came up with what Rohm and Haas internal documents called "a very fine method of controlling the bootleg situation." The innovator suggested that Rohm and Haas should mix industrial MM with arsenic. This wouldn't reduce the value of MM in industry, but it would surely deter people from making it into dentures! Rohm and Haas's legal department rejected this plan, but the company came up with an idea nearly as good: They planted a *rumor* that industrial MM was mixed with arsenic![2]

Although Rohm and Haas never implemented the poisoning idea, the U.S. government has. The government taxes alcohol but subsidizes ethanol fuel. To prevent arbitrage, that is, to prevent entrepreneurs from buying ethanol fuel and converting it to drinkable alcohol, the government requires that ethanol fuel be poisoned!

It's easier to prevent arbitrage of some products than of others. A masseuse, for example, may easily set different prices for different customers because it's difficult for a customer who buys a massage at the low price to resell it to another customer at the higher price. Services, in general, are difficult to arbitrage.

> **CHECK YOURSELF**
>
> > Why does a monopolist want to segment a market?
>
> > Would a price-discriminating firm set higher or lower prices for a market segment with more inelastic demand?
>
> > What is arbitrage? How does arbitrage affect the ability of a monopolist to price-discriminate?

Price Discrimination Is Common

Once you know the signs, price discrimination is easy to see. Movie theaters, for example, often charge less for seniors than for younger adults. Is this because theater owners have a special respect for the elderly? Probably not. More likely it's that theater owners realize that young people have a more inelastic demand for movies than seniors. Thus, theater owners charge a high price to young people and a low price to seniors. It would probably be even more profitable if theater owners could charge people who are on a date more than married people (no one likes to look cheap on a date). But it's easy for theater owners to judge age and not so easy for them to figure out who is on a date and who is married.

Students don't always pay higher prices, however. Stata is a well-known statistical software package. It costs a business $1,295 to buy Stata, but registered students pay only $145. Thus, it's not about age—the young sometimes pay more and sometimes pay less—it's about how age correlates with what businesses really care about, which is how much the customer is willing to pay.

Here's another example. Airlines know that businesspeople are typically less sensitive to the price of an airline ticket than are vacationers (i.e., businesspeople have more inelastic demand curves). An airline would like, therefore, to set a high price for businesspeople and a low price for vacationers, as illustrated in Figure 14.2.

But airlines can't very well say to their customers, "Are you flying on business? Okay, the price is $600. Going on a vacation? The price is $200." So how can airlines segment the market?

Airlines set different prices according to characteristics that are correlated with the willingness to pay. Vacationers, for example, can easily plan their trips weeks or months in advance. Businesspeople, however, may discover that they need to fly tomorrow. Thus, if a customer wants to fly to Tampa, Florida, in two weeks' time he or she is probably a vacationer and the airline will

FIGURE 14.2

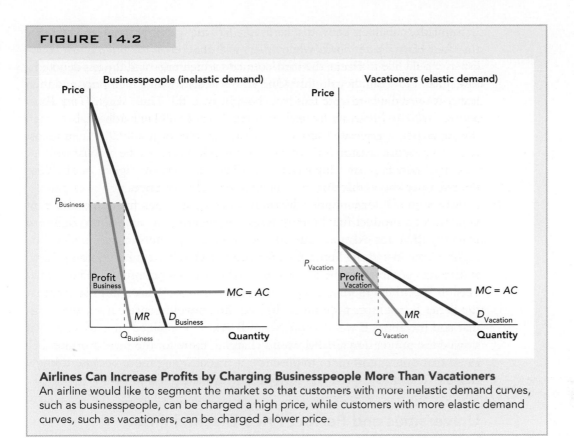

Airlines Can Increase Profits by Charging Businesspeople More Than Vacationers
An airline would like to segment the market so that customers with more inelastic demand curves, such as businesspeople, can be charged a high price, while customers with more elastic demand curves, such as vacationers, can be charged a lower price.

charge that person a low price, but if the customer wants to fly tomorrow, the price will be higher. On the day these words were written, U.S. Airways was charging $113 to fly from Washington, DC, to Tampa with two weeks' notice but more than three times as much, $395, to fly tomorrow. Except for the dates the flights were identical. Figure 14.3 illustrates how one airline charged many different prices for the same flight.

FIGURE 14.3

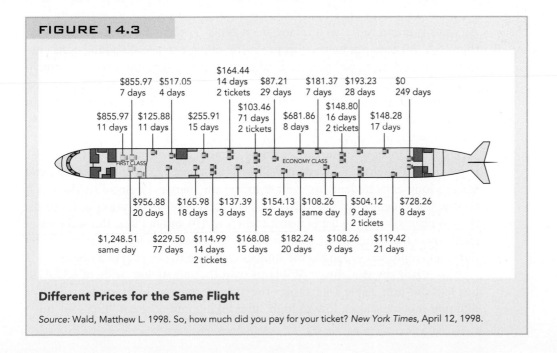

Different Prices for the Same Flight

Source: Wald, Matthew L. 1998. So, how much did you pay for your ticket? New York Times, April 12, 1998.

Similarly, publishers know that hard-core fans are willing to pay a high price for the latest Harry Potter book, while others will only buy if the price is low. Publishers would like to charge the hard-core fans a high price and the less devoted a low price. How can they do this? One way is to start with a high price and then lower it once the hard-core fans have bought their fill. Thus, when *Harry Potter and the Half-Blood Prince* hit the shelves, it retailed at $34.99 in hardback, but when the paperback was released about a year later, it sold for just $9.99. Does it cost more to produce a hardback? Yes, but not much more, maybe a dollar or two. The hard-core fans pay a higher price not because costs are higher, but because the publisher knows that they are willing to pay a higher price.

A more subtle form of price discrimination occurs when firms offer different versions of a product for the purpose of segmenting customers into different markets. IBM, for example, offered one of its laser printers in two models: the regular version and the Series E (E for economy). The regular version printed at 10 pages per minute, the Series E printed at 5 pages per minute. The regular version was much more expensive than the Series E. What's surprising is that the Series E cost more to produce. In fact, the only difference between the regular and the Series E was that the Series E printer contained an extra chip that slowed the printer down! IBM wasn't charging more for the regular printer because that printer cost more to produce; it was charging more because it knew that the demand for speed was correlated with willingness to pay.

Universities and Perfect Price Discrimination

Universities are one of the biggest practitioners of price discrimination, although they hide this practice under the blanket of "student aid." Student aid is a way of charging different students different prices for the same good. Consider Williams College, a small, prestigious liberal arts college. In 2001, some students at Williams paid the sticker price of $32,470, while others paid just $1,683 for exactly the same education. Why the big difference in price?

Part of the story is that Williams College was doing good by offering financial aid to students from poorer families. But Williams College was also doing well. To see why, notice that Williams College is a lot like an airline. If U.S. Airways is going to fly an airplane from New York to Los Angeles anyway, then U.S. Airways can increase its profits by filling extra seats so long as its customers are willing to pay the marginal costs of flying (say, the extra fuel costs). Of course, if a customer is willing to pay $800 to fly to LA., then U.S. Airways wants to charge that customer $800 and not less. But if the marginal cost of flying is $100, then U.S. Airways can increase its profits by filling an empty seat so long as the customer is willing to pay at least $101.

Williams College is a lot like an airline because if Ancient Greek History 101 is going to be taught anyway, then Williams can increase its profits by filling extra seats so long as its students are willing to pay the marginal costs of teaching. Of course, if a student is willing to pay $32,470 for a year of education at Williams, then Williams wants to charge that student $32,470 and not less. But if the marginal costs of teaching are $1,682 a year, then Williams can increase its profits by filling an empty seat so long as the student is willing to pay at least $1,683.

About half the students at Williams paid the full sticker price of $32,470, but half did not. Table 14.1 shows the average price paid by students in five different income classes, low to high, after taking into account "financial aid."

TABLE 14.1 Price Discrimination at Williams College, 2001–2002

Income Quintile	Family Income Range	Net Price After Financial Aid
Low	$0–$23,593	$1,683
Lower Middle	$23,594–$40,931	$5,186
Middle	$40,932–$61,397	$7,199
Upper Middle	$61,398–$91,043	$13,764
High	$91,044+	$22,013

Note: Students who did not apply for financial aid paid $32,470.
Source: Hill, Catharine B. and Gordon C. Winston. 2001. *Access: Net Prices, Affordability, and Equity at a Highly Selective College*. Williams College, DP-62.

The difference in price is extreme. Even the airlines, masters of price discrimination, can rarely charge some customers 20 times what they charge other customers. Williams has a big advantage over the airlines, however. Williams has an extraordinary amount of information about its customers.

To receive financial aid, Williams demands that students and their parents submit their tax returns to Williams. Williams, therefore, has very detailed information about the income of its customers, and it uses that information to set many different prices. Table 14.1 shows *average* prices within each income class, but, in fact, Williams divided prices even more finely, setting a different price, for example, to a student with family income of $30,000 than one with family income of $35,000. In theory, Williams could offer a different price to each one of it students, charging each student his or her maximum willingness to pay. This is what economists call **perfect price discrimination**.

Figure 14.4 on the next page shows how perfect price discrimination works in a market like education, where each customer buys one unit of the good. Alex values education the highest, Tyler the second highest, Robin the third highest, all the way down to Bryan who thinks that education has very little value. A firm that has a lot of information about Alex, Tyler, Robin, and Bryan can set four different prices, charging each of them their maximum willingness to pay (or, if you like, a penny less than their maximum willingness to pay). Thus, Alex is charged the most and Bryan the least.

Since a perfectly price-discriminating (PPD) monopolist charges each consumer his or her maximum willingness to pay, consumers end up with zero consumer surplus. All of the gains from trade go to the monopolist. This is bad for consumers but does have a beneficial side effect: Since the PPD monopolist gets all the gains from trade, the PPD monopolist has an incentive to maximize the gains from trade, and maximizing the gains from trade means no deadweight loss.

In Chapter 13, we showed that a single-price monopoly creates a deadweight loss, but this is not true for a perfectly price-discriminating monopoly. In Figure 14.4, notice that whenever a consumer's willingness to pay is higher than marginal cost, then that consumer is sold a unit of the good—but this means that the PPD monopoly produces the efficient quantity! In fact, the perfectly price-discriminating monopolist produces until $P = MC$ (i.e., Q^* units), exactly as does a competitive firm!

Under **perfect price discrimination (PPD),** each customer is charged his or her maximum willingness to pay.

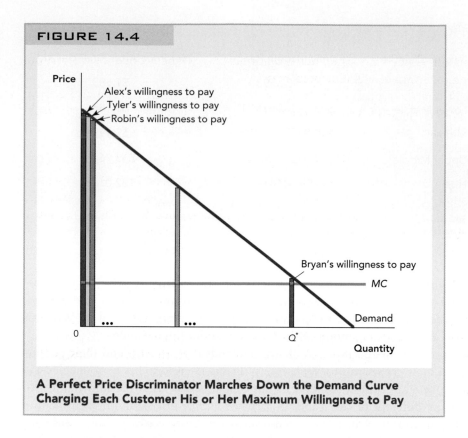

FIGURE 14.4

A Perfect Price Discriminator Marches Down the Demand Curve Charging Each Customer His or Her Maximum Willingness to Pay

Another way of seeing why the perfectly price-discriminating monopolist produces the efficient quantity is to remember that *all* firms want to produce until $MR = MC$. For a competitive firm, $MR = P$, so the competitive firm produces until $P = MC$. For a single single-price monopolist, $MR < P$, so the single-price monopolist produces less than the competitive firm. But what is MR for a PPD monopolist? It's P and thus the PPD monopolist also sets $P = MC$. Can you explain why as a PPD monopolist moves down the demand curve selling to additional customers, its MR is always equal to price?

Detailed information about its customers helps Williams College set each student's price close to that student's maximum willingness to pay, thus maximizing Williams's revenue. Ever wonder why many retailers ask for your zip code when they ring up your purchase? More information means more profit. Ever wonder why used car salespeople are so friendly? Sure, friendliness helps to sell cars, but what you think of as friendly talk is really a clever strategy to learn as much about you as possible so the salesperson can price accordingly. When buying a new car, one of the authors of this book always tells the salesperson he is a student. Alas, the ruse is becoming less believable as the years wear on.

CHECK YOURSELF

> Is the early bird special (eating dinner at a restaurant before 6:00 PM or 6:30 PM) a form of price discrimination? If so, what are the market segments? Can you think of another explanation for this type of pricing?

> Why is it much more expensive to see a movie in a theater than to wait a few months and see it at home on DVD? Can you give an explanation based on price discrimination?

Is Price Discrimination Bad?

Price discrimination certainly sounds bad, but we just showed that a perfectly price-discriminating monopolist produces more output than a single-price monopolist, and this is good so price discrimination can't always be bad. What about if price discrimination is imperfect? Does a monopolist that sets two (or a handful of) prices raise or lower total surplus? The answer is subtle, but there is a similar intuition to the case of the perfectly price-discriminating monopolist. Price discrimination is bad if the total output with price discrimination falls or stays the same, but if output increases under price discrimination, then total surplus will usually increase.

To see this, let's return to the case of Combivir in Europe and Africa. Suppose that GSK was forbidden from price discriminating so it had to set one world price. What world price would GSK set, and would this increase or decrease total surplus?

One possibility is that if forced to set a single price, GSK would lower the price enough so that some Africans could buy Combivir—for example, a price like P_{World} in Figure 14.1. A single price of P_{World} is better for Europeans since $P_{World} < P_{Europe}$, but it is worse for Africans since $P_{World} > P_{Africa}$. Thus, depending on exactly how much better off Europeans are and how much worse off Africans are at P_{World}, price discrimination could be better or worse than single pricing.

How likely is it, however, that GSK would lower the price to P_{World}? Two-thirds of the 630 million people living in Africa live on less than a dollar a day. Thus, even when GSK sells Combivir at close to its cost of 50 cents a pill, most Africans with AIDS cannot afford Combivir. GSK, therefore, cannot make up for a low price by selling large volumes of Combivir to Africans. Thus, if GSK cannot set two different prices, it will probably abandon the African market altogether and sell to the world at P_{Europe}. At P_{Europe}, only Europeans can afford to buy Combivir.

At the single price of P_{Europe}, are Europeans better off than with price discrimination? No, the price to Europeans hasn't changed and thus the quantity of Combivir consumed by Europeans is the same under both pricing systems. What about Africans? At the single price of P_{Europe}, Africans pay more for Combivir than with price discrimination and they consume less. Thus, in the most plausible case, forcing GSK to set a single price doesn't help Europeans but does hurt Africans. Alternatively stated, price discrimination in this case increases total surplus because price discrimination increases output—with price discrimination, Europeans consume as much Combivir as with a single price, but Africans increase their consumption from what it would be with a high single price.

Why Misery Loves Company and How Price Discrimination Helps to Cover Fixed Costs

In industries with high fixed costs, price discrimination has another benefit. To explain why, we ask a strange question. Imagine that there are two diseases that if left untreated are equally deadly. One of the diseases is rare, the other is common. If you had to choose, would you rather be afflicted with the rare disease or the common disease? Take a moment to think about this question because there is a definite answer.

It's much better to have the common disease because there are more drugs to treat common diseases than to treat rare diseases, and more drugs means greater life expectancy. Patients diagnosed with a rare disease are 45% more likely to die before the age of 55 than patients diagnosed with a more common disease.[*]

---

[*] "Rare" is defined as a disease in the bottom quarter of incidence in the United States in 1998; "common" is defined as a disease in the top quarter of incidence. See Lichtenberg, Frank R. and Waldfogel, Joel, June 2003, *Does Misery Love Company? Evidence from Pharmaceutical Markets Before and After the Orphan Drug Act*. NBER Working Paper No. W9750. Available at http://www.ssrn.com/abstract=414248.

The reason there are more drugs to treat common diseases is because the market is larger. Simply put, it costs about the same to develop a drug for a rare or a common disease but the revenues are much greater for a drug that treats a common disease. Thus, the larger the market, the more profitable it is to develop a drug for that market.

The fact that profits increase with market size explains why price discrimination can benefit *Europeans,* as well as Africans. We have already shown that Africans benefit from price discrimination because of lower prices. Europeans benefit because price discrimination increases the profit from producing pharmaceuticals, and more profit means more research and development, more new drugs, and greater life expectancy.

Pharmaceuticals are not the only industry with high fixed costs—airlines, chemicals, universities, software, and movies all have a similar cost structure. Low prices for vacationers, for example, can benefit business travelers because the extra profit that airlines earn from selling to vacationers encourages airlines to offer more flights to more places at more times. The synthetic fabric Kevlar is five times stronger by weight than steel and is used to make bulletproof vests as well as auto tires. As a bulletproof vest, Kevlar has few substitutes, but as tire belting, it has many. As a result, DuPont charges more for Kevlar used in vests than for Kevlar used in belting. If DuPont had to charge the same price in all markets, Kevlar might not be used for belting at all, and Du Pont would have lower profits and less incentive to innovate.

Tying and Bundling

Everyone knows that airlines charge different prices to different customers for the same flight. Senior citizen and student discounts are obvious. Universities advertise their scholarship policies—even if they don't always advertise that this is a way of increasing profit! But other types of price discrimination are more subtle and difficult to see. Let's take a look at tying and bundling, two types of price discrimination that are hidden to the untrained observer.

Tying

Why are printers so cheap and ink so expensive? As we write this chapter, one remarkable Hewlett-Packard (HP) photo printer/scanner/copier sells for just $69. A full set of color ink cartridges, however, will set you back $44. At that price, it almost pays to buy a new printer (which comes with a cartridge) every time you run out of ink! Clearly, HP is pricing its printers low and making its profit from selling ink. HP is not alone in pursuing this strategy. Xbox game consoles are priced below cost, and Xbox games are priced above cost. Cell phones are priced below cost and phone calls are priced above cost. Why?

Think of HP as selling not printers and ink, but the package good, "ability to print color photos." HP wants to charge a high price to consumers with a high willingness to pay and a low price to consumers with a low willingness to pay. Consumers with a high willingness to pay for the "ability to print color photos" probably want to print a lot of color photos. Consumers with a low willingness to pay probably want to print only the occasional color photo. By charging a high price for ink, HP is charging high willingness to pay consumers a high price. Yet, because the price of printers is low, consumers who have only a low willingness to pay are charged a low price.

HP's pricing scheme is especially brilliant because the price is so flexible. Instead of two prices, there are many: one for a consumer who prints 10 photos a month, another for a consumer who prints 15 photos a month, and yet another for a consumer who prints 100 photos a month.

For HP's scheme to work, it's critical that no one else but HP be allowed to sell ink for HP printers—HP must *tie* its printers to HP ink cartridges, which is why this form of price discrimination is called **tying**. If competitors could easily enter the market for ink, the price of ink would fall to marginal cost and HP's pricing scheme would fall apart. HP manages to keep competitors out of the market for ink in a clever way—the HP ink cartridge contains not just ink, but also a crucial and patented component of the printer head. Since other firms are forbidden by law from manufacturing the printer head, and since the head and the ink must be packaged together, HP manages to keep competitors out of the market for ink. Well, almost. There is an active market in *refilling* HP printer heads, which is much cheaper than buying them new.

> **Tying** occurs when to use one good, the consumer must use a second good that is sold (only) by the same firm. A firm can price-discriminate by tying two goods and carefully setting their prices.

HP's strategy illustrates both the benefits and costs of price discrimination. Price discrimination, as usual, may increase output by lowering the price to users who only want to print the occasional photo. Price discrimination also spreads the fixed costs of research and development—which are extensive for color photo printers—over more users, thus encouraging more innovation. But putting printer heads in the ink cartridge rather than in the printer probably raises the total cost of printing. Although there are some advantages to disposable printer heads, HP is spending the extra money not to benefit consumers but to keep competitors out of the ink business. Since the extra costs of production don't benefit consumers, they are a cost of price discrimination.

By the way, in addition to price discrimination, HP is probably also taking advantage of a bit of consumer irrationality. When comparing printers, consumers *should* look at the total price, printer plus ink, over the entire lifetime of the printer. But it takes some work to estimate the total price, and consumers who are shortsighted may focus on amazingly cheap printers rather than astonishingly expensive ink.

Bundling

Goods are **bundled** when they must be bought in a package. Nike doesn't sell right and left shoes individually, Nike only sells shoes in a right and left bundle.* Toyota doesn't sell engines, steering columns, and wheels, it sells a bundle called a car. As the examples suggest, most bundling is easily explained as a way to reduce costs. But why does Microsoft sell Word, Excel, Outlook, Access, and PowerPoint in a bundle called Microsoft Office?

> **Bundling** is requiring that products be bought together in a bundle or package.

Unlike buying a car piece by piece, it would not be difficult for consumers to buy the Office products individually and assemble them as they wanted. Almost every car buyer wants an engine and four wheels, but not every Office buyer wants Microsoft Access. So why does Microsoft bundle? Note that Microsoft does sell most Office products individually, but the sum of the individual prices far exceeds the price of the bundle, so most consumers buy Office.

---

* The difference between tying and bundling is that bundled goods are sold one to one. Every right shoe comes with a left shoe. Tied goods are sold one to many. Every HP printer is tied to a variable number of ink cartridges depending on consumer demand.

TABLE 14.2 Maximum Willingness to Pay for Word and Excel

	Amanda	Yvonne
Word	$100	$40
Excel	$20	$90

Bundling is a type of price discrimination. Suppose that we have two consumers, Amanda and Yvonne, whose maximum willingness to pay for Word and Excel is as given in Table 14.2.

Microsoft can sell each product individually or it can sell Word and Excel together as a bundle. Let's calculate profit for each possibility. To make our lives simple, we will assume that the marginal costs of production are zero (which is approximately true—it costs very little to write another Word CD).

If Microsoft sets prices individually, there are two sensible choices for the price of Word: $40 or $100. If Microsoft sets a price of $40 for Word, both Amanda and Yvonne will buy and profit will be $80. If Microsoft sets a price of $100, Amanda alone will buy but profit will be higher, $100. Similarly, Microsoft can sensibly sell Excel for $20 or $90. Profit is higher at a price of $90 because 2 × $20 = $40 < $90. If Microsoft sets prices individually, therefore, it will charge $100 for Word and $90 for Excel for a total profit of $190 = $100 + $90.

TABLE 14.3 Maximum Willingness to Pay for Office

	Amanda	Yvonne
Word	$100	$40
Excel	$20	$90
Office = Word + Excel	$120	$130

Now consider bundling Word and Excel and selling them as Office. What price to set? To calculate this, we need to know the maximum amount that Amanda and Yvonne will pay for Word plus Excel. We calculate this in Table 14.3.

Amanda is willing to pay up to $120 for the Office bundle and Yvonne is willing to pay up to $130. What is the profit-maximizing price for the Office bundle? Microsoft will set the bundle price at $120 and sell two Office bundles for a total profit of $240. What has happened to Microsoft's profit compared with when it set prices individually? When Microsoft priced Word and Excel individually, its profit was just $190. When Microsoft sells Word and Excel in a bundle called Office, its profits increase by $50 or 26% more. Why?

Notice that in this example bundling is equivalent to a sophisticated scheme of (almost) perfect price discrimination. At a bundle price of $120, we can think of Amanda as being charged $100 for Word and $20 for Excel, and Yvonne as being charged $40 for Word and $80 for Excel. But in order to implement this price discrimination scheme directly, Microsoft would have to know a lot about Amanda's and Yvonne's willingness to pay for Word and Excel and Microsoft would have to prevent Yvonne from buying Word at $40 and reselling it to Amanda (and similarly keep Amanda from reselling Excel to Yvonne). When Microsoft bundles, however, it's easier to price-discriminate because although Amanda and Yvonne place very different values on Word and Excel, they have similar values for Office. Microsoft, therefore, knows more about the demand for Office than about the demand for Word or Excel, and the more Microsoft knows about demand, the easier it is for Microsoft to price-discriminate.

As with other forms of price discrimination, bundling can increase efficiency especially when fixed costs are high and marginal costs are low. In our example, when Microsoft set prices individually, only Amanda bought Word and only Yvonne bought Excel. This is inefficient because Amanda values Excel at $40 and the costs of providing Excel is zero (and similarly for Yvonne and Word). When Microsoft bundles, Amanda and Yvonne buy both Word and Excel, which increases total surplus.

Total surplus without bundling is $190. What is total surplus with bundling? It's $250. Check that you understand where this number came from.

Furthermore, the costs of producing software are primarily the fixed costs of research and development. Bundling means that these fixed costs are spread across more consumers, which raises the incentive to innovate.

Bundling and Cable TV

Bundling is quite common. LexisNexis sells online access to a bundle of thousands of newspapers, journals, and references. Disneyland bundles many attractions and sells them for a single entrance fee. The buffet at China Garden is a bundle of food. Bundling, however, can be controversial. Cable TV operators sell television channels in a bundle. Recently, this practice has come under attack with many politicians arguing for "à la carte" pricing, that is, pricing by the channel. Critics of bundling complain that consumers should not be forced to pay for channels that they don't watch. The claim seems sensible at first, but does it add up? Would the critics also say that the buffet at China Garden forces consumers of kung pao chicken to pay for unwanted egg foo young?

Bundle pricing makes sense for cable operators because customers have a high willingness to pay for some channels and a low willingness to pay for other channels, but the high- and low-value channels differ by customer. The demand for the bundle, however, is more similar across customers. Since it costs the cable company very little to offer every channel to every customer, bundling can increase profit and efficiency. The idea is exactly the same as we showed with the Office example. In Table 14.3, change Word to the Food Network and Excel to Lifetime (and see also end-of-chapter Challenge question 1).

As usual, bundling is most likely to be beneficial in a high fixed cost, low marginal cost industry. Cable TV is a high fixed cost, low marginal cost industry. Over the last decade, for example, one cable operator, Comcast, spent $40 billion laying new cable. Once the cable is laid, the marginal cost of carrying another channel is low, especially with high bandwidth fiber optic cable. In cases like this, bundling doesn't cost the firm very much (and may even be cheaper than individual pricing), and by increasing profit, it increases the incentive to spend resources on the fixed costs of development.

MODERN PRINCIPLES: MICROECONOMICS

Tyler Cowen • Alex Tabarrok

Textbooks are bundles of chapters.

CHECK YOURSELF

> If cell phone companies were not allowed to tie cell phones with service plans, what do you predict would happen to the price of cell phones and what do you predict would happen to the price of cell phone calls?
> When is bundling likely to increase total surplus?

◻ Takeaway

Price discrimination—selling the same good to different customers at different prices—is a common feature of many markets. The most obvious form of price discrimination is when a firm sets different prices in different markets—as, for example, when GSK sells Combivir for a high price in Europe and a low price in Africa. Firms also price goods based on characteristics that are correlated with willingness to pay so student and senior discounts are a form of price discrimination, as are the different prices that airlines set for the same flight depending on how far in advance the flight is booked.

Price discrimination isn't always easy. To price-discriminate, the firm must prevent consumers who are charged a low price from reselling to consumers who would be charged a high price, that is, prevent arbitrage. Price discrimination also requires that the firm know a lot about its customers. The more the firm knows, the better it can price-discriminate. If the firm knew exactly how much each of its customers valued its product and it could prevent arbitrage, the firm could charge each customer that customer's maximum willingness to pay—this is called perfect price discrimination. Universities come closest to practicing perfect price discrimination because to provide scholarships, the university can demand a lot of information about the income of its students and their families and it's hard to resell an education.

Tying and bundling are less obvious forms of price discrimination. By setting a low price for printers and a high price for ink, HP is setting different prices for the "ability to print color photos"—a low price for those who print only occasionally and a high price for those who print often. Cell phones are priced below cost and cell phone calls are priced above cost for the same reason.

Bundling goods in a package can also be a form of price discrimination. When consumers place very different values on package components but similar values on the package, bundling can increase profits.

Firms want to price-discriminate because price discrimination increases profits. Price discrimination may also increase total surplus. Price discrimination is most likely to increase total surplus when it increases output and when there are large fixed costs of development. Price discrimination for pharmaceuticals, for example, lowers the price for consumers in poor countries (thus, increasing output) and, by increasing profits, price discrimination increases the incentive to research and develop new drugs.

□ CHAPTER REVIEW

KEY CONCEPTS

Price discrimination, p. 257

Arbitrage, p. 259

Perfect price discrimination, p. 263

Tying, p. 267

Bundling, p. 267

FACTS AND TOOLS

1. True or False? A business that price-discriminates will generally charge some customers more than marginal cost, and it will generally charge other customers less than marginal cost.

2. Two customers, Fred and Lamont, walk into Grady's Used Pickups. Who probably has a more inelastic demand for one of Grady's pickups: people like Lamont, who are good at shopping around, or people like Fred, who know what they like and just buy it?

3. Who probably has more elastic demand for a Hertz rental car: someone who reserves a car online weeks before a trip, or someone who walks up to a Hertz counter after he walks off an airplane following a 4-hour flight? Who probably gets charged more?

4. When arbitrage is easy in a market of would-be price discriminators, who is more likely to get priced out of the market: those with elastic demand or those with inelastic demand?

5. If Congress passed a privacy law making it illegal for colleges to ask for parents' tax returns, would that tend to help students from high-income families or students from low-income families?

6. Why would a firm hand out coupons for its products rather than just lowering the price? Here's a hint: At your school, what kind of students use coupons to buy their pizza? What kind of students *never* use coupons to buy their pizza?

7. Where will you see more price discrimination: in monopoly-type markets with just a few firms or in competitive markets with many firms? Why?

8. When will a monopoly create more output: when it is allowed to and can perfectly price-discriminate or when the government bans price discrimination?

9. Some razors, like Gillette's Fusion and Venus razors, have disposable heads. The razor comes with an initial pack with a razor handle plus three or four heads; after that, you need to buy refills separately.

   a. Where do you think Gillette gets more revenue: by selling the initial pack or by selling the refills?

   b. The next time you buy a new razor, are you going to spend more time looking at the price of the razor or at the price of the refills?

THINKING AND PROBLEM SOLVING

1. Subway, the fast-food chain, sells foot-long sandwiches for $5 each. However, Subway still sells 6-inch sandwiches for considerably more than $2.50 each, that is, at a higher price per inch of sub.

   a. Can you think of a way that in theory you could make money from Subway's pricing practices? Would this method work in practice? What does this tell you about the limits of arbitrage?

   b. In many of our price discrimination examples, we think that businesses try to break customers into two groups: "more price-sensitive" and "less price-sensitive." What kinds of Subway customers fit into the first group? Into the second?

   Busy lawyers with 20-minute lunches

   College students

   Health-conscious soccer moms

   Long-haul truck drivers

2. A dry cleaner has a sign in its window: "Free Internet Coupons." The dry cleaner lists its Web site, and indeed there are good discounts available with the coupons. Most customers don't use the coupons.

   a. What probably would be the main difference between customers who use the coupons and those who don't?

   b. Some people might think "The dry cleaner offers the coupons to get people in the door to try the place out, but then the customers will pay the normal high price afterward." But the coupons are always there, so even repeat customers can keep using the coupons. Is this a mistake on the business owner's part? *Hint:* Think about marginal cost.

3. a. When will a firm find it easier to price-discriminate: before the existence of eBay or afterward?

   b. Which of the two "principles of price discrimination" does this invoke?

4. As we saw in this chapter, drug companies often charge much more for the same drug in the United States than in other countries. Congress often considers passing laws to make it *easier* to import drugs from these low-price countries (it also considers passing laws to make it illegal to import these drugs, but that's another story).

   If one of these laws passes, and it becomes effortless to buy AIDS drugs from Africa or antibiotics from Latin America—drugs that are made by the same companies and have essentially the same quality controls as the drugs here in the United States—how will drug companies change the prices they charge in Latin America and Africa? Why?

5. Some people think that *businesses* create monopolies by destroying their competition, and there is certainly some truth to that. But as we learned from Obi-Wan Kenobi, "[Y]ou will find that many of the truths we cling to depend greatly on our own point of view." For instance, some people (Convenience Shoppers) love shopping at one particular store and will only switch stores when a product is outrageously expensive, while other people (Bargain Shoppers) will gladly spend hours looking through newspaper advertisements searching for the best deal.

   a. When both kinds of people, the Convenience Shoppers and the Bargain Shoppers, are shopping at the same Wal-Mart, who is more likely to stick to their prearranged shopping list, and who is more likely to splurge on a little something?

   b. Which group does Wal-Mart have monopoly power over? Which group does Wal-Mart have no monopoly power over?

c. Does this mean that the same shop can simultaneously be a "monopolist" to some customers and a "competitive firm" to other customers? Why or why not?

d. Does this mean that Darth Vader really *did* kill Anakin Skywalker?

6. Where are you more likely to see businesses "bundling" a lot of goods into one package: in industries with high fixed costs and low marginal costs (like computer games or moviemaking), or in industries with low fixed costs and high marginal costs (like doctor visits, where the doctor's time is expensive)?

7. Isn't it surprising that movies, with tickets that cost around $10, often use vastly more economic resources than stage plays where tickets can easily cost $100?

Compare, for example, a live stage performance of Shakespeare's *Hamlet* with a movie of *Hamlet*.

a. In which field is the marginal cost of one more showing lower: on stage or on screen?

b. "Bundling" in a movie or stage performance might show up in the form of adding special effects, expensive actors, or fancy costumes: Some customers might not be too interested in an Elizabethan revenge drama, but they show up to see Liam Neeson waving an authentic medieval dagger. Is it better to think of these extra expenses as "fixed costs" or "marginal costs"?

c. In which setting will it be easier for a business to cover its total costs: in a "bundled" stage production or in a "bundled" movie production?

8. When is a pharmaceutical company more likely to spend $100 million to research a new drug: when it knows it will be able to charge different prices in different countries or when it knows that it will be required to charge the same price in different countries? Why?

9. True or false? A price-discriminating business will sometimes be willing to spend money to make a product worse.

10. Let's calculate the profit from price discrimination. The average daily demand for dinners at Paradise Grille, an upscale casual restaurant, is as follows:

Demand for dinners by senior citizens:
$P = 50 - 0.5Q \quad MR = 50 - Q$

Demand for dinners by others: $P = 100 - Q$
$MR = 100 - 2Q$

Marginal cost = 10 in both cases

a. What is the profit-maximizing price for each group?

b. Translate this into real-world jargon: If you owned this restaurant, what "senior citizen discount" would you offer, in percent?

c. Ignoring fixed costs, how much profit would Paradise Grille make if it did this?

d. If it became illegal to discriminate on the basis of age, you would face only one demand curve. Adding up these two demand curves turns out to yield

$$P = 67 - \left(\tfrac{1}{3}\right)Q \quad MR = 67 - \left(\tfrac{2}{3}\right)Q$$

What are the optimal price and quantity in this unified market? Are the total meals sold in this discrimination-free market higher or lower than in part a?

e. What is the profit in this discrimination-free market?

11. At the Kennedy Center for the Performing Arts in Washington, DC, if you make a $120 donation per year, you are allowed to go to a small room before the concert and drink free coffee and eat free cookies. If you make a donation of $1,200 per year, you are allowed to go to a *different* small room before the concert and drink the *same* free coffee and eat the *same* free cookies. There are always a lot of people in both rooms before the concert: Why doesn't everybody just pay the $120 instead of the higher price?

CHALLENGES

1. In the table below, we consider how Alex, Tyler, and Monique would fare under à la carte pricing and under bundling for cable TV when there are two channels: Lifetime and the Food Network.

Alex and Tyler like to watch *Project Runway* so they each place a higher value on Lifetime than on the Food Network. Monique is practicing to be an Iron Chef in her second life so she places a higher value on the Food Network than on Lifetime.

Maximum Willingness to Pay for Cable TV			
	Alex	Tyler	Monique
Lifetime	10	15	3
The Food Network	7	4	9
The Bundle	15	19	12

a. If the channels are priced individually, the most profitable prices for the cable operator turn out to be 10 for Lifetime and 7 for the Food Network. At these prices, who buys what channel and how much profit is there?

b. Let's just check to see if these prices really are profit-maximizing. What would profit be if the cable company raised Lifetime to a price of 11 and Food Network to a price of 8?

c. At the profit-maximizing prices, how much total consumer surplus would there be for the three of them? (Recall that consumer surplus is just each customer's willingness to pay minus the amount each person actually paid.)

d. Now consider what happens under bundling: Customers get a take-it-or-leave-it offer of both channels or nothing at all. The profit-maximizing bundle price turns out to be 12, and at that price, Alex, Tyler, and Monique all subscribe. How much consumer surplus is there at this price? How much profit? And, most important, what would profit equal if the cable company raised the price to 13 instead?

2. Consider the following seating arrangement for a concert hall:

The front row only seats two people. Rows B–H, about 50 feet back from the front row, seat 20 people per row.

a. Would these front-row seats sell for more or for less than the front-row seats at a typical concert hall? Why?

b. Why don't we see concert halls set up like this?

3. a. In competitive markets in the long run, if there are two kinds of steaks, "regular" and "high-quality Angus beef," and the regular beef sells at a lower price, is this an example of price discrimination?

b. How is this different from the HP printer story in this chapter?

4. Amanda and Yvonne are thinking of going out to the movies. Amanda likes action flicks more, but Yvonne likes a little bit of romance. Warner Bros. is trying to decide what kind of movies to make this year. Should it make one movie for release this summer, an action flick with a romantic subplot, or should it make two movies for release this summer: an action flick and a romantic drama?

Here's the two friends' willingness to pay for the separate kinds of movies. As you can see, both Amanda and Yvonne are annoyed by the idea of a hybrid movie: Each would rather see her favorite kind of movie.

Maximum Willingness to Pay for a Movie Ticket		
	Amanda	Yvonne
Pure Action	$10	$2
Pure Romance	$2	$10
Action + Romance	$9	$9

Now, let's look at this from Warner Bros.' point of view. You're the mid-level executive who has to decide which project to green light. Your marketing people have figured out that there are 5 million people like Amanda and 5 million people like Yvonne in the United States, and they'll only see one film per summer. To make things simple, assume that the marginal cost of showing the movie one more time is zero, and that ticket prices are fixed at $8.

a. If the cost of producing any of the three films is $30 million, what should the studio do: make the two films or just the one hybrid film? Of course, the right way to find the answer is to figure out which choice would generate the most profit for Warner Bros.

b. Of course, the hybrid might cost a bit more to make. What if the hybrid costs $40 million to make, the pure action flick $30 million, and the romance a mere $15 million? What's the best choice now: one hybrid or two pure films?

c. Let's see how much prices would have to change for the answer to this question to change. Holding all else equal, how low would the cost of the pure romance film have to fall before the two-movie deal would get the green light?

d. (Hard) There's an underlying principle here: The "unbundled" two-movie deal won't get the green light unless its total cost is less than what? The answer is not a number—it's an idea. Is this likely to happen in the real world? Why or why not?

5. Think about the kind of 40-year-old who pulls out a faded, obviously expired student ID to get a discount ticket at a movie theater: What can you predict about his or her willingness to pay for a full-price movie? Is the movie theater making a mistake when it lets him or her pay the student price?

6. We mentioned that airlines charge much more for flights booked at the last minute than for flights booked well in advance, even for exactly the same flight. This is because people who tend to book at the last minute tend to have inelastic demand. Think of other characteristics that airlines use to vary their pricing: Do you think these characteristics are correlated with business travel or any other sort of inelastic demand? (If you don't fly too often, just ask someone who does: "What's the key to getting the lowest possible airfare?")

Solving Price Discrimination Problems with Excel (Advanced Section)

Excel's Solver tool can be used to solve difficult price discrimination problems. Imagine that there are two groups of customers with the following demand curves:

$$Q_1^D = 330 - 2 \times P_1$$
$$Q_2^D = 510 - 4 \times P_2$$

where Q_1^D is the quantity demanded by Group 1 when it faces price P_1 and Q_2^D is the quantity demanded by Group 2 when it faces price P_2. We could think of these markets as Europe and Africa or business travelers and vacationers, similar to the way we did in the text. The monopolist has the following costs:

$$\text{Costs} = 1{,}000 + Q^2$$

where Q is the quantity produced by the monopolist.

The monopolist's goal is simple: It wants to choose prices P_1 and P_2 in order to maximize its profits. We will assume that the two markets are distinct so arbitrage is not possible. Although the goal is simple, the solution is difficult. In fact, this problem is considerably more difficult than any of the problems we dealt with in the text. In the text, we assumed that marginal cost was constant (a flat *MC* curve). Assuming constant marginal costs simplified the problem because it meant that when the monopolist produced more in Market 1, the costs of producing another unit in Market 2 didn't change. In our problem here, marginal cost is increasing—which means that when the monopolist produces more in Market 1, its cost of producing an additional unit in Market 2 also increases. In an intermediate or graduate economics class, you would use calculus to solve a problem like this.

In the real world, business managers and entrepreneurs must solve problems like this every day and they don't all know calculus, so we will show you how to solve the problem using Excel. First, let's write down what we know. In Figure A14.1, we highlight the equation for Q_1^D, which we enter as "=330−2*B2". We put the price for Group 1 in cell B2. We want to find the profit-maximizing price for Group 1 but we don't know what it is, so for now we just put a zero in cell B2. The equation and price for Group 2 are entered similarly.

FIGURE A14.1

B3	▾	f_x =330-2*B2	
	A	B	C
1		Group 1	Group 2
2	Price	$0.00	$0.00
3	Quantity Demanded	330.00	510.00
4			

Now we enter the formula for the monopolist's cost. The total quantity produced by the monopolist is simply the quantity produced for Group 1 plus the quantity produced for Group 2. Thus, we can rewrite the monopolist's costs as

$$\text{Costs} = 1,000 + (Q_1^D + Q_2^D)^2$$

In Figure A14.2, we have entered the monopolist's costs in cell B5 as "=1000+(B3+C3)^2".

FIGURE A14.2

B5	f_x =1000+(B3+C3)^2

	A	B	C	
1		Group 1	Group 2	
2	Price	$0.00	$0.00	
3	Quantity Demanded	330.00	510.00	
4				
5	Monopoly Cost	$706,600.00		
6				

It is important to see that what matters here is the formula for costs; the number in the picture, $706,600.00, is simply the monopolist's costs if the monopolist set P_1 and P_2 at zero and produced everything its customers demanded at those prices!

Finally, we enter the formula for profits, as shown in Figure A14.3.

FIGURE A14.3

B6	f_x =B2*B3+C2*C3-B5

	A	B	C	
1		Group 1	Group 2	
2	Price	$0.00	$0.00	
3	Quantity Demanded	330.00	510.00	
4				
5	Monopoly Cost	$706,600.00		
6	Monopoly Profit	-$706,600.00		
7				

Profits are revenues minus costs so we enter into Excel ="B2*B3+C2*C3-B5", which is price times the quantity demanded for Group 1 plus price times quantity demanded for Group 2 minus total costs. Excel now has enough information to solve this problem. In Excel 2007, the Solver function is found under the Data tab (but you may first have to add-in the Solver application—see Excel help for instructions on how to do this). Clicking on the Solver button produces Figure A14.4.

FIGURE A14.4

	C6	f_x =B2*B3+C2*C3-B5							
	A	B	C	D	E	F	G	H	I
1		Group 1	Group 2						
2	Price	$0.00	$0.00						
3	Quantity Demanded	330.00	510.00						
4									
5	Monopoly Cost	$706,600.00							
6	Monopoly Profit	-$706,600.00							
7									
8									
9									
10									
11									
12									
13									
14									
15									
16									
17									
18									
19									
20									
21									
22									
23									
24									
25									
26									
27									

Solver Parameters

Set Target Cell: B6   Solve

Equal To: ⦿ Max   ○ Min   ○ Value of: 0   Close

By Changing Cells:

B2:C2   Guess

Subject to the Constraints: Options

Add

Change   Reset All

Delete   Help

Our target is profits so in the Solver box next to "Set Target Cell", we enter B6. We want a maximum of profits, so make sure the "Equal to" button is filled in on Max. Finally, we are going to maximize profits by changing prices, so in the box for "By Changing Cells", we enter "B2:C2". Now we click Solve and Excel finds the answer shown in Figure A14.5.

FIGURE A14.5

	B6	f_x =B2*B3+C2*C3-B5		
	A	B	C	D
1		Group 1	Group 2	
2	Price	$142.50	$123.75	
3	Quantity Demanded	45.00	15.00	
4				
5	Monopoly Cost	$4,600.00		
6	Monopoly Profit	$3,668.75		
7				

Excel tells us that the profit-maximizing prices are $142.50 for Group 1 and $123.75 for Group 2. At these prices, Group 1 customers buy 45 units, Group 2 customers buy 15 units, and monopoly profits are $3,668.75.

Once you understand the basic ideas, it's easy to make these models even more realistic by adding bells and whistles such as more groups. Notice that we have solved this problem with a combination of economic principles and practical skills (in this case, a bit of Excel know-how). An important lesson to learn is that this combination of principles and practical skills is very powerful and eagerly sought out by employers in a variety of fields.

15

Cartels, Oligopolies, and Monopolistic Competition

As oil prices neared a historic high in July 1979, President Jimmy Carter spoke to the nation. Quoting a concerned American, Carter said, "Our neck is stretched over the fence and OPEC has a knife." What is OPEC and what power did OPEC have to control the price of oil?

OPEC, which is short for the Organization of the Petroleum Exporting Countries, is a **cartel**, a group of suppliers who try to act together to reduce supply, raise prices, and increase profits. In other words, a cartel is a group of suppliers who try to act as if they were a monopolist.

We analyzed monopoly in Chapter 13 so we have a good understanding of what cartels are *trying* to achieve, but the question we address in this chapter is when will cartels be *able* to achieve their goal. As we will see, it's not easy for a group of firms to act as if they were a monopolist. But even when a group of firms is not able to coordinate or collude to act like a monopolist, prices are likely to be higher in an industry with a small number of firms than in a highly competitive market. We call an industry that is dominated by a small number of firms an **oligopoly**. Thus, we begin our chapter by discussing cartels, an oligopoly that acts like a monopolist, and then move to a more general discussion of oligopoly. Finally, we will take a look at **monopolistic competition**, a market in which there are many firms that sell similar but not identical products.

In this chapter, we also introduce a new tool: game theory. Game theory is the study of **strategic decision making**. An example illustrates what we mean. In Las Vegas, craps players make decisions, but poker players make strategic decisions. Craps is a dice game and deciding when and how much to bet can be complicated, but the outcome depends only on the dice and the bet and not on how other people bet. In contrast, poker is a game of strategy because a good poker player must forecast the decisions

A **cartel** is a group of suppliers that tries to act *as if* they were a monopoly.

An **oligopoly** is a market that is dominated by a small number of firms.

Monopolistic competition is a market with a large number of firms selling similar but not identical products.

Strategic decision making is decision making in situations that are interactive.

of other players, knowing that they in turn are trying to forecast his or her decisions. Game theory is used to model decisions in situations where the players interact.

Although we introduced game theory with an example from poker, a game in the usual sense of the word, game theory is used to study decision making in any situation that is interactive in a significant way. Game theory has also been used to study war, romance, business decisions of all kinds, evolution, voting, and many other situations involving interaction.

In this chapter, we use game theory to look at the economics of cartels.

Cartels

Figure 15.1 shows the price for a barrel of oil from 1960 to 2005.

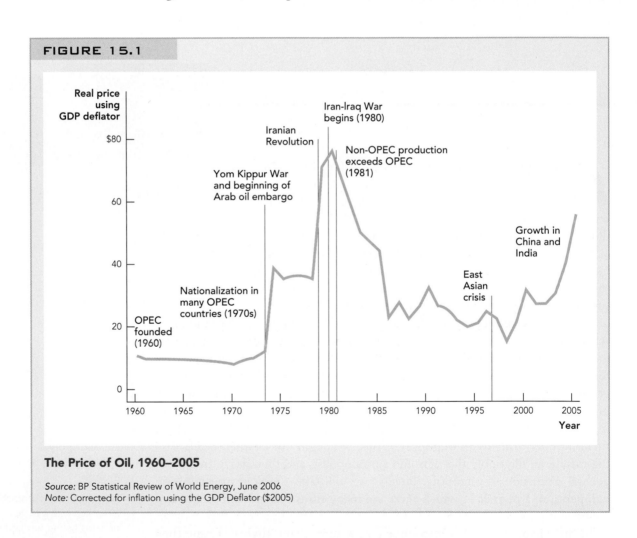

FIGURE 15.1

The Price of Oil, 1960–2005

Source: BP Statistical Review of World Energy, June 2006
Note: Corrected for inflation using the GDP Deflator ($2005)

The patterns are striking. The price of oil is very low and stable for several decades. From 1973 to 1974, the price of oil spikes upward dramatically. From 1979 to 1980, the price of oil spikes upward again. In 1985, the price of oil plummets. From the end of the 1990s to 2005, the price of oil mostly rose.

Why did the price of oil more than triple in 1973–1974, jumping from $8 a barrel to $27 a barrel? The answer is simple: Led by Saudi Arabia, a cartel of oil-exporting countries cut back on their production of oil.*

The left panel of Figure 15.2 shows a competitive market in a constant-cost industry so the supply curve is flat (the constant-cost assumption makes the analysis simpler but is not necessary); remember that in a competitive market each supplier earns zero economic profit. The right panel shows the *same market* but now run *as if* it were controlled by a monopolist; profits, shown in green, are maximized. A cartel is not a monopolist, but if all the firms in a market could be convinced to cut supply so that total supply fell from Q_c to Q_m, then each firm could share in the "monopoly" profits. Thus, a cartel is an organization of suppliers that tries to move the market from the left panel of Figure 15.2 to the right panel, that is, from "Competition" toward "As if Controlled by a Monopolist."

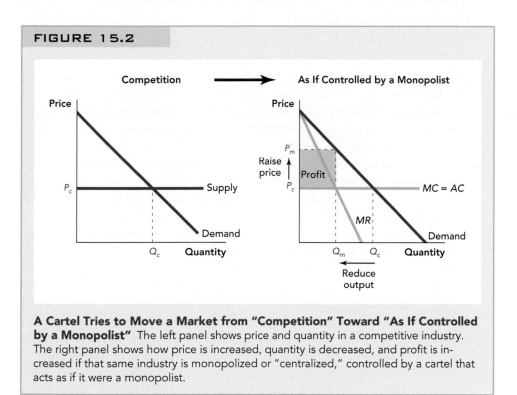

FIGURE 15.2

A Cartel Tries to Move a Market from "Competition" Toward "As If Controlled by a Monopolist" The left panel shows price and quantity in a competitive industry. The right panel shows how price is increased, quantity is decreased, and profit is increased if that same industry is monopolized or "centralized," controlled by a cartel that acts as if it were a monopolist.

Very few cartels can move an industry from competition to pure monopoly, but Figure 15.2 shows the basic tendency of cartels to reduce output and raise price.

It might seem from this short look at OPEC that cartels are all-powerful. But in reality few cartels—unless they have strong government support—have much control over market price for very long. A cartel is a deal in which businesspeople promise: "I will raise my price and cut back my production if you promise to do the same." But will the promise be kept?

---

* OPEC had been around since 1960, but until the early 1970s, it didn't have much success in raising the price of oil. OPEC became more powerful through the 1960s and 1970s as the participating countries nationalized oil fields and as more countries joined OPEC. In 1973, OPEC expanded from Iran, Iraq, Kuwait, and Saudi Arabia to add Qatar, Indonesia, Libya, the United Arab Emirates, Algeria, Nigeria, Ecuador, and Gabon. Ecuador left in 1992 but returned in 2007. Gabon left OPEC in 1995, Angola joined in 2007, Indonesia left in 2009.

Cartels tend to collapse and lose their power for three reasons:

1. Cheating by the cartel members
2. New entrants and demand response
3. Government prosecution and regulation

OPEC, although a relatively successful cartel by historical standards, could not keep the price of oil high for very long. By 1985, the price of oil plummeted from its previous heights of $75 per barrel, sometimes falling as low as $10 per barrel; occasionally a Persian Gulf country would sell its oil for as little as $6 a barrel. OPEC nations were unhappy, but there was little they could do to keep oil prices high.

How did this happen? To understand, let's turn to the first reason for why cartels collapse, namely cheating by the cartel members.

The Incentive to Cheat

OPEC nations have a great deal at stake in the oil market. For instance, when oil prices were relatively high, in 1981, Saudi Arabia pulled in $119 billion in oil revenue. By 1985, when the price of oil was much lower, the Saudis earned only $26 billion. So it's no surprise that oil-exporting nations might seek to work together to reduce production and raise prices. If the cartel succeeds, cartel members earn high profits on each barrel of oil that comes out of the ground.

But this same desire for profit makes the cartel fall apart. Members will cheat on the cartel agreement. That is, they will promise to reduce production, but when everyone else reduces production and the price of oil rises, some cartel members will cheat by producing more than they promised. If everyone else is keeping their promises, the cheaters will increase their profits. At first, only a few firms might cheat, but the more cheaters, the less profitable it is to reduce production and cheating will soon increase.

We can get another perspective on the incentive to cheat by comparing a monopolist with a cartel member. When a monopolist increases quantity beyond the profit-maximizing quantity, the monopolist hurts itself. But when a cartel cheater increases quantity beyond the profit-maximizing quantity, the cheater benefits itself and hurts *other cartel members*. We compare the incentive to lower price for a monopolist and for a member of a four-firm cartel in Figure 15.3.

When a monopolist lowers the price and increases its sales, it enjoys all of the gains from selling more (the green area in the left panel of Figure 15.3); but it also bears all of the losses from selling its previous output at a lower price (the red area). But if a cartel member cheats on the cartel, it enjoys all of the gains from selling more (the green area), but it bears only a fraction of the losses from a lower price (the red area in the right panel).

If a cheater hurts the other cartel members, not so many tears will be shed by the cheater. This is especially true for the OPEC cartel. Iran and Iraq, for example, fought a major war from 1980 to 1988, with more than 800,000 people killed. The war saw the use of poison gas, chemical weapons, and child soldiers as advance scouts to trigger land mines. While this war was going on, Iran and Iraq were both in OPEC. Each nation, in effect, was promising it would not undercut the other when it came to selling more oil at a lower price. Do you really think they felt obliged to keep their word?

And so have most cartels ended. The more successful the cartel is in raising member profits, the greater the incentive to cheat. And once a cartel falls apart, it is difficult to put it back together again. Everyone correctly expects cheating to be the norm.

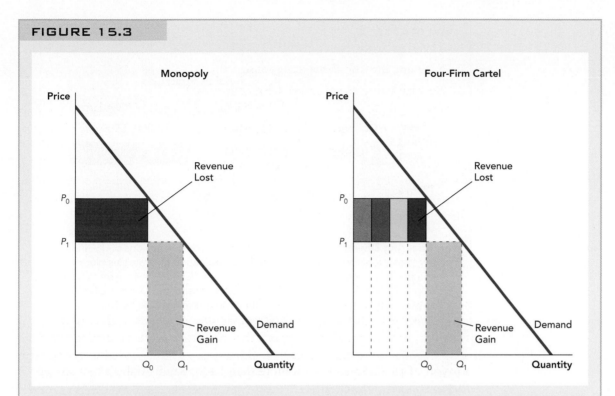

FIGURE 15.3

The Incentive to Cheat When a monopolist increases quantity from Q_0 to Q_1 it gets all of the revenues from the new sales (the green area) but it also bears all of the losses from the lower price on old sales (the red area). The red plus green area is equal to marginal revenue (see Chapter 11).

When a single firm in a four-firm cartel increases quantity from Q_0 to Q_1 it gets all of the revenues from the new sales (the green area), but the fall in price is spread across all firms in the industry in proportion to their sales so the cartel member loses only the much smaller red area. The cartel member, therefore, has a much larger incentive to increase output than does the monopolist.

No One Wins the Cheating Game It's useful to show the incentive to cheat in another way, using what is called a payoff table. With more than two firms, the payoff table would be quite complicated and hard to draw in two dimensions, but the same logic of cheating applies if there are just two firms. So imagine that the oil market is dominated by two large firms, Saudi Arabia and Russia.

Saudi Arabia has two choices or strategies, Cooperate (by cutting back production) or Cheat. These strategies are shown in Figure 15.4 by the rows of the payoff table. Russia also has the same two strategies, shown as the columns of the payoff table.

The two numbers in each box of the table are the payoffs to the players; the first number is the payoff to Saudi Arabia, the second to Russia. For instance, if both Saudi Arabia and Russia choose to cooperate by cutting back production, the payoff is $400 (million per day) to Saudi Arabia and $400 (million per day) to Russia. If Saudi Arabia cheats and Russia cooperates, then the payoff to Saudi Arabia is $500 and the payoff to Russia is $200.

Now let's see what the "players" will do in this "game." Consider the incentives faced by Saudi Arabia. If Russia cooperates, then Saudi Arabia can choose Cooperate and receive a payoff of $400 or choose Cheat and receive

I promise never to cheat on you.
Venezuelan President Hugo Chavez (left) hugs Saudi Crown Prince Abdullah bin Abdul Aziz Al Saud during an OPEC summit in 2000.

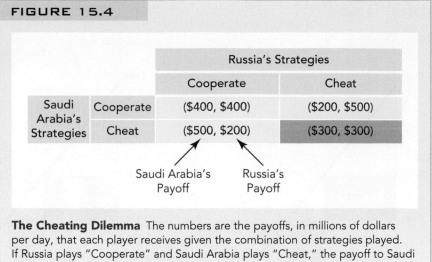

FIGURE 15.4

		Russia's Strategies	
		Cooperate	Cheat
Saudi Arabia's Strategies	Cooperate	($400, $400)	($200, $500)
	Cheat	($500, $200)	($300, $300)

Saudi Arabia's Payoff   Russia's Payoff

The Cheating Dilemma The numbers are the payoffs, in millions of dollars per day, that each player receives given the combination of strategies played. If Russia plays "Cooperate" and Saudi Arabia plays "Cheat," the payoff to Saudi Arabia is $500 and the payoff to Russia is $200. In this game, Cheat is a better strategy for each player no matter what the other player's strategy. Thus, the equilibrium of this game (shaded) is (Cheat, Cheat).

A dominant strategy is a strategy that has a higher payoff than any other strategy no matter what the other player does.

The prisoner's dilemma describes situations where the pursuit of individual interest leads to a group outcome that is in the interest of no one.

a payoff of $500. Since $500 is more than $400, Saudi Arabia's best strategy *if Russia cooperates* is to cheat.

What is Saudi Arabia's best strategy if Russia cheats? If Russia cheats, Saudi Arabia can cooperate and earn a payoff of $200 or Saudi Arabia can cheat and earn a payoff of $300. Cheat is again the more profitable strategy. A strategy that has a higher payoff than any other strategy, no matter what the other player does, is called a **dominant strategy**. In this setup, cheating is a dominant strategy for Saudi Arabia.

Cheating is also a dominant strategy for Russia. If Saudi Arabia cooperates, Russia earns $500 by choosing Cheat and $400 by choosing Cooperate. If Saudi Arabia cheats, Russia earns $300 by choosing Cheat and $200 by choosing Cooperate. Thus, both Saudi Arabia and Russia will cheat and we shade (Cheat, Cheat) to show that this is the equilibrium outcome of the game.

The logic is compelling but also surprising. When Saudi Arabia and Russia each follow their individually sensible strategy of Cheat, each receives a payoff of $300. If Saudi Arabia and Russia instead both chose to cooperate, a strategy that is not individually sensible, they will receive a higher payoff of $400. Thus, when Saudi Arabia acts in its interest and Russia acts in its interest, the result is an outcome that is in the interest of neither. That is a dilemma well verified by both theory and evidence.

The analysis we have just given of cartel cheating is part of a branch of economics called game theory and Figure 15.4 is one version of a very famous game called the **prisoner's dilemma**. The prisoner's dilemma describes situations where the pursuit of individual interest leads to a group outcome that is in the interest of no one.

To give another example of this phenomenon, the world's stock of fish is rapidly being depleted. To understand why, replace Saudi Arabia and Russia in Figure 15.4 with two large fishing firms or countries, say, the United States and Japan. Cooperate now means "produce less fish" (instead of less oil). If both players choose Cooperate, fishing revenue can be maximized and the stock of fish will be maintained for future generations. But if one player cooperates, the other has an incentive to cheat by overfishing. And, of course, if one player cheats, the other has an incentive to cheat as well. Each player has the same incentive and so both players cheat. That reduces the stock of fish below the best possible outcome and eventually it may deplete the stock completely. That's why so many people are concerned that the world is running out of many species of fish.

We will also have more to say about overfishing in Chapter 18.

New Entrants and Demand Response Break Down Cartels

Cheating is not the only reason why cartels fall apart. Usually, the high prices of a cartel will attract new entrants; of course, those entrants do not feel bound by previous agreements. For instance, the high price of OPEC oil encouraged a search for new supplies. Pemex, the Mexican oil company, had been a small player in the industry for many decades. But when oil prices went up, Mexico engaged in more searching, more drilling, and more oil production. In 2006, Mexico was the fifth leading oil producer in the world. Great Britain, the Netherlands, and many African nations also expanded their presence in oil markets. Africa will soon supply more oil than does Saudi Arabia, and Brazil may soon become a major producer as well.[1]

It is not just about oil. High oil prices led to more conservation, more interest in natural gas, more interest in solar energy, and many other adjustments. Taken together, these demand responses make it less profitable for OPEC member nations to increase the price of oil. Cartels will tend to be more successful when there are fewer substitutes for the cartelized good, which of course implies less elastic demand. As we know from Chapter 5, more substitutes are typically available in the long run than in the short run, so demand curves tend to become more elastic over time, thus limiting a cartel's power.

The fact that cartels are challenged by new entrants explains why it is typically easier to maintain a cartel in a natural resource than in a manufactured good. It's hard to stop entry into the production of a good that can be made anywhere in the world. In contrast, some natural resources are found in large quantities in only a few places, so if you control those places, you control the supply.

Oil and diamonds, two goods where cartels have been partially successful, are good examples of natural resources found in only a few places in the world (but see the sidebar on diamonds!). Similarly, Indonesia and Grenada, taken together, control 98% of the world's supply of nutmeg, a hard-to-replace spice used in many baking recipes. The nutmeg cartel has had some success. Copper, however, is a natural resource that is distributed more widely. The copper cartel (Intergovernmental Council of Copper Exporting Countries) controls no more than one-third of the world's copper reserves and, as a result, has not been able to raise prices in any significant manner. There are also good substitutes for copper in most uses, including plastic, aluminum, and recycled copper. The copper case is more typical than diamonds or oil.

It's not just natural resources that may be in limited supply. In some cases, the cartel may control access to some key input that cannot be easily duplicated. In these cases, individual firms may not wish to break with the cartel for fear that they will be cut off from the key input.

Is the diamond cartel forever?
Diamonds are found in only a few places in the world. As a result, for decades the De Beers cartel has been able to keep prices high. The diamonds pictured below, however, were not mined—they were *grown*. Man-made diamonds are as beautiful as natural diamonds—even an expert jeweler cannot tell them apart. Man-made diamonds could break the De Beers cartel.

COURTESY APOLLO DIAMOND

Major league sports, for example, are cartelized. For instance, major league basketball—the NBA—consists of 30 teams playing against one another. Those teams compete on the court but they collude off the court. They use the NBA league structure to keep down player salaries, using a "salary cap." The salary cap rules are complex, but in essence the league tells teams they cannot spend any more than a certain amount ($58 million in 2010–2011) without facing significant financial penalties ("the luxury tax"). Each team, in joining the league, agrees to limit how much it spends on players. This is a buyer's cartel, and the result is that professional basketball salaries are lower than they otherwise would be. Team owners make more money, but players make less money.

Any team that broke the cartel and paid players more would, in time, be kicked out of the league. Access to the league is the good that the cartel controls to keep its members from cheating. The Phoenix Suns are a wonderful team, but how much fun would it be to watch them beat up on some college players? Not much. Fans want to see the Suns play in the NBA and that is why the Suns have to heed the rules of the league (cartel).

Of course, the NBA cartel still has to attract the attention of the consumer. NBA games compete against collegiate sports, other professional sports, and of course many other activities, such as computer games, listening to music, or going out for a pickup game. In fact, consumers may benefit from the NBA cartel because the salary cap prevents rich teams from buying up all the great players and reducing the competition that consumers demand. It's this last reason that helps to explain another unusual aspect of the NBA cartel; unlike most other cartels, the NBA cartel is legal.

Government Prosecution and Regulation

The **antitrust laws** give the government the power to regulate or prohibit business practices that may be anticompetitive.

Most cartels have been illegal in the United States since the Sherman Antitrust Act of 1890. ("Trust" is simply an old word for monopoly. The **antitrust laws** are laws that give the government the power to prohibit or regulate business practices that may be anticompetitive.) In the early 1990s, for example, four firms controlled 95% of the world market for lysine, an amino acid used to promote growth in pigs, chickens, and cattle. The firms—Archer Daniels Midland (USA), Ajinomoto (Japan), Kyowa Hakko Kogyo (Japan), and Sewon America Inc. (South Korea)—held secret meetings around the world at which they agreed to act in unison to reduce quantity and raise prices.

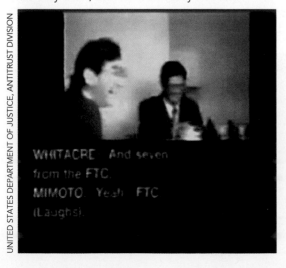

Members of the lysine cartel secretly meeting in Atlanta to fix prices laugh that the FBI and FTC will also be sending members to their meeting. Little did they know, the FBI had already arrived.

WHITACRE: And seven from the FTC.
MIMOTO: Yeah FTC
(Laughs).

UNITED STATES DEPARTMENT OF JUSTICE, ANTITRUST DIVISION

What the conspirators didn't know was that one of them was a mole. A high-ranking executive at ADM informed the FBI of the cartel. Working with FBI equipment, the mole videotaped meetings at which the conspirators discussed how to split the market and keep prices high. You can watch one of the conspiracy videos online by going to our textbook's resource bank (www.SeeTheInvisibleHandResourceBank.com), clicking on the title for this chapter and then scrolling to Cartels and the Informant!

With the evidence in hand, the FBI and the Department of Justice put the conspirators on trial. Three executives of Archer Daniels Midland, including the vice president, Michael D. Andreas, were fined and imprisoned. One of the Japanese executives was also sentenced to prison, but he fled the country and is currently a fugitive from U.S. law.

Government-Supported Cartels Governments don't always prosecute cartels and, in fact, sometimes they support cartels. In fact, most successful cartels operate with clear legal and governmental backing. Governments are the ultimate cartel enforcers because they can throw cheaters in jail. OPEC, for example, is a cartel of oil-exporting *governments*. In the United States, government-controlled milk cartels raise the price of milk. This cartel is extremely stable. Any seller who breaks it is fined or sent to jail.[2] In the past, the U.S. government has supported cartels in coal mining, agriculture, medicine, and other areas; some but not all of these restrictions have been lifted.

Government-enforced monopolies and cartels, however, are one of the most serious problems facing poor nations today. They plague Mexico, Russia, Indonesia, most of the poor nations in Africa, and many other locales. In Nigeria, it is common for police officers to set up roadblocks to extract bribes or for teachers to demand payoffs for good grades. Entrepreneurs who start new businesses sometimes find that the law (or threats of violence that the law does not prevent) forces them out of competition with the small number of so-called untouchable big men who have cartelized the major sectors of the economy.[3] Recent governments in Nigeria have tried to fight corruption but these problems are severe.

Got milk?
It will cost you more because of the government-controlled milk cartel.

S. KIRCHNER/PHOTOCUISINE/CORBIS

A government-supported cartel usually means higher prices, lower quality of service, and less innovation. People with new ideas find it harder or impossible to enter the market. Furthermore, people spend their energies trying to get monopoly or cartel privileges from governments, rather than innovating or finding new ways to service consumers. Governments become more corrupt. For these reasons, most economists oppose most government-enforced cartels. Those cartels are put in place to serve special interests—usually, the politically connected cartel members—rather than consumers or the general citizenry.

Summing Up: Successful and Unsuccessful Cartels

Recall that cartels collapse because of cheating by the cartel members, new entrants, demand response, and possible legal penalties. Thus, successful cartels occur when these factors are weak rather than strong. Cheating by cartel members is less profitable and easier to detect, for example, the fewer the firms that are in an industry. New entrants can be prevented when the good being cartelized is limited in supply or when the good can only be found in a few places in the world. It's easier and more profitable to cartelize goods with few substitutes; that is one reason De Beers spends so much money advertising that only a "Diamond Is Forever." Cartels will also be more successful if they are backed by government and the power of the law.

CHECK YOURSELF

> When Great Britain discovered large oil deposits in the North Sea, why didn't it immediately join OPEC?

> What is the surprising conclusion of the prisoner's dilemma?

Oligopolies

Cartels are difficult to form and maintain, but an oligopoly that fails to form a cartel is still very likely to maintain prices above competitive levels. In Figure 15.3, we showed how a cartel member has an incentive to cheat on the agreement by

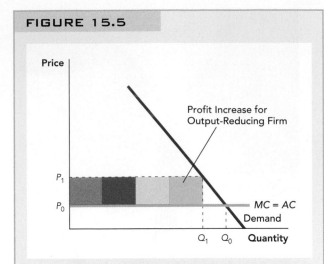

FIGURE 15.5

The Incentive to Raise Price Above Competitive Levels in an Oligopoly The competitive equilibrium is shown at P_0, Q_0. In the competitive equilibrium no firm makes an above-normal profit since $P = MC$. Even though no firm makes an above-normal profit, a competitive firm has no control over the price and thus cannot increase its profits by reducing output.

But a firm in a four-firm oligopoly who reduces quantity by the amount Q_0-Q_1 increases the market price to P_1 which is greater than MC. The increase in price increases the profits of the firm that cuts output (the green area), as well as increasing the profits of the other firms in the industry.

lowering price and producing more than the assigned quota. Exactly the same diagram shows why the price in an oligopoly is likely to be below the monopoly price. A firm in an oligopoly that produces more and cuts price earns all the gains for itself, but bears only a fraction of the costs. Thus, prices in an oligopoly are likely to be below monopoly levels, but how will prices in an oligopoly compare with competitive levels?

In Figure 15.5, we show how an oligopolist has an incentive to raise prices above competitive levels. Imagine first that the oligopolistic market is producing at competitive levels. Recall from Chapter 11 that this means the price is equal to marginal cost and no firm is making an above-normal profit. In Figure 15.5, the competitive price and quantity are P_0 ($=MC$) and Q_0. Now suppose that one firm in, say, a four-firm oligopoly were to cut output by $Q_0 - Q_1$, thus raising the price to P_1. At P_1, every firm in the industry is making a profit since $P_1 > MC$. In particular, even the firm that cut its output increased its profits since before it was making zero profits and now it is making positive profits, as shown by the green area.

In a competitive industry, no firm is able to influence the price, so a competitive firm has no incentive to reduce output. In an oligopoly, each firm is large relative to the total size of the market. Thus, a firm in an oligopoly has some influence over the price and therefore has an incentive to reduce output and increase price from the competitive level.

Figures 15.3 and 15.5 tell us that price in an oligopoly is likely to be below monopoly levels but above competitive levels. Moreover, we can also see that the more firms in the oligopoly, the greater the incentive to cut price from monopoly levels and the smaller the incentive to increase price above competitive levels. Thus, we can also predict that the more firms in an industry, the closer price will be to competitive levels.

Can we be more precise about pricing in an oligopolistic market? Economists have spent a lot of time on this question and developed many models of oligopolistic pricing. Famous models in this literature include those by Bertrand, Cournot and Nash, and Stackelberg. Each of these models has its uses, but it's difficult to say that one model is best for all purposes. A lot depends on factors specific to the industry; the right model for the auto industry might not be the right model for the soft-drink industry or the aircraft industry. The field of industrial organization has a lot more to say about the specifics of oligopoly. We turn now to a different form of market structure, monopolistic competition.

Monopolistic Competition

So far we've talked about competition, monopoly, cartels, and oligopoly, but a lot of situations illustrate an intermediate form, namely *monopolistic competition*. Monopolistic competition has one key feature of monopoly—the firm faces a downward-sloping demand curve and has some power to set price—but also

CHECK YOURSELF

> The auto industry is an oligopoly: It has a small number of very large firms. Why don't we call the auto industry a cartel?

> When a firm in an oligopoly reduces output, who gets most of the gains from the reduction: the firm that reduces output or the other firms in the industry?

some key features of competition, namely that there are many firms in the market and each firm earns zero profit (Chapter 11).

Most likely, you deal with monopolistically competitive markets every day. Let's say you drive to your favorite Chinese restaurant and you see that it's charging $9.55 for your favorite dish, kung pao shrimp. You might wonder what would happen if the restaurant suddenly raised the price to $10 or, for that matter, to just a penny more at $9.56. In a perfectly competitive market, there are plenty of very close substitutes for these shrimp and market demand would immediately go to zero. Yet, that hardly seems to be a realistic description of the restaurant world. Probably some customers would stop going to the restaurant, but many others would continue to frequent it and they would pay more for their beloved shrimp dish. That means the firm faces a downward-sloping demand curve.

At the same time, the people running the Chinese restaurant don't seem to be getting rich. They're doing OK but they're not buying the largest mansion in town. Few people find their prices outrageous, as some of the dishes are not much more expensive than those at McDonald's. No one thinks of calling them "capitalist exploiters."

Monopolistic competition takes the standard model of monopoly but allows for the free entry of competing business firms. That's a realistic assumption for a large number of economic sectors. The first Chinese restaurant in our town of Fairfax, Virginia, probably did have some monopoly power, but since that time many entrepreneurs have opened up competing establishments. Yahoo! lists 346 restaurants in or near Fairfax as serving some form of Chinese food.

As more restaurants open, the demand curve facing the former monopolist shifts down and to the left, as some of the previous customers start patronizing other restaurants. In Figure 15.6, we show this process. We begin on the left

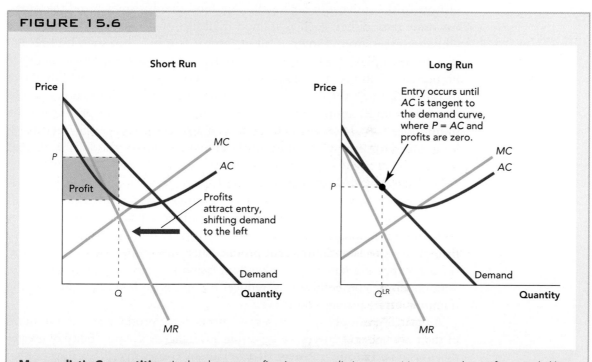

FIGURE 15.6

Monopolistic Competition In the short run, a firm in monopolistic competition can make profits exactly like a monopolist. In the long run, however, entry occurs, shifting the demand curve to the left/down until the demand curve is tangent to the AC curve. At this point the firm produces Q^{LR} and makes zero profits but $P > MC$.

when the first Chinese restaurant in Fairfax has a monopoly. As you know, a monopoly maximizes profit by producing the quantity such that $MR = MC$. Profit is given by $(P - AC) \times Q$ and is shown by the green rectangle. All of this is exactly the same as for monopoly that we discussed in Chapter 13. The difference comes in the long run. There are no barriers to entry preventing an entrepreneur from starting a new Chinese restaurant in Fairfax so monopoly profits attract entry. Entry reduces the demand for the original restaurant, shifting its demand curve left and down. The firm continues to make profits so long as price is greater than average cost, $P > AC$, but that means entry occurs so long as $P > AC$. The end result is that the demand curve is driven to the left and down until it becomes tangent to (just touching) the average cost (AC) curve. At this point, $P = AC$ and each firm in the industry is earning zero economic profits.

It's the entry of competing business firms that drives the move from the left side of Figure 15.6 to the right side.

Although producers under monopolistic competition don't earn high total profits, they still are charging prices above marginal cost, $P > MC$, as you can see in the right panel of Figure 15.6. When $P > MC$, output is not at the efficient level. Remember that the price P measures the value to consumers of one additional meal, and the MC curve at Q^{LR} tells us the cost of producing one additional meal. Thus, when $P > MC$, the value of an additional meal exceeds the cost of an additional meal and social surplus would be higher if the firm produced more. Production under monopolistic competition, just as with monopoly, is not perfectly efficient.

A monopolistic competitive firm is able to charge $P > MC$ because its product is slightly different than the product of other firms. Your authors have a favorite Chinese restaurant in Fairfax—China Star. It's where we take visitors to the university for lunch. The food there is spicier and the menu has some tasty dishes, such as scallion fried fish, that you can't find at other Chinese places around town. Call us fussy if you like, but such features are specific examples of what is called product differentiation. Since there are no perfect substitutes for China Star, it can price its scallion fried fish above marginal cost and yet not lose us as customers. Product differentiation also means that under monopolistic competition, a firm does not produce at the minimum of its AC curve. To see this in a picture, Figure 15.7 compares long-run output under monopolistic competition (on the left) with that under competition (on the right).

A competitive firm, sometimes also called a perfectly competitive firm, produces a product like oil that has perfect substitutes. As a result, the firm can't control the price of its product, and just to earn zero profits, it must produce at the output level that minimizes average costs. A monopolistic competitive firm produces a slightly different product than its competitors, and so it can reduce output and raise the price without losing all of its customers. But when a monopolistic competitive firm reduces output, it no longer produces at the minimum of its average cost curve.

Although monopolistic competitive firms don't produce at the minimum of their average cost curves, an offsetting advantage is the possibility of greater dynamism and product variety. If a restaurant comes up with a new recipe, for example, or some new and interesting décor, the demand curve for that restaurant's product will shift up and to the right and that restaurant will enjoy

FIGURE 15.7

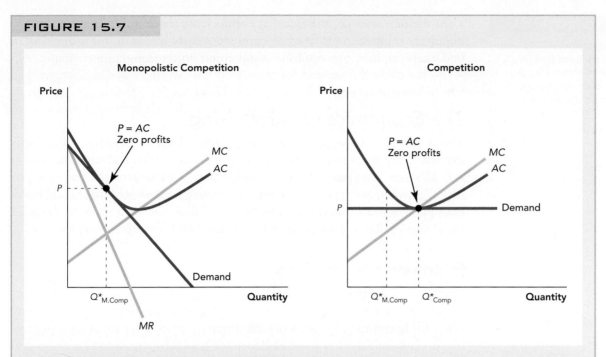

Comparing Monopolistic Competition and Competition In the long run, competitive and monopolistically competitive firms produce where $P = AC$ and earn zero profits. Each firm in monopolistic competition offers a slightly different product and so each firm faces a downward-sloping demand curve. As a result, firms under monopolistic competition charge prices above marginal cost, they produce a smaller quantity compared with competitive firms and Q^* is not at minimum average cost. In the case of competitive firms, each firm produces exactly the same product so there are perfect substitutes for each firm's products. As a result, the demand curve is perfectly elastic, production quantity is higher than under monopolistic competition, and output is at the point that minimizes average costs.

Note that for comparison we show the monopolistic competition output level, $Q^*_{M.Comp}$ and the competitive output level, Q^*_{Comp} in the right panel.

higher profits. Although there is more market power and monopoly in the meantime, usually in the longer run, consumers are better off from the new products and the better matching of products to tastes.

We can see both the benefits and the costs of monopolistic competition in the market for drinking water. Water is simple: It's uniform, and it's often available for free. So who would imagine that you could sell water by the glass for billions of dollars? And yet, bottled water products like Dasani, Fiji, and Voss sell some $60 billion worth worldwide. The fact that there are many producers of bottled water means that average costs of production are not minimized—bottled water would be cheaper if we could consolidate production in just a few firms, each of which would produce more. (And it would be even cheaper if we just used tap water.) On the other hand, many people do have a favorite brand of water so the product variety and experimentation of the industry does create value. Yes, sometimes we think this is a bit absurd—we have seen people buy bottled water at a restaurant instead of tap water even when the bottled water comes from exactly the same source! On the other hand, mineral water, sparkling water, and flavored waters, not to mention soft drinks, coffee, and tea (all mostly water), are different and it's hard to say how different is different enough to justify the extra costs.

As inefficiencies go, the fact that average cost is not minimized under monopolistic competition is typically considered fairly minor, but it is one way of understanding how monopolistic competition differs from competition.

The Economics of Advertising

The monopolistic competition model helps explain both the negative and the positive features of advertising. Perfectly competitive firms won't advertise because at $P = MC$ there is no gain from selling additional units of the product. But monopolies, oligopolies, and monopolistically competitive firms all wish to sell additional units and thus will attempt to use advertising to differentiate their products and build brand identity. These communications embody both information and persuasion.

Informative Advertising

Informative advertising is advertising about price, quality, and availability. Supermarkets, for example, send out newspaper supplements boasting of low prices for hamburger, apples, and milk. Price advertising is part of the competitive process, and there is good evidence for how advertising lowers prices and improves consumer welfare. In some states, for example, it used to be illegal for optometrists to advertise prices for eyeglasses; this restriction allowed economists to test the effect of advertising on prices. Would the states with advertising restrictions have lower prices for eyeglasses, on the theory that optometrists would save money if they didn't advertise and would pass on these lower costs to consumers? Or would states with restrictions on advertising have higher prices, on the theory that without advertising there would be less competition? The states that allowed price advertising for eyeglasses had systematically lower eyeglass prices; in other words, advertising improves the competitive process. The same pattern—lower prices where advertising is allowed—has been true for prescription drugs, retail gasoline prices, eye exams, and legal services.[4]

Other times, advertising promotes messages of quality, thereby informing consumers and also giving suppliers a better incentive to meet quality standards. Once it was discovered that high-fiber cereals may help prevent cancer, and such advertising was allowed by law, companies had (1) a greater incentive to produce and advertise high-fiber cereals and (2) consumers became better informed about the benefits of high-fiber cereals and they ate more of the healthier cereals.[5] These two processes were mutually reinforcing.

A lot of advertising is about telling people what's out there. As of 2010, it was more common to see advertisements for the iPad in Berlin than in Virginia, or for that matter, Silicon Valley. Why? Germans are less familiar with Apple products in the first place. Advertising tells customers about new products, what they do, and why they are beneficial.

Advertising as Signaling

Sometimes advertising doesn't appear to be about price, quality, or availability but the ad itself could be informative. If a new product debuts with a lot of accompanying advertising, consumers might infer that the seller expects the product to make a big splash, as with the iPad ads in Germany. The biggest piece of information is the ad itself. Apple was trying to get German consumers to think, either explicitly or implicitly, "If they're spending so much advertising on this new product, they must expect it to have a long and profitable life. There really is something to this iPad after all." That makes potential customers more interested in buying or at least sampling the product. Similarly, if a new movie or musical release is accompanied by a lot of ads, consumers will rationally infer that the producers expect the new product to hit it big; for a while, it seemed that *Avatar* commercials were everywhere. It might seem that the advertising creates the demand, but we also have to take into account that the firms who believe that their products are likely to be hits are the ones who have the biggest incentive to advertise. We'll discuss this kind of reasoning more in the section on "signaling" in Chapter 16 on knowledge goods.

Advertising as Part of the Product

It's obvious that a lot of advertising is simply about trying to change our minds and not about information at all. You can watch a Coca-Cola ad on YouTube that has no words, catchy music, lots of beautiful images including tumbling snowmen, no information about price, a cool dude pulling a Coke out of a vending machine, and at the end you see on the screen the simple words, "The Coke side of life".[6] Coke ads have been, well, vague for many years. Previous slogans include "The pause that refreshes," "Thirst knows no season," "Things go better with Coke," and "The real thing."[7] It's not so well known that Coca-Cola publicized the idea, through its ads, of Santa as an old man in a red suit, but that shows how central Coke ads have been to our national consciousness.[8] It's not obvious how these messages have anything to do with informing buyers about Coca-Cola, if only because just about everyone already has heard of Coke. Worldwide, for all brands, the company was spending $2.5 billion a year in advertisements in 2009. Like Apple, Coca-Cola is trying to nudge the market in the direction of monopoly, and away from a state of affairs where consumers view different soft drinks as close substitutes.[9]

Yet, is persuasion through advertising always such a bad thing? Persuasion can give us tastes that appear silly or unjustified to outside observers, such as when we believe that drinking a particular beer will make us more suave or more attractive to potential dates. Nonetheless, persuasion also can deepen our enjoyments and our memories.

Here's an example of how advertising gives us richer memories. In a blind taste test performed by researchers, the subjects reported roughly equal preferences for Coke and Pepsi. As part of the same test, the subjects were given one cup labeled as "Coke" and another cup, also containing Coke, but unlabeled. The subjects reported greater enjoyment from drinking the labeled cup and brain scans showed that they were activating the memory regions of their brain when they offered these reports. The researchers suspected that the subjects were associating Coke with fond images from ads or from earlier moments in their lives. It was not possible to replicate the same effect of "enhanced enjoyment from memory" when labeled and unlabeled Pepsi were put in the cups and sampled by subjects.

In other words, the very act of thinking about the Coke brand has resonance with a lot of customers.[10]

It's possible to read this story in two differing ways. Are the people who enjoy the Coke being "manipulated" or "tricked" by the advertisers? (If so, do your friends ever manipulate or trick you in the same way? Do you ever manipulate or trick them?) Or do the Coke ads mean many of us enjoy the Coca-Cola product more? Do the ads themselves enhance consumer welfare by turning a sweet, fizzy drink into something more? It's common that people bring their value judgments to bear on advertising, as some will condemn and others will praise persuasive ads; economic science itself does not give us a means of deciding which ads are good and which are bad, all things considered. What we do know is that persuasive advertising can create some market power by brand differentiation, but at the same time advertising also helps people enjoy a lot of products.

Advertising, whether informative or persuasive, also helps finance many useful goods and services. Why is Google available on the Web for free? Because the company earns income by selling click-through ads and thus doesn't need to charge users of a Web search. In fact, Google has an incentive to provide search services for free in order to maximize the number of people who will see the ads that it sells. Advertisements make newspapers and cable TV much cheaper than otherwise would be the case; for instance, a typical newspaper earns more from its ads than from its subscription revenue. In this sense, you, as a reader, benefit from ads even if you don't care about the advertised products. There was even a high-school calculus teacher in San Diego, who, when the school budget was cut, responded by selling ads on his classroom exams. The going rate was $10 for a quiz, $20 for a chapter test, $30 for a semester final.[11] Not everyone enjoys every ad, but advertising is an important part of what makes business work—at the most fundamental level, advertising is about bringing businesses and customers together.

☐ Takeaway

An oligopoly is a market dominated by a small number of firms. A cartel is an oligopoly that is able to maximize its joint profits by producing the monopoly quantity.

The OPEC cartel did not exhibit a long-term ability to control the price of oil. Most market cartels are not stable either. Either businesses cheat on the cartel agreement or new competitors enter the market. Governments break up some cartels, but they also enforce many other cartels. When you observe a harmful cartel, you should ask whether some governmental rule or regulation might be at fault. The prisoner's dilemma explains why cheating is common in cartels and more generally how individual interest can make cooperation difficult even when cooperation is better for everyone in the group than noncooperation.

Although firms in an oligopoly are unlikely to be able to produce the joint profit-maximizing quantity, neither are they likely to produce as much as in a highly competitive market. Prices in an oligopoly, therefore, tend to be below monopoly prices but above competitive prices.

In a monopolistically competitive industry, firms sell similar but differentiated products. As a result, each firm faces a downward-sloping demand curve but earns zero economic profit in long-run equilibrium.

Advertising can be informative as in advertising about price, quality, and availability. Advertising itself can also add to a consumer's understanding and enjoyment of a product by changing what the product means to them.

☐ CHAPTER REVIEW

Cartel, p. 279

Oligopoly, p. 279

Monopolistic competition, p.279

Strategic decision making, p. 279

Dominant strategy, p. 284

Prisoner's dilemma, p. 284

Antitrust laws, p. 286

FACTS AND TOOLS

1. Let's start off by working out a few examples to illustrate the lure of the cartel. To keep it simple on the supply side, we'll assume that fixed costs are zero so marginal cost equals average cost. We'll compare the competitive outcome ($P = MC$) to what you'd get if the firms all agreed to act "as if" they were a monopoly. In all cases, we'll use terms from the following diagram:

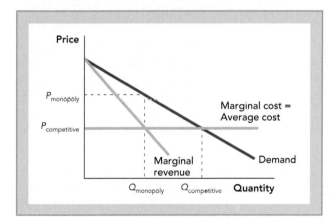

   a. First, let's see where the profits are. Comparing this figure with Figure 15.2, shade the rectangle that corresponds to monopoly profit.

   b. What is the formula for this rectangle in terms of price, cost, and quantity?

   c. Let's look at the market for one kind of apple: Gala. Assume that there are 300 producers of Gala apples and that $MC = AC = \$0.40$ per pound. In a competitive market, price will be driven down to marginal cost. Let's assume that when $P = MC$, each apple grower produces 2 million pounds of apples for a total market production of 600 million pounds. Now

imagine that the apple growers form a cartel and each agrees to cut production to 1 million pounds, which drives the price up to $0.70 per pound. Calculate profit per pound and total industry profit if the apple growers behave "as if" they were a monopoly and are able to produce according to the following table:

$P_{monopoly}$	$Q_{monopoly}$
$0.70/lb	300 million lb
Profit per pound$_{monopoly}$	Total industry profit$_{monopoly}$
_____	_____

   d. If a single apple grower broke from the cartel and produced an extra million pounds of apples, how much additional profit (approximately) would this apple grower make?

2. Take a look at the reasons why cartels collapse presented in this chapter. For each pair below, choose the case where the cartel is more likely to stick together.

   a. An industry where it's easy for new firms to enter vs. an industry where the same firms stick around for decades.

   b. When the government makes it legal for all the firms to agree on prices vs. when the government makes it illegal for all firms in an industry to agree on prices. (*Note:* The Sherman Antitrust Act made the latter generally illegal in 1890, but President Franklin Roosevelt's National Industrial Recovery Act temporarily legalized price-setting cartels during the Great Depression.)

   c. Cartels where all the industry leaders went to the same schools and live in the same neighborhood vs. cartels where the industry leaders don't really know or trust each other. (*Hint:* As Adam Smith said in the *Wealth of Nations,* "People of the same trade seldom meet together, even for merriment and diversion, but the conversation ends in a conspiracy against the public, or in some contrivance to raise prices.")

d. An industry where it's easy for a firm to sell a little extra product without anyone knowing (e.g., music downloads) vs. an industry where all sales are public and visible (e.g., concert tickets).

e. An industry where a high price spurs new production vs. an industry with highly inelastic supply.

3. The prisoner's dilemma game is one of the most important models in all of social science: Most games of trust can be thought of as some kind of prisoner's dilemma. Here's the classic game: Two men rob a bank and are quickly arrested. The police do not have an airtight case; they have just enough evidence to put each man in prison for one year, a slap on the wrist for a serious crime.

If the police had more evidence, they could put the men away for longer. To get more evidence, they put the men in separate interrogation rooms and offer each man the same deal: If you testify against your accomplice, we will drop all the charges against you (and convict the other guy of the full penalty of 10 years of prison time). Of course, if both prisoners take the deal, the police will have enough evidence to put both prisoners away and they will each get 6 years. And, as noted above, if neither testifies, both will get just 1 year of prison time. What's the best thing for each man to do?

In each cell in the table below, the first number is the number of years Butch will spend in prison, and the second is the number that Sundance will spend in prison given the strategies chosen by Butch and Sundance. If years in prison are minuses, then we can write up the problem like this:

		Sundance	
		Keep quiet	Testify
Butch	Keep quiet	(−1, −1)	(−10, 0)
	Testify	(0, −10)	(−6, −6)

a. If Sundance keeps quiet, what's the best choice (highest payoff) for Butch: keep quiet or testify?

b. If Sundance chooses testify, what's the best choice for Butch: keep quiet or testify?

c. What's the best choice for Butch? What's the best choice for Sundance?

d. Using the definition in this chapter, does Butch have a "dominant strategy"? If so, what is it?

e. What is your prediction about what will happen?

f. How does this help explain why the police never put two suspects in the same interrogation room? (Note the similarity between this question and the earlier Adam Smith quote.)

4. Your professor probably grades on a curve, implicitly if not explicitly. This means that you and your classmates could each agree to study half as much, and you would all earn the same grade you would have earned without the agreement. What do you think would happen if you tried to enact this agreement? Why? Which model in this chapter is most similar to this conspiracy?

5. In many college towns, rumors abound that the gas stations in town collude to keep prices high. If this were true, where would you expect this conspiracy against the public to work best? Why?

a. In towns with dozens of gas stations or in towns with less than 10?

b. In towns where the city council has many environmental and zoning regulations, making it difficult to open a new gas station, or in towns where there is lots of open land for development?

c. In towns where all the gas stations are about equally busy or in towns where half the gas stations are always busy and half tend to be empty?

6. Suppose you have a suit that needs altering, and you take it to three different tailors in the same mall to get an estimate of the cost of the alterations. All three tailors give you the exact same estimate of $25. What are two different explanations for the similarity of the price quotes? (*Hint:* One is consistent with competition and one is not.)

7. As this chapter pointed out, most cartels fail to successfully maximize profits by restricting output and raising prices because of the incentive to cheat. However, even a cartel that can achieve sustained cooperation is not guaranteed to succeed; "success" in raising prices can actually harm a cartel in the long run. Why is this?

8. Though its name can sometimes cause confusion for students, the market structure we call "monopolistic competition" is so named because it has some features of monopoly and some features of competition.

   a. In what ways is a monopolistically competitive market like a monopoly? In what ways is it like competition?

   b. Which of the outcomes of monopolistically competitive markets is a direct result of its monopoly-like features? Which outcome is a result of its competitive features? Can you summarize these results, so that they can be applied to product markets in general?

9. In a city like New York, the market for stand-up comedians is likely to be monopolistically competitive. Explain why this is. If the market is monopolistically competitive, then what can be said about prices, output, and profits in this market?

THINKING AND PROBLEM SOLVING

1. Usually, we think of cheating as a bad thing. But in this chapter, cheating turns out to be a very good thing in some important cases.

   a. Who gets the benefit when a cartel collapses through cheating: consumers or producers?

   b. Does this benefit usually show up in a lower price, a higher quantity, or both?

   c. Does cheating increase consumer surplus, producer surplus, or both?

   d. So, is cheating good for the cheaters or good for other people?

2. Firms in a cartel each have an incentive individually to lower the prices they charge.

   a. Suppose there was a government regulation that set minimum prices. Would this regulation tend to strengthen cartels, weaken them, or have no effect?

   b. Another way that one firm can cheat on a cartel is to offer a higher-quality product to consumers. Suppose there was a government regulation that standardized the quality of a good. Would this regulation tend to strengthen cartels, weaken them, or have no effect?

3. In the late fifteenth century, Europe consumed about 2 million pounds of pepper per year. At this time, Venice (ruled by a small, tightly knit group of merchants) was the major player in the pepper trade. But after Portuguese explorer Vasco da Gama blazed a path around Africa into the Indian Ocean in 1498, Venice found itself competing with Portugal's trade route. By the mid-sixteenth century, Europeans consumed 6 to 7 million pounds per year, much of it through Lisbon. After da Gama's success, the price of pepper fell.

   a. During the fifteenth century, was it likely that a cartel was restricting pepper imports? Why or why not?

   b. If the price of pepper before 1498 had been lower, would da Gama have been more willing or less willing to sail around South Africa's Cape of Good Hope? Why?

   c. Of the three reasons listed in this chapter for why cartels weaken, which one best explains the decline of Venice's influence on the world pepper trade?

   d. The ruling merchants of Venice had no political power in other parts of Europe. Why is that important in understanding how European pepper consumption more than tripled in just over half a century?

4. In 1890, Senator Sherman (of the Sherman Antitrust Act, which we mentioned earlier) pushed through the legislation that bears his name, which gave the government significant power to "bust up" cartels, presumably in order to increase output. More than a century later, economist Thomas J. DiLorenzo examined the industries commonly accused of being cartels and found those industries increased output by an average of 175% from 1880 to 1890—seven times the growth rate of the economy at the time.

   Suppose the industries were conspiring. Indeed, let's suppose that these cartels grew ever-stronger in the decade before the Sherman Act became law. If that were true, would we expect output in these industries to grow by so much? In other words, is DiLorenzo's evidence consistent with the standard story of the Sherman Antitrust Act?

5. In 2005, economist Thomas Schelling won the Nobel Prize in economics, in part for his development of the concept of the "focal point" in game theory. Focal points are a way to solve a coordination game. If two people both benefit by choosing the same option but cannot communicate, they will choose the most obvious option, called the focal point. Of course,

what's obvious will vary from culture to culture: whether to wear business attire or just shorts and a t-shirt, whether to use Apple or Microsoft products, whether to arrive at meetings on time or late. In all these cases, having a group agree on one focal point is more important than which particular focal point you all agree on. Therefore, people will look for cultural clues so that they can find the focal point. (*Note:* Schelling wrote two highly readable books that won him the Nobel Prize: *Micromotives and Macrobehavior* and *The Strategy of Conflict*.)

a. Suppose you are playing a game in which you and another player have to choose one of three boxes. You can't communicate with the other player until the game is over. One box is blue and the other two are red. If the two of you choose the same box, you win $50, otherwise, you get nothing. Which box do you choose: the blue box or one of the red boxes? Why?

b. Suppose that you and another player have to write down on a slip of paper *any* price in dollars and cents between $90.01 and $109.83. If you both write down the same price, you'll each win that amount of money. If your numbers don't match, you get nothing. Again, you can't communicate with the other player until the game is over. What number will both of you probably choose?

c. Many "slippery slope" arguments are really stories about focal points. In the United States during debates over banning guns or restricting speech, people will argue that *any* limitation follows a "slippery slope." What do they mean by that? (*Hint:* Attorneys often worry about "gray areas" and they prefer "bright line tests.")

d. Schelling used the idea of the focal point to explain implicit agreements on the limits to war. Poison gas, for example, was not used in World War II and the agreement was largely implicit. Since focal points have to be obvious, explain why there was no implicit agreement that "some" poison gas would be allowed, but "a lot" of poison gas would not be allowed.

6. Suppose the five landscapers in your neighborhood form a cartel and decide to restrict output to 16 lawns each per week (for a total of 80 lawns in the entire market) in order to keep prices high. The weekly demand curve for lawn-mowing services is shown below. Assume that the marginal cost of mowing a lawn is a constant $10 per lawn.

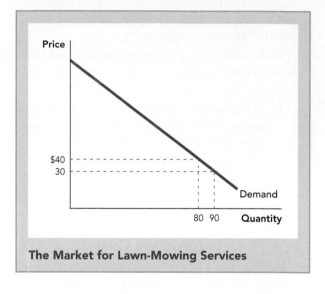

The Market for Lawn-Mowing Services

a. What is the market price under the cartel's arrangement? How much profit is each landscaper earning per week under this arrangement?

b. Suppose one untrustworthy landscaper decides to cheat and increase her own output by an additional 10 lawns. For this landscaper, what is the total increase in revenue from such behavior? What is the marginal revenue per lawn from cheating? Which is higher: the marginal revenue from the extra lawns, or the marginal cost?

c. Is it a good idea for the untrustworthy landscaper to cheat? What considerations, other than weekly profit, might enter into the landscaper's decision about whether to cheat?

7. Consider the demand schedule for Silly Bandz below. Assume that the marginal cost of producing a pack of Silly Bandz is a constant $0.50.

Price ($/pack of Silly Bandz)	Quantity Demanded (packs of Silly Bandz)
$3.50	0
$3.00	12
$2.50	24
$2.00	36
$1.50	48
$1.00	60

a. How many packs of Silly Bandz would be produced under a Silly Bandz monopoly?

b. If instead of a monopoly, a two-firm cartel controlled the Silly Bandz market, how many packs of Silly Bandz would each firm want to produce in order to maximize industry profits?

c. Determine whether it would be possible for one of the two firms in the cartel to earn higher profits by producing more than the industry profit-maximizing quantity you calculated in part b above.

8. As you read in the textbook, the requirements for an industry to be considered monopolistically competitive are that there are many firms and those firms are producing unique, or differentiated, products. One industry in which we find differentiated products is the recording industry. Not only are there many genres of music (iTunes lists almost 50), but within each genre there are countless artists, as well.

Over the past few decades, technology has reduced the fixed costs of recording and the marginal costs of distributing music. In 1979, for example, the average studio bill for an album was more than $30,000 ($170,000 in today's dollars). Nowadays, with digital recording technology, an artist or band can record an entire album for a few thousand dollars and the album can be distributed at low cost as MP3s on the Internet, with no record store involved.

a. What do you expect to happen to the music industry because of the evolution of much cheaper recording technology? What do you expect to happen to the number of recording artists?

b. Suppose there are initially only two recording artists in all of the record industry: the Decemberists (an indie rock band) and Yo-Yo Ma (a famous cellist). How many MP3s will they each be able to sell? Who would buy MP3s from the Decemberists? What about from Yo-Yo Ma? Will anybody buy MP3s from both?

c. Now suppose that another artist joins the industry: Isobel Campbell (an indie rock cellist!). What will happen to the demand curves for MP3s that the Decemberists and Yo-Yo Ma face? Will they keep all of their fans? Will they keep *any* of their fans? What do you think will happen to the total number of MP3s sold in the industry?

d. Generally speaking, as technology makes it cheaper and cheaper to produce MP3s, and as more and more bands join the music industry, what will happen to the total number of MP3s downloaded by music fans? What will happen to the MP3s sold by each individual band? What will happen to the profits of each band?

9. In a famous article on advertising,[12] Gary Becker and Kevin Murphy wrote about advertisements that run during television programs: "One can say either that advertising pays for the programming—the usual interpretation—or that programming compensates for the advertising, which is our preferred interpretation." Viewing ads during a television program (or hearing them during a radio broadcast) makes consumers worse off, so they must be compensated (with programming) for having experienced the ads. On the other hand, print ads in newspapers and magazines can be avoided by consumers, so these ads must make consumers better off; otherwise, no one would ever read them. Use this theory to answer the following questions:

a. Think about the different types of advertisements discussed in the chapter (informative, signaling, part of the product). Which type is more likely to appear on TV? Which type is more likely to appear in a newspaper or magazine? Often you'll see television commercials, especially for pharmaceuticals, that say: "See our ad in *such-and-such* magazine." What does this say about the difference between television and print ads?

b. Becker and Murphy wrote their article before TiVo and other DVR systems became popular. Nowadays, ads on television are avoidable (to a degree), just like ads in a newspaper. What impact do you think this new technology has on the types of ads you see on TV?

Can you see the influence of TIVO in this picture?

CHALLENGES

1. The French economist Antoine Cournot developed an interesting model of competition in an oligopoly that now bears his name. In a Cournot oligopoly, all of the firms know that the total output from all firms will determine the price (based on the downward-sloping market demand curve), but they make independent and simultaneous decisions about how much output to produce. Cournot developed this model after observing how a spring water duopoly (two firms) behaved. So let's look at a duopoly example.

   For each firm to decide how much to produce, it must make a guess about how much the other firm is going to produce. Also, the firms basically assume that once the other firm has decided how much to produce, it can't really change its decision.

   Here's an example. Suppose the market demand curve for gallons of fresh spring water looks like the one below and, to keep things simple, the marginal cost of spring water is zero. If Firm X believes that Firm Y is going to produce 100 gallons of spring water, for example, then Firm X knows that if it produces 0 gallons, the price will be $2.75; if it produces 100 gallons, the price will be $2.50, and so on. Basically, Firm X will face its own demand curve where all of the quantities are lower by 100.

Market Demand	
Price	Quantity demanded, in gallons
$3.00	0
$2.75	100
$2.50	200
$2.25	300
$2.00	400
$1.75	500
$1.50	600
$1.25	700
$1.00	800
$0.75	900
$0.50	1,000

Based on the demand schedule above, calculate the demand schedule that Firm X

would face if it suspected Firm Y was going to produce 0, 200, 400, or 600 gallons of spring water. Then, figure out the profit-maximizing amount of spring water for Firm X to produce in response. Fill in the table below.

If Firm Y produces...	...then Firm X should produce...
0 gallons	
200 gallons	
400 gallons	
600 gallons	

What you have just constructed is what economists would call Firm X's *reaction function*. Even though Firm X thought about the different choices Firm Y could make, Firm Y is not actually going to choose just any random level of output. In fact, Firm Y has its own reaction function, where it considers how best to respond to what it thinks Firm X is doing. Because both firms have the same zero marginal cost, the two reaction functions are symmetrical. (Thus, Firm Y's reaction function looks the same, only with "X" and "Y" switched.)

Graph the two reaction functions. Do you notice any points that stand out? Describe why this point represents an equilibrium for both firms.

2. The diagram below shows the monthly demand for hot dogs in a large city. The marginal cost (and average cost) is a constant $2 per hot dog.

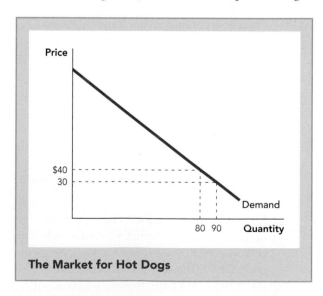

The Market for Hot Dogs

a. If the market for hot dogs is perfectly competitive, how many hot dogs will be sold per month, and at what price? Suppose there are 100 identical firms in this perfectly competitive market. How many hot dogs is each firm selling, and what are the profits for each firm?

b. Suppose the market was almost perfectly competitive, so that each firm has *some* very limited ability to change the price. What would happen if one of the firms in this market reduced its output by one-fifth, and no other firm changed its output? What would happen to the price of a hot dog? How much profit would the firm earn as a result?

c. Discuss the ability of one firm to reduce output and raise the market price if the market for hot dogs was instead an oligopoly made up of four firms, each initially producing 25,000 hot dogs per month. If only one firm reduced its output by a fifth, what would happen to the price of a hot dog? How much profit could this firm potentially earn?

d. Compare your answers for parts *b* and *c*. What does this tell you about the ability to earn profits in perfect competition vs. oligopoly?

16

Competing for Monopoly: The Economics of Network Goods

As of 2011, there were more than 750 million active users on Facebook. Why post your profile on Facebook? It's simple: Facebook is where everyone else posts a profile or goes to view profiles. If you are a teenager, unless you want to be a hermit, it is better to belong to the same network as your friends. Similarly, Match.com, the largest Internet dating service, claims to have over 20 million users.[1] If you are looking to date or marry, Match.com has the largest selection of potential partners and so you are most likely to use it.

Some markets involve building or coordinating a network, and those markets usually have some special properties. We wrote this book in Microsoft Word and not in some other software package. Why? It's not that we firmly believe that Word is superior to other programs. In fact, we've hardly tried most of the other programs. Instead, we knew that both of us had a copy of Word and we were both familiar with writing in Word. Even more important, we knew that our editor and publisher could work with Word files. Notice that we chose to use Word even though there are other software packages such as OpenOffice that are *free*.

In each of these examples, the value of the good depends on how many other people use the good. Facebook, Match.com, and Microsoft Word are all more valuable to one consumer when other consumers also use these goods. Thus, a **network good** is a good whose value to one consumer increases the more that other consumers use the good.

A **network good** is a good whose value to one consumer increases the more that other consumers use the good.

These examples hint at some of the interesting features of network goods that we will be exploring in this chapter. When networks are important, we typically see the following:

Features of Markets for Network Goods

1. Network goods are usually sold by monopolies or oligopolies.

2. When networks are important, the "best" product may not always win.

3. Standard wars are common in establishing network goods.

4. Competition in the market for network goods is "for the market" instead of "in the market."

By the way, did you notice the tension between features 1 and 4? Network goods are often sold by monopolies or oligopolies (feature 1), but competition *for* these markets can be intense (feature 4). In fact, the tension between these features of network-good markets has led to a debate about when the antitrust laws should be applied to network markets and when potential competition alone is enough to discipline monopolies. We will also be looking at this debate at greater length in this chapter. Let's look at each of these features in turn.

Network Goods Are Usually Sold by Monopolies or Oligopolies

Microsoft is one of the most profitable corporations on earth. Most of its profit comes from selling its operating system and software at prices above marginal cost. Microsoft can sell its products at prices above marginal cost not because those products are necessarily the best in some absolute sense but because most people want to use the same software as most other people. Microsoft products are, in most cases, the most likely to be compatible with other products and other readers, writers, and publishers.

The power of coordination in "Office-like" software is so strong that Microsoft can sell Office for hundreds of dollars even though there are *free* alternatives such as OpenOffice, Think Free Office, and Google Docs, all of which are roughly similar in quality to Office. But don't make the mistake of thinking that if one of these products became the dominant standard, we would all enjoy free software. The only reason these products are given away for free is that the owners hope to become the dominant standard so that they can charge a high price!

Sometimes the pressures for coordination are strong, but other factors mean that more than one firm can compete in the market. eBay is the market leader in online auctions and it uses its market power to charge higher prices than would occur in a standard competitive market. But there are a handful of other firms in the industry that offer slightly different features. Craigslist, for example, is able to compete with eBay because it offers buyers and sellers a way to buy and sell locally, which is especially useful for products that are expensive to ship. As we saw in the previous chapter, a market dominated by a small number of firms is called an oligopoly.

The market for Internet dating is an oligopoly simply because most people want to join large networks with many other people. But it's not a monopoly because Yahoo! Personals and eHarmony compete with the market leader Match.com by offering different matching algorithms. In addition, there are competing niche services, such as JDate.com (for those looking for a Jewish partner), but notice that JDate dominates its competitors within that niche.

The "Best" Product May Not Always Win

In markets with network goods, it's possible for the market to "lock in" to the "wrong" product or network. We can illustrate using a coordination game as shown in Figure 16.1, similar in structure to the prisoner's dilemma we showed in the previous chapter. Alex and Tyler are choosing whether to use software from Apple or Microsoft to write their textbook. Alex's choices or strategies are the rows, Tyler's are the columns. What Alex and Tyler most want to avoid is making different choices. If Alex chooses Microsoft and Tyler chooses Apple, it will be difficult for them to work together so their payoffs will be low, just (3,3). And the same thing is true if Alex chooses Apple and Tyler chooses Microsoft. Alex and Tyler receive the highest payoffs if both are using the same software. So, if Alex chooses Apple, it will make sense for Tyler to choose Apple, and vice versa. In other words, if Alex and Tyler both choose Apple, then neither will have an incentive to change his strategy.

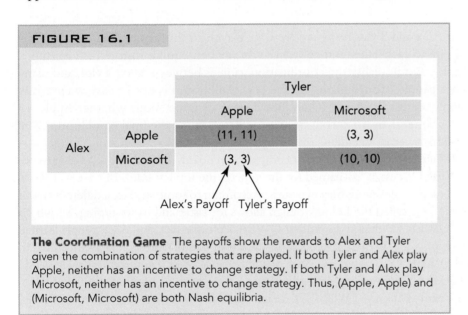

FIGURE 16.1

		Tyler	
		Apple	Microsoft
Alex	Apple	(11, 11)	(3, 3)
	Microsoft	(3, 3)	(10, 10)

Alex's Payoff   Tyler's Payoff

The Coordination Game The payoffs show the rewards to Alex and Tyler given the combination of strategies that are played. If both Tyler and Alex play Apple, neither has an incentive to change strategy. If both Tyler and Alex play Microsoft, neither has an incentive to change strategy. Thus, (Apple, Apple) and (Microsoft, Microsoft) are both Nash equilibria.

More formally, economists say a situation is an equilibrium if no player in the game has an incentive to change his or her strategy unilaterally. This is also called a **Nash equilibrium** after John Nash, the mathematician. His contributions to game theory resulted in a Nobel Prize, and his life story, detailing his struggle with mental illness, was featured in the movie *A Beautiful Mind*. The outcome (Apple, Apple) is an equilibrium because neither Alex nor Tyler has an incentive to change his strategy unilaterally, that is, given that Tyler chooses Apple, Alex wants to choose Apple and vice-versa.

But notice that (Apple, Apple) is not the only equilibrium in this **coordination game**. If Alex chooses Microsoft, then Tyler will also want to choose Microsoft, and vice versa. Thus, (Microsoft, Microsoft) is also an equilibrium strategy. The payoffs to the (Microsoft, Microsoft) equilibrium are slightly lower than the payoffs to the (Apple, Apple) equilibrium. Nevertheless, (Microsoft, Microsoft) is still an equilibrium because if Alex and Tyler do choose Microsoft, neither will have an incentive to switch. So which equilibrium, (Apple, Apple) or (Microsoft, Microsoft), will Alex and Tyler end up at?

A **Nash equilibrium** is a situation in which no player has an incentive to change his or her strategy unilaterally.

A **coordination game** is one in which the players are better off if they choose the same strategies than if they choose different strategies and there is more than one strategy on which to potentially coordinate.

The Dvorak keyboard.

Would you type faster?

If Alex and Tyler really are the only players in this game, they could probably talk to each other and coordinate on the best equilibrium, which is (Apple, Apple). But in reality the coordination game is between Alex, Tyler, and many other people. Coordinating on the best equilibrium is not so easy when many people are involved and when they do not all agree about whether Apple really is better than Microsoft. So what will determine the final equilibrium? The classic answer is "accidents of history."

It's an accident of history that computer keyboards are laid out according to the QWERTY design (so-named for the keys on the top left side). But is QWERTY the best possible layout for keyboards? According to some studies, a different layout of the keys called the Dvorak design allows for faster and easier typing. So why is the QWERTY design dominant? QWERTY came first, and once people learned to type on a QWERTY keyboard, typewriter manufacturers had an incentive to sell QWERTY typewriters. And, of course, once most manufacturers were selling QWERTY typewriters, it made sense to learn how to type on the QWERTY keyboard. Thus, the QWERTY design became "locked in." If you're wondering, QWERTY is the only way that your authors know how to type.

The QWERTY story needs to be taken with a grain of salt, however. The first study showing that the Dvorak layout was better than QWERTY was a 1944 study by the U.S. Navy. But who authored the 1944 study? None other than Lieutenant-Commander August Dvorak. Any guesses as to who created the Dvorak keyboard? Later studies have failed to show big advantages to either keyboard. Thus, it makes sense that few people bother to learn Dvorak even though it's now easy to reprogram a computer keyboard according to any design.★

When networks are important, product design isn't just about the stand-alone product, it is also about making sure the product fits into the rest of the industry and about making things easy for as many users as possible. Microsoft's competitors like Apple have at times arguably had the superior products in stand-alone terms, but Apple has not been better at ensuring widespread compatibility and an easy-to-use industry standard. Designing products that everyone can use will often mean a certain amount of simplification and a certain number of shortcuts. It is precisely the experts who will be most unhappy

★ The QWERTY story was made prominent by David, Paul A. 1985. Clio and the economics of QWERTY. *American Economic Review* 75: 332–337 and is criticized in Liebowitz, Stan J. and Stephen E. Margolis. 1990. The fable of the keys. *Journal of Law & Economics* 33(1): 1–25.

with a mass-compatible product. That is one reason why some people say "Microsoft is evil," but in part this charge is the result of wishful thinking that everyone could be an advanced computer user.

Standard Wars Are Common

More common than a coordination game in which a bad equilibrium becomes locked in is a standard war where there are two good equilibria but the players differ over which equilibrium is best.

In recent years, two groups of manufacturers battled over the standard for high-definition DVD discs. One group, led by Toshiba, supported the HD-DVD standard; the other group, led by Sony, supported Blu-ray. HD-DVD was a less complex and cheaper technology, but Blu-ray could store more information. Toshiba and Sony each wanted to win the standard war, but they also knew that consumers wouldn't buy either standard in large numbers until they were certain which standard would win the war. Thus, in Figure 16.2 we show that Toshiba is better off in the (HD-DVD, HD-DVD) equilibrium and Sony is better off in the (Blu-ray, Blu-ray) equilibrium, but neither company does well when there are two competing standards.

FIGURE 16.2

		Sony	
		HD-DVD	Blu-ray
Toshiba	HD-DVD	(10, 8)	(0, 0)
	Blu-ray	(0, 0)	(8, 10)

The Standard War There are two Nash equilibria in the standard war (shaded blue). Sony and Toshiba both prefer that they agree on a standard than having no standard at all, but Sony prefers the Blu-ray standard and Toshiba prefers the HD-DVD standard.

In the Blu-ray standard war, Toshiba and Sony battled to get content producers such as Disney, 20th Century Fox, and Universal and distributors like Wal-Mart and Netflix to sign on to one standard or the other. HD-DVD initially had the lead but Sony included Blu-ray players in the PlayStation 3, thus building an audience for its standard. More and more firms began to sign on to Blu-ray. After Warner Brothers announced in January 2008 that it would produce movies for Blu-ray exclusively, Toshiba threw in the towel and ended production of HD-DVD machines.

Competition Is "For the Market" Instead of "In the Market"

The Blu-ray wars illustrate another important feature of network goods, namely that competition occurs "for the market" rather than "in the market."

CHECK YOURSELF

> Compare the price of Blu-ray during its standard war with HD-DVD, and after. Do they differ? Why?

> Why don't you need actual prices to successfully answer the previous question?

For instance, once there is a winning standard, the losing standard can disappear quite quickly. It's also the case that a winning standard is not guaranteed to last forever or even for very long. Let's look at this in more detail.

Network goods are usually sold by monopolies or oligopolies, but what makes these markets different from standard monopolies and oligopolies is the ease and speed by which the monopoly can change hands. In 1988, the spreadsheet program Lotus 1–2-3 held a 70% share of the market, but it faced competition from Quattro Pro and Excel. At first Quattro Pro, with sales twice that of Excel, appeared to be gaining, but comparative reviews of all three programs gave the edge to Excel. By 1998, Excel had 70% of the market and Lotus 1–2-3 was heading toward irrelevance.

Microsoft Word is the dominant word processor today, but the authors of this book remember when WordStar and then WordPerfect were the market leaders. When it comes to network goods, consumer loyalties can switch quickly and this reintroduces significant competition into these markets. Currently, Facebook has more than 750 million members worldwide and it is the dominant social network. But less than five years ago, it was not clear whether MySpace, Friendster, or Facebook would become Number 1. Facebook eventually pulled away from the pack, as it offered a cleaner page, more and better apps, and better ability to tag and track your friends.[2]

One firm, or a handful of them, has dominated the market for network goods like spreadsheets, word processors, and social networking sites at each point in the history of their evolution, but the dominant firm has changed over time. We have had serial monopolies rather than a single, stable monopoly. Microsoft's share of the word processing and spreadsheet market appears to be strong today, but the history of this market reminds us that leaders can fall behind very quickly. Microsoft faces a number of web-based competitors that hope to dethrone the king. Google looks dominant in search, but Microsoft is betting that Bing will grab some market share. Facebook is growing, but Google+ is a potential threat. Maybe today's dominant firm will be dethroned, maybe not, but it's a mistake to think that a large market share, taken alone, implies that competition is absent. Competition for the market can dethrone market leaders very quickly.

Since Facebook and other network firms could be dethroned by a new entrant, these firms must make choices in light of *potential* competition. Markets in which potential competition disciplines firms are called contestable. Let's examine in more detail what makes a market contestable.

Contestable Markets

A market is **contestable** if a competitor could credibly enter and take away business from the incumbent.

A market is **contestable** if a competitor could credibly enter and take away business from the incumbent. Contestability does not require that such entry actually occur, only that it can potentially occur.

Contestability disciplines an incumbent firm even if the incumbent has a large market share because the mere threat of entry acts as a competitive force. For instance, Facebook is the dominant U.S. social network today, but fear of potential competitors motivates Facebook to keep its prices low (free!) and to keep advertising relatively unobtrusive. Potential competition is also leading Facebook to accept stronger privacy settings and to improve its interface to encourage games and apps for the site, such as FarmVille and YoVille. To the extent a market, even a network market, is contestable, it is hard for everyone to get locked into the wrong network, as was discussed above.

Contestability of a market rises to the extent:

1. Fixed costs of market entry are low, relative to potential revenue.

2. There are few or no legal barriers to entry.

3. The incumbent has no unique, hard-to-replicate resource.

4. Consumers are open to the prospect of dealing with a new competitor.

To put it more intuitively, the market for taco trucks is more contestable than the market for tacos in restaurants. Most markets are fairly contestable, as you can see by the turnover in corporate America.

A hard-to-contest market is piped water. Piped water is hard to contest because a competitor would need to lay a separate set of pipes to your home. Laying new pipe is very costly and involves difficult negotiations about which pipes have hook-up priority, rights of way, and so on. Most important, even if a potential competitor did enter this market, it would still be difficult to dethrone the incumbent because the incumbent could match any price offer made by the entrant. The result is that piped water is a natural monopoly (as we discussed in Chapter 13) and one that is stable through time. Since the piped water market has low contestability, a piped water monopolist might say to a Beverly Hills resident: "Pay $5000 this year, otherwise you don't get to take a shower." Consumers have a lot more to fear from a monopoly in piped water than a monopoly in, say, search. Thus, there is a case for regulation of monopolies that are not contestable, but it remains an open question (see below) whether or how government should regulate contestable monopolies.

The market for *mineral* water is more contestable because it's sold in bottles and not through pipes. A good Virginia supermarket will offer 10 or more brands of mineral water and new brands appear on the shelves every year. More important, even in the early days of mineral water in this country, when Perrier was a clear leading player, there was always potential competition and that held down retail prices. Shipping bottles of mineral water is more contestable than piping water because of the relationship between marginal cost and fixed cost. Laying pipes involves a high fixed cost (putting the pipes in is expensive) but a relatively low marginal cost, as running water through the pipes is quite cheap. As for shipping mineral water, a general network of roads and trucks is already in place and that network is not monopolized. It can be used by new entrants easily. Shipping mineral water involves low fixed costs and that means the incumbent firm doesn't have much of an advantage, so again that market is fairly contestable.

The general principle can be stated thus: To the extent fixed costs are high, a market tends to be less contestable and more easily monopolized. High fixed costs mean that entry is difficult and will be attempted only if expected revenue is large, to recoup the expenditures on those fixed costs.

Some markets become more contestable over time. In the early days of cell phones, few companies had good networks of connected towers and thus good reception. Today Verizon, AT&T, Sprint, T-Mobile, Cricket, Virgin Mobile, Boost Mobile, and others are in the market, with networks of varying degrees of quality but they all manage to attract customers. That increase in competition and contestability is one reason why cell phone calls have become progressively more affordable; between 1997 and 2010, when most other prices in the economy were rising, cell phone calls became more than 35% cheaper.[3]

Limiting Contestability with Switching Costs

Incumbent firms often try to limit the contestability of the markets they operate in. Facebook, for instance, encourages its users to load as many photos onto the site as possible. The company doesn't charge you for adding more photos, even though the viewing of those photos increases their server costs. Why does Facebook allow so many free photos? In part, they want to attract more users, but it's not just that. Facebook knows that if you load a lot of your photos onto their site, it will be more costly for you to switch to another networking site.

Switching costs are the costs of switching purchases from one firm to another. Firms sometimes try to raise switching costs to reduce competition for their customers.

If a new social networking site came along that was 3% better than Facebook, but all your photos were loaded onto your Facebook profile, would you switch? Maybe not. If you haven't kept copies of all those old photos, in a neat and organized way, you are especially unlikely to switch. Apple has pursued a similar strategy of increasing **switching costs** with its iPad, but they have gone further to make the export of content difficult. It is easy to download music, videos, TV shows, and other forms of media content onto your iPad. That makes more people want to buy an iPad, which can serve as a traveling movie theater, museum, and music hall, all in one. Yet once all that material is on your iPad, it is difficult to export it to other systems. You can't send it from your iPad to your television or to your personal computer or to your Blackberry, even though technologically, such transfers should be quite easy, if only the operating system would allow them. Apple wants to increase the costs of your switching to a competitor's product line.

Sometimes businesses use *customer loyalty plans* to increase switching costs and reduce contestability. A customer loyalty plan gives regular customers special treatment or a better price. The best-known customer loyalty plans are probably frequent flyer miles on airlines, but you will find customer loyalty plans at Barnes & Noble, at Starbucks, and at your local Giant and Safeway supermarkets.

Let's take the bookstore loyalty plans. If you buy enough books, you get some coupons good on future purchases. It's easy to see how those coupons limit contestability. Let's say you hold a few "30% off" coupons at your local book superstore and the time comes to do your Christmas shopping. You're most likely to go to that same book superstore. If you read in the paper that books are 10% off at a competing store, you won't be so impressed, compared with the 30% discount you are holding in your pocketbook. As you accumulate coupons over time, your mobility as a customer declines.

The trick is this: Suppose that Barnes & Noble, Amazon, and the other major booksellers *all* offer customer loyalty plans. Loyal customers of each of these companies feel good that they are getting valuable discounts, but once customers are loyal—that is, once they are locked in a bit—the different bookstores don't have to compete with each other quite as much. Loyalty creates monopoly power and each bookstore, facing a more inelastic demand curve, will raise prices. As a result, the net effect of discounts is higher prices! A cynic might say that exploitation is the price of loyalty.

When you cash in your coupons, you feel like a winner, but the reality is that you are being conned just a little. It does you no good, however, to stay out of the plans and refuse to use the coupons. If you refuse to join the loyalty plan, you lose the discounts. Furthermore, your refusal won't increase competition in the book market enough to get booksellers to lower their prices across the board. Customers are better off refusing to join the loyalty plan only if all or most of them refuse, in which case each bookseller will face a more elastic demand curve and prices will fall for everyone. Loyalty plans put customers in a type of prisoner's dilemma (Chapter 15)—it's good for a single customer to join the loyalty plan, but if all the customers join, the result is bad for them as a whole. As you know from the analysis of the prisoner's dilemma, however, it's going to be difficult to organize a mass boycott of loyalty plans.

By the way, limiting contestability is not the only motivation for customer loyalty plans; price discrimination (see Chapter 14) is another factor and that suggests a more positive take on such plans. People with lower incomes and more time on their hands are more likely to apply for the book discount cards and carry them in their wallet. The customer loyalty plans give those customers lower prices on some purchases, while still charging higher prices to the less careful customers or to the customers who are too busy earning money (and spending it) to keep track of a bunch of retail discount cards in their wallet. The bookstore ends up selling more books this way, and to the extent price discrimination is the basic motivation, customer loyalty plans aren't so bad.

Airline frequent flyer miles are another way to lock in customers; once you have accumulated a lot of miles on American or Delta, you can visit Hawaii or Paris for free. The lock-in is usually to the airline which is most dominant locally; for Alex and Tyler, that means United. The customers get some free flights, but overall competition is reduced and airline tickets are more expensive on average.

Like other customer loyalty programs, frequent flyer miles are motivated by more than one reason. They may be a form of price discrimination, as perhaps only the more budget-conscious travelers take the trouble to sign up for miles and cash them in, sometimes altering their flight plans to save the money. Over time, budget-conscious travelers, who redeem their miles conscientiously and thus get some free flights, pay lower average prices for flying than do non–budget-conscious travelers. Frequent flyer programs also encourage business travelers to sometimes take the more expensive flight; the traveler will get miles on the preferred airline but the employer will pay the higher price; the airline is indirectly "bribing" the employee to take advantage of the employer. Finally, firms may deliberately allow employees to keep their frequent flyer miles, even if it means paying for higher ticket prices come reimbursement time. It's one way of rewarding employees while skirting taxes (legally). Frequent flyer miles are tax-free as a means of compensation. If you really value the extra flights, you can save up to 40% in value by avoiding the taxation of ordinary monetary income and taking your marginal compensation in the form of miles. Frequent flyer miles are a good example of how, if you look closely at a business practice, you will see microeconomics everywhere.

Antitrust and Network Goods

In 2000, the Department of Justice brought a lawsuit against Microsoft, on the grounds that the company tried to monopolize operating systems and use its operating system to promote its other products. Windows, for example, was packaged with Internet Explorer, and this helped Internet Explorer replace Netscape as the leading market browser. In 1996, Netscape held 80% of the browser market according to some estimates, but by 2002, Internet Explorer had taken almost all of Netscape's market share.[4]

To be sure, it seems that Microsoft was guilty of "intent to monopolize," as defined by the antitrust laws. It is less clear that Microsoft's behavior made consumers worse off. Netscape's open-source spinoff, Firefox, is widely available today, as is Google's browser, Chrome, Apple's browser, Safari, and many others. Thus, there is considerable competition in this market. Switching to another browser is easy, but many of us don't bother because the quality of all browsers is high. More generally, during the 1990s, Microsoft prices fell and the software added many new features. For instance, Windows 95 and Windows XP were much more consumer friendly than their predecessors.

The dilemma facing the antitrust authorities is that we know the market for network goods will be dominated by a handful of firms. Thus, the question is not monopoly versus competition (in the sense of competition from many firms in the market), but rather it is one monopoly versus another. It's not obvious that consumers are better off when Netscape has a market share of 80% than when Internet Explorer has a market share of 80%. What is important is that competition *for the market* is not impeded. Regulators claim that Microsoft did impede competition for the market by giving away Internet Explorer for free in a bundle with Windows. Maybe, but that is a tough claim to either prove or to refute.

Microsoft settled with the government in 2001. The agreement was that the company would give its competitors the knowledge and technologies to produce software that would interact seamlessly with Windows.

Music Is a Network Good

Finally, network products aren't just found in high tech. Most people want to listen to music that is popular, so music is a network good. If you listen to music that is popular, you can swap songs with your friends, go to concerts together, and talk about the same people. Thus, music that is popular is a more valuable good; namely it offers more benefits to the listener than does music that is obscure.

In fact, an ingenious experiment by Duncan J. Watts, a sociologist at Columbia University, demonstrated that tastes in music have a strong social component.[5] Watts asked thousands of people to listen to and rate some bands that they had never heard of. If they liked a song, participants could download it for free. The trick was that some of the participants saw only the names of the songs and bands, but others also saw how many times the songs had previously been downloaded by other participants. If tastes in music are independent of what other people are listening to, knowing how many people had previously downloaded a song should be irrelevant. You should just download the songs you like, right?

But Watts discovered that the more downloads a song had, the more people wanted to download the song! So if a few early participants happened to like and download a song, that song got even more downloads. As a result, when participants saw previous downloads, accidents of history turned some songs and bands into big hits, while others languished. Even more surprisingly, when Watts ran his experiment again and again, the songs that turned into hits were different every time!

So what does this mean? Well, look at two of the principles we outlined above for network industries, namely that the best product may not always win and that standard wars are important. You'll find both of those phenomena in music markets. Some bands catch a lucky break and become popular fairly quickly. That popularity feeds on itself so a small head start is turned into a big market advantage even if the band is not necessarily the "best." Was Britney Spears ever that good an entertainer? Standard wars occur when different groups, singers, or genres compete to be seen as the market leader and thus attract the patronage of all those looking to support what is popular. Stars can rise or fall quickly depending on public perceptions of popularity. As with other network goods, at any one point in time a handful of entertainers dominate the airwaves and make the most revenues. But a large market share today is no guarantee of popularity in the future so older stars fear being dethroned by hot, young new stars.

◻ Takeaway

Network goods exist when many different users wish to share the same system or product; Microsoft Word and Facebook are examples. In these cases, we usually find monopolies or oligopolies because of the advantages offered when many customers can share one common system. Sometimes a firm may achieve market power by selling or creating a network good. Once such networks take off, they become large very rapidly and tend to be sold by one or only a handful of major firms. Since networks often grow rapidly and offer significant revenue potential, many entrepreneurs will try to set the standard for the network, thus leading to standard wars.

Sometimes customers will end up "locked in" to the wrong network, or at least users will disagree as to whether the better network has won out. There is a coordination problem involved in switching from one network to another, since virtually everyone must make a coordinated change. The end result is that often not everyone is happy with the dominant network.

Still, network markets often are highly competitive, as different firms compete to be the dominant player. This competition induces them to upgrade their products, make them more convenient, and introduce innovations, as we have seen from Facebook. It is common that a new market leader will leapfrog the old leader and replace it. The more contestable the market, the greater the incentive for product improvement and the less likely that customers will be locked into the wrong network. Businesses often take actions to deliberately increase switching costs, as we observe with customer loyalty programs, such as frequent buyer discounts or frequent flyer miles on airlines.

CHECK YOURSELF

> Does a firm with an established network good, such as Microsoft Office, face competition? Why or why not?

> Consider the Blu-ray versus HD-DVD competition. Why is it useful for you to wait before purchasing when standards are not set? What do you predict will happen to sales once standards *are* set?

◻ CHAPTER REVIEW

KEY CONCEPTS

Network good, p. 303

Nash equilibrium, p. 305

Coordination game, p. 305

Contestable markets, p. 308

Switching costs, p. 310

FACTS AND TOOLS

1. Antitrust laws make certain "anticompetitive" practices illegal because these practices raise prices and reduce output, which reduces the total amount of consumer surplus. Explain why antitrust action may not be helpful or necessary in markets that are:

   a. Characterized by network goods

   b. Highly contestable

2. Explain the difference between competition "in the market" and competition "for the market." What impact does each kind of competition have on prices and output in a market? Is one better than the other? How does the distinction make the application of antitrust laws more complicated?

3. LinkedIn is an online professional networking site, much like Facebook or MySpace, except that it's for connecting with classmates and colleagues to create networks that may be helpful in, among other things, finding job opportunities. The site boasts more than 100 million members (as of March 2011) and claims to be the "world's largest professional network on the Internet." What made LinkedIn the largest professional network site? Since it is already the largest, does that mean LinkedIn will always be the largest? Why or why not?

4. For each of the pairs below, determine which business is more likely to operate in a contestable market, and explain why.

   a. The only clothing store in a small town vs. the only natural gas provider in a small town

   b. The only clothing store in a small town vs. the only cable TV provider in a small town (What recent technologies makes *b* different from *a*?)

   c. De Beers diamond mining vs. H&R Block tax preparation services

5. In the following three games, is each a coordination game or a prisoner's dilemma? The best way to check is to see if there is exactly one Nash equilibrium; another way is to see if there is a dominant strategy for each player. To keep it a little challenging, we won't give the actions obvious labels that might give away the answer. Higher numbers are always better:

a.

		Player B	
		Left	Right
Player A	Up	(3, 3)	(5, 5)
	Down	(5, 5)	(1, 1)

b.

		Player B	
		Left	Right
Player A	Up	(100, 100)	(600, 50)
	Down	(50, 600)	(500, 500)

c.

		Player B	
		Left	Right
Player A	Up	(8, 6)	(7, 5)
	Down	(3, 0)	(9, 9)

6. The mantra of Amazon.com CEO Jeff Bezos is "Get big fast." As we saw in Chapter 13 on monopoly, one reason to "get big fast" is because in some industries the firm's average cost will plummet as the firm expands—so size helps on the supply side. In this chapter, network effects illustrated how size helps on the demand side. With this in mind, explain the following real-world drives to get big fast: Do you think it's mostly about increasing returns or mostly about network effects? Explain why:

   a. Second Life, an online virtual world, lets people use many of its features for free. To use the best features, you have to pay for it.

   b. Likewise, Match.com, the online dating site, lets people post profiles, look at other people's profiles, and even get mail from other members for free. To send an email to a member, you have to pay.

   c. Adobe Acrobat Reader is free, but the software to create sophisticated Adobe documents is not.

   d. King Gillette (real name) gave away his first disposable razor blades in 1885. They came free with the purchase of a box of Cuban cigars.

   e. Amazon.com itself.

THINKING AND PROBLEM SOLVING

1. If you get a crack in your windshield, you can take your car to an auto-glass repair shop where they will gladly try to repair your windshield, so you can avoid having to replace it. They guarantee their work, too; if the repair is not successful, they will allow you to apply the money you already paid for the unsuccessful repair toward the purchase of a new windshield. Sounds terrific, but how does this strategy relate to the material in the chapter? If all auto-glass repair shops employ this strategy, what impact do you think this has on the price of a new windshield?

2. Every so often, rumors float around Facebook claiming that the social networking site is going to begin charging its users a small monthly fee. So far, those rumors have always turned out to be false.

   a. Do you use Facebook? If so, how much would you be willing to pay per month for access to Facebook? (If you don't use Facebook—as unlikely as that is nowadays— how much do you imagine the typical user would be willing to pay to use it?)

b. Besides the price itself, what else would determine whether it was worth it to you to pay for Facebook? Is your response independent of others' responses?

c. Do you think Facebook ever will charge users a fee? What are some reasons Facebook might do this? What are some arguments against this idea?

3. Deciding which side of the road to drive on is a kind of coordination game. In some countries, people drive on the right side of the road, and in other countries (notably the United Kingdom and some of its former colonies), they drive on the left. These customs developed hundreds of years ago. If there were a single world standard, car companies could save some money by not having to produce both left and right types and cars would be a little bit cheaper. Why do you think it is that these customs persist? In other words, what keeps the world "locked in" to two separate kinds of cars?

4. Suppose you and your friend Amy work together to develop a unique magic trick that either of you could perform alone. It turns out to be a tremendously popular trick and both of you make it big as professional magicians. Suppose you decide to conspire together and limit the number of performances featuring the trick. If both of you do only one show a week, each of you earns a profit of $10,000 for that show. If both of you do five shows a week, each of you earns a total profit of $6,000. If one does a single show while the other does five shows, the former gets a profit of $1,000 and the latter gets a profit of $15,000.

a. Use the information above to complete the table below. (*Hint:* It'll look a lot like Figure 15.4.)

		Amy	
		1 show	5 shows
You	1 show	,	,
	5 shows	,	,

b. Suppose Amy does one show. What is your preferred strategy?

c. Suppose Amy does five shows. What is your preferred strategy?

d. What is your dominant strategy?

e. Suppose you do one show. What is Amy's preferred strategy?

f. Suppose you do five shows. What is Amy's preferred strategy?

g. What is Amy's dominant strategy?

h. What is the Nash equilibrium?

i. Magicians are famously hesitant to reveal the secrets behind their magic, even to other magicians. Based on what you've learned in this question, why do they act like this? Is letting other magicians in on your secrets an optimal strategy?

5. Consider the shipping container (the large box that stacks on cargo ships and attaches to trucks). If all containers are the same size and design, then the container can pass seamlessly between ships, trains, trucks, and cranes along the way. Today, the standard dimensions are 8 feet wide, 8.5 feet tall, and 40 feet long. (The recent book *The Box* tells the surprisingly gripping tale of how this size came to be the standard, and how it has cut the cost of shipping worldwide.) Let's see how this standard dimension illustrates the meaning of "Nash equilibrium."

a. Suppose an inventor created a new shipping container that was slightly cheaper to make, as well as stronger, but it *had* to be 41 feet long. Keeping the idea of standardization in mind, would this inventor be successful? Why or why not?

b. Suppose a container manufacturer reduced the strength of the end walls of his containers (saving him $100 per container made). Although this makes no difference to containers on a boat, containers on a train are at risk as the container bumps against the flatcar when the train hits the brakes. Who would tend to oppose these weaker, cheaper containers: the company whose products are stored in the container, the train companies who transport the goods, or both?

c. Why does Federal Express, the overnight delivery company, require everyone to use FedEx packaging for most shipments?

6. It's more efficient to go shopping when everyone else is shopping: This is one explanation for the rise of Christmas as a shopping season. Even many people who don't celebrate Christmas do a lot of shopping and gift-giving during this season. At the other extreme, a "dead mall" is one of the dreariest sights of modern consumer capitalism. Let's see how a pleasant shopping experience is a network good.

Facebook for those without computers.

a. Part of the pleasure of walking through a mall is the pleasure of seeing and being seen. When will you see more people at the mall: in the months before Christmas or at other times? So if you like seeing people, when will *you* tend to go to the mall? (This is an example of the "multiplier effects" so common in economics.)

b. When you were in high school (or perhaps middle school), you may have spent time hanging out at a mall. How was the mall like Facebook, MySpace, or other social networking Web sites?

c. Malls will spend more money on decorations and entertainment when they can spread this cost over a large number of consumers. Again, when will you expect to see more of these extra expenses: in the months before Christmas or at other times?

d. If Christmas is so great for malls, why don't they have Christmas every month, spending money on decorations and singers all the time? Of course, they *try* to do this with Easter and back-to-school and Valentine's Day, and so forth, but why do these attempts fail so miserably compared with the big success of Christmas? Answer in the language of network goods. (*Hint:* Once there's a big chunk of the population committed to using Facebook, what's the benefit to setting up another pseudo-Facebook?)

CHALLENGES

1. Prisoner's dilemmas are common in real life, but not all real-life games are as dismal as the prisoner's dilemma. One game, known as "stag hunt," describes situations where cooperation is possible but fragile. The philosopher Jean-Jacques Rousseau described the game. He said that a lot of social situations are like going hunting with a friend: If you both agree to hunt for a large male deer (a stag), then you each have to hold your positions near each end of a valley so that the animal can't escape. If you both hold to your positions, then you will almost surely get your kill. If one hunter wanders off to hunt the easier-to-find rabbit, however, then the stag will almost surely get away. Rabbit hunting works fine as a solo sport, but to catch a deer, you need a team effort. This is the usual way of writing the game:

		Hume	
		Hunt Stag	Hunt Rabbit
Rousseau	Hunt Stag	(5, 5)	(0, 3)
	Hunt Rabbit	(3, 0)	(3, 3)

a. If Rousseau is quite sure that Hume will hunt stag, will he also hunt stag?

b. If Rousseau is quite sure that Hume will hunt rabbit, will Rousseau still hunt stag?

c. There are two Nash equilibria here: What are they? (Check by looking in each box and asking, "Would one player unilaterally change his choice between rabbit and stag? If so, this isn't an equilibrium.")

d. Of these two equilibria, economists call one the "payoff-dominant equilibrium" and the other the "risk-dominant equilibrium." You can figure out which is which by the process of elimination. What do you think is the biggest risk that might push someone to choose the "risk-dominant equilibrium"?

e. Is this a coordination game or is there a dominant strategy?

f. In the coordination games we looked at in previous questions, if you failed to coordinate, things turned out badly. Is that the case here?

g. Anytime someone says, "I'll do it as long as I'm not the only one," they're probably describing a stag hunt. Wearing a cocktail dress to a dinner party, making a solid team effort, keeping your lawn mowed—all might be examples of stag hunts. In a stag hunt, if you think the other players are nice, then you'll want to be nice yourself. But if you suspect they're not nice, you'll probably just be a "rugged individualist" and go hunt the rabbit on your own. With this in mind, think of two more examples of stag hunt situations on your own.

(For an excellent, somewhat technical treatment of how people might agree to hunt stag across many areas of life, see Skyrms, Brian. 2004. *The Stag Hunt and the Evolution of Social Structure.* Cambridge, UK: Cambridge University Press. Skyrms is a philosopher who uses the tools of game theory to investigate important social questions.)

2. We mentioned research by Liebowitz and Margolis that poked some holes in the QWERTY story. In particular, they emphasized that in the age when typing first became common, many corporations had large "typing pools," dozens of women (rarely men) who just typed up other people's handwritten notes. If DVORAK had really been faster than QWERTY, then these corporations could have saved millions of dollars in hourly wages by just retraining their workers with a few days on a DVORAK keyboard. In other words, individuals might choose the wrong standard, but big firms have a tendency to grab the easy money, especially when it's measured in the millions of dollars. That gives these big players a strong incentive to pick the best standard.

   a. With this in mind, which major market players might have pushed for the Blu-ray DVD standard? In other words, which organizations might have a lot of experts on staff to check every detail of the competing high-definition DVD formats? Which organizations would also care about choosing the format consumers would actually prefer two or three years down the road?

   b. In future standard wars, do you expect most of the early sales efforts to be directed at regular consumers or instead at "power users," owners of big retail chains, and other gatekeepers?

3. Why doesn't everyone just switch to one language?

4. Nobel Laureate Paul Krugman once asked, "Who would enter a demolition derby without the incentive of a prize?" (Source: Krugman, Paul. 1998. Soft microeconomics: The squishy case against you-know-who. *Slate.* www.slate .com/id/1933/. Posted April 24, 1998.)

   a. The "demolition derby" he was talking about was the battle over Internet browsers: Many enter the battle, but only one (or two) survive. But let's take his story literally: If there were two cars in a demolition derby, and each car costs $20,000 to build, and one car will be to-tally destroyed, how big will the prize probably have to be to get two people to enter if there's a 50–50 chance of losing all your investment?

Netscape?

   b. What if we want a really good demolition derby: one where 10 of these cars compete but only one survives. About how big will the prize have to be now?

   c. Let's draw the lesson for network goods: Since competition in network good markets is competition "for the market," then it's like winning a prize in a demolition derby. If there's a fixed price of starting up a new social networking Web site (you need so many computers, so many nerds, so many advertisers), then when would you see a lot of firms competing for the prize: when the prize is large or when the prize is small? Thus, if we want a lot of competition *for the market,* do we necessarily want to restrict the profits of the winner?

5. The market for college textbooks is an interesting one. One thing that makes it unique is that the person who chooses the textbook (the professor) is not the person who purchases the textbook (the student). Therefore, much of a textbook publishing company's marketing is geared toward college professors. Most publishers of economics textbooks have developed (or have partnered with other companies to provide) online homework-management systems. The one that goes with this textbook is called *EconPortal*, as you may already know if your professor is using it. Explain how a homework-management system might benefit a professor. What impact might a homework-management system have on switching costs?

6. Imagine that two players are competing over a valuable resource. Each player has two options. He or she can either be aggressive and demand the entire resource, or the player can offer to split the resource equally. The literature uses the word "Hawk" to describe the aggressive

behavior, and the word "Dove" to describe the sharing behavior. If two Hawks meet, then both will demand the resource, neither will give in, and there will be a fight. If a Hawk meets a Dove, the Hawk will take the resource and the Dove will get nothing. If two Doves meet, the resource will be shared equally.

Assume that the value of the resource is 60; the cost of losing a fight is 100; and if two Hawks fight, each of them has a 50% chance of losing.

Here's the payoff matrix:

		B's Strategies	
		Hawk	Dove
A's Strategies	Hawk		
	Dove		

a. Oops! The payoffs are missing. You'll have to fill them in. Remember, if there's a fight, there is a 50% chance of winning 60 but also a 50% of losing the fight, which has a payoff -100. What's the expected outcome? If both animals choose Dove, assume that they peacefully split the resource. If one is a Hawk and the other is the Dove, the Hawk gets the resource, and the Dove receives nothing

b. Explain why (Hawk, Dove) and (Dove, Hawk) are both Nash equilibriums.

c. The Hawk-Dove game is often used to discuss international relations. Can you explain why a country might like to be perceived as a Hawk? What are the dangers of being a Hawk? What are the dangers of being a Dove?

d. Biologists also use game theory to understand animal behavior, but they interpret the strategies a little differently. Instead of allowing an animal to choose a strategy, they assume that x percent of animals in a population will always play Hawk and $100 - x$ percent of animals in a population will always play Dove, and they also assume that animals will meet randomly.

Biologists argue that if Hawk has an expected higher payoff than Dove, then Hawks will outcompete Doves so that over time, evolution will increase the percentage of animals playing Hawk. Similarly, if Dove has a higher payoff, then over time, evolution will increase the percentage of animals playing Dove.

Can you find a strategy that is *evolutionarily stable*; that is, can you find a strategy where the percentage of animals playing Hawk and Dove is stable over time?

Here are two hints: Let x be the percentage of animals playing Hawk. If 0% percent of animals play Hawk ($x = 0$%) and thus all play Dove, is that evolutionarily stable? If all animals play Hawk ($x = 100$%), is that evolutionarily stable?

17

Labor Markets

Ajanitor in the United States earns about $10 an hour; a typical janitor in India earns less than $1 an hour. Why is there such a difference? Why does one person earn so much more than the other? After all, janitors in both countries do many of the same things: They clean windows and floors, scrub toilets, remove trash, and so forth.

If you think the differences in wages have to do with supply and demand, you are on the right track.

Wages are determined in the market for labor just like other prices are determined.

In this chapter, we look more deeply at the factors underlying the demand for labor and the supply of labor. A deeper understanding explains how wages are determined at a fundamental level, why most Americans earn so much by global standards, why education raises wages, whether and how much labor unions help workers, and how discrimination still shapes labor markets today.

The Demand for Labor and the Marginal Product of Labor

A firm is willing to hire a worker when the worker increases the firm's revenues more than the firm's costs. Economists call the increase in revenue created by hiring an additional worker the **marginal product of labor (MPL)**. The increase in costs created by hiring an additional worker is, for a competitive firm, simply the worker's wage (including the cost of other compensation like health benefits). Thus, we can say that a firm is willing to hire a worker when the marginal product of labor is greater than the wage.

The **marginal product of labor (MPL)** is the increase in a firm's revenues created by hiring an additional laborer.

When the Boston Celtics traded for Kevin Garnett, they went from a mediocre record of 24 wins and 58 losses to having the best record in the NBA. Not only did the Celtics win more games when they hired Garnett, their attendance increased and they sold more merchandise. In the long run, the value of their TV contract was much higher, too. When the Celtics hired Garnett, their revenues increased by a lot—Kevin Garnett had a high marginal product—that's why the Celtics were willing to pay Garnett nearly $24 million a year.

McDonald's considers marginal product when the company hires people to keep its restaurants clean and in good running order. No one wants to eat in a restaurant that looks unclean so a cleaner restaurant increases profit. But how clean is clean enough? At some point, cleanliness costs more than it's worth. Thus, to maximize profit, *McDonald's will hire janitors so long as the increase in revenue from hiring an additional janitor exceeds the janitor's wage.*

To make that more concrete, let's consider the marginal product of labor as we vary the number of janitors, as in Table 17.1.

TABLE 17.1 The Marginal Product of Labor

Number of Cleaners	Task	Marginal Product of Labor (MPL per hour)
One	Clean restrooms, once a day.	$35
Two	Empty trash.	$30
Three	Clean restrooms, second time in a day.	$24
Four	Wash floors.	$20
Five	Pick up outside trash.	$16
Six	Clean restrooms, third time in a day.	$12
Seven	Clean windows.	$11
Eight	Remove gum from the bottom of tables.	$8

You'll notice a few things about these numbers. First, the marginal product of labor generally declines as more labor is hired. If there is one janitor, he or she will focus on the most important tasks so the marginal product of labor is high. As McDonald's adds janitors, each subsequent janitor is assigned to a less important task so the marginal product of labor falls.

We can see from Table 17.1 that if McDonald's hires three janitors, then the marginal product of labor (per hour) is $24. If McDonald's hires four janitors, the marginal product of labor is $20, and so forth. But how many janitors will McDonald's hire? That depends on the wage.

If a janitor's wage is above $35 an hour, then McDonald's will hire zero janitors. If the wage falls to, say, $32 an hour, McDonald's will compare the additional revenues from hiring a janitor (the MPL), $35 an hour, to the cost of hiring the janitor, $32 an hour. Since the MPL is greater than the wage W, McDonald's will make the hire. If the wage falls to $28, McDonald's will hire a second janitor. If the wage falls to $22, McDonald's will hire a third janitor and so forth.

Notice that when the wage falls, McDonald's hires more janitors and assigns them to less important tasks, so as the wage falls, so does the MPL. The wage and the marginal product of labor will always be very close together since McDonald's will keep hiring workers so long as the MPL is greater than W.

If we know the marginal product of labor, we can derive the demand curve for labor. In Figure 17.1, for example, we show McDonald's demand curve for janitors. From the figure and from Table 17.1, you can see that if the wage is $10, then McDonald's will hire seven janitors.

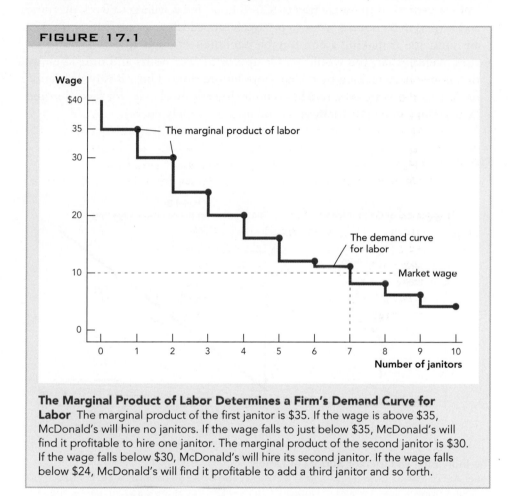

FIGURE 17.1

The Marginal Product of Labor Determines a Firm's Demand Curve for Labor The marginal product of the first janitor is $35. If the wage is above $35, McDonald's will hire no janitors. If the wage falls to just below $35, McDonald's will find it profitable to hire one janitor. The marginal product of the second janitor is $30. If the wage falls below $30, McDonald's will hire its second janitor. If the wage falls below $24, McDonald's will find it profitable to add a third janitor and so forth.

Of course, we still have not explained what determines the wage. To do that, we need to remember that many firms demand janitors, so the wage of janitors will be determined by the *market* demand and supply of janitors. But don't worry, the market demand for janitors is very similar to McDonald's demand for janitors. At a high wage, only some firms (and some consumers, such as the very wealthy) will demand janitors. As the wage falls, more and more firms will demand janitors and each firm will demand more janitors, as we saw with McDonald's. Thus, the market demand for cleaners is downward-sloping, as usual.

Supply of Labor

The market supply curve for labor will be upward-sloping, again as usual. In other words, high wages encourage a greater supply of labor. That's intuitive but we do have to take into account one complication. An *individual's* labor supply curve need not slope upward throughout its range. When Bruce Springsteen was

CHECK YOURSELF

> Why does the marginal product of labor fall as more workers are hired?

paid $100 a night, he toured constantly just to pay the rent. Now that he is paid hundreds of thousands of dollars a night, Springsteen tours less often. If his wage is already high, even Joe the cleaner might decide that he would prefer spending more time with his family to working more hours at an even higher wage rate.

Figure 17.2 illustrates. In Panel A, if the wage is between $7 and $16 an hour, Joe works 40 hours a week, so over this range Joe's supply curve for labor is vertical. If the wage rises to $20 an hour, Joe is willing to work overtime and he puts in 50 hours a week (a positively sloped labor supply curve). At $20 an hour, Joe is making a comfortable income—enough so that if his wage rises even further, Joe would prefer to work fewer hours and instead enjoy the money he is making by taking more leisure time. Thus, it is quite plausible that as the wage rises to $28 an hour, Joe asks his bosses for less overtime (a negatively sloped or backward-bending labor supply curve).

FIGURE 17.2

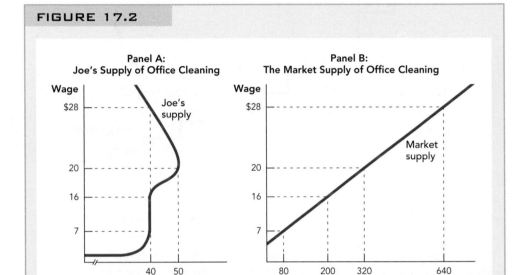

The Individual and Market Supply of Labor
Panel A: For a wage between $7 and $16 an hour, Joe works 40 hours a week. For $20 an hour, however, Joe is willing to work 50 hours a week, but as the wage increases, Joe takes more of his income in the form of leisure and works less—thus, over a higher range, Joe's labor supply curve may be backward-bending.
Panel B: The labor supply curve for the market is positively sloped throughout because even if Joe works less as the wage rises (over some range), many other workers enter the office cleaning industry as the wage rises.

Although Joe's supply curve for labor could have a zero, positive, or even negative slope, the market supply curve for labor is very likely to be positively sloped. Why? Let's go back to when Joe was earning $7 an hour and putting in 40 hours a week. When the wage rises to $16 an hour, Joe doesn't work more hours; but, at a higher wage, Mary, who was working in the restaurant business, is likely to switch to office cleaning. Thus, in Panel B, we show the market supply of janitors. When the wage increases, the market supply increases for two reasons: First, some workers—although not all—are likely to work more as the wage increases. Second, and more important, when the wages of janitors increase, that attracts workers from other industries. Together, these two factors mean that even if some individuals supply less labor at a higher wage, a higher wage increases the quantity of labor supplied overall.

Thus, an upward-sloping *market* supply curve is the normal situation.

We can now put together the supply and demand for janitors in the usual fashion to represent the market for janitors.

In the United States, there are about 4.2 million janitors, each working about 40 hours a week (168 million hours a week in total) and earning an average wage of $10 an hour. Thus, the market for janitors can be represented in Figure 17.3. As usual, the price (wage) is found at the intersection of the demand for janitors and the supply of janitors.

By the way, recall that we said earlier that the wage and the marginal product of labor will always be very close together. That is because a firm will keep hiring workers so long as the MPL is greater than W. When we think about many firms and many workers, it often simplifies things to say that the MPL $= W$. Thus, we know that in the United States, the marginal product of a janitor is about $10 an hour.

FIGURE 17.3

Market Demand for Janitors The price of labor (wage) is determined in the market for labor. In this case, the wage of janitors is determined by the demand and supply of janitors.

CHECK YOURSELF

> Why might an individual's supply of labor curve be backward-bending? Explain.

Labor Market Issues

Now that we know the basic principles underlying the demand and supply of labor, let's turn to some specific questions and issues that our principles can help us to understand.

Why Do Janitors in the United States Earn More Than Janitors in India Even When They Do the Same Job?

The short answer for why janitors in the United States earn more for the same type of work as janitors in India is that the janitors in the United States are working for very productive firms, such as McDonald's. The productivity of American firms and offices in general raises the marginal product of labor and thus the wages of American janitors. Indian janitors might work as hard or harder than American janitors but they are less productive and have lower wages because they work in a less productive economy.

Let's look at the differences between the typical American and Indian office building a little more closely. The American office building has more and better equipment, more fax machines, more computers, and more copiers. Overall, there is more capital invested in the American workplace, and American office workers, on average, are better-educated than office workers in India. That makes the American office building more productive. The American office building also has a better marketing department, longer global reach for its sales force, and greater investment in building up the brand name of the product. Most important, the American office is producing a more valuable product.

Since it's more valuable to keep a productive workplace clean than to keep a less productive workplace clean, the wages of American janitors are higher than those in India.

To put it in a single sentence, the American janitor gets the benefit of productivity in many other sectors of the American economy. A typical janitor in India might earn less than $1,000 per year. That same worker, if he wins the green card lottery and comes to the United States, might instead earn over $20,000 in a similar job or even up to $30,000, depending on location and hours. It's not that he has suddenly learned new cleaning techniques, but rather, that he is working in a more productive economy.

There is no doubt that you are a very productive person—perhaps you know how to use a computer, have some artistic talents, and write well. Now look around the world—how much would these skills earn you in another country? Your skills are yours alone, but your wage is determined not by your skills alone but by the productivity of the entire economy.

Of course, wages are about supply as well as demand. India has more workers than the United States, but what's more important than India's total population is that India has a great many low-skilled workers who eagerly compete for the job of janitor. A much greater proportion of Indians than Americans, for example, would consider a cleaning job in a modern office building to be a very attractive job. Since many Indians compete for the job of janitor, the wages of janitors are pushed down.

Figure 17.4 shows the two reasons why the wages of janitors are lower in India than in the United States. First, the demand for janitors is higher in

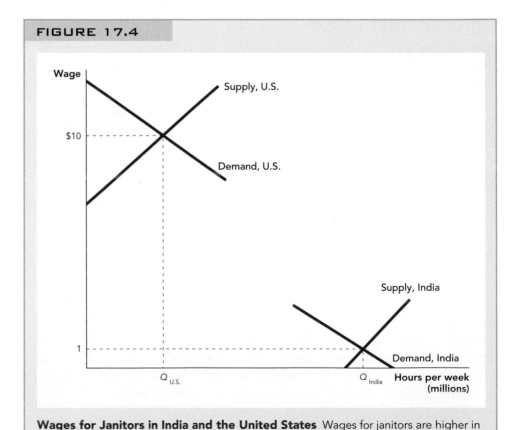

FIGURE 17.4

Wages for Janitors in India and the United States Wages for janitors are higher in the United States than in India because (1) U.S. firms overall are more productive than Indian firms, which raises the demand for janitors, and (2) the supply of low-skilled labor is much larger in India than in the United States.

the United States because U.S. firms are more productive than firms in India overall. Second, the supply of low-skilled labor in India is higher than in the United States.

Human Capital

Americans are fortunate to work in a productive economy. But high wages are not just the result of fortunes of birth. Wages within America differ greatly from worker to worker so let's look at some of the reasons why.

Some workers have higher wages than others because they have more human capital. Physical capital is tools like computers, bulldozers, and 3D printers. **Human capital** is tools of the mind, the stuff in people's heads that makes them productive. Human capital is not something we are born with—it is produced by investing time and other resources in education, training, and experience.

Human capital is tools of the mind, the stuff in people's heads that makes them productive.

Of course, investing in human capital usually costs money; it costs not just what a doctor spends on medical school tuition but what he or she could have earned during those eight years in medical school, namely opportunity cost. But, in general, investments in human capital bring a good return in the United States. In recent years, college graduates have made almost twice as much as high school graduates.

The left panel of Figure 17.5 shows annual wages by education level. Clearly more education, on average, brings a higher wage.

The right panel shows that the return to a college education has been rising over time. College pays off much more now than ever before. The top line is

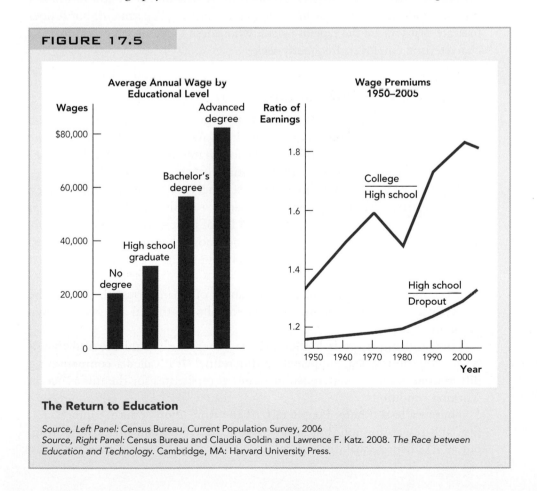

FIGURE 17.5

The Return to Education

Source, Left Panel: Census Bureau, Current Population Survey, 2006
Source, Right Panel: Census Bureau and Claudia Goldin and Lawrence F. Katz. 2008. *The Race between Education and Technology.* Cambridge, MA: Harvard University Press.

the ratio of the wages of college graduates to that of high school graduates, or the "college wage premium." The bottom line reflects how much it is worth to have a high school diploma, relative to dropping out. The returns to education are rising across the board, but nowadays college is especially important.

Why is the return to human capital rising so strongly? Some economists believe that the ability to work with computers has made an education more valuable than in times past. Another hypothesis is that bottlenecks in the U.S. system of grade-school education are lowering student quality and thus limiting the flow of new people into the ranks of the college-educated, thus raising the return to a college education. It's also the case that technology and greater competition from developing countries have limited or reduced wage growth for Americans with low skills. In any case, it's more important to finish college than it used to be, at least in terms of the wages you can expect to earn.

We should also mention that the return to education is not just about human capital. Have you ever wondered why an art history major earns a higher income than a high school graduate even though neither works in the field of art history? An employer may want to hire someone with a college degree not because of anything he or she learned at college but because the very fact that this individual earned a degree signals to the employer something good about the job candidate, namely that he or she has enough intelligence, competence, and conscientiousness to earn a college degree. For the same reasons, if you have ever completed an Ironman triathlon, you might want to subtly indicate that on your résumé (say, under interests) even if the job you are applying for requires no athletic ability. Competing in an Ironman triathlon doesn't increase your productivity at managing an advertising department, but it does indicate that you are the type of person who doesn't give up easily and that is a characteristic employers frequently seek.

Compensating Differentials

The supply of labor depends on the real wage, but the real wage of a job includes not just the monetary pay but also how much fun the job is. Some people work for nice bosses; others work for tyrants. Some jobs are dangerous; others are very safe. Some jobs are interesting; others are a bore.

Right now being a fisherman is the most dangerous job in the United States, more dangerous than being a police officer or a firefighter. There are a lot of accidents out on the water. Most of all, a lot of people just slip and fall overboard. Being a truck driver is dangerous, too, mostly because of road accidents. That's why those professions earn relatively high wages, especially given that they do not demand a college degree.[1]

It's simple supply and demand. The danger of a dangerous job reduces the supply of labor, pushing the supply curve for labor to the left and up, as shown in Figure 17.6.

The resulting wage is higher than it otherwise would be, and that is what economists call a compensating differential. It is called a **compensating differential** because a difference in wages compensates for the difference in working conditions.

A **compensating differential** is a difference in wages that offsets differences in working conditions.

There's a lesson here. People talk all the time about wanting interesting, fun, and rewarding jobs but *beware*: Being an accountant might be boring, but all else being equal, that's a sign of higher wages. Being a musician is fun but most musicians don't make a lot of money. The higher wage of accountants compensates for the lack of fun or, equivalently, the greater fun of being an artist compensates for the lack of money.

To see this in more detail, consider the following principle: *Similar jobs must have similar compensation packages.* Imagine that being an accountant and a musician requires similar amounts of skill, education, training, and so forth. Now what would happen if musicians were paid higher wages than accountants? Higher wages *and* more fun can't be beat so the supply of musicians will increase and the supply of accountants will decrease. But the increased supply of musicians will drive down the wages of musicians and the decreased supply of accountants will drive up the wages of accountants. In fact, musician wages will fall and accountant wages will rise until a typical young person deciding on a career will be more or less indifferent: Higher wages and less

FIGURE 17.6

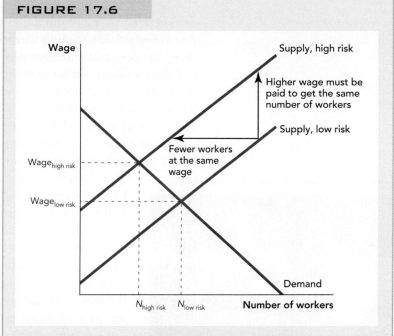

Riskier Jobs Pay More, All Else Being Equal Increased risk reduces the supply of labor—that is, the supply curve for labor shifts up and to the left—increasing the wage.

fun equal lower wages and more fun. Figure 17.7 illustrates the main idea.

Every job has a different combination of wages, benefits, fun, risk, and other conditions. Some workers will choose jobs with less risk but lower wages, while others will prefer jobs with more risk but higher wages. In fact, workers who choose the less risky jobs are "buying" safety with a reduction in their wages. Now consider, who is more likely to buy safety, a rich worker or a poor worker?

FIGURE 17.7

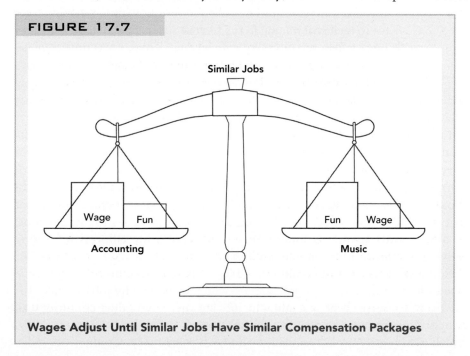

Wages Adjust Until Similar Jobs Have Similar Compensation Packages

The rich buy more safety for the same reason they buy more BMWs—buying safety is one of the things that money is good for! We've already noted that being a fisherman is a dangerous job. It should come as no surprise that many of these fishermen are recent immigrants to the United States. But it's not the immigrants from wealthy Sweden who take the fishing jobs. Instead, it's poor immigrants from Honduras who concentrate in the fishing trade. These poorer immigrants need the money the most and are less willing to buy safety by taking jobs with lower wages.

The same reasoning explains why jobs in the United States are much safer than similar jobs in poorer countries. Workers in the United States use their wealth to buy more smoke detectors, fire extinguishers, and airbags on their cars and they also "buy" more job safety. Thus, one of the most important reasons why job safety increases over time is economic growth.

In other words, workers become less willing to accept risk as economic growth makes them wealthier. You might take a dangerous job if you need the money to feed your family, but not if you need the money to feed your family at *The French Laundry*, one of the best and most expensive restaurants in the United States.

Government regulation has improved the quality of American jobs, as well (see below), but increasing wealth and the profit incentive are the main drivers behind this process. Are you surprised that the pursuit of profit leads to *greater* job safety? Remember that firms must pay workers to take on higher risks, the compensating differentials we talked about earlier. But the process works the other way just as well—when firms make jobs safer, they can pay lower wages, thus increasing their profits.

Coal mining is a tough job anywhere, but in China the death rate per ton of coal is more than 100 times higher than in the United States.

Take a job like coal mining. An American coal miner will earn between $50,000 to $80,000 annually—let's say for purposes of argument, $70,000.[2] If that sounds like a pretty good wage to you, it is because coal mining is not especially fun. But how much would wages have to be if coal mining in the United States were as dangerous as in China, where the mortality rate per ton of coal is 100 times higher? Coal miners might demand $100,000 to take on the extra risk. That's an extra $30,000 per coal miner per year that firms would have to pay because of riskier working conditions. If the mining company can make the mines safer for less than that, obviously their incentive is to invest in safety.

Economists have estimated how much more firms must pay American workers to take on risk and the numbers are very large, by one estimate $245 billion in recent years. In comparison, OSHA (the Occupational Safety and Health Administration), which oversees workplace safety, levies fines every year of about $150 million. These numbers imply that fear of government fines is not that big a cost, compared with having to pay higher wages for riskier jobs. In other words, market competition—employers luring laborers by paying wages—is the major factor in making jobs safer.

So, as workers become wealthier and less willing to take on risk, firms have greater incentives to increase job safety—which explains why jobs are safer today than they were in the past and why jobs are safer in wealthier countries than in poorer countries. The pursuit of profit doesn't always lead to greater safety, which is why government regulation also has a role to play. Compensating differentials give firms an incentive to increase safety only if workers *know* that a job is risky. If workers don't know about or underestimate risk, they won't demand higher wages. A government agency like OSHA can help to ensure that firms do not hide job risks. Even more important, in the United States, firms are required to buy workers' compensation insurance—which pays workers for on-the-job injuries. Crucially, the premiums that firms must pay to buy this insurance are *experienced-based*, which means that the more injuries a firm has, the more it must pay for insurance. Thus, workers' compensation programs give firms an incentive to reduce risk so they can save money on insurance. Since the insurance premiums a firm must pay are based on actual injuries, this incentive works even when workers do not know or underestimate risk.

Do Unions Raise Wages?

It is commonly suggested that unions are a fundamental reason why wages are so high in some countries and so low in other countries. Yet, the evidence does not bear out this view. The more unionized countries do not obviously have higher levels of wages. For instance, the United States and Switzerland have much lower levels of unionization (12% and 25%, respectively, as of 2011) than does most of Western Europe, where unionization rates can run between 30% and 80%. Yet, the United States and Switzerland have equally high or higher wage levels.

It is true that wages in unionized jobs tend to be higher than in nonunionized jobs for similar workers. Studies that compare the wage of unionized electricians to the wages of nonunionized electricians, for example, typically find that unionized electricians have wages about 10% to 15% higher than nonunionized electricians. But this doesn't mean that unions could raise wages in all jobs because the primary method that unions use to raise wages is to reduce industry employment.[3]

If you are wondering how unions raise wages and reduce employment, it is easy to see on a supply and demand graph. By restricting their membership and threatening to strike unless employers hire union labor, unions reduce the supply of labor to an industry. The reduction in labor supply shifts the supply curve for labor to the left and up, as shown in Figure 17.8. Notice that the reduction in the supply of labor increases wages but reduces employment from $N_{\text{without union}}$ to $N_{\text{with union}}$.

Unions can be beneficial in ensuring that employees are treated fairly and by improving labor/management relations, but the main reason that unions raise wages is through restricting the supply of labor. In this respect, a union is quite similar to a cartel, like those we discussed in Chapter 15. The OPEC oil cartel raises the price of oil by restricting the supply of oil and unions raise the wages of labor by restricting the supply of labor.

Unions also can lower wages, although this effect is more difficult

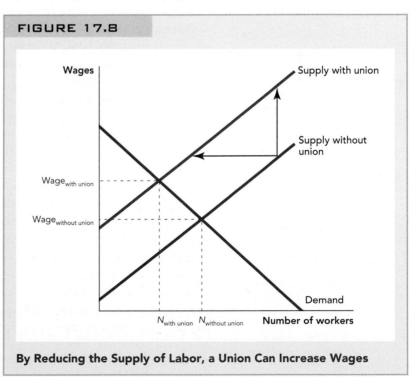

FIGURE 17.8

By Reducing the Supply of Labor, a Union Can Increase Wages

to see. First, consider what happens to the workers who are not hired in the unionized industry—these workers must seek employment in other industries, which increases the supply of labor to those other industries and drives wages down. Second, unions sometimes bring strikes and work stoppages, which can slow down an entire economy. For instance, the British economy was highly unionized from 1970 to 1982; this coincided with Britain's period of long economic decline relative to other nations.[4] In 1970, dockworkers were on strike for so long that it shut down almost all of Britain's main ports. Coal miners went on strike in 1972, which led to a shortage of electricity. A three-day workweek was implemented for a short time to save power. In 1974, the miners went on strike again and a shortened workweek was implemented again. Ten years later, the British experienced another strike that lasted for almost one year. Prime Minister Margaret Thatcher limited the government-supplied privileges of the British unions during the 1980s. Since that time, Britain has grown rapidly and is now a wealthier country than the more unionized France or Germany.

You've probably also experienced or heard about work stoppages in professional sports (baseball players struck in 1972, 1980, 1981, 1985, and 1994–1995; the NBA lockouts of 1998–1999 and 2011; the NFL strike of 1987), or you may remember the Hollywood writer's strike of 2007–2008. When they don't broadcast your favorite TV shows, the quality of your cable TV package goes down, or in other words its real price goes up. That means that the real wages of everyone buying cable TV are worth that much less. That's just one small example, but enough work stoppages of this kind and the entire economy is much poorer. So labor unions can hurt workers just as they can help them; it's just that the help is immediately evident, while the harm is longer-term and harder to see.

When people think of unions, the longshoreman's union or a union of electricians often comes to mind, but it's important to remember that doctors, lawyers, dentists, accountants, and other professionals have their own type of union, called a professional association. The American Medical Association (AMA), for example, works to restrict the supply of physicians for the same reason that an electrician's union works to reduce the supply of electricians. It's very difficult to get into a medical school, for example. The AMA says that restricting the supply of physicians is necessary to maintain high standards. Maybe that is true, but restricting the supply of physicians also maintains high wages. The AMA lobbies for laws that make competing against physicians more difficult; for instance, they restrict the procedures that can be legally performed by nurse practitioners, midwives, chiropractors, and pharmacists and they make it more difficult for foreign-educated physicians to practice in the United States. As noted, the AMA says that restrictions are necessary to maintain quality and there is some truth to this claim, but as always, you should be somewhat skeptical when members of a group claim that their high wages are good for you!

The bottom line is this: Unions can raise the wages of particular classes of workers, but unions are not the fundamental reason why wages are high in the wealthy countries.

How Bad Is Labor Market Discrimination, or Can Lakisha Catch a Break?

We all think we know what discrimination is. Discrimination is *bad*. Discrimination is what racists and bigots do. And, yes, that is partly right: Discrimination often is morally objectionable. It's also true that there are different types of discrimination and not all discrimination is motivated by prejudice. Let's take a closer look at two major types of discrimination, statistical discrimination and preference-based discrimination.

Statistical Discrimination

Let's say you are walking down a dark alley, late at night, in the warehouse district of your city. Suddenly, you hear footsteps behind you. You turn around and you see an old lady walking her dachshund. Do you breathe a sigh of relief? Probably. Would you breathe the same sigh of relief if you saw an angry young man in a dark leather jacket, muttering to himself? What if he was holding a knife? What if he was walking with his two-year-old daughter in a baby stroller?

One way of reading this story is to claim that you are discriminating against young men, relative to old ladies, or relative to young men with baby girls at their side. Another way of describing this story is that you are using information rationally. An angry young man in a leather jacket is far more likely to mug you than is an old lady walking her dachshund. Maybe both descriptions capture some aspect of the reality, but suddenly discrimination isn't so simple a concept anymore.

Statistical discrimination is using information about group averages to make conclusions about individuals. Not every young man in a leather jacket walking the warehouse district late at night is a mugger and not every young man with a baby girl at his side is safe, but that's the way to bet. Although statistical discrimination is a useful shorthand for making some decisions, it also causes people to make many errors. There are some people with whom they refuse to deal but really ought to. They may refuse to hire some people who deserve the job. We gave one example of this earlier—employers may not look carefully at workers without college degrees, even though some of these workers are just as intelligent and industrious as those with college degrees. It is called statistical discrimination because, in essence, the employer is treating the worker as an abstract statistic. Even though statistical discrimination is not motivated by malice, its long-run consequences can be harmful to the penalized groups.

Over time, markets tend to develop more subtle and more finely grained ways of judging people and judging job candidates. An employer can give prospective employees multiple interviews and psychological tests, Google previous histories or writings, look up people on Facebook, ask for more references, and so on, all to get an accurate picture of the person. Eventually, these practices break down the crudest methods of statistical discrimination but, of course, some statistical discrimination always remains.

Statistical discrimination tends to be most persistent when people meet in purely casual settings with no repeat interactions, such as in a dark alley late at night. It is profit-seeking employers, who make money from finding and keeping the best workers, who have the greatest incentive to overcome unfairness.

Preference-Based Discrimination

A second kind of discrimination—preference-based discrimination—is based on a plain, flat-out dislike of some group of people, such

Statistical discrimination is using information about group averages to make conclusions about individuals.

How many times a day do you discriminate?

TIMOTHY TADDER/CORBIS

as a race, religion, or gender. We're going to lay out three different kinds of preference-based discrimination: discrimination by employers, discrimination by customers, and discrimination by employees. The first of these is easiest for a market economy to overcome while the last is the most difficult to solve.

Discrimination by Employers

When most people think of discrimination, they think of an employer with bigoted tastes. Some employers just don't want to hire people of a particular race, ethnicity, religion, or gender. If this discrimination is widespread, the wages of people who are discriminated against will fall since the demand for their labor falls. But fortunately, this kind of discrimination, if taken alone, tends to break down for two reasons: Employer discrimination is expensive to the employer and it leaves the bigot open to being outcompeted.

Imagine, for example, that black workers are widely discriminated against and thus that their wages are lower than those of white workers. Say that a firm can hire white workers for $10 an hour or equally productive black workers for $8 an hour. Imagine that the firm needs 100 workers. If it hires black workers instead of white workers, the firm can increase its profits by $2 per hour per worker. Thus, by hiring black workers, the firm can increase its profits by $1,600 per day ($2 saving per hour for 100 workers for 8 hours a day), $8,000 per week (5 days a week), or $400,000 in a year (50 working weeks). That's a lot of money to give up just so the employer can indulge his or her prejudice.

Even if some employers discriminate, that gives other employers a chance to hire black workers and increase their profits. As profit-hungry employers compete for underpaid, discriminated against workers, the wages of those workers will rise until wages are close to marginal product for all workers, as we described above.

In 1947, Brooklyn Dodgers General Manager Branch Rickey hired Jackie Robinson to be the first black player in modern major league baseball. Robinson already had extensive experience in what were then called the Negro Leagues, and he proved to be an immediate star. Robinson won the Rookie of the Year award and then in his third season he won the MVP award. The first black player in the American League, Larry Doby, proved to be a star for the Cleveland Indians. The baseball teams that moved first to hire black players had a competitive advantage and eventually all teams had to follow, whether or not they were run by bigots.

An All-Star Game to Remember (left to right): Roy Campanella, Larry Doby, Don Newcombe, and Jackie Robinson, 1949.

BETTMANN/CORBIS

Of course, that story is about baseball, but it applies to the broader world of business, as well. If employer-driven discrimination is unjustly depressing the wages of a group of people, you can make money by hiring them.

If the pursuit of profit raises wages so that all workers earn their marginal product, why do women earn less than men? It's often said, for example, that women earn about 80 cents per dollar earned by men. The trouble with this widely reported statistic, however, is that it compares the wages of all women with those of all men—the statistic does not mean that a woman with the same qualifications earns less than a man for doing the same job.

One factor lowering wages for women as a group is that women tend to have less job experience than men of the same age because they sometimes leave the job force, typically to take care of children. In fact, if we compare the wages of single men and single women, single women earn just as much as single men. Married women without children also earn about as much as married men without children.

Men may also have specialized in higher-paying fields and they take more dangerous jobs. Remember those coal miners we discussed earlier with an average wage of $70,000? Most of them are men, perhaps because women prefer jobs with lower wages but less risk.

Over time, women have moved toward higher-paying sectors (more lawyers and economists, for instance) and there has been a long decline in the birth rate. Since women are having fewer children and they are having their children at later ages, that is helping women earn higher wages.

Nevertheless, some discrimination against women may yet remain, but it is probably more subtle than employer discrimination. We need to look at the roles of customers and employees to better understand other forms of discrimination.

Discrimination by Customers   When the customers drive discrimination, owners are not always so keen to hire undervalued, victimized workers. If employing underpaid black workers upsets the customers, it's not a surefire way for an employer to earn more money.

Let's revisit the story of Jackie Robinson and Branch Rickey, discussed earlier. You might wonder why Branch Rickey hired Robinson in 1947 but not 1946. It's not that one day Branch Rickey stopped being prejudiced against African Americans; he may not have been prejudiced in the first place. Rather, in 1947, Rickey sensed that his ticket-buying customers were ready for the idea of watching a black man play baseball in a Brooklyn Dodgers uniform. The lesson is that sometimes discrimination comes from the customers of a business, not always from the owners or managers.

Or, let's consider a lunch counter or hamburger joint in the Deep South in 1957, before the civil rights movement had much influence. Part of the problem was that state laws did not allow mixed-race establishments. But part of the problem came from customers, as well. At that time, many white customers didn't like the idea of eating a hamburger while sitting next to a black man. These white customers demanded separate facilities, so usually, there were separate lunch counters and separate restaurants for white and black people in many parts of the United States. The entrepreneur running the lunch counter may or may not have been racist, but in any case the preferences of his customers encouraged him to discriminate and to keep out black patrons.

Don't make the mistake of thinking customer-based discrimination has vanished from modern America. It's usually done in a more subtle manner, but many country clubs, restaurants, and other businesses try to encourage "the right kind of customers." They're not always concerned about race per se, but often they seek customers who dress a certain way, have the right kind of jobs, come from the right part of town, and so on. The result is sometimes de facto segregation, even though the restaurant or country club owner is simply responding to the preferences of his consumers for a particular cultural style or "feel."

By the way, the decline of employer-based discrimination, through market forces, also tends to weaken customer-based discrimination. Marketplace transactions bring different groups into regular contact with each other. Many white people who started listening to black music on the jukebox in the 1950s, or who saw Jackie Robinson play baseball, started asking themselves what was so wrong with integrated lunch counters. Discrimination is also weakened by economic growth more generally. For instance, declining costs of production make it possible for businesses to take more chances. If a small town has only two lunch counters, maybe neither will take a chance with integration. If the town grows and also the costs of starting a new business fall, suddenly there are seven lunch counters. Maybe one will experiment with integration. In the long run, no successful market economy has succeeded in maintaining formal segregation on a widespread basis.

Discrimination by Employees Customers and employers aren't the only possible sources of discrimination. Sometimes workers don't want to mix with people from different groups. In India, many workers don't want to work alongside Dalits, workers from a low caste who are considered impure. In the United States, some firefighters—rightly or wrongly—don't want women to have equal status in the firehouse. Similarly, some men in the armed forces don't think that women should serve in combat and some men are looked on with suspicion if they want to work at a day-care center.

The profit incentive doesn't necessarily break down discrimination of this kind. An employer in India who hires Dalits, for example, may find that he has to pay other workers a higher wage to compensate them for the negative of working with Dalits. As a result, it's cheaper to discriminate than to hire everyone equally. Similarly, if you hire a woman into an all-male firehouse that doesn't want women, morale may fall and some men may leave for other jobs. As a result, employers are less likely to hire a person, even a productive person, from the victimized group.

Of course, an employer might hire only Dalits, or if women are not welcome in firehouses, an employer may set up an entirely new firehouse, one equipped with women and nonprejudicial men, but starting from scratch in this fashion isn't always so easy to do.

Discrimination of this kind can be self-reinforcing and difficult to identify. If it's unpleasant for women to work in firehouses, then many women who want to be firefighters won't want to work in firehouses. Few women are hired but employers might say that's because few women are applying. Maybe it won't look like discrimination at all, but discrimination will still be a force at work.

Discrimination by Government So far we've been talking about discrimination in markets but it's important to remember that governments discriminate, too. Government is sometimes part of the problem rather than part of the solution. We've already mentioned that pro-segregation policies in the American South, before the civil rights movement, often came from governments. Governments required separate hospitals for black and white patients, separate public and private schools, separate churches, separate cemeteries, separate public restrooms, and separate restaurants, hotels, and train service. Before prosegregation laws were passed after the Civil War, many parts of the South were moving (albeit sometimes hesitantly) toward more integration.

The best-known example of widespread government segregation was the apartheid system of South Africa, which was enforced from 1948 until the early 1990s. ("Apartheid" is a word in the Afrikaaner language; it translates literally as "apartness.") Under this arrangement, black people had to live in special areas and could not compete with white workers for many jobs. But this highly unjust situation was enforced by government laws, and enacted by white minority governments (black citizens also couldn't vote). Once those laws were removed, black people moved into many jobs and received higher wages. Many forms of implicit segregation continue in South Africa, but some of the most egregious examples of discrimination have fallen away. Many employers are happy to hire the most productive workers they can find, regardless of the skin color or ethnic background of those workers.

Why Discrimination Isn't Always Easy to Identify

Two economists had a neat idea. They sent around two sets of identical résumés. On one set of résumés, the names were quite traditional and did not identify the background of the person applying. An applicant named "John Smith," for instance, could be either white or black. The second set of résumés had more unusual names on them—names like "Lakisha Washington" or "Jamal Jones." As you may know, those are names closely associated with African Americans. Names can tell you a lot about who a person is. In recent years, more than 40% of the black girls born in California were given names that, in those same years, not one of the roughly 100,000 white newly born California girls was given.*

The result was striking: The resumes with the black names received many fewer interview requests. The job applicants with the "whiter" names received 50% more calls.

But that is not the end of the story. Steven Levitt (of *Freakonomics* fame) and Roland Fryer (a Harvard professor and an African American) set out to test how much African American names really mattered in the long run for earnings. It seems that having a "black name" does not appear to hurt a person's chances in life, once the neighborhood that person comes from is controlled for. In other words, the number of interviews a person gets at first may not matter so much in the long run. Levitt and Fryer consider two possibilities. It may be that the so-called black names get fewer interviews, but they end up with jobs of equal quality. Alternatively, people with African-American–sounding names may have fewer chances in white communities but greater chances in black communities; the two tendencies might balance each other out.

One point to note is that in the résumé experiment, by far the most common outcome of submitting a résumé, for both the white and black candidates and regardless of name, was not receiving any interview requests at all. The lesson is that just about everyone can expect a lot of rejection before they find the job that is right for them.

Other economists have tested labor market discrimination in the world of sports. Basketball teams, it seems, do not discriminate against black players. Depending on how racial categories are defined, about 75% to 80% of the NBA is black, which includes African Americans, Africans, and Brazilians of African descent. If anything, there has been statistical discrimination against (usually white) European players, who are sometimes considered "soft on defense." In baseball, large numbers of players from the Dominican Republic have ended up as shortstops, including superstars Miguel Tejada and Alex Rodriguez (before moving to third base) and more recent notables Jose Reyes and Hanley Ramirez.

* That is from Bertrand, Marianne and Sendhil Mullainathan. 2004. "Are Emily and Greg More Employable than Lakisha and Jamal? A Field Experiment on Labor Market Discrimination." *The American Economic Review*, 94(4):991–1013. For the earnings study, see Fryer, Jr., Roland G. and Steven D. Levitt. 2002. "The Causes and Consequences of Distinctively Black Names." *Quarterly Journal of Economics*, 119(3):767–805.

Did the man on the left get the better deal?

Did you know that good-looking people earn more, even if they have the same job credentials? That's right, good-looking people earn about 5% more. Tall people earn more, too, again if they are compared with shorter people with the same paper credentials. Under one account, an extra inch in height translates into a 1.8% increase in wages.[*]

But these studies also show just how difficult it is to identify true discrimination. For instance, maybe tall people are paid more because they are more self-confident and not because anyone discriminates against shorter people. One study found that what best predicts wages, in this context, is *the height a man had at the time of high school* and not the height he ends up with as an adult. So if you were a tall person in high school, maybe that built up your self-confidence and makes you a better leader today, even if you stopped growing while your friends kept on getting taller.[†]

One question is why employers might prefer to hire tall people and to pay them more. One possibility is simply that the employer has an unreasonable preference against shorter people. Another possibility is that the employer is subconsciously tricked into thinking the taller leader is better, without ever realizing it. Yet another option is that the taller leader really is better (for the firm), because subordinates are more likely to pay that person respect. Again, we don't know the right answer, and this illustrates just how difficult it is to estimate the scope of labor market discrimination.

In many cases, market forces have succeeded in making some discrimination go away, or at least markets have minimized some of the bad effects of discrimination. But few people doubt that discrimination remains a feature of our world today.

CHECK YOURSELF

> From a profit-making perspective, why is employer discrimination just plain dumb?
> Of the three types of discrimination—employer, customer, employee—which has been affected most by market economies? Which has been affected least? Why?

☐ Takeaway

It is no accident that workers in some countries earn much more than workers in other countries. Workers in wealthy, high-wage countries work with more physical capital, they have more education and training (human capital), and they work in a more efficient and flexible setting. Those are the fundamental reasons why wages are high.

The theory of compensating differentials explains why fun jobs pay less and dangerous jobs pay more. As wealth increases, workers become more willing to give up money for safety and so job safety increases over time and is higher in wealthier countries than in poorer countries.

Unions can raise some workers' wages, often at the expense of other workers, but unions are not a fundamental reason why wages are high in wealthy countries.

At least two kinds of discrimination occur in labor markets, statistical discrimination and preference-based discrimination. Markets tend to break down discrimination over time, because profit-seeking employers are looking to hire the most productive workers. Nonetheless, this force is imperfect and often discrimination persists.

[*] For a survey of this literature, see Engemann, Kristie M. and Michael T. Owyang. April, 2005. "So Much for That Merit Raise: The Link between Wages and Appearance." *The Regional Economist.* http://www.stlouisfed.org/publications/re/2005/b/pdf/appearance.pdf
[†] Persico, Nicola; Andrew Postlewaite, and Dan Silverman. 2004. "The Effect of Adolescent Experience on Labor Market Outcomes: The Case of Height." *Journal of Political Economy,* 112(5):1019–1053.

□ CHAPTER REVIEW

KEY CONCEPTS

Marginal product of labor (MPL), p. 319

Human capital, p. 325

Compensating differential, p. 326

Statistical discrimination, p. 331

FACTS AND TOOLS

1. In Chapter 3, we listed six important demand shifters. Since the demand for labor is like the demand for any other good, those same factors apply here. Let's look at factors that might shift the demand for janitors at the McDonald's we discussed. For each case below, state whether labor demand will rise or fall, and also state which of the six factors seems to be causing the shift in demand.

   a. A new junior high school opens up across the street from the McDonald's.

   b. Customers become much more concerned about clean restaurants: They'll walk out if there's dirt on the floor.

   c. As robots like the Roomba vacuum cleaner become cheaper, the McDonald's buys some robots to do half of the janitors' work.

2. Now let's do the same with shifts in Joe's labor supply from Figure 17.2. We listed five important supply shifters in Chapter 3. For each example below, state whether you think Joe's labor supply will tend to increase or decrease as a result of the change, and state which of the five factors seem to cause the supply shift.

   a. The government raises Joe's income tax rate, so now he pays 20% of his wages to the government instead of the old 10%.

   b. The price of comfortable work shoes falls dramatically. Now, his feet won't ache nearly as much after a full day of work.

   c. While in Las Vegas for the weekend, Joe wins a $1 million jackpot.

3. Let's apply the idea of compensating differentials to janitorial jobs. Suppose there are two quite similar restaurants in the same town, OrangeBee's and the City Inn. Both have the same demand for janitorial labor. But all the janitors in town know that it's much more fun to work at City Inn.

   a. Which restaurant will pay a higher wage for janitors? Why?

   b. Which restaurant will hire more janitors? Why?

4. According to the theory of compensating differentials, which low-skilled jobs in the United States will tend to pay the most:

   a. The safe jobs or the dangerous jobs?

   b. The fun jobs or the boring jobs?

   c. The dead-end jobs or the first-rung-on-the-ladder jobs?

5. As we mentioned, OSHA fines companies for unsafe workplaces. At the same time, the labor market also "fines" companies that give their workers dangerous jobs. The fines of the marketplace are larger than the U.S. government's fines by about what factor: a factor of 10, of 100, of 1,000, or of 10,000?

6. The director of human resources at ToyCo is hiring new engineers. She's got a stack of 250 applications, and she's going to do a little research. She sits down and does a little cyber-snooping on all 250, and she finds the following:

   i. Of the 150 who have Facebook pages, 50 are holding a bottle of beer in their profile photo, and 100 aren't.

   ii. Of the 100 who have their own websites, 20 have more than two typos.

   iii. Of the 150 who have Facebook pages, 25 have at least two friends who have apparently spent time in prison, according to a quick check of public records.

   a. Each of these are cases of sending bad signals. In each case, describe what you think these might be signals of.

   b. In each case, is the bad signal 100% correct? For example, is every applicant with three or four typos on their personal website worse than every applicant with an error-free page?

   c. In each case, is the bad signal probably better or probably worse than having no signal at all? In other words, should the bad signal get at least a little bit of weight in the balance if the HR director's only goal is to hire the best workers?

7. It is commonly said that women earn 80 cents for every dollar that a man earns, even when doing the same job. Let's assume this is literally true in order to see how an entrepreneur would respond to this fact.

   a. Netrovia, a battery manufacturer, has an all-male workforce. It pays $10 million per year in salary to these men, and has annual profits of $1 million. You've just been hired as an outside consultant to help Netrovia raise its profits. Your advice is to fire all the men and replace them with women. If Netrovia followed your advice, what would Netrovia's salary costs fall to? How much would this decision raise Netrovia's profits?

   b. After your success at Netrovia, you start getting a lot more consulting jobs. You give the same advice to all the companies looking to boost profits: Fire your men and hire an all-female workforce for 20% less. What will this do to the demand for female labor? And what will this tend to do to women's wages?

8. Michael Lynn, a social psychologist in Cornell's School of Hotel Administration, has spent years studying tipping (his homepage has well-tested advice on how to increase your tips). He finds that men tip more when they have a female server, while women tend to tip more when they have a male server. This sounds a lot like discrimination by customers.

   a. If this is a fact, who will tend to apply for jobs waiting tables at truck stops: mostly men or mostly women?

   b. If this is a fact, who will tend to apply for jobs waiting tables at steakhouses: mostly men or mostly women?

   c. If this is a fact, who will tend to apply for jobs waiting tables at vegetarian restaurants: mostly men or mostly women?

   d. In these three cases, does your experience match up with what this simple theory predicts? If there's a contradiction, what do you think the simple model is missing?

9. True or false?

   a. The marginal product of labor is the amount of extra profit that a firm will earn if it hires one more worker.

   b. The benefit of having a college education has increased since the 1960s.

   c. The wage gap between high school graduates and high school dropouts has fallen since the 1960s.

   d. By definition, a labor supply curve cannot have a negative slope.

   e. Compensating differentials is a government program that pays injured workers.

   f. The main reason that an immigrant earns more when he moves from Algeria to France is because the French have strong labor unions.

   g. If customers are racist and sexist, then self-interest will tend to push entrepreneurs to engage in racist and sexist hiring.

   h. If some employers are bigots but others are not, the bigoted employers will be able to hire good workers for less money and will tend to drive the fair-minded employers out of business.

THINKING AND PROBLEM SOLVING

1. Construction jobs in New Chongqing pay $20 per hour. The job isn't that safe: a lot of sharp objects, a lot of ways to fall off a building. The city council of New Chongqing decides to set some job safety regulations for the construction industry. Let's assume that the government enforces these new regulations effectively and fairly, so that half as many workers get hurt on the job. Let's also assume that the city council makes the taxpayers pay the cost of making these jobs safer, so there's no noticeable shift in the labor demand curve.

   a. After these new job safety regulations come into effect, will workers be more willing to take these jobs than before or less willing than before?

   b. Is that like a rise in the supply of labor or like a fall in the supply of labor?

   c. Let's put it all together: What will these job safety regulations do to the wage for construction jobs in New Chongqing?

   d. What principle from this chapter does this illustrate?

   e. In the United States, OSHA doesn't make taxpayers pay the cost of making jobs safer. Instead, OSHA requires employers to spend the money themselves to make their firm's jobs safer. Thus, OSHA requirements work like a tax on labor demand. What would this probably do to the demand curve for construction labor: Would it increase or decrease construction labor demand?

2. One way to think about wages for different jobs is to see it as another application of the law of one price. We came across this law when we discussed speculation in Chapter 7, and it came up again when we discussed international trade in Chapter 9. The basic idea is that the supply of workers will keep adjusting until jobs that need the same kinds of workers earn the same wage. If *similar* workers earned *different* wages, then the workers in the low-paid jobs would reduce their labor supply, and the workers in the high-paid jobs would face more competition from those low-paid workers.

Let's look at 100 computer programmers who are trying to decide whether to work for one of two companies: Robotron or Korrexia. To keep things simple, assume that both companies are equally fun to work for, so you don't need to worry about compensating differentials here. The marginal product of labor (per additional hour of work) is in the table below:

Number of Programmers per Firm	Robotron's MPL	Korrexia's MPL
10	$200	$110
20	$150	$80
30	$120	$60
40	$110	$50
50	$80	$40
60	$60	$20
70	$50	$10
80	$40	$0
90	$20	$0
100	$10	$0

a. These two firms are the whole market for programmer labor. In the table below, estimate the programmer demand curve by adding up the quantity of programmers demanded at each wage. For example, at a wage of $80 per hour, Robotron would hire 50 workers (since the first 50 workers have a MPL $\geq$80) and Korrexia 20, so the total demand is 70 workers.

Wage	Number of Programmers Demanded
$200	10
$150	
$120	
$110	
$80	50 + 20 = 70
$60	
$50	
$40	
$20	
$10	

b. The programmers in this town are going to work at one of these two places for sure: Their labor supply is vertical, or in other words, perfectly inelastic, with supply = 100. So, what will the equilibrium wage be? Just as in Figure 17.1, the numbers may not work out exactly—so use your judgment to come up with a good answer.

c. Now, head back to the first table: About how many programmers will work at Robotron and how many at Korrexia? Again, use your judgment to come up with a good answer.

d. Suppose 50 more programmers come to town. What will the wage be now? And how many will work at each firm?

3. We've seen what happens when job safety regulations are imposed. Now let's see what happens when they're taken away.

a. If a radical free-market, antiregulation government comes to power in the land of Pelerania, and it begins dismantling job safety regulations, what will this tend to do to the supply of labor for dangerous jobs in Pelerania: Will it increase or decrease?

b. Will that push wages in dangerous jobs up or down?

c. What will this do to the supply of labor in safer jobs? And to the number of people working in safer jobs?

d. Overall, will employers have to pay for their decision to offer dangerous jobs, or will they have a free lunch handed to them by the new government?

4. As we saw, unions can raise wages in a sector of the economy by restricting the number of workers in that sector. Let's see what tends to happen to the workers who don't get jobs in those favored unionized sectors. We'll recycle the computer programmer data to illustrate:

Number of Programmers per Firm	Robotron's MPL	Korrexia's MPL
10	$200	$110
20	$150	$80
30	$120	$60
40	$110	$50
50	$80	$40
60	$60	$20
70	$50	$10
80	$40	$0
90	$20	$0
100	$10	$0

a. As before, there are 100 workers. In 2084, after decades of complaining about low wages, the programmers at Robotron have a secret-ballot vote and form a union. Their new union bargains for a wage of $80 per hour, and the newly unionized programmers are very excited. How many workers will Robotron hire at the new, higher wage?

b. How many Robotron workers just got laid off? Compare your answer to part a against the answer to question 2c to find out.

c. A natural choice for the other programmers is to look for work at Korrexia: As before, the remaining workers have perfectly inelastic labor supply, so all 100 workers are going to work at one of the two firms. What's the wage for the nonunion Korrexia workers? How many programmers work for Korrexia?

d. You might think that one solution is to unionize both firms and lift wages for all the programmers. If the unions negotiate a high-wage contract and unionized wages

rise to $110 at both firms, how many of the 100 workers will have jobs?

5. Suppose that we tax CEO salaries very highly, as some are proposing in the United States. What is your prediction about CEO perks such as jets and in-house chefs?

6. a. The average person doesn't like working the night shift. According to the theory of compensating differentials, are night-shift wages probably higher or lower than day-shift wages?

b. Most companies do their high-skilled work during the day shift: The big meetings, the major deliveries, the crucial repair work—all get done during the day. As a result, firms prefer to hire workers with more human capital during day-shift work, and they prefer to hire less-skilled workers at night. According to the theory of human capital, are night-shift wages probably higher or lower than day-shift wages?

c. Just based on these two theories, will night-shift work pay more than day-shift work on average, will it pay less on average, or can't you tell with the information given?

d. Economist Peter Kostiuk, in a 1990 article in the *Journal of Political Economy*, wanted to see whether the theory of compensating differentials was true for U.S. workers. He had information on the wages, education backgrounds, and work experience of U.S. workers, and he knew whether they worked the day shift or the night shift. On average, those who worked the night shift actually earned about 4% *less* than workers on the day shift. Is this probably because of compensating differentials, or is it probably because of human capital differences?

e. Kostiuk then used statistical techniques to simulate how much a typical low-skilled worker would earn if he were switched from the day shift to the night shift. The answer? The low-skilled worker would earn 44% *more* money, on average. Is this 44% wage increase caused by lower supply of night-shift labor, or is it caused by a higher demand for night-shift labor?

7. True or false? Morticians are paid lower wages than other workers because very few people want to work with dead bodies.

8. One way that Jim Crow segregation laws operated was by providing worse government

schools for black students. This widened the human capital gap between black workers and white workers (this human capital gap has narrowed dramatically since the successes of the 1960s civil rights movement). Would this form of government segregation tend to increase statistical discrimination on the basis of race or lower it? How can you tell?

9. In the United States, it's legal to work for free: We call this an "unpaid internship."

   a. Why will college students take these zero-wage jobs when they could get a minimum wage job instead?

   b. Which idea in this chapter does this sound like?

   c. Just for thought: Why do you think federal law allows people to work for free, but not for $1 per hour? Is it just an oversight on the part of government, or do you think there's some grand design at work?

CHALLENGES

1. In the decades after the Civil War, most streetcar companies in the South discriminated against one class of citizens: smokers. Customers who wanted to smoke had to ride in the back of the car. Around 1900, many governments in the South passed laws mandating segregation by race instead. As Jennifer Roback documented in the *Journal of Economic History* in 1986, many streetcar operators protested against this new form of segregation. Assuming that these entrepreneurs were driven by self-interest alone rather than a desire for equality, why would they do that?

2. We mentioned that "a [college] degree signals. . . something good about the job candidate, namely that they have enough intelligence, competence, and conscientiousness to earn a college degree." This view, put forward by Nobel laureate Michael Spence, is unsurprisingly known as the signaling theory of education. Taken to the extreme, signaling theorists say that you suffer through college not because you get valuable job skills, but only because it's a good way to prove that you were *already* smart and capable before you started college.

   a. Suppose you want to prove this theory wrong: You want to show that college courses really do make you a better worker, just like the human capital theorists say. How would you go about proving that? Remember, just showing that college graduates earn more isn't evidence!

   b. If that's too difficult, at least explain why the following plausible-sounding tests of human capital vs. signaling aren't very good tests at all:

      i. Looking at wages of people with degrees compared with people without degrees

      ii. Comparing wages for people whose parents can afford college with wages for people whose parents can't afford college.

3. In a market economy, firms with more workers can make and sell more output—that goes without saying. The marginal product of labor tells you how much extra revenue each extra worker generates. Economists tend to use one particular equation to sum up the link between workers, revenue, and the marginal product of labor: We call it the production function. Let's practice with it just a little here.

   a. At Dunder Mifflin, the hourly revenue production function works like this:

$$\text{Revenue} = 100 \times \sqrt{(\text{\# of semi-skilled workers})}$$

   This is a way of saying that in order to sell product, you actually need workers to do work. Use this formula to fill out the total revenue column below.

Number of Workers	Total Revenue	Marginal Product of Labor
0	$0	N/A
1	$100	$100
2	$141	$41
3		
4		
5		

   b. As we mentioned in the chapter, the marginal product of labor is the extra revenue that's generated by each extra worker. It's the change in revenue from adding one more worker. Fill out that column, as well.

c. If the market wage for semiskilled workers is $25 per hour, how many workers should Dunder Mifflin hire?

4. In Chapter 8, we analyzed a minimum wage in the usual way, as a price floor, and we showed that a minimum wage creates unemployment. Now suppose that firms must pay the minimum wage but they can adjust the working conditions, such as increasing the pace of work, reducing lunch breaks, cutting back on employee discounts, and so forth. Will the minimum wage create (as much) unemployment if firms adjust in this way? *Hint*: Think of the balance in Figure 17.7.

18

Public Goods and the Tragedy of the Commons

Armageddon almost happened on September 29, 2004. We aren't talking about the final battle described in the Bible, but what happened in *Armageddon* the movie. In *Armageddon,* an asteroid is discovered to be on a collision course with Earth and NASA recruits a group of roughneck oil drillers to rocket into space, deflect the asteroid, and save civilization. *Armageddon* the movie is a bit absurd, but it got a few things right. Even an asteroid the size of an apartment building would hit Earth with the force of a 4-megaton nuclear bomb. On September 29, 2004, an asteroid called Toutatis, 2.9 *miles* long by 1.5 *miles* wide, narrowly missed Earth. If Toutatis had hit, it would have meant the end of civilization.

The probability of death by asteroid is remarkably high, by some calculations about the same as death by passenger aircraft crash. How can this be? Although the probability of an asteroid hitting Earth is very small, a lot of people would be killed if one did hit, so the probability of death by asteroid is much larger than most people imagine. It doesn't happen very often but watch out when it does.[*]

Let's assume that we have convinced you that the danger from an asteroid collision is real and thus that asteroid deflection would be a valuable good to have. Markets provide us with all kinds of valuable goods like food, clothing, and cell phones, but you can't buy asteroid deflection in the market. Even if everyone were to become convinced of the benefits of asteroid deflection, you

Toutatis: Harbinger of Armageddon?

---

[*] Everyone dies from something. In the United States, the probability of death by car crash is about 1 in 100 and the probability of death by commercial airplane crash is about 1 in 20,000. Chapman and Morrison (1994) estimate that the probability of death by asteroid collision is also about 1 in 20,000. See Chapman, Clark and David Morrison. 1994. Impacts on the earth by asteroids and comets: Assessing the hazard. *Nature* **367**: 33–40.

probably will *never* be able to buy asteroid deflection in the market. To see why, we need to take a closer look at some of the common properties of ordinary goods and some of the special properties of asteroid deflection.

When you spend $100 on a new pair of jeans, you get the exclusive use of a new pair of jeans. If you don't spend $100 on a new pair of jeans, you are excluded from using the jeans. In other words, the $100 makes a big difference in whether or not you get the jeans. That's obvious.

Now consider paying $100 toward asteroid deflection. What do you get for your $100? There are really only two situations to consider: Either enough other people pay for asteroid deflection so that the asteroid will be deflected even without your $100 or so few other people pay that the asteroid will not be deflected even with your $100.★ Either way, your $100 makes no appreciable difference to the amount of asteroid deflection that you will receive. In other words, you get the same amount of asteroid deflection whether you pay or don't pay.

Since your $100 doesn't get you more asteroid deflection but it does get you a new pair of jeans, most people will buy the jeans rather than the asteroid deflection. As a result, we see a lot of firms selling jeans and none selling asteroid deflection. That's a problem because asteroid deflection is an important threat to everyone on the planet.

Jeans are an example of a private good. Asteroid deflection is an example of what economists call a public good, a good that markets are unlikely to produce in efficient quantities. Let's look more closely at these terms and the differences between jeans and asteroid deflection.

Four Types of Goods

Jeans are different from asteroid deflection for two reasons. First, as we said, people are willing to pay for jeans because paying makes the difference between getting the jeans or not—non-payers can be cheaply excluded or prevented from consuming jeans. But people aren't willing to pay for asteroid deflection because paying makes no appreciable difference to how much asteroid deflection you consume—non-payers cannot be excluded from consuming the benefits of asteroid deflection. When a person can cheaply be prevented from using a good, economists say the good is excludable. When a person cannot be cheaply prevented from using a good, economists say the good is **nonexcludable**. Jeans are excludable; asteroid deflection is nonexcludable.

The second reason why asteroid deflection is different from jeans is that when one person is wearing a pair of jeans, it's not easy for a second person to wear the same jeans. But two people can enjoy the benefits of the same asteroid deflection. In fact, billions of people can enjoy the benefits of the same asteroid deflection. But don't try fitting a billion people into the same pair of jeans!

When one person's use of a good reduces the ability of another person to use the same good, economists say the good is rival. When one person's use of a good does not reduce the ability of another person to use the same good, economists say the good is **nonrival**. Jeans are rival; asteroid deflection is nonrival.

These two factors, whether a good is excludable or nonexcludable and whether it is rival or nonrival, can be used to divide goods into four types, as in

A good is **nonexcludable** if people who don't pay cannot be easily prevented from using the good.

A good is **nonrival** if one person's use of the good does not reduce the ability of another person to use the same good.

★ The probability that your $100 makes the difference between a successful asteroid deflection and an unsuccessful asteroid deflection is so small that we can ignore it.

TABLE 18.1 Four Types of Goods

	Excludable	Nonexcludable
Rival	**Private Goods**	**Common Resources**
	Jeans	Tuna in the ocean
	Hamburgers	The environment
	Contact lenses	Public roads
Nonrival	**Nonrival Private Goods**	**Public Goods**
	Cable TV	Asteroid deflection
	Wi-Fi	National defense
	Digital music	Mosquito control

Table 18.1. We have already given an example of a private good, a good that is excludable and rival. Jeans are a private good, hamburgers and contact lenses are other familiar examples. We have also given one example of a public good, a good that is nonexcludable and nonrival. Asteroid deflection is nonexcludable and nonrival. National defense is another example. Let's take a closer look at the differences between private and public goods and then we will examine the other two categories of goods, nonrival private goods and common resources.

Private Goods and Public Goods

Private goods are excludable and rival. Since private goods are excludable, they can be provided by markets—someone who doesn't pay, doesn't get; so there is an incentive to pay for and thus to produce these goods. Furthermore, since the goods are rival, excludability doesn't result in inefficiency—in a competitive market the only people who will be excluded from consuming a private good are the people who are not willing to pay what it costs to produce the good, and that's efficient.

Public goods are nonexcludable and nonrival. Since public goods are nonexcludable, it's difficult to get people to pay for them voluntarily. Markets, therefore, will tend to underprovide public goods.

Public goods are also nonrival, which means that one person's use doesn't reduce the ability of another person to use the good. As a result, 7 billion people can be protected from an asteroid strike for the same cost as protecting 1 million people. Since public goods are nonrival, the losses from the failure to provide these goods can be especially large.

Let's look at another public good, mosquito control. Mosquitoes are annoying insects. With the spread of the West Nile virus in the United States, they are also dangerous. Mosquitoes can be killed by spraying, but spraying just one house won't do much good for its owners because mosquitoes from other areas will quickly repopulate any small region, so you have to spray a city or neighborhood. But who will pay to spray a city or neighborhood? If some people do pay, then many others are likely to **free ride,** sit back and enjoy the benefits without contributing to their share of the costs. Fewer mosquitoes mean fewer mosquitoes for everyone, not just those who pay for mosquito control. If a lot

Private goods are excludable and rival.

Public goods are nonexcludable and nonrival.

A **free rider** enjoys the benefits of a public good without paying a share of the costs.

The English philosopher Thomas Hobbes (1588–1679) explained under what conditions individuals might voluntarily give up their rights.

I authorise and give up my right of governing myself to this man, or to this assembly of men, on this condition; that thou give up, thy right to him, and authorise all his actions in like manner.
—Leviathan, *Chapter 17*

A **forced rider** is someone who pays a share of the costs of a public good but who does not enjoy the benefits.

of people free ride, then mosquito control will be underprovided by the market even though it is a valuable good.

The benefits of public goods provide an argument for taxation and government provision. By taxing everyone and producing the public good, government can make people better off. Many cities and counties, for example, pay for mosquito control from government tax revenues. National defense is another example of a public good that would be difficult to provide voluntarily but is provided by government.

It may seem paradoxical that people can be made better off by requiring them to do something that they would not choose to do voluntarily, but the paradox can be resolved. Imagine that there are a million people, all of whom want national defense, but none of whom chooses to voluntarily contribute to national defense because of the incentive to free ride. Now imagine that this group is offered the following plan: "The government will tax each of you and use the proceeds to pay for national defense but only if you all agree to the plan." It's quite possible that even though none contribute voluntarily, all will agree to be taxed, *so long as everyone else is also taxed.*

Of course, just because everyone *can* be made better off by taxation does not mean that everyone *will* be made better off. Some people want more national defense, some people want less, pacifists want none. So, taxation means that some people will be turned into **forced riders,** people who must contribute to the public good even though their benefits from the public good are low or even negative.

What quantity of the public good should the government produce? In principle, the government should produce the amount that maximizes consumer plus producer surplus or the total benefits of the public good minus the total costs. But, in practice, figuring this out is very difficult. The total benefit of a public good, for example, is the sum of the benefits to each individual. But some individuals value the public good more than others and there is no easy way to finding out exactly how much each person values the good.

We showed in Chapter 4 that (under certain conditions) a market automatically produces the quantity of a good that maximizes consumer plus producer surplus. We now know that one of the required conditions is that the good be a private good, a good that is rival and excludable. Unfortunately, no one has yet discovered a workable process that, as if guided by an "invisible hand," produces optimal amounts of nonrival and nonexcludable goods, that is, public goods.

Voting and other democratic procedures can help to produce information about the demand for public goods, but these processes are unlikely to work as well at providing the optimal amounts of public goods as do markets at providing the optimal amounts of private goods (see Chapter 19 for more). Thus, we have more confidence that the optimal amount of toothpaste is purchased every year ($2.3 billion worth in recent years) than the optimal amount of defense spending ($660 billion) or the optimal amount of asteroid deflection (close to $0). In some cases, we could get too much of the public good with many people being forced riders, and in other cases, we could get too little of the public good. Nevertheless, since the market fails to provide public goods, we are probably fortunate that government can provide public goods even if the method is imperfect.

One final point about public goods: A public good is *not* defined as a good produced in the public sector. If the government started to produce jeans, for example, that does not make jeans a public good. The government does produce mail delivery even though mail delivery is not a public good. Similarly, asteroid deflection is a public good even though, as of yet, the government does not produce very much asteroid deflection.

CHECK YOURSELF

> What happens if government provides more of a public good than is efficient? Who is hurt? Who benefits? Use national defense as an example.

Nonrival Private Goods

Nonrival private goods are goods that are excludable but nonrival. A television show like *True Blood*, for example, is excludable—you must buy HBO to watch the show, at least in its first run—but it's also nonrival because when one person watches, this does not reduce the ability of another person to watch. Clearly, markets can provide goods that are excludable but nonrival, but they do so at the price of some inefficiency. HBO prohibits some people from watching *True Blood*, for example, even though they would be willing to pay the cost (close to zero for an additional viewer) but not the price (say, $25.99 a month).

Nonrival private goods are goods that are excludable but nonrival.

In practice, the inefficiency from the underprovision of most nonrival private goods like television, music, and software is not that big a deal. The fixed costs of producing these goods must be paid somehow and we do not want to lose the diversity, creativity, and responsiveness provided by markets.

Entrepreneurs are constantly looking for ways to turn nonexcludable, nonrival goods such as television into nonrival, private (excludable) goods such as cable television, so that they can be provided at a profit. Furthermore, entrepreneurs can sometimes find clever ways of profiting from nonrival goods *even without relying on exclusion*.

The Peculiar Case of Advertising

Radio and television are peculiar goods because although they are public goods, nonrival *and* nonexcludable, they are provided in large quantities by markets. How is this possible? When radio first appeared, no one could figure out how to make a profit from it and most people thought that government provision would be necessary if people were to benefit from this amazing discovery. After much experimentation, however, entrepreneurs did discover how to give radio away for free (the efficient solution) and yet still make a profit—they discovered advertising. Advertisers pay for the costs of programming that is then given away for free.

Advertising, of course, is not a perfect solution to the problem of nonexcludability and nonrivalry, but for radio and broadcast television, it has worked fairly well. Advertising works so well that some nonrival goods are provided without exclusion even when exclusion would be cheap. Google, for example, spends billions of dollars indexing the Web and developing search algorithms and then it offers its product to anyone in the world for free. Google could exclude people who don't pay for its service, but Google has discovered that selling advertising and providing its services for free is more profitable.

Finally, Wi-Fi is an interesting example of a nonrival but potentially excludable public good because it is currently provided in just about every possible manner. Wi-Fi is sold by private firms like Sprint who exclude non-payers by requiring security codes. Other firms offer Wi-Fi for free but only if you watch advertising. Cafés such as Panera Bread offer free Wi-Fi to help attract customers. Wi-Fi is also given away by people who choose not to close their access points. In Philadelphia, the government taxes citizens to pay for the network and then offers free access. Each of these methods has its advantages and disadvantages.

Common resources are goods that are nonexcludable but rival.

The **tragedy of the commons** is the tendency of any resource that is unowned and hence nonexcludable to be overused and undermaintained.

Common Resources and the Tragedy of the Commons

Common resources are goods that are nonexcludable but rival. An example is tuna in the ocean. Until they are caught, the tuna are unowned—hence nonexcludable—and it's difficult to prevent anyone from fishing for tuna. But tuna are not public goods since when one person catches and consumes a tuna, that leaves fewer tuna for other people. The result of nonexcludability and rivalry is often the **tragedy of the commons**, overexploitation and undermaintenance of the common resource. As a result of the tragedy of the commons, tuna are being driven toward extinction.

Since 1960, the tuna catch has decreased by 75% (see Figure 18.1). The southern bluefin is highly prized as sushi and demand has increased as sushi has become more trendy. The increase in demand and the decrease in the catch have driven up prices so a single choice tuna can now fetch $50,000 or more at the Tokyo fish market. As a result of the high price, corporations hunt tuna across the oceans in fast ships using satellites, sophisticated radar, and on-board helicopters. The sad truth is that so many fish are caught, various types of sushi may soon become a thing of the past.

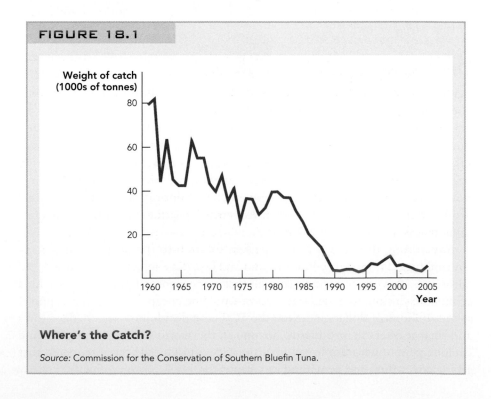

FIGURE 18.1

Weight of catch (1000s of tonnes)

Where's the Catch?

Source: Commission for the Conservation of Southern Bluefin Tuna.

Tuna isn't the only fish headed toward extinction. A 2006 paper in *Science* estimated that if the long-term trend continues, *all* of the world's major seafood stocks will collapse by 2048. Already nearly 30% of seafood species have collapsed (defined as a decline in the catch of 90%). As seafood species decline so do all the species that depend on them in the food chain. Overfishing is draining the oceans of fish.

The Difference Is Ownership

Chickens
(owned, not endangered)

"Chickens of the Sea"
(unowned, endangered)

Overfishing, however, is not primarily caused by increased demand. People like to eat chickens even more than they like to eat tuna but chickens are not going extinct. Why not? The difference is that chickens are owned and tuna, "chickens of the sea," are unowned.

To see why ownership means that chickens are plentiful and tuna are scarce, let's take a closer look at the incentives of fishermen and chicken ranchers.

Everyone, including the fishermen whose livelihoods depend on tuna, knows that tuna are being fished to extinction. So, you might think that the logical thing for a tuna fisherman to do is to fish less. But that's not correct. If Haru, a Japanese tuna fisherman, fishes less, will there be more tuna for him to catch in the future? No; if Haru fishes less, that just leaves more tuna for other fishermen to catch—fishing less doesn't help Haru because he doesn't own the tuna until it's in the hold of his ship. Since Haru doesn't own the tuna in the ocean, he has no way of securing the fruits of his restraint.

Compare the incentives facing Haru with those facing Frank Perdue, the legendary chicken entrepreneur. Will Frank Perdue ever let his chickens go extinct? Of course not. Perdue makes money from his chickens, so to maximize profits, he will keep his stock of chickens healthy and growing. If Perdue "overfishes" his chickens, he pays the price. If Perdue exercises restraint and grows his flock, he gets the benefit. In short, Frank Perdue will never kill the chicken that lays his golden eggs.

The problem of overfishing is one example of the *tragedy of the commons*, the tendency for any resource that is unowned to be overused and undermaintained. The theory goes back at least to Aristotle who in criticizing Plato's idea of raising children in common said "that which is common to the greatest number has the least care bestowed upon it."[1]

Do you live with other students? Take a look at your kitchen—that's the tragedy of the commons. Other examples of the tragedy of the commons include the slaughter of the open-range buffalo during the nineteenth century, deforestation in the African Sahel region, and the hunting of elephants to near extinction.

The tragedy of the commons applies especially strongly to resources like fish, forests, and agricultural land because these resources must be carefully maintained to remain useful. But when resources are unowned, the users do not have strong incentives to invest in maintenance because maintenance mostly creates an external benefit, not a private benefit. In other words, the fisherman who throws the small fish back mostly increases other people's future catch, not his own. The tragedy of the commons is thus a type of externality problem like those we examined in Chapter 10.

The tragedy of the commons

We typically call something a *tragedy* of the commons when the lack of maintenance is so severe, that exploitation is pushed beyond the point where the resource reproduces itself. To maintain a healthy stock of fish, for example, the yearly catch of fish must be no more than the yearly increase in fish population. If a population of 100 fish grows by 10% every year, then fishermen can catch 10 fish *forever*. But if the fishermen catch just one more fish, 11 fish per year, the stock of fish will be extinct in just 26 years. (See the appendix for a proof.) So, the fishermen who overfish are not just driving the fish into extinction, they are driving *their own way of life* into extinction— that's a tragedy.

Happy Solutions to the Tragedy of the Commons

The tragedy of the commons can sometimes by averted in small groups. Small tribes and villages have avoided the tragedy of overfishing a lake or overgrazing a pasture through the enforcement of norms. A tribe member who takes too many fish from the common lake will be shunned, like someone who litters in a public park. A tribe member who exercises restraint and throws the small fish back will be respected. Tragedy of the commons problems, however, are more difficult to solve when a lot of unrelated people have access to the common good.

Command and control and, more recently, tradable allowances have been used to solve tragedy of the commons problems, just as they have been used to solve other externality problems, as we discussed in Chapter 10. When fishing stocks have neared depletion, for example, governments have tried command and control solutions like limiting the number of fishing boats. To protect their salmon fishery, British Columbia limited the number of boats in 1968. Unfortunately, the scheme did not work well because the fishermen installed more powerful engines and better electronics for finding fish— this is often called "capital stuffing" because the fishermen stuffed their boats with expensive capital so those boats could be more effective. As a result of capital stuffing, the value of the typical fishing boat tripled in just 10 years; not surprisingly, the salmon fishery continued to decline. Similar problems have occurred when governments have restricted the number of days that fishing is allowed.

New Zealand pioneered an alternative approach in 1986 with individual transferable quotas (ITQs). ITQs are just like the pollution allowances that we looked at in Chapter 10; the owner of an ITQ has the right to catch a certain tonnage of fish. The sum of the individual ITQs adds up to the total allowable catch, which is set by the government.[2] ITQs can be bought and sold and the government does not restrict the types of boats or equipment that the fishermen use so resources are not wasted by capital stuffing.

The ITQ system has been very successful. Figure 18.2 shows that after the ITQ system was put into place, the fish catch in New Zealand increased—in other words, preventing the fishermen from overfishing *increased* the amount of fish that they caught! This may seem paradoxical but it's just a reminder of why the tragedy of the commons is a tragedy—when each fisherman chooses to fish rather than restrain themselves, the net result is less fish for everyone.[*]

---

[*] Thus, the tragedy of the commons can also be understood as a prisoner's dilemma, which we introduced in Chapter 15.

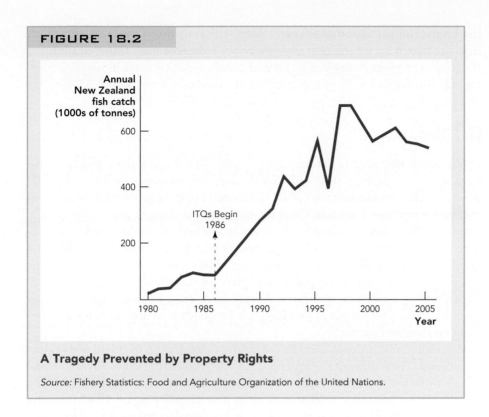

FIGURE 18.2

A Tragedy Prevented by Property Rights

Source: Fishery Statistics: Food and Agriculture Organization of the United Nations.

New Zealand was able to create an ITQ system and rescue its fishery because most of the New Zealand fish live and spawn within 200 miles of New Zealand's shore—the economic zone that international law assigns exclusively to New Zealand. Thus, the New Zealand government was able to create property rights and exclude anyone who didn't have the right to fish (i.e., an ITQ) from catching fish within its waters. Property rights in other common resources such as African elephants have also been created and have resulted in substantial improvements.

Unfortunately, it's not easy to create property rights in all common resources. Southern bluefin tuna, for example, migrate throughout the Pacific, and some have been tagged and tracked across thousands of miles of ocean. So any solution to the tragedy of the tuna commons will require a multicountry agreement. That's not impossible. In the 1970s, scientists discovered that certain chemicals commonly used in aerosols could disrupt the ozone layer, which protects the earth from UV-B radiation. Protecting the ozone layer is a public good since it is nonexcludable and nonrival. Fortunately, an international treaty called the Montreal Protocol has been signed by 195 of the 196 United Nations member states and it restricts the use of chemicals that damage the ozone layer. The treaty is widely regarded as the most successful environmental treaty as emissions of ozone-depleting chemicals have declined and the ozone layer has begun to recover.[3]

Similarly, if there were world agreement, technology could be used to tag tuna and create property rights, but as we know from our discussion of the Coase theorem in Chapter 10, the more parties required to make an agreement, the greater the transactions costs and the less likely a solution. Moreover, rather than working to create property rights or restrict fishing to sustainable levels, most major governments today subsidize fishing extensively, which is making the tragedy of the commons worse. Thus, the tragedy of the tuna commons may not have a happy solution any time soon, either for sushi lovers or for tuna.

□ Takeaway

Public goods are valuable but markets will often undersupply these goods. As we have seen, "nonexcludability" and "nonrivalry" are important qualities of public goods, but nonexcludability is usually the more important problem. Nonrival but excludable goods such as cable TV or digital music can often be provided privately. Although there may be some inefficiency when non-payers are excluded, private provision does allow for entrepreneurship and market discovery. When a good is nonexcludable, however, demanders don't have an incentive to pay for the good and, as a result, suppliers don't have an incentive to supply the good. That's why, for instance, the world doesn't have enough protection against an asteroid strike. The benefit of providing public goods is an argument for government taxation and supply.

A resource that is nonexcludable but rival will tend to be overused and undermaintained. The tragedy of the commons explains many of the major environmental problems facing the world today. Sometimes there are creative solutions to the tragedy of the commons, such as instituting new property rights. Unfortunately, creating property rights is not automatic and may require extensive understanding of economic principles and agreement among many of the world's governments.

In short, many of the world's problems arise when property rights to goods are either not possible, not protected, or not easily implemented.

□ CHAPTER REVIEW

KEY CONCEPTS

Nonexcludable, p. 344

Nonrival, p. 344

Private good, p. 345

Public good, p. 345

Free rider, p. 345

Forced rider, p. 346

Nonrival private good, p. 347

Common resources, p. 348

Tragedy of the commons, p. 348

FACTS AND TOOLS

1. Take a look at the following list of goods and services:

   Apples

   Open-heart surgery

   Cable television

   Farm-raised salmon

   Yosemite National Park

   Central Park, New York City

   The Chinese language

   The idea of calculus

   a. Is each item on the list excludable or nonexcludable? Sometimes the border is a little fuzzy, but justify your answer if you think there's any ambiguity.

   b. Rival or nonrival?

   c. Based on your answers to parts a and b, sort each good or service into one of the four categories from Table 18.1.

   d. How do you exclude people from a park?

2. Which of the following are free riders, which are forced riders, and which are just people paying for public goods?

   a. In Britain, Alistair pays a tax to support the British Broadcasting Corporation. He doesn't own a radio or TV.

b. Monica pays her local property taxes and state income taxes. Police patrol her neighborhood regularly.

c. Richard, a young boy in 1940s Los Angeles, jumps on board the streetcar without paying.

d. In the United States, Sara pays taxes to fund children's immunizations. She lives out in the forest, has no family, and rarely sees other people.

e. In Japan, Dave, a tourist from the United States, enjoys the public parks.

3. a. Is education—a college course, for instance—excludable?

b. Is education a rival good? That is, if your class has more students, do you get a worse education on average? Do students (and parents) typically prefer smaller class sizes? Do professors typically prefer smaller classes? Does it usually cost more for a school to educate more students?

c. According to the standard economists' definition of a public good—the definition we use in this chapter—is education a public good?

d. Into which of the four categories from Table 18.1 does education seem to fit best?

4. Emeril says, "In my economics class, I learned that the only way to fund public goods was to have the government tax citizens to pay for those goods. Is that what you learned?"

Rachel responds, "Actually, in my class, we used *Modern Principles,* and we learned that there are other ways to fund public goods, like _____." Complete Rachel's statement.

5. a. American bison onced freely roamed the Great Plains. In the 1820s, there were some 30 million bison in the United States but a survey in 1889 counted just 1,091. Why were the bison driven to near extinction? How were the bison like tuna?

b. At some restaurants and grocery stores, you can buy bison burgers, made from farm-raised bison. Is this good news or bad news if we want more bison around?

6. a. The nation of Alphaville has been hunting its deer population to extinction. The government decrees strict limits on the number of hunters, and on the number of rounds of ammunition that each hunter can take into the hunt. Hunters, like fishermen,

are a creative lot: What will "capital stuffing" look like in this case?

b. What would an individual transferable quotas (ITQ) system look like in this case?

c. Do real governments use quotas like this to control deer populations? If you don't know the answer, just ask your classmates: There's probably a hunter or two in your course.

7. This chapter noted that chickens and the "chicken of the sea" (tuna) are fundamentally different in terms of population though they are both food. Indeed, chickens are eaten far more than tuna, and chickens are abundant compared with their ocean-living cousins.

a. What difference between these two species does this chapter identify as the explanation for this seemingly strange puzzle?

b. As population and prosperity have increased, the demand for chicken has increased. What happens to the price of chickens as a result? Why?

c. Because of the rules humans have concerning chickens, what happens to the number of people raising chickens as a result of the price change? Why? What happens to the number of chickens? Why?

d. What happens to the price of tuna as population and prosperity increase? Why?

e. Because of the rules humans have concerning tuna, what happens to the number of people harvesting tuna as a result of the price change? Why?

8. a. Why did the fish catch *increase* in New Zealand after the amount that each fisherman could catch was *limited* by a quota?

b. Given your answer to part a, would an individual fisherman in New Zealand want to catch more fish than he's allowed, if he knew no one would ever catch him?

c. So given your answer to part b, does the New Zealand system depend on government enforcement to work, or will individual fishermen agree out of self-interest to abide by the ITQ?

THINKING AND PROBLEM SOLVING

1. In 2008, Jean Nouvel won the Pritzker Architecture Prize (the highest prize in architecture). One of his most notable works is the Torre Agbar (pictured), a breakthrough skyscraper that lights up each night thanks to more than 4,000 LED devices—a pricey but purely cosmetic feature.

ATLANTIDE PHOTO TRAVEL/CORBIS

a. Many people enjoy looking at the Torre Agbar. Just considering that enjoyment, how would you classify the Torre Agbar: rival or nonrival? Why?

b. The Torre Agbar is the third tallest building in Barcelona. For the purposes of enjoying its illuminated façade, would you classify the building as an excludable or nonexcludable good? Why?

c. Based on your answers, is the LED façade a public good?

d. Companies often hire architects like Nouvel to create beautiful buildings that are expensive to design, build, and maintain, yet they cannot charge people to look at them. This chapter offered one possible explanation for this puzzle. What's the explanation and how does it help justify the construction of a widely enjoyed building? (*Hint:* The building is the headquarters for Grupo Agbar, a company dedicated to the distribution and treatment of water in countries all over the world. For most of you, this is the first time you've heard of this company.)

2. a. "A public good is just a good that provides large external benefits." Discuss.

b. "A tragedy of the commons occurs when using a good causes massive external costs." Discuss. In parts a and b, compare the definitions from Chapter 10 with those from this chapter.

3. a. Has the rise of the Internet and file sharing turned media such as movies and music into public goods? Why?

b. Taking your answer in part a into account, would government taxation and funding of music improve social welfare? In your answer, at least *mention* some of the practical difficulties of doing this.

4. We mentioned that the tragedy of the commons is a form of prisoner's dilemma, something we saw back in Chapter 15. As is so often the case in economics, the same model can apply to many different settings. Let's recycle Facts and Tools question 5b from Chapter 16 just to emphasize the point:

		Player B	
		Left	Right
Player A	Up	(100, 100)	(600, 50)
	Down	(50, 600)	(500, 500)

a. We have given you very generic strategies: up, down, left, and right. Relabel the matrix so the game applies to fishermen and the tragedy of the commons.

b. Which set of strategies would give the fishermen the highest joint payoff?

c. Which set of actions would be equivalent to the following choice: "One fisherman decided not to conserve and to catch more than his fair share." (There are two correct answers here.)

d. Which set of actions is the one and only Nash equilibrium? How would you describe it in terms of these two fishermen?

5. As we've already mentioned, the line between "public good" and "private good" is genuinely blurry. Electronic tolls on roadways are making excludability a little bit easier every year. In your view, should we continue to think of roads as public goods? (To be more accurate, we really should say, "Should we continue to think of *travel* on uncongested roads as public goods?")

6. The massive stone faces that pepper Easter Island puzzled people for centuries. What happened to the civilization that erected these faces? A clue is that the island currently has no trees. Trees would have been necessary to roll

the stones and to make boats to bring the stones to the island. Archeological digs have discovered the island *did* have trees very long ago, but it's believed that the natives used up all the trees until they had no choice but to leave. Can you think of an explanation for why people would behave in this way? The following questions may suggest an answer.

JAMES L. AMOS/CORBIS

   a. Who bore the cost of planting new trees? Who benefited from planting new trees?

   b. As the population of the island grew, what happened to the number of trees? Why?

   c. Biologist Jared Diamond, writing on the subject of trees in Easter Island, asked, "What were they thinking when they cut down the last palm tree?"[4] What do you think the person who cut down that last palm tree was thinking, if he acted like a person facing a tragedy of the commons?

7. Economists typically remind people to weigh the costs of an action against the benefits of that action. Let's invent some examples where it's just too expensive or too risky to solve the very real problems discussed in this chapter.

   a. It's possible that it would just cost too much to defend the earth from asteroids, where the best option, all things considered, is just to hope for the best. Invent an extreme example where this is the case—your example might take place in a world with different technology, different type of government, and so forth.

   b. What about saving the tuna? Invent an example where the best option is to just let the fishermen do what they want, even if tuna go extinct.

CHALLENGES

1. a. Two girls are sharing a cold chocolate milk, as in the picture below. How long do you think it will take them to drink all the milk? How long would it take if each girl had her own glass and half the milk? Can you see a problem when the girls drink from a common glass?

SEAN JUSTIC/CORBIS

   b. What is going on in this picture of the East Texas oil field in 1919? Can you see the problem?

AMERICAN PETROLEUM INSTITUTE PHOTOGRAPH AND FILM COLLECTION, ARCHIVES CENTER, NATIONAL MUSEUM OF AMERICAN HISTORY, SMITHSONIAN INSTITUTION

   c. Why did we put these two questions together? (*Hint:* A speech from the movie *There Will Be Blood* gets at the same question—it's based on a 1924 speech by U.S. Senator Albert Fall of New Mexico.)

2. Some media companies (especially in music and movie industries) run ads claiming that downloading or copying media is the same thing as stealing a CD or DVD from a store. Let's see if this is the case.

a. Is a DVD a nonrival good? Why or why not?

b. Suppose someone stole a DVD from a retail outlet. Regardless of how that person values the DVD, does the movie company lose any revenue as a result of the theft? Why or why not?

c. Suppose someone illegally downloaded a movie instead of purchasing it. Also suppose that person placed a high value on the movie (he or she valued it more than the price required to purchase it legally). Does the movie company lose any revenue as a result of the theft? Why or why not?

d. Suppose someone illegally downloaded a movie instead of purchasing it. Also suppose that person placed a low value on the movie (he or she valued it less than the price required to purchase it legally). Does the movie company lose any revenue as a result of the theft? Why or why not?

e. How is illegally downloading media like retail theft and how is it not?

3. The economic theory of public goods makes a very clear prediction: If the benefits of some action go to strangers, not to yourself, then you won't do that action. Economists have run dozens of experiments testing out this prediction. Nobel laureate Elinor Ostrom sums up the results in a 2000 article in the *Journal of Economic Perspectives.*

A typical "public goods game" is quite simple: Everyone in the experiment is given, say, $5 each, theirs to take home if they like. They're told that if they donate money to the common pool, all the money in the pool will then be doubled. The money in the pool will then be divided equally among all players, whether they contributed to the pool or not. That's the whole game. Let's see what a purely self-interested person would do in this setting. (*Hint:* A public goods game is just like a prisoner's dilemma, only with more people.)

a. If there are 10 people playing the game, and they all chip in their $5 to the pool, how much will be in the pool *after* it doubles?

b. So how much money does each person get to take home if everyone puts their money in the pool?

c. Now, suppose that you are one of the players, and you've seen that all 9 other players have put in all their money. If you keep your $5, and the pool money gets divided up equally among all 10 of you, how much will you have in total?

d. So are you better or worse off if you keep your money?

e. What if none of the nine had put money into the pot: If you were the only one to put your money in, how much would you have afterward? Is this better or worse than if you'd just kept the money yourself?

f. So if you were a purely self-interested individual, what's the best thing to do regardless of what the other players are doing: Put all the money in, put some of it in, or put none of it in? (Answer in percent.) Do the benefits of donating go to you or to other people?

g. If people just cared about "the group," they'd surely donate 100%. In part f, you just said what a purely self-interested person would do. In the dozens of studies that Ostrom summarizes, people give an average of 30% to the common pool. So, are the people in these studies closer to the pure self-interest model from part f, or are they closer to the pure altruist model of human behavior?

4. Canada's Labrador Peninsula (which includes modern-day Newfoundland and most of modern-day Quebec) was once home to an indigenous group, the Montagnes, who, in contrast to their counterparts in the American Southwest, established property rights over land. This institutional change was a direct result of the increase in the fur trade after European traders arrived.[5]

a. Before European traders came, the amount of land in the Labrador Peninsula far exceeded the indigenous people's needs. Hunting animals specifically for fur was not yet widely practiced. What can you conclude about the relative scarcity of land or animals? Why?

b. Before the European arrival, land was commonly held. Given your answer in part a, did the tragedy of the commons play out for the indigenous Montagnes? (Remember, air is also commonly held.)

c. Once the European traders came, the demand for fur increased. Do you expect the tragedy of the commons to play out under these circumstances? Why or why not?

d. The Montagnes established property rights over the fur trade, allocating families' hunting territory. This led to rules ranging from when an animal is accidentally killed in a neighbor's territory to laws governing inheritance. Why did the Montagnes create property rights only after the Europeans traders came?

5. It's one of the ironies of American history that when the pilgrims first arrived at Plymouth Rock, they promptly set about creating a communal society in which all shared equally in the produce of their land. As a result, the pilgrims were soon starving to death.

Fortunately, "after much debate of things," Governor William Bradford ended the corn commons, decreeing that each family should keep the corn that it produced. In one of the most insightful statements of political economy ever written, Bradford described the results of the new and old systems.

> [Ending the corn commons] had very good success, for it made all hands very industrious, so as much more corn was planted than otherwise would have been by any means the Governor or any other could use, and saved him a great deal of trouble, and gave far better content. The women now went willingly into the field, and took their little ones with them to set corn; which before would allege weakness and inability; whom to have compelled would have been thought great tyranny and oppression.
>
> The experience that was had in this common course and condition, tried sundry years and that amongst godly and sober men, may well evince the vanity of that conceit of Plato's and other ancients applauded by some of later times; that the taking away of property and bringing in community into a commonwealth would make them happy and flourishing; as if they were wiser than God. For this community (so far as it was) was found to breed much confusion and discontent and retard much employment that would have been to their benefit and comfort. For the young men, that were most able and fit for labour and service, did repine that they should spend their time and strength to work for other men's wives and children without any recompense. The strong, or man of parts,

> had no more in division of victuals and clothes than he that was weak and not able to do a quarter the other could; this was thought injustice. The aged and graver men to be ranked and equalized in labours and victuals, clothes, etc., with the meaner and younger sort, thought it some indignity and disrespect unto them. And for men's wives to be commanded to do service for other men, as dressing their meat, washing their clothes, etc., they deemed it a kind of slavery, neither could many husbands well brook it. Upon the point all being to have alike, and all to do alike, they thought themselves in the like condition, and one as good as another; and so, if it did not cut off those relations that God hath set amongst men, yet it did at least much diminish and take off the mutual respects that should be preserved amongst them. And would have been worse if they had been men of another condition. Let none object this is men's corruption, and nothing to the course itself. I answer, seeing all men have this corruption in them, God in His wisdom saw another course fitter for them.

(*Source:* Bradford, William. *Of Plymouth Plantation, 1620–1647.* Edited by Samuel Eliot Morison. New York: Modern Library, 1967.)

a. Imagine yourself a pilgrim under the communal (commons) system. If you worked hard all day in the fields, would that increase your share of the food by a lot or a little? Describe the incentive to work under the communal system.

b. Under this system, what type of good was the pilgrim's harvest?

c. According to Bradford, the communal system "retard[ed] much employment that would have been to their benefit and comfort." Why would the communal system reduce something that would have been to the pilgrim's benefit? How would you describe this using the tools of economics?

d. According to Bradford, what happened to the amount of food produced and the amount of labor after the communal system was abolished and workers got to keep a larger share of what they produced?

e. Read Bradford's statement carefully. What other effects did the communal system create? (Note that economists typically ignore these kinds of effects.)

The Tragedy of the Commons: How Fast?

We can use a simple spreadsheet to see how quickly common resources can become tragically overexploited and ruined. Suppose that we start with a stock of 100. This could be 100 million fish or 100 thousand elephants, or 100 units of agricultural quality or other common resource. Let's suppose that this resource grows or reproduces itself by 10% every year. We can then set up our spreadsheet as shown in Figure A18.1. The key cell is Cell B3, which contains the formula =B2*(1+$C$2)−$D$2. This formula takes the stock of fish in the previous year from cell B2, multiplies it by 1 plus the growth rate in Cell C2 (using the dollar signs to make sure that this cell reference stays the same when we copy it elsewhere), and then subtracts the annual catch or usage in Cell D2 (which we initially set at 10) to get the stock in this year.

FIGURE A18.1

	B3	▾	f_x	=B2*(1+$C$2)-$D$2	
	A	B	C	D	
1	Year	Stock	Natural Growth Rate	Annual Catch	
2	1	100	0.10	10	
3	2	100			
4	3	100			
5	4	100			
6	5	100			
7	6	100			
8	⋮	⋮			
9					
10					

We now copy and paste Cell B3 into Cells B4 onward. It's fairly obvious that if a stock of 100 fish grows by 10% every year, then a catch of 10 is sustainable forever and this is what our spreadsheet indicates.

What is more surprising is how quickly an increase in the catch can drive a stock to extinction. If we change the annual catch in Cell D2 to 11, for example, we get the result in Figure A18.2.

FIGURE A18.2

	A	B	C	D
1	Year	Stock	Natural Growth Rate	Annual Catch
2	1	100	0.10	11
3	2	99		
4	3	97.9		
5	4	96.69		
6	5	95.359		
7	6	93.8949		
8	7	92.28439		
9	8	90.51283		
10	9	88.56411		
11	10	86.42052		
12	11	84.06258		
13	12	81.46883		
14	13	78.61572		
15	14	75.47729		
16	15	72.02502		
17	16	68.22752		
18	17	64.05027		
19	18	59.4553		
20	19	54.40083		
21	20	48.84091		
22	21	42.725		
23	22	35.9975		
24	23	28.59725		
25	24	20.45698		
26	25	11.50267		
27	26	1.652941		
28	27	-9.18177		
29				

Notice that the decline starts slowly, but by year 27 the stock of fish has gone negative; that is, the fish are extinct. You can experiment with different assumptions about growth rates and catches to see how long stocks can be sustained under different scenarios.

19

Political Economy and Public Choice

If you have read this far, you may now be asking "What's wrong with the world?" Economists tend to favor free and competitive markets and to be skeptical about policies like price controls, tariffs, command and control regulation, and high inflation rates. Yet around the world, markets are often suppressed, monopolies are supported, and harmful policies, such as those listed above, are quite common. Why do the arguments of economists fall on deaf ears?

One possible answer is that politicians are right to reject mainstream economics. As we explore in Chapter 20, some people do argue that mainstream economics ignores important ethical values. Or perhaps mainstream economics is simply wrong about economics. Of course, that is not our view, so you will have to seek other books to judge that question for yourself. A third answer to what's wrong with the world and the one we will explore in this chapter is . . . can you guess? Bad incentives.

To say it once again (but never enough times!), incentives matter. A good incentive system aligns self-interest with the social interest. In Chapters 7 and 10, we explored the conditions under which markets do and do not align self-interest with the social interest. It's now time to turn to government. The critical question is this: When does the self-interest of politicians and voters align with the social interest and when do these interests collide? This question is at the heart of political economy or **public choice**, which is the study of political behavior using the tools of economics.

We will begin this chapter looking at some of the major institutions and incentives that govern the behavior of voters and politicians in a democracy. As we will see, democracies have many problems, including voter ignorance, control of politics by special interests, and political business cycles. Yet, to quote Winston Churchill, "No one pretends that democracy is perfect or all-wise. Indeed, it has been said that democracy is the worst form of government except all those other forms that have been tried from time to time."[1]

Public choice is the study of political behavior using the tools of economics.

361

Thus, in the latter half of the chapter, we look at nondemocracies and some of the reasons why nondemocracies have typically failed to produce either wealth or political or economic liberty for their citizens.

Let's begin with voters and the question: "Do voters have an incentive to be well informed about politics?"

Voters and the Incentive To Be Ignorant

Knowledge is a good thing, but sometimes the price of knowledge is too high. Imagine that your professor changed the grading scheme. Instead of awarding grades based on individual performance, your professor averages test scores and assigns the same grade to everyone. Will you study more or less under this new grading scheme? We think that most people would study less because studying now has a lower payoff. Let's say that before the change an extra few hours of studying would raise your grade by 10 points. What is the payoff to studying under the new system? Imagine that there are 100 people in your class. Then the same hours of studying will now raise your grade by just 10/100 or 0.1 points.★ Studying doesn't pay under the second system because your grade is mostly determined by what other people do, not by what you do.

Now let's apply the same idea to politics. When you choose a politician, does studying have a high payoff? No. Studying position papers, examining voting histories, and listening to political speeches is sometimes entertaining, but it doesn't offer much concrete return. Even when studying changes your vote, your vote is very unlikely to change the outcome of the election. Studying politics doesn't pay because the outcome of any election is mostly determined by what other people do, not by what you do.

Economists say that voters are **rationally ignorant** about politics because the incentives to be informed are low.

> **Rational ignorance** occurs when the benefits of being informed are less than the costs of becoming informed.

It's not hard to find evidence that Americans are uninformed about politics. Consider the following questions. Who is the speaker of the U.S. House of Representatives? Who sings "Poker Face?" Be honest. Which question was it easier for you to answer? And which question is more important? (At the time of writing, John Boehner was speaker of the House. "Poker Face" was a Lady Gaga hit.)

Not knowing who the speaker of the House is might not be critical, but Americans are equally uninformed or worse—misinformed—about important political questions. For example, in one survey Americans were asked to name the two largest sources of government spending out of the following six choices.

> Welfare

> Interest on the federal debt

> Defense

> Foreign aid

> Social Security

> Health care

Amazingly, 41% named foreign aid as one of the two biggest programs. But foreign aid is by far the smallest program of the six listed. Do you know

★ It's possible that some people could study more under the new system. Under the old system, studying only raises an individual's grade, but under the new system, it raises everyone's grades! Thus, if there are some super-altruistic students, they might study more under the new system. We have not met many such students. Have you?

the correct answers? The two biggest programs are defense and Social Security. Americans were not even close to the correct answers; for instance, the second most popular choice was welfare, which is at least a large program although still much smaller than defense and Social Security.[2]

Similarly, by their own admission, most Americans know "not much" or "nothing" about important pieces of legislation such as the USA Patriot Act. Most Americans cannot estimate the inflation rate or the unemployment rate to within five percentage points. Hundreds of surveys over many decades have shown that most Americans know little about political matters. Of course, we'd all like to change that—we are glad you are reading this book!—but in the meantime it is simply a fact. And it appears to be a fact that is not easily changed.

Why Rational Ignorance Matters

Ignorance about political matters is important for at least three reasons. First, if voters don't know what the USA Patriot Act says or what the unemployment rate is, then it's difficult to make informed choices. Moreover, voters who think that the unemployment rate is much higher than it actually is are likely to make quite different choices than if they knew the true rate. The difficulty is compounded if voters don't know the positions that politicians take on the issues, and it is worse yet if voters don't know much about possible solutions to problems such as unemployment. Voters are supposed to be the drivers in a democracy, but if the drivers don't know where they are or how to get to where they want to go, they are unlikely to ever arrive at their desired destination.

Second, voters who are rationally ignorant will often make decisions on the basis of low-quality, unreliable, or potentially biased information. Not everyone has read a good principles of economics textbook and those who haven't are likely to vote in ways that are quite different than someone who is better informed.* It's not really surprising, for example, that better-looking politicians get more votes even if good looks have nothing to do with policy. Once again, we should not expect too much in the way of wise government policy when voters are rationally ignorant.

The third reason that rational ignorance matters is that not everyone is rationally ignorant. Let's look at this in more detail.

Special Interests and the Incentive To Be Informed

Let's return to the sugar quota that we discussed in Chapter 9. As you may recall, the government restricts how much sugar can be imported into the United States. As a result, the U.S. price of sugar is about double the world price. American consumers of candy, soda, and other sweet goods pay more for these goods than they would if the quota was lifted. Why does the government harm sugar consumers, many of whom are voters?

Although sugar consumers are harmed by the quota, few of them even know of the quota's existence. That's rational because even though the quota costs consumers more than a billion dollars, the costs are diffused over millions

CHECK YOURSELF

> Would you expect more rational ignorance about national issues among national voters or about local issues among local voters? Make an argument for both possibilities.

---

* For a superb treatment of this issue, see Caplan, Bryan. 2007. *The Myth of the Rational Voter: Why Democracies Choose Bad Policies.* Princeton, NJ: Princeton University Press.

of consumers, costing each person about $5 or $6 per year. Even if sugar consumers did know about the quota, they probably wouldn't spend much time or effort to oppose it. Will you? After all, just writing a letter to your local newspaper opposing the quota might cost $5 or $6 in time and trouble, and what's the probability that your letter will change the policy?

Sugar consumers, therefore, won't do much to oppose the quota but what about U.S. sugar producers? U.S. sugar producers benefit enormously from the quota. As we saw in Chapter 9, if the quota were lifted, most sugar producers in Florida would be outcompeted by producers in Brazil where better weather makes sugar cheaper to produce. But with the quota, U.S. producers are shielded from competition and sugar farming in Florida becomes very profitable. Moreover, although there are millions of sugar consumers, sugar production is concentrated among a handful of producers. Each producer benefits from the quota by millions of dollars.

TABLE 19.1 Special Interests Are Rationally Informed

Senators on the Agriculture Committee, 2008	Donations from the American Crystal Sugar PAC (2006–2008)
Tom Harkin, D-IA	$15,000
Sherrod Brown, D-OH	$15,000
Saxby Chambliss R-GA	$10,000
Mitch McConnell, R-KY	$10,000
Robert Casey, Jr., D-PA	$10,000
E. Benjamin Nelson, D-NE	$8,000
Amy Klobuchar, D-MN	$7,000
Patrick J. Leahy, D-VT	$6,000
Max Baucus, D-MT	$6,000
Pat Roberts, R-KS	$3,000
Kent Conrad, D-ND	$2,000
Ken Salazar, D-CO	$2,000
Debbie Stabenow, D-MI	$1,000
Richard G. Lugar, R-IN	
Thad Cochran, R-MS	
Blanche Lincoln, D-AR	
Lindsey Graham, R-SC	
Norm Coleman, R-MN	
Mike Crapo, R-ID	
John Thune, R-SD	
Charles Grassley, R-IA	

Source: Federal Election Commission data compiled by OpenSecrets.org.

Sugar producers, unlike sugar consumers, have a lot of money at stake so they are *rationally informed*. The sugar producers know when the sugar quota comes up for a vote, they know who is on the House and Senate agricultural committees that largely decide on the quota, they know which politicians are running for reelection and in need of campaign funds, and they act accordingly. Table 19.1, for example, lists the members of the Senate Agricultural Committee in 2008 and the amount of money from 2006 to 2008 that they received from the American Crystal Sugar Political Action Committee (PAC), an industry lobby group in favor of the sugar quota.

As you can see, 13 of the 21 senators on the Agricultural Committee (perhaps not coincidentally just over a majority!) received money from the American Crystal Sugar PAC. Many senators on the committee *also* received money from the American Sugar Cane League, the Florida Sugar Cane League, the American Sugarbeet Growers Association, and the U.S. Beet Sugar Association! Nor is that the end of the story. The owners and executives of the major players in the sugar industry also donate campaign funds as individuals. The "sugar barons" José and Alfonso Fanjul, for example, head Florida Crystals Corporation, which is one of the country's largest sugar cane growers. The Fanjuls donate money to the Florida Sugar Cane League and they give money to politicians in their own names. Interestingly, José directs most of his support to Republicans, while his brother Alfonso supports Democrats. Do you think there is a difference of political opinion between the two brothers? Or can you think of another explanation for their pattern of donations? Other Fanjul brothers, wives, daughters, sons, and even sisters–in–law are also active political contributors.

One Formula for Political Success: Diffuse Costs, Concentrate Benefits

▶▶ SEARCH ENGINE

Extensive information on campaign contributions can be found at www. OpenSecrets.org.

The politics behind the sugar quota illustrate one formula for political success: Diffuse costs and concentrate benefits. The costs of the sugar quota are diffused over millions of consumers, so no consumer has much of an incentive to oppose the quota. But the benefits of the quota are concentrated on a handful of producers; they have strong incentives to support the quota. So, the sugar quota is a winning policy for politicians. The people who are harmed are rationally ignorant and have little incentive to oppose the policy, while the people who benefit are rationally informed and have strong incentives to support the policy. Thus, we can see one reason why the self-interest of politicians does not always align with the social interest.

The formula for political success works for many types of public policies, not just trade quotas and tariffs. Agricultural subsidies and price supports, for example, fit the diffused costs and concentrated benefits story. It's interesting that the political power of farmers has *increased* as the share of farmers in the population has *decreased*. The reason? When farmers decline in population, the benefits of, for example, a price support become more concentrated (on farmers) and the costs become more diffused (on nonfarmers).

The benefits of many government projects such as roads, bridges, dams, and parks, for example, are concentrated on local residents and producers, while the costs of these projects can be diffused over all federal taxpayers. As a result, politicians have an incentive to lobby for these projects even when the benefits are smaller than the costs.

Consider the infamous "Bridge to Nowhere," a proposed bridge in Alaska that would connect the town of Ketchikan (population 8,900) with its airport on Gravina Island (population 50) at a cost to federal taxpayers of $320 million. At present, a ferry service runs to the island but some people in the town complain that it costs too much ($6 per car). If the town's residents had to pay the $320 million cost of the bridge themselves—that's $35,754 each!—do you think they would want the bridge? Of course not, but the residents will be happy to have the bridge if most of the costs are paid by other taxpayers.

As far as the residents of Ketchikan are concerned, the costs of the bridge are *external costs*. Recall from Chapter 10 that when the costs of a good are paid for by other people—rather than the consumers or producers of the good—we get an inefficiently large quantity of the good. In Chapter 10, we gave the example of a firm that pollutes—since the firm doesn't pay all the costs of its production, it produces too much. The same thing is true here, except the external cost is created by government. When government makes it possible to push the costs of a good onto other people—to *externalize the cost*—we get too much of the good. In this case, we get too many bridges to nowhere.

The bridge to nowhere is not unique. Representative John Carter (R-Texas), who sits on the House Military Construction Appropriations Subcommittee, included nearly $7 million in funding for a physical fitness center at Fort Hood, which lies within his district. It may be a good idea to provide a physical fitness center for the troops at Fort Hood—but they already have six! One of the fitness centers includes two co-ed saunas, three racquetball courts, an eight-lane, 25-meter swimming pool, and much more.

Given that Fort Hood already has six fitness centers, the benefits of another center are likely to be less than the cost. But since the benefits are concentrated and the costs are diffused over many taxpayers, the project is funded anyway. Special interest provisions like this are very common. Can you guess who supported the $2 million grant for the Charles B. Rangel Center for Public Service? And which senator included $7.5 million in funding for the Harkin Grant Program for the Iowa Department of Education?

The formula for political success works for tax credits and deductions, as well as for spending. The federal tax code, including various regulations and rulings, is more than 60,000 pages long and it grows every year as politicians add special interest provisions. Tax breaks for various manufacturing industries, for example, have long been common, but in 2004, the term "manufacturing" was significantly expanded so that oil and gas drilling as well as mining and timber were included as manufacturing industries. The new tax breaks were worth some $76 billion to the firms involved. One last-minute provision even defined "coffee roasting" as a form of manufacturing. That provision was worth a lot of *bucks* to one famous corporation.

Every year Congress inserts many thousands of special spending projects, exemptions, regulations, and tax breaks into major bills. A multibillion dollar lobbying industry works the system on behalf of their clients, and it is not unusual for those lobbies, in essence, to propose and even write up the details of the forthcoming legislation. In 1975, there were more than 3,000 lobbyists, by 2000 the number had expanded to over 16,000, and by the late 2000s there were more than 35,000 lobbyists—all to lobby just 535 politicians (435 representatives and 100 senators) and their staff. Many lobbyists are former politicians who find that lobbying their friends can be very profitable.

When benefits are concentrated and costs are diffuse, resources can be wasted on projects with low benefits and high costs. Consider a special interest group that represents 1% of society and a simple policy that benefits the special interest by $100 and costs society $100. Thus, the policy benefits the special interest by $100 and it costs the *special interest* just $1 (if you are wondering where that came from, $1 is 1% of the total cost to society). The special interest group will certainly lobby for a policy like this.

But now imagine that the policy benefits the special interest by $100 but costs society twice as much, $200. The policy is very bad for society, but it's still good for the special interest, which gets a benefit of $100 at a cost (to the lobby) of only $2 ($2 is 1% of the total social costs of $200). Indeed, a special interest representing 1% of the population will benefit from any policy that transfers $100 in its favor, even if the costs to society are nearly 100 times as much!

If each policy, taken on its own, wastes just a few million or billion dollars worth of resources, the country will be much poorer. A country with many inefficient policies will have less wealth and slower economic growth. No society can get rich by passing policies with benefits that are less than costs.

In extreme situations, an economy can falter or even collapse when fighting over the division of the pie becomes more profitable than making the pie grow larger. The fall of the Roman Empire, for instance, was caused in part by bad political institutions. As the Roman Empire grew, courting politicians in Rome became a more secure path to riches than starting a new business. Toward the end of the empire, the emperors taxed peasant farmers heavily. Rather than spending the money on roads or valuable infrastructure, the activities that had made Rome powerful and

Many small distortions can tie a giant down.

rich, tax revenues were used to pay off privileged insiders and to placate the public in the city of Rome with "bread and circuses." When the empire finally collapsed in 476 CE, the tax collector was a hated figure and the government enjoyed little respect.[3]

Voter Myopia and Political Business Cycles

We turn now from the microeconomics of political economy to an application in macroeconomics. Rational ignorance and another factor, voter myopia, can encourage politicians to boost the economy before an election in order to increase their chances of reelection.

Presidential elections appear to be fought on many fronts. Candidates battle over education, war, health care, the environment, and the economy. Pundits scrutinize the daily chronicle of events to divine how the candidates advance and retreat in public opinion. Personalities and "leadership" loom large and are reckoned to swing voters one way or other. When the battle is done, historians mark one personality and set of issues as having won the day and reflected the "will of the voters."

But economists and political scientists have been surprised to discover that a simpler logic underlies this apparent chaos of seemingly unique and momentous events. Over the past 100 years, the American voter has voted for the party of the incumbent when the economy is doing well and voted against the incumbent when the economy is doing poorly. Voters are so responsive to economic conditions that the winner of a presidential election can be predicted with considerable accuracy, even if one knows nothing about the personalities, issues, or events that seem, on the surface, to matter so much.

The green line in Figure 19.1 shows, for each presidential election since 1948, the share of the two-party vote won by the party of the incumbent (that is, a

CHECK YOURSELF

> President Ronald Reagan set up a commission to examine government and cut waste. It had some limited success. If special interest spending is such a problem, why don't we set up another federal commission to examine government waste? Who would push for such a commission? Who would resist it? What will be its prospects for success?

> A local library expanded into a new building and wanted to establish a local history collection and room. The state senator found some state money and had that contributed to the library. Who benefits from this? Who ultimately pays for it?

FIGURE 19.1

Economic Conditions in an Election Year Predict Presidential Votes

Notes:
Vote share predicted using growth in disposable income in year of election, inflation in year of election, and a measure of how long the incumbent party has been in office.
Actual vote share is the share of the two-party vote captured by the party of the presidential incumbent.

share greater than 50% usually means the presidency stayed with the incumbent party and a share less than 50% usually means the presidency switched party). The blue line is the share of the two-party vote predicted by just three variables: growth in personal disposable income (per capita) in the year of the election, the inflation rate in the year of the election, and a simple measure of how long the incumbent party has been in power. Notice that these three variables alone give us great power to predict election results. (But the model did not predict the 2004 election well. Why do you think this might have been the case?)

More specifically, the incumbent party wins elections when personal disposable income is growing, when the inflation rate in the election year is low, and when the incumbent party has not been in power for too many terms in a row. Personal disposable income is the amount of income a person has after taxes. It includes income from wages, dividends, and interest but also income from welfare payments, unemployment insurance, and Social Security payments. The inflation rate is the general increase in prices. The last variable, a measure of how long the incumbent party has been in power, reduces a party's vote share. Voters seem to get tired or disillusioned with a party the longer it has been in power, so there is a natural tendency for the presidency to switch parties even if all else remains the same.

Figure 19.1 tells us that voters are responsive to economic conditions, but more deeply it tells us that voters are surprisingly responsive to economic *conditions in the year of an election*. Voters are myopic—they don't look at economic conditions over a president's entire term. Instead, they focus on what is close at hand, namely economic conditions the year of an election. Politicians who want to be reelected, therefore, are wise to do whatever they can to increase personal disposable income and reduce inflation in the year of an election even if this means decreases in income and increases in inflation at other times. Is there evidence that politicians behave in this way? Yes.

One of the most brazen examples comes from President Richard Nixon. Just two weeks before the 1972 election, he sent a letter to more than 24 million recipients of Social Security benefits. President Nixon's letter read:

Higher Social Security Payments

Your social security payment has been increased by 20 percent, starting with this month's check, by a new statute enacted by Congress and signed into law by President Richard Nixon on July 1, 1972.

The President also signed into law a provision that will allow your social security benefits to increase automatically if the cost of living goes up. Automatic benefit increases will be added to your check in future years according to the conditions set out in the law.

Of course, higher Social Security payments must be funded with higher taxes, but Nixon timed things so that the increase in payments started in October but the increase in taxes didn't begin until January, that is, not until after the election! Nixon was thus able to shift benefits and costs so that the benefits hit before the election and the costs hit after the election.

To be fair, President Nixon's policies were not unique or even unusual. Government benefits of all kinds typically increase before an election while taxes hardly ever do—taxes increase only after an election!

Using 60 years of U.S. data, Figure 19.2 shows the growth rate in personal disposable income in each quarter of a president's 16-quarter term. Growth is much higher in the year before an election than at any other time in a president's term. In fact, in an election year personal disposable income grows on average by 3.01% compared with 1.79% in a nonelection year. The difference is probably not due to chance.

Inflation also follows a cyclical pattern, but since voters dislike inflation, it tends to decrease in the year of an election and increase after the election. These patterns have been observed in many other countries, not just the United States. We also see political patterns at lower levels of politics. Mayors and governors, for example, try to increase the number of police on the streets in an election year, so that crime will fall and people will feel safer.

There are a limited number of things that a president can do to influence the economy, so presidents do not always succeed in increasing income during an election year. Presidents can influence transfers and taxes much more readily than they can influence pure economic growth. This is one reason why cyclical patterns are more difficult to see in GDP statistics than they are in personal disposable income.

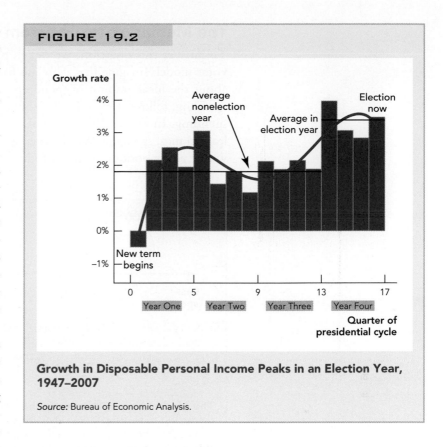

FIGURE 19.2

Growth in Disposable Personal Income Peaks in an Election Year, 1947–2007

Source: Bureau of Economic Analysis.

Two Cheers for Democracy

You might be wondering by now: Why isn't everything from the federal government handed out to special interest groups and why aren't politicians always reelected? Do the voters ever get their way? In fact, voters in a democracy can be very powerful. If you want to think about when voters matter most and when lobbies and special interests matter most, turn to the idea of incentives.

When a policy is specialized in its impact, difficult to understand, and affects a small part of the economy, it is likely that lobbies and special interests get their way. Let's say the question is whether the depreciation deduction in the investment tax credit should be accelerated or decelerated. Even though this issue is important to many powerful corporations, you can expect that most voters have never heard of the issue and that it will be settled behind closed doors by a relatively small number of people.

But when a policy is highly visible, appears often in the newspapers and on television, and has a major effect on the lives of millions of Americans, the voters are likely to have an opinion. The point isn't that voter opinions are always well informed or rational, but that voters do care about some of the biggest issues such as Social Security, Medicare, and taxes and when they do care, politicians have an incentive to serve them. But how exactly does voter opinion translate into policy? After all, opinions are divided, so which voters will get their way in a democracy?

CHECK YOURSELF

> If voters are myopic, will politicians prefer a policy with small gains now and big costs later, or a policy with small costs now but big gains later?

The Median Voter Theorem

To answer this question, we develop a model of voting called the median voter model. Imagine that there are five voters, each of whom has an opinion about the ideal amount of spending on Social Security. Max wants the least spending, followed by Sofia, Inez, Peter, and finally Alex who wants the most spending. In Figure 19.3, we plot each voter's ideal policy along a line from least to most spending. We also assume that each voter will vote for the candidate whose policy position is closest to his or her ideal point.

FIGURE 19.3

The Median Voter Theorem Each voter has an ideal policy, marked by an x, on the less to more spending line. Voters will vote for the candidate whose policy is closest to their ideal. The median voter is the voter such that half of the other voters want more spending and half of the other voters want less spending—Inez is the median voter. Under majority rule, the ideal policy of the median voter will beat any other policy. Consider any two candidate policies, such as those of Candidate D and Candidate R. Candidate D will receive two votes (Max and Sofia) and Candidate R will receive three votes (Inez, Peter, and Alex). But Candidate R's position can be beaten by a policy even closer to the ideal policy of the median voter, such as that of Candidate D'. Over time, competition pushes both candidates toward the ideal policy of the median voter, which is the only policy that cannot be beaten.

The median voter is defined as the voter such that half of the other voters want more spending and half want less spending. In this case, the median voter is Inez, since compared with Inez, half of the voters (Paul and Alex) want more spending and half the voters (Max and Sofia) want less spending.

The **median voter theorem** says that under these conditions, the median voter rules! Or to put it more formally, the median voter theorem says that when voters vote for the policy that is closest to their ideal point on a line, then the ideal point of the median voter will beat any other policy in a majority rule election.

Let's see why this is true and, as a result, how democracy will tend to push politicians toward the ideal point of the median voter. First, consider any two policies such as those adopted by Candidate D and Candidate R. Which policy will win in a majority rule election? Max and Sofia will vote for Candidate D since D's policy is closer to their ideal point than R's policy. But Inez, Peter, and Alex will vote for Candidate R. By majority rule, Candidate R will win the election. Notice that of the two policies on offer, the policy closest to that of the median voter's ideal policy won the election.

The **median voter theorem** says that when voters vote for the policy that is closest to their ideal point on a line, then the ideal point of the median voter will beat any other policy in a majority rule election.

Most politicians don't like to lose. So in the next election Candidate D may shift her position, becoming Candidate D'. By exactly the same reasoning as before, Candidate D' will now win the election. If we repeat this process, the only policy that is not a *sure loser* is the ideal point of the median voter (Inez). As Candidates D and R converge on the ideal point of the median voter, there will be little difference between them and each will have a 50% chance of winning the election.*

The median voter theorem can be interpreted quite generally. Instead of thinking about less spending and more spending on Social Security, for example, we can interpret the line as the standard political spectrum of left to right. In this case, the median voter theorem can be interpreted as a theory of democracy in a country such as the United States where there are just two major parties.

The median voter theorem tells us that in a democracy what counts are noses—the number of voters—and not their positions per se. Imagine, for example, that Max decided he wanted even less spending or that Alex decided he wanted even more spending. Would the political outcome change? No. According to the median voter theorem, the median voter rules, and if the median voter doesn't change, then neither does policy. Thus, under the conditions given by the median voter theorem, democracy does not seek out consensus or compromise or a policy that maximizes voter preferences, on average—it seeks out a policy that cannot be beaten in a majority rule election.

The median voter theorem does not always apply. The most important assumption we made was that voters will vote for the policy that is closest to their ideal point. That's not necessarily true. If no candidate offers a policy close to Max's ideal point, he may refuse to vote for anyone, not even the candidate whose policy is (slightly) closer to his own ideal. In this case, a candidate who moves too far away from the voters on her wing may lose votes even if her position moves closer to that of the median voter. As a result, this type of voter behavior means that candidates do not necessarily converge on the ideal point of the median voter.

We have also assumed that there is just one major dimension over which voting takes place. That's not necessarily true either. Suppose that voters care about two issues, such as taxes and war, and assume that we cannot force both issues into a left-right spectrum (so knowing a person's views about taxes doesn't necessarily predict much about his or her views about war). With two voting dimensions, it's very likely that there is *no* policy that beats every other policy in a majority rule contest, so politics may never converge on a stable policy.

To understand why a winning policy sometimes doesn't exist, consider an analogy from sports. Imagine holding a series of (hypothetical) boxing matches to figure out who is the greatest heavyweight boxer of all time. Suppose that Muhammad Ali beats Lennox Lewis and Lewis beats Mike Tyson but Tyson beats Muhammad Ali. So who is the greatest of all time? The question may have no answer if there is more than one dimension to boxing skill, so Ali has the skills needed to beat Lewis and Lewis has the skills needed to beat Tyson, but Tyson has the skills to beat Ali. In a similar way, when there is more than one dimension to politics, no policy may exist that beats every other policy. In terms of politics, the result may be that every vote or election brings a new

---

* In terms of the game theory we discussed in Chapters 15 and 16, the ideal policy of the median voter is the only policy that cannot be beaten by another policy and thus the only Nash equilibrium of a two-candidate game is for both candidates to choose this policy.

winner, or alternatively, constitutions and procedural restrictions may slow down the rate of political change. The U.S. Constitution, for example, requires that new legislation must pass two houses of Congress and evade the president's veto, which is more difficult than passing a simple majority rule vote.

As a predictive theory of politics, the median voter theorem is applicable in some but not all circumstances. The theorem, however, does remind us that politicians have substantial incentives to listen to voters on issues that the voters care about. This is a powerful feature of democracy, although of course the quality of the democracy you get will depend on the wisdom of the voters behind it.

Democracy and Nondemocracy

Our picture of democracy so far has been a little disillusioning, at least compared with what you might have learned in high school civics. Yet when we look around the world, democracies tend to be the wealthiest countries, and despite the power of special interests, they also tend to be the countries with the best record for supporting markets, property rights, the rule of law, fair government, and other institutions that support economic growth.

Figure 19.4 graphs an index meant to capture good economic policy, called the economic freedom index (with higher numbers indicating greater economic freedom) on the horizontal axis against a measure of the standard of living on the vertical axis (gross national income per capita in 2007). The figure shows two things. First, there is a strong correlation between economic freedom and a higher standard of living. Second, the countries that are most democratic (labeled "Full democracies" and shown in red) are among the wealthiest counties in the world and the countries with the most economic freedom. The only

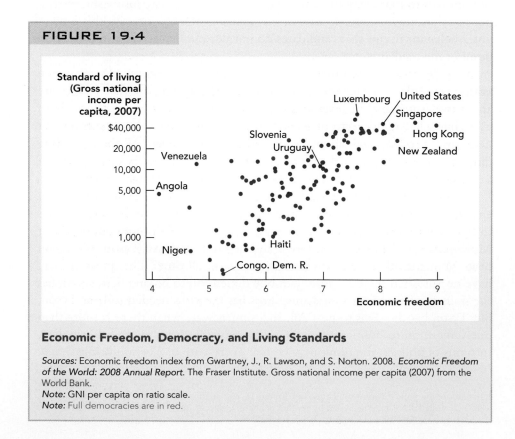

FIGURE 19.4

Economic Freedom, Democracy, and Living Standards

Sources: Economic freedom index from Gwartney, J., R. Lawson, and S. Norton. 2008. *Economic Freedom of the World: 2008 Annual Report.* The Fraser Institute. Gross national income per capita (2007) from the World Bank.
Note: GNI per capita on ratio scale.
Note: Full democracies are in red.

interesting exceptions to this rule are Singapore and Hong Kong, both of which score very highly on economic freedom and the standard of living but that are not quite full democracies.

Notice, however, that in part there is an association between democracy and the standard of living because greater wealth creates a greater demand for democracy. When citizens have satisfied their basic needs for food, shelter, and security, they demand more cerebral goods, such as the right to participate in the political process. This is exactly what happened in South Korea and Taiwan, two countries that became more democratic as they grew wealthier. Many people think that China may become a more democratic country as it grows wealthier; we will see. But it's not just that wealth brings democracy. Democracy also seems to bring wealth and favorable institutions. Democracies must be doing something right. We therefore need to examine some of the benefits of democratic decision making.

We've already discussed rational ignorance under democracy, but keep in mind that public ignorance is often worse in nondemocracies.[4] In many quasi-democracies and in nondemocracies, the public is not well informed because the media are controlled or censored by the government.

In Africa, for example, most countries have traditionally banned private television stations. In fact as of 2000, 71% of African countries had a state monopoly on television broadcasting. Most African governments also control the largest newspapers in the country. Government ownership and control of the media are also common in most Middle Eastern countries and, of course, the former Communist countries controlled the media extensively.

Control of the media has exactly the effects that we would expect from our study of rational ignorance in democracies—it enables special interests to control the government for their own ends. Greater government ownership of the press, for example, is associated with lower levels of political rights and civil liberties, worse regulation (more policies like price controls that economists think are ineffective and wasteful), higher levels of corruption, and a greater risk of property confiscation. The authors of an important study of media ownership conclude that "government ownership of the press restricts information flows to the public, which reduces the quality of the government."[5]

Citizens in democracies may be "rationally ignorant," but on the whole they are much better informed about their governments than citizens in quasidemocracies and nondemocracies. Moreover, in a democracy, citizens can use their knowledge to influence public policy at low cost by voting. In a democracy, knowledge is power. In nondemocracies, knowledge alone is not enough because intimidation and government violence create steep barriers to political participation. Many people just give up or become cynical. Other citizens in nondemocracies fall prey to propaganda and come to accept the regime's portrait of itself as a great friend of the people.

The importance of knowledge and the power to vote for bringing about better outcomes is illustrated by the shocking history of mass starvation.

Democracy and Famine

At first glance, the cause of famine seems obvious—a lack of food. Yet the obvious explanation is wrong or at least drastically incomplete. Mass starvations have occurred during times of plenty, and even when lack of food is a contributing factor, it is rarely the determining factor of whether mass starvation occurs.

Many of the famines in recent world history have been intentional. When Stalin came to power in 1924, for example, he saw the Ukrainians, particularly the relatively wealthy independent farmers known as kulaks, to be a threat. Stalin collectivized the farms and expropriated the land of the kulaks, turning them out of their homes and sending hundreds of thousands to gulag prisons in Siberia.

Agricultural productivity in Ukraine plummeted under forced collectivization and people began to starve. Nevertheless, Stalin continued to ship food out of Ukraine. Peasants who tried to escape starving regions were arrested or turned back at the border by Stalin's secret police. Desperate Ukrainians ate dogs, cats, and even tree bark. Millions died.[6]

The starvation of Ukraine was intentional and it's clear that it would not have happened in a democracy. Stalin did not need the votes of the Ukrainians and thus they had little power to influence policy. Democratically elected politicians will not ignore the votes of millions of people.

Even unintentional mass starvations can be avoided in democracies. The 1974 famine in Bangladesh was not on the scale of that in Ukraine, but still 26,000 to 100,000 people died of mass starvation. It was probably the first televised starvation, and it illustrates some important themes in the relationship between economics and politics.

Floods destroyed much of the rice crop of 1974 at the same time as world rice prices were increasing for other reasons. The flood meant that there was no work for landless rural laborers who in ordinary years would have been employed harvesting the rice.

The lower income from work and the higher rice prices, taken together, led to starvations. Yet in 1974, Bangladesh in the aggregate did not lack for food. In fact, food per capita in 1974 was at an all-time high, as shown in Figure 19.5.

Mass starvation occurred not because of a lack of food per se, but because a poor group of laborers lacked both economic and political power. Lack of economic power meant they could not purchase food. Lack of political power meant that the elites then running Bangladesh were not compelled to avert the famine. Bangladesh continued to pursue bad economic policies; for instance, government regulations made it very difficult to purchase foreign exchange so it wasn't easy for capitalists to import rice from nearby Thailand or India. In fact, rice was even being smuggled out of Bangladesh and into India to avoid price controls and other regulations.

Amartya Sen, the Nobel Prize-winning economist and philosopher, has argued that whether a country is rich or poor, "no famine has taken place in the history of the world in a functioning democracy." The precise claim can be disputed depending on how one defines "functioning democracy" but the lesson Sen draws is correct:

Perhaps the most important reform that can contribute to the elimination of famines, in Africa as well as in Asia, is the enhancement of democratic practice, unfettered newspapers and—more generally—adversarial politics.[7]

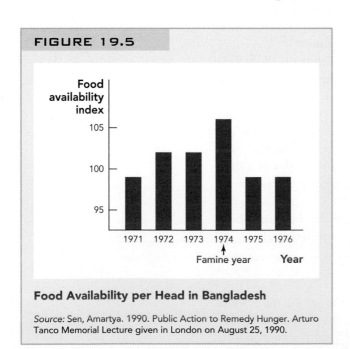

FIGURE 19.5

Food Availability per Head in Bangladesh

Source: Sen, Amartya. 1990. Public Action to Remedy Hunger. Arturo Tanco Memorial Lecture given in London on August 25, 1990.

Economists Timothy Besley and Robin Burgess have tested Sen's theory of democracy, newspapers, and famine relief in India.[8] India is a federal democracy with 16 major states. The states vary considerably in their susceptibility to food crises, newspaper circulation, education, political competition, and other factors.

Besley and Burgess ask whether state governments are more responsive to food crises when there is more political competition and more newspapers. Note that both of these factors are important. Newspapers won't work without political competition and political competition won't work without newspapers. Knowledge and power together make the difference.

Besley and Burgess find that greater political competition is associated with higher levels of public food distribution. Public food distribution is especially responsive in election and pre-election years. In addition, as Sen's theory predicts, government is more responsive to a crisis in food availability when newspaper circulation is higher. That is, when food production falls or flood damage occurs, governments increase food distribution and calamity relief

Democracy, newspapers, and famine relief.

more in states where newspaper circulation is higher. Newspapers and free media inform the public and spur politicians to action.

Democracy and Growth

Democracies have a good record for not killing their own citizens or letting them starve to death. Not killing your own citizens or letting them starve may seem like rather a low standard, but many governments have failed to meet this standard so we count this accomplishment as a serious one favoring democracies. Democracies also have a relatively good record for supporting markets, property rights, the rule of law, fair government, and other institutions that promote economic growth, as we showed in Figure 19.4.

One reason for the good record of democracies on economic growth may be that the *only* way the public as a whole can become rich is by supporting efficient policies that generate economic growth. In contrast, small (nondemocratic) elites can become rich by dividing the pie in their favor even if it means making the pie smaller.

Let's first recall why small groups can become rich by dividing the pie in their favor even when this means the pie gets smaller. Recall the special interest group that we discussed earlier that made up 1% of the population. Consider a policy that transfers $100 to the special interest at a cost of $4,000 to society. Will the group lobby for the policy? Yes, because the group gets $100 in benefits but it bears only $40 of the costs (1% of $4,000).

By definition, oligarchies or quasi-democracies are ruled by small groups. Thus, the rulers in these countries don't have much incentive to pay attention to the larger costs of their policies as borne by the broader public. The incentives of ruling elites may even be to promote and maintain policies that keep their nations poor. An entrenched, nondemocratic elite, for example, might not want to support mass education. Not only would a more educated populace compete with the elite, but an informed people might decide that they don't need the elite any more and, of course, the elite know this. As a result, the elites will often want to keep the masses weak and uninformed, neither of which is good for economic growth or, for that matter, preventing starvation.

But now let's think about a special interest that represents 20% of society. Will this special interest be in favor of a policy that transfers $100 to it at a cost of $4,000 to society? No. The special interest gets $100 in benefits from the transfer but its share of the costs is now $800 (20% of $4,000), so the policy is a net loser even for the special interest. Thus, the larger the group, the greater the group's incentives to take into account the social costs of inefficient policies.

Large groups are more concerned about the cost to society of their policies simply because they make up a large fraction of society. Thus, large groups tend to favor more efficient policies. In addition, the more numerous the group in charge, the less lucrative transfers are as a way to get rich. A small group has a big incentive to take $1 from 300 million people and transfer it to themselves. But a group of 100 million that takes $1 from each of the remaining 200 million gets only $2 per person. Even if you took one hundred times as much, $100, from each of the 200 million people and gave it to the 100 million, that's only $200 each. Pretty small pickings. It's usually better for a large group to focus on policies that increase the total size of the pie.

In other words, the greater the share of the population that is brought into power, the more likely that policies will offer something for virtually everybody, and not just riches for a small elite.

The tendency for larger groups to favor economic growth is no guarantee of perfect or ideal policies, of course. As we have seen, rational ignorance can cause trouble. But on the big questions, a democratic leader simply will not want to let things become too bad. That's a big reason why democracies tend to be pretty good—although not perfect—for economic growth.

CHECK YOURSELF

> The free flow of ideas helps markets to function. How does the free flow of ideas help democracies to function?

□ Takeaway

Incentives matter, so a good institution aligns self-interest with the social interest. Does democracy align self-interest with the social interest? Sometimes. On the negative side, voters in a democracy have too little incentive to be informed about political matters. Voters are rationally ignorant because the benefits of being informed are small—if you are informed, you are more likely to choose wisely at the polls, but your vote doesn't appreciably increase the probability that society will choose wisely, so why bother to be informed? Being informed creates an external benefit because your informed vote benefits everyone, but we know from Chapter 10 that goods with external benefits are underprovided.

Rational ignorance means that special interests can dominate parts of the political process. By concentrating benefits and diffusing costs, politicians can often build political support for themselves even when their policies generate more costs than benefits.

Incumbent politicians can use their control of the government to increase the probability that they will be reelected. Politicians typically increase spending before an election and only increase taxes after the election. Voters pay attention to current economic conditions even when the prosperity is temporarily and artificially enhanced at the expense of future economic conditions.

Our study of political economy can usefully be considered a study of government failure that complements the theory of market failure we presented in Chapter 10 on externalities and Chapter 13 on monopoly. When markets fail to align self-interest with the social interest, we get market failure. When the institutions of government fail to align self-interest with the social interest, we get government failure. No institutions are perfect and trade-offs are everywhere—this is a key lesson when thinking about markets and government.

A close look at democracy can be disillusioning, but the record of democracies on some of the big issues is quite good. It's hard for politicians in a democracy to ignore the major interests of voters. And if things do go wrong, voters in a democracy can always "throw the bums out" and start again with new ideas. Partially as a result, democracies have a good record on averting mass famines, maintaining civil liberties like free speech, and supporting economic growth. Most of all, democracies tend not to kill their own citizens, who after all are potential voters.

□CHAPTER REVIEW

KEY CONCEPTS

Public choice, p. 361

Rational ignorance, p. 362

Median voter theorem, p. 370

FACTS AND TOOLS

1. Which of the following is the smallest fraction of the U.S. federal budget? Which are the two largest categories of federal spending?

   Welfare

   Interest on the federal debt

   Defense

   Foreign aid

   Social Security

   Health care

2. **a.** How many famines have occurred in functioning democracies?

   b. What percentage of famines occurred in countries without functioning democracies?

3. Around 130 million voters participated in the 2008 U.S. presidential election. Imagine that you are deciding whether to vote in the next presidential election. What do you think is the probability that your vote will determine the outcome of the election? Is it greater than 1%, between 1% and 0.1%, between 0.1% and 0.01%, or less than 0.01% (i.e., less than 1 in 10,000)?

4. If a particular government policy—like a decision to go to war or to raise taxes—only works when citizens are informed, is that an argument for that policy or against that policy?

5. True or false?

   a. During Bangladesh's worst famine, average food per person was much lower than usual.

   b. Democracies are less likely to kill their own citizens than other kinds of governments.

   c. Surprisingly, newspapers aren't that important for informing voters about hungry citizens.

   d. Compared with dictatorship or oligarchy, democracies have a stronger incentive to make the economic pie bigger.

   e. Compared with most other countries, full democracies tend to put a lot of restrictions on markets and property rights.

   f. When it comes to disposable income, American presidents seem to prefer "making a good first impression" rather than "going out with a bang."

   g. When the government owns most of the TV and radio stations, it's motivated to serve the public interest, so voters tend to get better, less-biased information.

6. The "median voter theorem" is sometimes called the "pivotal voter theorem." This is actually a fairly good way to think of the theorem. Why?

7. Let's walk through the median voter theorem in a little more detail. Consider a town with three voters, Enrique, Nandini, and Torsten. The big issue in the upcoming election is how high the sales tax rate should be. As you'll learn in macroeconomics (and in real life), on average, a government that wants to do more spending has to bring in more taxes, so "higher permanent taxes" is the same as "higher government spending." Enrique wants low taxes and small government, Nandini is in the middle, and Torsten wants the biggest town government of the three. Each one is a stubborn person, and his or her favorite position—what economic theorists call the "ideal point"—never changes in this problem. Their preferences can be summed up like this, with the x denoting each person's favorite tax rate:

   a. Suppose there are two politicians running for office, N and O. Who will vote for N? Who will vote for O? Which candidate will win the election?

   b. O drops out of the campaign after the local paper reports that he hasn't paid his sales taxes in years. P enters the race, pushing for higher taxes, so it's N vs. P. Voters prefer the candidate who is closest to them, as in the text. Who will vote for N? Who will vote for P? Who will win? Who will lose?

c. In part b, you decided who was heading for a loss. You get a job as the campaign manager for this candidate just a month before election day. You advise her to retool her campaign and come up with a new position on the sales tax. Of course, in politics as in life, there's more than one way to win, so give your boss a choice: Provide her with two different positions on the sales tax, both of which would beat the would-be winner from part b. She'll make the final pick herself.

d. Are the two options you recommended in part c closer to the median voter's preferred option than the loser's old position, or are they further away? So in this case, is the median voter theorem roughly true or roughly false?

8. Perhaps it was in elementary school that you first realized that if everyone in the world gave you a penny, you'd become fantastically rich. This insight is at the core of modern politics. Sort the following government policies into "concentrated benefits" and "diffuse benefits."

a. Social Security

b. Tax cuts for families

c. Social Security Disability Insurance for the severely disabled

d. National Park Service spending for remote trails

e. National Park Service spending on the National Mall in Washington, DC

f. Tax cuts for people making more than $250,000 per year

g. Sugar quotas

The trail to Half Dome: diffuse benefits?

GALEN ROWELL/CORBIS

THINKING AND PROBLEM SOLVING

1. David Mayhew's classic book *Congress: The Electoral Connection* argued that members of Congress face strong incentives to put most of their efforts into highly visible activities like foreign travel and ribbon-cutting ceremonies, instead of actually running the government. How does the rational ignorance of *voters* explain why *politicians* put so much effort into these highly visible activities?

2. An initiative on Arizona's 2006 ballot would have handed out a $1 million lottery prize every election: The only way to enter the lottery would be to vote in a primary or general election. How do you think a lottery like this would influence voter ignorance?

3. We mentioned that voters are myopic, mostly paying attention to how the economy is doing in the few months before a presidential election. If they want to be rational, what should they do instead? In particular, should they pay attention to all four years of the economy, just the first year, just the last two years, or some other combination?

4. In his book *The Myth of the Rational Voter*, our GMU colleague Bryan Caplan argues that not only can voters be rationally ignorant, they can even be rationally irrational. People in general seem to *enjoy* believing in some types of false ideas. If this is true, then they won't challenge their own beliefs unless the cost of holding these beliefs is high. Instead, they'll enjoy their delusion.

Let's consider two examples:

a. John has watched a lot of Bruce Lee movies and likes to think that he is a champion of the martial arts who can whip any other man in a fight. One night, John is in a bar and he gets into a dispute with another man. Will John act on his beliefs and act aggressively, or do you think he is more likely to rationally calculate the probability of injury and seek to avoid confrontation?

b. John has watched a lot of war movies and likes to think that his country is a champion of the military arts that can whip any other country in a fight. John's country gets into a dispute with another country. John and everyone else in his country go to the polls to vote on war. Will John act on his beliefs and vote for aggression, or do you think he is more likely to rationally calculate the probability of defeat and seek to avoid confrontation?

5. In the television show *Scrubs*, the main character J. D. is a competent and knowledgeable doctor. He also has very little information outside of the field of medicine, admitting he doesn't know the difference between a senator and a representative and believes New Zealand is near "Old Zealand."

   a. Suppose J. D. spends some time learning some of these common facts. What benefits would he receive as a result? (Assume there are no benefits for the sake of knowledge itself.)

   b. Suppose instead J. D. spends that time learning how to diagnose a rare disease that has a slight possibility of showing up in one of his patients. What benefits would he receive as a result? (Again, assume there are no benefits for the sake of knowledge itself.)

   c. Make an *economic* argument that even given your answer to question b, voters have too little incentive to be informed about political matters.

6. Driving along America's interstates, you'll notice that few rest areas have commercial businesses. Vending machines are the only reliable source of food or drink, much to the annoyance of the weary traveler looking for a hot meal. Thank the National Association of Truck Stop Operators (NATSO), who consistently lobby the U.S. government to deny commercialization. They argue:

   > Interchange businesses cannot compete with commercialized rest areas, which are conveniently located on the highway right-of-way. . . Rest area commercialization results in an unfair competitive environment for privately-operated interchange businesses and will ultimately destroy a successful economic business model that has proven beneficial for both consumers and businesses.[9]

The sorrow of a land without burgers.

STEVE CRAFT/CORBIS

   a. How does NATSO make travel more expensive for consumers?

   b. Do you think most Americans have heard of NATSO and the legislation to commercialize rest stops? How does your answer illustrate rational ignorance? Do you think that the owners of interchange businesses (i.e., restaurants, gas stations, and other businesses located near but not on highways) have heard of NATSO?

   c. Why does NATSO often succeed in its lobbying efforts despite your answer to part a? *Hint:* What is the concentrated benefit in this story? What is the diffused cost?

7. The following figure shows the political leanings of 101 voters. Voters will vote for the candidate who is closest to them on the spectrum, as in the typical median voter story. Again as usual, politicians compete against each other, entering the "political market" just as freely as firms enter the economic market back in Chapter 11.

   a. Which group of voters will get their exact wish: the group on the left, the center-left, the center-right, or the right?

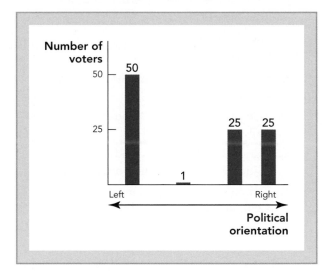

   b. Now, four years later, it's time for a new election. Suppose that in the meantime, the two right-leaning groups of voters have merged: The 25 center-right voters move to the far right, forming a far-right coalition. In the new election, whose position will win now?

   c. As you've just seen, there's a "pivotal voter" in this model. Who is it?

8. Let's rewrite a sentence from the chapter concerning the Roman Empire: "As the American Empire grew, courting politicians

in Washington became a more secure path to riches than starting a new business." Does this seem true today? If it started happening, how would you be able to tell? In your answer, put some emphasis on market signals that could point in favor or against the "decadent empire" theory. (*Hint:* By some measures, Moscow has the highest real estate prices in the world, and it's probably not due to low housing supply.)

CHALLENGES

1. Is rational ignorance the whole explanation for why voters allow programs like the sugar quota to persist? Perhaps not. In the early 1900s, the government of New York City was controlled by a Democratic Party organization known as Tammany Hall. In a delightful essay entitled "Honest Graft and Dishonest Graft" by George Plunkitt, one of the most successful politicians from the Tammany machine, he argued that voters actually approve of these kinds of government-granted favors. (The essay and the entire book, *Plunkitt of Tammany Hall: A Series of Very Plain Talks on Very Practical Politics,* are available for free online.)

   For example, Plunkitt said that ordinary voters like it when government workers get paid more than the market wage: "The Wall Street banker thinks it is shameful to raise a [government] clerk's salary from $1500 to $1800, but every man who draws a salary himself says, 'That's all right. I wish it was me.' And he feels very much like votin' the Tammany ticket on election day, just out of sympathy."

   a. Plunkitt said this in the early 1900s. Do you think this is more true today than it was back then, or less true? Why?

   b. If more Americans knew about the sugar quota, do you think they would be outraged? Or would they approve, saying, "That's all right, I wish it was me"? Why?

   c. Overall, do you think that real-world voters prefer a party that gives special favors to narrow groups, even if those voters aren't in the favored group? Why?

2. a. When a drought hits a country, and a famine is possible, what probably falls more: the demand for food or the demand for haircuts? Why?

   b. Who probably suffers more from a deep drought: people who own farms or people who own barbershops? (*Note:* The answer

is on page 164 of Sen's summary of his life's work, *Development as Freedom.*)

   c. Sen emphasizes that "lack of buying power" is more important during a famine than "lack of food." How does Sen's barber story illustrate this?

3. Political scientist Jeffrey Friedman and law professor Ilya Somin say that since voters are largely ignorant, that is an argument for keeping government simple. Government, they say, should stick to a few basic tasks. That way, rationally ignorant voters can keep track of their government by simply catching a few bits of the news between reruns of *Two and a Half Men*.

   a. What might such a government look like? In particular, what policies and programs are too complicated for today's voters to easily monitor? Just consider the U.S. federal government in your answer.

   b. Which current government programs and policies are fairly easy for modern voters to monitor? What programs do you think that you and your family have a good handle on?

   c. Are there easy replacements you can think of for the too complex programs in part a? For instance, cutting one check per farmer and posting the amount on a Web site might be easier to monitor than the hundreds of farm subsidies and low-interest farm loans that exist today.

4. We mentioned that the median voter theorem doesn't always work, and sometimes a winning policy doesn't exist. This fact has driven economists and political scientists to write thousands of papers and books, both proving that fact and trying to find good workarounds. The most famous theoretical example of how voting doesn't work is the Condorcet paradox. The Marquis de Condorcet, a French nobleman in the 1700s, wondered what would happen if three voters had the preferences like those below. Three friends are holding a vote to see which French economist they should read in their study group. Here are their preferences:

	Jean	Marie	Claude
1st choice	Walras	Bastiat	Say
2nd choice	Bastiat	Say	Walras
3rd choice	Say	Walras	Bastiat

a. They vote by majority rule. If the vote is Walras vs. Say, who will win? Say vs. Bastiat? Bastiat v. Walras?

b. They decide to vote in a single-elimination tournament: Two votes and the winner of the first round proceeds on to the final round. This is the way many sporting events and legislatures work. Now, suppose that Jean is in charge of deciding in which order to hold the votes. He wants to make sure that his favorite, Walras, wins the final vote. How should he stack the order of voting to make sure Walras wins?

c. Now, suppose that Claude is in charge instead: How would Claude stack the votes?

d. And Marie? Comment on the importance of being the agenda setter.

(In case you think these examples are unusual, they're not. Any kind of voting that involves dividing a fixed number of dollars can easily wind up the same way—check for yourself! Condorcet himself experienced another form of democratic failure: He died in prison, a victim of the French Revolution that he supported.)

5. In the previous question, you showed that sometimes there may be no policy that beats every other policy in a majority rule election and, as a result, the agenda can determine the outcome. In the previous question, all of the policy choices on the agenda were as good as any other, but this is not always the case. Imagine that three voters, L, M, and R, are choosing between seven candidates. The preferences of the voters are given in the following table. Voter M, for example, likes Grumpy the best and Doc the least.

Preferences for President of Voters L, M, R			
	Voter L	Voter M	Voter R
1st Choice	Happy	Grumpy	Dopey
2nd Choice	Sneezy	Dopey	Happy
3rd Choice	Grumpy	Happy	Sleepy
4th Choice	Dopey	Bashful	Sneezy
5th Choice	Doc	Sleepy	Grumpy
6th Choice	Bashful	Sneezy	Doc
7th Choice	Sleepy	Doc	Bashful

a. Imagine that we vote according to a given agenda starting with Happy vs. Dopey. Who wins? We will help you with this one.

Voter L ranks Happy above Dopey, so voter L will vote for Happy. Voter M prefers Dopey to Happy, so voter M will vote for Dopey. Voter R ranks Dopey above Happy so voter R will vote for Dopey. So _____ wins.

b. Now take the winner from part a and match him against Grumpy. Who wins?

c. Now take the winner from part b and match him against Sneezy. Who wins?

d. Now take the winner from part c and match him against Sleepy. Who wins?

e. Now take the winner from part d and match him against Bashful. Who wins?

f. Finally, take the winner from part e and match him against Doc. Who wins?

g. We have now run through the entire agenda so the winner from part f is the final winner. Here is the point. Look carefully at the preferences of the three voters. Compare the preferences of each voter for Happy (or Grumpy or Dopey) with the final winner. Fill in the blank: Majority rule has led to an outcome that _____ regards as worse than some other possible outcome. The answer to this question should shock you.

This question is drawn from the classic and highly recommended introduction to game theory, *Thinking Strategically* by Avinash K. Dixit and Barry J. Nalebuff (New York: W.W. Norton, 1993).

6. In the 1998 Minnesota gubernatorial election, there were three main candidates: Norm Coleman (the Republican), Jesse "The Body" Ventura (an Independent), and Hubert Humphrey (the Democrat). Although we can't know for certain, the voters probably ranked the candidates in a way similar to that found in the table below. The table tells us, for example, that 35% of the voters ranked Coleman first, Humphrey second, and Ventura third; and 20% of the voters ranked Ventura first, Coleman second, and Humphrey third; and so forth.

Minnesota Gubernatorial Election, 1998				
Rank	35%	28%	20%	17%
1	Coleman	Humphrey	Ventura	Ventura
2	Humphrey	Coleman	Coleman	Humphrey
3	Ventura	Ventura	Humphrey	Coleman

a. Suppose the election is by plurality rule, which means that the candidate with the most first place votes wins the election. Who wins in this case?

b. In Challenge question 4, you were introduced to the Marquis de Condorcet. Today, voting theorists call a candidate a Condorcet *winner* if he or she can beat every other candidate in a series of 1:1 or *"face-off"* elections. Question 4 showed you that in some cases, there is no Condorcet winner. What about in the gubernatorial election of 1998?

c. A Condorcet winner beats every other candidate in a face-off. A Condorcet loser loses to every other candidate in a face-off. Was there a Condorcet loser in the 1998 Minnesota gubernatorial election (given the preferences we have estimated)?

Jesse "The Body" Ventura. Who are you calling a loser?

20

Economics, Ethics, and Public Policy

Is it okay to export pollution from rich to poor countries? Larry Summers said not only that it was okay when he was chief economist at the World Bank, but also that exporting pollution should be encouraged. Summers, if you don't already recognize the name, is one of the best economists of his generation, and a former president of Harvard, secretary of the Treasury, and lead advisor to President Obama. In a memo to some of his colleagues, Summers wrote:

> Just between you and me, shouldn't the World Bank be encouraging *more* migration of the dirty industries to the LDCs [Less Developed Countries]? . . .

> The measurements of the costs of health impairing pollution depend on the foregone earnings from increased morbidity and mortality. From this point of view a given amount of health impairing pollution should be done in the country with the lowest cost, which will be the country with the lowest wages. I think the economic logic behind dumping a load of toxic waste in the lowest wage country is impeccable and we should face up to that.*

Unfortunately for Summers, his memo didn't remain "just between you and me." When it was leaked to the press, there was a firestorm of controversy, not just against Summers but against economics and the type of "impeccable" economic reasoning that Summers found convincing.

If you found Larry Summers's memo disturbing, what about some of the ideas of Nobel Prize–winning economist Gary Becker? Becker says that we should legalize the trade in human kidneys. In fact, in a survey, Robert Whaples found that 70% of the economists he surveyed (128 members of the American

---

* The Summers memo can be widely found online.

Kidney for sale! Kidney for sale!

OWEN FRANKEN/CORBIS

Economic Association) agreed or strongly agreed with this idea.[1] Right now more than 75,000 Americans are waiting for kidney transplants. Many of them will die; others will undergo painful and exhausting dialysis for three days a week, four hours a day. The hospital waiting lists run for five years or more to get a kidney from a willing donor. In case you didn't know, the law won't allow kidneys to be bought and sold, so at a price of zero we have a severe kidney shortage (see Chapter 8 for a discussion of how price controls work).

Becker says that to alleviate the shortage, we should allow people to sell their kidneys (you only need one of the two you have). Many citizens of poorer countries would be willing to sell their kidneys for a few thousand dollars or less; in fact, some of these people are selling their kidneys on the black market right now.

Thus, we have two outstanding economists: one of whom says we should export pollution *to* poor countries, while the other says we should import kidneys *from* poor countries. No doubt, these two economists would probably also agree with each other!

Positive economics is describing, explaining, or predicting economic events.

Normative economics is recommendations or arguments about what economic policy should be.

Economists sometimes draw a distinction between positive economics and normative economics. **Positive economics** is about describing, explaining, or predicting economic events. For instance, if a quota restricts imports of sugar, the price of sugar will increase and people will buy less sugar. That's true whether or not we think that sugar is good for people. **Normative economics** is about making recommendations on what economic policy should be. Is a sugar quota a good policy? That depends on what we think is good and who we think counts most when we measure benefits and costs.

Not all of this chapter is economics—much of it touches on ethics and morals—but it is still important material for understanding economics as a broader approach to the world. First, economics has limitations and you need to know what they are. It helps to know which ethical values are left out of economic theory. Second, sometimes you will hear bad or misleading arguments against economics, and you need to know those, too, and where they fall short.

We warn you, however, that in this chapter our primary goal is to raise questions rather than provide answers. And, we try not to present our own normative claims. Instead, we consider the normative claims made by other people, especially critics of economics, and how they intersect with the positive economics that you have learned already.

The Case for Exporting Pollution and Importing Kidneys

The case for exporting pollution and importing kidneys is actually a familiar one: Trade makes people better off. One person wants the kidney more than the money; the other wants the money more than the kidney. Both people can be made better off by trade.

Similarly, it's not surprising that the rich are willing to pay the poor to take some of their pollution. On the margin, the rich value health more than money and the poor value money more than health, so both can be made better off by trade.

What's wrong with these trades? Plenty, according to many people who argue that economic reasoning ignores important values. Economists, it has been said, know the price of everything and the value of nothing.

Some of the objections to standard economic reasoning that we will examine are:

1. The problem of exploitation
2. Meddlesome preferences
3. Fair and equal treatment
4. Cultural goods and paternalism
5. Poverty, inequality, and the distribution of income
6. Who counts? Should some count for more?

Let's consider each in turn. You can think of these as the major reasons why not everyone thinks that voluntary exchanges are, in every case, a good idea.

Exploitation

Is the seller of a kidney being exploited? To focus on the difficult issues, let's assume that the seller is of good mind and fully informed about all the risks of donating a kidney. Even in this situation, many people argue that someone selling a kidney is being exploited. Dr. Francis Delmonico, a transplant surgeon and prominent opponent of kidney sales, argues that "payments eventually result in the exploitation of the individual. It's the poor person who sells."[2]

Delmonico is correct that a poor person is more likely to sell a kidney than a rich person. But does this mean that the poor person who sells a kidney is being exploited? Let's consider three cases.

> Case 1: Alex buys a kidney from Ajay.

> Case 2: Alex pays Ajay to clean his house.

> Case 3: George Mason University pays Alex to grade exams.

In all three cases, the seller would not sell if he were wealthier. So are the sellers (Ajay in the first two cases and Alex in the third) being exploited? We may feel that there is something different about selling a kidney, but it's difficult to see the dividing line that separates exploitation from exchange. Many people in rich and poor countries alike take jobs that involve significant risks. The yearly mortality rate for commercial fishermen in Alaska, for example, is seven times higher than the mortality rate for donating a kidney—so why is donating a kidney different than fishing in Alaska?[3]

One response is that for a poor person the money is exploitative because the circumstances of a poor person give them little choice but to sell things they would rather keep. But consider which of the three following cases is most exploitive:

> Case 1: Someone asks you to donate a kidney but offers you nothing in return.

> Case 2: Someone offers you $5,000 to donate a kidney.

> Case 3: Someone offers you $500,000 to donate a kidney.

Few people would say that case 1 involves exploitation. But what about case 2 and case 3? If case 2 is exploitative, then case 3 must be even more exploitative—after all, the temptation to sell is many times greater. In fact, many more people, including a great many people in rich countries, would accept an offer of $500,000 to sell one of their kidneys. But it seems odd to say that case 3 is the *most* exploitative case. The usual story is that buyers exploit sellers by offering them too little, not too much! But if bigger offers are less exploitive, then case 2 can't be exploitative either because case 2 is case 1 plus some money and how can offering someone more be a way to exploit them?

If someone offered you $500,000 to sell your kidney, would you feel exploited? Probably not. After all, you could always say no. But if case 3 doesn't exploit *you*, it's hard to see how case 2 exploits Ajay. Maybe Ajay needs the money more than you but imagine, for example, that 10% of the people in India would accept $5,000 for a kidney and 12% of people in the United States would accept $500,000 for a kidney. Does this make the larger offer more exploitive?

Keep in mind that everyone agrees that abject poverty is itself a problem. Overall, it would be better if people had access to clean water, good health care, and more wealth. The issue is whether it's wrong to offer to buy things from the poor just because they are poor. We will be returning to the issue of poverty and the distribution of income further below.

One more point: We assumed for the sake of argument that the seller of the kidney was of good mind and understood all the risks. One possible response is to say that no one ever understands the risks well enough to make trades like this. If that is the case, however, then we ought to ban gifts of kidneys as well as sales. In fact, thousands of people voluntarily give one of their kidneys away every year and we generally regard such people as heroes. But we don't allow anyone to buy or sell a kidney, despite the fact that doing so could save many thousands of lives.

Meddlesome Preferences

Even if exploitation isn't an issue, many people have a gut feeling that trading kidneys for money is just wrong. How much should this gut feeling count when thinking about justice?

Consider this: Is it okay to eat a horse? Not in California. Millions of Californians voted for a law that says, "No restaurant, cafe, or other public eating place may offer horsemeat for human consumption." The market in horsemeat is open, however, in Europe and Japan where you'll find horse on the menu at many restaurants. In Japan, it's even common to find raw horsemeat for sale, as a kind of sushi. The National Horse Protection League doesn't want anyone eating horses—especially foreigners—so it took out full-page ads in the *New York Times* to lobby for a ban on the export of horses to save them from a "brutal fate designed to feed foreign coffers."

In America the horse is, so to speak, a sacred cow (unlike in India where the cow is a sacred cow). So should horsemeat be banned? And if horsemeat is banned because people don't like the idea of someone eating horses, should kidney sales be banned because some people don't like the idea of someone trading kidneys? And what about homosexuality, interracial dating, or various religious practices that do not meet with anything close to universal approval? Often these practices offend someone, so how much should these meddlesome preferences count?

Preferences over what other people do, even when those other people don't interfere in any direct way with what you do, are sometimes called meddlesome preferences. It's often difficult to resolve meddlesome preferences with other values that are considered important, such as liberty, rights, or religious freedom. We, Alex and Tyler, don't usually put much normative weight on meddlesome preferences (we think that "live and let live" should be more popular), but that's one of our value judgments, not anything intrinsic to being economists.

Fair and Equal Treatment

The notion of fair and equal treatment also can run up against the value of trade and efficiency. Consider some of the programs to make mass transit accessible to disabled passengers. In New York City, it has long been the case that buses are capable of accepting passengers in wheelchairs. In essence, the bus "kneels down" until the wheelchair can board and then the bus elevates again.

Equipping buses in this fashion was very costly. A study commissioned by Ed Koch, the mayor of New York City at the time of bus conversion, estimated that it would have been cheaper for each wheelchair user or severely handicapped person to take a taxi than refit all buses. Not only would it have cost less, but it would have been more convenient, as well. But would that have been the right thing to do? On one side of the equation stands the virtue of efficiency. Taxpayers would have saved money and disabled people, if they took taxis, would have had easier and more luxurious transport options. But defenders of the bus investments claimed that the principle of "equal treatment" was more important than buying each disabled person free taxi trips for life. Even if the taxpayers and disabled people both agreed that taxis were preferable, the critics were saying that more is involved in mass transit than getting a person from place A to place B. Mass transit was, in part, about the sacred value of equal treatment and not making people feel different or disadvantaged.

Economics cannot answer questions about the sacred and the profane, but these issues underlie many arguments about public policy. When thinking about tradeoffs, we need to be aware of the resulting tensions and subtleties, many of which are ethical in nature.

The French government sees a dark side to American culture.

Cultural Goods and Paternalism

A closely related issue is whether governments should support some goods even when the public isn't willing to pay for them. The French government, for example, spends 1.5% of French GDP a year subsidizing culture and related "higher values."[4] The implicit judgment is that culture is "more valuable" than what people will otherwise spend their money on, and that government is a better judge of "what is best" than are private individuals, at least for these particular sums of money.

The French also place a minimum quota on how many French-language movies must be shown on TV, specifically 40% of the total. For a while, there was even a French ministry of rock 'n' roll, to support the production of French-language popular music. Again, the goal has been to give people something different from what they otherwise would have chosen.

The government tried to give the French people French rock 'n' roll instead of the American and British rock 'n' roll that the French people were buying. Supporters of the policy say that subsidizing French culture is valuable in its own right, and that the aesthetic judgments of the marketplace should not be the final ones.

The pragmatic criticism of French policy is to argue that these subsidy schemes tend to be counterproductive and wasteful. Maybe French movies would be more successful if they had to appeal to French consumers rather than to the French bureaucrats who hand out the subsidies. The more philosophical criticism is that people should be allowed to spend their money as they choose. In the latter view, freely chosen values have a moral worth of their own that is to be respected.

Of course, it is not just the French who give special support to some cultures and not others. The American government exempts the Amish, a small religious community living predominantly in Ohio, Pennsylvania, and Indiana, from many forms of taxation and compulsory education. America's approximately 300 Indian reservations have a special legal status, in part because the U.S. government takes special care to preserve those cultures. The U.S. federal government also spends money supporting the arts (though the American government spends less than does the French government), in part, because some people want to encourage a higher quality of art than they think will arise through the marketplace and voluntary charity. In fiscal 2010, the U.S. budget for the National Endowment for the Arts was just over $167 million.

Poverty, Inequality, and the Distribution of Income

Perhaps the problem with kidney sales and exporting pollution to poor countries is not trade per se, but the poverty and inequality that make the trade happen. We might accept that when a poor person sells a kidney to a rich person, both are made better off, but still rue the fact that the poor person is poor.

But what is a just distribution of income? How much is owed to the poor? How much is owed to the rich? Questions like these are at the heart of many debates about foreign aid, trade, taxation, health care, and immigration, to name just a few controversial areas.

Many economists have turned to moral philosophy to seek support for their normative policy judgments, and three views have proven especially influential: John Rawls's maximin principle, utilitarianism, and Robert Nozick's entitlement theory of justice. These three views have very different implications for how we, as citizens, should judge the distribution of income and the status of voluntary marketplace transactions.

Rawls's Maximin Principle

Rawls's maximin principle says that justice requires maximizing the benefits going to society's most disadvantaged group.

John Rawls's *A Theory of Justice*, published in 1971, argued that questions of income and wealth distribution are keys for evaluating social policy. Rawls, a Harvard philosopher, laid out the **maximin principle**, namely that a government should (without violating people's basic rights) maximize the benefits going to society's most disadvantaged group. The notion of "maximizing the minimum" led to the phrase "maximin." For Rawls, doing well by the worst-off group is more important than improving the lot of better-off groups. Rawls deliberately rejects the economist's idea of tradeoffs, instead concluding that the worst-off group should be the clear first priority.

Society	Red	Blue	Green	Average Income
A	100	100	100	100
B	150	100	50	100
C	600	600	99	433
D	1096	102	101	433

Rawls's argument for making the worst-off the first priority is that if no one knew what position they held in society, that is, if people were behind a "veil of ignorance," then they would want a rule that maximized the position of the worst-off, just in case they turned out to be the worst-off! In economic terms, Rawls believed that people were extremely risk-averse.

To see how maximin works in practice, consider a simple example with three people, Red, Blue, and Green.

Now let's compare Society A where Red, Blue, and Green have equal incomes of 100 to Society B where the respective incomes are 150, 100, and 50. Rawls's maximin principle implies that Society A is better or more just than Society B because the worst-off person in Society B, Green, has more income in Society A. Notice that the only difference between Society A and B is that income is more equally distributed in A than in B; average income is identical so it doesn't seem unreasonable to prefer Society A to Society B.

But now let's compare Society A with Society C. In Society C, Red and Blue are much better off than in Society A and Green is slightly worse off. Notice that average income in Society C is more than four times as high as in Society A. Which society would you rank as the better society? Which society does maximin rank more highly? The maximin principle says that Society A is better than Society C because the worst-off person in Society C, Green, is better off in Society A. The maximin principle says that the extra income of Red and Blue counts for nothing; only the income of the least well-off person counts.

It's sometimes said that the maximin principle favors societies with more equal division of incomes but that is not necessarily true. Let's compare Society A with Society D. Even though income is perfectly egalitarian in Society A, the maximin principle says that Society D is better because, once again, the income of the least well-off person is higher. The maximin principle even prefers Society D to Society C, even though Society C has a more equal division of the same average income.

The maximin principle is influential among philosophers but less so among economists who, as you know, tend to think in terms of tradeoffs between values. A little bit less income for the worst-off might be acceptable if it comes with a big enough gain to others. Lower average income might be acceptable if income is a little bit more equally divided, and so forth.

Utilitarianism

Under **utilitarianism**, we try to implement the outcome that brings the greatest sum of utility or "happiness" to society. The best known utilitarian philosopher today is Peter Singer, whom you also may know as an advocate of animal rights.

Utilitarianism is the idea that the best society maximizes the sum of utility.

When it comes to redistribution, a utilitarian approach tries to determine which people have the greatest need for some additional income. For instance, an extra dollar for a poor person may go toward a doctor's visit, but an extra dollar for a rich person may just go toward buying an extra silk tie. The poor person probably gets greater happiness from the extra dollar. The utilitarian is likely to suggest that some amount of money be redistributed from rich people toward poor people. Unlike Rawls, however, utilitarians are not always trying to make the poorest people as well off as possible. Utilitarians advocate redistributing income only up to the point where the marginal change in utility created from the redistribution is positive. They try to maximize the total sum of utility, not the utility of the worst-off person. So, in principle, utilitarianism (unlike maximin) allows the poor to undergo some extra suffering, provided that suffering is outweighed by enough gains elsewhere in the economy.

What might limit the amount of wealth a utilitarian would redistribute from rich to poor? Incentives! Taking money away from richer people decreases their incentive to earn, so more redistribution could reduce overall wealth by enough to reduce total utility. A utilitarian recipe therefore might involve only a modest amount of redistribution, especially if people are very responsive to incentives. Utilitarianism will also take into account the incentive effects of redistribution on the poor. Giving dollars to poor people is not always the best way to improve their welfare. As Milton Friedman once said, if you pay people to be poor, you're going to have a lot of poor people.

Some rich people have a very high marginal utility of wealth. Should we give them more?

Notice the usual assumption in economics is that a dollar gain is a dollar gain no matter who gets the dollar, so utilitarianism needs to make assumptions that extend beyond those of economic theory. Economic theory does not assume that a dollar is worth more to a poor man than to a rich man and standard economic tools don't give us any easy way to measure happiness or utility. In fact, many economists believe that comparing the happiness of two people is not very scientific. We might think that the poor person gets more happiness than the rich person from an extra dollar of wealth, but perhaps the poor person is a monk who neither needs nor wants money, while the rich person really does desire another silk tie. Maybe the rich person is rich precisely because he loves money and worked very hard to get it. We aren't saying that this is the case; we are only pointing out that there is no natural unit of measurement of utility and human beings have very different preferences.

Most economists do believe in a safety net and a welfare state to take care of the poor people in a wealthy society. But this belief doesn't have to be rooted in any very strict comparison of utilities between rich people and poor people. Economists frequently portray the social safety net as a way of obtaining insurance against bankruptcy, major health-care problems, and other bad outcomes. If you think that insurance has value, and that private markets might not provide this insurance on their own (this claim has been debated), that provides some case for a social safety net. Utilitarians go further, however, and try to offer very specific recipes for just how much money should be transferred from the rich to the poor.

Robert Nozick's Entitlement Theory

Whether we accept Rawls's maximin principle or prefer utilitarianism or choose almost any other theory of justice, one thing is clear. There is no guarantee that the distribution of income generated by market forces will be anything like what these theories describe as the just distribution. Most theories of justice, therefore, will call for some amount of taxation and redistribution, using the force of government. One of the few exceptions is Robert **Nozick's entitlement theory of justice**, which is also known as a libertarian theory of justice.

Robert Nozick, another Harvard philosopher, laid out a moral system very different from that of Rawls. Nozick was far more sympathetic to the market economy than was Rawls, and he outlined a defense of the market in a 1974 book called *Anarchy, State, and Utopia*. Nozick argued that the pattern of the distribution of income was irrelevant. What mattered was whether income differences were *justly acquired* and thus Nozick focused on the process by which income is distributed.

Nozick argued that if John wishes to trade with Mary, that decision should be up to John and Mary alone, provided they do not infringe on the rights of others. In the words of Nozick, all capitalist acts between consenting adults should be allowed. Nozick admitted and indeed emphasized that such trades, performed on a cumulative basis, would result in different and indeed unequal outcomes and opportunities for people, but he saw nothing wrong with those inequalities. Nozick went further and positively endorsed those inequalities that resulted from freely chosen market transactions, devoid of coercive force or fraud.

Nozick offered a classic rebuttal to Rawlsian and other theories of justice. Nozick said let's imagine that one day we create a world in which the distribution of wealth is exactly as described by some theory of justice. Let's say the distribution of wealth is exactly like that described by *your* theory of justice. Now, Nozick said, imagine someone like J. K. Rowling, the author of the Harry Potter book series (Nozick actually used the example of Wilt Chamberlain, the basketball star of the 1960s and 1970s).

Rowling, let us say, writes another Harry Potter book and she offers to sell a copy to anyone who is willing to buy. Of course, many people are very willing to buy Rowling's book, and so person by person money is transferred from book buyers to Rowling. Rowling becomes very rich so at the end of the day (she is the first author ever to become a billionaire by writing), the distribution of wealth will be very different than at the beginning of the day, when by assumption all was just. Yet how can the new distribution of wealth, the one with a very rich J. K. Rowling, be unjust? No one's rights were violated in the process and indeed everyone, including both the fans and Rowling, was made better off every time Rowling sold a book. All that has happened has been voluntary, peaceful trade. A just and rightful trade, Nozick's theory would imply. So why should any outsider disapprove of the resulting pattern of wealth?

Note that this example is not fanciful: When she wrote her first book, J. K. Rowling was an unemployed single mother living on welfare. Today her income is thousands of times higher than that of her average fan.

Nozick's example is a direct criticism of the view that equality of outcome is important. Nozick argues that what we should care about is the justness of the process that leads to differences in wealth—theft is bad and should be condemned and rectified, but voluntary, peaceful trade should not be condemned even when it leads to large differences in wealth.

In the libertarian account, what is just is to respect an individual's rights. One way to think of libertarian rights is that they are "side constraints" on possible government actions. The libertarian view corresponds to some common

Nozick's entitlement theory of justice says that the distribution of income in a society is just if property is justly acquired and voluntarily exchanged.

intuitions. For instance, as we discussed above, many people in the world need kidneys; otherwise, they will die or require dialysis. Thus, many people need a kidney and you have two good ones. But you need only one kidney to live and be healthy. Is it okay to take a kidney from you, against your will? Is it okay to draft your kidney for the greater good? Is it okay to redistribute kidneys?

If you believe the answer to that question is no, you have taken one big step toward the libertarian theory of justice. If you want to think about the next step, a libertarian would ask, if it's not okay to draft your kidney, why is it okay to draft your whole body? And if redistributing kidneys is wrong, isn't redistributing income wrong for similar reasons?

Philosophers continue to debate the relevance of the perspectives of Rawls, utilitarianism, and Nozick, among other ideas. One contribution of the economist is simply to insist that people should be more focused on producing rather than redistributing wealth. Moral philosophers sometimes write as if all the goods were just sitting there on the table ready to be divvied up, but economists know this isn't true. Economists usually stress the importance of producing the wealth in the first place.

Who Counts? Immigration

KAREN KASMAUSKI/CORBIS

Does his well-being count?

When economists evaluate a public policy like trade or immigration, they tend to count the benefits and costs to all individuals equally regardless of where they live. But this isn't always how politics works. Usually, national governments weigh the preferences of their citizens more heavily, usually much more heavily, than they do the preferences of foreigners.

Immigration is the most salient current issue where the preferences of citizens are counted for much more than the preferences of foreigners. Some people argue that immigration hurts U.S. citizens because low-skilled immigrants reduce the wages of low-skilled Americans. Other people argue that immigrants add to the U.S. economy through their entrepreneurship and their willingness to work at very tough jobs.

On net, careful studies indicate that immigration has some positive and some negative effects, but the U.S. economy is so large that overall immigration is not such a big issue—economists who support and oppose immigration agree on this conclusion. People debate the pluses and minuses of additional immigration, and often this is an emotional issue; but again, no matter what your view, the net cost or benefit is likely small relative to the entire U.S. economy.[5]

So let's assume that immigration is either a small benefit or a small cost to U.S. citizens. Everyone agrees, however, that immigration is a huge benefit to the immigrants. The typical Mexican immigrant today comes from a small village in Chiapas, Guerrero, Oaxaca, or some other very poor part of Mexico. People in those villages usually earn no more than a dollar or two a day. If they come to the United States, they can earn $10 an hour or more. Of course, they send a lot of this money home to their families. Remittances, most of which come from the United States, are Mexico's number one leading "import" industry. Remittances often make the difference between hunger and plenty, or between a collapsing village and a revitalized one. Immigration matters a great deal to the approximately 400,000 Mexicans who cross the border every year and to those who would come if it were easier to do so.

So, if the United States is making decisions about its immigration policy, how much should it weigh the benefits accruing to Mexicans from immigration? We're talking not just about the Mexicans who arrive in this country (some of whom may become citizens), but also the Mexicans back home receiving the remittances. Economics tends to be cosmopolitan in its implications as it treats all people equally, no matter where those people live. If the gains to foreigners are counted as much as the gains to nationals, then Mexican immigration into the United States will look especially beneficial. But again, not everyone buys the presumption that foreigners should count for as much as the welfare of U.S. citizens. A presidential candidate who held that assumption as a campaign platform would be unlikely to win election.

Foreign aid is another policy issue where we must ask whether our government should be looking after American citizens or people in other countries. In reality, the amount of money the American government spends on foreign aid is very low. The exact sum is difficult to determine, because in the government budget, "foreign aid" and "military assistance" are not completely distinct categories. But, by standard accounts, formal measures of foreign aid amount to less than $30 billion per year, or less than 1% of the federal budget.[6] Of course, simply sending money to other countries does not always make them better off; often foreign aid is captured by corrupt elites or used for bad ends. Still you could say the same about some of the money the U.S. government spends at home! The point is this: It remains within the voters' power to have the federal government spend less money on American citizens and more money on needy people overseas. Why not just drop some dollar bills from a helicopter, flying over a poor country?

Whether we should do this will depend, in part, on your views as to "who counts?" and "how much?"

Economic Ethics

When economists recommend ideas like exporting pollution or paying for kidneys, they are often said to be ignoring ethics. Economists sometimes agree, perhaps with a bit of pride! But a closer look shows that this is not true. Even though the predictions of economics are independent of any ethical theory, there are ethical ideas behind normative economic reasoning. An economist who rejects the idea of exploitation in kidney purchases, for example, is treating the seller of kidneys with respect—as a person who is capable of choosing for him or herself even in difficult circumstances.

Similarly, economists don't second-guess people's preferences very much. If people like wrestling more than opera, then so be it; the economist, acting as economist, does not regard some preferences as better than others. In normative terms, economists once again tend to respect people's choices.

Respect for people's preferences and choices leads naturally to respect for trade—a key action that people take to make themselves better off. As we saw in Chapter 10 on externalities, economists recognize that trade can sometimes make the people who do not trade worse off. Nonetheless, the basic idea that people can make decisions and know their own preferences leads economists to be very sympathetic to the idea of noncoercive trade.

Economists also tend to treat all market demands equally, no matter which person they come from. Whether you are white or black, male or female, quiet or talkative, American or Belgian, your consumer and producer surplus count for the same in an economic assessment of a policy choice.

None of this is to say that economists are always right in their ethical assumptions. As we warned you in the beginning, this chapter has more questions than answers. But the ethical views of economists—respect for individual choice and preference, support for voluntary trade, and equality of treatment—are all ethical views with considerable grounding and support in a wide variety of ethical and religious traditions. Perhaps you have heard that Thomas Carlyle, the Victorian-era writer, called economics the "dismal science." What you may not know is that Carlyle was a defender of slavery and he was attacking the ethical views of economics. Economists like John Stuart Mill believed that all people were able to make rational choices; that trade, not coercion, was the best route to wealth; and that everyone should be counted equally, regardless of race. As a result, Mill and the laissez-faire economists of the nineteenth century opposed slavery, believing that everyone was entitled to liberty. It was these ethical views that Carlyle found dismal.[*] We beg to differ.

☐ Takeaway

Economics stresses the core idea of gains from trade. Yet in many circumstances, not everyone approves of gains from trade, mostly for ethical reasons. Not everyone thinks that kidneys should be bought and sold and not everyone thinks that pollution should be exported to poor countries. Intuitions about fairness, equitable treatment, distribution, and other matters often clash with the economic notion of increasing gains from trade.

We respect the distinction between positive economics—predicting what will happen—and normative judgments—what should be done. So we haven't tried to answer these ethical dilemmas or give you our sense of the best possible ethical theory. But we do know that you need to understand something about these debates, at least if you wish to make sense of the debates over economics in the real world. Not everyone respects the economic idea of gains from trade and we've tried to give you some idea why.

[*] The Secret History of the Dismal Science is discussed in an excellent article of that title by David M. Levy and Sandra J. Peart available online at http://www.econlib.org/library/Columns/LevyPeartdismal.html#.

☐ CHAPTER REVIEW

KEY CONCEPTS

Positive economics, p. 386

Normative economics, p. 386

Rawls's maximin principle, p. 390

Utilitarianism, p. 391

Nozick's entitlement theory of justice, p. 393

FACTS AND TOOLS

1. a. In this chapter, we never actually defined "exploitation." What is one dictionary definition of the word?

b. Decide whether the six cases of alleged exploitation we discussed earlier in the chapter fit your dictionary's definition. Yes, this will involve quite a bit of personal judgment, as will most of this chapter's questions.

  c. In your opinion, does the dictionary definition go too far or not far enough when it comes to labeling some voluntary exchanges as exploitation?

2. Of the three ethical theories we discuss (Rawlsian, utilitarian, and Nozickian), which two are most different from the third? In what way are the two different from the third?

3. One of Nozick's arguments against utilitarianism was the "utility monster": a person who *always* gets enormous happiness from every extra dollar, more happiness than anyone else in society. If such a person existed, the utilitarian solution would be to give all the wealth in society to Nozick's utility monster; any other income distribution would needlessly waste resources. This possibility was appalling to Nozick. Nozick's argument is intentionally extreme, but we can use it as a metaphor to think about the ethics of real-world income redistribution.

  a. Do you know any utility monsters in your own life: people who get absurdly large amounts of happiness from buying things, owning things, going places? Perhaps a family member or someone from high school?

  b. Do you know any utility misers? That would be people who don't get much pleasure from anything they do or anything they own, even though they probably have enough money to buy what they want.

  c. In your view, would it be ethical for the government to distribute income from real-world utility misers to real-world utility monsters? Why or why not?

4. a. Just thinking about yourself, if you did not know in advance whether you were a Red, Blue, or Green person, would you rather live in society A, B, C, or D that are discussed in the Rawl's section of the chapter? Why?

  b. Which society would you like least? Why?

5. Rawlsians support government income redistribution to the worst-off members of "society." If "society" means the whole world, how much redistribution might be involved? In other words, what fraction of people in the rich countries might have to give most of their income to people in the poorest countries?

Keep in mind that the poorest Americans have clean water, guaranteed food stamps, and free health care, while billions of people around the world lack such guarantees.

6. Would a "global utilitarian" (someone who values the utility of everyone in the world equally, without giving more weight to people in their own country) who lives in America want more immigrants from poor countries or more immigrants from rich countries? Why?

THINKING AND PROBLEM SOLVING

1. To a Rawlsian, would the world be better off without the Harry Potter novels and one additional billionaire?

2. Some people say that the right to equal treatment has no price. But it seems that most people don't really believe that: Those are just polite words that we tell one another. Consider the following cases:

  a. What if it costs $10 million per kneeling bus?

  b. What if it costs $10,000 to hire translators to translate ballots into a rare language spoken by fewer than 10 voters?

  c. What if it costs the lives of dozens of police officers to ensure the right of a persecuted minority to vote?

  d. At these prices, is the right to equal treatment too expensive for society to buy it? In each case, describe what you think the exact price cutoff should be (in dollars or lives), and briefly explain how you came to that decision. Why not twice the price? Why not half?

3. The line between "having a meddlesome preference" and "recognizing an externality" is not always clear. Both are ways of saying, "What you're doing bothers me." As we used it in this chapter, a "meddlesome preference" is something that reasonable people should just not worry about so much. By contrast, "recognizing an externality" is a way of advancing the subject for public discussion and perhaps even for a vote. In the town you grew up in, which of the following issues were considered things that should be left to individuals and which were things that should be put up for a vote? Is there a good way of distinguishing between the two?

  a. The amount of pollution emitted by a local factory

b. How much noise would be allowed after 11 PM

c. Whether siblings should be allowed to marry, even if it is consensual

d. Where liquor stores could be located

e. How people should dress in public

f. How many children someone should have

4. Let's see how a utilitarian dictator would arrange things for Adam, Eve, and Lilith. One heroic assumption that utilitarians make is that you can actually compare happiness and misery across different people: In reality, brain scans are making this easier to do but it's still a lot of guesswork. Let's suppose that this utilitarian dictator has 8 apples to distribute: The table below shows the utility that each person receives from their first apple (a lot), but extra apples give less extra happiness (apples give diminishing marginal utility, in economic jargon).

Utility per Apple	Adam	Eve	Lilith
1st	1,000	600	1,200
2nd	140	500	200
3rd	20	400	100
4th	1	300	50

a. So, if the dictator wants to maximize the sum of Adam, Eve, and Lilith's utility, how many apples does each person get?

b. If instead, Lilith received 2,000 units of utility from the first apple, how would this change the optimal utilitarian distribution?

5. a. The "trolley problem" is a famous ethical puzzle created by Philippa Foot: You are the conductor of a trolley (or subway or streetcar or train) that is heading out of control down a track. Five innocent people are tied to the track ahead of you: If you run over them, they will surely die. If you push a lever on your trolley, it will shift onto another track, where one unfortunate person is tied up. Either you *let* five people die or you *choose* to kill one person: Those are your only choices. Which will you choose and why? Which ethical view from this chapter best fits your reasoning? (If you Google "trolley problem," you will find many other interesting ethical dilemmas to debate with your friends.)

b. Another ethical dilemma sounds quite different: You are a medical doctor trying to find five organ donors to save the lives of five innocent people. A new patient comes in for a checkup, and you find that this patient has five organs exactly compatible with the five innocent people. Do you kill the one innocent patient to save the lives of five innocents? Suppose you will never get caught: Perhaps you live in a country where people don't care about such things. Is this the same dilemma? Is it the same dilemma from a utilitarian perspective?

6. What do you think best describes the reason that trade in recreational drugs is illegal: fear of exploitation, meddlesome preferences, notions of fairness, paternalism, concerns about equality, or some other factor?

7. Based on the tools from this chapter, how could a person reasonably justify a ban on gambling?

8. Compare a Rawlsian view with a utilitarian view on the question of whether it should be legal to copy movies and music freely.

CHALLENGES

1. Should responsible adults be allowed to sell a kidney? Why or why not? If so, what restrictions would you place on such sales, if any?

2. a. In your view, when should governments enforce a "live and let live" rule: on issues that matter most to people (e.g., matters of life and death, matters of how much income to give to the government, matters of religion, matters of sexuality) or on the issues that matter least to people (e.g., what flavors of spices are permitted at the dinner table, what kind of clothing is acceptable in public)?

b. Europeans fought a lot of wars in the 1500s over the right to meddlesome preferences. Thinking back on your history courses, what preferences did Europeans want to meddle with?

c. What was the usual argument given in the 1500s for why it was right to meddle with other people's preferences?

3. Philosopher Alastair Norcross poses the following question. Suppose that 1 billion people are suffering from a moderately severe headache that will last a few hours. The only way to alleviate their headache is for one person to die a horrible death. Can the death of this one person ever be justified in a cost-benefit sense?

4. If the rich countries were able to send individual cash payments to people in poor countries, bypassing possibly corrupt governments, would you let rich countries pay people in poor countries to take their high-polluting factories? If so, how high would the annual payment have to be per family? If not, why not?

5. You would probably sacrifice yourself to save all of humanity, but you probably wouldn't sacrifice yourself to save the life of one random stranger. What number is your cutoff: How many lives would you have to save for you to voluntarily face sure death?

6. Some people feel inequality is justified if the people with unequal outcomes accepted risks voluntarily; it was simply the case that some won and some lost. Imagine two people, each spending $10,000 on lottery tickets, but only one of them wins. We end up with one poor person and one multimillionaire.

Is this inequality better or worse than if one person is born into a rich family and the other is born into a poor family? What exactly is the difference and why?

7. Sometimes poor countries have a lot of people; India has more than 1 billion residents. Indians are relatively poor, and we know that as families become wealthy, they tend to limit their number of children. So, a much wealthier India, over time, would probably have much fewer than 1 billion inhabitants. Would this make for a better India or a worse India? Although each Indian would have much more, there would be fewer Indians. As a result, is there any argument for keeping India poor, so as to have a higher number of people? If not, why not? In general, what can economics tell us about the ideal number of people in a society? Anything at all?

8. Let's say that Tom, who is 25 years old, wants to smoke a cigarette. Consider the following two situations.

   a. Tom is smoking. Suddenly, the government comes along and tells Tom that he cannot do this. The government claims that Tom is inflicting an "external cost" on other human beings. Is this a good policy or bad policy?

   b. Tom is smoking a cigarette at home with no one else around. Suddenly, the government comes along and tells Tom that he cannot do this. The government claims that Tom is inflicting an "external cost" on another human being. Tom asks who this might be? The government says that the 65-year-old Tom will be harmed by the smoking-today-Tom. The government claims that today-Tom isn't doing enough to look out for the well-being of future-Tom. Does this argument make any sense? Is it ethically correct? If so, can and should we trust our government to make these decisions for our future selves?

21

Managing Incentives

A good social system aligns self-interest with the social interest. A successful organization aligns self-interest with the organization's goals.

Organizations—businesses, governments, teams—whose members face incentives that conflict with its goals won't last very long. It's often not easy, however, to align incentives and goals. Incentives are powerful but they can misfire, which is why the topic of this chapter, incentive design, is important.

Incentives matter—this is one of the key lessons of this book—but getting the incentives right is not always easy. Managers of businesses and sports teams, voters, politicians, parents, all must think about and choose incentives. This chapter is all about getting the incentives right and what happens when we get the incentives wrong.

Lesson One: You Get What You Pay For

Every May, Chicago public school students take a standardized test. Students are used to being tested, graded, and rewarded accordingly, but beginning in May 1996, teachers and principals had a lot more than usual on the line: Schools with low scores would be closed, teachers reassigned, and principals fired. The idea, of course, was to give educators stronger incentives to work harder and better. If grading was good for the students, why not for the teachers?

Stronger incentives do give teachers and principals an incentive to put in extra hours and search for better teaching methods. But how else can teachers raise the grades of their students? Here's a hint: Some students also use this method. That's right—they cheat. Indeed, teachers can cheat a lot better than students because they know which answers are correct! Two economists who understand incentives, Brian Jacob and Steven Levitt (the latter of *Freakonomics* fame), started to look carefully at test data and asked: Would teachers really cheat to raise student grades?[1] Sure enough, Jacob and Levitt found odd patterns in the data—students who got easy answers wrong and difficult answers right, groups of students who had exactly the same right and wrong answers, and students who received high grades during a test year but low grades the year after. Most telling for an economist was that the indicators of cheating were much stronger after the penalty for low-performing schools went into effect than before!

Perhaps you think that teachers' cheating to raise student grades is a good idea! But it wasn't what the proponents of strong incentives for teachers had in mind. Not all teachers cheated, but cheating was surprisingly common. Jacob and Levitt estimated that cheating occurred in at least 4% to 5% of classrooms. Other researchers have found that after the introduction of strong incentives, a lot more students are declared learning disabled.[2] Why? Test scores of students called "learning disabled" are usually not counted when it comes to rewarding teachers and principals.

Does all this mean that strong incentives for teachers are a bad idea? Not necessarily. Students who learn more, earn more. If strong incentives for teachers do increase true scores, even by a small amount, maybe it's a good idea even if some of the better scores are due to cheating.[3]

A similar example of incentives for cheating comes from corporate finance. In the 1980s, chief executive officers (CEOs) were given much stronger incentives to increase their firm's stock price. Instead of being paid a straight salary, they were awarded stock options. These are complicated financial instruments, but what you need to know is that they pay off only if the stock rises above a certain price. As with strong incentives for teaching, strong incentives encouraged CEOs to work harder and smarter. It also encouraged them to cheat by manipulating earnings reports to make their firms appear more profitable than they really were. Enron and the other scandals of the 1990s and first decade of the 2000s were, in part, the result. Were strong incentives worth it? If the shareholders believed that on average the costs of cheating exceeded the benefits of encouraging harder work, they would offer their CEOs fewer options and other strong incentives. But so far most of these incentives have stayed in place, albeit with more monitoring of potentially bad behavior.

Shareholders, however, are not the only ones who can be harmed when a company like Enron or Lehman Brothers collapses, so their choice of CEO incentive scheme may not reflect everyone's interests and may not be best for society as a whole. (Recall our discussion of externalities in Chapter 10.) Incentive schemes, for example, that give executives big bonuses for very good performance but don't penalize them very much for very bad performance can encourage executives to take on too much risk. In part for this reason, investment banks such as Bear Stearns and Lehman Brothers took on lots of risk in mortgage securities, and when they collapsed, that helped lead to the financial crisis of 2008. Executive compensation, therefore, has become a subject of political controversy. We will return to executive compensation later on in this chapter.

When designing an incentive scheme, remember this: You get what you pay for. That sounds good but there is a problem. What if what you pay for is not exactly what you want? If you pay for higher test scores, you will get higher test scores. But test scores are an imperfect measure of what you really want—more productive teachers and more knowledgeable students. What you pay for is higher stock prices, but what you really want is a more profitable firm. Usually, stock prices reflect a firm's fundamental value, but even the market can be fooled sometimes!

The closer "what you pay for" is to "what you want," then the more you can rely on strong incentives. Careful design of an incentive scheme can narrow the gap between what you want and what you can pay for. After Jacob and Levitt published their results, the administrators of Chicago Public Schools, to their credit, fired some teachers, and instituted new procedures to make cheating more difficult. After the Enron scandal, investors demanded more independent financial audits. The stronger the incentives, the more it pays to invest in careful measurement and auditing, and vice versa.

If you can't bridge the gap between "what you pay for" and "what you want," then weak incentive schemes can be better than strong incentive schemes.

Prisons for Profit?

Should the management of prisons be contracted out to the private sector? The owners of a private firm have a strong incentive to cut costs and improve productivity because they get to keep the resulting profits. If a public prison cuts costs, there is more money in the public treasury but no one gets to buy a yacht, so the incentive to cut costs is much weaker.

In 1985, Kentucky became the first state to contract out a prison to a for-profit firm. Private prisons today hold about 120,000 prisoners in the United States, about 8% of all prisoners. Should efficient private prisons replace inefficient public prisons? Three economists—Oliver Hart, Andrei Shleifer, and Robert Vishny (HSV)—say no. HSV don't question that the profit motive gives private prisons stronger incentives than public prisons to cut costs—HSV say that's the problem! Suppose that we care about costs but we also care about prisoner rehabilitation, civil rights, and low levels of inmate and guard violence. What we pay for is cheap prisons, but what we want is cheap but high-quality prisons. If we can't measure and pay for quality, then strong incentives could encourage cost cutting at the expense of quality.

The principle is a general one, a strong-incentive scheme that incentivizes the wrong thing can be worse than a weak-incentive scheme. One car dealer in California advertises that its sales staff is not paid on commission.[4] Why would a store advertise that its sales staff do not have strong incentives to help you? The answer is clear to anyone who has tried to buy a car. High-pressure dealers who pounce on you the moment you enter the showroom and bombard you with high-pressure sales tactics ("I can get you 15% off the sticker, but you have to act NOW!") may sell cars to first-time buyers, but the strategy is too unpleasant to win many repeat customers. Car dealers who rely on repeat business usually prefer a low-pressure, informative sales staff.

Private prisons in the United States hold about 8% of all prisoners. England and Wales (9%) and Australia (17%) also have some private prisons.

COURTESY EVERETT COLLECTION

In theory, a car dealer could have strong incentives *and* repeat business by paying its sales staff based on their "nice" sales tactics, but in practice, it's too expensive to monitor how salespeople interact with clients. Cheating by the sales staff would be difficult to detect and thus would be common. Paying the sales staff a salary instead of a commission calms them down a bit. Of course, there is a price to be paid for weak incentives. Imagine that Joe's Honda pays its sales staff on commission, while Pete's Subaru pays its staff a straight salary. Which dealership do you expect to be open late at night and on Sundays?

What about prisons? Are HSV correct that weak-incentive public prisons are better than strong-incentive private prisons? Not necessarily. HSV assume that cutting quality is the way to cut cost. But sometimes higher quality is also a path to lower costs. Low levels of inmate and guard violence, for example, are likely to reduce costs. And respect for prisoner's civil rights? That can save on legal bills. When quality and cost-cutting go together, a private firm has a strong incentive to increase quality.

HSV may also underestimate how well quality can be measured. Measuring output pays off more when incentives are high. Unsurprisingly, therefore, private prison companies and government purchasers have made extensive efforts to measure the quality of private prisons.

Finally, don't forget that weak incentives reduce the incentive to cut costs but they don't increase the incentive to produce high quality! Public prisons might use their slack budget constraints to offer high-quality rehabilitation programs, or they might instead offer prison guards above-market wages. Which do you think is more likely?

Nevertheless, whether HSV are right or wrong about private prisons, their argument is clever. The usual argument against government bureaucracy is that without the profit incentive, public bureaucracies won't have an incentive to cut costs. HSV suggest this is exactly why public bureaucracies may sometimes be better than private firms.[5]

Piece Rates vs. Hourly Wages

A majority of workers are paid by the hour but a significant number are paid by the piece. An hourly wage pays workers for their inputs (of time); a **piece rate** pays workers directly for their output. Agricultural workers, for example, are often paid by the number of pieces of fruit or vegetable that they pick. Garment workers are often paid per item completed. Salespeople are often paid, in part, by the number of sales that they make. When should workers be paid by the hour and when should they be paid by the piece?

Piece rates increase the incentive to work hard and can work well when output is easy to measure so "what you pay for" is close to "what you want." Piece rates are common in agricultural work because it's easy to measure the number of apples picked and this is close to what the employer wants. Even in agricultural work, however, the employer wants not just apples but ripe and unbruised apples so piece rates usually require some form of quality control. Piece rates do not work well when quality is important but quality control is expensive.

In the early days of computing, IBM paid its programmers per line of code. Can you see the problem? When IBM paid by the line, IBM programmers produced lots of code, but in their rush to earn more money, the programmers

A **piece rate** is any payment system that pays workers directly for their output.

often wrote low-quality code. IBM's incentive scheme rewarded what was measurable—lines of code—at the expense of what IBM really wanted but what was difficult to measure, high-quality code. IBM quickly stopped paying its workers by the line and switched to hourly wages. Hourly wages reduced the incentive to work hard, but hourly wages also reduced the incentive to rush the work before it was ready.

The advantage of piece rates is that, if used properly, they can greatly increase productivity. The auto-glass installer Safelite Glass Corporation switched from an hourly wage system to a piece rate in 1994. Safelite was able to handle the quality control issue by linking every job with a worker so that if a quality problem arose, the worker who was responsible for that windshield installation had to fix it on his or her own time. Productivity quickly improved by an astonishing 44%.[6] About half of the increase in productivity was due to the same workers working harder, including lower absenteeism and fewer sick days, but the other half of the productivity increase was due to another important effect of piece rates. A piece rate system attracts more productive workers.

Consider two firms, one of which pays workers according to a piece rate, the other pays workers an hourly wage. Now consider two workers, one of whom can install five windshields a day, the other just three. Which worker will be attracted to which firm? The piece rate firm will attract the more productive worker because piece rates give productive workers a chance to earn more money. The hourly wage plan will attract workers who are relatively less productive or even "lazy."

The differences between workers in productivity can be surprisingly large. One California wine grower switched from paying grape pickers by the hour to paying by the pound. Previously, the firm had paid its workers $6.20 per hour. Under piece rates the average pay was effectively $6.84 per hour, about the same as before, but some workers were making as much as $24.85 an hour.

When some workers are more productive than other workers, piece rates will tend to increase inequality in earnings. Under the hourly wage, every grape picker earned $6.20 an hour. Under the piece rate, some earned $6.84, while others earned $24.85. Information technology is making it easier to measure the output of all kinds of workers, not just grape pickers. As a result, performance pay (piece rates, commissions, bonuses, and other rewards tied directly to output) is becoming more common in the U.S. economy and this is one important reason why the inequality of earnings has also increased.[7]

The increase in effective pay under piece rates explains why both firms and employees can benefit from piece rates. Under hourly wages, workers don't have an incentive to work harder even when they can do so at low cost. Piece rates benefit productive workers by giving them an opportunity to use their skills to make more money. Piece rates also benefit firms by increasing productivity more than wages.

Even though firms and workers can both benefit from piece rates, piece rates are sometimes not implemented because of issues of distrust. Workers fear that if they respond to a new piece rate plan by increasing productivity (and thus wages), the firm will respond by reducing the piece rate in the next period (e.g., paying less per pound of grapes picked). In the old Soviet Union, factory managers who increased productivity in response to new incentives were often denounced because their increased performance proved that they had

CHECK YOURSELF

> Lincoln Electric is a firm famous for using piece rates. Lincoln Electric also has a policy of guaranteed employment. How are these two policies related?

> In the United States, restaurant customers have the option of adding a tip to the restaurant bill. In much of Europe, a "tip" is added on automatically. Where would you expect waiters to be more attentive?

previously been lazy! Of course, this greatly reduced the incentive to increase productivity. Similarly, workers won't work harder if they expect that higher productivity will be punished with lower piece rates. Firms that want to introduce piece rates must build trust with their workers.

Lesson Two: Tie Pay to Performance to Reduce Risk

Consider an auto dealer who wants to motivate her sales staff. Let's assume that all the auto dealer cares about is sales, so she is not worried that strong incentives will make her sales staff too pushy. Are strong incentives now the best? Maybe not.

Auto sales depend on more than hard work. Sales also depend on factors the staff has no control over, such as the price and quality of the car, the price of gas, and the state of the economy. If the sales staff has strong incentives, they are going to do great when the economy is booming but poorly when the economy is in a recession.

When sales vary for reasons having little to do with hard work, strong incentives may be more expensive than they are worth. Most people don't like risk. Which would you prefer, $100 for sure or a gamble that pays $200 with probability 0.5 and $0 with probability 0.5? Gambling in Las Vegas can be fun but most people will prefer $100 for certain over a gamble with the same expected payoff. Similarly, suppose that there are two jobs: Job 1 pays $100,000 a year for sure, job 2 pays $200,000 in a good year but just $0 in a bad year. Suppose also that good and bad years are equally likely, so, on average, job 2 also pays $100,000 a year. Which job would you prefer? If the wages are the same on average most people will prefer job 1, the less risky job. How high would the average wage have to be for you to prefer job 2? $110,000, $150,000, $175,000? The precise number is less important than the principle: The riskier payments are to workers, the more a firm must pay, on average. Thus, if a firm's sales staff has to bear the risk of a bad economy on a low-quality car, they will demand a big bonus for every sale. But if staff members demand a big bonus, what is left over for the owner? If the sales staff is sufficiently afraid to face these risks, the owner and the staff might not be able to agree on a mutually profitable strong incentive plan.*

Weak incentives insulate the sales staff from risk. If the owner is better able than the sales staff to bear the risk of a recession (perhaps because she is wealthier), weak incentives may be mutually profitable. In essence, the owner can sell the staff "recession insurance" by paying them with a fixed or nearly fixed salary. The sales staff "buy" the insurance by accepting smaller bonuses but, of course, their pay stream is more stable.

Bearing the risk of a recession might be worth it if hard work from the sales force is also the critical factor in sales. But if the state of the economy is a significant determinant of sales, then strong incentives have created risk with very little motivational advantage. Imagine if rewards were based solely on luck—what incentive would there be to exert effort? Similarly, if rewards are mostly based on luck, the incentive to exert effort will be low and many potential employees won't want to face those risks at a price the owner is willing to pay.

---

* Or worse, the sales staff may be eager to sell cars when the economy is good but the staff may quit the day the economy turns sour.

Tournament Theory

When sales depend heavily on outside factors such as the state of the economy, tying bonuses to sales will reward or penalize agents for outcomes that are often beyond their control—thus, shifting risk to the agent but giving the agent little incentive to exert effort. One way a manager can reduce an agent's risk is to tie rewards more closely to actions that a sales agent does control. A surprising way to do this is to pay bonuses based not on a sales agent's absolute number of sales but on their sales relative to other agents—for example, giving a bonus to the sales agents with the highest, second highest, and third highest sales. For obvious reasons, economists call a compensation scheme in which pay is based on relative performance, a **tournament.**

If they are used cleverly, tournaments can tie rewards more closely to actions that an agent controls, thereby improving productivity and pay. To see how a tournament works in the business world, let's start with sports, an area where we are all used to thinking about tournaments.

Imagine a golf game in which players are paid based on the total number of strokes to finish the course (by the nature of golf, fewer strokes mean better play and thus higher payments). If the weather is bad, scores will be high and agents won't earn very much even if they work hard. If the weather is good (clear day, no wind), scores will be low and agents will earn a lot even if they don't work very hard. Either way, when players are paid based on their absolute scores, random forces—such as the weather—will influence how much the players earn.

Now imagine that players are playing in a tournament with a fixed number of prizes, which of course is usually the case. The fixed number of prizes means that the players are competing *against one another* rather than against some external standard of achievement. Since every player plays with the same weather, the weather no longer influences rewards. Thus, a tournament limits the amount of risk from the external environment. A lot of sporting events, not just golf, are organized in the form of tournaments. Tournaments are also common in the business world.

For instance, paying sales agents based on relative sales will reduce environment risk, risk from external factors that are common to all the agents. When sales agents are paid based on relative sales, factors that the agents do not control such as the state of the economy, the quality of the product, and the price of competing products will no longer influence agent rewards. *Here is the key*: When factors that an agent doesn't control no longer influence rewards, then factors that an agent does control—factors like effort—become more important determinants of rewards. Thus, pay for relative performance such as that used in a tournament can reduce risk and tie rewards more closely to actions that an agent controls. This will mean harder work, less risk, more output, and higher pay.

Improving Executive Compensation with Pay for Relative Performance

A good compensation scheme ties rewards to actions that an agent controls. How would you use the idea of *pay for relative performance* to tie executive pay more closely to actions that executives control?

> A **tournament** is a compensation scheme in which payment is based on relative performance.

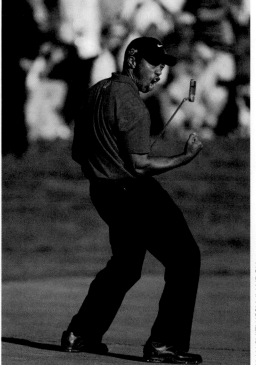

ALAN SMITH/CSM /LANDOV

Bonus!

Today, a large fraction of an executive's pay is tied to the stock price of his or her firm. When the value of the firm rises, executives are often able to cash in stock options at profitable prices. But many factors other than executive effort or ability influence the price of a stock. When the economy does well, for example, the price of most stocks goes up. Similarly, when the price of oil goes up, the stock price of firms in the oil industry tends to go up—and surprisingly, so does the pay of executives in the oil industry, despite the fact that these executives have no control over the price of oil.[8] Of course, when the price of oil falls, these executives are paid less, despite the fact that they may be working as hard, or harder, than ever. The bottom line is that quite a bit of executive pay appears to be based on luck. But payment based on luck is not a good compensation scheme on either the upside or downside.

Is there a better way to pay executives? Instead of paying based on how well their stock performs, how about paying executives based on how well their stock performs *relative to other firms in the same industry?* If executives were paid based on relative performance, they wouldn't reap big windfall profits when the industry boomed (due to no virtue of their own) but neither would they necessarily be paid less when the industry declined (due to no fault of their own).

Pay for relative performance seems to make a lot of sense but it has not been widely adopted. As a result, some observers suspect that the complicated stock option schemes currently used to reward executives are less about creating incentives than about creative accounting that takes advantage of shareholders who do not closely monitor how much the executives are being paid. Interestingly, firms that have at least one very large shareholder—and thus at least one shareholder with an incentive to monitor the firm closely—do appear to base more executive pay on relative performance.[9]

In recent times, the American economy has experienced another problem with compensating senior managers, especially in banking and finance: Sometimes the incentive is to take too many "long tail" risks, namely risks that rarely go bad, but when they do, they go very, very bad. Let's say a bank manager encourages his staff to make risky mortgage loans that go bad only once every 30 years, but when they do, they endanger the very existence of the bank and perhaps even the banking system. Most of the time the risks pay off, the bank prospers, and the managers get a nice bonus. Sooner or later, however, the mortgages go bad and the bank ends up insolvent or in need of a government bailout. How much do the managers suffer? Usually, they don't have to give back their old bonuses and often the worst thing that happens—if that—is they are fired. In 2008, two investment banks, Bear Stearns and Lehman Brothers, went bankrupt. This wasn't good for their managers, but over the 2000–2008 period, they had already pulled out about $1.4 billion (Bear Stearns) and $1 billion (Lehman Brothers) in cash bonuses and equity sales.[10] Thus, even though these managers took on huge risks, they still profited handsomely. Many of them found other jobs or retired on their previous bonuses, so the penalties to discourage excess risk-taking aren't so strong. Prior to the financial crisis of 2007–2009, the U.S. financial system took too many risks of this nature. It remains to be seen whether better incentives can be designed to overcome this problem.

Environment Risk and Ability Risk

A tournament insulates rewards from risks due to outside factors that are common to all the players but it adds another type of risk called ability risk. Imagine that you had to compete in a golf game against Tiger Woods. Would you put in more effort if you were paid based on the number of strokes or if you were paid based on who wins the game? The probability that you could beat Tiger Woods at golf is so low that if all you cared about was money, it would make sense to give up right away—why exert effort in a hopeless cause? Of course, for the same reason, Tiger Woods won't need to try very hard either!

Remember, an ideal incentive scheme ties rewards to factors that an agent controls, such as effort. But winning at golf takes more than effort, it also takes ability. As far as an agent is concerned, someone else's ability is just like the weather or the state of the economy; it's not under his or her control. A golf tournament between players with highly unequal abilities doesn't tie rewards to effort, it ties rewards to ability and that often causes people to shirk and slack. Thus, tournaments work best when the risk from the outside environment is more important than ability risk.

Tournaments can be structured to reduce ability risk. At a professional golf tournament, for example, players play in rounds with the weakest players being eliminated in early rounds, so when the final and most important round is played, the players have similar abilities. Similarly, tournaments are often split into age classes or experience classes (beginner, intermediate, expert) so that abilities are similar and each player has a strong incentive to work hard. In amateur but serious golf games, when players of different ability compete together, the high-ability players will often be handicapped, which makes competition more intense for all the players. A manager who wants a lot of effort will also structure tournaments so that rewards are closely tied to effort. A manager, for example, might create junior and senior sales positions with tournaments played within each class of employee.

Tournaments in business might seem a bit unusual but they are quite common. About one third of U.S. corporations evaluate employees based on relative performance.[11] Under the hard-nosed CEO Jack Welch, managers at General Electric were required to divide employees into three groups—the top 20%, the middle 70%, and the bottom 10%—with the bottom 10% often being shown the door. Even when employees are not explicitly rewarded based on relative performance, tournaments are often implicit. Lawyers, for example, compete to earn the prize of becoming a partner. Becoming the president of a corporation is a lot like winning a tournament. Imagine that a corporation has eight vice presidents and one president—the vice presidents compete to become the next president. The fact that moving up the corporate ladder is like competing in a tournament may also shed some light on the large salaries and perks of many corporate presidents. Personal chefs, corporate jets, and lavish parties might be a sign of the abuse of power but the perks of presidency may also motivate the eight vice presidents. In part, corporate presidents are paid a lot to motivate those beneath them.

Tournaments are wonderful at encouraging competition but sometimes competition can be too fierce. In a tournament, when one player falters, the others gain, so tournaments can discourage cooperation. One corporate vice president might be unwilling to mentor another if she sees a competitor waiting to take away her job. Thus, as usual, compensation schemes must be carefully designed to balance a variety of goals.

Tournaments and Grades

Let's apply some of the insights from tournament theory to a competition that you are very familiar with: the competition for grades. Some professors

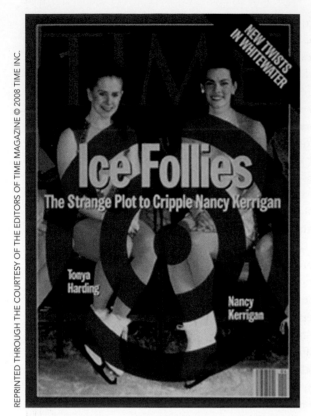

Tournaments can encourage too much competition.

grade on a curve, while others use an absolute scale. When a professor "grades on a curve," there are a fixed number of "prizes," A's, B's, C's, for each class. The competition for grades becomes a tournament.

The costs and benefits of being graded on a curve are just like the more general analysis of tournaments. Grading on a curve reduces environment risk but increases ability risk. Can you think of some examples of environment risk? Suppose that your professor is hard to understand—perhaps the professor has an accent or teaches the material too quickly or is simply not a good teacher (unlike us!). Fortunately, if the professor grades on a curve, his or her bad performance doesn't mean you have to fail. Bad teaching will reduce how much you learn but bad teaching harms everyone's performance. If the professor grades on a curve, bad teaching need not reduce your grade or reduce your incentive to study.

A bad teacher who grades on an absolute scale, however, is double trouble. First, bad teaching means that you won't learn much. Second, if the grading is on an absolute scale, not learning much means that even if you work hard, you will get a low grade. There isn't much incentive to work hard in that case.

Grading on a curve, however, does have disadvantages—grading on a curve means that you will be competing directly with the other students in the class. If you happen to be in a class with a handful of super-brilliant students, it's like golfing against Tiger Woods (unless *you* are the academic Tiger Woods). Even if you learn a lot and work hard, you won't get a high grade and that reduces your incentive to study.

Grading on a curve, therefore, creates better incentives to study when the big risk is that the professor will be bad (an environment risk), but it reduces the incentive to study when students are of very different abilities (ability risk). Grading on an absolute scale creates better incentives to study when students are of very different abilities (ability risk), but reduces the incentive to study when the big risk is that professors will be bad (environment risk).

What are some other effects of grading on a curve? Remember, tournaments tend to reduce cooperation. If your professor grades on a curve, other students might be less willing to help you with your homework (or you might be less willing to help them!). Study groups will probably be less common. Some students might even try to sabotage other students. Tournaments can also encourage the wrong kinds of cooperation. If a professor grades on a curve, in theory all the students could get together and agree not to study very much. This probably wouldn't be a problem in a large class, but if two sales agents regularly compete for the "salesman of the month" award, they could collude to reduce effort and rotate the prize between them.

Here's another problem for you to think about. Suppose that the environment risk is not bad professors but rather difficult material. Imagine, for example, that some classes are more difficult than other classes (quantum physics 101 vs. handball 101). If you really wanted to learn a little about quantum physics, but you were afraid of reducing your GPA, what type of grading system would you prefer? And to ask the classic economist's question: under what conditions? See Thinking and Problem Solving question 6 for further discussion of this question.

Lesson Three: Money Isn't Everything

Incentives are powerful, but not all powerful incentives are for money. If you want to keep business or school club meetings short, make everyone stand until the meeting is over. All of a sudden the cost of talking is higher so people have an incentive to talk less.

In addition to money, other powerful rewards include the feeling of identification and belonging that comes from being part of a team, the joy that comes from a job well done, and the status that comes from success on one's own terms. Intrinsic motivation is when you want to do something simply for feelings of enjoyment and pride. Ideally, firms would like their employees to be motivated by intrinsic rewards like pride in a job well done, as well as extrinsic rewards like money.

A good manager will get workers to enjoy doing what the manager wants. One way of doing this is to encourage workers to identify with the corporation and its goals in the same way that sports fans identify with their team. Many workers, for example, are given shares of stock in the company they work in. Currently, about 20 million American employees own a part of their employers.[12] Since most workers don't have much control over the value of the entire company, this doesn't make sense as a monetary incentive. But workers are more likely to identify with their company if they are also part owners of their company. Workers who identify with their company see corporate success as their success. Bostonians celebrated when the Red Sox won the World Series even though the fans didn't receive any monetary rewards. In a company with strong worker identification, high profits are a cause for celebration even if the workers don't receive raises. Workers who identify with their company are more likely to see themselves in the same boat as other workers and to think and act more like a team or sometimes even like a family. This is also why many companies run staff retreats or invest in a softball team.

Successful businesses take great care to create the right **corporate culture.** Corporate culture is the shared collection of values and norms that govern how people interact in an organization or firm. Sometimes it is said that corporate culture is "how things get done around here."

The American military is one of the most successful creators of a powerful "corporate culture." In the military, a team member may sacrifice his or her life for the sake of the team. Business corporations can rarely rely on this intensity of identification, but a strong corporate culture can help workers improve. Recall that one of the big problems with monetary incentives is that the firm can't always measure what it wants and a firm that can't measure quality, for example, may be worried about creating strong incentives for quantity. But a firm with workers who value high quality for its own sake can have the best of both worlds—high quantity and high quality. Corporate culture helps firms incentivize what is difficult to measure.

CHECK YOURSELF

> At one prominent university, a professor's first name and middle initial are "Harvey C." Undergraduates refer to him as "Harvey C-minus" because he is a notoriously hard grader. What are this professor's incentives to be known as a hard grader? What type of students does he attract? Who does he encourage to stay away? Why might this professor not want to grade on a curve?

> How can a tournament create too much competition? Isn't competition a good thing?

Corporate culture is the shared collection of values and norms that govern how people interact in an organization or firm.

Corporate culture is, in part, responsible for the ascendancy of Walmart, starting in the 1970s. In the 1970s, CEO Sam Walton spent several days a week visiting each store. He typically would gather the employees together in a rousing corporate cheer. He then walked around the store and encouraged people to tell him what the problems were or what the company was doing wrong. Most managers were encouraged to visit stores and find out what was on the minds of workers. The flow of useful information up to the bosses became a company norm, and workers grew more and more willing to share what they knew. When something in the company went wrong, usually the mistake was discovered quickly and there was someone ready to set it right.

In other cases, corporate culture malfunctions. As Walmart was growing, Kmart, one of its main competitors, was on the road to bankruptcy. At Kmart, employees tended to hide problems from managers rather than volunteer solutions. Usually, control was centralized and the attitude was that the home office knows best. Each time the company had a problem, it looked for a "quick fix" rather than going to the root of the difficulty. The tradition of failure bred on itself and members of the company simply did not work together very well. Kmart has come out of bankruptcy but it remains unclear whether the company enjoys much of a future. Most customers vote with their feet and go to Walmart.[13]

The importance of morale and good relations extends beyond the business corporation. You can see these same principles at work in your everyday life.

Intrinsic and extrinsic motivation can work together but not always. When intrinsic motivation is strong, people are sometimes insulted by offers of money. If you ask a friend to give you a ride to the airport, the friend would probably say yes (well, *some* friends . . . maybe not all of your friends). Offer your friend $20 for a ride and all of a sudden the friend feels like a taxi driver, not a friend. The friend who might have done it for free will turn down the job for $20. In one advice column, a woman complained that her husband promised to "pay her by the pound" to lose weight (the advice column did not say whether the husband was an economist). This marriage probably was not a happy one, and we should not expect this proposed transaction to succeed.

Similarly, it is not always possible to pay a son or a daughter to do the dirty dishes. Nagging doesn't always work well either but paying money can be worse. When the parents pay money, the daughter feels less familial obligation. Once she says to herself "Doing the dishes is a job for money," the daughter is no more obligated to do her parent's dishes than she is to get a job at a restaurant to do other people's dishes.

In these cases, payment causes external motivation to replace internal motivation. Yet for some tasks, internal motivation is what gets the job done, and in these cases payment can be counterproductive.

Note that payment from a restaurant will get the same daughter to show up for work on time. Having her own job—which is a signal of adulthood and independence—is "cool" and makes the daughter feel like a grown-up. Money from parents, which feels like an allowance for tots, or feels like a means of parental control, will not boost the daughter's internal motivation to do the dishes.

The lesson is this: Monetary rewards are most effective when they are supported by intrinsic motivation and measures of social status. Good entrepreneurs understand these connections, and they design their workplaces so that money, intrinsic motivation, and status incentives work together. Money can't buy you love, however, and sometimes love is the incentive that makes family and personal relationships work well. Money can't buy you duty or honor either, so even within firms and other organizations such as the military, monetary incentives must be used with care. Understanding when extrinsic and intrinsic rewards complement one another and when they are at odds is today more of an art than a science. Questions like these are on the cutting edge of social psychology and behavioral economics.

CHECK YOURSELF

> Is Christmas wasteful? Instead of presents, wouldn't it be more efficient to give cash that can be used to buy what the recipient really wants? Why don't we see cash gifts more often?

> Some parents and increasingly some schools are using cash to pay students for good grades. Good idea or not?

□ Takeaway

Incentives are a double-edged sword. When aligned with the social interest, incentives can be powerful forces for good but misaligned incentives can be equally powerful forces for bad. One of the goals of economics is to understand what institutions generate good incentives.

On a less grand level, getting the incentives right is an important goal of managers who want to motivate employees, stockholders who want to motivate managers, parents who want to motivate children, and consumers who want to motivate real estate agents, physicians, or lawyers among many others.

In this chapter, we discussed three lessons to help get the incentives right. Lesson one is: You get what you pay for, but what you pay for is not always what you want. Sometimes the gap between what you pay for and what you want arises because the incentive plan is badly designed. More often the gap arises because measuring exactly what you want is difficult, so you must pay for something that is more easily measurable but is not exactly what you want. When the gap between what you pay for and what you want is large, strong incentives can be worse than weak incentives. As it becomes easier to measure things like quality, however, strong incentive plans are becoming more common.

Lesson two is: Tie pay to performance to reduce risk. Strong incentives put more risk on agents from factors beyond their control, and to bear this risk, the agents will demand greater compensation. Sales agents on commission, for example, bear the risk that the economy goes into a downturn or that the product they sell is of low quality. As a result of this increased financial risk, sales agents on commission must be paid higher average wages than sales agents on salary. A firm must ask whether the strong incentives created by commissions increase sales enough to justify the higher average wages.

A good incentive plan will reduce unnecessary risk by tying rewards to actions that an agent controls and that are effective in increasing output. Different incentive plans like commissions, bonuses, and tournaments impose different types of risks on agents. Which incentive plan is best will depend on which risks are most important.

Lesson three is that money isn't everything. In addition to earning money, workers want to enjoy their work, identify with a team, and be respected. Successful corporations provide these rewards, as well as monetary rewards. Monetary rewards can be paid only for what is measurable, but a successful corporate culture can help firms incentivize what is difficult to measure. Monetary rewards are most effective when they are supported by intrinsic motivation and measures of social status.

▢ CHAPTER REVIEW

KEY CONCEPTS

Piece rate, p. 404

Tournament, p. 407

Corporate culture, p. 411

FACTS AND TOOLS

1. This chapter had three big lessons. Each of the following situations illustrates one and (we think) only one of those lessons. Which one?

   a. Militaries throughout the world give medals, citations, and other public honors to members of the military who excel in their duties.

   b. People tip for good service after their meal is concluded.

   c. Real estate agents work on commission, but office managers at a real estate office are paid a straight salary.

   d. In Pennsylvania in 2009, two judges received $2.6 million in bribes from a juvenile prison. The more people they sent to jail, the more they received from the prison owners. What tipped off prosecutors was that the judges were sentencing teens to such harsh sentences for relatively minor crimes. One teenager was sent to prison for putting up a Facebook page that said mean things about her school principal; another accidentally bought a stolen bicycle. (Both judges pled guilty.)

2. An American church sends 10 missionaries to Panama for three years to find new converts. Every six months, the missionary with the most new converts gets to be the supervising missionary for the next six months. This basically means that he or she gets to drive a car, while the other 9 have to walk or ride bicycles. Clearly, this is a tournament. Now consider the following two cases. For which case will the church's incentive plan work best? (Hint: Think about ability risk vs. environment risk.)

   Case 1: Missionaries specialize in different regions: Some stay in rich neighborhoods for the whole six months, others stay in poor neighborhoods for the whole six months.

   Case 2: Missionaries move from region to region every few weeks, so that all missionaries spend a little time in every kind of Panamanian neighborhood.

3. Punishments can be an incentive, not just rewards. Consider an assembly line. Why wouldn't you necessarily want to reward the fastest worker on the assembly line? What other incentive system might work?

4. The basketball player Tim Hardaway was once promised a big bonus if he made a lot of assists. Can you think of any problems that such an incentive scheme might cause? Many professional athletes get a bonus if they win a championship. Is this kind of incentive better or worse than a basketball player's bonus for assists? Why?

5. Let's return to Big Idea Four (thinking on the margin) back in Chapter 1. Why are calls to give harsher penalties to drug dealers and kidnappers often met with warnings by economists?

6. Why are salespeople so much more likely than other kinds of workers to be paid on a "piece rate" (i.e., on commission)? What is it about the kind of work they do that makes the high-commission + low-base-salary combination the equilibrium outcome?

7. Unlike in the previous question, sometimes, piece rates don't work so well. Why might the following incentive mechanisms turn out to be more trouble than they're worth?

   a. An industrial materials company pays welders by the number of welds per hour. Of course, the company only pays for necessary welds.

   b. A magazine publisher pays its authors to write "serial novels" one chapter at a time. The authors are paid by the word (common in the nineteenth century: This is how Dickens and Dostoyevsky made their livings).

8. The typical corporate executive's incentive package offers higher pay when the company's stock does well. One proposal for such executive merit pay is to instead pay executives based on whether their firm's stock price does better or worse than the stock price of the average firm in their own industry. Does this proposal solve an environment risk problem or an ability risk problem? How can you tell?

THINKING AND PROBLEM SOLVING

1. In 1975, economist Sam Peltzman published a study of the effects of recent safety regulations for automobiles. His results were surprising: Increased safety standards for automobiles had no measurable effect on passenger fatalities. Pedestrian fatalities in automobile accidents, however, increased. (This is now known as the Peltzman effect and has been tested repeatedly over the decades.)

   a. Why might more *pedestrians* be killed when a car has *more* safety features?

   b. Economists have looked for ways out of Peltzman's dilemma. Here's one possible solution: Gordon Tullock, our colleague at George Mason, has argued that cars could have long spikes jutting out of the steering column pointed directly at the driver's heart. Keeping Peltzman's paper and the role of incentives in mind, would you expect this safety mechanism to result in an increase, decrease, or no change in automobile accident fatalities? Why?

   c. Would a pedestrian who never drives or rides in cars tend to favor Tullock's solution? Why or why not?

2. One reason it's difficult for a manager to set up good incentives is because it's easy for employees to lie about how they'll respond to incentives. For example, Simple Books pays Mary Sue to proofread chapters of new books. After an author writes a draft of a book, Simple sends chapters out to proofreaders like Mary Sue to make sure that spelling, punctuation, and basic facts are correct.

   As you can imagine, some books are easy to proofread (perhaps Westerns and romances), while others are hard to proofread (perhaps engineering textbooks). But what's difficult or easy is often in the eye of the beholder: Simple can't tell which books are particularly easy for Mary Sue to proof, so they have to take her word for it. Let's see how this fact influences the publishing industry.

   In the figure below, $Q^\star$ is the number of chapters in the new book *Burned: The Secret History of Toast.* It's a strange mix of chemistry and history, so Simple isn't sure how Mary Sue will feel about proofing it. The marginal cost curve shows Mary Sue's true willingness to work: The more chapters she has to read, the more you have to pay her. If Simple offers to pay her $50 per chapter, as shown, she'll actually finish the job.

   a. If Mary Sue wants to bluff, claiming that the book is actually painful to read, what is that equivalent to?

      Supply curve shifting left

      Supply curve shifting right

      Demand curve shifting down

      Demand curve shifting up

      Once you decide, make the appropriate shift in the figure above.

   b. The publisher just *has* to have Mary Sue proof all $Q^\star$ chapters of *Burned:* All its other proofreaders are busy. The publisher will pay what it needs to for her to finish the book. This is the same as another curve shift in a certain direction: Draw in this shift in the figure above.

   c. What did Mary Sue's complaining do to her price per chapter? What did it do to her work load?

   d. (Bonus) You've seen how Mary Sue's bluffing influenced the outcome. What are some things that Simple might do to keep this from happening?

3. Who do you think is in favor of forbidding baseball player contracts from including bonuses based on playing skill? Owners or players? Why?

4. In the short, readable classic *Congress: The Electoral Connection,* David Mayhew uses the basic ideas of incentives and information as a pair of lenses through which to view members of Congress. What he saw was quite simple: The urge for reelection drives everything. Thus, members are driven by self-interest to give the voters in their home district as much as possible. Of course, voters face the same problem in judging members of Congress that any manager faces when evaluating an employee: Some outputs are harder to measure than others, so voters focus on measurable outputs. With that in mind, what will voters be most likely to care about? Choose one from each pair and briefly explain why you made that choice.

   a. How many dollars come to the district for new hospitals and highways vs. how many dollars are spent on top-secret military research.

   b. How well the member behaved in private meetings with Chinese leaders vs. how the member sounded on *Meet the Press.*

   c. How well the member did in reforming the Justice Department vs. how well the member did at the Turkey Toss back in the district last Thanksgiving.

   (As you've seen, voters' focus on the visible can easily drive the member's entire career. Mayhew's book was an important early work in "public choice," the use of basic microeconomic ideas like self-interest and strategy to study political behavior. For more on the topic, Kenneth Shepsle and Mark Bonchek's short textbook *Analyzing Politics* is highly recommended. See also Chapter 19 of this textbook.)

5. In the movie business, character actors are typically paid a fixed fee, while movie "stars" are typically paid a share of the box office revenues. Why the difference? Try to give *two* explanations based on the ideas in this chapter.

6. Let's return to the question we posed in the chapter: Suppose that the big environment risk is not bad professors but rather hard material. Imagine, for example, that some classes are more difficult than other classes (quantum physics 101 vs. handball 101). If you really wanted to learn a little about quantum physics but you were afraid of reducing your GPA, you'd face a tough choice. A curve is better for you than an absolute scale, but even if your professor grades on a curve, you're probably still sitting in a class with other well-trained physics majors. Let's see if we can find a work-around.

   a. At your school, are there certain times of the day when the less serious, more fun-loving tend to take their classes? If so, what time is that? If you sign up for a section scheduled then, you might look better on the curve.

   b. Some schools offer simplified (we won't say "dumbed down") versions of some hard courses. Does your school offer anything like this? If so, does it allow majors to take the same sections as the nonmajors? How is this sorting related to tournament theory?

   c. If you were a professor, which teaching schedule would you rather have: two sections where the majors and nonmajors are mixed together, or one section with the majors, and one with the nonmajors?

7. When an accused defendant is brought before a judge to schedule a trial, the judge may release the defendant on his or her "own recognizance" or the judge may demand that the defendant post bail, an amount of cash that the defendant must give to the court and that will be forfeited if the defendant fails to appear. Many defendants don't have the cash, so they borrow the money from a bail bondsperson. So if the defendant fails to appear, the bail bondsperson is out the money, unless the defendant is recaptured within 90–180 days. To recover their money, a bail bondsperson will hire bail enforcement agents, also known as bounty hunters, to track down the missing defendant. If the bounty hunters don't find the defendant, they don't get paid.

DAVID HOWELLS/CORBIS

This Dog knows how to hunt.

a. If defendants released on their own recognizance fail to appear, they are pursued by the police, but if they are released on bail borrowed from a bondsperson and they fail to appear, they will be pursued by bounty hunters. Which type of defendant do you think is more likely to fail to appear, and which type is more likely to be recaptured if they do fail to appear? Why?

b. Perhaps surprisingly, bounty hunters tend to be quite courteous and respectful even to defendants who have tried to skip town. Can you think of one reason why?

8. a. Why do so many charitable activities like marathons, walks, and 5K runs give the participants "free" t-shirts, wristbands, hats, bumper stickers, and so forth?

b. Charitable organizations could probably make a lot of money for their cause by selling these items on their Web sites, but you usually have to actually attend the "2012 Cancer Run" to get the "2012 Cancer Run" t-shirt. Why?

9. Waiters and waitresses are generally paid very low hourly wages and receive most of their compensation from customer tips.

a. As the owner of a restaurant, what do you want from your wait staff?

b. Which element of a waiter's or waitress' compensation—the hourly wage or the tips—represents a method of "tying pay to performance"?

c. Which element of a waiter's or waitress' compensation—the hourly wage or the tips—plays the role of "insurance" that the restaurant owner provides for the wait staff? Against what are the waiters and waitresses being insured?

d. Theoretically, a restaurant owner could pay workers a higher wage, raise menu prices, and make the restaurant strictly tip-free. Or, the owner could eliminate the wage, reduce menu prices, and encourage greater tipping by alerting customers to the fact that the wait staff do not earn an hourly wage. What are the potential pros and cons (from the point of view of the restaurant owner) of each system?

10. In early 2004, Donald Trump took the idea of using a tournament for hiring executives to a whole new level with the premiere of the TV show *The Apprentice*. On the show, a group of contestants compete for a position running one of Trump's many companies for a starting annual salary of $250,000. Generally speaking, on each episode, the contestants are divided up into teams and compete to most successfully complete some business-related task, and a member of the losing team is eliminated.

a. Contestants for *The Apprentice* are carefully auditioned and screened, to make sure that each contestant has the skills necessary to do well on the show. Why do you think this screening is done? What kind of risk is being eliminated by this audition process? What would happen if there was one contestant who, right from the beginning, demonstrated more potential and greater capabilities than the other contestants?

b. Though only one contestant will end up with the job at the conclusion of the show, each must try to prove his or her worth to Trump by performing well in the team challenges. What impact do you think the tournament structure of this "ultimate job interview" has on these team challenges?

c. Some of the challenges can be quite demanding, and the contestants often work very hard. Wouldn't it be easier if they all shirked the challenge rather than working hard? Trump would still (presumably) have to choose one of them as the winner—and chances are it would be the same person whether everybody worked hard or not. Why are the contestants not likely to all agree to stop trying so hard?

CHALLENGES

1. Let's tie together this chapter's story on incentives with Chapter 15's story about cartels. Suppose your economics professor grades on a curve: The average score on each test becomes a B–. If all of the students in your class form a conspiracy to cut back on studying, point out how this cartel might break down just like OPEC's cartel breaks down during some decades.

2. What type of systems in the United States help overcome the incentives of physicians to order medically unnecessary tests?

3. In his path-breaking book *Managerial Dilemmas,* political scientist Gary Miller says that a good corporate culture is one that gets workers to work together even when they face prisoner's dilemmas (we discussed the prisoner's dilemma in detail in Chapter 15). In a healthy corporate culture, you feel guilty if you're being lazy while your buddy is working. Let's sum up "guilt" as simply as possible: It's some number "X" that represents how you feel. These figures are adapted from Figure 15.4.

		Stan	
		Work	Shirk
Kyle	Work	(4, 4)	(2, X)
	Shirk	(X, 2)	(3, 3)

a. What does X have to be in order to keep this from being a prisoner's dilemma? Answer with a range (e.g., greater than 12.5, less than −2).

b. Now, there are two Nash equilibria in this problem. What are they? Using the language of Chapter 15 and 16, what kind of game has this just become?

c. There's an idea buried in the questions from Chapter 16 that will "point" Stan and Kyle toward the best possible outcome. What is it? (Keep in mind that a good corporate culture can help with this part, too.)

4. a. Many HMOs pay their doctors based, in part, on how many patients the doctor sees in a day. What problems does this incentive system create?

b. If HMOs pay their doctors a fixed salary, what problems does this incentive system create?

c. Ideally, we would like to pay doctors based on how long their patients live! What problems exist in implementing this type of system?

5. In most big cities, taxicab fares are fairly standardized, and they are regulated by local governments. For the sake of simplicity, assume that a cab driver works for a licensed taxicab company, and he or she pays a fixed daily fee for the use of the taxi; all fares and tips go to the driver.

a. In Atlanta, GA, meter rates are $2.50 for the first 1/8 mile and $0.25 for each additional 1/8 mile. What are the benefits of allowing cab drivers to charge fares based on the number of miles driven? In other words, what good behavior is encouraged—or what bad behavior is discouraged—by this? What are the possible drawbacks?

b. In addition to the meter rates above, there is a $21 per hour waiting fee. Why do you think there is a waiting fee? If cab drivers could not charge a waiting fee, how might that change their behavior? What if cab drivers were always just paid an hourly wage of $21 per hour? What would be the benefits and drawbacks of this payment scheme?

c. For some fairly standard trips in Atlanta, there are flat fees. A trip from the airport to anywhere downtown, for example, is always $30 (plus $2 for each additional person). What are the potential benefits and drawbacks of this kind of compensation scheme? Why might a city require this payment scheme for trips from the airport?

d. In the chapter, we talked about the importance of the gap between *what you pay for* and *what you want*. What is it that Atlanta's City Council and taxi customers *want* from the cab drivers in Atlanta? Which basis for cab fares (miles, hours, trips) comes closest to closing the gap between what is *wanted* and what is *paid for*?

22

Stock Markets and Personal Finance

In 1992, television reporter John Stossel decided to challenge the experts of Wall Street. As a student, Stossel had taken classes from economist Burton Malkiel whose book *A Random Walk Down Wall Street* claimed that the money and fame that went to stock-picking gurus were a sham and a waste. According to Malkiel: "A blind-folded monkey throwing darts at a newspaper's financial pages could select a portfolio that would do just as well as one carefully selected by experts."[1]

Instead of using a monkey, Stossel himself threw darts at a giant wall-sized version of the stock pages of the *Wall Street Journal*. Stossel followed his portfolio for nearly a year and compared the return with the portfolios picked by major Wall Street experts. Stossel's portfolio beat 90% of the experts! Not surprisingly, none of the experts would speak to him on camera about their humiliating loss. The lesson, according to Stossel, is that if you are paying an expert a lot of money to pick your stocks, it is probably you who are the monkey.

In this chapter, we explain why Stossel's amusing experiment is backed up by economic theory and by many careful empirical studies. We will also be giving you some investment advice in this chapter. No, we can't promise you the secret to getting rich. Most of the get rich quick schemes sold in books, investment seminars, and newsletters are scams. Economics, however, does provide some important lessons for investing wisely. We won't tell you how to get rich quick, but we can perhaps help you to get richer slowly.

Throughout this chapter, we emphasize a core principle of economics: There's no such thing as a free lunch. That's just another way of saying that you shouldn't expect something for nothing, or trade-offs are everywhere. Let's see how the principle applies to personal finance.

Better than the experts?

Passive vs. Active Investing

Many people invest in the stock market through a mutual fund. A mutual fund pools money from many customers and invests the money in many firms, in return, of course, for a management fee. Some of these mutual funds, called "active funds," are run by managers who try to pick stocks—these mutual funds often charge higher than average fees. Other mutual funds are called "passive funds" because they simply attempt to mimic a broad stock market index such as Standard and Poor's 500 (S&P 500), a basket of 500 large firms broadly representative of the U.S. economy.

Figure 22.1 shows that in a typical year passive investing in the S&P 500 Index beats about 60% of all mutual funds. In any given year, some mutual funds beat the index, but what is telling is that the funds that beat the index are different nearly every year! In other words, the funds that beat the index in one year probably just got lucky that year. One study that looked over 10 years found that passive investing beat 97.6% of all mutual funds![2] Overall, it is clear that very few mutual fund managers can consistently beat the market averages.

FIGURE 22.1

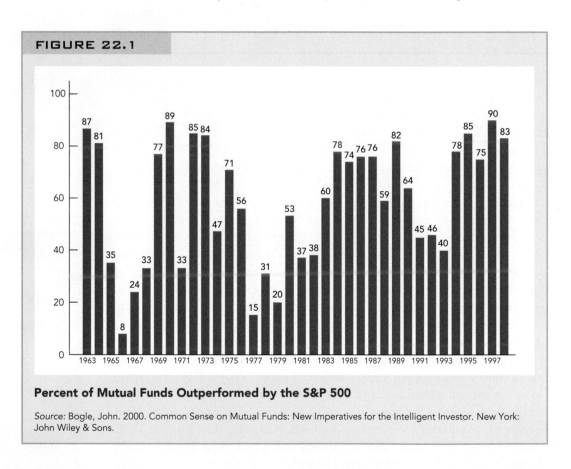

Percent of Mutual Funds Outperformed by the S&P 500

Source: Bogle, John. 2000. Common Sense on Mutual Funds: New Imperatives for the Intelligent Investor. New York: John Wiley & Sons.

It is possible that a very small number of experts can systematically beat the stock market. Sometimes Warren Buffett, who promotes long-term investing for value, is cited as an example of a person who sees farther than the rest of the market. He started out as a paperboy and worked his way up to $52 billion by purchasing undervalued stocks.

Some economists even think that Buffett, and a few others like him, just got lucky. If enough people are out there trying to pick stocks, you're going to have a few who get lucky many times in a row. Take a look at Figure 22.2. At the top

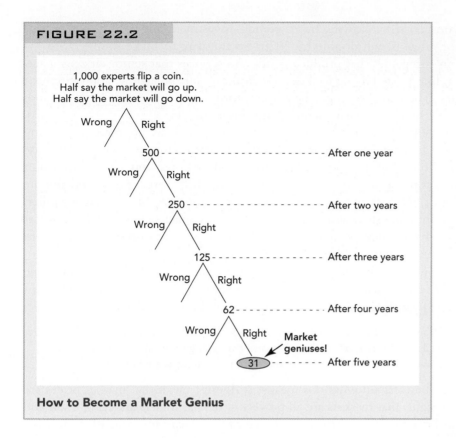

FIGURE 22.2

1,000 experts flip a coin.
Half say the market will go up.
Half say the market will go down.

Wrong / Right

500 - After one year

Wrong / Right

250 - - - - - - - - - - - - - - - - - After two years

Wrong / Right

125 - - - - - - - - - - - - - - After three years

Wrong / Right

62 - - - - - - - - - - - - After four years

Wrong / Right   **Market geniuses!**

31 - - - - - - - After five years

How to Become a Market Genius

of the figure, we start out with 1,000 experts, each of whom flips a coin to predict whether the market will go up in the following year or down. After one year, 500 of the experts will turn out to be right. After two years, 250 experts will have been right two years in a row. At the end of five years, just 31 out of 1,000 experts will have been right five years in a row. The experts who get it correct every time will be lauded as geniuses on CNBC and their advice will be eagerly sought. But the reality is that they just got lucky.

Is Buffett skilled or lucky? We're not so sure, but we do know this: Right now there is a small industry of people following the moves of Warren Buffett, trying to guess what he will say and do next. It is harder and harder for Buffett to get a big jump on the rest of the stock market. Even if Buffett could beat the market at first, it is not so clear he can beat the market any longer.

Warren Buffett: Genius investor or lucky as a monkey?

CHIP SOMODEVILLA/GETTY IMAGES

Why Is It Hard to Beat the Market?

These results aren't just an accident. Nor is it a statement about the stupidity of mutual fund managers. We know a few of these managers and most of them are pretty smart. Rather, the difficulty of beating the stock market is a tribute to the power of markets and the ability of market prices to reflect information.

Think about it this way: For every buyer of a stock, there is a seller. The buyer thinks the price is going up, the seller thinks the price is going down. There is a disagreement. On average, who do you think is more likely to be correct, the buyer or the seller? Of course, the answer is neither. But if on average buyers and sellers have about the same amount of information, stock picking can't work very well.

Consider the following bit of pseudo-investment advice. The number of senior citizens will double by 2020. So the way to make money is to invest in companies that produce goods and services that senior citizens want, things like assisted living facilities, medical care for the elderly, and retirement homes. The baby boom can be a boom for you, If You Invest Now! Sounds plausible right? So, what's wrong with this argument?

All the premises in the argument are true: The baby boomers are retiring and the demand for goods and services that senior citizens want will increase in the future. But investing in firms that produce goods and services for senior citizens is not a sure road to riches. Why not? If it were, why would anyone sell his or her stock in these firms? Remember, for every buyer there is a seller. If you think the stock is a good buy, why is the seller selling? It's not a secret that the baby boomers are retiring so the stock price of firms that are likely to do well in the future *already* reflects this information.

The **efficient markets hypothesis** says that the prices of traded assets reflect all publicly available information.

Since for every buyer there is a seller, you can't get rich by buying and selling on *public information*. This idea is the foundation of what is called the **efficient markets hypothesis**. The best-known form of this hypothesis states:

> The prices of traded assets, such as stocks and bonds, reflects all publicly available information. Unless an investor is trading on inside information, he or she will not systematically outperform the market as a whole over time.

Let's be clear on what this means. It doesn't mean that market prices are always right, that markets are all powerful, or that traders are calm, cool, and rational people. It just means it is difficult for ordinary investors (that probably means you, too!) to systematically outperform the market, again unless a trader has inside information—information that no one else has. It's restating our above point that you might as well throw darts at the stock pages as try to figure out which companies will beat the market. The efficient markets hypothesis is just another way of saying there is no such thing as a free lunch.

So what happens if you do have some information that no one else has, then can you make money in the stock market? Yes, but you have to act very quickly. Within *minutes* of the news that the Russian nuclear power plant at Chernobyl had melted down, shares in U.S. nuclear power plant companies tumbled, the price of oil jumped, as did the price of potatoes. Why potatoes? Clever traders on Wall Street figured out that the disaster at Chernobyl meant that the Ukrainian potato crop would be contaminated, so they bought American potato futures to profit from the coming rise in prices. The traders who acted quickly made a lot of money, but as they bought and sold, prices changed and signaled to other people that something was going on. Quite quickly, the inside information became public information and the opportunities for profit evaporated.

The only way you can take advantage of information that other people don't have is to start buying or selling large numbers of shares. But once you start the buying or selling, the rest of the market knows something is up. That is why secrets do not last very long in the stock market and that is another reason why it is so hard to beat the market as a whole.

Some people believe that they have found exceptions to the efficient markets hypothesis. For instance, it is commonly believed that you can make more money by buying stocks when prices are low, or by buying right after prices have fallen. That sounds good, doesn't it? Buying at lower prices. It feels like what you do when you go to Walmart. But a stock isn't like buying a lawn chair or a banana. The value of a stock is simply what its price will be in future periods of time. The banana, in contrast, you can simply eat for pleasure, no matter what the future price of bananas. Often lower prices mean that prices are going to stay low or fall even more and that means lower returns on owning stocks. Some studies find that you can do slightly better with your investments by buying right after prices have fallen. But do you know what? If you adjust those higher returns to account for the broker commissions that you have to pay for the extra trading, the higher returns pretty much go away.

A field of study known as "technical analysis" looks for much deeper patterns in stock and asset prices. Maybe you've heard on the financial news that stocks have "broken through a key support point," or "moved into a new trading range." If you dig deeper, you will find a claim that stock prices exhibit predictable mathematical patterns. For instance, if a stock hovers in the range of $100 a share but does not exceed that level, and one day goes over $100, it might be claimed that the stock is now expected to skyrocket to a much higher level. Hardly. One nice thing about studying the stock market is that there is a lot of very good data. One team of economists studied 7,846 different strategies of technical analysis. Their conclusion was that none of them systematically beat the market over time.[3]

For most investors, the efficient markets hypothesis looks like a pretty good description of reality.

How to Really Pick Stocks, Seriously

Okay, you probably can't beat the market without a lot of luck on your side. But we do still have four pieces of important advice. *Very* important advice. If you apply this advice over the course of your life, you will probably save thousands of dollars, and if you become rich, you may save millions of dollars. (Suddenly, this textbook seems like a real bargain!) No, we don't have a get rich quick formula for you, but there are a few simple mistakes you can avoid to your benefit and at no real cost, other than a bit of time and attention. Let's go through each piece of advice in turn.

Diversify

The first secret to picking stocks is to pick lots of them! Since picking stocks doesn't work well, the "secret" to wise investing is to invest in a large basket of stocks—to diversify. Diversification lowers the risk of your portfolio, how much your portfolio fluctuates in value over time.

By picking a lot of stocks, you limit your overall exposure to things going wrong in any particular company. When the energy company Enron went bankrupt in 2001, many Enron employees had put most of their life's wealth in . . . can you guess? . . . Enron stock. That's a huge mistake, whether you work at the company or not. If you put all your eggs in one basket, it is a disaster if the handle on that basket breaks. Instead, you should buy many different stocks, in many different sectors of the economy, and, yes, in many countries, too. You'll end up with some Enrons, but you'll also have some big winners, such as Google and Microsoft. And if Google and Microsoft have become Enrons and gone under since this book was published, well, that is just further reason why you should diversify!

Modern financial markets have made diversification easy. Mutual funds let you invest in hundreds of stocks with just one purchase. And since stock picking doesn't work well, diversification has no downside—it reduces risk without reducing your expected return.

CHECK YOURSELF

> Is it better to invest in a mutual fund that has performed well for five years in a row or one that has performed poorly for five years in a row? Use the efficient markets hypothesis to justify your answer.

We are focusing on diversification across stocks but there are all kinds of risks in the world and you should diversify across as many as possible. U.S. stocks, for example, tend to fluctuate in value along with the growth rate of the U.S. economy. You can reduce this source of risk by including a large number of international firms in your portfolio. Bonds, art, housing, and human capital (your knowledge and skills) all have associated returns and risks, and for a given amount of return, you minimize your risk by diversifying across many assets.

If you accept the efficient markets hypothesis, and you accept the value of diversification, your best trading strategy can be summed up very simply. It is called **buy and hold**. That's right, buy a large bundle of stocks and just hold them. You don't have to do anything more. You will be diversified, you will not be trying to beat the market, and you can live a peaceful, quiet life.

Some of the simplest ways to buy and hold mean that you replicate the well-known stock indexes. Just for your knowledge, here are a few of those indexes:

The Dow Jones Industrial Average (or the Dow for short) is the most famous stock price index. The Dow is composed of 30 leading American stocks, each of these counted equally, whether the company is large or small. The Dow is not a very diversified index.

The Standard and Poor's 500 (S&P 500) is a much broader index of stock prices than the Dow; as the name indicates, it consists of the prices of 500 different stocks. Unlike in the Dow, the larger companies receive greater weight in the index than the smaller companies. The S&P 500 is a better indicator of the market as a whole than the Dow.

The NASDAQ Composite Index averages the prices of all the companies traded on NASDAQ, or National Association of Securities Dealers Automated Quotations. This usually amounts to a few thousand securities; as of 2011, there were 2,872 securities, but, of course, the number changes all the time. The NASDAQ index gives especially high weight to small stocks and high-tech stocks, at least relative to the Dow or the S&P 500.

Notice that diversification changes our understanding of what makes a stock risky, or not risky. You might at first think that a risky stock is one whose price moves up and down a lot. Not exactly. If investors are diversified, and indeed most of them are, their risk depends on how much their portfolio moves up and down, not how much a single stock moves up and down. A single stock might move up and down all the time but still an overall diversified portfolio won't change in value much if some of your stocks are moving up, while others are moving down.

According to finance economists, the riskiest stocks are those that move up and down in harmony with the market. For instance, many real estate stocks are risky because they are highly cyclical. They move up a lot when times are good (and the rest of the market is high) and they move down a lot when times are bad. When a recession comes, a lot of people just can't afford to buy a new house. In contrast, for an example of a relatively safe stock, consider Walmart, the discount outlet. When bad times come, yes, Walmart loses some business. But Walmart also gains some business because people who used to shop at Nordstrom now have less money and some of them will now shop at Walmart. In this regard, Walmart is partly protected from business downturns.[4] Many health-care stocks are safe in a similar way. Even if times are bad, you're probably not going to postpone that triple bypass operation; if you do, you won't be around to see when times are good again. In other words, if you care about the risk of a stock, don't just look at how the price of that stock moves. Look at how the price varies with the rest of the market. In the language of finance economists or statisticians, the riskiest stocks are those with the highest *covariance* with the market as a whole.

To **buy and hold** is to buy stocks and then hold them for the long run, regardless of what prices do in the short run.

The lesson here is that if you are worried about risk, think about your portfolio as a whole, rather than obsessing over any single stock. Or let's be more specific: If you are going to become an aerospace engineer, don't buy a lot of stock in aerospace companies. The value of your human capital—which is worth a lot—is already tied up in that industry. Don't make your overall portfolio riskier by putting more eggs in that basket. If anything, buy stocks that do well when aerospace does poorly. More generally, finance theorists say that the least risky assets *for you* are assets that are *negatively correlated* with *your portfolio*. What this means is that you should try to buy assets that rise in value when the rest of your portfolio is falling in value. Are you afraid that high energy prices will cripple the prospects for your career? Buy stock in a company that builds roads in Saudi Arabia. If oil prices stay high, the gains of that road-building company will partially offset your other losses. The lesson applies to more than stocks. If you become a dentist, you run the risk that a new technology will eliminate cavities. So try to limit your risk by diversifying your portfolio: Marry an optician or an engineer, not another dentist!

Avoid High Fees

We have some other advice for picking stocks. Avoid investments and mutual funds that have high fees or "loads," as they are sometimes called. It simply isn't worth it.

Let's say for instance that you wish to invest in the S&P 500. Some funds charge management and administrative fees of 0.09% of your investment, but other funds can charge up to 2.5% per year for what is really the same thing! Table 22.1 shows some of the different options for investing in the S&P 500 and their expense ratios (in 2008), the yearly percentage of your investment that you must pay in fees to the fund's managers.

The funds with the higher fees don't give you much of value in return. The lesson is simple: Don't pay the higher fees!

TABLE 22.1 Don't Pay Higher Fees for the Same Service

S&P Index Fund	Expense Ratio
Vanguard 500 Index Mutual Fund Admiral Shares (VFIAX)	0.09%
Fidelity Spartan 500 Index Mutual Fund (FSMKX)	0.10%
State Street Global Advisors S&P 500 Index Fund (SVSPX)	0.16%
United Association S&P 500 Index Fund II (UAIIX)	0.16%
USAA S&P 500 Index Mutual Fund Member Shares (USSPX)	0.18%
Schwab S&P 500 Index Fund—Select Shares (SWPPX)	0.19%
Vantagepoint 500 Stock Index Mutual Fund Class II Shares (VPSKX)	0.25%
T. Rowe Price Equity Index 500 Mutual Fund (PREIX)	0.35%
California Investment S&P 500 Index Mutual Fund (SPFIX)	0.36%
MassMutual Select Indexed Equity A (MIEAX)	0.67%
MassMutual Select Indexed Equity N (MMINX)	0.97%
ProFunds Bull Svc, Inv (BLPSX)	2.50%

Often when your broker calls you up to make a stock purchase, that purchase involves a relatively high fee (have you ever wondered why the broker is making the call?). Before buying or selling a stock in these circumstances, you should ask what the fee is to make the transaction. Understand the incentives of the person you are dealing with and that means understand that the broker usually earns more, the greater the number of transactions he or she can get you to make. Might that explain why he or she is telling you to buy or sell? Or maybe this really is a "once in a lifetime opportunity."

Even small fees can add up to large differences in returns over time. Let's say you are investing $10,000 over 30 years. If you invest with a firm that charges 0.10% a year in fees and the stock market gives a real return of 7% a year, then in 30 years you will have earned $74,016. If you invest in a firm that charges 1% a year, then in 30 years you will have about $57,434. The higher fees cost you $16,582 and, as we showed above, you probably got nothing for your extra fees. Small differences in growth or loss rates, when compounded over time, make for a big difference. The same is true for your portfolio.

That brings us to a corollary principle, to which we now turn.

Compound Returns Build Wealth

If one investment earns a higher rate of return each year than another investment, in the long run that makes a big difference. Imagine you buy a well-diversified portfolio of stocks and every year you reinvest all of your dividends. A simple approximation, called the rule of 70, explains how long it will take for your investment to double in value given a specified rate of return.

Rule of 70: If the rate of return (annual percent increase in value including dividends) of an investment is x%, then the doubling time is $70/x$ years.

Table 22.2 illustrates the rule of 70 by showing how long it takes for an investment to double in value given different returns. With a return of 1%, an investment will double approximately every 70 years (70/1 = 70). If returns increase to 2%, the value of your investment will double every 35 years (70/2 = 35). Consider the impact of a 4% return. If this rate of return is sustained, then the value of an investment doubles every 17.5 years (70/4 = 17.5). In 70 years, the value doubles 4 times, reaching a level 16 times its starting value!

The rule of 70 is just a mathematical approximation but it bears out the key concept that when compounded, small differences in investment returns can have a large effect. To make this more concrete, if you have a long time horizon, you probably should invest in (diversified) stocks rather than bonds.

In the long run, stocks offer higher returns than bonds. Since 1802, for example, stocks have had an average real rate of return of about 7% per year, while bonds have paid closer to 2% per year.[5] Using our now familiar rule of 70, we know that money that grows at 7% a year will double in 10 years, but money that grows at 2% a year won't double for 35 years. Alternatively, growing at 7% a year, $10,000 will return $76,122 in 30 years, but if it grows at 2% a year, the return will be only $18,113.

Stocks, however, have the potential for greater losses than do bonds because bond holders and other creditors are always paid before shareholders. You are unlikely to lose much money if you buy high-grade corporate or government

TABLE 22.2 Years to Double Using the Rule of 70

Annual Return, %	Years to Double
0	Never
1	70
2	35
3	23.3
4	17.5

bonds, but the stock market is highly volatile and it does periodically crash. Nonetheless, in American history stocks almost always outperform bonds over any 20-year time period you care to examine, including the period of the Great Depression and World War II. Stocks are usually the better long-term investment.

Of course, that doesn't mean that everyone should invest so heavily in stocks. In any particular year, or even over the course of a month, week, or day, stocks can go down in value quite a bit. If you are 80 years old and managing your retirement income, you probably shouldn't invest much in stocks. If you have to send your twins to college in two years' time, you might want some safer investments, as well. Nor does the past necessarily predict the future—just because stocks outperformed bonds in the past doesn't mean that will continue to happen. Remember to diversify!

The No Free Lunch Principle, or No Return Without Risk

The differences between stocks and bonds, as investment vehicles, reflect a more general principle. There is a systematic **trade-off between return and risk**. Figure 22.3, for example, shows the trade-off between return and risk on four asset classes. U.S. T-bills are safe but have low returns. You can get a higher return by buying stock in a group of large firms such as in the S&P 500, but the value of those firms fluctuates a lot more than the value of T-bills, so to get the higher return, you need to bear higher risk.*

The **risk-return trade-off** means higher returns come at the price of higher risk.

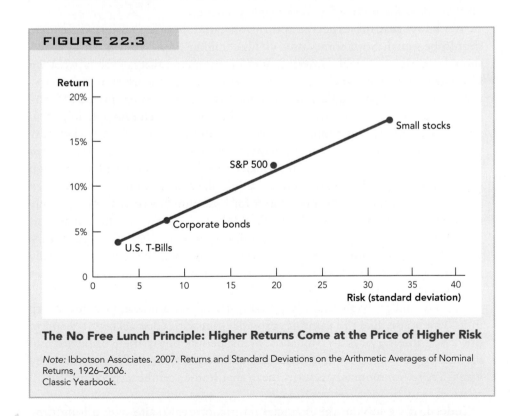

FIGURE 22.3

The No Free Lunch Principle: Higher Returns Come at the Price of Higher Risk

Note: Ibbotson Associates. 2007. Returns and Standard Deviations on the Arithmetic Averages of Nominal Returns, 1926–2006.
Classic Yearbook.

---

* We measure risk using the standard deviation of the portfolio return. The standard deviation is a measure of how much the return tends to fluctuate from its average level: thus, the larger the standard deviation, the greater the risk. A rule of thumb is that there is a 68% probability of being within ±1 standard deviation of the mean return. For the S&P 500, for example, the mean return is about 12% and the standard deviation is about 20% so in any given year, there is a 68% probability that the return will be between −8% and 32%. Of course, there is a 32% probability that something else could happen! But beware! The rule of thumb is only an approximation. Risk in the real world can rarely be modeled with perfect mathematical accuracy.

If you want even more risk than an investment in the stock market, numerous schemes give you a chance of making a killing. The simplest of such strategies is to take all your money, fly to Las Vegas, and bet on "black" for a spin of the roulette wheel. Yes, there is a 47.37% chance that you double your wealth. That's a high return, sort of. Sadly, there is also a 52.63% chance that you will lose everything you have, including your credit rating and the trust of your spouse and children. That's what we call high risk.

Remember this story when you hear about a high-flying "hedge fund" or other fancy investment device. It's easy to generate high returns for a few years by getting lucky and doubling down (betting all your winnings again). Take a look again at Figure 22.2. Higher returns come at the expense of higher risk.

This no free lunch principle can help you evaluate some other investments, as well. Let's say you come into a tidy sum of money and you start wondering whether you should invest in art. Overall, should you expect art to be a better or inferior financial investment, compared with the market as a whole?

A lot of people—probably most people—buy art because they want to look at it. They enjoy hanging it on their walls. In the language of economics, art yields "a nonmonetary return," which is just our way of saying it is fun to look at. Now suppose that investments in art earned just as high a return as investments in stocks. In that case, art would be fun to have on the wall *and* would be an excellent investment. But wait, that sounds like a free lunch doesn't it? So what does the no free lunch principle predict?

We know that the expected returns on different assets, adjusted for risk, should be equal. So if some asset yields a higher "fun" return, those assets should, on average, yield a lower financial return. And that is exactly what we find with art. On average, art underperforms the stock market by a few percentage points a year. You can think of the lower returns as the price of having some beautiful art on your wall. Again, it's the no free lunch principle in action.

This kind of analysis applies not just to art but also to real estate. Let's say you want to buy a home. Can you expect superior or inferior financial returns over time? This question is a little trickier than the art question because two different and opposing forces operate. Let's look at each in turn.

First, a home tends to be a risky asset for most purchasers. Let's say you buy a $300,000 home by putting down $200,000 and borrowing the remainder. That home is probably a fairly big chunk of your overall wealth and it puts you in a relatively nondiversified position. That's risk, people don't usually like risk, and as we saw above, riskier assets earn, all other things equal, higher expected returns (the risk-return trade-off).

Second, and probably more important, if you buy a house, you get to live in it. The house, like the painting, provides you with personal services and in this case those services are valuable. Many people enjoy their backyard and the feeling of owning a home and being able to paint the walls any color they want. These nonmonetary returns mean that houses can be expected to pay a relatively low financial return.

Indeed, if we look at the financial returns on real estate over a long time horizon, it turns out they are fairly low. In fact, for long periods of time, the average financial rate of return on real estate is not much different than zero. One lesson is that houses must be lots of fun!

If you want to see that the downside of real estate investments is not just a recent phenomenon, take a look at Figure 22.4.

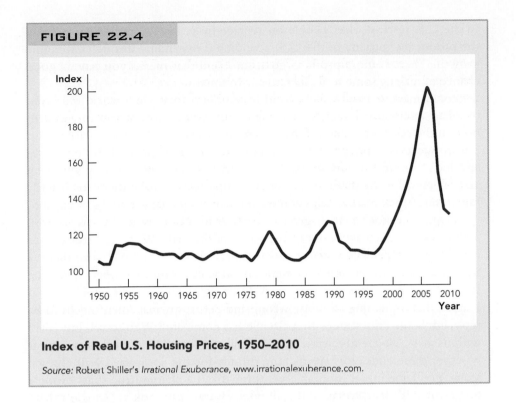

FIGURE 22.4

Index of Real U.S. Housing Prices, 1950–2010

Source: Robert Shiller's *Irrational Exuberance*, www.irrationalexuberance.com.

In the 50 years from 1947 to 1997, real housing prices hardly changed at all with some blips upward in the late 1970s and late 1980s. Beginning in 1997, a housing boom pushed prices well above any before seen in U.S. history. As you probably know, however, since 2006 prices have tumbled and may be even lower by the time you read this book.

The lesson is that most of the time a house is a good place to live but not a good place to invest. When prices started to rise in 1997 and kept rising year after year, many people thought that real estate was the investment of the century—"they ain't making any more," people said. But the no free lunch principle tells us that precisely because houses are a good place to live, we should not also expect them to be a good investment. All other things equal, fun activities yield lower financial returns than non-fun activities.

When prices rose, some people got lucky and made a killing, but other people tried to do the same and ended up bankrupt. So don't expect to make a killing in the real estate market, and remember to diversify! One more point. Are you one of these people who doesn't like to mow the lawn? Do you dread the notion of choosing homeowner's insurance or worrying about when your roof will fall in? The lesson is simple: Don't buy a house, you won't have fun, and the financial returns won't make it worth your while.

Other Benefits and Costs of Stock Markets

Throughout this chapter, we've recommended against gambling with all or most of your money. We've recommended buy and hold, based on a diversified portfolio. But hey, maybe some of you are into gambling. You know what? If you want to take risk for the sake of risk alone, the U.S. stock market offers the best odds in the world, better than Las Vegas and better than your local bookie.

CHECK YOURSELF

> How does investing in stocks of other countries help to diversify your investments?

> Many people dream of owning a football or baseball team. Would you expect the return on these assets to be relatively high or low?

In the U.S. stock market, people on average make money and that is because the productive capacity of the U.S. economy is expanding through economic growth. There is more profit to go around and that means you have a good chance of making some really lucrative investments.

Stocks markets have uses beyond investment. First, new stock and bond issues are an important means of raising capital for new investment (investment now in the economic sense of increasing the capital stock). Stock markets also reward successful entrepreneurs and thus encourage people to start companies and look around for new ideas. The founders of Google are now very rich and selling company shares to the stock market helped make them so. A well-functioning stock market helps companies such as Google get going or expand.

Second, the stock market gives us a better idea of how well firms are run. The stock price is a signal about the value of the firm. When the stock price is increasing, especially when it is increasing relative to other stocks, this is a signal that the firm is making the right investments for future profits. When the stock is declining, especially when it is declining relative to other stocks, this is a signal that something has gone wrong and perhaps management needs to be replaced. Some critics allege that Google has dominated Web search but failed with its maps, blog search services, and email accounts. It is not necessarily clear whether these endeavors are making money for the company. Will Google make YouTube into a profitable venture? Are the charges true that "Google has lost it"? It's hard to say in the abstract. But we can look at Google's share price and see if it is going up or down. Market prices give the public a daily report on whether the managers of a company are succeeding or failing.

Third, stock markets are a way of transferring company control from less competent people to more competent people. If a group of people think they know the right way to run a company, they can buy it and put their money where their mouth is, so to speak. Maybe a company should be merged, broken up, or simply taken in a new direction. The stock market is the ultimate venue where people bid for the right to make these decisions.

Bubble, Bubble, Toil, and Trouble

It's worth pointing out that stock markets (and other asset markets) have a downside, namely that they can encourage speculative bubbles. A speculative bubble arises when stock prices rise far higher, and more rapidly, than can be accounted for by the fundamental prospects of the companies at hand. Bubbles are based in human psychology and often they are hard to understand. Nobel Prize-winning economist Vernon Smith, whom you met in Chapter 4, has found that speculative bubbles and crashes occur in experimental markets, even when traders are given enough information to easily calculate an asset's true value.[6] Inexperienced traders are more prone to bubbles, but even experienced traders can fall for bubbles when the trading environment changes. Speculative bubbles and crashes have significant costs, as we discuss below, so economists are trying to better understand bubbles and how market institutions can be designed to help avoid bubbles.

During the dot.com era, circa 2000, many Internet or dot.com stocks had very high prices even though many of these companies had never earned a dime of profit or for that matter any revenue. Many of the tech stocks were listed on the NASDAQ stock exchange. As you can see in Figure 22.5, in the space of five years the NASDAQ Composite Index more than tripled from a monthly average of about 1,200 to over 4,000 before

FIGURE 22.5

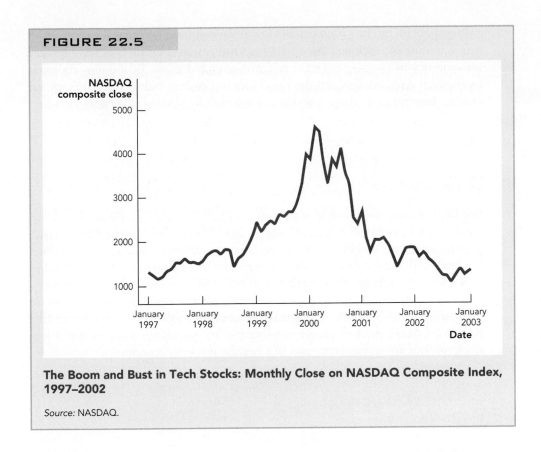

The Boom and Bust in Tech Stocks: Monthly Close on NASDAQ Composite Index, 1997–2002

Source: NASDAQ.

falling back down again. Many people made a lot of money on the ride up and many people—maybe the same people, maybe others—lost a lot of money on the ride down.

If you can spot speculative bubbles on a consistent basis, yes, you can become very wealthy. But, of course, a speculative bubble is usually easier to detect with hindsight than at the time. Microsoft and Google might have looked like speculative bubbles, too; the only problem is that they never burst. Betting too soon that high prices will end is also one way to go bankrupt.

Speculative bubbles, and their bursting, can hurt an economy. During the rise of the bubble, capital is invested in areas where it is not actually very valuable. A second wave of problems comes when the bubble crashes. Lower stock prices (or lower home prices) mean that people feel poorer and so they will spend less. The collapse of the bubble also means that workers must move from one sector to another, such as from high tech to retailing, or from real estate to export industries. Shifting labor from one sector of an economy to another creates labor adjustment costs.

We saw both of these problems with the dot.com bubble and the real estate bubble leading up to the crash of housing prices in 2007–2008. During the dot.com boom years, for example, we invested too much in stringing fiber-optic cable across the world's oceans—cable that later proved to be unprofitable. Similarly, during the housing boom we invested too much in houses that later were abandoned. In addition, the boom in housing prices led banks to be much too lax about the value of financial assets backed by portfolios of mortgages. When housing prices started to fall and people began to default on their mortgages, the value of these asset-backed securities plummeted and banks found themselves nearing bankruptcy. To stave off bankruptcy, these banks cut back on lending, transmitting problems in the housing markets to the wider economy and helping to generate the lengthy recession beginning in late 2008.

CHECK YOURSELF

> The Federal Reserve has been criticized for not stepping in and bursting the housing bubble, which would have prevented the housing collapse. Do you think this criticism is valid, based on what you read in this section?

Yes, bubbles can be a problem, but few people doubt that we are better off with active trading in stock and asset markets. One partial solution is to have greater transparency in assessing the value of companies and assets. Economists continue to research asset markets and the possibility of limiting bubbles and subsequent crashes. But, for now, there is no surefire solution for getting rid of asset bubbles.

☐ Takeaway

We have stressed some simple and practical points. It is difficult for an investor to consistently beat the market over long periods. You are well advised to diversify your investments. Avoid fees and try to generate a high compound return over time. Understand that the promise of higher returns is often accompanied by higher risk.

Viewed as a whole, stock markets and other trading markets give investors a chance to earn money, diversify their holdings, express opinions on the course of the market, and hedge risks. Stock markets also play a role in financing innovative new firms. Stock markets appear to be subject to speculative bubbles, but active stock markets are an important part of a healthy growing economy.

☐ CHAPTER REVIEW

KEY CONCEPTS

Efficient markets hypothesis, p. 422

Buy and hold, p. 424

Risk-return trade-off, p. 427

FACTS AND TOOLS

1. Before we plunge into the world of finance, let's review the rule of 70. Suppose your rich aunt hands you a $3,000 check at the end of the school year. She tells you it's for your education. But what should you *really* do with that extra money? Let's see how much it would be worth if you saved it for a while.

   a. If you put it in a bank account earning 2% real annual return on average, how many years would it take before it was worth $6,000? Until it was worth $12,000?

   b. If you put it in a Standard and Poor's 500 (S&P 500) mutual fund earning an average 7% real return every year, how many years would it take before it was worth $6,000? Until it was worth $12,000?

   c. Suppose you invest a little less than half your money in the bank and a little more than half in a mutual fund, just to play it somewhat safe, so that you can expect a 5% real return on average. How many years now until you reach $6,000 and $12,000?

2. Let's do something boring just to drive home a point: Count up the number of years in Figure 22.1 in which more than half of the mutual funds managed to beat the S&P 500 index. (Recall that the Standard and Poor's 500 is just a list of 500 large U.S. corporations—it's a list that overlaps a lot with the Fortune 500.) What percentage of the time did the experts actually beat the S&P 500?

3. Consider the supply and demand for oranges. Orange crops can be destroyed by below-freezing temperatures.

   a. If a weather report states that oranges are likely to freeze in a storm later this week, what probably happens to the demand for oranges *today*, before the storm comes?

   b. According to a simple supply-and-demand model, what happens to the price of oranges today given your answer to part a.

   c. How does this illustrate the idea that stock prices *today* "bake in" information about *future* events? In other words, how is a share of Microsoft like an orange? (*Note*: Wall Street people often use the expression "That news is already baked into the price" when they talk about the efficient markets hypothesis.)

4. In the United States, high-level corporate officials have to publicly state when they buy or sell a large number of shares in their own company. They have to make these statements a few days after their purchase or sale. What do you think probably happens (choose a, b, c or d below) when newspapers report these true "insider trades"? (*Note*: The right answer according to theory is actually true in practice.)

   a. When insiders sell, prices rise, since investors increase their demand for the company's shares.

   b. When insiders sell, prices fall, since investors increase their demand for the company's shares.

   c. When insiders sell, prices fall, since investors decrease their demand for the company's shares.

   d. When insiders sell, prices rise, since investors decrease their demand for the company's shares.

5. Let's see how fees can hurt your investment strategy. Let's assume that your mutual fund grows at an average rate of 7% per year—before subtracting off the fees. Using the rule of 70:

   a. How many years will it take for your money to double if fees are 0.5% per year?

   b. How many years will it take for your money to double if fees are 1.5% per year (not uncommon in the mutual fund industry)?

   c. How many years to double if fees are 2.5% per year?

6. a. If you talk to a broker selling the high-fee mutual fund, what will he or she probably tell you when you ask them, "Am I getting my money's worth when I pay your high fees?"

   b. According to Figure 22.1, is your broker's answer likely to be right most of the time?

THINKING AND PROBLEM SOLVING

1. Your brother calls you on the phone telling you that Google's share price has fallen by about 25% over the past few days. Now you can own one small slice of Google for only $430 a share (the price on the day this question was written). Your brother says he is pretty sure the stock is going to head back up to $600 very soon and you should buy.

   Should you believe your brother? *Hint:* Remember someone is selling shares whenever someone else is buying.

2. In most of your financial decisions early in life, you'll be a buyer, but let's think about the incentives of people who sell stocks, bonds, bank accounts, and other financial products.

   a. Walking in the shopping mall one day, you see a new store: the Dollar Store. Of course, you've seen plenty of dollar stores before, but none like this one: The sign in the window says, "Dollars for sale: Fifty cents each." Why will this store be out of business soon?

   b. If business owners are self-interested and fairly rational people, will they ever open up this dollar store in the first place? Why or why not?

   c. This dollar store is similar to stories people tell about "cheap stocks" that you might hear of on the news. Fill in the blank with any prices that make sense: "If the shares of this company were really worth _____, no one would really sell it for _____."

3. How is "stock market diversification" like putting money in a bank account?

4. Warren Buffett often says that he doesn't want a lot of diversification in his portfolio. He says that diversification means buying stocks that go up along with stocks that go down; but he only wants to buy the stocks that go up! From the point of view of the typical investor, what is wrong with this reasoning?

5. You own shares in a pharmaceutical company, PillCo. Reading the Yahoo! Finance Web site, you see that PillCo was sued this morning by users of PillCo's new heart drug, Amphlistatin. PillCo's stock has already been trading for a few hours today.

   a. When the bad news about the lawsuits came out, what probably happened to the price of PillCo shares within just a few minutes?

   b. According to the efficient markets hypothesis, should you sell your shares in PillCo now, a few hours after the bad news came out?

c. In many statistical studies of the stock market, the best strategy turns out to be "buy and hold." This means just what it sounds like: You buy a bunch of shares in different companies and hold them through good times and bad. People often have a tough time with the "bad" part of "holding through good times and bad." What does your answer to part b tell you about this idea?

CHALLENGES

1. What is so bad about bubbles? If the price of Internet stocks or housing rises and then falls, is that such a big problem? After all, some people say, most of the gains going up are "paper gains" and most of the losses going down are "paper losses." Comment on this view.

23

Consumer Choice

In this chapter, we take a deeper look at how rational consumers choose. In previous chapters, we analyzed a fairly simple choice. What should a consumer do when the price of a good falls? Buy more! That was easy. In this chapter, we look at more complicated choices such as whether a consumer should shop at Costco. Costco, like Sam's Club or BJ's, offers lower prices, but to shop there, you have to pay a membership fee. How much will consumers be willing to pay to shop at Costco? As you might imagine, this is a key question for Costco managers!

We will also be looking at how much labor a worker should supply in response to a lower wage. In our chapter on labor supply, we pointed out that a worker might respond to a lower wage by working less (called the substitution effect) or the worker might choose to work more to make up for the shortfall in income at the lower wage (the income effect). In this chapter, we introduce two new tools—budget constraints and indifference curves—that will help us understand in greater detail the substitution and income effects, and how consumers and workers choose when faced with complicated decisions.

How to Compare Apples and Oranges

Despite being warned not to, consumers do compare apples and oranges. In fact, consumers have to compare apples, oranges, and every other good if they are to spend their limited budget wisely.

Apples and oranges both produce value or, in economic terms, "utility" for the consumer. We call the increase in utility generated by an additional apple the **marginal utility** of an apple and denote it MU_A. To simplify, we will assume that marginal utility is diminishing. **Diminishing marginal utility** means that the first apple is great, the second good, the third not bad, and so on.

Marginal utility is the change in utility from consuming an additional unit.

Diminishing marginal utility means that each additional unit of a good adds less to utility than the previous unit.

435

FIGURE 23.1

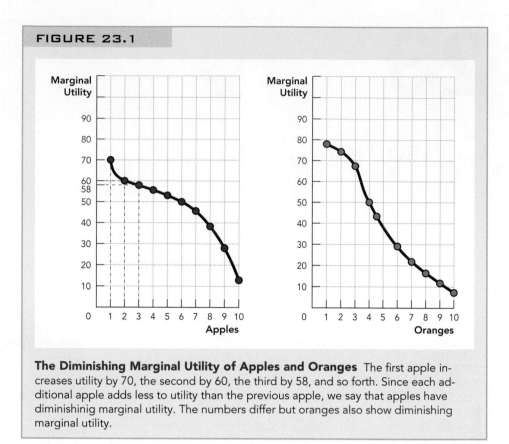

The Diminishing Marginal Utility of Apples and Oranges The first apple in-creases utility by 70, the second by 60, the third by 58, and so forth. Since each ad-ditional apple adds less to utility than the previous apple, we say that apples have diminishinig marginal utility. The numbers differ but oranges also show diminishing marginal utility.

Figure 23.1, for example, shows a marginal utility curve for apples on the left and a marginal utility curve for oranges on the right. In the figure, the mar-ginal utility of the first apple is 70 "utils," the second is 60 utils, the third is 58 utils, and so forth.

But apples and oranges aren't free. There is a price for apples, which we write as P_A, and there is a price for oranges, which we write as P_O. A consumer might love oranges more than any other fruit, but if the price of oranges is high, that consumer may prefer to consume apples. The real problem a con-sumer faces, therefore, is not to choose apples and oranges directly, but to choose how many dollars to spend on apples and how many dollars to spend on oranges. Apples and oranges are two alternative ways of generating utility from dollars. So how should a consumer allocate her dollars between apples and oranges?

As usual, the way to solve this problem is to think on the margin. Each additional dollar allocated to apples generates a certain amount of utility. For example, if the marginal utility of an apple is 70 and the price of apples is $2 per apple, then the marginal utility per dollar spent on apples is 35. More generally, the marginal utility per dollar spent on apples is $\dfrac{MU_A}{P_A}$. To simplify, if we suppose that $P_A = P_O = \$1$, then we can use the same figure as before, except now the axis is in terms of marginal utilities per dollar.

So which combination of apples and oranges maximizes utility? It's easiest to begin with a bundle that doesn't maximize utility. Once we understand why such a bundle doesn't maximize utility, the solution to the problem will become clear.

FIGURE 23.2

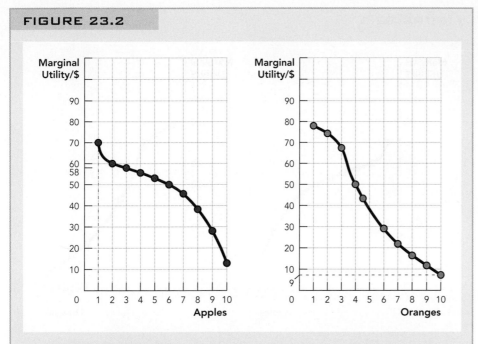

Diminishing Marginal Utility The curves now show the marginal utility per dollar of spending on apples and oranges. Imagine that apples and oranges are $1 each and the consumer spends her entire budget of $10 on oranges. The 10th dollar of spending on oranges increases utility by 9. If the consumer spent one dollar less on oranges (−9 utils) and one dollar more on apples (+70 utils), the consumer's total utility would increase by 61.

Consider Figure 23.2 and suppose that the consumer has $10 in income and she buys 10 oranges and no apples. From the right panel, we can see that the 10th orange is generating 9 utils per dollar. Now consider how much utility would be generated by consuming one dollar less of oranges and one dollar more of apples. From the left panel, we can see that the first dollar spent on apples will generate 70 utils. Thus, by consuming one fewer orange (−9 utils) and one more apple (+70 utils), the consumer can get an increase of 61 utils in total utility.

Keep following this logic. Should the consumer consume 9 oranges and 1 apple? No. Notice that the marginal utility per dollar of the second apple exceeds the marginal utility per dollar of the ninth orange, so the consumer can increase total utility by shifting another dollar of consumption away from oranges and toward apples.

In other words, if the marginal utility per dollar of apples is higher than the marginal utility per dollar of oranges, then the consumer gets more "bang from a buck" spent on apples than on oranges. Thus, she should buy more apples and fewer oranges:

$$\text{If } \frac{MU_A}{P_A} > \frac{MU_O}{P_O}\text{, then buy more apples and fewer oranges.}$$

By exactly the same logic, if the marginal utility of apples were less than that of oranges, then the consumer gets more bang from a buck spent on oranges. Thus, she should buy fewer apples and more oranges, that is,

$$\text{If } \frac{MU_A}{P_A} < \frac{MU_O}{P_O}\text{, then buy fewer apples and more oranges.}$$

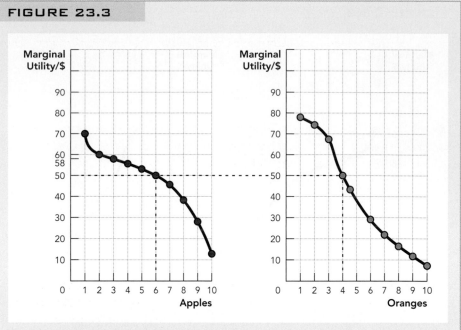

FIGURE 23.3

How to Maximize Utility To maximize utility, choose the quantity of apples and oranges such that the marginal utility per dollar of apples is equal to the marginal utility per dollar of oranges, $\frac{MU}{P_A} = \frac{MU}{P_O}$.

Putting these two conditions together, we find that there is only one condition when the consumer cannot increase utility by adjusting her spending, that is, only one condition when the consumer is maximizing utility:

$$\text{If } \frac{MU_A}{P_A} = \frac{MU_O}{P_O}, \text{ then utility is maximized.}$$

Figure 23.3 shows that if one follows this logic, the point of maximum utility for the consumer is to consume 6 apples and 4 oranges.

We have derived our rule for just two goods, but the idea is perfectly general. Thus, to maximize utility, the **optimal consumption rule** says a consumer should allocate his or her spending so the marginal utility per dollar is equal for all purchases:

$$\frac{MU_A}{P_A} = \frac{MU_O}{P_O} = \frac{MU_i}{P_i} = \cdots \frac{MU_z}{P_z}$$

The **optimal consumption rule** says that to maximize utility, a consumer should allocate spending so that the marginal utility per dollar is equal for all purchases.

Even if you don't consciously think of the "marginal utility per dollar of an apple" as a specific number, the rule tells us that to maximize utility, we should spend our bucks until the bang from a buck is the same for all purchases.

The Demand Curve

The optimal consumption rule also gives us an informal explanation for why a consumer's demand curve slopes downward. Suppose that the consumer is currently maximizing utility, so the two-goods version of the optimal consumption rule says:

$$\frac{MU_A}{P_A} = \frac{MU_O}{P_O}$$

Now imagine that the price of apples P_A increases. An increase in P_A means that apples now provide less utility per dollar, so we have $\dfrac{MU_A}{P_A} < \dfrac{MU_O}{P_O}$. But recall our rule from above:

If $\dfrac{MU_A}{P_A} < \dfrac{MU_O}{P_O}$, then buy fewer apples and more oranges.

We can see that an increase in the price of apples leads to the consumer buying fewer apples. The optimal consumption rule therefore gives us a foundation for demand curves based on individual choice.

The optimal consumption rule is an intuitive and useful way of thinking about how consumers choose to allocate their dollars, but we have derived the rule informally and in a form that makes it difficult to make specific predictions. It's not obvious from the optimal consumption rule, for example, how changes in income affect choices. We also showed how an increase in P_A means that a consumer should buy fewer apples and more oranges, but we didn't say much about whether or when the dominant effect is fewer apples and when the dominant effect is more oranges. The theory, as we presented it, also puts this strange idea of "utils" front and center even though no one has ever seen a util. We can fix all of these problems and produce a richer, more complete theory by developing consumer choice theory a bit more formally. Fortunately, the optimal consumption rule will continue to hold true even in our richer model.

The Budget Constraint

Imagine that there are only two goods as before, but just for variety, we will switch to gasoline and pizza. Gasoline is $2 per gallon and pizzas are $10 per pizza. Let's suppose also that the consumer has $100 of income. Figure 23.4 on the next page shows the consumer's **budget constraint**, namely all of the bundles of gasoline and pizza that the consumer can afford given his income and prices. For example, the consumer could buy 50 gallons of gas and 0 pizzas, or 10 pizzas and 0 gallons of gas, or any consumption bundle along the line connecting these two points. The consumer cannot afford bundles that are "outside" the budget constraint. For example, the consumer cannot afford the red bundle of 40 gallons and 6 pizzas. (How much income would the consumer need to afford this bundle?)

In addition to the points along the budget constraint, the consumer can also afford any point that is "inside" the budget constraint, such as the green point of 10 gallons and 4 pizzas. If the consumer bought this bundle of goods, however, he would spend $60 ($2 × 10 + $10 × 4), leaving him with $40 in income. Note, however, that in this model, there are only two goods and no future periods so saving doesn't have any benefits. Thus, a consumer will always want to purchase a consumption bundle that lies on the budget constraint.

The budget constraint depends on the consumer's income and also on the prices of gasoline and pizza. Let's look at income first. Imagine, for example, that the consumer had $140 of income. Now the consumer could purchase any of the consumption bundles shown in Figure 23.5 on the next page.

Notice that with $140 in income, the consumer can now afford the red consumption bundle (40 gallons of gasoline, 6 pizzas) that he could not afford with $100 income. More generally, an increase in income pushes the budget constraint outward, parallel to the old budget constraint.

A **budget constraint** shows all the consumption bundles that a consumer can afford given their income and prices.

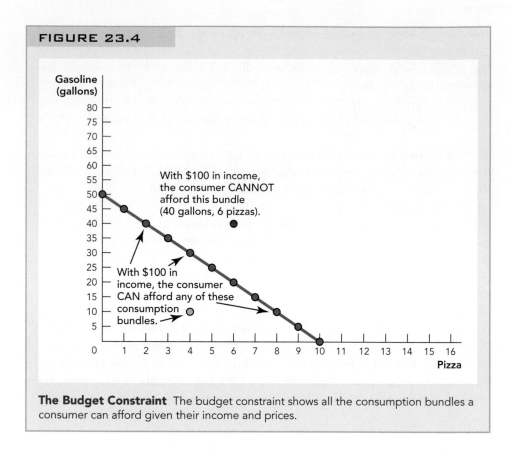

The Budget Constraint The budget constraint shows all the consumption bundles a consumer can afford given their income and prices.

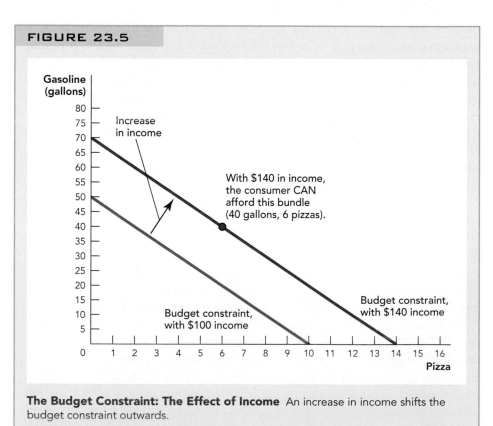

The Budget Constraint: The Effect of Income An increase in income shifts the budget constraint outwards.

Now let's look at how changes in prices affect the budget constraint. Assume that the consumer has $100 in income and the price of gasoline is $2 per gallon, but now there is a sale on pizzas so the price falls to $5 per pizza. If the consumer spends all of his money on gasoline, he can still purchase 50 gallons of gasoline and 0 pizzas so the point on the vertical axis remains the same. If he spends all his money on pizza, however, he can now afford 20 pizzas. Thus, as shown in Figure 23.6, a fall in the price of pizzas *rotates* the budget constraint outward along the horizontal axis.

As you might expect from the figure, the slope of the budget constraint is closely related to the prices of pizza and gasoline. The slope of the budget constraint, the rise/run, tells us the trade-off between gasoline and pizza, that is, how many gallons of gasoline the consumer can afford if he buys 1 fewer pizza. When the price of a pizza is $10 and the price of a gallon of gas is $2, the consumer can afford 5 more gallons of gasoline when he purchases 1 fewer pizza, so the slope of the budget constraint is $\frac{P_{Pizza}}{P_{Gas}} = \frac{\$10}{\$2} = 5$. The slope of the budget constraint is also called the relative price. In this case, the relative price of pizza to gas is 5. To be precise, the slope of the budget constraint is -5, which reflects the fact that to get more gasoline, the consumer must purchase *fewer* pizzas, but economists often drop the negative sign for convenience (mathematicians, however, would be horrified at this practice).

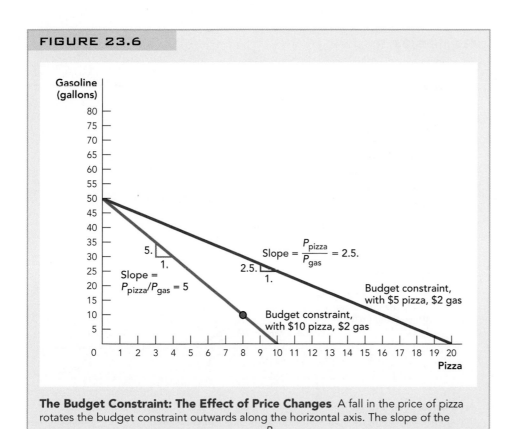

FIGURE 23.6

The Budget Constraint: The Effect of Price Changes A fall in the price of pizza rotates the budget constraint outwards along the horizontal axis. The slope of the budget constraint is equal to the price ratio $\frac{P_{Pizza}}{P_{Gas}}$.

When the price of pizza falls to $5 per pizza, the consumer can afford 2.5 additional gallons of gasoline when he purchases 1 fewer pizza, so the slope of the budget constraint falls to $\frac{P_{Pizza}}{P_{Gas}} = \frac{\$5}{\$2} = 2.5$. We can now draw a consumer's budget constraint for any income and set of prices. We know that the consumer will choose a consumption bundle somewhere along the budget constraint, but to say more about the exact consumption bundle, we need to say more about preferences.

Preferences and Indifference Curves

Consider a particular consumption bundle, say, bundle *A* in Figure 23.7. Now let's find all the bundles that the consumer regards as *just as good as* bundle *A*. If bundle *A* is just as good as bundle *B*, we say the consumer is indifferent between bundle *A* and bundle *B*, or equivalently, we say that bundle *A* and bundle *B* give the consumer an equal amount of utility. An indifference curve connects all the bundles that give the consumer an equal amount of utility and so we have drawn an indifference curve in Figure 23.7 that shows all the consumption bundles which give an equal amount of utility to bundle *A*.

We have drawn an indifference curve in Figure 23.7 that is curved inward. Let's explain why this is a plausible shape for indifference curves. Notice that

CHECK YOURSELF

> Draw a consumer's budget constraint when the consumer has an income of $100, $P_{Gas} = \$2$, and $P_{Pizza} = \$10$. Now draw the new budget constraint when income = $80.

> Draw a consumer's budget constraint when the consumer has an income of $100, $P_{Gas} = \$2$, and $P_{Pizza} = \$10$. Now draw the new budget constraint when $P_{Gas} = \$4$.

> In 1970, the price of pizza is $2.50 and the price of a gallon of gas is $0.50. In 2010, the price of pizza is $10 and the price of a gallon of gas is $2. Has the relative price of pizza changed?

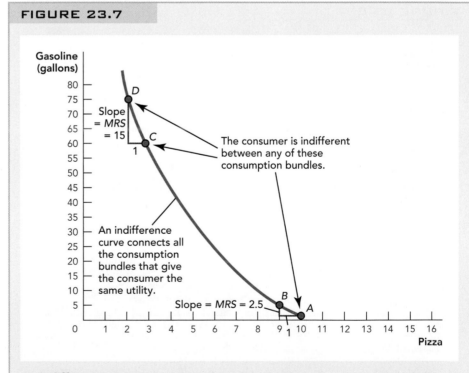

FIGURE 23.7

An Indifference Curve An indifference curves connects all consumption bundles that give the consumer the same utility. At point *A* the consumer has lots of pizza and only a little gasoline so they are willing to give up 1 pizza in return for just 2.5 gallons of gas. At point *C* the consumer has lots of gasoline and not so much pizza so to give up 1 pizza they require an additional 15 gallons of gasoline to remain indifferent.

bundle *A* has 10 pizzas and 0 gallons of gas—that's an awful lot of pizza and not so much gas, or at least not so much gasoline. Since the consumer has a lot of pizza at bundle *A*, he probably would be willing to give up a pizza to get just a few gallons gasoline, say, 2.5 gallons for 1 pizza, which would place the consumer at bundle *B*. The number of gallons per pizza that the consumer requires to remain indifferent is called the **marginal rate of substitution (MRS)** and is given by the slope of the indifference curve (noting once again, that we have dropped the negative sign).

But now consider bundle *C*. At bundle *C*, the consumer has fewer pizzas and more gas than at bundle *A*, so to remain indifferent, the consumer now requires 15 additional gallons of gasoline to give up 1 pizza. As the consumer gives up more pizza and gets more gasoline, pizza becomes more valuable and gasoline less valuable, so the consumer requires more and more gasoline in return for the same number of pizzas. Graphically, what this behavior implies is an indifference curve that is curved inward.

In Figure 23.8, we illustrate a second indifference curve that shows all the consumption bundles that have the same utility as consumption bundle *Y*. What is the relationship between the *ABCD* indifference curve and the *XYZ* indifference curve? Compare consumption bundles *C* and *Y*. Consumption bundle *Y* has more gasoline and more pizza than consumption bundle *C*, so we can say for sure that consumption bundle *Y* has higher utility or is more preferred than consumption bundle *C*. But how does consumption bundle *C* compare with consumption bundle *Z* (which has more gasoline but fewer pizzas) or consumption bundle *X* (which has more pizzas but less gasoline)? We know that bundle *Y* is preferred to *C* but we also know that the consumer

The **marginal rate of substitution (MRS)** is the rate at which the consumer is willing to trade one good for another and remain indifferent. The MRS is equal to the slope of the indifference curve at that point.

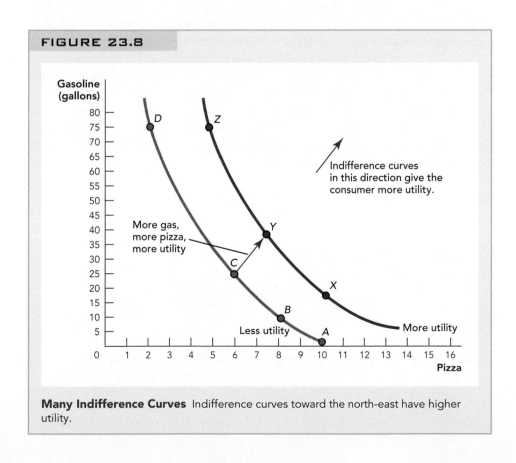

FIGURE 23.8

Many Indifference Curves Indifference curves toward the north-east have higher utility.

CHECK YOUR SELF

> Use an argument similar to the one we used in the last paragraph to show that (1) indifference curves can never cross and (2) indifference curves must have a negative slope.

is indifferent between X, Y, and Z, so it follows that bundles X and Z are also preferred to bundle C. In fact, through a similar argument, we can say that any consumption bundle on XYZ is preferred to any consumption bundle on ABCD. This means that indifference curves toward the north-east of the diagram give the consumer more utility, so the consumer wants to be as far to the north-east as possible.

Optimization and Consumer Choices

Now that we understand budget constraints and preferences, we can find the consumer's optimal consumption bundle. We know that the consumer must be on (or inside) the budget constraint and the consumer wants to be on the indifference curve that is the farthest to the north-east. Thus, to find the optimal consumption bundle, we look for the consumption bundle that is on the highest indifference curve but still on the budget constraint. Figure 23.9 illustrates.

Notice from Figure 23.9 that at the optimal bundle, the slope of the indifference curve is equal to the slope of the budget constraint. This is not an accident but a requirement. To see why, try to "push" an indifference curve as far as you can toward the north-east while still keeping at least one point on the budget constraint. The point of maximum utility is found where the indifference curve has been pushed so far it just touches the budget constraint.

More formally, consider the point labeled "Possible but not optimal." This point is on the consumer's budget constraint, which explains why it is possible. Why isn't this point optimal? At Possible but not optimal, the slope of the indifference curve is 2, which means that the consumer needs just 2 additional gallons of gas to be indifferent to giving up 1 pizza. The slope of the budget constraint is 5, which means that the consumer can get 5 gallons of gas if he gives up 1 pizza—that's more gas than he requires to be indifferent! Thus at Possible but not optimal, the consumer can increase his utility by buying more gas and fewer pizzas and therefore this point cannot be optimal. In fact, what we have just shown is that the consumer can always do better if the slope of the indifference curve is different from the slope of the budget constraint.

Thus, remembering that the slope of the indifference curve is the MRS and the slope of the budget constraint is the price ratio, we can write that the optimal consumption bundle is found where

$$\text{slope of indifference curve} \equiv MRS = \frac{P_{\text{Pizza}}}{P_{\text{Gas}}} \equiv \text{slope of budget constraint}$$

Perhaps you are wondering how $MRS = \dfrac{P_{\text{Pizza}}}{P_{\text{Gas}}}$ relates to the optimal consumption rule that we stated earlier:

$$\frac{MU_{\text{Pizza}}}{P_{\text{Pizza}}} = \frac{MU_{\text{Gas}}}{P_{\text{Gas}}}$$

or rearranging

$$\frac{MU_{\text{Pizza}}}{MU_{\text{Gas}}} = \frac{P_{\text{Pizza}}}{P_{\text{Gas}}}$$

Can you guess what we are going to say next? Correct, it turns out that $MRS = \dfrac{MU_{\text{Pizza}}}{MU_{\text{Gas}}}$ so fortunately, our two conditions for optimal consumption,

$$\frac{MU_{\text{pizza}}}{P_{\text{pizza}}} = \frac{MU_{\text{gas}}}{P_{\text{gas}}} \text{ and } MRS = \frac{P_{\text{pizza}}}{P_{\text{gas}}},$$ are really just two ways of writing the same thing.★

FIGURE 23.9

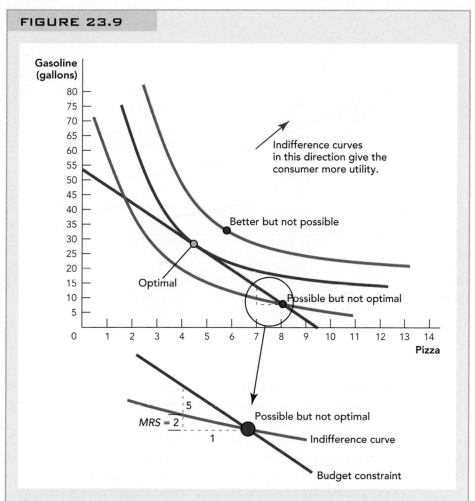

The Consumer's Optimum The figure at top shows that the optimal consumption bundle is found where the budget constraint is just tangent to an indifference curve. At this point the slope of the indifference curve is equal to the slope of the budget constraint, $MRS = \frac{P_{\text{Pizza}}}{P_{\text{Gas}}}$. The Better but not possible bundle has more gasoline and more pizza than the bundle labeled Optimal but it is not on the budget constraint and thus not affordable.

At the Possible but not optimal bundle the $MRS = 2$ and the slope of the budget constraint, $\frac{P_{\text{Pizza}}}{P_{\text{Gas}}} = 5$. What this means is that the consumer will accept 2 gallons of gas to give up 1 pizza but the market is willing to give the consumer 5 gallons of gas if they give up 1 pizza—that is a good deal! The consumer, therefore, will trade pizza for gas until the $MRS = \frac{P_{\text{Pizza}}}{P_{\text{Gas}}}$.

★ The proof is slightly involved but not difficult. Suppose that we take away from a consumer a small amount of pizza, $\triangle_{\text{Pizza}}$, and we give him in return a small amount of gas, $\triangle_{\text{Gas}}$; then the change in total utility, $\triangle U$, from this exchange is $\triangle U = -\triangle_{\text{Pizza}} \times MU_{\text{Pizza}} + \triangle_{\text{Gas}} \times MU_{\text{Gas}}$. Along an indifference curve, total utility is constant, so $\triangle U = 0$ and thus $-\triangle_{\text{Pizza}} \times MU_{\text{Pizza}} + \triangle_{\text{Gas}} \times MU_{\text{Gas}} = 0$. Then rearrange to find $\triangle_{\text{Gas}}/\triangle_{\text{Pizza}} = MU_{\text{Pizza}}/MU_{\text{Gas}}$. But $\triangle_{\text{Gas}}/\triangle_{\text{Pizza}}$ is the MRS, the slope of the indifference curve, so we have shown that $MRS = MU_{\text{Pizza}}/MU_{\text{Gas}}$.

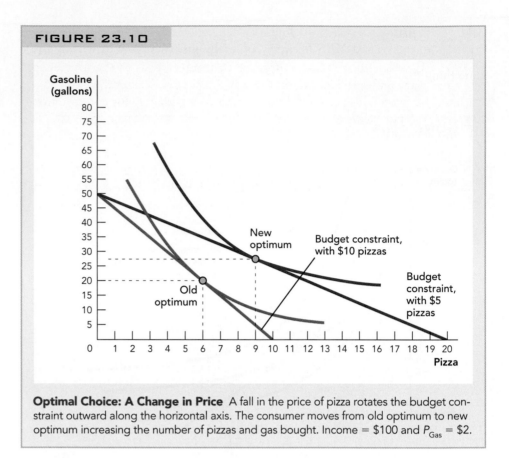

FIGURE 23.10

Optimal Choice: A Change in Price A fall in the price of pizza rotates the budget constraint outward along the horizontal axis. The consumer moves from old optimum to new optimum increasing the number of pizzas and gas bought. Income = $100 and P_{Gas} = $2.

Now that we know how to find the consumer's optimal consumption bundle, we can show how the optimal bundle changes as income and prices change. Figure 23.10, for example, shows how a consumer responds to a decrease in the price of pizzas from $10 to $5. When P_{Pizza} = $10 and P_{Gas} = $2, the consumer maximizes utility by choosing 6 pizzas and 20 gallons of gas at the point labeled "Old optimum." As we showed in Figure 23.6, a decrease in the price of pizzas rotates the budget constraint along the horizontal axis. With the new budget constraint, the consumer chooses 9 pizzas and 27.5 gallons of gas at the point labeled "New optimum."

Notice that a fall in the price of pizza increases the number of pizzas purchased, but in this example it also increases the number of gallons of gasoline consumed. At first, this result may seem confusing: Why should a fall in the price of pizza increase the consumption of gasoline? The reason is that a fall in the price of pizza has two effects, the income effect and the substitution effect. Let's now explain these two effects.

The Income and Substitution Effects

When the price of pizza was $10, the consumer bought 6 pizzas for a total pizza spending of $60. When the price of pizza falls to $5, the consumer can buy 6 pizzas for $30, so the drop in the price of pizza gives the consumer an additional $30 to spend. With greater income, the consumer may choose to spend more money on pizza *and* more money on gas. More generally, a fall in the price of a good means the consumer's income goes further than before, so a fall in price is in some ways similar to an increase in income.

A price change is more than a change in income, however. Imagine that the price of pizza falls from $10 to $5, which, as we said, gives the consumer an extra $30 to spend. Feeling richer, the consumer heads to the market to buy more pizza and gasoline, but on the way a pickpocket takes the extra $30. Without the extra income, should the consumer still change his consumption bundle? Yes. The price of pizza has fallen relative to the price of gas and the consumer should take advantage of this change in relative prices by consuming more pizza. Of course, if the consumer has been pickpocketed on the way to market, the only way he can consume more pizza is by consuming less gasoline. Even so, the consumer will be better off by substituting pizza for gasoline in response to the change in relative prices. Remember, the optimal consumption rule says that to maximize utility, we need $\dfrac{MU_{\text{Pizza}}}{P_{\text{Pizza}}} = \dfrac{MU_{\text{Gas}}}{P_{\text{Gas}}}$, but if the consumer was maximizing utility before the price change, then after the P_{Pizza} falls, it must be that $\dfrac{MU_{\text{Pizza}}}{P_{\text{Pizza}}} > \dfrac{MU_{\text{Gas}}}{P_{\text{Gas}}}$, and this tells us that after P_{Pizza} falls, the consumer should buy more pizza and less gas.

Thus, a change in price causes consumers to change their consumption bundle for two reasons, *the income effect* and the relative price, or *substitution effect*. In Figure 23.11, we show how to decompose the total effect of a price change into the income and substitution effects. The fall in the price of pizza causes

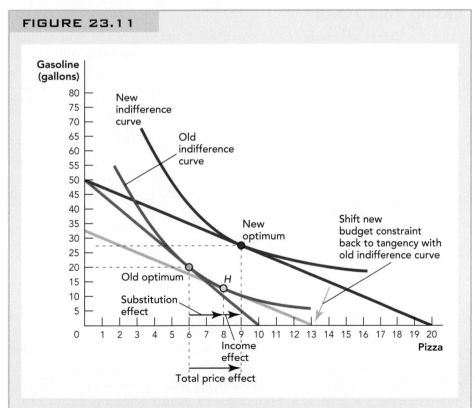

FIGURE 23.11

Income and Substitution Effects To decompose the total effect of a price change into the income and substitution effects, shift the new budget constraint back until it is just tangent to the old indifference curve (at *H*).

The substitution effect is given by change in consumption along the old indifference curve from the Old optimum to point *H*. The income effect is given by the change in consumption from point *H* to the New optimum.

the consumer to shift from buying 6 pizzas at the old optimum to buying 9 pizzas at the new optimum. This is the total effect of the price change. To decompose the total effect, we take the new budget constraint, which reflects the new relative prices, and we shift it back toward the origin until it is tangent to the old indifference curve at point *H*. The shifting back of the budget constraint is like the pickpocket we describe earlier—we reduce the consumer's income until the consumer has the same utility level (is on the same indifference curve) as before the price change.★

We can now define the substitution and income effects more precisely. The **substitution effect** is the change in consumption caused by a change in relative prices holding the consumer's utility level constant. Thus, in Figure 23.11, the substitution effect is the change in consumption from Old optimum to point *H*. The **income effect** is the change in consumption caused by the change in purchasing power from a price change. Thus, in Figure 23.11, the income effect is given by the movement from *H* to New optimum.

The **substitution effect** is the change in consumption caused by a change in relative prices holding the consumer's utility level constant.

The **income effect** is the change in consumption caused by the change in purchasing power from a price change.

Applications of Income and Substitution Effects

We have now developed the key tools that we need to better understand consumer and worker choice. Let's begin with some applications of income and substitution effects.

Losing Your Ticket

Have you ever bought a concert or movie ticket and then lost it? When should you buy another ticket? If you lost your ticket, you probably feel foolish or angry. Many of us react emotionally in a situation like this, and perhaps we decide that fate is against us and that we weren't really meant to see the concert or movie anyway. The better course of action, however, can be determined by some cooler thinking and a little economics.

Let's say you lose a movie ticket on which you spent $10. What is the price if you wish to buy another ticket? It's still $10. You are still comparing the movie against other uses for the $10. In terms of the substitution effect, the price hasn't changed so there should be no change in your assessment. Either the movie is worth giving up $10 worth of other goods or it is not.

What about the income effect? Well, you're out the $10 and thus you are poorer. That's a fairly small negative income effect. If you're really poor, though, it might induce you to make fewer purchases, including movie ticket purchases. But for most people, the income effect should be very small, so small that it can be safely ignored. Thus, if the ticket cost $10, you should buy another ticket.

Alternatively, let's say you lose a Lady Gaga concert ticket, which cost you $200 on eBay. There is still no change in the price, at least assuming that the price on eBay hasn't changed, so the logic of substitution still says buy another ticket. But now the negative income effect is larger than in the case of the movie ticket. It shouldn't bother a well-off person, but some of you will feel noticeably poorer and you may wish to reconsider buying another concert ticket for $200.

★If you are following very closely, you may notice that our pickpocket leaves the consumer with just enough income to purchase the old bundle at the point labeled "Old optimum" but our graphical pickpocket takes a little bit more. The first version of the income effect is called the Slutsky income effect, while the second is called the Hicks income effect after its originators. For a small price change, the difference between these two versions of the income effect is slight and can be ignored, which is what we do here.

The motto of the story: If you lose cheap tickets, replace them for sure. If you lose expensive tickets, you need to compare the income effect with the substitution effect. For a sufficiently wealthy person, even the loss of an expensive concert ticket shouldn't create a very big income effect. Poorer people may wish to think twice.

How Much Should Costco Charge for Membership?

Costco, one of the largest retailers in the world, offers low prices on many consumer goods. But to shop at Costco, you have to join the Costco "club" and pay a yearly membership fee. How much should Costco charge for membership?

To answer this question, let's create a budget constraint and indifference curve diagram with income on the vertical axis and goods you can buy at Costco on the horizontal axis. Without Costco membership, the consumer faces the blue budget constraint in Figure 23.12, labeled "Without Costco Membership," and consumes the No Costco bundle. Costco members pay

FIGURE 23.12

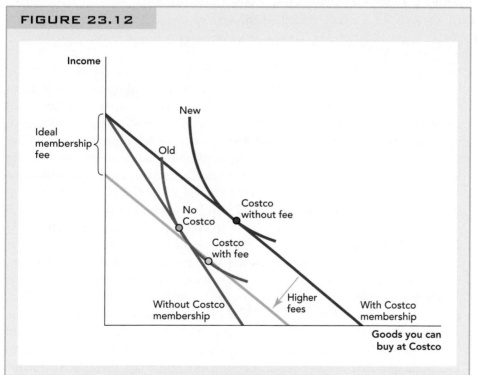

How Much Should Costco Charge for Membership? Without Costco membership the price ratio is given by the slope of the Without Costco membership budget constraint and the consumer chooses the bundle at No Costco. If the consumer joins Costco they can buy the goods that Costco sells at lower prices so the budget constraint rotates out. With no membership fee the consumer would consume the bundle at Costco without fee.

Costco would like to charge as high a membership fee as possible. The membership price is a decrease in the consumer's income so we can ask how much income can we take from the consumer and still leave the consumer at least as well off as without membership?

The Ideal membership fee (from Costco's point of view!) is the reduction in income that keeps the consumer on their old indifference curve. With the ideal membership fee the consumer consumes the bundle at Costco with fee.

lower prices, so if there were no membership fee, Costco members would face the red budget constraint, labeled "With Costco membership," and consume the Costco without fee bundle.

Costco, however, wants to charge as high a membership fee as possible. How much can the retailer charge? The membership fee is equivalent to a decrease in the consumer's income, so another way of asking this question is to ask how much can we decrease the consumer's income and still leave the consumer at least as well off with Costco membership as without it? If we shift the green budget line, which reflects the lower prices at Costco, back toward the origin, we can shift the line until it is tangent to the old indifference curve at the point labeled "Costco with fee." At Costco with fee, the consumer is indifferent between joining Costco, paying the fee, and enjoying the lower prices, and not joining Costco, saving on the fee, but paying higher prices. Since income is on the vertical axis, we can easily read the ideal membership fee off the graph.

Costco charges $50 for membership. This may not seem like a lot, but in 2010 membership fees earned Costco revenues of $1.7 billion dollars, which exceeded its profits of $1.3 billion. Costco, therefore, is very concerned with setting the ideal membership fee.

Labor Supply

In Chapter 17, we discussed how a worker's labor supply curve can be backward-bending; that is, a decrease in the wage could cause a worker to work more. At first, this might seem surprising. Why would a worker work more hours when the payoff to working is going down? To see the intuition, imagine a janitor, perhaps an immigrant from a developing country, whose wage falls. The janitor may choose to work more hours in response to the lower wage, because at a lower wage, he needs to work more hours to make enough money to put his children through college. Similarly, when the Beatles were young and unknown, they were paid low wages but they played 4 to 5 sets a day, 7 days a week in German strip clubs, just to make ends meet. As their fame grew, so did their wages and the Beatles responded by playing fewer hours. Eventually, they stopped touring altogether, and a few years after that, they split up completely.

More generally, remember that a lower wage has two effects: the substitution effect and the income effect. When the wage decreases, that's the same as a decrease in the price of leisure so the substitution effect says you should "buy" more leisure by working fewer hours. When the wage decreases, however, that also makes you poorer. The income effect says that when your income falls, you should buy fewer (normal) goods including leisure.

Notice that the substitution and income effects work in opposite directions in this case. If the substitution effect dominates, the worker works fewer hours when the wage rate falls. If the income effect dominates, the worker works more hours when the wage rate falls.

In Figure 23.13, we explain the basics of the income-leisure model of labor supply. We put income on the vertical axis and leisure on the horizontal axis. We will think about daily labor supply so the maximum number of hours of leisure is 24. Imagine that the wage is $20 an hour. If the worker chooses 24 hours of leisure (0 hours of work), she earns $0. If the worker chooses 0 hours of leisure (24 hours of work), she earns $480 a day. The budget constraint labeled $w = \$20$, therefore, shows all the income-leisure possibilities

FIGURE 23.13

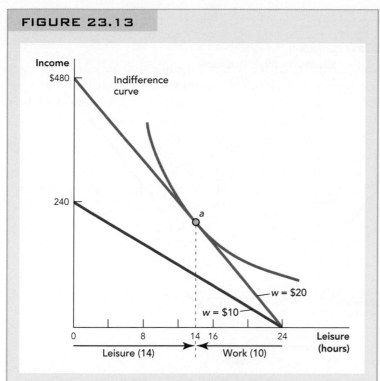

The Income-Leisure Model of Labor Supply Leisure is measured on the horizontal axis moving toward the right so work hours are measured toward the left. Suppose the wage is $20 an hour. If the worker chooses 24 hours of leisure they earn $0. If the worker chooses 0 hours of leisure (24 hours of work) they earn $480. The blue budget constraint thus shows all the income-leisure possibilities open to the worker when the wage is $20 an hour. At the optimal choice the worker chooses 14 hours of leisure (10 hours of work).

The red budget constraint shows all the income-leisure possibilities open to the worker when the wage is $10 an hour.

open to the worker when the wage is $20 an hour. As usual, the optimum is found where the budget constraint is tangent to the indifference curve. At point *a*, the worker chooses 14 hours of leisure (10 hours of work).

Suppose the wage is cut to $10 an hour. If the worker chooses 24 hours of leisure, she still earns $0, but if the worker chooses 0 hours of leisure (24 hours of work), her take-home pay falls to $240. The budget constraint labeled $w = $10, therefore, shows all the income-leisure possibilities open to the worker when the wage is $10 an hour. The worker will choose a new point (not shown) on the new budget constraint.

In Figure 23.14, we use this model to show how a decrease in the wage can decrease or increase labor supply. In the top-left panel, the worker chooses 14 hours of leisure (10 hours of work) when the wage is $20 an hour. A decrease in the wage causes the worker to increase leisure to 16 hours (8 hours of work). We haven't drawn the substitution and income effects in the diagram (we leave that as an exercise), but since the total effect of the decrease in wages is a decrease in labor supply, we know that in this case the substitution effect dominates. The top-right panel translates the same information into a labor supply diagram.

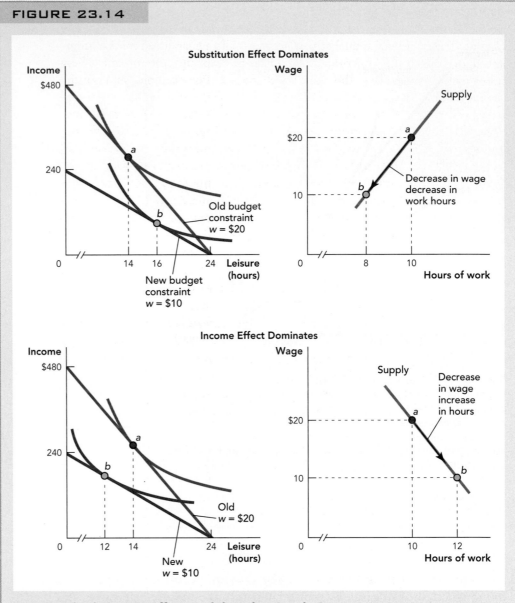

FIGURE 23.14

Income and Substitution Effects and the Labor Supply Curve A decrease in the wage can cause a worker to work fewer or more hours depending on the balance of the substitution and income effects. In the top-left panel the substitution effect (not shown) dominates, so a decrease in the wage from $20 to $10 increases leisure from 14 hours a day to 16 (i.e., a decrease in work from 10 to 8 hours). The same information is shown in the top-right panel but translated into a labor supply diagram. When the substitution effect dominates we get a positively sloped supply curve.

In the bottom-left panel a decrease in the wage from $20 to $10 causes the worker to decrease leisure hours from 14 hours a day to 12 (i.e., an increase in work hours from 10 to 12 hours). The same information is translated into a labor supply diagram in the bottom-right panel. When the income effect dominates we get a negatively sloped or "backward-bending" supply curve.

In the bottom–left panel, the worker chooses 14 hours of leisure (10 hours of work) when the wage is $20 an hour. A decrease in the wage causes the worker to decrease leisure to 12 hours (12 hours of work). Since the total effect of the decrease in wage is an increase in labor supply, we know that in this case the income effect dominates. The bottom–right panel shows that over this wage range, the worker has a backward–bending labor supply curve.

Labor Supply and Welfare Programs

Let's use the income-leisure model to examine the labor supply effects of welfare programs. The traditional model of welfare works like a guaranteed minimum income under which the government subsidizes or "tops up" the income of any worker who earns less than the guaranteed amount. For example, suppose the guaranteed minimum income for an individual is $10,000 a year; in that case, an individual with yearly earnings of $6,000 would receive $4,000 in welfare payments.

The economics of this program are shown in Figure 23.15. We use the same setup as before only now we measure leisure and work on a yearly basis in days rather than on a daily basis in hours. Before the welfare program, the worker faces the No welfare budget constraint and chooses 125 days of leisure (240 days of work.) The guaranteed minimum income expands the worker's opportunities. In particular, the worker now has the option of taking the guaranteed income and 365 days of leisure. The worker pictured earns more utility by taking the option of the guaranteed minimum income and the 365 days of leisure. Not every worker will take the guaranteed minimum income, but every worker who does take the option will reduce work effort.

We can explain why the guaranteed minimum income reduces work effort in a second way. Consider again how a guaranteed minimum income of $10,000 works. If a worker earns $2,000, she receives $8,000 in welfare for a total of $10,000. If a worker earns $4,000, she receives $6,000 in welfare for a total of $10,000. If a worker earns $7,000, she receives $3,000 in welfare for a total of $10,000. Do you see a pattern? Under the guaranteed minimum income, for every $1 in income that the worker earns, the government subtracts

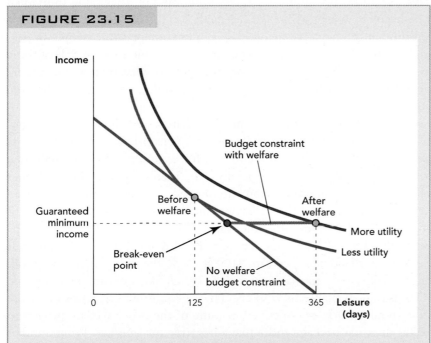

FIGURE 23.15

Labor Supply Effects of the Guaranteed Minimum Income The guaranteed minimum income is a welfare program that tops up income so that everyone receives at least the guaranteed amount. Before the program the worker chooses Before welfare with 125 days of leisure (240 days of work). With the guaranteed minimum income the worker chooses After welfare and consumes the guaranteed minimum income and 365 days of leisure.

$1 in welfare so the worker's take-home pay doesn't change. Thus, under the guaranteed minimum income, a worker faces a 100% tax rate until he is earning more than $10,000 a year (the break-even point). Thus, under a guaranteed minimum income, many workers will choose to work 0 hours. How much would you work if you faced a 100% marginal tax rate?

On the one hand, most people feel that a welfare program is necessary to help those in need. On the other, we don't want to discourage work effort. Even a low-paying job, for example, may lead to a higher-paying job in the future. The trade-off between ethics and the disincentive effects of welfare programs have bedeviled policymakers for decades. In fact, for hundreds of years, economists like Adam Smith and John Stuart Mill have worried about this problem.[1]

Several resolutions to this trade-off have been suggested, none of which is perfect. We will mention two briefly. One possibility is to focus on the 100% tax rate faced by people on welfare. Instead of reducing the welfare payment by $1 for every $1 of earnings, how about reducing payments by, say, $0.50 for every dollar of earnings? This is called a negative income tax (NIT) program. Under a negative income tax, for example, a worker who works 0 hours would receive $10,000 in welfare for a total of $10,000. But a worker who earned $4,000 would receive $8,000 in welfare (not $6,000 as before) for a total of $12,000. In this way, some of the incentives to work are restored for those receiving welfare.

Unfortunately—precisely because the program is more generous—the negative income can encourage more people to reduce labor supply at least somewhat and to take at least some welfare, even if they are able to work. Under the traditional guaranteed income program, for example, a worker who was earning, say, $14,000 a year might refuse the option of $10,000 a year and 365 days of leisure, but under a negative income tax, that same individual might be happy to accept $12,000 a year with 200 days of leisure.

Even though the negative income tax can encourage some people to partially reduce their hours of work, it encourages everyone to have at least some kind of job. If having a job, even a part-time job, is what matters for gaining experience, learning skills, moving up the work ladder, and so forth, then the NIT may work acceptably well.

Another approach is to limit how much welfare a person can accept or put various requirements on welfare recipients. If a person knows in advance that welfare is available only for a limited time, for example, he or she will treat welfare as more of an insurance program to be used only in bad times rather than as a guaranteed minimum income to be used as an alternative to work.

In practice, the United States has pursued both of these approaches to various degrees. The Earned Income Tax Credit (EITC), for example, supplements the wages of low-wage workers. For instance, depending on your income and other factors, if you earn $100 at work, the government tops it off, through the tax system, to make it worth $120. Unlike a negative income tax, the EITC is only available to workers. The EITC, however, helps offset the incentive to quit work, as contained in some of the other welfare programs, and makes the total package more like a negative income tax. From another direction, the Personal Responsibility and Work Opportunity Reconciliation Act (PRWORA) of 1996 put limits on welfare. Under PRWORA, a person can receive only 5 years of welfare benefits over his or her lifetime, and after 2 years on welfare, recipients must work at least 30 hours a week.

Both of these programs appear to have been relatively successful at encouraging welfare recipients to enter the job force. Analyzing the incentive and disincentive effects of welfare programs continues to be an active area of research for economists.

□ Takeaway

Economists use the language of prices and marginal utilities to analyze consumer decisions and, in general, consumers choose to allocate their dollars so the marginal utility per dollar of all purchases is equalized. To maximize utility, allocate dollars such that

$$\frac{MU_A}{P_A} = \frac{MU_O}{P_O} = \frac{MU_i}{P_i} = \dots \frac{MU_z}{P_z}$$

This equation may look tough, but it simply reflects what happens when consumers allocate their money wisely.

The budget constraint represents how much money a consumer has to spend and the prices that the consumer faces. If we put together a budget constraint and information about consumer preferences—as expressed in the form of indifference curves—we can solve for a consumer's optimal consumption bundle. This is a standard economic story, namely that preferences and constraints come together to shape an outcome.

The concepts of income and substitution effects, and more generally preferences and constraints, are useful for analyzing many economic problems. This includes how labor supply responds to welfare programs, how much Costco should charge for membership, and whether you should replace a lost concert ticket.

□ CHAPTER REVIEW

KEY CONCEPTS

Marginal utility, p. 435

Diminishing marginal utility, p. 435

Optimal consumption rule, p. 438

Budget constraint, p. 439

Marginal rate of substitution (MRS), p. 443

Substitution effect, p. 448

Income effect, p. 448

FACTS AND TOOLS

1. The table at right shows the marginal utility a consumer receives from the weekly consumption of On-Demand movie rentals and Thai takeout meals. One On-Demand movie rental costs $5, and Thai takeout costs $10 per meal. Suppose this consumer is currently (for some reason) eating Thai takeout 10 times per week and is spending all of her $100 income, so that she has no money left over for movie rentals. Is the consumer maximizing utility?

On-Demand Movies	Marginal Utility	Thai Takeout Meals	Marginal Utility
1	50	1	50
2	30	2	45
3	20	3	40
4	15	4	35
5	10	5	30
6	8	6	25
7	6	7	20
8	4	8	15
9	2	9	10
10	1	10	5

2. Imagine that for the past two years, you've consumed only two goods: lattes and scones. As you're probably aware, prices tend to go up over time. If the price of your latte increased from

$2 to $3 over the last two years, and the price of scones increased from $1.50 to $2.25, what impact would this have on your budget constraint if your $240 weekly take-home pay didn't change at all over the same two-year period? Draw both budget constraints on the same set of axes. What if you were able to negotiate a raise to $360 per week? Draw this final budget constraint on the same set of axes as the first two. How does your final budget constraint compare with your original budget constraint from two years ago?

3. You learned in the chapter that the process of utility maximization involves a comparison of marginal utilities per dollar, which are calculated as marginal utility divided by price. Consider two goods that most people consume at least some of during their lives: apples and cars.

   a. If utility maximization was only about marginal utility (not marginal utility per dollar), which good (apples or cars) would consumers want to consume? Would they ever consume the other good?

   b. If utility maximization was only about price (as opposed to marginal utility divided by price), which good (apples or cars) would consumers want to consume? Would they ever consume the other good?

   c. Given your answers to parts a and b, and given the observation that some people eat apples *and* drive cars, explain why utility maximization involves a comparison of marginal utility *divided* by price, and not just one or the other.

4. Fill in the blanks below with either "good X" or "good Y," where good X is measured on the *x*-axis and good Y is measured on the *y*-axis.

   a. If the price of _____ is $8 and the price of _____ is $12, then the price ratio (also the slope of the budget constraint) is 1.5.

   b. A price ratio of 1.5 means that the consumer is able to trade 1 unit of _____ for 1.5 units of _____.

   c. If another unit of _____ would give a consumer 20 extra units of utility, and another unit of _____ would give a consumer 10 extra units of utility, then the marginal rate of substitution for this consumer is equal to 2.

   d. A marginal rate of substitution of 2 means that, from the consumer's point of view, 1 more unit of _____ is as good as 2 more units of _____.

   e. If the price ratio is 1.5 and the marginal rate of substitution is 2, then the market values _____ more than the consumer does, and the consumer values _____ more than the market does. In this case, the consumer ought to buy less of _____ and more of _____.

5. Suppose Haya has $120 of income left each week after she pays her bills and puts some money away in a savings account, and she has two ways to spend this extra money: go to the movies, which costs $18 including popcorn and a soda, or go out to a club with several friends, which costs $33 including the cover charge and drinks. Assuming these are her only two choices to spend the extra money, what can you say about the following bundles of going to the movies and clubbing? Which of these could possibly be the utility-maximizing bundle?

   a. 3 movies and 2 nights out at the club

   b. 2 movies and 3 nights out at the club

   c. 2 movies and 2 nights out at the club

6. The utility-maximizing bundle of goods is found at the point of tangency between the budget constraint and an indifference curve. In the diagram below, the utility-maximizing bundle is the one labeled point K. There are two different, but equally important, ways to interpret this point.

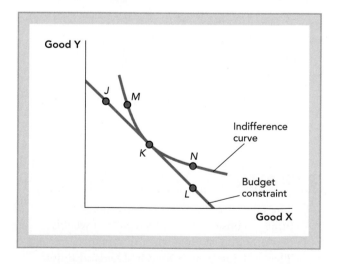

   a. Of the three points on the consumer's budget constraint (J, K, and L), what makes K special?

   b. Of the three points on the consumer's indifference curve (M, K, and N), what makes K special?

7. Is marginal utility always diminishing? Consider playing cards. If playing cards were purchased one at a time, what would be true about the marginal utility of the 51st playing card compared with the marginal utility of the 52nd playing card? Why do you think it's okay for economists to assume that marginal utility diminishes? How does the concept of marginal utility explain why playing cards are not sold individually, but only as entire 52-card decks?

THINKING AND PROBLEM SOLVING

1. Suppose we wanted to investigate the saving and borrowing behavior of consumers. It's not that difficult to extend our basic model. We can use the same framework as before, but define our two goods as "consumption in period 1" (horizontal axis) and "consumption in period 2" (vertical axis).

   a. Construct a budget constraint for a consumer who earns $50 in income in period 1 and $150 of income in period 2. Label this point E for the "Endowment" point. Assume that he can choose to save some income in period 1 to be used in period 2, or to borrow some income from period 2 to use in period 1. (Let's imagine the consumer saves the money by putting it in a piggy bank and can borrow money from his parents, who don't charge interest.)

   b. For the consumer in the situation described above, do you think he would consume at his endowment point or would he borrow or save?

2. In Major League Baseball, teams in the American League use a designated hitter (DH) to bat in place of the pitcher, while teams in the National League require their pitchers to bat. Sports economists have noted that in the National League, batters are hit by pitches 15% less often than in the American League. Can you use the concepts from this chapter to explain this behavior from the point of view of the pitcher's utility-maximizing decision about whether to throw pitches high and inside (where they are more likely to hit the batter)?

3. Consider Facts and Tools question 2. Explain the income and substitution effects of the price changes on your optimal consumption bundle when the latte and scone prices increased, but your income did not.

4. With inferior goods (like ramen noodles), the income effect works in the opposite direction from the income effect discussed in the text. If a consumer feels richer, she would buy less of an inferior good. If she feels poorer, more.

   a. Suppose that a consumer eats two different foods: potatoes and meat. Potatoes are inferior and meat is a luxury. Describe both the income and substitution effects on the consumer's optimal choice of potatoes and meat if the price of potatoes were to rise. Put the two effects together. What can you conclude?

   b. What if you knew for sure that the substitution effect dominated the income effect? What would happen to the consumer's optimal choices for potatoes and meat?

   c. What if instead you knew that the income effect dominated the substitution effect? What would happen in this case? Why is this result a bit unusual?

5. eMusic is a popular subscription MP3 Web site. For a monthly membership fee, you can download MP3s for a price that's about half of what MP3s cost at iTunes or Amazon. Consider someone with $50 worth of income to spend on entertainment each month and who can choose to buy MP3s or "other stuff"—with a price equal to $1 per unit, so that other stuff is measured in dollars. Create budget constraints for each of the different eMusic membership plans. Prices have been rounded to make things simpler. (To simplify things, we'll assume that the consumer will use his entire eMusic balance each month, even though eMusic members don't have to do this. We'll also just think about MP3 singles, not albums.)

   a. No membership: The consumer has to purchase MP3s from another Web site, at $1 each.

   b. eMusic Basic: For $12/month, the consumer gets 24 MP3 downloads. After that, the consumer would have to buy MP3s at another Web site for $1 each.

   c. eMusic Plus: For $16/month, the consumer gets 34 MP3 downloads. After that, the consumer would have to buy MP3s at another Web site for $1 each.

d. eMusic Premium: For $21/month, the consumer gets 46 MP3 downloads. After that, the consumer would have to buy MP3s at another Web site for $1 each.

e. eMusic Fan: For $32/month, the consumer gets 73 MP3 downloads. After that, the consumer would have to buy MP3s at another Web site for $1 each.

Which plan do you think will be most popular? Which will be the least popular? Although eMusic has hundreds of thousands of members, most people are not members of eMusic. What must be true about their indifference curves? How many MP3s do these people download per month?

6. In this chapter, we focused a lot on budget constraints, but time is an additional constraint that consumers face. Jackson has $40 per week to spend on leisure activities. He likes to bowl and to play racquetball. Bowling costs $4 per game, and a day pass to the racquet club costs $8. Jackson only has 7 hours of leisure time per week, and both bowling and racquetball each take 1 hour per game. Construct Jackson's budget constraint and his time constraint on the same diagram. Consider each of the consumption bundles below that could possibly be Jackson's utility-maximizing bundle. How does each of these bundles relate to Jackson's two constraints?

a. Bowling twice per week and playing racquetball four times per week

b. Bowling four times per week and playing racquetball three times per week

c. Bowling six times per week and playing racquetball once per week

CHALLENGES

1. This chapter argues that the ideal membership fee from Costco's point of view would leave consumers indifferent between shopping at Costco and shopping elsewhere. Do you think most of the shoppers at Costco are indifferent? What prevents Costco from setting its ideal fee?

2. Refer to Thinking and Problem-Solving question 1. In that question, we assumed that the consumer earned $50 in period 1 and $150 in period 2, and that saving and borrowing were both interest-free. Let's see if we can't add even more real-life detail to this problem.

a. Draw a new budget constraint for the consumer if the period 1 income remains at $50, but the period 2 income falls to $100. Use the ideas of income and substitution effects to describe how this change would affect the optimal choice of the consumer.

b. Now let's add another wrinkle: an interest rate. We'll use the same endowment point from Thinking and Problem-Solving question 1. Construct a budget constraint for a consumer that can earn 20% interest by saving money in period 1 for use in period 2, but also has to pay 20% interest to borrow money from period 2 for use in period 1. (These interest rates are high so that the impact is obvious on your graph; the results will still hold—although less dramatically—with lower interest rates.) What is the substitution effect of the addition of the interest rate? The income effect is more complicated, because it depends on the consumer's preferences, which could be revealed by the pre-interest-rate behavior.

c. In December 2010, the average interest rate on money market and savings accounts was 0.7%, but the average rate on a variable-rate credit card was 14.4%. Obviously, the assumption above that the interest rate is the same for borrowers and savers is not very realistic. Again, using more dramatic interest rates, can you construct a budget constraint for a consumer with the same initial endowment from above who faces a 1% interest rate for saving and a 50% interest rate for borrowing? What do you notice about this budget constraint?

3. Currently, if you join Columbia House's DVD club, you get 3 DVDs for $1 each, but you have to commit to buying at least 3 more DVDs at $20 each over the next year. Suppose the normal market price of a DVD is $16.

a. Construct two budget constraints: one for a consumer who joins Columbia House and another for a consumer who doesn't. Assume that both consumers have $100 worth of income. Place income on the vertical axis just as in Figure 23.12.

b. What kind of consumer is likely to get more utility from joining Columbia House? What kind of consumer would not?

c. If Columbia House wanted to charge an additional membership fee to generate more revenue, what would be the maximum it could charge for membership?

4. There are two special cases that might result in indifference curves that look a little different from the ones discussed in the text.

   a. If two goods are perfect substitutes, that means the consumer would always be willing to trade one for the other in a certain, fixed proportion. In this case, the MRS would be constant, which means that indifference curves would be straight lines. Suppose a consumer's MRS between two goods X and Y is a constant 2.5, which means that the consumer is always willing to give up 1 unit of good X for 2.5 units of good Y. If the consumer has $180 in income to spend, the price of good X is $20 per unit, and the price of good Y is $10 per unit, what is this consumer's utility-maximizing bundle of X and Y? Answer the question by thinking it through and then show with a diagram (including a budget constraint and an indifference curve) why your answer works.

   b. If two goods are perfect complements, indifference curves have a very unusual shape. Let's see if you can reason through this one. Consider left and right shoes. For most people, having left shoes alone (or right shoes alone) does not really provide any utility; rather, people get utility from having a pair of shoes that they can wear. In this case, left and right shoes are perfect 1:1 complements. Can you figure out what indifference curves would look like in such a case? To do this, it might be helpful to think about questions like the following: If someone has 4 right shoes and 4 (matching) left shoes, what's the marginal utility of an extra right shoe? If a consumer had to compare the bundles (4 left shoes, 4 right shoes), (4 left shoes, 5 right shoes), and (7 left shoes, 4 left shoes), how would these bundles rank? Would any of these bundles be better than the others?

Appendix A

Reading Graphs
and Making Graphs

Economists use graphs to illustrate both ideas and data. In this appendix, we review commonly used graphs, explain how to read them, and give you a few tips on how you can make graphs using Microsoft Excel or similar software.

Graphs Express Ideas

In economics, graphs are used to express ideas. The most common graphs we use throughout this book plot two variables on a coordinate system. One variable is plotted on the vertical or y-axis, while the other variable is plotted on the horizontal or x-axis.

In Figure A.1, for example, we plot a very generic graph of variable Y against variable X. Starting on the vertical axis at Y = 100, you read across to the point at which you hit the graph and then down to find X = 800. Thus, when Y = 100, X = 800. In this case, you can also see that when X = 800, then Y = 100. Similarly, when Y = 60, you can read from the graph that X = 400, and vice versa. As you may recall, the slope of a straight line is defined as the rise over the run or rise/run. In this case, when Y rises from 60 to 100, a rise of 40, then X runs from 400 to 800, a run of 400, so the slope of the line is 40/400 = 0.1. The slope is positive, indicating that when Y increases so does X.

Let's now apply the idea of a graph to some economic concepts. In Chapter 3, we show how a demand curve can be constructed from hypothetical data on the price and quantity demanded of oil. We show this here as Figure A.2.

The table on the left of the figure shows that at a price of $55 per barrel buyers are willing and able to buy 5 million barrels of oil a day (MBD), or more simply at a price of $55, the quantity demanded is 5 MBD. You can read this information off the graph in the following way. Starting on the vertical axis, locate the price of $55. Then look to the right for the point where the

FIGURE A.1

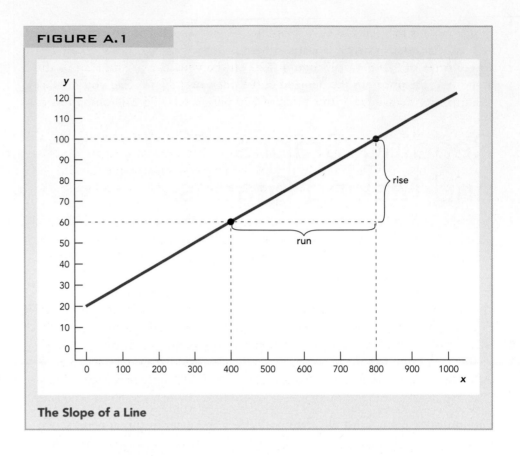

The Slope of a Line

FIGURE A.2

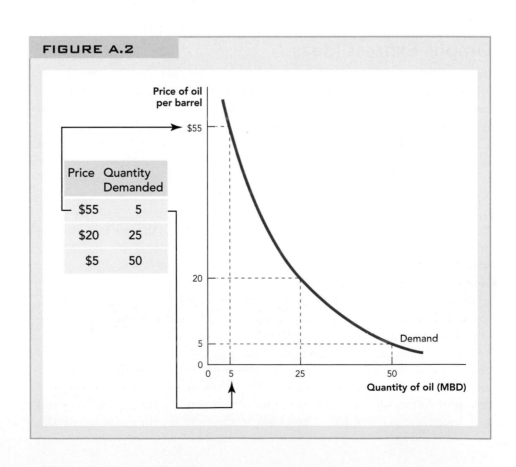

$55 price hits the demand curve: looking down from this point, you see that the quantity demanded is 5 million barrels of oil per day. How about at a lower price of $20 per day? Start at $20 on the vertical axis and read to the right until the price hits the demand curve, then read down. Can you see that the quantity demanded at this price of $20 per barrel is 25 million barrels of oil per day?

We said that graphs express ideas, so what is the idea being expressed here? The most important fact about a demand curve is that it has a negative slope, that is, it slopes downward. This tells us the important but simple idea that as the price of a good falls, the quantity demanded increases. This is key: as the price of a good such as oil falls, people demand more of it.

A demand curve is a description of what *would happen* to the quantity demanded as the price of a good changed *holding fixed all other influences on the quantity of oil demanded.* (In this sense, demand curves are hypothetical and we rarely observe them directly.)

The quantity of oil demanded, for example, depends not just on the price of oil but on many other factors such as income or the price of other goods like automobiles and population, to name just a few of many influences. Today's demand curve for oil, for example, depends on today's income, price of automobiles and population. Imagine, for example, that average income today is $10,000, the price of an average automobile is $25,000 and world population is 7 billion. The blue curve in Figure A.3 shows the demand curve for oil under these conditions. Note that there are also many other influences on the demand for oil that we don't list but that are also being held fixed. Most importantly, if any of these conditions changes then the demand curve for oil will shift.

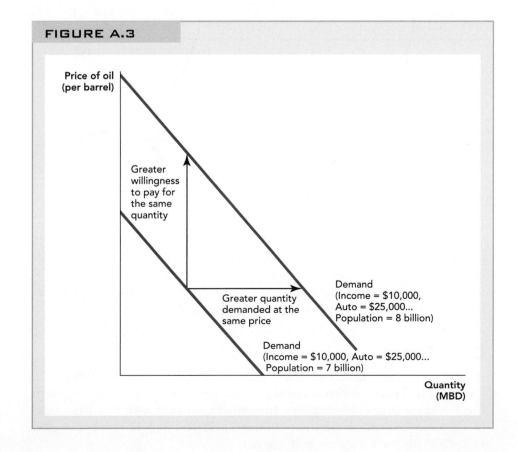

FIGURE A.3

If world population increases to 8 billion, for example, there will be a new demand curve for oil. With a greater population, there will be more barrels of oil demanded at every specific price so the demand curve will shift to the right. Equivalently, as the population increases, there will be a greater willingness to pay for any given quantity of oil so the demand curve will shift up. Thus, we say that an increase in demand is a shift in the curve up and to the right shown by the red curve in Figure A.3. Chapter 3 explains in greater detail how a demand curve shifts in response to changes in factors other than price.

What is important to emphasize here is that a demand curve is drawn holding fixed every influence on the quantity demanded other than price. Changes in any factor that influences the demand for oil other than price will produce a new demand curve.

One more important feature of two variables graphed in a coordinate system is that these figures can be read in two different ways. For example, as we mention in Chapter 3, demand curves can be read both horizontally and vertically. Read "horizontally," you can see from Figure A.4 that at a price of $20 per barrel demanders are willing and able to buy 25 million barrels of oil per day. Read "vertically," you can see that the maximum price that demanders are willing to pay for 25 million barrels of oil a day is $20 per barrel. Thus, demand curves show the quantity demanded at any price or the maximum willingness to pay (per unit) for any quantity.

FIGURE A.4

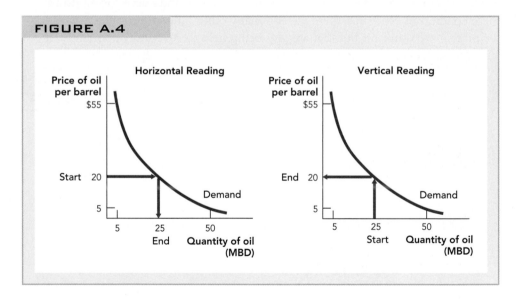

It may seem difficult at first to interpret these graphs, but as you will see, graphs are amazingly useful for thinking about difficult economic problems. It's like learning to drive a car—at first it's not easy and you will make some mistakes but once you learn how to drive your ability to do things and go places increases enormously. The same thing is true with graphs!

Data Graphs

As well as expressing ideas, graphs can also be used to illustrate data. For example, GDP can be broken down according to the national spending identity into these components: Consumption, Investment, Government Purchases, and Net Exports (Exports minus Imports), that is, $GDP = Y = C + I + G + NX$. U.S. GDP for 2007 is shown in Table A.1.

TABLE A.1 U.S. GDP 2007 (in billions of dollars)	
Category	GDP
Consumption	9,710.2
Investment	2,130.4
Government	2,674.8
Net Exports	−707.8
GDP (Total)	13,807.6

Source: Bureau of Economic Analysis

If you type the components into Excel, as shown in Figure A.5, you can use the sum function to check that the components do add up to GDP.

Highlighting the data in columns A and B and clicking Insert > Column > Clustered Column and (with a few modifications to add axis titles and to make the graph look pretty), we have the graph on the left side of Figure A.6.

The graph on the right side of Figure A.6 shows exactly the same data only on the right side we chose Stacked Column (and we switched the rows and columns). Sometimes one visualization of the data is more revealing than another so it's a good idea to experiment a little bit with alternative ways of presenting the same data. But please don't get carried away with adding 3D effects or other chart junk. Always keep the focus on the data, not on the special effects.

FIGURE A.5

B7			f_x	=SUM(B2:B5)
	A	B	C	D
1	Category	GDP		
2	Cons	9710.2		
3	Inv	2130.4		
4	Govt	2674.8		
5	NX	-707.8		
6				
7	GDP (Total)	13807.6		
8				

FIGURE A.6

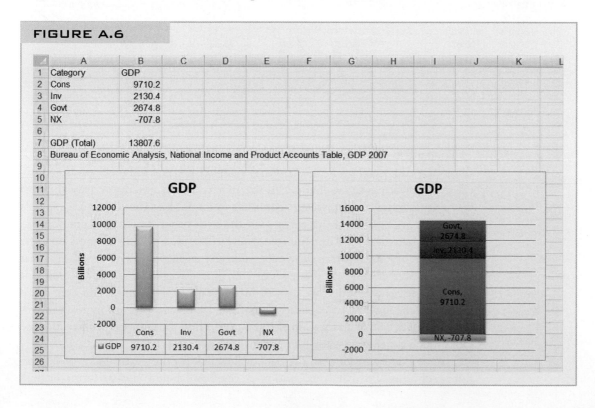

In this book, we explain the economics of stocks, bonds, and other invest-ments. A lot of financial data is available for free on the web. We used Yahoo! Finance, for example, to download data for the value of the S&P 500 Index on the first trading day of the month from 1950 to the end of 2000. The data is graphed in Figure A.7.

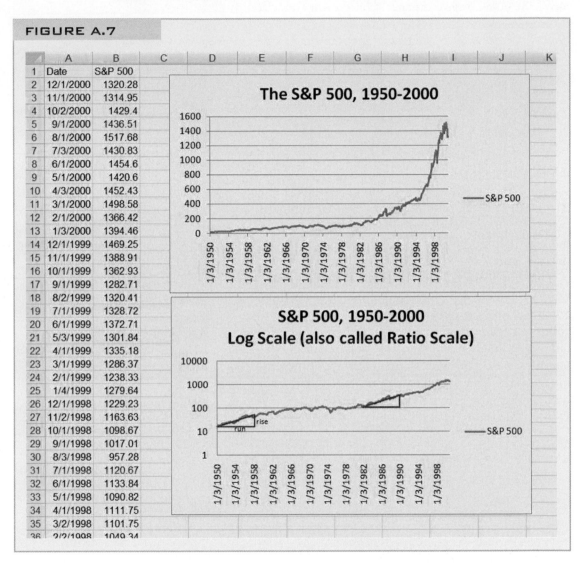

FIGURE A.7

To graph the S&P 500 data, we used a line graph. The top graph in Figure A.7 shows the data graphed in the "normal" way with equal distances on the verti-cal axis indicating equal changes in the index. That's not necessarily the best way to graph the data, however, because a quick look at the top figure suggests that stock prices were rising faster over time. In other words, the graph looks pretty flat between 1950 and approximately 1980, after which it shoots up. The appearance of faster growth, however, is mostly an illusion. The problem is that when the S&P 500 was at the level of 100, as it was around 1968, a 10 percent increase moves the index to 110, or an increase of 10 points. But when the index is at the level of 1,000, as it was around 1998, a 10 percent increase moves the index to 1,100, or an increase of 100 points. Thus, the same percentage increase looks much larger in 1998 than in 1968.

To get a different view of the data, right-click on the vertical axis of the top figure, choose "Format Axis" and click the box labeled "Logarithmic Scale," which produces the graph in the bottom of Figure A.7 (without the red triangles, which we will explain shortly).

Notice on the bottom figure that equal distances on the vertical axis now indicate equal percentage increases or ratios. The ratio 100/10, for example, is the same as the ratio 1,000/100. You can now see at a glance that if stock prices move the same vertical distance over the same length of time (as measured by the horizontal distance) then the percentage increase was the same. For example, we have superimposed two identical red triangles to show that the percentage increase in stock prices between 1950 and 1958 was about the same as between 1982 and 1990. The red triangles are identical so over the same 8-year period, given by the horizontal length of the triangle, the run, the S&P 500 rose by the same vertical distance, the rise. Recall that the slope of a line is given by the rise/run. Thus, we can also say that on a ratio graph, equal slopes mean equal percentage growth rates.

The log scale or ratio graph reveals more clearly than our earlier graph that stock prices increased from 1950 to the mid-1960s but were then flat throughout the 1970s and did not begin to rise again until after the recession in 1982. We use ratio graphs for a number of figures throughout this book to better identify patterns in the data.

Graphs are also very useful for suggesting possible relationships between two variables. In the macroeconomics section, for example, we present evidence that labor employment laws in much of Western Europe that make it difficult to fire workers also raise the costs of hiring workers. As a result, the percentage of unemployment that is long term in Europe tends to be very high. To show this relationship, we graphed an index called the "rigidity of employment index," produced by the World Bank. The rigidity of employment index summarizes hiring and firing costs as well as how easy it is for firms to adjust hours of work (e.g., whether there are restrictions on night or weekend hours). A higher index number means that it is more expensive to hire and fire workers and more difficult to adjust hours. We then graphed a country's rigidity of employment index against the share of a country's unemployment rate that is long term (lasting more than a year).

The data for this graph are shown in Figure A.8.

FIGURE A.8

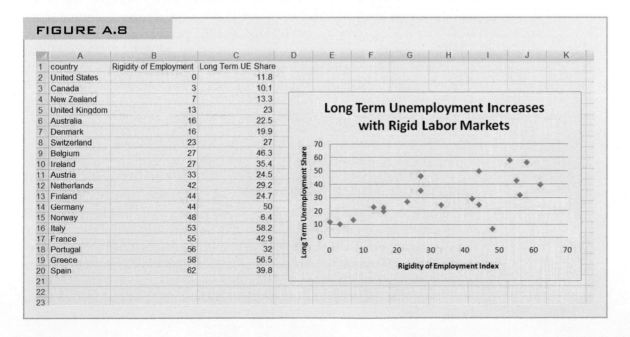

	A	B	C	D	E	F	G	H	I	J	K
1	country	Rigidity of Employment	Long Term UE Share								
2	United States	0	11.8								
3	Canada	3	10.1								
4	New Zealand	7	13.3								
5	United Kingdom	13	23								
6	Australia	16	22.5								
7	Denmark	16	19.9								
8	Switzerland	23	27								
9	Belgium	27	46.3								
10	Ireland	27	35.4								
11	Austria	33	24.5								
12	Netherlands	42	29.2								
13	Finland	44	24.7								
14	Germany	44	50								
15	Norway	48	6.4								
16	Italy	53	58.2								
17	France	55	42.9								
18	Portugal	56	32								
19	Greece	58	56.5								
20	Spain	62	39.8								
21											
22											
23											

Long Term Unemployment Increases with Rigid Labor Markets

Long Term Unemployment Share (vertical axis: 0–70)

Rigidity of Employment Index (horizontal axis: 0–70)

We can do something else of interest with this data. If you right-click on any of the data points in the figure, you will get the option to "Add Trendline." Clicking on this and then clicking the two boxes "Linear" and "Display Equation on Chart" produces Figure A.9 (absent the red arrow, which we added for clarity).

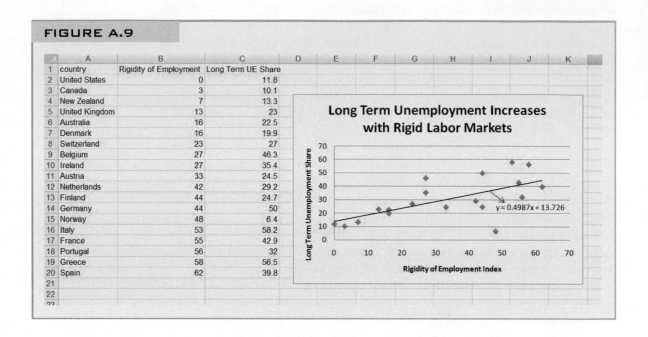

FIGURE A.9

	A	B	C
1	country	Rigidity of Employment	Long Term UE Share
2	United States	0	11.8
3	Canada	3	10.1
4	New Zealand	7	13.3
5	United Kingdom	13	23
6	Australia	16	22.5
7	Denmark	16	19.9
8	Switzerland	23	27
9	Belgium	27	46.3
10	Ireland	27	35.4
11	Austria	33	24.5
12	Netherlands	42	29.2
13	Finland	44	24.7
14	Germany	44	50
15	Norway	48	6.4
16	Italy	53	58.2
17	France	55	42.9
18	Portugal	56	32
19	Greece	58	56.5
20	Spain	62	39.8

The black line is the linear curve that "best fits" the data. (Best fit in this context is defined statistically; we won't go into the details here but if you take a statistics class you will learn about ordinary least squares.) Excel also produces for us the equation for the best-fit line, $Y = 0.4987 \times X + 13.726$. Do you remember from high school the formula for a straight line, $Y = m \times X + b$? In this case m, the slope of the line or the rise/run is 0.4987 and b, the intercept, is 13.726. The slope tells us that a 1 unit increase in the rigidity of employment index (a run of 1) increases the share of unemployment that is long term by, on average, 0.4987 percentage points (a rise of 0.4987). Using the equation, you can substitute any value for the index to find a predicted value for the share of long-term unemployment. If the rigidity of employment index is 15, for example, then our prediction for the long-term unemployment share is $21.2065 = 0.4987 \times 15 + 13.726$ If the index is 55, our prediction for the long-term unemployment share is $41.1545 = 0.4987 \times 55 + 13.726$.

Graphing Three Variables

In our international trade chapter, we present evidence that child labor decreases with increases in GDP per capita. Figure A.10 shows a subset of that data. We put our X variable, real GDP per capita, in column B and our Y variable, the percentage of children ages 10–14 in the labor force, in column C. In column D, we have the total number of children in the labor force. In Burundi, a larger fraction (48.5 percent) of the children are in the labor force than in India (12.1 percent), but

FIGURE A.10

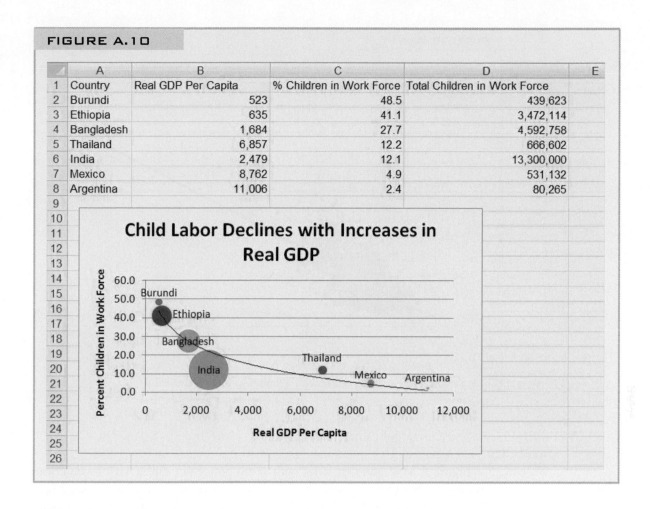

	A	B	C	D	E
1	Country	Real GDP Per Capita	% Children in Work Force	Total Children in Work Force	
2	Burundi	523	48.5	439,623	
3	Ethiopia	635	41.1	3,472,114	
4	Bangladesh	1,684	27.7	4,592,758	
5	Thailand	6,857	12.2	666,602	
6	India	2,479	12.1	13,300,000	
7	Mexico	8,762	4.9	531,132	
8	Argentina	11,006	2.4	80,265	

since Burundi is a small country, the total number of children in the labor force is larger in India. To understand the problem of child labor, it's important to understand both types of information so we put both types of information on a graph.

Excel's bubble chart will take data arrayed in three columns and use the third column to set the area of the bubble or data point. In Figure A.10, for example, India has the largest number of children in the labor force and so has the bubble with the largest area. The area of the other bubbles is in relative proportion so Mexico's bubble is 1/25th the size of India's bubble because there are 1/25th as many children in the labor force in Mexico as in India. (Unfortunately, Excel doesn't label the bubbles automatically so we added these by hand.)

Cause and Effect

Do police reduce crime? If so, by how much? That's a key question that economists and criminologists are interested in understanding because local governments (and taxpayers) spend billions of dollars on police every year and would like to know whether they are getting their money's worth. Should they spend less on police or more? Unfortunately, it's surprisingly difficult to answer this question. To illustrate why, Figure A.11 shows the relationship between crime per capita and police per capita from across a large number of U.S. cities.

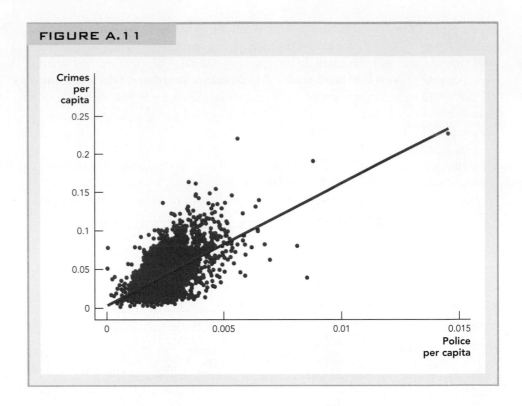

FIGURE A.11

Figure A.11 shows that cities with more police per capita have more crime per capita. Should we conclude that police cause crime? Probably not. More likely is "reverse causality," crime causes police—that is, greater crime rates lead to more hiring of police. We thus have two chains of potential cause and effect, more police reduce crime and more crime increases police. Unfortunately, you can't tell much about either of these two potential cause-and-effect relationships by looking at Figure A.11, which shows the correlation between police and crime but not the causation. But if you want to estimate the value of police, you need to know causation not just correlation. So what should you do?

The best way to estimate how much police reduce crime would be to take say 1,000 roughly similar cities and randomly flip a coin dividing the cities into two groups. In the first group of cities, double the police force and in the second group do nothing. Then compare crime rates over say the next year in cities with and without an increase in police. If the cities with an increase in police have lower rates of crime, then you can safely ascribe this difference to the effect of police on crime. What makes the correlation evidence in Figure A.11 difficult to interpret is that increases in crime sometimes cause increases in police. But if you increase the number of police randomly, you eliminate the possibility of this "reverse causality." Thus, if crime falls in the cities that have *random increases in police,* the cause is most plausibly the increase in police. Similarly, if crime were to increase in cities that have random decreases in police, the cause is most plausibly the decrease in police.

Unfortunately, randomized experiments have at least one big problem—they are very expensive. Occasionally, large randomized experiments are done in criminology and other social sciences but because they are so expensive we must usually look for alternative methods for assessing causality.

If you can't afford a randomized experiment, what else can you do? One possibility is to look for what economists call quasi-experiments or natural experiments. In 1969, for example, police in Montreal, Canada, went on strike and there were 50 times more bank robberies than normal.[1] If you can think of the strike as a random event, not tied in any direct way to increases or decreases in crime, then you can be reasonably certain that the increase in bank robberies was caused by the decrease in police.

The Montreal experiment tells you it's probably not a good idea to eliminate all police, but it doesn't tell you whether governments should increase or decrease police on the street by a more reasonable amount, say 10 percent to 20 percent. Jonathan Klick and Alex Tabarrok use another natural experiment to address this question.[2] Since shortly after 9/11, the United States has had a terror alert system run by the Department of Homeland Security. When the terror alert level rises from "elevated" (yellow) to "high" (orange) due to intelligence reports regarding the current threat posed by terrorist organizations, the Washington, D.C. Metropolitan Police Department reacts by increasing the number of hours each officer must work. Because the change in the terror alert system is not tied to any observed or expected changes in Washington crime patterns, this provides a useful quasi-experiment. In other words, whenever the terror alert system shifts from yellow to orange—a random decision with respect to crime in Washington—the effective police presence in Washington increases. Klick and Tabarrok find that during the high terror alert periods when more police are on the street, the amount of crime falls. Street crime such as stolen automobiles, thefts from automobiles, and burglaries decline especially sharply. Overall, Klick and Tabarrok estimate that a 10 percent increase in police reduces crime by about 3 percent. Using these numbers and figures on the cost of crime and of hiring more police, Klick and Tabarrok argue that more police would be very beneficial.

Economists have developed many techniques for assessing causality from data and we have only just brushed the surface. We can't go into details here. We want you to know, however, that in this textbook when we present data that suggests a causal relationship—such as when we argue in the international trade chapter that higher GDP leads to lower levels of child labor—that a significant amount of statistical research has gone into assessing causality, not just correlation. If you are interested in further details, we have provided you with the references to the original papers.

Appendix A Questions

1. We start with a simple idea from algebra: Which of the graphs at the top of the next page have a positive slope and which have a negative slope?

2. When social scientists talk about social and economic facts, they usually talk about a "positive relationship" or a "negative relationship" instead of "positive slope" or "negative slope." Based on your knowledge, which of the following pairs of variables tend to have a "positive relationship" (a positive slope when graphed), and which have a negative relationship? (Note: "Negative relationship" and "inverse relationship" mean the same thing. Also, in this question, we're only talking about correlation, not causation.)

   a. A professional baseball player's batting average and his annual salary.

   b. A professional golfer's average score and her average salary.

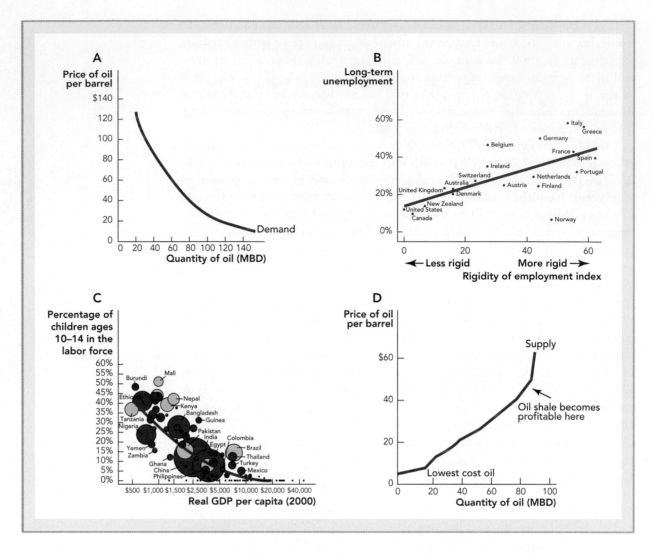

c. The number of cigarettes a person smokes and her life expectancy.

d. The size of the car you drive and your probability of surviving a serious accident.

e. A country's distance from the equator and how rich its citizens tend to be. (For the answer, see Robert Hall and Charles Jones. 1999. Why Do Some Countries Produce so Much More Output per Worker than Others? *Quarterly Journal of Economics*. 114: 83–116.)

3. Let's convert Klick and Tabarrok's research on crime into a simple algebra equation. We reported the result as the effect of a 10 percent increase in police on the crime rate in Washington, D.C. In the equation below, fill in the effect of a 1 percent increase in the police on the crime rate:

The percent change in crime = ____ * The percent change in police officers

4. Let's read the child labor graph [A.10] horizontally and then vertically:

a. According to the trendline, in a typical country with 10 percent of the children in the labor force, what's the real GDP per person?

b. According to the trendline, when a country's GDP per person is $2,000, roughly what percentage of children are in the labor force?

5. Let's take another look at the ratio scale, and compare it to a normal scale.

   a. In Figure A.7, which one is presented in ratio scale and which in normal scale?

   b. In the top graph, every time the S&P 500 crosses a horizontal line, how many points did the S&P rise?

   c. In the bottom graph, every time the S&P 500 crosses a horizontal line, how many *times* higher is the S&P?

6. As a scientist, you have to plot the following data: The number of bacteria you have in a large petri dish, measured every hour over the course of a week. (Note: *E. coli* bacteria populations can double every 20 minutes) Should this data be plotted on a ratio scale and why?

7. Educated people are supposed to point out (correctly) that "correlation isn't proof of causation." This is an important fact—which explains why economists, medical doctors, and other researchers spend a lot of time trying to look for proof of causation. But sometimes, correlation is good enough. In the following examples, take the correlation as a true fact, and explain why the correlation is, all by itself, useful for the task presented in each question.

   a. Your task is to decide what brand of car to buy. You know that Brand H usually gets higher quality ratings than Brand C. You don't know what causes Brand H to get higher ratings—maybe Brand H hires better workers, maybe Brand H buys better raw materials. All you have is the correlation.

   b. Your task is to hire the job applicant who appears to be the smartest. Applicant M has a degree from MIT, and applicant S has a degree from a typical state university. You don't know what causes MIT graduates to be smarter than typical state university graduates—maybe they start off smarter before they get to MIT, maybe their professors teach them a lot, maybe having smart classmates for four years gives them constant brain exercise.

   c. Your task is to decide which city to move to, and you want to move to the city that is probably the safest. For some strange reason, the only fact you have to help you with your decision is the number of police per person.

8. If you haven't practiced in a while, let's calculate some slopes. In each case, we give two points, and you can use the "rise over run" formula to get the right answer.

   a. Point 1: x = 0, y = 0. Point 2: x = 3, y = 6

   b. Point 1: x = 6, y = −9. Point 2: x = 3, y = 6

   c. Point 1: x = 4, y = 8. Point 2: x = 1, y = 12

9. We mentioned that a demand curve is a hypothetical relationship: It answers a "what if" question: "What if today's price of oil rose (or fell), but the average consumer's income, beliefs about future oil prices, and the prices of everything else in the economy stayed the same?" When some of those other features change, then the demand curve isn't fixed any more: It shifts up (and right) or left (and down). In Figure A.3, we showed one shift graphically: Let's make some changes in algebra:

The economy of Perovia has the following demand for oil:

$$\text{Price} = \text{B} - \text{M} \times \text{Quantity}$$

When will B tend to be a larger number:

a. When population in Perovia is high or when it is low?

b. When the price of autos in Perovia is high or when it is low?

c. When Perovian income is high or when it is low?

10. Using the raw data from this chapter, use Excel to replicate simple versions of any two of our graphs. Figures A.6, A.7, A.9, and A.10 all provide the data you'll need. If you're adventurous, feel free to search out the newest GDP data and S&P 500 data on the Bureau of Economic Analysis (BEA) website and Yahoo! Finance, respectively.

Appendix B

Solutions to Check Yourself Questions

Here are suggested answers to the Check Yourself questions found within the chapters.

Chapter 2

Page 21

1. Specialization increases productivity because it increases knowledge.

2. If people can't trade for other goods, they won't specialize in producing just one good. Thus, trade is necessary if people are to benefit from specialization.

3. Alex Rodriguez has a comparative advantage in playing baseball, but Harry has a comparative advantage in mowing Alex's lawn because Harry faces a much lower opportunity cost in mowing lawns than Alex Rodriguez does.

Chapter 3

Page 34

1. As the income of Indian workers rises, this will lead to an increase in the demand for automobiles. At first as income rises, workers may demand more charcoal bricks for heating, but charcoal bricks are a dangerous and unpleasant way to heat a home so as income increases beyond a certain level, workers will demand fewer charcoal bricks. Thus, a good can be a normal good over some levels of income and an inferior good over other (usually higher) levels of income.

2. As the price of oil rises, some people will substitute mopeds for automobiles so the demand for mopeds will increase.

Page 40

1. Improvements in chip-making technology have driven down the costs of this input so the supply of computers increases, meaning that the supply curve for computers shifts to the right/down.

2. The ethanol subsidy lowers the cost of producing ethanol, therefore increasing the supply of ethanol (the supply curve for ethanol shifts to the right/down).

Chapter 4

Page 49

1. If the demand for large trucks and SUVs falls unexpectedly, auto companies will find that at the current price they have a surplus of trucks and SUVs. The quantity supplied is greater than the quantity demanded so they will lower prices in order to sell already manufactured trucks and SUVs.

2. Sellers have produced too many clothes if they have them available at outlet malls where price discounts are the norm. Sellers are cutting their prices to reduce the surplus and move the clothes out the door.

Page 52

1. As the price of cars goes up, the least-valued wants will be the first to stop being satisfied. For example, parents may be more reluctant to buy their teenage sons and daughters a new automobile.

2. If telecommunication firms overinvest in fiber-optic cable, for example, they will have to lower the price of using fiber-optic lines. For example, a company such as Verizon will offer fiber-optic Internet and phone connections at discount prices. The ensuing losses from price cutting will dampen future investment in fiber-optic cable. More generally, firms invest in order to make a profit. If firms overinvest, they will take losses, which give them an incentive to invest carefully.

Page 56

1. If flooding destroys some of the corn and soybean crops, these crops will have a decrease in supply. This decrease in supply will lower the equilibrium quantity and increase the equilibrium price.

2. If resveratrol (from Japanese knotweed) increases life expectancy in fish, people might think it will have the same effect in humans, and so more people will demand it, increasing demand. This will increase the price of Japanese knotweed, and will lead to an increase in the quantity grown.

3. The demand for hybrid cars will increase as the price of gas increases, that is, the demand curve shifts to the right/up. We show this in Figure 4.7: Think of the New Demand as the demand for hybrids when the price of gas is high and the Old Demand as the demand for hybrids when the price of gas is low. The price of hybrids will rise with an increase in demand, especially in the short run.

Page 60

1. The price of oil rose in 1991 primarily because of a supply shock, the Persian Gulf War. (It would also be okay to label this as a demand shock because the demand for oil increased when people expected that the war would reduce the future supply of oil.) Bonus points if you recognized both possibilities.

2. From 1981 to 1986, the price of oil fell steadily. The higher price in the preceding years encouraged exploration, which several years later led to increased supply, especially from non-OPEC sources.

Chapter 5

Page 75

1. There are more substitutes for a brand than a general product category, so there are more substitutes for Dell computers than for computers. When there are more substitutes, demand is more elastic, so demand is more elastic for Dell computers than for computers.

2. An elasticity of demand of 0.1 is an inelastic demand. With inelastic demand, revenue and price move together. Thus, if the price of eggs increases, total revenue will increase. Bonus points if you said that with an elasticity of 0.1, when price goes up by 10%, quantity goes down by 1% so revenues (= $P \times Q$) increase by approximately 9%.

3. A fashionable clothing store might raise its prices by 25% if it thought there was inelastic demand for its products: The increase in price on everything would more than make up for the decrease in sales (quantity).

Page 82

1. Supply is usually not very elastic in the short run. In the case of computer chips, a factory can run 24 hours per day and pay overtime, but it takes years to build a new factory. In the long run, supply is more elastic because over time a computer chip firm can respond to increased demand by building new factories.

2. Manhattan is an island with very little land available for development so the supply of housing in Manhattan is very inelastic. In contrast, there is lots of unbuilt land available in the Des Moines area so the supply is more elastic. The same increase in demand will increase the price more when the supply is inelastic than elastic—thus the same increase in demand will increases prices more in Manhattan than in Des Moines.

Chapter 6

Page 103

1. Because demand for insulin is highly inelastic, the users of insulin are likely ultimately to pay a government insulin tax. Producers of insulin have some ability to produce other products and so can escape the tax more readily.

2. The government would rather tax items that have relatively inelastic demands and supplies rather than elastic demands and supplies because the deadweight loss from taxation is lower when supply and demand are inelastic.

Page 106

1. Because of the ethanol subsidy, the quantity supplied of ethanol increases. The subsidy increases the price received by the ethanol producers (corn growers) and lowers the price paid by ethanol users. The relative amount received by producers vs. that paid by buyers depends on the relative elasticities of demand and supply.

2. Government subsidies for college education increased the demand for education. The supply of education, however, is relatively inelastic, especially at elite colleges. Thus, the benefits of the subsidy flow to suppliers, that is, the price paid to suppliers increases by more than the price paid by buyers falls. Much of the subsidy ends up raising the incomes of professors! Perhaps this is one reason that many professors argue for subsidies to education.

Chapter 7

Page 115

1. If farmers receive a higher price for turning corn into ethanol, they will supply more of their corn for ethanol production. Thus, the (opportunity) cost of supplying corn for cornbread will increase and there will be a decrease in the supply of corn for cornbread. As a result, the price of cornbread will increase and customers will consume less, perhaps substituting toward cheaper items such as regular bread.

2. During the housing boom, the use of lumber skyrocketed, as did the supply of a lumber by-product, sawdust. The increase in the supply of sawdust caused a fall in the price of sawdust. Since a lot of sawdust is used in bedding milk cows, this reduced the cost of producing milk. When the housing boom collapsed, less lumber was produced so less sawdust was produced and the price of sawdust rose, which increased the cost of producing milk and thus the price of milk. Markets are linked in non-obvious ways. Who would have thought the housing and milk markets were linked so closely?

Page 118

1. We aren't peanut experts either but the highest value of peanuts is probably in its use as a food; furthermore, there are fewer substitutes for peanuts in paint, varnish, and furniture polish, where the peanut has some unique properties, than in insecticides or soap or finally bird feed. So let's rank the use of peanuts from highest- to least-valued use as follows: food, paint, varnish, furniture polish, insecticides, soap, and bird feed. Any ranking you have is fine—the point is that there is a ranking.

2. If there is a peanut crop failure in a large producer such as China, the price of peanuts and peanut products will rise and people will substitute away from peanuts in their least-valued uses. Thus, we would expect fewer

peanuts used in bird feed, soap, and insecticides, which will free up more peanuts for use in the higher-valued categories. Thus, as the price of peanuts rises, there is a reallocation of peanuts from lower- to higher-valued uses. It's important to recognize that the best way of figuring out which uses are higher-valued is to see what happens when the price rises.

Page 119

1. No central planner could possibly know or understand all of the links between products so the messaging system is unlikely to send the right information. But let's suppose that the *information problem* was solved. Even if the government sent the right messages, there would still be an *incentive problem*. What incentives would producers and consumers have to obey the messages? In contrast, the price system sums up all of the links between products in one number, the price, and it provides an incentive to pay attention to the price. Thus, the price system solves the information problem and the incentive problem, which is why we say that a price is a signal wrapped up in an incentive.

2. If firms do not have to face bankruptcy, they can continue with poor products, practices, and efforts. The fear of bankruptcy is a spur to innovate and grow, but the fear has to be backed up by the reality.

Page 122

1. In hindsight, it is clear that Lehman Brothers was engaged in wishful thinking. Speculators, with their money on the line, did not believe the Lehman forecasts. Companies can have a tendency to look at things in the best possible way and to ignore reality, and speculators provide a market vote (a reality check).

Chapter 8

Page 141

1. Price ceilings set below equilibrium prices cause shortages. Price ceilings set above equilibrium prices have no effects.

2. A price control reduces the incentive to respond to shifts in demand, thus resources become misallocated according to essentially random factors. For example, it costs much more to ship oil from Alaskan oil fields to refineries on the East Coast than on the West Coast. Price ceilings did not let that difference become factored in the price, and therefore reduced the incentive to ship oil to where it was most needed so shortages could be worse in some areas than in others.

Page 145

1. If landlords under rent control have an incentive to do only minimum upkeep, deteriorating buildings inevitably accompany rent control. Only major repairs are made. Tenants with dripping faucets may never get a response from landlords, and have to fix it themselves. At a minimum,

they will have to wait, maybe until the drip becomes something larger and so has an effect on the landlord's water bill.

2. Vested interests will fight any attempt at rolling back rent control, and these vested interests become powerful over time. It's especially difficult to eliminate rent controls because tenants (people who already have an apartment) don't care much about the shortage—they do not have to find a new apartment every week. In contrast, buyers of gasoline have to deal with the shortage every time they need a fillup so it may be easier to get rid of price controls on oil than on apartments.

Page 147

1. Price ceilings cause shortages. Universal price controls cause shortages across the economy, with no obvious pattern. Sometimes one product is in abundance, at other times there are shortages. A rational response when there are products that face inexplicable shortages is to buy as much as possible when possible: buy as much toilet paper now because who knows when it will come available again? In other words, hoarding is a standard response to universal price controls. Hoarding is wasteful because it implies a misallocation of resources. Some people, for reasons of luck (or influence), may have a lot of toilet paper while others have none. If trade were allowed, people would experience gains from trade and products would gravitate to their highest value uses.

2. The Soviet Union also faced surpluses of goods as well as shortages because under universal price controls there was no incentive to get products to the places at the times that they had the highest value uses. As a result, goods would be misallocated and production and consumption would be chaotic. One week a farm might get enough oil to deliver its chickens to the city and in that week the city shops would get a lot of chickens as the farm dumped its accumulated stock. A few weeks later there might be no oil available and chickens would disappear from the shops.

Page 152

1. A price floor set above the equilibrium price leads to surpluses. Because the European Union price floor for butter is above the equilibrium price, the EU has created a surplus of butter which the government must buy. The surplus has been so large that it has been called a butter mountain.

2. The U.S. price floor for milk, set above the equilibrium price, has led to a surplus of milk. The government has dealt with the surplus by buying the surplus and giving away milk and dairy products produced from milk (such as cheese) to schools. This accounts for the low or zero price you paid for milk at most schools.

Chapter 9

Page 165

1. Domestic producers gain from a tariff and domestic consumers lose.

2. Trade protectionism leads to wasted resources because it shifts production from the lowest-cost producers to higher-cost producers.

3. You hear more often about people who gain from trade restrictions than people who lose because the gains from trade restrictions are concentrated on a few winners, while the losses are diffused over many losers. Even though the total gains are smaller than the total losses, the concentrated benefits mean that the winners have a greater incentive to argue for trade restriction than the losers do to argue against it.

Page 170

1. The movement of the garment trade overseas has been a net benefit for the United States because clothing is now much cheaper for U.S. consumers and U.S. workers specialize in the fields in which they are most productive.

2. If the U.S. government subsidized the Silicon Valley computer industry, it would encourage more computer chip manufacturing, but at a higher cost (production would not be as efficient). This would be a waste of resources. Foreign competitors would be pushed out of the industry. Consumers of computer chips would benefit from the subsidy, but they would benefit by less than the cost to U.S. taxpayers.

Chapter 10

Page 181

1. If the government overshoots and sets a Pigouvian tax that is too high, it will result in an equilibrium quantity that is lower than the efficient equilibrium. A tax that is too high will create a deadweight loss from too few trades. If the tax is much too high, it can be worse than leaving the externality alone.

2. If the government undershoots and provides a subsidy that is too low, the equilibrium quantity will be lower than the efficient equilibrium. In this case, there will be an undersupply.

Page 183

1. Using the Coase theorem, a solution to the prospect of elderly neighbors complaining about your party is to buy the elderly couple tickets to a movie or to a night away at a hotel. Transaction costs are low in this case: You can easily contact your neighbors and you might even pay for the gift by collecting contributions from the partygoers.

2. A solution to the polluting factory problem depends on the transactions costs. Are there many neighbors or only a few? Are the victims of the pollution located nearby or are they spread out? Is it clear whether the factory has the right to pollute, say, because it was there first and everyone moved into the area knowing about the pollution? Transaction costs are key here, because even if the factory has the right to pollute, if you can negotiate with your neighbors, you may be able to pay off the factory if it has certain property rights.

Page 188

1. A falling price for tradable pollution allowances tells us that the value of the allowance has fallen. This means that the costs of eliminating pollution have fallen—perhaps because of technological developments in clean energy.

2. If a local government sets tradable allowances for pollution in the neighborhood, some groups that would press for a large total quantity of allowances would be the big polluters: chemical factories, meat-processing plants, sometimes automobile repair shops. Some groups that would press for a smaller total quantity of allowances would be homeowners, parents sending their children to local schools but who live outside of the immediate vicinity, the elderly. Unfortunately, there is no theorem that says the rough-and-tumble of the political process will result in an efficient equilibrium. If the political process gets it approximately right and the externality is serious, the tradable allowance system will improve social welfare but this is not guaranteed.

Chapter 11

Page 195

1. In a competitive market, if a firm prices its product above the market price, no one will buy the firm's product. Why should anyone pay more for the same product? In a competitive market, if a firm prices its product below the market price, it will sell everything it produces, but why should it set price below the market price when it can sell the same amount at the market price?

2. Demand for a competitive firm's product is perfectly elastic, portrayed as a horizontal demand curve for the firm's product. It can sell all it wants at the competitive price.

3. If there is more than one firm in the industry, then the demand for a particular firm's product is always more elastic than the demand for the product itself. The demand for each stripper well's oil is very elastic even though the demand for oil is inelastic because there are very good substitutes for the oil from a particular firm, namely the oil from any other firm.

Page 200

1. When the firm in Figure 11.2 produces 4 barrels rather than 3, $33 in additional profit is made. Going from 7 to 8 barrels, no additional profit is made. Going from 8 to 9 barrels, profit falls to $-$ $40. Looking at the figure, $MR = MC$ when the quantity produced is 8 barrels. At this quantity, marginal profit is $0.

Page 203

1. Profit equals (price minus average cost) times quantity, $\pi = (P - AC) \times Q$. Another way of saying this is that profit per unit is price minus average cost (the cost for each unit), and profit per unit times the number of units sold gives you total profits.

2. Assuming that the firm produces the optimal quantity (found where $P = MC$), then at *any* price greater than average cost, the firm is making a profit and at *any* price less than average cost, the firm is taking a loss.

Page 205

1. Just because the price of a barrel of oil reaches $65 does not mean that the firm should undertake to spend $100 million to drill an oil well. The price easily could drop. The firm should project the price of oil over the life of the oil well to carefully determine revenues, and then see if it will make a lifetime profit considering its total costs. If lifetime profits are negative, the firm should not enter. Even when lifetime profits are positive, the firm should not necessarily invest right away—the firm may be better off waiting for a time to gather more information.

Page 210

1. In the early stages, an automobile manufacturing industry is a decreasing cost industry because as the industry expands, it can draw on economies of scale both in auto manufacturing and in steel, plastic, and other input industries. Economies of scale, however, don't increase forever, so once the industry matures, it becomes an increasing cost industry. Today, for example, the automobile industry is an increasing cost industry because greater demand for autos means an increased demand for steel and plastic, which will drive up the price of steel and plastic, thus increasing costs in the auto industry.
2. The U.S. film industry is clustered around Hollywood because the central location leads to lower costs. Perhaps only in Hollywood could a movie director easily arrange to interview four movie stars in a single afternoon.

Chapter 12

Page 226

If Sandy's MC is higher than Pat's MC, total costs can be reduced by producing a little bit less on Sandy's farm and a little bit more on Pat's farm.

Page 228

1. In competitive markets, profits are a signal for new firms to enter. It is as if entrepreneurs see a sign flashing "Profits, Profits, Profits."
2. In competitive markets, because a firm has no control over price, its best opportunity for profits is to keep its costs low.

Chapter 13

Page 239

1. As a firm with market power moves down its demand curve, the price it can charge on all units moves down as well.
2. A firm with market power prefers to face an inelastic demand curve because the more inelastic the demand curve, the more the firm with market power can raise its price above marginal cost. See Figure 13.4 for a display of this.

Page 241

1. A monopolist always prices its product above the price of an equal cost competitive firm.

2. A monopolist always produces less than an equal cost competitive firm because this way it produces more profit than a competitive firm.

Page 243

1. Apple has market power and plausibly it encourages innovation. Pharmaceutical companies have an incentive by the patent system to use market power to innovate. One can argue that many utilities have market power but do not seem to be great innovators. The U.S. Postal Service has market power but does not seem to innovate much.

2. The prize for a new cancer drug should be calculated by taking the number of people expected to die of cancer over a long period, then multiplying this by the presumed willingness of people with cancer to pay for a cure, discounted for payments received over a long period, minus the probable cost of research and the low marginal cost of producing the drug. The size of the prize is likely to be enormous.

Page 249

1. If regulators controlled the price at $P = AC$ (and AC is at point a), the monopolist would produce where the AC curve crosses the demand curve. At this price, the monopolist would make zero (normal) profits and the quantity would be greater than the monopoly quantity, although still not as high as the efficient quantity.

2. Telephones used to be a natural monopoly because it was much cheaper for one firm to lay one set of lines and serve everyone than to have competing phone companies. Today, cell phones have broken the natural land-line monopoly because cell towers cost much less to create than telephone poles and wires so it makes sense to have multiple, competing operators. In this way, technology can quickly abolish what was once a natural monopoly.

Page 250

1. Major league baseball and professional football restrict the entry of competitors in local areas, thus supporting the market power of these local teams. With market power, teams raise prices, without the fear that competitors will see the higher prices as opportunities to enter. In this case, prospective teams face more than just barriers to entry in the form of high entry costs: The teams are prohibited from entering by the leagues.

2. Barriers to entry are strong when they are mandated and enforced: The U.S. Postal Service still has a monopoly on delivering first-class mail because by law other firms must charge three times as much as the Postal Service if they wish to deliver a letter. Of course, the prevalence of email has made this monopoly less valuable. In contrast to this, when Congress took away the U.S. Postal Service's monopoly on the delivery of parcels, competitors such as UPS and FedEx jumped in and took over much of

the market. People still send parcels through the Postal Service, but often not when delivery needs to be fast and guaranteed. NBA basketball restricts entry just as major league baseball does, and that looks to be fairly permanent for the near term, though the league may let additional teams enter over time.

Chapter 14

Page 260

1. If a monopolist segments a market, it can price-discriminate between the different segments and so raise its profits.

2. When demand is more inelastic, the price-discriminating firm would set higher prices. Remember that elasticity = escape. People with inelastic demand find it harder to escape and so will pay more.

3. Arbitrage is taking advantage of price differences for the same good in different markets by buying low in one market and selling high in another market. When the monopolist price-discriminates by setting a low price in one market and a high price in another, it creates a potential arbitrage opportunity. In order to profitably price-discriminate, the monopolist must prevent this arbitrage.

Page 264

1. The early bird special is a form of price discrimination if people who want to eat at a later time have a more inelastic demand curve. This could be true, for example, if people who want to eat at a later hour are wealthier (perhaps because they are working long hours!). An alternative explanation is that the restaurant's marginal costs increase as the restaurant becomes more crowded—thus, restaurants charge more during peak hours. In the first case the markup of price over marginal cost increases in the later evening, in the second the firm's costs and price both increase in the later evening. It's not obvious which explanation is correct!

2. People who want to see movies right after the movies are released have a more inelastic demand for them than people who are willing to wait for the movies to be released as a DVD. Movie theaters know this and set their prices relatively high for those who cannot wait (have an inelastic demand). For the same reason, books are more expensive when they are first released in hardback, than later when they are released in paperback. The increased costs of producing a hardback are trivial compared to the difference in price.

Page 266

1. Price discrimination is likely to increase total surplus if output increases.

2. Price discrimination helps industries with high fixed costs because profits increase with market size. Simply, more market segments means that the price-discriminating firm can extract more consumer surplus. This leads to higher prices, which fund the high fixed costs. Universities have high fixed costs. The ability for a university to price-discriminate

means it can attract more paying students to its campus and so pay for its high fixed costs.

Page 269

1. Tying cell phones to service plans is a type of price discrimination whereby high demanders (long talkers) are charged more. If cell phone companies were not allowed to tie cell phones with service plans, the price of cell phones likely would rise and the price of phone calls likely would fall. This would be good for people who want to talk a lot but bad for people who want to use their cell phone only occasionally. Profits for the cell phone companies would also fall, so there would be fewer funds to pay for the fixed costs of building cell phone towers and infrastructure.

2. Bundling is likely to increase total surplus in high fixed cost, low marginal cost industries because without some form of price discrimination, it's difficult to provide these goods at optimal levels.

Chapter 15

Page 287

1. When Great Britain found oil in the North Sea, it could obtain the benefits of OPEC (the cartel price) without any of the disadvantages of joining the cartel, such as limiting production. Why join?

2. The surprising conclusion of the prisoner's dilemma is that there are situations when the pursuit of individual interest leads to a group outcome that is in the interest of no one. Think of three cases. First, the "invisible hand" is a metaphor for the idea that under the right circumstances the pursuit of self-interest can lead to the social interest. Second, theft is an intermediate case where the pursuit of self-interest benefits one's self but not the social interest. Third, the prisoner's dilemma reminds us that in some circumstances when everyone pursues their self-interest, the result can be against the interest of everyone!

Page 288

1. Though individual auto firms try to act as if they are monopolies, they do not band together in an attempt to raise prices and cut back on quantities. Such banding together is illegal in the United States. It is not illegal in various places in the world.

2. When a firm in an oligopoly reduces output, it shares equally in the gains from the reduction with the other firms.

Page 292

1. Monopolistic competitors earn zero economic profits in the long run and they produce above-minimum average cost. This categorization tells us that McDonald's, Burger King, and Wendy's over the long term will earn zero economic profits, with costs higher than the minimum of average costs.

2. Monopolistic competitors produce differentiated products. In the eyes of the consumer, a hamburger is not the same at these firms.

Page 294

1. Wood is practically the same everywhere as far as building houses is concerned. Windows are a differentiated product. Thick and double-paned windows with various cold-stopping features are manufactured for northern climates. There may be a benefit for an individual firm to advertise differentiated products, unlike similar products such as wood.

2. Famous athletes' endorsement of sports products that they use informs us that the product is of superior quality. If the product has nothing to do with sports, the endorsement signals quality rather than provides information.

Chapter 16

Page 307

1. The prices of Blu-ray and HD-DVD during the standard war were similar because each company kept prices low in the hope of driving out the other. Once Blu-ray won, its price went up because the company used its market power.

2. Economic theory can let you make strong predictions in certain cases.

Page 311

1. Your old cell phone provider prevents you taking your address list to a new cell phone from a new cell phone provider as a way of setting up high switching costs in an attempt to prevent you from changing your service.

2. Google is in a contestable market because it would be fairly easy for a competitor to enter the search market, as Microsoft has done with its Bing search engine.

Page 313

1. A firm with an established network good such as Microsoft Office faces competition or potential competition for the market. Network monopolies can last for a long time but then evaporate very quickly.

2. It is useful to wait until standards are set because you don't want to be the person or firm who has chosen what turns out to be the loser: You will face diminished support and product offerings. Once standards are set, there is little risk of picking a loser and so sales should burst forward.

Chapter 17

Page 321

1. The marginal product of labor falls as more workers are hired because the first worker will focus on the most important tasks, and so the marginal

product of labor will be high. The next worker will focus on the next important tasks, but these tasks will not be as important as the first worker tackled, so the marginal product of labor will not be as high as for the first worker. As more workers are hired, they do progressively less important tasks, so their marginal product falls relative to the first workers.

Page 323

1. An individual's labor supply curve might be backward-bending because at some point, individuals might prefer more leisure to working more, even at a higher wage. In other words, one of the things that people may buy more of when their wage goes up is leisure.

Page 330

1. An increase in mine safety would lower the wages of miners because mine workers are paid extra money to undertake their risky jobs. Making the job less risky would increase the number of people willing to be miners and thus would drive down wages.

2. Firms will pay for human capital improvements if the firm can reap the benefit. Training on a firm's specific inventory techniques will help the firm, but this is a skill that it is difficult for a worker to take to other firms, so the firm need not pay a higher wage to individuals with specific training. In this sense, the firm reaps the benefit of this training exclusively. In contrast, an MBA provides skills that can be used by many firms, so an individual with an MBA can earn a higher wage at other firms. In order to benefit from training an individual with general skills, the firm must keep the individual around at the lower wage long enough to recover its costs. Thus, the time requirement helps the firm recover a large portion of its investment in the worker.

Page 336

1. Employer discrimination is dumb or at least costly from a profit-making perspective because hiring equally good workers at a lower wage increases profit.

2. Market economies have had the most effect on eliminating discrimination by employers because the profit motive is a powerful incentive—notice that the more employers discriminate against minorities, the greater the profit from hiring a minority worker. Market economies have had some success in mitigating customer discrimination because market transactions bring different groups into regular contact with each other and thereby break down barriers. Market economies have had the toughest time eliminating employee discrimination because this type of discrimination can be self-reinforcing.

Chapter 18

Page 347

1. If government provides more of national defense than is efficient, it is pulling resources away from other, more valuable goods and having

taxpayers bear the burden. People with a very strong preference for national defense would benefit as well perhaps as those involved in providing national defense.

Page 348

1. Advertising could be used to pay for the upkeep of public parks. Advertising could be seen in obvious places such as signs by entryways to the park, on garbage cans, or on the sides of refreshment stands. If there is a music bandshell or a stage (in larger parks), advertising could be seen on the sides of these structures. Notice that under the Adopt-a-Highway program, there is advertising on roads that supports road cleanup.

2. Airports charge for Wi-Fi because they can make money from it by excluding non-payers. Since more Wi-Fi users don't (usually) increase congestion by appreciable amounts, it would be more efficient to allow open access.

Page 352

1. Small communities find it easier to deal with common resource problems than states or nations because they have an easier time enforcing norms (standards of behavior) that reduce free riding. Even so, the more unrelated people that have access to a common good, the harder it is to deal with common resource problems.

2. The establishment of property rights can help solve the tragedy of the commons because people who have property rights have no incentive to overuse a resource. The tragedy of the commons occurs because people have an incentive to overuse common resources: to get theirs before someone else takes it.

Chapter 19

Page 363

1. National voters have a smaller chance of influencing the election than do local voters, which suggests that people have a greater incentive to be informed about local issues. On the other hand, local issues are less important than national issues and there is less free information (e.g., from Jon Stewart) about local issues than about national issues, which suggests local voters would be even more rationally ignorant than national voters.

Page 367

1. Because of the benefits that special interests receive from current programs, they would fight against the establishment of a commission to examine federal waste. If the commission was set up, these special interests would then try to "capture" the commission: argue that their specific programs were needed, and exert political pressure to keep these programs. The bearers of the costs of these programs—the taxpayers—are too large and diverse a group to zero in on any particular program. The commission idea might be popular, but the chance of its success is low.

2. The beneficiaries of the local history collection at the library are the users of the collection. Ultimately, the taxpayers of the state pay for it. Benefits are concentrated on a small group, while the costs are spread over a large body of people (the taxpayers). Don't be surprised if the reading room is named after the state senator!

Page 369

1. If voters are myopic, politicians could prefer a policy with small gains now and big costs later (let's get reelected and maybe someone else will have to deal with the large costs down the road) than a policy with small costs now and large gains later (why jeopardize my chance to get reelected?). For these reasons, dealing with a large potential problem, such as the fiscal sustainability of Medicare, is often put off until the last minute when the solutions are much more difficult and costly.

Page 377

1. The free flow of ideas helps democracies function by getting alternatives out and on the table. Voters will always be rationally ignorant to some extent, but the more information that is out there and available at low cost, the more voters will be informed, at least about the big issues. Debate and dissent can improve the quality of ideas. The free flow of information reduces the possibility of corruption. New ideas help democracies adapt to changing conditions.

Chapter 21

Page 406

1. Workers sometimes fear that if they work harder under a piece rate system, they will work themselves out of a job. Lincoln's policy of guaranteed employment reassures workers that productivity will always work to their advantage, not to their detriment.

2. It is sometimes said that the word tips stands for "To Insure Prompt Service." Certainly, the idea is that restaurant customers will give bigger tips the better the service, thus giving waiters an incentive to be attentive. Thus, we would predict that waiters would be less attentive in Europe where the "tip" is typically automatic than in America where it usually is not.

Page 411

1. Professors have an incentive to be known as a hard grader because this reputation will keep away all but the serious students and maybe also all but the brightest students. Grading on a curve would encourage the usual diverse spectrum of students, from serious to indifferent and from smart to struggling.

2. In a tournament, one worker's gain is another's loss. Sometimes tournaments can encourage too much competition by discouraging cooperation.

If a firm wants its sales staff to work together to land sales, for example, then it would not want a strong tournament scheme. Professors who want their students to work together on projects should not grade on a curve.

Page 413

1. A famous paper in economics calculated that, on average, $10 spent on gifts was worth only $8 to the gift recipients. In other words, when your Uncle gives you $10 in cash, you get $10 worth of utility, but when your Uncle gives you a $10 pair of socks, on average, you get only $8 worth of utility. Thus, according to the author of the study, Joel Waldfogel, Christmas wastes billions of dollars. Even though most people understand this idea when it is explained to them, we don't see a big shift to giving cash. Why not? Perhaps gift giving is valuable precisely because it is challenging. If you spend $10 giving something to someone that they value for $50, this shows how much you must really understand and care for them. Or perhaps we want the gift giver to buy something for us that we would not have bought for ourselves. Or perhaps people give gifts to signal something about themselves. Giving someone a CD of Bach sonatas says something about *you* that a gift of $15 does not. Understanding the answer to this question may tell us a lot about social life. See Waldfogel, Joel. 1993, December. The deadweight loss of Christmas. *The American Economic Review* **83**(5): 1328–1336.

2. Maybe. Maybe not. If we pay for grades, some people worry that this will stifle the love of learning and perhaps send the message that getting good grades is like a job that the student is free to quit at any time. A number of experiments are currently under way testing these ideas.

Chapter 22

Page 423

1. According to the efficient markets hypothesis, one cannot consistently beat the market. Therefore, past performance is not a good guide to future success. On average, mutual funds that have performed well in the past are no more likely to perform well in the future than mutual funds that performed poorly in the past.

Page 429

1. Investing in the stocks of other countries helps to diversify your investments because the economies of other countries do not always rise and fall at the same time as the U.S. economy. If all economies tended to rise and fall together, there would not be any large benefits in diversifying across countries.

2. If many people dream of owning a football or baseball team, it is likely that the rewards to owning one go beyond monetary rewards. Thus, the monetary return on these assets is likely to be relatively low.

Page 432

1. This question is being hotly debated by many economists. It can be said that identifying and bursting bubbles is more difficult than it looks. How does the Federal Reserve know when there is a bubble? Increases in prices do not necessarily signify a bubble. Even if it can be said to be fairly certain that a bubble is present, how does the Federal Reserve burst the bubble while avoiding widespread collateral damage?

GLOSSARY

absolute advantage the ability to produce the same good using fewer inputs than another producer

accounting profit total revenue minus explicit costs (compare with economic profit)

antitrust laws laws that give the government the power to regulate or prohibit business practices that may be anticompetitive

arbitrage the practice of taking advantage of price differences for the same good in different markets by buying low in one market and selling high in another market

average cost the total cost of producing a given quantity divided by that quantity, $AC=TC/Q$

barriers to entry factors that increase the cost to new firms of entering an industry

budget constraint all the consumption bundles that a consumer can afford given their income and prices

bundling the requirement that products be bought together in a bundle or package

buy and hold the practice of buying stocks and then holding them for the long run, regardless of what prices do in the short run

cartel a group of suppliers that tries to act *as if* they were a monopoly

Coase theorem the principle that if transactions costs are low and property rights are clearly defined, private bargains will ensure that the market equilibrium is efficient even when there are externalities

common resources goods that are nonexcludable but rival

comparative advantage the ability to produce a good or service at a lower opportunity cost than another producer

compensating differential a difference in wages that offsets differences in working conditions

complements two goods for which a decrease in the price of one leads to an increase in the demand for the other

constant cost industry an industry in which industry costs do not change with greater output; shown with a flat supply curve

consumer surplus the consumer's gain from exchange, or the difference between the maximum price a consumer is willing to pay for a certain quantity and the market price

consumer surplus (total) an amount measured by the area beneath the demand curve and above the price up to the quantity traded

contestable market a market with many potential entrants

coordination game game in which the players arc better off if they choose the same strategies than if they choose different strategies and there is more than one strategy on which to potentially coordinate

corporate culture the shared collection of values and norms that govern how people interact in an organization or firm

deadweight loss the total of lost consumer and producer surplus when not all mutually profitable gains from trade are exploited

decreasing cost industry an industry in which the industry costs decrease with an increase in output; shown with a downward sloping supply curve

demand curve a function that shows the quantity demanded at different prices

diminishing marginal utility each additional unit of a good adds less to utility than the previous unit

dominant strategy a strategy that has a higher payoff than any other strategy no matter the strategies of other players

economic growth the growth rate of real GDP per capita

economic profit total revenue minus total costs including implicit costs

economies of scale the advantages of large-scale production that reduce average cost as quantity increases

efficient equilibrium the price and quantity that maximizes social surplus

efficient market hypothesis the claim that the prices of traded assets reflect all publicly available information

efficient quantity the quantity that maximizes social surplus

elasticity of demand $= \dfrac{\%\Delta Q_D}{\%\Delta P}$ a measure of how responsive the quantity demanded is to a change in price

elasticity of supply $=\dfrac{\%\Delta Q_S}{\%\Delta P}$ a measure of how responsive the quantity supplied is to a change in price

elimination principle the principle that in a competitive market, above-normal profits are eliminated by entry and below-normal profits are eliminated by exit

equilibrium price the price at which the quantity demanded is equal to the quantity supplied

equilibrium quantity the quantity at which the quantity demanded is equal to the quantity supplied

explicit cost is a cost that requires a money outlay

external benefit a benefit received by people other than the consumers or producers trading in the market

external cost a cost borne by people other than the consumers or the producers trading in the market

externalities external costs or external benefits; costs or benefits that fall on bystanders

fixed costs costs that do not vary with output

forced rider someone who must pay a share of the costs of a public good but who does not enjoy the benefits

free rider someone who consumes a public good without paying a share of the costs

futures standardized contracts to buy or sell specified quantities of a commodity or financial instrument at a specified price with delivery set at a specified time in the future

great economic problem problem of how to arrange our limited resources to satisfy as many of our wants as possible

human capital tools of the mind, the stuff in people's heads that makes them productive

implicit cost a cost that does not require an outlay of money

incentives rewards and penalties that motivate behavior

income effect the change in consumption caused by the change in purchasing power from a price change

increasing cost industry an industry in which industry costs increase with greater output; shown with an upward sloped supply curve

inferior good a good for which demand decreases when income increases

inflation an increase in the general level of prices

long run the time after all exit or entry has occurred

marginal cost, MC, $\frac{\Delta TC}{\Delta Q}$, the change in total cost from producing an additional unit

marginal product of labor (MPL) the increase in a firm's revenues created by hiring an additional laborer

marginal rate of substitution (MRS) the rate at which the consumer is willing to trade one good for another and remain indifferent. The MRS is equal to the slope of the indifference curve at that point

marginal revenue, MR, $\frac{\Delta TR}{\Delta Q}$, the change in total revenue from selling an additional unit

marginal utility the change in total utility from consuming an additional unit

market power the power to raise price above marginal cost without fear that other firms will enter the market

median voter theorem the principle that when voters vote for the policy that is closest to their ideal point on a line, then the ideal point of the median voter will beat any other policy in a majority rule election

monopolistic competition a market with a large number of firms selling similar but not identical products

monopoly a firm with market power

Nash equilibrium a situation in which no player has an incentive to change strategy unilaterally

natural monopoly a situation when a single firm can supply the entire market at a lower cost than two or more firms

network good a good whose value to one consumer increases the more that other consumers use the good

nonexcludable when people who don't pay cannot easily be prevented from using the good, the good is nonexcludable

nonrival (or nonrivalrous) goods when one person's use of the good does not reduce the ability of another person to use the same good, the good is nonrival

nonrival private goods goods that are excludable but nonrival

normal good a good for which demand increases when income increases

normative economics recommendations or arguments about what economic policy should be

Nozick's entitlement theory of justice theory that says that the distribution of income in a society is just if property is justly acquired and voluntarily exchanged

oligopoly a market dominated by a small number of firms

opportunity cost the value of opportunities lost when a choice is made

optimal consumption rule rule holding that to maximize utility, a consumer should allocate spending so that the marginal utility per dollar is equal for all purchases

perfect price discrimination (PPD) the situation that exists when each customer is charged his or her maximum willingness to pay

piece rate any payment system that pays workers per unit of output

Pigouvian subsidy a subsidy on a good with external benefits

Pigouvian tax a tax on a good with external costs

positive economics describing, explaining, or predicting economic events

prediction market a speculative market designed so that prices can be interpreted as probabilities and used to make predictions

price ceiling a maximum price allowed by law

price discrimination the selling of the same product at different prices to different customers

price floor a minimum price allowed by law

prisoner's dilemma situations where the pursuit of individual interest leads to a group outcome that is in the interest of no one

private cost a cost paid by the consumer or the producer

private goods goods that are excludable and rival

producer surplus the producer's gain from exchange, or the difference between the market price and the minimum price at which a producer would be willing to sell a particular quantity

producer surplus (total) an amount measured by the area above the supply curve and below the price up to the quantity traded

production possibilities frontier all the combinations of goods that a country can produce given its productivity and supply of inputs

protectionism the economic policy of restraining trade through quotas, tariffs, or other regulations that burden foreign producers but not domestic producers

public choice is the study of political behavior using the tools of economics.

public goods goods that are nonexcludable and nonrival

quantity demanded the quantity that buyers are willing and able to buy at a particular price

quantity supplied the quantity that sellers are willing and able to sell at a particular price

rational ignorance when the benefits of being informed are less than the costs of becoming informed it is rational to be ignorant

Rawls's maximin principle principle that justice requires

maximizing the benefits going to society's most disadvantaged group

rent control a price ceiling on rental housing

risk-return trade-off higher returns come at the price of higher risk

shortage a situation in which the quantity demanded is greater than the quantity supplied

short run the period before exit or entry can occur

social cost the private cost plus the external cost

social surplus consumer surplus plus producer surplus plus everyone else's surplus

speculation the attempt to profit from future price changes

statistical discrimination discrimination using information about group averages to make conclusions about individuals

strategic decision making decision making in situations that are interactive

substitutes two goods for which a decrease in the price of one leads to a decrease in demand for the other

substitution effect the change in consumption caused by a change in relative prices holding the consumer's utility level constant

sunk cost a cost that once incurred can never be recovered

surplus a situation in which the quantity supplied is greater than the quantity demanded

switching costs the costs of switching purchases from one firm to another. Firms sometimes try to raise switching costs to reduce competition for their customers

tariff a tax on imports

total cost the cost of producing a given quantity of output

total revenue price times quantity sold: $TR = P \times Q$

tournament a compensation scheme in which payment is based on relative performance

trade quota a restriction on the quantity of goods that can be imported: imports greater than the quota amount are forbidden or heavily taxed

tragedy of the commons the tendency of any resource that is unowned and hence nonexcludable to be overused and undermaintained

transaction costs all the costs necessary to reach an agreement

tying a form of price discrimination in which one good, called the base good, is tied to a second good called the variable good

utilitarianism the idea that the best society maximizes the sum of utility

variable costs costs that vary with output

zero profits or normal profits the condition when $P = AC$; at this price the firm is covering all of its costs including enough to pay labor and capital their ordinary opportunity costs

REFERENCES

Chapter 1 Notes

1. Quoted in **Christopher, Emma.** 2007. "The Slave Trade is Merciful Compare to [this]": Slave traders, convict transportation and the abolitionists. In **Christopher, E., C. Pybus, and M. Rediker** (eds.), *Many Middle Passages*, Chap. 6, pp. 109–128. Berkeley, CA: University of California Press.

2. **Chadwick, Edwin.** 1862. Opening address of the British Association for the Advancement of Science. *Journal of the Statistical Society of London* **25**(4): 502–524.

3. **Chadwick,** *op. cit.*

4. On the impact of new drugs, see **Lichtenberg, Frank.** 2007. The impact of new drugs on U.S. longevity and medical Expenditure, 1990–2003. *American Economic Review* **97**(2): 438–443.

5. **Celis III, William.** December 28, 1991. Study finds enrollment is up at colleges despite recession. *The New York Times.*

Chapter 2 Notes

1. On this point, see **Sowell, Thomas.** 1980. *Knowledge and Decisions.* New York: Basic Books. And see also Chapter 4 of **Reisman, George.** 1996. *Capitalism: A Treatise on Economics.* Ottawa, IL: Jameson.

2. **Smith, Adam.** August 2, 2006. *An Inquiry into the Nature and Causes of the Wealth of Nations.* Edited by Edwin Cannan, Book IV, II. 2.11. Indianapolis, IN: Library of Economics and Liberty. http://www.econlib.org/library/Smith/smWN13.html. Originally published London: Methuen, 1904 [1776].

3. See **Paley, Amit R.** May 15, 2006. Homework help, from a world away: Web joins students, cheap overseas tutors. *The Washington Post,* A01. http://www.washingtonpost.com/wp-dyn/content/article/2006/05/14/AR2006051401139_pf.html. See also **Bray, Hiawatha.** March 28, 2006. Online tutoring pays off at home, abroad. *The Boston Globe.*

4. **Boudreaux, Donald J.** 2008. *Globalization.* Westport, CT: Greenwood Press.

Chapter 3 Notes

1. On changing U.S. demographics and their impact on the economy, see **Kotlikoff, Laurence J. and Scott Burns.** 2004. *The Coming Generational Storm.* Cambridge, MA: MIT Press.

2. *International Herald Tribune.* http://www.iht.com/articles/ap/2007/07/31/business/EU-FIN-MKT-Oil-Prices.php.

3. **Information Resources, Inc.** September 16, 2005. *Times and Trends.*

4. **Paleontological Research Institution.** http://www.priweb.org/ed/pgws/history/spindletop/lucas_gusher.html.

5. See information available at the **U.S. Energy Information Administration** Web site. http://www.eia.gov/.

6. On the costs of oil production, see **Joint Economic Committee, United States Congress.** *OPEC and the High Price of Oil.* http://www.house.gov/jec/publications/109/11–17–05opec.pdf.

Chapter 4 Notes

1. **Smith, Vernon.** 1991. Experimental economics at Purdue. In **Smith, V.** (ed.), *Papers in Experimental Economics.* Cambridge, UK: Cambridge University Press. Originally appeared in **Horwich, G. and J. P. Quirk** (eds.), *Essays in Contemporary Fields of Economics.* Lafayette, IN: Purdue University Press, 1981.

2. **Conover, Ted.** July 2, 2006. Capitalist roaders. *New York Times Magazine,* pp. 31–37, 50.

Chapter 5 Notes

1. See **International Money Fund.** 2005. *World Economic Outlook—2005.* Washington, DC: IMF. See, in particular, Chap. 4.

2. On the elasticity of demand for oil, see **Cooper, John C. B.** 2003. Price elasticity of demand for crude oil: Estimates for 23 countries. *OPEC Review* **27**(1): 1–8. On the elasticity of demand for Minute Maid orange juice, see **Capps, Oral Jr. and H. Alan Love.** 2002. Econometric considerations in the use of electronic scanner data to conduct consumer demand analysis. *American Journal of Agricultural Economics* **84**(3): 807–816.

3. On the elasticity of demand for illegal drugs, see **Cicala, Steve J.** 2005. The demand for illicit drugs: A meta-analysis of price elasticities. Working paper, University of Chicago. On the elasticity of demand for cigarettes, see **Keeler T. E., T. W. Hu, P. G. Barnett, and W. G. Manning.** 1993. Taxation, regulation, and addiction: A demand function for cigarettes based on time-series evidence. *Journal of Health Economics* **12**(1): 1–18.

4. On the elasticity of supply for cocoa, see **Burger, K.** 1996. *The European Chocolate Market and the Effects of the Proposed EU Directive.* Amsterdam: Economic and Social Institute, Free University. For the elasticity of supply of coffee, see **Akiyama, T. and P. Varangis.** 1990. The impact of the international coffee agreement on producing countries. *World Bank Economic Review* **4**(2): 157–173.

5. For details on the national program, see **Office of the Press Secretary, White House.** April 28, 2000. *President Clinton Announces Gun Buyback Partnership with the District of Columbia.* http://clinton4.nara.gov/textonly/WH/New/html/20000428.html. Also from the Washington police, see http://mpdc.dc.gov/mpdc/cwp/view,a,1242,Q,546745,mpdcNav_GID,1541,mpdcNav,%7C,.asp. HUD's gun buyback program ended in 2001, although buybacks continue in many cities. In 2006, for example, the Boston Red Sox donated a substantial sum to help Boston's buyback program. See **Boston Red Sox.** July 1, 2006. *Red Sox Make $25,000 Donation to City's Gun Buyback Program.* http://boston.redsox.mlb.com/NASApp/mlb/news/press_releases/press_release.jsp?ymd=20060701&content_id=1532641&vkey=pr_bos&fext=.jsp&c_id=bos.

6. **Callahan, C., F. Rivara, and T. Koepsell.** 1994. Money for guns: Evaluation of the Seattle gun buy-back program. *Public Health Reports* **109**: 472–477.

7. **Welch, William M.** March 17, 2008. Critics take aim at gun buybacks. *USA Today.*

8. See **Mullin, Wallace P.** 2001. Will gun buyback programs increase the quantity of guns? *International Review of Law and Economics* **21**: 87–102.

9. For a review of some of the evidence on a variety of crime fighting policies, see **Levitt, Steven D.** 2004. Understanding why crime fell in the 1990s: Four factors that explain the decline and six that do not. *Journal of Economic Perspectives* **18**(1): 163–190.

10. For Williams's story, see **Gavel, Doug.** September 28, 2000. Sophomore skips orientation to free 4,000 slaves in Sudan. *Harvard University Gazette.* For Denver schoolchildren, *PBS OnlineNewsHour.* May 31, 1999. Jim Lehrer on the crisis in the Sudan. http://www.pbs.org/newshour/bb/africa/jan-june99/sudan.html.

11. **Miniter, Richard.** July 1999. The false promise of slave redemption. *The Atlantic Monthly* **284**(1): 63–71. http://www.theatlantic.com/issues/99jul/9907sudanslaves.htm. Note that although the Miniter article contains some useful information, it is a confused account of economics. Miniter argues that a low price for slaves means the slave traffickers are being driven out of business and high prices mean that slavery is profitable, but one has to ask why the price is low or high. High prices driven by increased demand from slave redeemers is a good sign because it means the slave redeemers are outbidding potential slave traffickers.

12. It is also possible to make predictions about quantities using two similar formulas.

13. The proof of these formulas is not difficult, but a bit more advanced than is necessary for this textbook. For a proof, see **McAfee, Preston.** 2006. *Introduction to Economic Analysis.* http://www.introecon.com.

14. **Office of the Press Secretary, White House.** http://www.whitehouse.gov/news/releases/2005/11/20051103-10.html.

15. The Klick and Tabarrok and Gruber articles use advanced statistical techniques to argue that the increase in police causes the decrease in crime and the increase in giving causes the decrease in attendance. For more details, see **Klick, J. and A. Tabarrok.** 2005. Using terror alert levels to estimate the effect of police on crime. *Journal of Law and Economics* **48**(1): 267–280. Also, **Gruber, Jonathan.** 2004. Pay or pray? The impact of charitable subsidies on religious attendance. *Journal of Public Economics* **88**(12): 2635–2655.

Chapter 6 Notes

1. Information about George Steinbrenner and the disappearing estate tax may be found in *The New York Times.* July 14, 2010. Steinbrenner heirs may save millions on estate tax. On estate taxes in Australia, see **Wojciech, Kopczuk and Joel Slemrod.** 2003. Dying to save taxes: Evidence from estate-tax returns on the death elasticity. *Review of Economics and Statistics* **85**(2): 256–265. The influence of the tax system on births is discussed in **Leonhardt, David.** December 20, 2006. To-do list: Wrap gifts. Have baby. *The New York Times.* Also, **Dickert-Conlin, Stacy and Chandra Amitabh.** 1999. Taxes and the timing of births. *Journal of Political Economy* **107**(1): 161–177.

Chapter 7 Notes

1. http://www.aboutflowers.com/press_b3b.html.

2. Ecuador and Colombia also export millions of roses to the United States.

3. See **Hennock, Mary.** 2002. Kenya's flower farms flourish. *BBC News Online.* http://news.bbc.co.uk/1/hi/business/1820515.stm. For more on Kenya and the Dutch flower market, refer to **McMillan, John.** 2002. *Reinventing the Bazaar.* New York: W.W. Norton. Also **Wijnands, Jo.** 2005. *Sustainable International Networks in the Flower Industry: Bridging Empirical Findings and Theoretical Issues.* The Hague: International Society for Horticultural Science.

4. For more information, see **Wikipedia.** Ethanol fuel in Brazil. http://en.wikipedia.org/wiki/Ethanol_fuel_in_Brazil, for more information.

5. See *The New York Times.* July 8, 2006. Ethanol is the new real estate. Page B5.

6. **American Petrochemical Institute.** *Oil Facts.* http://classroom-energy.org/teachers/oilfacts.pdf.

7. See **Williams, Scott.** 2006. Asphalt prices stalling budgets. *Milwaukee Journal Sentinel.* http://www.jsonline.com/story/index.aspx?id=434330.

8. **Smith, Vernon.** 1982. Microeconomic systems as an experimental science. *American Economic Review* **72**: 923–955.

9. **Federal Highway Administration.** 1993. *A Study of the Use of Recycled Paving Material.* Document no. FHWA-1993-RD-93-147. Washington, DC: FHWA.

10. **Roll, Richard.** 1984. Orange juice and weather. *American Economic Review* **74**(5): 861–880.

11. For much more on prediction markets and how they can be used to make decisions, see **Hanson, Robin D.** 2002. Decision markets. In **Alexander Tabarrok** (ed.), *Entrepreneurial Economics: Bright Ideas from the Dismal Science,* pp. 79–85. Oxford: Oxford University Press. Also **Hanson, Robin.** 20XX. Shall we vote on values, but bet on beliefs? *Journal of Political Philosophy.*

12. On polls versus prediction markets, see **Berg, J. E., R. Forsythe, F. D. Nelson, and T. A. Rietz.** 2001. Results from a dozen years of election futures markets research. In C. A. Plott and V. Smith (eds.), *Handbook of Experimental Economic Results.* http://www.biz.uiowa.edu/iem/archive/BFNR_2000.pdf. Also **Berg, J. E., F. Nelson, and T. A. Rietz.** 2003. Accuracy and forecast standard error of prediction markets. Working paper, Tippie College of Business, Iowa City. http://www.biz.uiowa.edu/iem/archive/forecasting.pdf.

Chapter 8 Notes

1. A 2″ × 4″ refers to the pre-planed dimensions, which after planing, are typically $1\frac{3}{4}″ \times 3\frac{3}{4}″$; with price controls, the average size fell to $1\frac{5}{8}″ \times 3\frac{5}{8}″$. See Thomas Hall. 2003. *The Rotten Fruits of Economic Controls and the Rise From the Ashes: 1965–1989.* University Press of America.

2. *Business Week.* February 16, 1974. Page 122. Quoted in Bradley (1996, p. 1635).

3. Prices were frozen at levels no higher than the May 25, 1970, price or a price at which 10% or more of transactions took place in the 30 days prior to August 14, 1971. Some adjustments for seasonal differences were allowed for some products, such as fashion items, but not for oil. See **Bradley, Robert Jr.** 1996. *Oil, Gas and Government: The U.S. Experience.* Vol. 2. Lanham, MD: Rowman & Littlefield. See especially pp. 1607–1608.

4. See **Hall, Thomas E.** 2003. *The Rotten Fruits of Economic Controls and the Rise from the Ashes, 1965–1989.* New York: University Press of America.

5. **Bradley, Robert Jr.** 1996. *Oil, Gas and Government: The U.S. Experience.* Vol. 1. Lanham, MD: Rowman & Littlefield.

6. See *The Washington Post.* November 26, 1973. Steps ordered by Nixon to meet energy crisis. Page A12.

7. *Time.* December 10, 1973. The shortage's losers and winners.

8. **Grayson, Jackson C.** February 6, 1974. Let's end controls—completely. *The Wall Street Journal,* p. 14.

9. See Bradley (1996, pp. 477, 515).

10. As assessed in 1999. See **Glaeser, E.** 2002. Does rent control reduce segregation? NBER working paper, Washington, DC.

11. **Lindbeck, Assar.** 1972. *The Political Economy of the New Left.* New York: Harper & Row. See especially p. 39.

12. Quoted in **Block, Walter.** August 29, 2006. Rent control. In **David R. Henderson** (ed.), *The Concise Encyclopedia of Economics.* Indianapolis, IN: Liberty Fund, Library of Economics and Liberty. http://econlib.org/library/Enc/RentControl.html.

13. **Glaeser, Edward L. and Erzo F. P. Luttmer. 2003.** The misallocation of housing under rent control. *American Economic Review* **93**(4): 1027–1046.

14. For a recent discussion, see **Arnott, Richard.** 1995. Time for revisionism on rent control? *The Journal of Economic Perspectives* **9**(1): 99–120.

15. On housing vouchers, see **Olsen, Ed.** 20XX. Housing programs for low-income households. In **Robert Moffitt** (ed.), *Means-Tested Transfer Programs in the U.S.* Chicago: University of Chicago Press.

16. **Chandrasekaran, Rajiv.** December 9, 2003. Fueling anger in Iraq. *The Washington Post.* Page A01.

17. *Ibid.*

18. Drawn from **Smith, Hedrick.** 1976. Consumers: The art of queuing. In *The Russians.* New York: Ballantine Books.

19. Data are from the **Bureau of Labor Statistics.** 2005. *Characteristics of Minimum Wage Workers.* Washington, DC: BLS. http://www.bls.gov/cps/minwage2005.htm.

20. For a listing and abstract of many studies on the minimum wage, see **U.S. Congress Joint Economic Committee.** *50 Years of Research on the Minimum Wage.* Recent studies include **Neumark, D. and W. Wascher.** 1992. Employment effects of minimum and subminimum wages: Panel data on state minimum wage laws. *Industrial and Labor Relations Review* **46**(1): 55–81. **Deere, D., K. M. Murphy, and F. Welch.** 1995. Employment and the 1990–1991 minimum-wage hike. *American Economic Review* **85**(2): 232–237. Not all studies find a significant reduction in employment. See **Card, David and Alan B.** September 1994. Minimum wages and employment: A case study of the fast-food industry in New Jersey and Pennsylvania. *American Economic Review* **84**: 772–793 for a well-designed study that challenges the conventional wisdom.

21. **Bureau of Labor Statistics,** *op. cit.*

22. On the minimum wage in Puerto Rico in 1938, see **Rottenberg, Simon.** 1981. Minimum wages in Puerto Rico. In **Simon Rottenberg** (ed.), *The Economics of Legal Minimum Wages,* pp. 327–339. Washington, DC: American Enterprise Institute. Also **Rustici, Thomas.** 1985. A public choice view of the minimum wage. *Cato Journal* **5**(1): 103–131.

Beginning in 1974, the Puerto Rican minimum wage was raised in steps to the U.S. level, creating a repeat of the experiment of 1938. The results were the same. Freeman and Freeman estimate that the increase in the minimum wage reduced the number of jobs in Puerto Rico by 8 to 10%. See **Freeman, Alida Castillo and Richard B Freeman.** June 1991. *Minimum Wages in Puerto Rico: Textbook Case of a Wage Floor?* Washington, DC: National Bureau of Economic Research.

23. On deregulation, see **Peltzman, Sam.** 1989. The economic theory of regulation after a decade of deregulation. Brookings Papers on Economic Activity. *Microeconomics:* 1–59.

24. On deregulation, see **Morrison, Steven A. and Clifford Winston.** 1986. *The Economic Effects of Airline Deregulation.* Washington, DC: Brookings Institution.

Chapter 9 Notes

1. On the environmental cost of sugar production, see **Schwabach, Aaron.** 2002. How protectionism is destroying the Everglades. *National Wetlands Newsletter* **24**(1): 7–14.

2. See **Bellamy, Carol.** 1997. *The State of the World's Children—1997.* New York: Oxford University Press and UNICEF. http://unicef.org/sowc97/.

3. See **Edmonds, Eric V. and Nina Pavcnik.** January 2006. International trade and child labor: Cross-country evidence. *Journal of International Economics:* 115–140.

4. On the Food for Education program, see **Ahmed, A. and C. del Nino.** 2002. *The Food for Education Program in Bangladesh: An Evaluation of Its Impact on Educational Attainment and Food Security.* FCND DP No. 138. Washington, DC: International Food Policy Research Institute. Also **Meng, Xin and Jim Ryan.** 2003. Evaluating the Food for Education Program in Bangladesh. Working paper, Australian National University, Australia South Asia Research Centre.

5. On the 1918 flu, see **Barry, John M.** 2005. *The Great Influenza: The Epic Story of the Deadliest Plague in History.* New York: Penguin. On policy for a future pandemic, see **Cowen, Tyler.** 2005. Avian flu: What should be done. Working paper, Mercatus Center, George Mason University, Arlington, VA. http://mercatus.org/repository/docLib/20060726_Avian_Flu.pdf.

6. Quoted in **Norberg, Johan.** 2003. *In Defense of Global Capitalism.* Washington, DC: Cato Institute.

7. **Johnson, Bradford.** 2002. Retail: The Wal-Mart effect. *McKinsey Quarterly* (1): 40–43.

Chapter 10 Notes

1. On the external cost of antibiotic use, see **Elbasha, Elamin H.** 2003. Deadweight loss of bacterial resistance due to overtreatment. *Health Economics* 12: 125–138.

2. **Meade, J. E.** 1952. External economies and diseconomies in a competitive situation. *Economic Journal* **62**: 54–67. On the market for pollination, see **Cheung, Steven N. S.** 1973. The fable of the bees: An economic investigation. *Journal of Law and Economics* **16**: 11–33. Also for a recent description of the market in the United States, see **Sumner, Daniel A. and Hayley Boriss.** 2006. Bee-conomics and the leap in pollination fees. *Agricultural and Resource Economics Update* **3**(9): 9–11.

3. *Consumer Reports.* June 2007. Washers and dryers: Dirty laundry.

4. The elasticity of demand for electricity is about −0.5, so a 2% increase in the price would reduce consumption by about 1%.

5. For a good overview of the acid rain program, see the EPA's recent *Acid Rain Program Progress Report*. http://www.epa.gov/airmarkets/progress/progress-reports.html.

Chapter 11 Notes

1. For information on stripper wells, see **U.S. Department of Energy.** *Marginal & Stripper Well Revitalization.* http://www.fossil.energy.gov/programs/oilgas/marginalwells/#.

2. **Bernstein, William J.** *A Splendid Exchange: How Trade Shaped the World.* New York: Atlantic Monthly Press, 2008. See p. 62.

3. MPAA. http://mpaa.org/press_releases/2005%20tms%20report.pdf.

4. New Providence. http://www.redorbit.com/news/entertainment/499053/bookish_britain_overtakes_america_as_top_publisher/.

Chapter 12 Notes

1. **Schumpeter, Joseph.** 1975 [1942]. *Capitalism, Socialism and Democracy.* New York: Harper. See, in particular, pp. 82–85.

2. Based on data from 1972 to 1992 in **Adams, William J.** 1993. TV program scheduling strategies and their relationship to new program renewal rates and rating changes. *Journal of Broadcasting and Electronic Media* **37:** 465–475. The renewal rate is probably lower today as there are more television stations and viewers are more difficult to keep.

Chapter 13 Notes

1. On deaths due to AIDS, see http://www.cdc.gov/hiv/graphics/mortalit.htm. On the efficacy of antiretrovirals, see **Weller I. V. and I. G. Williams.** 2001. ABC of AIDS: Antiretroviral drugs. *British Medical Journal* **322**(7299): 1410–1412. And, on developing countries, **Severe, P., et al.** 2005. Antiretroviral therapy in a thousand patients with AIDS in Haiti. *New England Journal of Medicine* **353**(22): 2325–2334. Also **Lichtenberg, Frank.** 2003. The effect of new drugs on HIV mortality in the U.S., 1987–1998. *Economics and Human Biology* **1:** 259–266.

2. On the cost of AIDS drugs in the United States, see http://www.aids.about.com/od/hivmedicationfactsheets/a/drugcost.htm.

3. On the number of people worldwide with AIDS, see **UN-AIDS.** 2006. *Report on the Global AIDS Epidemic.* http://unaids.org/en/HIV_data/2006GlobalReport/default.asp.

4. On the cost of Combivir, see http://www.money.cnn.com/magazines/fortune/fortune_archive/2006/09/18/8386170/index.htm?postversion=2006090806 and http://news.bbc.co.uk/1/hi/business/2981015.stm, and further below on patents and differential pricing.

5. See **Pepper, Daniel.** September 18, 2006. Patently unfair. *Fortune.* http://money.cnn.com/magazines/fortune/fortune_archive/2006/09/18/8386170/index.htm?postversion=2006090806.

6. It's possible to prove why the MR shortcut is true using calculus. Let the demand curve be written in the form $P = a - bQ$ so the slope is b. Total revenue is $P * q = TR = aQ - bQ^2$. Marginal revenue is the derivative of total revenue with respect to quantity or $MR = \frac{dTR}{dQ} = a - 2bQ$. Notice that the slope of the MR curve is $2b$, twice the slope of the demand curve.

7. American Airlines reservation Web site.

8. **DiMasi, Joseph A., Ronald W. Hansen, and Henry G. Grabowski.** 2003. The price of innovation: New estimates of drug development costs. *Journal of Health Economics* **22**(2): 151–185.

9. One study suggests that a 10% decline in price will lead to at least a 5% decline in the number of new drugs. See also **Vernon, John.** 2005. Examining the link between price regulation and pharmaceutical R&D investment. *Health Economics* **14**(1): 1–17.

10. **North, Douglass C.** 1981. *Structure and Change in Economic History.* New York: W.W. Norton. See p. 164.

11. **Kremer, M.** 1998. Patent buyouts: A mechanism for encouraging innovation. *Quarterly Journal of Economics* 113: 1137–1167.

12. See **Hazlett, Thomas W. and Matthew L. Spitzer.** 1997. *Public Policy towards Cable Television: The Economics of Rate Controls.* AEI.

13. On the $3,900 price, see **Berthelsen, Christian.** June 2, 2001. Duke admits overcharging utilities $3,880 bill per megawatt hour. *San Francisco Chronicle.* http://www.sfgate.com/cgi-bin/article.cgi%3Ffile%3D/chronicle/archive/2001/06/02/BU238492.DTL%20.

14. For good reviews of the California energy crisis, see **Borenstein, Severin.** 2002. The trouble with electricity markets: Understanding California's restructuring disaster. *Journal of Economic Perspectives* **16**(1): 191–211. See also **Congressional Budget Office.** 2001. *Causes and Lessons of the California Electricity Crisis.* http://www.cbo.gov/ftpdocs/30xx/doc3062/CaliforniaEnergy.pdf. And **Weare, Christopher.** 2003. *The California Electricity Crisis: Causes and Policy Options.* San Francisco: Public Policy Institute of California.

15. On Apple's market share, see *Business Week.* February 9, 2006. SanDisk surprise. http://www.businessweek.com/technology/tech_stats/mp3s060209.htm.

Chapter 14 Notes

1. Information on the Combivir smuggling operation can be found in **Irving, Richard.** February 21, 2005. AIDS drugs to Africa rebranded in drive to beat racket. *The Times.* http://www.business.timesonline.co.uk/tol/business/markets/africa/article516982.ece. On an earlier ring busted in 2002, see **Syal, Rajeev.** December 28, 2002. Scandal of Africa's AIDS drug re-sold to Britain. *Telegraph.* http://www.telegraph.co.uk/news/main.jhtml?xml=/news/2002/12/29/waids29.xml. See also **Morais, Richard C.** 2004. Pssst. . . Wanna buy some augmentin? *Forbes.* http://www.forbes.com/free_forbes/2004/0412/112.html.

2. See **R. Preston McAfee.** 2002. *Competitive Solutions: The Strategist's Toolkit.* Princeton, NJ: Princeton University Press.

Chapter 15 Notes

1. http://www.nationmaster.com/graph/ene_oil_pro-energy-oil-production. According to the *CIA World Factbook 2007*, combined production from African countries amounts to approximately 9,062,000 and Saudi Arabian production is about 9,475,000.

2. See, for example, **Morgan, Dan, Sarah Cohen, and Gilbert M. Gaul.** December 10, 2006. Dairy industry crushed innovator who bested price-control system. *Washington Post.* http://www.washingtonpost.com/wp-dyn/content/article/2006/12/09/AR2006120900925.html. Also http://www.findarticles.com/p/articles/mi_m3778/is_1991_August/ai_12056311.

3. On police road barriers, see **Polgreen, Lydia.** November 29, 2005. As Nigeria tries to fight graft, a new sordid tale. *The New York Times.* On grade selling, see **Goldman, Antony.** 1997. Same Salary, three lifestyles: Corruption's toll on Nigeria. *Christian Science Monitor.* As an example of cartelization, see **Gabriel, Omoh, Lukat Binniyat, Yemi Adeoye, and Victor Ahiuma-Young.** 2008. *PPMC Cartel, Politicians Responsible for Soaring Diesel Price.* Nigeria: Vanguard. http://www.allafrica.com/stories/200807140212.html.

4. See **Bagwell, Kyle.** 2007. The economic analysis of advertising. In **Mark Armstrong and Robert H. Porter** (eds.), *The Handbook of Industrial Organization,* Vol. III, p. 1745. Amsterdam: Elsevier and North Holland.

5. **Ippolito, Pauline M. and Alan D. Mathios.** Autumn 1990. Advertising and health choices: A study of the cereal market. *RAND Journal of Economics* **21**(3): 459–480.

6. http://www.youtube.com/watch?v=R1NnyE6DDnQ.

7. http://www.beautifullife.info/advertisment/history-of-coca-cola-in-ads/.

8. http://en.wikipedia.org/wiki/Coca-Cola.

9. http://www.thecoca-colacompany.com/contactus/faq/advertising.html.

10. **McClure, Samuel M., Jian Li, Damon Tomlin, Kim S. Cypert, Latane M. Montague, and P. Read Montague.** October 14, 2004. Neural correlates of behavioral preference for culturally familiar drinks. *Neuron* **44**: 379–387.

11. http://www.marginalrevolution.com/marginalrevolution/2008/12/advertising-mar.html.

12. https://www.chicagobooth.edu/capideas/win98/BeckMurph.htm.

Chapter 16 Notes

1. http://www.match.com/help/aboutus.aspx.

2. See, for instance, http://www.mashable.com/2007/06/10/facebook-hammers-myspace-on-almost-all-key-features/.

3. BLS includes an index of the cost of cellular service in the CPI. This is calculated based on changing costs of specific plan items and takes account of required contracts terms, etc. For more detail, consult http://www.bls.gov/cpi/cpifactc.htm if you are interested.
   December 1997: 100
   December 2000: 71.7
   December 2005: 65.7
   September 2010: 62.5
   From **Bureau of Labor Statistics.** December 2005. Table 28, Historical Consumer Price Index for Urban Wage Earners and Clerical Workers (CPI-W): U.S. City Average, by Commodity and Service Group and Detailed Expenditure Categories. http://www.bls.gov/cpi/cpid0512.pdf. And **Bureau of Labor Statistics.** September 2010. Table 3, Consumer Price Index for all Urban Consumers (CPI-U): U.S. City Average, Detailed Expenditure Categories. http://www.bls.gov/cpi/cpid1009.pdf.

4. http://www.cc.gatech.edu/gvu/user_surveys/survey-10-1996/graphs/use/Browser_You_Expect_To_Use_In_12_Months.html. Exact estimates vary; see http://en.wikipedia.org/wiki/Usage_share_of_web_browsers.

5. **Watts, Duncan J., Salganik, M. J., and P. S. Dodds.** 2006. Experimental study of inequality and unpredictability in an artificial cultural market. *Science* **311**: 854–856.

Chapter 17 Notes

1. On dangerous professions, see, for instance, http://www.forbes.com/2007/08/13/dangerous-jobs-fishing-lead-careers-cx_tvr_0813danger.html.

2. Here is one estimate of coal miner earnings: http://www.washingtonpost.com/wp-dyn/content/discussion/2006/01/04/DI2006010401171.html.

3. For one estimate of the union wage premium, see http://psi.org.uk/docs/2003/research/emp-union-wage-premium-us-uk.pdf.

4. Data from http://oecd.org for union members and employees.

Chapter 18 Notes

1. From Aristotle, *Politics,* Book II, Chap. III, 1261b. **Jowett, Benjamin** (trans.). 1885. *The Politics of Aristotle.* With Introduction, Marginal Analysis, Essays, Notes, and Indices. 2 vols. Oxford: Clarendon Press. See Vol. 2.

2. The system was later modified so the ITQs gave rights to a certain share of the total allowable catch.

3. See **World Meteorological Organization.** 2007. *Scientific Assessment of Ozone Depletion: 2006.* Global Ozone Research and Monitoring Project Rept. No. 50. Geneva, Switzerland: http://www.esrl.noaa.gov/csd/assessments/2006/report.html.

4. http://greatchange.org/footnotes-overshoot-easter_island.html.

5. **Demsetz, Harold.** 1967. Towards a theory of property rights. *AER* **57**: 2.

Chapter 19 Notes

1. **House of Commons.** November 11, 1947. Official Report, 5th Series, Vol. 444, cc. 206–207.

2. **Kaiser/Harvard Program on the Public and Health/Social Policy Survey.** January 1995.

3. See, for instance, **DeLorme, Charles D., Stacey Isom, and David R. Kamerschen.** April 2005. Rent seeking and taxation in the ancient Roman Empire. *Applied Economics* **37**: 705–711. http://ideas.repec.org/a/taf/applec/v372005i6p705-711.html.

4. **Leeson, Peter T.** 2008. Media freedom, political knowledge, and participation. *Journal of Economic Perspectives* **22**(2): 155–169.

5. **Djankov, S., C. McLiesh, T. Nenova, and A. Shleifer.** 2003. Who owns the media? *Journal of Law and Economics* **46**(2): 341–381.

6. See **Conquest, Robert.** 1987. *Harvest of Sorrow.* New York: Oxford University Press.

7. **Sen, Amartya.** August 2, 1990. *Public Action to Remedy Hunger.* Arturo Tanco Memorial Lecture. http://thp.org/reports/sen/sen890.htm.

8. **Besley, T. and R. Burgess.** 2002. The political economy of government responsiveness: Theory and evidence from India. *Quarterly Journal of Economics* **117**(4): 1415–1452.

9. http://www.natso.com/AM/Template.cfm?Section=Top_NATSO_Issues&Template=/CM/ContentDisplay.cfm&ContentID=7700&FusePreview=True&WebsiteKey=e91dcade-9ead-43ab-b6bc-c608fd2a3c34.

Chapter 20 Notes

1. Working paper, personal communication, from Robert Whaples.

2. **Meckler, Laura.** November 13, 2007. Kidney shortage inspires a radical idea: Organ sales. *Wall Street Journal.* Page A1.

3. The commercial fishing mortality rate derives from http://www.cdc.gov/niosh/fishfat.html. Kidney donation mortality rate from **Matas A. J., S. T. Bartlett, A. B. Leichtman, and F. L. Delmonico.** July 2003. *American Journal of Transplantation* 3(7): 830–834.

4. http://www.time.com/time/printout/0,8816,1686532,00.html.

5. For one source, see http://www.whitehouse.gov/cea/cea_immigration_062007.html.

6. On measures of foreign aid, see, for instance, http://www.online.wsj.com/public/article/SB1149642372278733311-9VLg4BPCPl76mawIeC92XypcO_E_20060706.html?mod=tff_main_tff_top.

Chapter 21 Notes

1. **Jacob, Brian A. and Steven D. Levitt.** August 3, 2003. Rotten apples: An investigation of the prevalence and predictors of teacher cheating. *Quarterly Journal of Economics* **118:** 843–878.

2. **Figlio, David N. and Lawrence S. Getzler.** 2002. Accountability, ability and disability: Gaming the system. NBER working paper 9307, Washington, DC.

3. For a calculation along these lines, see **Kane, T. and D. O. Staiger.** 2002. The promise and pitfalls of using imprecise school accountability measures. *Journal of Economic Perspectives* **16**(4): 91–114.

4. http://www.toyota101.com/No_Commission.aspx.

5. For more on private prisons, see **Tabarrok, Alexander** (ed). 2003. *Changing the Guard: Private Prisons and the Control of Crime.* Oakland, CA: The Independent Institute.

6. **Lazear, Edward P.** 2000. Performance pay and productivity. *AER* **90**(5): 1346–1361.

7. **Lemieux, T. W., Bentley MacLeod, and Daniel Parent.** 2007. Performance pay and wage inequality. NBER working paper 13128, Washington, DC.

8. **Bertrand, Marianne and Sendhil Mullainathan.** 2001. Are CEOs rewarded for luck? The ones without principals are. *Quarterly Journal of Economics* **116:** 901–932.

9. *Ibid.*

10. **Bebchuk, Lucian A., Alma Cohen, and Holger Spamann.** November 24, 2009. The wages of failure: Executive compensation at Bear Stearns and Lehman 2000–2008. *Yale Journal on Regulation* **27:** 257–282.

11. *Business Week.* January 9, 2006. The struggle to measure performance.

12. On employee ownership of stock, see **National Center for Employee Ownership.**

13. http://nceo.org/library/widespread.html.

14. On Walmart, see **Vance, Sandra S. and Roy V. Scott.** 1994. *Wal-Mart: A History of Sam Walton's Retail Phenomenon.* New York: Twayne. On Kmart, see **Turner, Marcia Layton.** 2003. *K-Mart's Deadly Sins: How Incompetence Tainted an American Icon.* New York: John Wiley & Sons.

Chapter 22 Notes

1. **Malkiel, Burton.** 1996. *A Random Walk Down Wall Street.* 6th ed. New York: W. W. Norton. See, in particular, p.24.

2. For a comprehensive review of efficient markets and the performance of mutual fund managers, see **Hebner, Mark T.** 2007. *Index Funds: The 12 Step Program for Active Investors.* Irvine, CA: IFA.

3. See **Marshall, Ben, Rochester Cahan, and Jared Cahan.** March 2008. Does intraday technical analysis in the U.S. equity market have value? *Journal of Empirical Finance:* 199–210.

4. On the relatively safe nature of Walmart, see, for instance, this analysis: http://www.slate.com/id/2185221/.

5. **Siegel, Jeremy J.** January/February 1992. The equity premium: Stock and bond returns since 1802. *Financial Analysts Journal* **48**(1): 28–38.

6. **Smith, Vernon L., Gerry L. Suchanek, and Arlington W. Williams.** 1988. Bubbles, crashes, and endogenous expectations in experimental spot asset markets. *Econometrica* **56**(5): 1119–1151. And **Hussam, Reshmaan N., David Porter, and Vernon L. Smith.** 2008. Thar she blows: Can bubbles be rekindled with experienced subjects? *American Economic Review* **98**(3): 924–937.

Chapter 23 Notes

1. For a good discussion, see **Persky, Joseph.** 1997. Retrospectives: Classical family values: Ending the poor laws as they knew them. *The Journal of Economic Perspectives* **11**(1): 179–189.

Appendix A Notes

1. **Clark, Gerald.** 1969. "What Happens When the Police Go On Strike." *New York Times Magazine,* November 16, sec. 6: 45, 176–185, 187, 194–195.

2. **Klick, Jonathan, & Alexander Tabarrok.** 2005. "Using Terror Alert Levels to Estimate the Effect of Police on Crime." *Journal of Law & Economics,* 48(1): 267–280.

INDEX

Note: Page numbers followed by f refer to figures; those followed by n refer to footnotes; those followed by t refer to tables.

A decrease in supply increases price and reduces quantity.

An increase in demand increases price and quantity.

At any price above the equilibrium price, there will be a surplus. A surplus will push prices down unless a price control (floor) makes it illegal to lower prices.

At any price below the equilibrium price, there will be a shortage. A shortage will push prices up unless a price control (ceiling) makes it illegal to raise prices.

A decrease in demand decreases price and quantity.

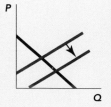

An increase in supply decreases price and increases quantity.

Elasticity

The elasticity of demand is a measure of how sensitive the quantity demanded is to a change in price.

$$E_d = \frac{\text{Percentage Change in Quantity Demanded}}{\text{Percentage Change in Price}} = \frac{\%\Delta Q_{demanded}}{\%\Delta\text{Price}} = \frac{\dfrac{Q_{before} - Q_{after}}{(Q_{before} + Q_{after})/2}}{\dfrac{P_{before} - P_{after}}{(P_{before} + P_{after})/2}}$$

Inelastic Demand

$|E_d| < 1$

Quantity is not very Sensitive to Price

Revenue and price move in same direction.

$R = P \times Q$

Elastic Demand

$|E_d| > 1$

Quantity is very Sensitive to Price

Revenue and price move in opposite directions.

$R = P \times Q$

Monopoly

Marginal Revenue, MR, is the change in total revenue from selling an additional unit.

Marginal Cost, MC, is the change in total cost from producing an additional unit.

To maximize profit, a firm produces until $MR = MC$.

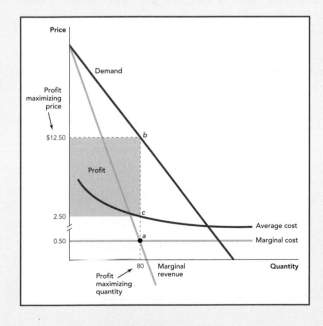

The more inelastic the demand, the greater the monopoly markup of P over MC.

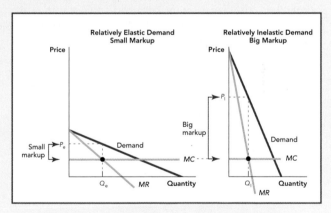

The Principles of Price Discrimination

1a. If the demand curves are different, it is more profitable to set different prices in different markets than a single price that covers all markets.

1b. To maximize profit the firm should set a higher price in markets with more inelastic demand.

2. Arbitrage makes it difficult for a firm to set different prices in different markets, thereby reducing the profit from price discrimination.

MICROECONOMICS ESSENTIALS

Externalities

An **external cost** is a cost paid by people other than the consumer or the producer trading in the market: for example, pollution creates an external cost. When external costs are significant, output is too high.

An **external benefit** is a benefit received by people other than the consumers or producers trading in the market; for example, flu shots create an external benefit. When external benefits are significant, output is too low.

Labor Markets

In a competitive market, firms will hire workers until the marginal product of labor equals the wage, $MPL = W$.

Incentives and Labor Markets

Three lessons of good incentive design:

1. You get what you pay for but what you pay for is not always what you want.
2. Tie pay to performance to reduce risk.
3. Money isn't everything.

A **compensating differential** is a difference in wages that offsets differences in working conditions.

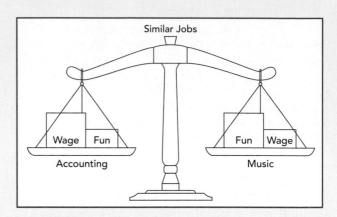

Public Goods and Tragedy of the Commons

A **good is nonexcludable** if people who don't pay cannot be easily prevented from using the good.

A **good is nonrival** if one person's use of the good does not reduce the ability of another person to use the same good.

A **free rider** enjoys the benefits of a public good without paying a share of the costs.

A **forced rider** is someone who pays a share of the costs of a public good but who does not enjoy the benefits.

The **tragedy of the commons** is the tendency of any resource that is unowned and hence nonexcludable to be overused and undermaintained.

The Four Types of Goods

	Excludable	Nonexcludable
Rival	**Private Goods**	**Common Resources**
	Jeans	Tuna in the ocean
	Hamburgers	The environment
	Contact lenses	Public roads
Nonrival	**Nonrival Private Goods**	**Public Goods**
	Cable TV	Asteroid deflection
	Wi-Fi	National defense
	Digital music	Mosquito control